ESSENTIALS
of
MARKETING RESEARCH

ESSENTIALS
of
MARKETING RESEARCH

WILLIAM R. DILLON
University of South Carolina

THOMAS J. MADDEN
University of South Carolina

NEIL H. FIRTLE
Leggett Lustig Firtle, Inc.

Irwin
McGraw-Hill

Boston, Massachusetts   Burr Ridge, Illinois   Dubuque, Iowa
Madison, Wisconsin   New York, New York   San Francisco, California   St. Louis, Missouri

Executive editor: Rob Zwettler
Developmental editor: Andy Winston
Marketing manager: Scott J. Timian
Project editor: Karen Smith
Production manager: Bob Lange
Cover designer: Jeanne M. Rivera
Cover illustrator: Karen Watson
Art manager: Kim Meriwether
Photo research coordinator: Patricia A. Seefelt
Compositor: Carlisle Communications, Ltd.
Typeface: 10/12 Bembo
Printer: Von Hoffmann Press

Library of Congress Cataloging-in-Publication Data

Dillon, William R.
    Essentials of marketing research / William R. Dillon, Thomas J. Madden, Neil H. Firtle.
        p.   cm. — (The Irwin series in marketing)
    Includes bibliographical references and indexes.
    ISBN 0-256-08112-3
    1. Marketing research.   I. Madden, Thomas J.   II. Firtle, Neil H.
III. Title.   IV. Series.
    HF5415.2D537   1993   92–30863
    658.8 ′3 — dc20

Printed in the United States of America
    6 7 8 9 0 VH 9 8 7

— *To my dearest wife Heidi and to Tinkerbell—if there is a place after this, I will be on the lookout for both of you*

— *In memory of Werner S. Noberini*

— *To two great new products—my children, Bridget and Kathleen*

THE IRWIN SERIES IN MARKETING

Consulting Editor Gilbert A. Churchill, Jr.
University of Wisconsin, Madison

Alreck and Settle
The Survey Research Handbook
Second Edition

Belch and Belch
Introduction to Advertising and Promotion
Second Edition

Berkowitz, Kerin, Hartley, and Rudelius
Marketing
Third Edition

Bernhardt and Kinnear
Cases in Marketing Management
Fifth Edition

Bingham and Raffield
Business to Business Marketing Management
First Edition

Bovee and Arens
Contemporary Advertising
Fourth Edition

Boyd and Walker
Marketing Management: A Strategic Approach
First Edition

Boyd, Westfall, and Stasch
Marketing Research: Text and Cases
Seventh Edition

Burstiner
Basic Retailing
Second Edition

Cadotte
The Market Place: A Strategic Marketing Simulation
First Edition

Cateora
International Marketing
Eighth Edition

Churchill, Ford, and Walker
Sales Force Management
Fourth Edition

Cole
Consumer and Commercial Credit Management
Ninth Edition

Cravens
Strategic Marketing
Third Edition

Cravens and Lamb
Strategic Marketing Management Cases
Fourth Edition

Crawford
New Products Management
Third Edition

Dillon, Madden, and Firtle
Essentials of Marketing Research
First Edition

Dillon, Madden, and Firtle
Marketing Research in a Marketing Environment
Second Edition

Engel, Warshaw, and Kinnear
Promotional Strategy
Seventh Edition

Faria, Nulsen, and Roussos
Compete
Fourth Edition

Futrell
ABC's of Selling
Third Edition

Futrell
Fundamentals of Selling
Fourth Edition

Hawkins, Best, and Coney
Consumer Behavior
Fifth Edition

Kurtz and Dodge
Professional Selling
Sixth Edition

Lambert and Stock
Strategic Logistics Management
Third Edition

Lehmann and Winer
Analysis for Marketing Planning
Second Edition

Lehmann
Marketing Research and Analysis
Fourth Edition

Levy and Weitz
Retailing Management
First Edition

Mason, Mayer, and Wilkinson
Modern Retailing
Sixth Edition

Mason, Mayer, and Ezell
Retailing
Fourth Edition

Mason and Perreault
The Marketing Game
Second Edition

McCarthy and Perreault
Basic Marketing: A Global-Managerial Approach
Eleventh Edition

McCarthy and Perreault
Essentials of Marketing
Fifth Edition

Peter and Olson
Consumer Behavior and Marketing Strategy
Third Edition

Peter and Donnelly
A Preface to Marketing Management
Fifth Edition

Peter and Donnelly
Marketing Management: Knowledge and Skills
Third Edition

Quelch and Farris
Cases in Advertising and Promotion Management
Third Edition

Quelch, Dolan, and Kosnik
Marketing Management: Text and Cases
First Edition

Smith and Quelch
Ethics in Marketing
First Edition

Stanton, Spiro, and Buskirk
Management of a Sales Force
Eighth Edition

Thompson and Stappenbeck
The Marketing Strategy Game
First Edition

Walker, Boyd, and Larreche
Marketing Strategy: Planning and Implementation
First Edition

Weitz, Castleberry, and Tanner
Selling: Building Partnerships
First Edition

In the preface to the first edition of *Marketing Research in a Marketing Environment*, we noted that the proliferation of textbooks provided teachers with an increased number of texts from which to choose. In *Essentials of Marketing Research* we provide another option to the marketing research teacher.

Essentials of Marketing Research was motivated by a desire to expose undergraduate students to the theory and practice of marketing research with a view toward teaching students how to be effective managers of the marketing research function. Our approach in this textbook is, in principle, similar to *Marketing Research in a Marketing Environment* in the sense that we have continued to emphasize the problem-oriented nature of marketing research and how marketing research activities are actually implemented by professional marketing researchers. *Essentials* is ideally suited for an introductory undergraduate marketing research course. In this textbook we take a more general, macro-oriented approach to presenting the essential tools and techniques of marketing research, which we view as consistent with the needs of students who will eventually become users of marketing research as opposed to marketing research practitioners.

ORGANIZATION

Essentials of Marketing Research is divided into six parts.

Part I, Marketing Research Environments, consists of three chapters. The first chapter introduces the student to the area of marketing research by discussing the relationship(s) between marketing researchers and other marketing professionals. The second chapter presents the relationship of marketing research to the marketing planning process. The section concludes with Chapter 3, which describes what we call the research cycle. The research cycle high-lights several different types of marketing research studies that are likely to be conducted for the various stages in the product life cycle.

Part II, Acquiring Data: An Overview, consists of five chapters. This section considers the tools and techniques that can be used to collect marketing research data. Chapter 4 presents traditional sources of secondary data. The next chapter, Chapter 5, opens with a discussion of the newer on-line CD-ROM type data bases and closes with a presentation of syndicated sources of marketing research data. The major suppliers of syndicated sources are discussed with a presentation of the recent single-source type data. Chapter 6 is devoted to qualitative interviewing methods with emphasis on focus group interviews. Chapter 7 discusses survey interviewing methods and provides a critical comparative evaluation of the various methods. The last chapter in the section, Chapter 8, presents the most commonly used experimental designs and a discussion of causality.

Part III, Sampling Theory and Practices, consists of two chapters. The first chapter discusses the sampling process basically from a nontechnical perspective. Sampling estimates are described but the emphasis is on the use and understanding of sampling rather than sampling theory. The second chapter in the section, Chapter 10, discusses issues related to sample size determination.

Part IV, Measurement, Scaling, and Questionnaire Design, contains three chapters. The first chapter, Chapter 11, presents the basic concepts of measurement scales and presents the most commonly used comparative and non-comparative scaling methods. The chapter also contains a discussion of multiple-item scales such as the semantic differential. Chapter 12 presents a discussion of the issues that should be considered when designing a questionnaire. Chapter 13 presents issues involved with the fielding of a study and the steps that are necessary for processing marketing research data.

Part V, Data Analysis, consists of four chapters. The first chapter in the section, Chapter 14, presents basic data analysis methods such as descriptive statistics and graphical analyses. Chapter 15 is devoted soley to the issues of hypothesis testing. Chapter 16 presents common hypothesis tests for nominal and interval data for single versus multiple sample designs. The last chapter in the section, Chapter 17, presents a standard discussion of correlation and regression techniques.

Part VI, Presenting the Research and Ethical Issues, contains two chapters. The first chapter in the section describes a typical marketing research presentation and discusses a number of issues related to the writing of a marketing research report and the oral presentation of the results. Chapter 19 is devoted to ethical issues in marketing research.

KEY FEATURES

There are a number of features that we believe will allow the student to better understand the role of marketing research.

1. *Part-Opening Executive Profiles* offer special insights by experienced marketing professionals. The profiles, which address both product and service marketing, help clarify how research interacts with other marketing functions.
2. *From the User's Perspective* boxes offer brief business anecdotes to add texture and interest to each chapter. Once again, students are offered the opportunity to learn from real business experiences.
3. *Chapter-Opening Vignettes* offer a variety of marketing narratives that emphasize the place of research and its ability to lead to marketing success or, in several instances, how it didn't lead to success.
4. *Part-Ending Cases* feature high profile companies such as Campbell's Soup and Rold Gold Pretzels.

SUPPLEMENTS

We have prepared all of the supplements that accompany this textbook. In doing so, we have attempted to provide elements and features of value to the inexperienced as well as experienced instructor.

Instructor's Manual

The most important features include:

— *Author comments.* These describe the author's rationale for the major topics presented in each chapter.
— *Learning objectives.* The learning objectives that appear at the beginning of each chapter are reproduced.
— *Key terms and concepts.* The key terms and concepts that appear throughout the textbook are reproduced.
— *Lecture notes.* A detailed outline of each chapter is provided.
— *Transparency masters.* Key exhibits, tables, and figures appearing in the textbook are reproduced as $8\frac{1}{2}'' \times 11''$ transparency masters. Transparency masters are also provided for supplemental material not appearing in the textbook. The suggested spot for the use of each of these is provided within the teaching suggestions.
— *Teaching suggestions.* These hints and ideas indicate how the authors would organize and present the material appearing in each chapter. Suggestions for where to integrate the transparency masters are also provided.
— *Answers to end-of-chapter problems.* Detailed answers to every question are provided.
— *Case notes.* For instructors who decide to use any or all of the case studies in the text, a detailed set of case notes is provided.

Test Bank. The test bank contains an extensive array of questions, categorized by chapter. In addition, correct answers are provided.

CompuTest. All questions appearing in the test bank are reproduced in Irwin's CompuTest test-generation system, for use with the IBM PC and compatible computers. The test-generation system provides the following features:

1. Individual test items can be added or deleted.

2. Individual test items can be edited.

3. A shuffle option is provided that allows different versions of the same examination.

4. Ample documentation is included.

Software

A unique set of contemporary interactive software programs are available to adopters. The software is pedagogical in nature and designed to enhance students' understanding of the concepts and techniques discussed throughout the textbook. Six individual modules are available:

1. The SAMPLE module demonstrates selected concepts related to drawing simple and stratified samples.

2. The SCALE module takes students through various types of monadic and comparative rating scales. Asking students to rate a set of brands on different types of scales enables them to gain an appreciation for the issues involved in selecting a rating instrument.

3. The ACA module illustrates how conjoint analysis works in an interactive PC environment. The module utilizes the Adaptive Conjoint Analysis (ACA) system developed by Richard Johnson of Sawtooth Software, Inc.

4. The QUADMAP module is a system for analyzing top-box importance ratings along with top-box ratings of a brand on a number of salient attributes. This type of analysis, referred to as *quadrant analysis*, is discussed in Chapter 14.

5. The ASCID module is a marketing decision support system for perceptual mapping. A unique feature of this system is the ability to position new objects in an existing perceptual space.

6. The FORCAST module is designed to demonstrate how the more popular forecasting techniques work.

7. The MARITZSTATS module is an interactive statistical analysis system for testing hypotheses concerning means and proportions for one or multiple independent/dependent samples. It also includes an option for determining sample sizes.

Color Transparencies

There are 75 acetates, many of which include material and sources that do not appear in the textbook.

Videos

Focus group sessions are featured; they provide real life experiences.

ACKNOWLEDGMENTS

This textbook has benefited from the hard work and dedication of a number of individuals who have been involved in this project. First, we would like to acknowledge the contributions of those individuals who reviewed the manuscript at various stages of development. Their suggestions and constructive criticisms have greatly improved the treatment and presentation. We sincerely thank each of them for their generous efforts.

Joe Ballenger
Stephen F. Austin State University

Pam Scholder Ellen
Georgia State University

Gopala K. Ganesh
University of North Texas

Timothy A. Longfellow
Illinois State University

William Mulvaney
Central Michigan University

Michael F. O'Neill
California State University-Chico

Diana Grewal
University of Miami

Douglas R. Hausknecht
University of Akron

Roy Howell
Texas Tech University

Elizabeth K. LaFleur
Nicholls State University

Susan M. Petroshius
Bowling Green State University

Harlan E. Spotts
Northeastern University

J. K. Stuenkel
Central Michigan University

Several individuals associated with Irwin deserve a special acknowledgment. We have worked with our developmental editor, Andy

Winston, for several years. His dedication to detail and helpful comments are most appreciated. On this project we have had the opportunity to work with Rob Zwettler and appreciate his administrative acumen. The production staff, Karen Smith and Pat Peat, have been fastidious and professional. We gratefully acknowledge their contribution. Permissions for the various material appearing in the textbook were secured by Ms. Harriet Stockanes. The presentation of material was enormously enhanced by the talents of Beverly Hincks, who was responsible for researching and obtaining the photographs in this textbook.

Several individuals at the College of Business Administration, University of South Carolina, deserve special thanks. Our secretaries Ruth Ford, Jennie Smyrl, and Edie Beaver devoted many hours in the preparation of manuscript. We owe Ruth a special thanks for her willingness to master PCTex. Though at times her frustration was raised to new heights, through sheer tennacity, hard work, and an unwillingness to give up, she always managed to win the fight. Several students also contributed greatly. Carol Fiske, Judith Spios, Shannon Craft, and Robert McCardle assisted in a variety of tasks instrumental in the development of the material.

All of our marketing colleagues at the College of Business Administration deserve thanks, especially our program director, Donald G. Frederick.

We would be remiss if we did not take the opportunity to thank all of the marketing research companies discussed in Chapter 5 who provided supportive materials.

Finally, we would like to thank the marketing research professionals who so graciously provided their time in preparing the comments that open each of the major sections of the textbook.

William R. Dillon
Thomas J. Madden
Neil H. Firtle

BRIEF CONTENTS

CONTENTS

ESSENTIALS
of
MARKETING RESEARCH

MARKETING RESEARCH ENVIRONMENTS

PETER HARRIS
DIRECTOR OF MARKETING RESEARCH
METROPOLITAN TRANSPORTATION AUTHORITY

Marketing research is helping government break new ground in service delivery and policy development.

"Government has been, in many ways, one of the least accountable areas of the service sector; and this is ironic given the fact that government exists in this country for the people," says Peter Harris, director of marketing research with New York City's Metropolitan Transportation Authority (MTA).

"Despite the fact that MTA is about as pure a service as one can imagine, I think it's fair to say that the public has perceived MTA over the past several decades as a fairly entrenched bureaucracy," Harris says. "The way the agency approaches its business is changing dramatically. Marketing research is playing an important role in that change. The chairman has made it a top priority to make our operations customer driven."

Specifically, the research program is used in three ways: to support marketing programs, to help customer drive operations, and to support policy development. The research is both tactical and strategic. Tactical initiatives have ranged from how to disseminate bus informa-tion to taking surveys of what people would like to see in new prototype trains. Strategic initiatives range from using research to help set priorities for the capital program to developing market-based service improvement strategies.

MTA's research department conducts regular tracking surveys — primarily through telephone interviews but also through seat drops on trains and station intercepts — to find out what customers think of service and the overall transit environment. The surveys have indicated that customers' most important concern is personal security, followed by the reliability and frequency of service, and the overall station environment.

"We share that information with our operating agencies, and task forces develop initiatives to respond," Harris says. Extensive research has been conducted on the issue of personal security, including an evaluation of the impact of policing initiatives on public perceptions and the design of new station features such as passenger alarm systems and two-way communication devices.

The research department then follows up with evaluative research. In this case, the department asked customers

as they walked through the stations if they noticed the new features, liked them, or had ideas on how to improve the stations. That information is shared with the station department.

"Our research department is proactive, but we also solicit ideas from the operating departments. After we discuss with an operating department the issues that concern them, they might come back to us and request a project, or we may propose a project to them," Harris says of his department's relationship to other departments. "We also do policy research, which tends to be on broader issues like fare policy."

MTA has several types of retainer contracts with outside full service market research firms, telephone interviewing firms, transportation planning firms, and qualitative research firms. "We typically send out scopes of work for projects to vendors in one or more of these categories," Harris says, adding that all work is selected on the basis of competitive proposals.

Rarely does the department simply hand over a project to a consultant. "We are very involved," Harris says. "Our research has to be customized to our situation."

Harris believes that careers in market research in government will keep opening up because it is such a new field. Although research had been done in the past, it was ad hoc and rarely focused on customer satisfaction or tactical programs designed to address customer concerns. "The use of marketing research on policy issues such as how to increase the sense of personal safety, or how people feel about social issues like the homeless and panhandlers—these are newer to government," he says.

"In this way, policy that is informed by research better serves the public, makes government more accountable and responsive, and better serves a democratic society," Harris says.

Peter Harris graduated with a B.A. in Humanities from The New School for Social Research in New York. After a period of working primarily for governmental agencies and political candidates, he served as a financial analyst for the New York State Financial Control Board. In 1983 he joined the Metropolitan Transportation Authority, becoming its Director of Marketing Research in 1988.

3

Marketing Research Environments

BREWERS TAP NEW BRANDS

Beer sales this year are likely to remain as flat as a brew left open on a sun-baked picnic table, most industry experts agree.

Once able to rely almost exclusively on population growth to fuel their business, major brewers face the prospect of aging baby boomers who are cutting back during their middle-age years.

For most companies that leaves one choice: Roll out more brands, and make it snappy.

"Ultra," "light," "genuine," "dry," "draft," and "nonalcoholic" are the magic words these days in the battle for market share. And recent stunning successes in some of those categories—such as that of Miller Genuine Draft—have forced other companies to concoct their versions.

"All of the major brewers have been launching new brands forever," said Robert Joanis, director of development for third-place Adolph Coors Co. "What's a relatively new phenomenon is that they're launching national brands and pouring a lot of money behind them after just a very short period of test-marketing.

"There's the risk of being accused of taking a 'me too' strategy, but when a category comes along, you have to come up with one that competes," he said.

Nine new products that were introduced after 1987—three nonalcoholic beers and six regular beers—experienced strong growth, with Bud Dry Draft leading the pack. It sold 3.2 million barrels in that time, according to *Impact*, a newsletter on the alcohol beverage industry.

Five of those beers—Bud Dry, Busch Light, Genuine Draft Light, Keystone, and Keystone Light—and two non-alcoholic beers, Sharp's and O'Doul's, were launched nationwide in 1990. They accounted for 8.77 million, or almost 5 per-

Top beer brands

In percent of 1991 U.S. sales

Miller Lite 10.3&
Coors Light 6.4
Bud Light 5.0
Busch 4.5
Milwaukee's Best
Miller Genuine Draft 3.9
Old Milwaukee 3.2
Miller High Life 3.1
Coors 1.9
Busch Light 1.9
Budweiser 25.6%
Other 25.6%

TWIST

©Copyright 1991 Knight-Ridder Tribune, Inc.

New brands last year gained volume at the expense of the traditional premium beers at the five leading brewers, according to *Impact*.

The three top brands behind number-one seller Budweiser—Miller Lite, Coors Light, and Bud Light—were introduced within the past 17 years. And last year, 43.8 percent of the beer sold in the United States consisted of products introduced after 1972. The remaining 56.2 percent were traditional beers, according to Robert S. Weinberg, a former executive with the leading brewer, Anheuser-Busch Co.

cent, of the 189.9 million barrels of domestic beer shipped to distributors that year, according to *Beer Marketer's Insights*.

Source:©Copyright 1991, Chicago Tribune Company, all rights reserved, used with permission.

INTRODUCTION

Rolling out new product types and varieties to maintain or enhance a firm's market position is not unique to the beer industry. Today most firms face stiff competition from domestic as well as international sources. Many firms face rapidly changing marketing conditions. The U.S. beer industry is a case in point. The need for timely and accurate information on competitive factors is essential for developing effective marketing strategy. As we will see, marketing research provides a hedge against the adverse effects that might accompany changes in a firm's competitive environment by providing management with information that can reduce the uncertainty inherent in decision making. Through marketing research a brewer, for example, can monitor the market place and determine the relative appeal of "ultra light" or "genuine draft" products with a view toward reducing the risk of rolling out new product varieties.

In this chapter we explain what marketing research is all about. We begin with a discussion that emphasizes the importance of understanding a company's customers. Next we define marketing research and describe the environments in which marketing research takes place. We then explain the principal parties involved in conducting marketing research.

UNDERSTANDING CONSUMER NEEDS AND WANTS

Marketing Concept
A marketing strategy that preaches that success comes through customer satisfaction.

A thorough understanding of customer needs and wants is essential in developing effective marketing strategies. This position is consistent with the **marketing concept** which preaches success through customer satisfaction. Marketing research provides the information that firms need to practice the marketing concept.

To see how this might work in another context, consider Fred, a typical automobile commuter:

> Fred drives to work early each morning. The trip takes about one hour. On the way he usually picks up coffee and a doughnut, which he eats while driving. Fred listens to traffic reports, and he consults his maps if an alternative route is suggested. Whenever possible, he uses the exact-change lanes on the tollway, and consequently he likes to be able to reach his correct change with his left hand.[1]

Fred's habits suggest what he might like in a car. Several specific product features come to mind. Attractive features to him might be a place to put his coffee and doughnut without fear of mess or spilling, a map pocket handy to the driver, and a coin storage tray at the left corner of the dashboard. Among the less specific, but presumably equally important, product features would be good gas economy, dependability, good visibility for changing lanes, good acceleration for merging, a comfortable and roomy driver's seat that won't wrinkle his suit, a smooth ride that doesn't spill coffee, and an effective heating and air-conditioning system that will make the one-hour trip to and from the office comfortable.

Future automobile end-benefits may include telephones.

The point of this example is that the context in which Fred uses his car each day influences the product features that he will tend to want in an automobile. Drivers who commute by public transport and who use their cars primarily for leisure time activities will undoubtedly find other product features, such as a roof rack or a large spacious trunk, more desirable.

Marketing research can identify the end benefits that people desire. We will refer to needs and wants as **end benefits.** You can think of a product or service as being made up of a number of end benefits. Product features or attributes deliver the end benefits. Failure to understand product features in terms of the end benefits that they satisfy, as well as identifying the customers who find such end benefits most desirable, is a leading cause of poor market performance. Consider, for example, the plight of domestic automobile manufacturers. In 1990 Toyota Motor Co. of Japan surpassed Chrysler Corp. as the third leading seller of automobiles in the United States.

END BENEFITS
Product features that satisfy consumers' needs and wants.

UNDERSTANDING MARKETING RESEARCH

In 1986 the board of directors of the American Marketing Association endorsed the following definition of marketing research:

> Marketing research is the function that links the consumer, customer, and public to the marketer through information—information used to identify and define marketing opportunities and problems; generate, refine, identify, and evaluate marketing actions; monitor marketing performance; and improve understanding of marketing as a process. Marketing research specifies the information required to address these issues; designs the method for collecting information; manages and implements the data collection process; analyzes the results; and communicates the findings and their implications.[2]

Put simply, **marketing research** helps the marketing manager to make better informed and less risky marketing decisions. Accordingly, the information obtained through marketing research must be objective, impartial, current, translatable, and relevant. Marketing research involves the systematic gathering, recording, processing, and analyzing of marketing

MARKETING RESEARCH
Activities involving the systematic gathering, recording, processing, and analyzing of marketing data.

data, which—when interpreted—will help the marketing manager uncover opportunities and reduce the risks in decision making.

Let us now take a closer look at how marketing research information is used and the activities involved when conducting a marketing research study.

Marketing Research Information

The information collected by conducting marketing research is used to: (1) identify and define marketing opportunities and problems; (2) generate, refine, and evaluate marketing actions; (3) monitor marketing performance; and (4) improve the understanding of marketing as a process.

Marketing research can help the marketing manager to[3]

1. *Learn the values of the high-profit customers.* In the sales of many products and services, the '80/20 Rule' applies—20 percent of the customers generate 80 percent of the profits. Marketing research can help the manager identify which customers are its best, or "core," customers and understand the values and perceptions that distinguish these customers from others. Marketing research information can help in designing marketing strategies to better satisfy these customers and strengthen their ties to the company.

2. *Analyze customer purchase patterns.* Evaluating the sales of individual products and services should not be undertaken in a vacuum. Marketing research information can help the marketing manager to understand purchasing patterns. For example, a particular product or service may not be profitable but may be valued by many of the firm's core customers. This product or service may in fact form a strong bond between those customers and the company.

3. *Continually monitor customers.* The behavior of customers changes over time. Companies use marketing research information to stay one step ahead of their core customers. Marketing research information can contribute to the development of institutionalized systems and practices that virtually eliminate production defects and service breakdowns.

4. *Develop product strategy.* Marketing managers must be concerned not only with how to market a product or service but also with whether the product or service should be marketed in the first place. Marketing research information provides a framework for analyzing the potential profitability of new products or services before a decision to launch is made.

Marketing Research Activities

At the heart of marketing research is the collection and dissemination of information. The practice of marketing research involves a number of activities. Specifically, marketing researchers, in cooperation with marketing managers' perform and/or supervise the following activities:

1. *Define the research problem.* Perhaps the most important responsibility of marketing researchers is to assure that the problem facing the company is accurately and precisely defined. Symptoms, for example, declining sales or market share, are not problems. Problem formulation is discussed in Chapter 2. The nature of the problem facing

the firm will determine the type of study to conduct. Various types of marketing research studies are discussed in Chapter 3.

2. *Specify the information required.* Having defined the problem the marketing researcher must determine what kind of information will best meet the research objectives. The marketing researcher may decide to use information that has been already collected by the firm or information that is in the public domain. This kind of information is called secondary data. The marketing researcher can decide to collect data from the firm's customers. This kind of information is called primary data. Secondary information sources are discussed in Chapters 4 and 5.

3. *Design the method for collecting the needed information.* There are a variety of ways for collecting marketing research information. For example, information obtained from customers of a firm can be collected via a mail, telephone, or personal interview. Some marketing research firms maintain consumer panels, consisting of individuals who have agreed to provide purchasing and media viewing behavior. Chapters 5 through 8 provide details on various aspects of collecting marketing research information.

4. *Decide on the sampling design.* The marketing researcher must determine the qualifications for being in a study. The sampling design must result in the proper sample of respondents being selected. A variety of different sampling designs are open to researchers. Sampling issues are discussed in Chapters 9 and 10.

5. *Design the questionnaire.* The marketing researcher generally has the primary responsibility for constructing the data collection instrument. The instrument must be designed to be easily administered and understood by the respondent. Chapters 11 and 12 present material on measurment issues and questionnaire construction.

6. *Manage and implement the data collection.* An important activity that the marketing researcher is responsible for is the overseeing of the data collection process. Among other things, the marketing researcher must provide instructions for training interviewers and procedures for controlling the quality of the interviewing. Fielding the questionnaire and preparing the information collected for analysis are discussed in Chapters 13 and 14, respectively.

7. *Analyze and interpret the results.* The marketing researcher has the primary responsibility for analyzing the information that has been collected and for interpreting the results. The analysis plan follows closely from the research objective of the study. Approaches for analyzing marketing research data are discussed in Chapters 15 through 17.

8. *Communicate the findings and implications.* The results of a marketing research study must be disseminated. The marketing researcher is responsible for providing a written report and generally an oral presentation to management. Chapter 18 provides tips for presenting the results of a marketing research study.

MARKETING RESEARCH ENVIRONMENTS

Exhibit 1–1 diagrams the principal organizations that make up the marketing research community, separated into principal internal, principal external, and facilitating external parties. The internal parties are persons and

Exhibit 1—1

Overview of Marketing
Research Environments

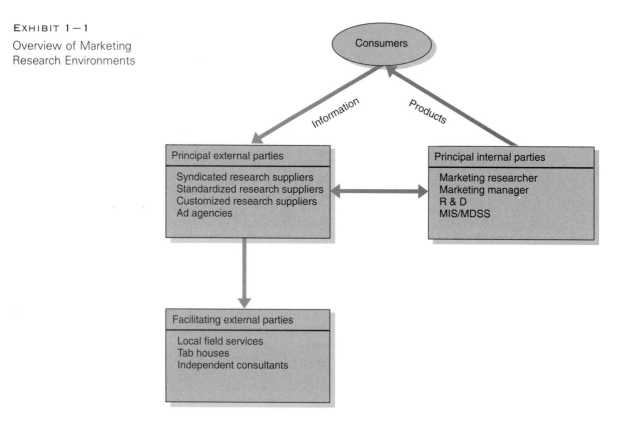

departments that are part of a firm's organizational structure. These include the marketing researcher, the marketing manager; the research and
development department (R&D); and management information services
(MIS), which includes marketing decision support systems (MDSS).

The principal external parties are organizations and individuals outside
of the firm that are hired to provide marketing research functions and
that interact directly with principal internal parties within the firm.
These include various types of suppliers and advertising agencies. Suppliers and ad agencies subcontract marketing research activities to local
field services, tabulation houses, and independent consultants; these are
all referred to as facilitating external parties.

Exhibit 1–1 gives us a way to describe the interrelationships among
these parties and the basic marketing research functions they provide.

Principal Internal Parties

Let us begin with the marketing research department. Marketing research
is a staff function, similar to legal, personnel, and accounting functions.
Thus, the marketing researcher does not have the power to dictate or
control line function activities. Put simply, the marketing researcher's role
is to advise. Accordingly, compelling arguments presented persuasively are
the marketing researcher's most important weapons.

At the head of the marketing research department is the director of marketing research, who reports directly to the vice president of marketing services. Reporting to the director of marketing research are a number of group managers, often titled associate directors. Associate directors or group managers are responsible for overseeing the marketing research activities for specific groups of products, say, carbonated soft drinks or health-care products. Under each associate director or group manager is a marketing research manager who oversees the senior and junior research analysts who are assigned to particular products and/or services (see Exhibit 1–2).

Marketing research budgets are controlled by marketing managers. Consequently they must approve the study. When the manager identifies a possible reason for initiating a study, the manager will contact the marketing research department. The product or service category or the nature of the problem determines which marketing researcher is assigned to the project. Once a marketing researcher has been assigned, the marketing manager and the researcher then operate as a team, although the marketing researcher is primarily responsible for designing the research.

The marketing researcher must understand the environment in the industry, and how the marketing manager views the problem that he or she is facing. Knowing the industry environment and viewing the problem from the marketing manager's perspective are critical to identifying the key variables that the marketing research manager should focus on. Also, a knowledge of the corporate culture is important since it determines how decisions are made. Such knowledge can increase the chance that research results are accepted and correctly implemented.

Both the marketing manager and the marketing researcher interface with the *R&D department* and the *MIS/MDSS department*. R&D provides technological support and advice and plays an instrumental role in product design decisions. MIS/MDSS provide computer-based technology—databases and software—enabling the marketing manager and marketing researcher to access information needed for strategic and tactical decisions.

Principal External Parties

Four principal parties outside the organization play an important role in shaping marketing research activities: (1) syndicated research suppliers, (2) standardized research suppliers, (3) customized research suppliers, and (4) advertising agencies. The first three parties are commonly referred to as marketing research suppliers and are distinguished by the unique nature of the services they provide. These parties interface with the marketing manager and the marketing researcher and provide services that cannot be found within the organization.

Marketing research suppliers.   The main business of **marketing research suppliers** is research—they are the primary data gatherers and analysts who execute marketing research studies. There are literally thousands of marketing research suppliers, ranging from small one- or two-person firms to extremely large multinational corporations. Table 1–1 gives worldwide and U.S. marketing

MARKETING RESEARCH
SUPPLIERS
Independent companies that execute marketing research studies.

EXHIBIT 1—2
Organization Chart for a Corporate Marketing Research Department

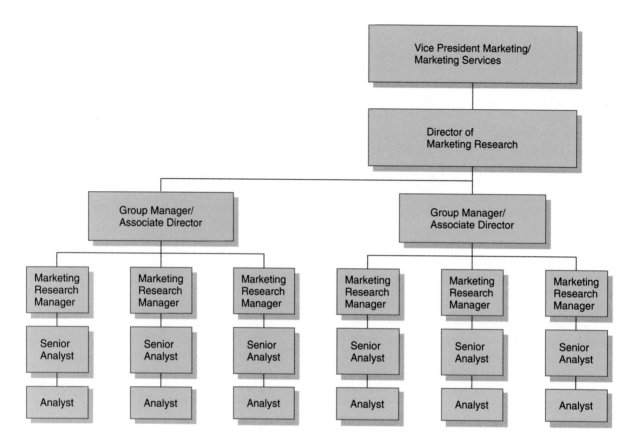

research revenues for the top 50 marketing research suppliers for 1990. Leading the field is Nielsen, with estimated total (U.S. and worldwide) revenues of $1,200 million. A distant second is IMS International, Inc., with estimated revenues of $509 million.

The reasons for using outside research services are simple: Compared to internal providers, marketing research suppliers

FULL SERVICE SUPPLIER
A marketing research company that can and usually does carry out all aspects of a research project.

1. Provide economies of scale by offering specialized services that could be provided internally only at considerable cost.
2. Are less subject to internal politics.
3. Provide greater flexibility in terms of scheduling.

LIMITED SERVICE SUPPLIER
A marketing research company that specializes in one or more marketing research activities.

There are two basic types of suppliers. A **full service supplier** can carry out all aspects of a research project; questionnaire design, preparation and production, interviewing, research design, data processing, and analysis and interpretation. A **limited service supplier** specializes in one or more marketing research activities and may not offer the full range of marketing research services.

Marketing research suppliers provide three broad categories of service: (1) syndicated research services, (2) standardized research services, and (3) customized research services.

1. **Syndicated research services.** Companies that provide information from common pools of data to different clients are in the syndicated research service business. For example, you are probably familiar with A.C. Nielsen's television viewing service, which estimates audience share of prime-time programming. Suppliers who offer syndicated research services tend to be among the largest in the marketing research business. All four of the top marketing research suppliers listed in Table 1–1 provide mainly syndicated services. Details on most of the major syndicated research services will be provided in Chapter 5.

SYNDICATED RESEARCH SERVICE
A marketing research company that provides information from common pools of data.

2. **Standardized research services.** Standardized research is research conducted for different clients using the same research design. Advertising testing techniques, for example, are frequently standardized so that the results from one study can be compared to those obtained in another study. Such comparability across studies generally leads to the development of "norms," which then provide the basis for evaluating all studies.

STANDARDIZED RESEARCH SERVICE
A marketing research company that uses the same research design for different clients.

3. **Customized research services.** Almost all marketing research suppliers offer tailor-made, one-of-a-kind studies for particular clients. Customized marketing research studies probably constitute the largest number of studies conducted, but not the most significant in terms of dollar billings. Among the major marketing research suppliers offering customized research services are Westat, Inc., The M/A/R/C Group, Maritz Marketing Research, Inc., The NPD Group, and Burke Marketing Research.

CUSTOMIZED RESEARCH SERVICE
A marketing research company that provides one-of-a-kind studies.

Advertising agencies.   The marketing manager and marketing researcher often work with the **advertising agency** that currently handles the firm's account (or a particular brand of the firm). There must be coordination between the research activities for a product or service and current and future advertising campaigns. Some advertising agencies maintain their own marketing research departments, although the emphasis placed on marketing research varies greatly. In most instances, the agency's marketing researcher acts as an internal consultant.

ADVERTISING AGENCY
A firm whose primary responsibility is to create and develop effective communication material and, in the course of such activities, interact with the client's marketing research department and/or provide marketing research support.

Local field services.   **Field services** are firms that are hired to collect data, that is, administer interviews. These firms are dispersed in communities throughout the United States. A field service can be a single proprietorship where the owner acts in the capacity of field supervisor. This person hires interviewers from the pool of available interviewers in the area based on who will be interviewed, the type of interview, and the number of interviews to complete. The field supervisor assembles the interviewers, briefs them, and coordinates their efforts while in the field. Most field service firms are free-lance and frequently do work for more than one marketing research supplier.

FIELD SERVICE
A marketing research company that specializes in activities involved in collecting data.

The director of field services at the marketing research supplier selects the field service to use. Some of the larger marketing research suppliers have their

TABLE 1–1

Top 50 Research Organizations

Rank 1991	Rank 1990	Organization	Headquarters	Phone	Total Research Revenues (millions)*	Percent Change from 1989†	Revenues from Outside United States ($ millions)	Percent from Outside United States ($ millions)
1	1	Nielsen	Northbrook, IL.	(708) 498-6300	$1,200.0‡	9.0%‡	$708.0‡	59.0%‡
2	2	IMS International, Inc.	New York, NY	(212) 371-2310	509.0‡	14.0%‡	330.1‡	65.0%‡
3	4	Information Resources Inc.	Chicago, IL.	(312) 726-1221	207.7	24.6%‡	23.9	11.5%
4	3	The Arbitron Co.	New York, NY	(212) 887-1300	187.8‡	—		
5	5	Westat, Inc.	Rockville, MD.	(301) 251-1500	87.2	17.0%		
6	7	Maritz Marketing Research Inc.	St. Louis, MO	(314) 827-1610	59.6	12.0%		
7	6	The M/A/R/C Group	Las Colinas, TX	(214) 506-3400	56.1	-1.4%		
8	11	The NPD Group	Port Washington, NY	(516) 625-0700	48.8	20.5%	11.7	24.0%
9	8	NFO Research Inc.	Greenwich, CT	(203) 629-8888	45.6	-1.3%		
10	14	Walsh America/PMSI	Scottsdale AZ	(602) 391-4600	44.0	32.1%		
11	10	Elrick & Lavidge Inc.	New York, N.Y.	(212) 682-1221	43.8	1.3%		
12	12	Market Facts Inc.	Arlington Heights, IL	(708) 590-7000	40.7	1.2%		
13	9	MBR Group Ltd.	London, England	(44-81) 579-5500	37.3	-8.0%		
14	13	Walker Group	Indianapolis, IN	(317) 843-3939	32.5	9.8%	1.6	4.9%
15	—	MAI U.S. Information Group	Livingston, NJ	(201) 716-0500	32.3	2.5%		
16	16	Intersearch Group	Horsham, PA	(215) 657-6400	28.3	12.8%		
17	15	Burke Marketing Research	Cincinnati, OH	(513) 684-7500	25.5	1.0%	0.6	2.3%
18	20	The National Research Group Inc.	Los Angeles, CA	(213) 856-4400	25.0	13.6%	3.8	15.0%
19	18	Chilton Research Services	Radnor, PA	(215) 964-4660	23.5	4.0%		
20	21	Louis Harris and Associates Inc.	New York, NY	(212) 689-9600	22.8	4.6%	13.7	60.0%
21	19	The BASES Group	Covington, KY	(606) 655-6000	22.7	15.8%	1.1	5.0%
22	27	Abt Associates Inc.	Cambridge, MA	(617) 492-7100	22.5	46.1%		
23	22	Research International Ltd.	London, England	(44-71) 235-1588	21.2	6.5%	4.2	19.8%
24	17	Starch INRA Hooper, Inc.	Mamaroneck, NY	(914) 698-0800	21.1	-7.0%		
25	24	Millward Brown Inc.	Naperville, IL	(708) 505-0066	19.7	11.4%		
26	30	J.D. Power & Associates	Agoura Hills, CA	(818) 889-6300	18.0	29.5%		
27	23	ASI Market Research Inc.	New York, NY	(212) 807-9393	17.1	-13.2%		
28	26	M.O.R.-PACE	Farmington Hills, MI	(313) 737-5300	16.2	1.3%	1.0	6.0%
29	29	Creative & Response Research Svcs.	Chicago, IL	(312) 828-9200	15.1	4.2%		

Rank	Prev.	Company	Location	Phone	Revenue ($ mil.)	Growth⁺		
30	31	Custom Research Inc.	Minneapolis, MN	(612)542-0800	$ 14.9	11.2%		
31	32	National Analysts	Philadelphia, PA	(215)496-6800	14.5%	9.1%		
32	33	Decision Research Corp.	Lexington, MA	(617)861-7350	14.0	8.0%		
33	35	Data Development Corp.	New York, NY	(212)633-1100	13.1	9.2%		
34	36	Total Research Corp.	Princeton, NJ	(609)520-9100	12.2	16.3%	$ 2.4	20.0%
35	—	Strategic Research & Consulting	Maumee, OH	(419)893-0029	12.2	14.0%		
36	37	Lieberman Research West Inc.	Los Angeles, CA	(310)553-0550	10.8	10.1%		
37	34	The Wirthlin Group	McLean, VA	(703)556-0001	9.9	-22.7%	0.2	1.0%
38	38	Conway/Milliken & Associates	Chicago, IL	(312)787-4060	9.9	7.6%		
39	49	The Vandervee Group, Inc.	Fort Washington, PA	(215)616-7200	9.2	39.4%		
40	41	Guideline Research Corp.	New York, NY	(212)947-5140	9.2	15.0%		
41	39	Response Analysis Corp.	Princeton, NJ	(609) 921-1333	8.8	4.0%		
42	40	ICR Survey Research Group	Media, PA	(215)565-9280	8.6	1.4%		
43	43	McCollum/Spielman Worldwide	Great Neck, N.Y.	(516)482-0310	8.4	10.5%	0.3	4.0%
44	48	Field Research Corp.	San Francisco, CA	(415)392-5763	8.4	23.5%		
45	42	Newman-Stein Inc.	New York, NY	(212)777-2700	8.0	1.3%		
46	—	Market Strategies Inc.	Southfield, MI	(313)261-9550	7.3	6.4%		
47	44	Research Data Analysis Inc.	Bloomfield Hills, MI	(313)332-5000	6.8	-4.2%		
48	—	Nordhaus Research Inc.	Southfield, MI	(313)827-2400	6.8	11.5%		
49	47	CTL Research Associates Inc.	New York, NY	(212)779-1990	6.7	-1.5%		
50	—	FRC Research Corp.	New York, NY	(212)696-0870	6.5	-1.3%		
		Subtotal, top 50 §			3,137.3	9.7%	1102.6	35.1%
		All other (103 CASRO member companies not included in top 50) §			295.6	1.7%		
		Total (153 organizations)			3,432.9	0.0		

*Total revenues that include nonresearch activities for some companies are significantly higher.

⁺Rate of growth from year to year has been adjusted so as not to include revenue gains from acquisition.

‡Estimate.

§Total revenues of 103 survey research firms—over and beyond those listed in top 50 list—that provide financial information, on a confidential basis, to the Council of American Survey Research Organizations (CASRO).

Source: Council of American Survey Research Organizations (CASRO). Reprinted with permission.

own field services, especially in the areas of central-location telephone interviewing and mall-intercept personal interviewing.

Facilitating External Parties

Marketing research suppliers and ad agencies subcontract with a number of other types of companies who perform many of the activities necessary to implement and complete a marketing research study. These companies facilitate the research function. Among the more important facilitators are (1) field services, (2) tabulation houses, and (3) independent consultants.

TAB HOUSE
A marketing research company that specializes in tabulating and analyzing marketing research data.

Tabulation houses.   **Tab (tabulation) houses** are firms dedicated to statistical analysis and computation. Tab houses are responsible for ensuring that the data collected are coded properly and can be transferred onto magnetic tape or diskette. They also provide specialized programming assistance and have libraries of statistical software programs for performing statistical analysis and generating cross-tabulations of data. Selection of a tab house is based primarily on cost and turnaround. The marketing research supplier selected to execute the research generally decides on which tab house to use.

INDEPENDENT CONSULTANTS
Individuals with specialized skills that assist marketing research companies on specific projects.

Independent consultants.   **Independent consultants** are individuals with unique and specialized marketing research skills. The sponsoring firm or the marketing research supplier hires independent consultants to assist them on specific research projects. These marketing research professionals could be academicians from universities or business schools.

Current Trends

Some restructuring of the industry is changing established practices. On the corporate side, mergers and acquisitions coupled with the impact of new technologies, especially in the area of syndicated services, have created considerable turmoil. The trend has also been away from large advertising

Coding the questionnaire

Using computer terminals for direct data entry

marketing research departments. Agency marketing research departments have been downsized, and fewer resources are being devoted to supporting marketing research activities.[4] Agency marketing researchers more and more service their own creative groups' needs rather than their clients' needs. Finally, on the supplier side, there seems to be a growing distinction between marketing research suppliers that provide custom research services and those providing technology-based market information systems.

SUMMARY

We introduced several concepts basic to marketing research. Our main focus was that marketing research provides information that helps the marketing manager and product engineer to think explicitly about who their customers are and what product features are most important. The formal definition of marketing research that we used emphasizes that marketing research links the consumer and marketer through information. We outlined the environment in which marketing research takes place and the principal parties that conduct marketing research activities.

KEY CONCEPTS

Marketing Research

Marketing Research Activities

End Benefits

Marketing Research Suppliers

Standardized Research Services

Customized Research Services

Syndicated Data Companies

Tab Houses

Advertising Agencies

Local Field Services

Consultants

REVIEW QUESTIONS

1. Describe the set of end benefits relevant to a student who is considering the following purchase decisions:
   a. Purchasing a PC for college use.
   b. Choosing a vacation site for spring break.
   c. Renting an apartment for the school year.
   Relate each end benefit identified to one or more product features.

2. In explaining why large firms with experienced managers often "miss the boat" on new opportunities, former General Electric executive John B. McKitterick made the following comment:

   So the principal task of management function in following the marketing concept is not so much to be skillful in making the customer do what suits the interests of the business as to be skillful in conceiving and then making the business do what suits the interests of the customer.[5]

   The sentiments voiced by Mr. McKitterick embody what has been labeled the *marketing concept*. Discuss how marketing research relates to the marketing concept.

3. If companies have in-house marketing research departments, how can they justify going outside to hire marketing research expertise?

4. List the primary functions of each of the internal and external parties involved in the marketing research function.

ENDNOTES

1. The preceding scenario and the discussion that follows come from the work of John Hauser and Robert Klein, "Without Good Research, Quality Is a Shot in the Dark," *Marketing News 22* (January 4, 1988), pp. 1–2.

2. "AMA Board Approves New Marketing Definition," *Marketing News* (March 1, 1985), pp. 1, 14.

3. Adapted from Robert S. Duboff, "Bottom Line Marketing," *Mercer Management Quarterly* vol. VIII, no. 1 (Spring 1992), pp. 5–7.

4. William D. Neal, "Researchers Can Have a Say in Their Destiny," *Marketing News,* November 4, 1990, p. 4.

5. John B. McKitterick, "What Is the Marketing Concept?" *The Frontiers of Marketing Thought and Action,* American Marketing Association (Chicago: 1957), pp. 71–82.

The Marketing Research Planning Process

NOVEL MICROWAVE DINNERS ARE TASTY—AND LIKELY TO FAIL WITHOUT A QUICK FIX

Most of the thousands of food products introduced this year will flop. Many deserve to. They're misconceived, poorly marketed, me-too items that offer consumers little new.

Every so often, though, one emerges that's innovative and tastes better than the competition. And even then, the chances of survival are slim.

Hidden Valley frozen microwave entrees seem to be such a product. Slipped into test markets early this year by HVR Co., a unit of Clorox Co., the food takes novel advantage of microwave oven technology. Instead of simply thawing and reheating precooked fare, Hidden Valley turns the appliance into a steamer. Consumers must add water—a paper measuring cup is included—but the result is crisp vegetables, al dente pasta, tasty meats, and flavorful sauces. Moreover, cooking time is shortened.

Yet the line is limping along in test markets and seems unlikely to make it without changes. "None of them is setting the world on fire," says Ed Snaza, head buyer at Country Club Markets in suburban Minneapolis. "They're slow," agrees Tim Heyman, head grocery perishable buyer for Wetterau, Inc.'s Pittsburgh division. Hidden Valley's other test markets are Indianapolis and Ft. Wayne,

Indiana, where grocers report mixed results.

The tale of why this promising product is going awry could be textbook material for marketers everywhere. Consider:

Wrong Category. Few areas are as crowded, or costly to enter, as frozen foods. Spurred by the microwave-cooking phenomenon, heat-and-eat foods quickly became a $4 billion-a-year market, although it seems to be slowing; tonnage grew only 4 percent last year, the National Frozen Food Association says.

"There's too much new stuff coming out," says Doug Kleven, explaining why the Lunds, Inc., store he manages in Minneapolis's lake district carries only three of Hidden Valley's 10 entrees. Besides the usual array of meat-and-macaroni dishes, the store's freezers are packed with exotic eating alternatives, from Howlin' Coyote black bean chili to Vietnamese egg rolls.

Wrong Product. Growth in frozen foods is in the low-fat, low-calorie end, as illustrated by the impressive debut of ConAgra's Healthy Choice line. "Anything that has 'light' on it seems to do very well," says Roger Robbe, corporate director of frozen foods and dairy for Super Valu Stores, Inc., a big Minnesota-based food distributor.

But while Kraft recently augmented its frozen lineup with Eating Right lower-calorie entrees, Hidden Valley opted for flavor. Several of its entrees even contain butter. Its macaroni and cheese, which comes with cubes of cheddar, contains 572 calories; the lowest-calorie item is seafood scampi, at 310 calories, and grocers say it's the most popular. By comparison, Healthy Choice entrees top out at 280 calories.

Wrong Turf. Frozen meals are a veritable Muscle Beach patrolled by four giants: ConAgra, the Kraft General Foods unit of Philip Morris Cos., Nestle S.A.'s Stouffer unit, and Campbell Soup Co. They leave little room for interlopers.

A recent survey of Minneapolis and St. Paul supermarkets found graphic evidence of that. Often the Hidden Valley line was lost amid rows of Big Four fare. Of the 350 frozen-food shelves in one Rainbow Foods store in St. Paul, Hidden Valley had just two. Stouffer, on the other hand, had 28, ConAgra 25, Campbell 24, and Kraft 19.

Wrong Brand Name. For most people Hidden Valley means salad dressing mixes, not frozen foods. Moreover, the competition vastly outspends Hidden

Valley to build brand identity. (The Clorox name doesn't appear anywhere on the entrees' packages.)

Wrong Packaging. Alongside its competition, Hidden Valley's package appears to be smaller and to contain less food. Grocery-trade sources say the size was partly intended to make better use of limited freezer space, and Hidden Valley officials say the package size and shape are vital to the steaming technology. Still, Mr. Heyman of Wetterau thinks the package is deterring sales. Also, because consumers add 2.5 ounces of water to each package, the pre-steamed weight on the label is less than its rivals' weight.

Wrong Advantage. Shopping pulse taker Mona Doyle, president of Consumer Network, Inc., applauds Hidden Valley's use of steam cooking as a "right-on approach" that should attract buyers. But she worries that requiring consumers to add water and stir the cooked ingredients may be asking too much.

"This doesn't sound like it's totally mindless," she says. "If they're otherwise engaged and tired, people wouldn't want to bring very much to it."

Despite the hurdles, Hidden Valley entrees may still make it. Wetterau's Mr. Heyman says the company recently held a "brainstorming" session about what it should do. (He suggested reshaping the package and cutting the price.) Once the consumer gets the product home, "she'll understand it's a good value," he believes.

Source: Richard Gibson, *The Wall Street Journal,* July 12, 1991, p. B1. Reprinted by permission of *THE WALL STREET JOURNAL,* © 1991 Dow Jones & Company, Inc. All Rights Reserved Worldwide.

INTRODUCTION

Unfortunately, even novel products may not succeed. In the case of Hidden Valley's line of frozen foods it appears that consumers have not been convinced of the benefits of the new steaming technology. A legitimate question to ask: How could Hidden Valley have been so wrong in evaluating consumer reactions to their new frozen food line? Undoubtedly, this line of frozen food products was subjected to consumer testing. Poorly formulated research, however, could conceivably provide an explanation. For example, the research conducted by Hidden Valley may have concentrated on the effects of the new steaming technology, which produces tastier dinners, to the exclusion of other product features (e.g., calories, size, and convenience of preparation) that consumers apparently evaluate less favorably.

Previous success in rolling out new products is also not a guarantee of future successes. Take, for example, the case of 7UP Gold.[1] The Seven Up Co. had been very successful with the launch of Cherry 7UP. So in 1988 the Seven Up Co. management team decided to launch another new variety, 7UP Gold. Unfortunately, the Seven Up Co.'s sure-fire strategy (see Box 2–1) wasn't so sure-fire afterall, and this product has been written off by the company. The image problems of 7UP Gold should have been identified long before the product was rolled out. Apparently, the research conducted by the Seven Up Co. concentrated on taste alone, ignoring the fit of this product with the parent brand. The research conducted by the Seven Up Co. undoubtedly indicated that 7UP Gold had a taste that people liked but failed to investigate whether people could understand the total concept of a brownish-colored, caffeinated 7UP variety. Here again, the research problem was poorly formulated.

Successful products come about from understanding consumer decision making and through careful planning based on solid research. This chapter discusses both these issues with particular emphasis on developing the stages in planning a marketing research study. Because every marketing

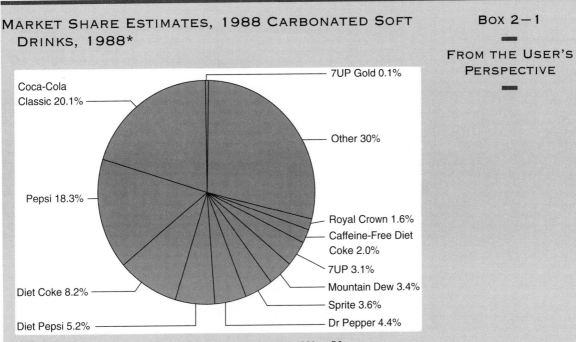

MARKET SHARE ESTIMATES, 1988 CARBONATED SOFT DRINKS, 1988*

BOX 2—1

FROM THE USER'S PERSPECTIVE

7UP Gold 0.1%
Coca-Cola Classic 20.1%
Other 30%
Pepsi 18.3%
Royal Crown 1.6%
Caffeine-Free Diet Coke 2.0%
7UP 3.1%
Mountain Dew 3.4%
Sprite 3.6%
Diet Coke 8.2%
Dr Pepper 4.4%
Diet Pepsi 5.2%

Source: Maxwell Consumer Reports, *New York Times*, February 11, 1989, p. B6.

Filled with optimism after their success in rolling out Cherry 7UP, the Seven-Up Co.'s management decided to roll out another new product, 7UP Gold, in the spring of 1988. Seven-Up's executives, along with Seven-Up's bottlers and distributors, thought they would have another hit because they followed what seemed to them a sure-fire strategy: Test the flavor to make sure people like it; sell it under the brand name of an established brand; and back it with $10 million in advertising.

Unfortunately, for Seven-Up, this strategy didn't work. Since its introduction, 7UP Gold has captured only one tenth of 1 percent of the market, and it has been written off by the company.

What was the reason for this failure? Probably several factors. First, the company that established its product as the "Un-Cola" gave 7UP Gold a brownish hue. Second, in contrast to its advertising, which emphasized the end benefit of a caffeine-free beverage, 7UP Gold did contain caffeine. Finally, partly because of the success of Cherry 7UP, the company rolled out 7UP Gold without extensive test marketing.

The general consensus among Seven-Up executives, bottlers, and distributors is that 7UP Gold was simply misunderstood by consumers. Consumers perceive 7UP products as clear, clean, and crisp beverages that have no caffeine. The name Gold was selected because of its connotation of high quality; in addition, 7UP Gold had a distinctive flavor that tasted like ginger ale with a cinnamon-apple overtone and a caffeine kick, a situation that is similar to Dr. Pepper and Mountain Dew which do not fit into an established category, and it needed a name that did not attempt to define the taste. Unfortunately, a dark-colored, caffeinated 7UP did not fit the usual 7UP image, and it was something consumers could not understand.

*This discussion is based on D. C. McGill, "7UP Gold: The Failure of a Can't-Lose Plan," Copyright ©1989 by The New York Times Company. Reprinted by permission.

EXHIBIT 2—1
The Research Process

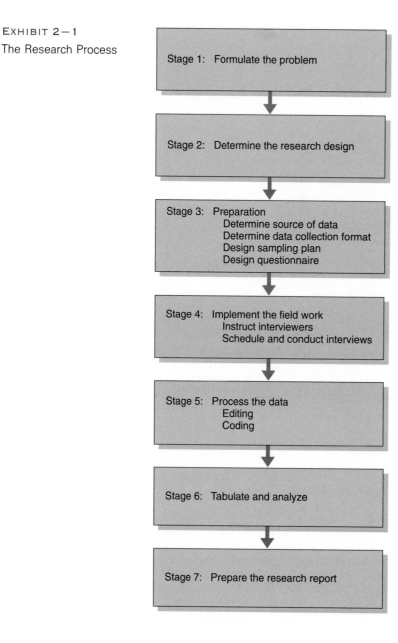

Stage 1:   Formulate the problem

Stage 2:   Determine the research design

Stage 3:   Preparation
                Determine source of data
                Determine data collection format
                Design sampling plan
                Design questionnaire

Stage 4:   Implement the field work
                Instruct interviewers
                Schedule and conduct interviews

Stage 5:   Process the data
                Editing
                Coding

Stage 6:   Tabulate and analyze

Stage 7:   Prepare the research report

RESEARCH PROCESS

Sequence of stages that provides a general framework to follow when implementing a marketing research study.

research problem is in some way unique, the steps undertaken in planning a particular research study will vary. However, there is a sequence of stages called the **research process** that provides a general framework to follow when designing and implementing a research study (see Exhibit 2–1). The remainder of this chapter is devoted to overviewing this process. The chapter concludes with a discussion of marketing research proposals and illustrates how firms may request competitive bids from suppliers for conducting specific types of studies.

STAGE 1: FORMULATE THE PROBLEM

The research problem can come about from a desire to either (1) solve a current problem (e.g., decreasing market share), or (2) pursue an opportunity (e.g., the growth of convenience-oriented microwavable products). Precise definition of the problem aids in understanding the information that will be needed and helps in formulating research objectives. If the problem is well formulated and the objectives of the research are precisely defined, then the likelihood of designing a research study that will provide the necessary information in an efficient manner is greatly increased. The end result of **problem formulation** should be a precise statement of the objectives of the research to be conducted and a set of research questions.

There are two fundamental components in formulating a problem. The first is the **research objective.** Ideally, this is a short, perhaps even a single sentence, description of the purpose of the marketing research effort, which provides the focus of everything that is to follow. The second component is made up of a set of **research questions** that immediately flow from the research objective and which will be answered by the research to be conducted. It is important to emphasize that symptoms of the problem (e.g., declining sales) should not be confused with what the problem actually is (i.e., the reasons why sales are declining).

Research objectives and questions evolve from a process of give and take by the marketing researcher and the client/decision maker. It is important to understand the relationships between these two parties.

PROBLEM FORMULATION

A precise statement of the objectives of the research to be conducted.

RESEARCH OBJECTIVE

A short description of the marketing research effort that provides the focus of the marketing research activities to follow.

RESEARCH QUESTIONS

A list of questions that follows from the research objective that will be answered by the study.

Researcher and Client

To accurately formulate the problem, marketing researchers must understand their role and relationships to their client. Of course, there must be good communication between the researcher and the client. To understand the nature of the decisions managers face and what they hope to learn from the research is essential. However, to properly diagnose the problem, the researcher cannot solely rely on the information provided by the client, since the client may tend to be myopic, may misunderstand or misinterpret the situation, and may not disclose all relevant information.

> The marketing researcher, like the doctor, is responsible for an accurate diagnosis. Again like the doctor, the marketing researcher cannot fulfill his [her] responsibility without some help from the client. It is with respect to this issue that one of the most frequent and crucial errors made in marketing research occurs. When the research director allows the project to be based on the client's request for specific information he [she] not only allows the client to diagnose the cause of the problem but to specify a prescription for the cure as well. The doctor's responsibility is to cure the patient; the marketing researcher's responsibility is to solve the client's problem. In each case the cure may or may not have any relationship to the information presented by the patient.[2]

The situation is somewhat complicated by the fact that generally the client controls the research budget. Political conflicts are, unfortunately, a reality of the workplace. The marketing researcher must fight against do-ing "politically correct" research and research designed to justify decisions or programs that have been previously implemented.

It is often useful to ask the client for a tentative problem definition statement. If the client has difficulty in formulating a tentative problem definition statement, the marketing researcher can assist the process by asking questions: What is the basic problem here? Why do you feel that a research study should be implemented? In many instances the tentative problem statement may be too broad for a single study; for example, how can profitability be improved? Of course, problems that are broadly framed can be attacked through a series of marketing research projects. In any event, the tentative problem definition statement and the information provided by clients are only the first step in formulating the problem.

Once a tentative problem definition statement has been framed, the marketing researcher would—as a first step—ask more detailed questions of the client/decision maker. Such questions could include the following categories:

1. Available knowledge—What do we know?
2. Anticipated actions—How will the results of this study be used?
3. Alternative scenarios—If the results indicate outcome X as opposed to outcome Y, how will this influence your decision?
4. Actionable information—What type of information will allow you to take action?

Exhibit 2–2 presents two examples of how the research objective and the set of research questions can be framed in particular problem settings. In problem setting A, the research questions recognize the competitive aspects of the category. At issue is not only the likely volume and market share of the new product but also its effects on existing products. The research questions also consider the questions of whether the market is segmented with respect to consumer preferences and end benefits sought. Similarly, in problem setting B, the research questions recognize that per-ceptions of service delivery can vary by the meal occasion.

From Exhibit 2–2 we see that research questions are often posed in terms of hypotheses. For example, is speed of delivery or price more important in the decision to use an overnight carrier? In essence, relevant forms of research questions include: Who . . .?, What . . .?, Why . . .?, When . . .?, Where . . .?, and How . . .? These types of questions can be put into perspective through situation analysis.

Situation Analysis

SITUATION ANALYSIS
Taking stock of where a company has been, where it is now, and where it is likely to end up following current plans.

The essence of **situation analysis** is taking stock of where you've been, where you are, and where you are likely to end up, if you follow existing plans and if current trends continue. The organization's past and current marketing programs, the state of the market and current competition, and consumer reaction to these factors all play a vital role in helping the re-searcher and manager both recognize potential opportunities and problems and develop appropriate new strategies. Situation analysis involves scan-

---

Problem Setting A: A Consumer Package Goods Firm

Project:	A major package goods firm is deciding on whether to continue development of a new "hard candy" product. The new product is a line extension offering a distinctive new ingredient which should be attractive to at least some category users. Brand managers want to collect information on the likely success of the new product.
Research Objective:	To determine the likely market success of a new "hard candy" product containing ingredient X and its relation to existing products.
Possible Research Questions:	1. What volume and market share will the new product achieve when it is rolled out nationally? 2. What trial rate can be expected? 3. Will the new product cannibalize existing products in our line? 4. Which existing products does the new product draw its share from? 5. Are there segments of consumers who have a greater likelihood of trying the new product? 6. Are there segments of consumers who are particularly attracted to the new ingredient?

Problem Setting B: A Fast Food Chain

Project:	The corporate management of a national fast food chain wanted to determine whether customer perceptions of service are uniform across their franchises. The parent corporation has followed a policy of minimizing variation in services provided. The intent of management is to assess whether customer perceptions of services is consistent with corporate standards.
Research Objective:	To evaluate customers' perceptions of the services provided by franchise operators and to identify areas that need attention.
Possible Research Questions:	1. What is the relevant set of service features that franchises should be evaluated on? 2. What is the perceived value of each service feature? 3. Do perceptions of services vary by meal? 4. Does the value of a service feature vary by meal? 5. Are there regional differences across franchises in terms of services provided? 6. What factors contribute to any differences that are observed?

---

ning (1) the general environment, (2) the firm's product markets, (3) the firm's customers, and (4) the firm's marketing programs.

The general environment. The first step in situation analysis is to understand the environment. The environment includes the general state of the economy, the economic situation of the industry, and the condition of the company in that industry. Industries and particular sectors of the economy face different economic conditions. Take, for example, the automobile industry. Though U.S. auto sales were growing in the latter half of the last decade, this period was also marked by increased competitive pressure from Japanese automobile manufacturers.

A comparative analysis of the position of a company within its industry can often be revealing. Consider the situation of the Pontiac Division of General Motors in the early 1980s.[3] In 1968 the GTO was named *Motor Trend's* "Car of the Year," and Pontiac's sales reached an all-time high. However, by 1981 Pontiac had fallen to fifth position in U.S. industry sales.

Product markets.   Understanding competitive product markets is perhaps the most fundamental issue facing a firm. Assessing the strengths and weaknesses of the array of competing products in the markets that a firm serves is an important step in clarifying the problem.

Product markets need to be understood in terms of some basic and fundamental indicators. Among other things, the product markets that a firm serves should be evaluated in terms of (1) product types, varieties, and brands; (2) sales volume and trends; (3) growth rate; (4) market share; (5) competitive vulnerability; and (6) rate of return on investment.

Exhibit 2–3 shows a spatial representation of the product market in which Pontiac is competing. Spatial representations of this kind are called **perceptual product maps.** The map shows two dimensions, represented by the X-axis and the Y-axis, labeled according to how customers evaluate the automobile types in the market—in this case, conservative/family-oriented versus expensive, sporty-oriented and high price/upscale luxurious versus low price/practical. Perceptual maps let us see the relative positions of a set of brands, in this case automobile types, on a set of evaluative dimensions that describe the perceptions that people hold. Pontiac's success in the 1960s rested on the youthful sports car market. In assessing Pontiac's product line in 1981, Pontiac executives concluded that the once-successful image of sporty, youthful vehicles had been abandoned. The arrow in the exhibit indicates where in this perceptual space Pontiac would like to be positioned. From this perceptual map, Pontiac executives concluded that by 1981 people were relatively neutral and just didn't get excited about Pontiac products.

Customer markets.   In addition to its product markets, a firm must also understand the customers that it currently serves as well as the customers that it wishes to serve. *Customer markets* refer to subgroups of customers that desire the same set of end benefits in the products they purchase.

Evaluating a firm's customer markets amounts to doing a sort of customer audit. Among other things, this means that customer markets should be evaluated in terms of (1) demographic factors, for example, age, gender, income, and education; (2) lifestyle patterns, for example, interests, opinions, and activities; (3) usage patterns and behaviors, for example, what products are being used, who is using the product, in what usage contexts, and frequency of use; (4) preferences for specific end benefits (for example, what is more important, price or quality); and (5) price sensitivity (for example, how deal-prone our customers are).

By 1981 Pontiac executives had a clear understanding of their current customer markets. Pontiac's product line had attracted an older customer, a segment accounting for under 20 percent of all new car sales. From its product market assessment, Pontiac executives knew that regaining the sporty youthful image that had made the division successful in the 1960s meant placing new emphasis on segments of the population that desired performance and handling ability in the design and manufacture of their vehicles. In contrast to its current customer base, Pontiac executives decided to concentrate on a relatively younger, better-educated, and higher-income segment of the population. This target group was between 25 and 44 years old and as of 1981 had a median household income of $32,000.

PERCEPTUAL PRODUCT MAPS

Graphical diagrams showing consumers perceptions of products or services.

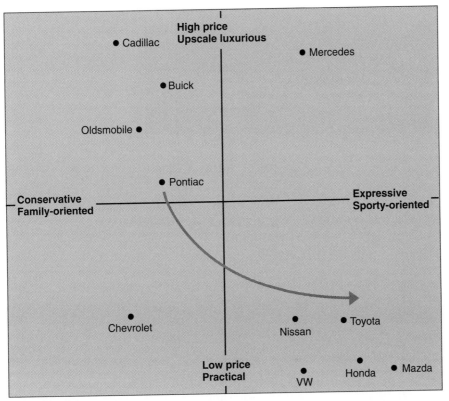

EXHIBIT 2—3

Pontiac Division:
Perceptual Map, 1981

Source: Peter Langenhorst, "Pontiac Division of General Motors (A)," The Colgate Darden Graduate School of Business Administration, University of Virginia, 1987.

Marketing programs. Situation analysis of marketing programs should include assessment of a variety of past and current strategic elements. Among other things, (1) advertising and promotional programs; (2) pricing practices; and (3) relationships with dealers, wholesalers, and retailers should be evaluated.

Pontiac executives knew by 1981 that they would have to reshape their marketing programs. Their assessment was that current marketing programs simply confused both consumers and dealers about the positioning of and end benefits offered by the Pontiac product line. Through understanding their product and customer markets and the types of marketing programs currently in place, Pontiac researchers were able to design a program of research studies aimed at turning Pontiac sales around through positioning Pontiac products as expressive and sporty (see the arrow in Exhibit 2–3). The various research projects completed by Pontiac led to many changes. In 1982 it introduced the redesigned Firebird, accompanied by a clear and consistent advertising campaign linking Pontiac to excitement and to the sporty, youthful image that buyers had previously associated with Pontiac. The overall strategy was to use image/specialty cars to sell its lower-priced models. Consistent with this strategy, in 1987 Pontiac redesigned one of its standard cars, the Bonneville, to fit the image of sporty, expressive vehicles. Today, the Bonneville is still linked to excitement (Exhibit 2–4).

STAGE 2: DETERMINE THE RESEARCH DESIGN

Having formulated the problem, the researcher must determine an appropriate research design. The choice of an appropriate research design will depend on (1) the value of the information provided by alternative courses of action and (2) the requirements of the research objective and research questions.

Valuing Alternative Courses of Action

As part of determining the appropriate research design the researcher must identify alternative courses of action and evaluate the information that each alternative course of action would provide. Faced with a particular research question, there will likely be several different options that the researcher can follow. In addition to recognizing the options that are available, the researcher must be able to value the information provided in relation to the cost of obtaining it.

As an example, consider the decision to introduce a new product.[4] There are several research options available to the researcher. One option, of course, is to roll the new product out without extensive testing. However, as we have seen in the case of 7UP Gold, this can be extremely risky. The brand manager responsible for the new product may be considering the following two-phase approach:

— Phase 1. On the basis of a pretest market study, make a go/no-go decision concerning the new product on the basis of its estimated market share and/or volume.
— Phase 2. If the phase 1 decision is to go, then initiate a test-market study and use the volume projection to make a final decision as to whether the new product should be launched nationally.

The brand manager responsible for this new product presented this test strategy to the marketing researcher assigned to this category. Being experienced in test market studies, the researcher knew that considerable amounts of resources would be needed. Test market studies involve introducing the new product in selected geographical markets to evaluate sales; such studies typically cost millions of dollars. Similar to test market studies, pretest market studies are designed to weed out product failures prior to test marketing and are considerably less expensive than test market studies, because they do not involve actually introducing the product in specific geographical markets. The researcher also knew, however, that without test marketing programs the risk of product failure would be much greater.

The researcher thought that, if the various alternatives could in some way be valued, a more intelligent decision could be made concerning what test marketing programs to implement, if any. The researcher decided to do some detective work. Based on internal secondary data on previous new-product launches, the researcher learned that profits from new products having been subjected to both a pretest market and a test market study averaged about $28.5 million dollars. For new products that were launched without conducting a pretest market or a test market study, profits were considerably lower, averaging about $16.75 million dollars.

Based upon this information, the researcher concluded that the value of implementing both a pretest market and a test market study is approximately $11.75 million dollars.

$$\$28.5 - 16.75 = \$11.75$$

From previous new-product launches, the researcher also determined that profits for new products launched with only a pretest market study averaged about $20 million dollars. Comparing this profit level to those obtained without initiating any test marketing program, the researcher valued a pretest market study at $3.25 million dollars.

$$\$20.0 - 16.75 = \$3.25$$

For those new products launched solely on the basis of test market results (that is, without any pretest market study), profits averaged about $25.25 million dollars. Thus, the researcher valued the information provided by test market studies at $8.5 million dollars.

$$\$25.25 - 16.75 = \$8.5$$

Thus, the researcher concluded that the available evidence clearly supports initiating test marketing programs. However, the researcher wondered about the wisdom of conducting both types of tests: Should a test market study be initiated given that a pretest market study has already been performed? Yes, since the incremental profit contributed from conducting a test market study after a pretest market study has been performed is $5.25 million.

$$\$8.5 - 3.25 = \$5.25$$

This simple example illustrates how a researcher might handle a difficult and complex question. Remember, the purpose of marketing research is to provide managers with information that reduces their uncertainty about the outcomes of specific courses of action. Marketing research, however, involves the commitment of resources, both labor and dollars. The actual value of information depends on three factors: (1) the likelihood of making a correct decision on the basis of the information collected, (2) the relative profitability of the alternative decisions, and (3) the cost of acquiring the information.

Research Objective Requirements

As we discussed earlier, problem formulation is important because it determines the information that will be needed. Information needs determine the objectives of the research and, in large measure, what kind of research design is most appropriate. The way the problem is formulated with respect to the research objective and accompanying research questions places certain demands on the research design.

In certain instances, the research problem to be solved is rather broad or vague. In such cases, the research designs must be flexible to permit the researcher to exercise judgment concerning possible areas and tactics of investigation. For example, although the Campbell Soup Company has tried to convince consumers that "soup is good food," increasing numbers of consumers have been shunning canned soup because of its high sodium content. More frustrating, however, is the fact that Campbell has had a low-sodium line on the market for years, but consumers have been unmoved.[5] In addressing the problem of why low-sodium soups have not had greater market penetration, the marketing researcher will probably have to conduct research that will give some ideas about and insights into the problem. One way to proceed is to interview small groups of soup consumers to find out about their experiences with, and reactions to, low-sodium soups. When the researcher knows relatively little about the issue being investigated, *exploratory research designs* are most appropriate. **Exploratory research designs** provide the marketing researcher with ideas and insights about a broad or relatively vague problem. Such designs allow a more precise statement of the problem to be formulated, which in turn will allow causal or descriptive research designs to be used.

In certain instances, the research problem to be solved is more specific in the sense that the marketing researcher and client/decision maker are aware of those factors that may be contributing to the problem. In such instances, the research design must allow the researcher to focus on specific aspects of the product or on the relationship between those factors thought to be contributing to the problem. For example, having determined that soup consumers don't believe low-sodium soups are not much different from soups having normal sodium content, Campbell might initiate a study to develop demographic and lifestyle profiles of those people who are currently buying low-sodium and health-conscious products and their perceptions of the benefits offered by such products with particular emphasis on why a low-sodium appeal is more believable in certain product categories. When the researcher knows something about the problem being addressed, *descriptive research designs* are often employed. **Descriptive research designs** generally involve attempts to determine the frequency with which something happens or the extent to which two or more variables are related.

Finally, in certain instances, the research problem to be solved is clearly and specifically identified. In such instances, the research design must allow the researcher to assess the exact relationship between factors thought to contribute to the problem. For example, having determined that soup consumers are confused about what low sodium actually means, Campbell might initiate a study to determine which of two advertisements produce greater change in consumers' understanding of the benefits of specific levels of sodium and their perceptions of products with different sodium levels. The purpose of this study is to test the informational effect of the two advertisements with a view toward determining which advertisement is superior. When the researcher wants to test specific hypotheses about those factors thought to contribute to the problem being investigated, *causal research designs* are often employed. **Causal research designs** generally involve attempts to determine the extent to which changes in one variable cause changes in some other variable. Experimental designs, which are the subject of Chapter 8, are frequently used when the objective of the research is to assess cause-and-effect relationships among variables.

CAUSAL RESEARCH DESIGNS
Research designs that attempt to determine the extent to which changes in one variable cause changes in another variable.

STAGE 3: PREPARATION

The preparation stage of the research process entails a number of activities. The researcher must (1) identify who will supply the information (the source), (2) determine how the needed information will be obtained, (3) design the sampling plan, and (4) design the data collection instrument. All of these activities precede going into the field.

Determine Source of Data

The first question facing the researcher is whether the problem at hand will require *secondary data sources* or *primary data sources* of information.

Secondary data sources already exist and can be found in libraries or other public institutions. The government represents a large depository of information that can be accessed to solve marketing research problems. One government agency that recently updated its information is the Census Bureau, which completed the 1990 U.S. census. Another source of secondary information can be found within the firm itself. Accounting, sales, and other departments within the firm can provide valuable information that can be accessed to solve marketing research problems. Marketing research suppliers who offer syndicated services are also sources of secondary data. Chapters 4 and 5 provide additional details on sources of secondary data.

SECONDARY DATA SOURCES
Data that already exists and can be found in libraries or other public institutions or found within the firm itself.

More often than not, the research problem being investigated will require information that is not readily available, or if available, the information is not in a suitable form. In such instances, the researcher will have to collect the necessary information directly. **Primary data** are information that has been collected specifically for the research problem at hand. For example, though some kinds of secondary information, such as income and population changes, may be useful to the marketing researcher in attempting to forecast first-year volume for a new-product introduction, primary data on how well the new product will sell in specific geographical

PRIMARY DATA
Information collected specifically for the research problem at hand.

regions are necessary in order to accurately predict what first-year volume would be if the new product were rolled out nationally. The need to collect primary data brings with it a number of accompanying activities. Many of the remaining chapters are devoted to issues and practices surrounding primary data collection.

Determine Data Collection Method

If the decision is to collect primary data, then the researcher will need to determine the appropriate method of collecting the data. Primary data can be collected through such *qualitative interviewing techniques* as direct observation, in-depth interviews, or focus group interviews. Alternatively, the researcher can use *survey interviewing methods,* which usually involve the use of a structured questionnaire. Qualitative data collection methods are relatively unstructured forms of interviewing and generally involve small numbers of respondents. In contrast, more structured interviewing formats (e.g., having an individual fill out a questionnaire) are generally used in survey research involving larger numbers of respondents where the objectives of the research require that survey results be projectable to the wider population.

Design Sampling Plan

There are three basic steps in designing a sampling plan. First, the researcher must precisely define who should participate in the study. Second, the researcher must devise a method for identifying and reaching those eligible to participate in the study. And third, the researcher must determine how many respondents to include.

SAMPLE
Subset of a population to be studied.

The term **sample** is used to denote the particular subset of the population that has been selected to participate in the study. The sample can consist of individuals, households, firms, homeowners, doctors, weightlifters, or any other segment of the population. However, determining who is eligible to participate in the study at hand may not be as clear-cut as it might first appear.

Consider the case of a manufacturer of rug cleaning products who is contemplating marketing a new line of rug cleaning products designed specifically for households with dogs and cats. In designing a study, say, to investigate the viability of this concept, the researcher will have to decide the type of household to include in the sample. Should it be made up of households that have carpets? Or perhaps the sample should be restricted to households with carpets and a dog or cat, or to households with carpets and pets *and* who have had their carpets cleaned within the last 18 months. The decision as to which sample of households to include is determined by the objectives of the study; so again it is important that the problem be precisely defined.

The researcher must devise a way to identify those who are eligible to participate in a study. This can be accomplished in a variety of ways. For example, mailing lists or telephone directories are two vehicles for iden-

Personal interviews sometimes use a city-block map of houses to select a sample.

tifying and reaching sample prospects. The way in which the researcher goes about identifying the sample has important consequences for the representativeness of the information obtained. When mailing lists and telephone directories are used, for example, the sample selected may not be representative of the population as a whole, since only those individuals whose names appear in the mailing list or those whose phone numbers are listed in the directory can be included in the sample. A sampling plan is used to ensure that a *representative* sample of the target population is obtained. We discuss various sampling designs in Chapter 9.

The final step in designing the sampling plan is to determine the size of the sample, that is, how many individuals, households, institutions, and so on, to sample. The size of the sample is influenced by several factors.

Obviously, the amount of dollars allocated to the research study at hand plays an important role. The length of the interview and the type of interviewing method used also play a role since the cost of collecting data will be greater the longer the interview, with costs varying depending on whether a mail, telephone, or personal interview is used. Finally, the research objectives influence what size sample will be representative. Sampling issues are discussed in Chapters 9 and 10.

Design Questionnaire

The final activity before entering the field to collect the necessary information is to design the questionnaire. The form of the questionnaire depends on the decisions that have been made up to this point. The nature of the problem and the data collection method, along with the chosen sampling design, all influence how the questionnaire will be structured and the format of the questions asked. For example, a questionnaire can be administered with the aid of a computer, by means of the telephone, and with or without the presence of an interviewer. The target sample of respondents may be adults between the ages of 18 and 54, or children 12 years of age. Researchers must take into account these considerations, as well as others, when designing the questionnaire. Questionnaire design considerations are discussed in Chapter 11.

STAGE 4: IMPLEMENT THE FIELDWORK

Implementing and completing the fieldwork involves a number of activities. As we discussed in Chapter 1, local field service firms handle the day-to-day activities for collecting the data. These firms are hired by marketing research suppliers to collect the needed information. Usually, the marketing research supplier has a "field department" that is responsible for coordinating and overseeing the activities of the local field services being used. The following briefly describes some of the activities that are necessary in fielding a study. Additional details are presented in Chapter 13.

Instruct Interviewers

Before the data can be collected, the interviewers must be properly acquainted with various aspects of the study. Field instructions are prepared by the research supplier and sent to the local field services. These instructions generally provide details on how the questionnaire should be administered and often provide instructions on a question-by-question basis.

Schedule and Conduct Interviews

The field department also prepares another set of instructions, this time covering how the fieldwork should be organized and controlled. These instructions typically go to interviewing supervisors and, among other things, provide guidance concerning (1) how to screen respondents, (2) sample quotas, and (3) when and where the sample should be selected. For example, if the plan is to intercept individuals while they are shopping at local malls, the instructions would cover which malls are to be used, how many individuals are to be intercepted at each mall, and where in the mall prospective respondents are to be intercepted.

STAGE 5: PROCESS THE DATA

There are two necessary and important functions that must be performed before data collected in the field can be analyzed. These include (1) check-in and editing and (2) coding and transcription. The following briefly describes each of these functions. Further details will be presented in Chapter 13.

Editing

After a completed questionnaire is received from the field, it must be inspected to determine whether it is acceptable for use in the study. A number of problems can cause a completed questionnaire to be excluded, for example, (1) portions of the questionnaire, or key questions, may be

Scheduling interviews

left unanswered, (2) questions may have been answered improperly, or (3) the questionnaire may have been completed by someone who should have been excluded from participating.

The **editing** process involves reviewing completed questionnaires for maximum accuracy and precision. Response consistency and accuracy are the primary concerns. When two answers are inconsistent—for example, the respondent indicates no familiarity with the test brand, but also indicates that the brand was purchased on the last shopping trip—it may be possible to determine which, if either, of the responses is correct by examining other responses. When this is not possible, both answers are usually discarded.

With respect to accuracy, the person responsible for editing concentrates on signs of interviewer bias or cheating, for example, common patterns of responses across different questionnaires for the same interviewer. In addition to these concerns, editing is also concerned with (1) response legibility, (2) response clarity, and (3) response completeness.

EDITING
Refers to evaluating the accuracy and precision of the questionnaires.

Coding

Coding involves (1) assigning numerical values (codes) to represent a specific response to a specific question and (2) designating the location of all responses appearing in the data file. Assigning numerical codes to each answer provided by a respondent is necessary so that the data collected can be analyzed by a computer.

A data file contains the coded responses of all the respondents who have participated in the survey. For example, consider the following question.

Which of the following categories best describes your total household income before taxes in 1992?

CODING
Assigning numerical values to represent specific responses to specific questions.

Less than $10,000	1	⎫
$10,000–$14,999	2	⎬ Codes
$15,000–$24,999	3	⎪
$25,000 or more	4	⎭

In the data field, a response of "less than $10,000" would be represented by a "1." In order for a computer to be able to properly read the data, the computer must be told where in the data file each answer resides. This involves specifying the row and column position(s) of each question in the data file. Data files are stored on magnetic tape or disk. Details on coding questionnaires and related data file issues are discussed in Chapter 13.

STAGE 6: TABULATE AND ANALYZE

The penultimate phase of the research process involves what can generally be referred to as *tabulation and data analysis.* Here, interest centers on reporting and interpreting relationships among the key questions that respondents have answered. As we indicated in Chapter 1, a tabulation house is generally responsible for analyzing the data, although the marketing researcher and supplier bear the responsibility for interpretation.

TABULATION

Orderly arrangement of data in a table or other summary format.

One basic component of the analysis phase is the tabulation plan. A **tabulation** refers to the orderly arrangement of the data in a table or other summary format by counting the frequency of responses to each question. For example, the researcher may wish to tabulate responses to the question dealing with how many units of a brand have been purchased by each respondent by the income of the respondent. The researcher, in consultation with the supplier, generally specifies what tables will be run. Chapters 13 and 14 provide details on various aspects of tabulating the data.

In addition, the researcher may also wish to perform other types of analyses. These analyses would allow the researcher to form specific conclusions about the research problem at hand that cannot be easily gleaned from a simple tabulation of the data. For example, the researcher may wish to test specific hypotheses about the relationships among key variables. Statistical analysis procedures are discussed in Chapters 15 through 17.

STAGE 7: PREPARE THE RESEARCH REPORT

The results of marketing research must be effectively communicated to management. Presenting the results of a marketing research study to management generally involves a formal written research report as well as an oral presentation. Needless to say, the report and presentation are extremely important. First, they are important because the results of marketing research are often intangible. After the study has been completed and a decision is made, there is very little physical evidence of the resources such as time, money, and effort that went into the project. Thus, the written report and oral presentation represent one physical source of "documentation."

Second, and perhaps more important, the written report and oral presentation are typically the only aspects of a study that many marketing executives are exposed to. Consequently, the overall evaluation of the research project rests on how well this information is communicated.

Finally, the quality of the written report and oral presentation ultimately reflects favorably or unfavorably upon the research supplier who conducted the study and ultimately determines whether that particular supplier will be used in the future. Chapter 18 provides several suggestions and guidelines for preparing written reports and oral presentations. Some guidelines to consider are: (1) think of your audience, (2) be concise yet complete, and (3) understand the results and draw appropriate conclusions.

RESEARCH PROPOSALS

Two formal documents are used to summarize the marketing research planning process. The first is called a *request for proposal.* In response to the request for proposal, a formal *research proposal* is prepared.

RFPs

Requests for Proposals (RFPs) are written documents that formally invite marketing research suppliers to submit a formal research proposal describing how the research study should be conducted. RFPs are prepared by corporate marketing research departments. The usual practice is to distribute the RFP to suppliers that have been used by the firm in the past. RFPs should present pertinent information regarding (1) background of the marketing problem, (2) objectives of the research, (3) sample design considerations, (4) timing, and (5) selection criteria and criteria weights. Exhibit 2–5 presents a typical RFP.

RFPs
Documents inviting research suppliers to submit research proposals.

Rarely will the corporate marketing research department disclose the budget it has allocated to the project. However, the RFP should contain sufficient information to allow suppliers to set a reasonable price for conducting the study. Typically, given the objectives of the study and information on the sampling design, suppliers can accurately price the study.

The solicitation of research proposals should meet ethical standards regarding (1) proposal content, (2) conditions governing submission, and (3) ownership rights. The Council of American Survey Research Organizations (CASRO) has provided ethical guidelines for the solicitation of proposals (see Exhibit 2–6).

Finally, as mentioned above, the RFP should also include a statement concerning the criteria on which the various proposals will be evaluated, along with the weights associated with each criterion. For example, Exhibit 2–5 indicates that 30 percent of the evaluation will be based on the expertise of the supplier in conducting market studies, 25 percent on the comprehensiveness of the proposal's content, 30 percent on the technical competency of the proposal, and 15 percent on the cost component.

The Research Proposal

A **research proposal** is a formal written document that describes the marketing problem, the purpose of the study, and provides a somewhat detailed outline of the research methodology. The form and length of

RESEARCH PROPOSAL
Document that describes the marketing problem, the purpose of the study, and the research methodology.

EXHIBIT 2—5

Request for Proposal

Background:	Our low-salt and unsalted crackers now account for 7.2 percent of total cracker sales, providing $119.3 million in sales and 88.6 million pounds in volume in 1992. The low-salt and unsalted crackers vary in importance to the parent brand. Our established entry into the low-salt and unsalted category now accounts for 23 percent of total brand volume while our most recent entry accounts for 9 percent of total brand volume. However, with the recent success of our low-salt crackers, competitive entries have begun to appear.
	In order to continue to build our low-salt cracker business and to effectively defend these brands against new competitive entries, a better understanding of consumers' usage of low-salt and unsalted crackers and their attitudes is needed.
Objective:	The objective of this research is to better understand the overall dynamics (i.e., behavioral and attitudinal) of the low-salt/unsalted cracker market. More specifically, the research will help answer the following key marketing questions.

— What are the behavioral (purchase and usage) dynamics within the low salt/unsalted cracker market?
— What is the attitudinal framework for low-salt/unsalted products?
— What demographic and attitudinal factors are best associated with product usage?

Sampling Frame:	Minimum sample of 150 users (past 3 months) of each of the following low-salt/unsalted brands:

Krispy (unsalted tops).

Premium (both low-salt and unsalted tops).

Ritz.

Town House.

Wheat Thins.

Zesta (unsalted tops).

Timing Selection Criteria:	The study should be completed within 20 weeks of its starting point. Proposals submitted will be evaluated according to the following criteria:

Supplier skills/expertise	30
Comprehensiveness	25
Technical competency	30
Cost	15

research proposals vary greatly. Some research proposals are over 20 pages, and others are as short as a single page. Exhibit 2–7 presents a research proposal written in response to the RFP shown in Exhibit 2–5.

Though the exact form of the proposal is also variable, most research proposals contain the following elements.

Background and problem/opportunity definition. A research proposal should provide relevant background for the proposed study. Specifically, the proposal should precisely define the problem at hand. In the research proposal shown in Exhibit 2–7, for example, the background indicates that although the firm's low-salt and unsalted crackers have been successful, they are likely to face increasing competitive pressures in the near future.

A.   Proposal content.

Research firms that are asked to submit cost estimates should be given a complete set of specifications (written, if possible) covering the following items where applicable or known:

a. Tasks to be performed by the client and by the contractor.
b. Description of questionnaire (or questionnaires) by (1) number of questions, by type of question—i.e., open-ended, single response closed-end, multiple response closed-end, etc.; or (2) duration of interview in minutes plus number of open-ended questions.
c. Estimated incidence (percent) and description of incidence groups.
d. Sample design and universe.
e. Household selection/respondent selection.
f. Percent of data entry that will be verified.
g. Type of edit/clean utilized, i.e., clean to questionnaire versus machine clean.
h. Number of banners and banner points for tabulation.
i. Number of cross-tabs.
j. Total copies of reports and/or tabs.
k. Special hand-tabs required.

B.   Conditions governing submission of proposals.

Proposals are prepared in response to a client request, entirely at the expense of the research company.

These should be submitted to the requesting client only. If that client does not authorize the work, the proposal may be submitted to other prospective clients, unless so doing would reveal confidential information.

C.   Ownership rights related to proposals.

Absent a contrary agreement between the prospective contractor and the prospective client:

Proposals prepared at the expense of a prospective contractor.

a. Such proposals are the property of the company that prepared them, and they may not be used by a prospective client in any way to its benefit without the permission of the prospective contractor.
b. Any part of proposal content, including questions or a questionnaire (which is constructed by the prospective contractor), are the property of the research company that prepared them.
c. Proposals prepared wholly or in substantial part at the expense of a prospective client are the property of the company that has requested and paid for them, and they are considered to be "reports."

Source: CASRO. Used with permission.

EXHIBIT 2—6

CASRO's Ethical Standards for Solicitation of Proposals

In general, a useful starting point is to define why the research is being undertaken, what the study is designed to measure, and how the information will be used.

Objectives.   A research proposal should provide a clear explanation of the study's objectives and value. For example, in the research proposal shown in Exhibit 2–7, the stated objectives are to investigate consumers' usage of and attitudes toward low-salt and unsalted crackers.

Research method.   Choice of the appropriate research methodology involves important and interdependent decisions. Major decisions include:

— Selection of the sample—who and how many respondents to include.

— Selection of the data collection method—whether to use primary or secondary data; whether to conduct mail, telephone, or personal interviews.

EXHIBIT 2—7

Marketing Research
Project Proposal

Category:	Low-salt crackers
Project:	Market study
Objectives:	In order to continue to build low-salt/unsalted cracker business and to effectively defend these brands against new competitive entries, a better understanding of consumers' usage of low-salt/unsalted crackers and their attitudes toward low-salt/unsalted crackers is needed.
Research Method:	A two-phase research study (screening and follow-up) will be conducted among households who are members of the supplier's mail panel.
Screening Phase:	In order to address the marketing questions outlined above, it will be necessary to obtain a basic sample of low-salt/unsalted cracker users and readable samples (N = 150 in follow-up phase) for each of the brands of interest.
Sampling Frame:	Screening questionnaires will be mailed to a nationally balanced sample of 36,000 panel member households. Within each household, men and women, age 18 or older, will complete the questionnaire. Returns are expected from 25,200 individuals, which is a response rate of 70 percent. A random sample of 2,000 of these respondents will be fully processed in the second phase of the study.
Follow-Up Phase:	In the follow-up phase, an extensive self-administered survey will be mailed to individuals having certain characteristics (i.e., category/specific brand usage) as identified in the screening phase.
Analysis:	Analysis will include standard cross-tabular analyses plus a number of multivariate statistical techniques (specifically a segmentation analysis) in order to help answer key research questions. For example, 1. What is the underlying need structure within the low-salt cracker market? 2. How is the market segmented in terms of usage dynamics? 3. What are the (particular brand's) strengths and weaknesses among its franchise?
Action Standard:	Not applicable.
Cost:	The cost for conducting the study as specified within this proposal will be $121,500 ± 10% ($28,500 for screener and $93,000 for follow-up). This cost includes sample selection, questionnaire production, first-class postage (out and back), reminder postcards (follow-up study only), respondent incentives (follow-up study only), data processing (up to 12 cards and 6 open ends), four banners of tabulations at the follow-up phase, all necessary multivariate statistical analyses, and one presentation or report.
Timing:	Scheduling for the study will be as follows:

	Weeks Elapsed (from start of field, August 3)
Screeners returned	4
Phase I data available	7
Phase II commences	8
Phase II data collection ends	12
Phase II data available	16
Draft presentation available	20

— Evaluation of the design—how the research methodology being proposed is going to be implemented and how it will meet the objectives of the study.

In Exhibit 2–7 the proposed research design methodology involves a two-phase screening and follow-up procedure that utilizes the supplier's mail panel. Notice that the research proposal is rather specific concerning the approach to be used and the anticipated completion rates. Consequently, the client knows exactly what will be done and what they are getting for their money.

Information to be obtained. The research proposal must express crucial decisions relating to:

— Measurement content—what should be measured.
— Measurement technique—how we should measure it.

Notice that the measurement content and technique to be used in the low-salt/unsalted cracker market study are both defined precisely in Exhibit 2–7. Cracker usage information and purchase dynamics will be measured, as well as the importance attached to brand-related end benefits for specific usage situations. Where appropriate, the research proposal specifies the type of measurement scales to be used.

Analysis. The analysis section of the research proposal provides a description of how the data collected will be analyzed. It can contain a description of the tabulation plans, indicating the scope and nature of the cross-tabulations to be run, for example, usage by age. In addition, it must also describe whether other types of statistical analyses will be performed. For example, in the research proposal described in Exhibit 2–7, the supplier has indicated that a segmentation analysis will be performed.

Action standard. The **action standard** for the research proposal clearly defines the performance criterion to be applied. How the research results are judged is ultimately tied to the study's purpose and objectives, and it also influences the choice of an analysis technique. Action standards provide an *a priori* means for evaluating survey results. When action standards are used, the interpretation of the data is less subject to political pressure. Notice that in the project proposal shown in Exhibit 2–7, no action standards are specified. Market studies typically do not lend themselves to explicit performance criteria since the objective of such studies is to describe competitive relationships, as opposed to judging the superiority of one brand over another.

If we were considering a project proposal for, say, a concept test concerning new snack food ideas, an appropriate action standard might be:

> Those concepts that have been selected by at least one-third of the respondents will be singled out for further testing.

ACTION STANDARD
Statement in the research proposal that clearly defines the performance criterion to be applied to the results of the study.

Cost and timing. A research proposal will include a statement of the estimated project cost and a schedule that outlines deadlines for various aspects of the project. Exhibit 2–7 indicates that the data collected will be available to the client 16 weeks from August 3, the beginning of the field operation, and will cost $121,500, plus or minus the customary 10 percent contingency factor.

SUMMARY

The research process provides a general framework to follow when designing and implementing a research study. In this chapter we have explained each stage in the research process. Each stage was described in terms of a number of research activities that must be completed. In addition, we also considered how firms request competitive bids from marketing research suppliers for conducting specific types of studies. In response to requests for proposals, suppliers prepare formal written documents outlining how the research study would be conducted. Each major component of the research proposal was explained and illustrated.

KEY CONCEPTS

Research Process
Problem Formulation
Research Objective
Research Questions
Situation Analysis
Exploratory Research Designs

Descriptive Research Designs
Causal Research Designs
Sources of Data
Sampling Plan
Questionnaire Design
Instructing Interviewers

Editing
Coding
Tabulating and Analysis
Report Writing
Research Proposal
Request for Proposals

REVIEW QUESTIONS

1. At the beginning of this chapter we discussed the plight of Hidden Valley microwave dinners. On the basis of the information provided:
   a. Perform situation analysis.
   b. Formulate the problem statement.
   c. Determine what type of information sources appear most appropriate.
   d. Identify some alternative courses of action that HVR Co. should possibly consider.
2. Develop a research objective and set of research questions for a study to revive 7UP Gold.

3. Discuss the differences between exploratory, descriptive, and causal research designs; and give specific illustrations of the type of research objective and accompanying set of research questions that are consistent with each design.
4. For each stage in the research process, develop a set of questions that a researcher should attempt to answer.

ENDNOTES

1. The following discussion is based on D. C. McGill, "7UP Gold: The Failure of a Can't-Lose Plan," New York Times, February 11, 1989, pp. 17, 26.
2. Robert W. Joselyn, Designing the Marketing Research Project (New York: Petrocelli/Charter, 1977), pp. 25–26.
3. The material pertaining to Pontiac discussed in this and subsequent sections of the chapter is excerpted from Peter Langenhorst, "Pontiac Division of General Motors (A)," The Colgate Darden Graduate School of Business Administration, University of Virginia, 1987.
4. The material following is adapted from G. L. Urban, G. M. Katz, T. E. Hatch, and A. J. Silk, "The ASSESSOR Pre-Test Market Evaluation Systems," Interfaces, December 1983, pp. 55–56.
5. Kathleen Deveny and Richard Gibson, "Food Giants Hope New 'Healthy' Soups Will Be Ingredients of Financial Success," The Wall Street Journal, September 4, 1991, p. B1.

The Marketing Research Cycle

PERRIER FINDS MYSTIQUE HARD TO RESTORE

The fizz is gone.

In February, Source Perrier S.A. voluntarily recalled Perrier worldwide after traces of benzene, a suspected carcinogen, were found in some bottles. By mid-July, the water was again available throughout most of the United States. But the protracted absence unleashed competitive forces that have broken the once-invincible import's stranglehold over the U.S. imported bottled water market.

Today, Perrier is a brand in deep water. Evian has replaced it as the top-selling imported bottled water, with Perrier's sales at just 60 percent of pre-recall levels. The brand's plight would probably be less severe, marketing experts say, had it not been for the evasiveness and strategic blunders of Perrier officials on both sides of the Atlantic.

Perrier officials in the United States vow the brand will regain 85 percent of its sales by the end of 1991, a goal critics say is wishful thinking. Its share of the imported bottled water market has sunk to 20.7 percent from 44.8 percent. And the brand's sales plunged 42 percent this year to $60 million. Perrier Group of America expects to report a sales gain for this year of 3.7 percent to $630 million, but that is largely because of the strong performance of such domestic brands as Calistoga and Poland Spring.

A host of rival brands — Saratoga, La-Croix, Quibell — have reaped minor windfalls in the aftermath of the contamination debacle. But the biggest winner is BSN S.A.'s Evian, a nonsparkling water. The aggressive marketing and advertising campaign Evian has waged since Perrier's recall has been so successful that "it's unlikely that Perrier will recover its number-one imported position in the near term," says Michael Bellas, president of Beverage Marketing Corp., a consulting firm.

Perrier distributors say the brand has been especially unsuccessful in staging a comeback in bars and restaurants, which formerly accounted for about 35 percent of its sales. And Perrier Group of America has resorted to unprecedented discounting this holiday season, which risks cheapening the brand's image.

It isn't the fear of benzene that has led many former loyalists to eschew the water. (Memory of the incident has all but faded, Perrier research confirms.) Rather, the contamination crisis exposed a fundamental flaw: Consumers tended to pick Perrier out of inertia and a perceived lack of alternatives, not any true product preference.

Thus, when Perrier essentially gave consumers a mandate to sample other waters, the floodgates opened. "Consumers got out of the habit of seeing

CHAPTER
OBJECTIVES

INTRODUCE
the concept of a research life
cycle.

DISCUSS
the three primary stages of
the research life cycle:
prelaunch, rollout, and
established markets.

UNDERSTAND
the types of marketing
research activities that are
conducted throughout the
research life cycle.

Perrier and began buying other things," says Tom Pirko, president of BevMark Inc., a consulting firm. "Perrier broke people's purchase-decision behavior."

Ronald V. Davis, chief executive of Perrier Group, calls what befell the familiar green bottles "unprecedented" in consumer product history. The raison d'etre of the brand—purity—was called into question, and Perrier itself was to blame. Afterward, the company could do little other than slap a "nouvelle production" label on every bottle to reassure customers. And the luxury product got reintroduced just as the economy was weakening.

"When the marketing gurus look back, they'll say this company came up against pretty formidable odds and did OK," the upbeat Mr. Davis declares. "We could have been dead."

Even before the crisis hit, Perrier was already at a difficult juncture in the United States. New entrants were crowding the American market, and the brand's sales had peaked. When the benzene incident arose, Perrier compounded its troubles by taking a whimsical view of the crisis. Gustave Leven, chairman of Source Perrier, even joked about the recall at a news conference.

In the United States, Perrier's crisis strategy was similarly glib. During the recall, to keep consumers lusting after

a brand they couldn't find, Burson-Marsteller, Inc., created a radio and print campaign that took a frothy tone and ducked the reasons for the brand's absence.

Then, just as the brand started to resurface in New York in mid-April, Perrier suffered other blows. The Food and Drug Administration made Perrier drop the words "naturally sparkling" from its labels. The Federal Trade Commission also began investigating the purity claims Perrier makes in its advertising. (Perrier contends the matter will be resolved.)

The biggest setback, however, was the time it took to relaunch the brand in the U.S. market, which accounts for about one fourth of the 1.4 billion bottles that Perrier sells each year. Initially, plain

Perrier was supposed to be back in the United States by mid-May; because of production snafus, it arrived in mid-July. Perrier's flavored versions have resurfaced even more slowly.

"The brand was out of sight and mind too long," says Richard Winger, a partner at Boston Consulting Group. "To come back into mind is extraordinarily difficult if the product is built on image, but isn't intrinsically superior."

Marketing experts say Perrier's U.S. purveyors are further eroding the brand's mystique by pursuing a highly visible discount strategy, which includes a buy-two, get-one-free offer. In supermarkets, bottles that used to fetch $1.09 to $1.19 are now going for 89 to 99 cents.

"If you want to rebuild the brand, you need to rebuild its mystique," says Mr. Winger of Boston Consulting Group. "They would have been better off with a premium strategy that maintains the integrity of Perrier's pricing at the cost of a slower volume build."

Some ad men also say the signature Gallic wit of Perrier's advertising is out of sync with the brand's increasingly middle-brow appeal. With its "Earth's First Soft Drink" ads from Waring & LaRosa, Perrier's marketing men have returned to the brand's original campaign, which played well to trendy drinkers. (A new Waring & LaRosa campaign will start next spring.)

Kim Jeffrey, Perrier's senior vice president of marketing, says Perrier has always engaged in heavy promotional activity at Christmas time and denies the brand is vying for Middle America. A huge $20 million was spent purely on advertising to rebuild the brand's mystique this year, he says, adding, "Perrier is a very upscale product and will remain that way."

But in a clear sign of its vanishing cachet, Perrier is either no longer stocked in many watering holes or must share its place with other rivals. Perrier research in 10 big markets suggests the water is now in 40 percent of food service accounts, compared with 65 percent before the recall.

Source: Alix M. Freedman, *The Wall Street Journal,* December 12, 1990, p. B1. Reprinted by permission of *THE WALL STREET JOURNAL,* © 1990 Dow Jones & Company, Inc. All Rights Reserved Worldwide.

INTRODUCTION

The woes of Perrier illustrate the worst-case scenario of a successful, established brand being thrown into a state of shock. As we have seen, Perrier's current market condition was precipitated by, but not completely due to, the fear of benzene. Competitive forces were bound to surface eventually. But without the contamination crisis, Perrier's loss of market share probably would not have been as quick or as severe.

Perrier's research needs are now very different from when the water was first distributed in the United States. This chapter deals with that subject: the changing configuration of research needs that brands face as they or their markets mature.

Most of you are probably familiar with the *product life cycle* concept. The product life cycle divides a product's evolution by sales patterns over time into four stages: *introduction, growth, maturity, decline.* Although a product's research needs are cyclical as well, the idea of a *research life cycle* is not so widely recognized.

RESEARCH CYCLE
Acknowledges that specific kinds of research projects are conducted as a product moves through its life cycle.

Research results from the need to anticipate, understand, or respond to changes in the marketplace. The **research cycle** acknowledges the fact that as products move through their life cycle they have unique research needs.

Dividing the research life cycle into prelaunch, rollout, and established market stages specifically matches research activities with the unique needs of a product. After discussing the idea of a research life cycle, we describe a variety of different marketing research studies that are implemented at various stages as a product or service moves from prelaunch, to national rollout, and into established markets.

THE RESEARCH CYCLE

As we indicated, while the concept of the product life cycle is widely accepted, the idea of a research life cycle is not so commonly recognized. Yet to develop effective marketing strategies, marketing researchers must recognize the connection between the product and research life cycles.

Exhibit 3–1 depicts this relationship. Notice that the product follows a sales pattern over time from introduction through growth and maturity to decline. Prior to the introduction stage comes a precommercialization period, though it is not specifically included as one of the four life cycle stages. Over the course of the cycle, the marketing research needs of the product change correspondingly. The research cycle, which can be divided into prelaunch, rollout, and established markets, recognizes such changes and specifically matches research activities to the unique needs of a product during each stage in its life cycle.

Prelaunch Stage

The **prelaunch phase** of the research life cycle is characterized by research activities aimed at assisting the marketing manager in developing and introducing (i.e., rolling out) new and improved products that can compete successfully in the marketplace. For many firms, the development and successful rollout of new products and services are essential for the continued financial health of the organization. All the marketing research activities undertaken in the prelaunch stage are designed to ensure that a national rollout, if undertaken, will be successful in matching or exceeding management's performance objectives.

PRELAUNCH PHASE
That stage in the research life cycle characterized by research activities aimed at assisting the marketing manager in developing and introducing new and improved products that are likely to be successful in the marketplace.

The different types of research activities undertaken in the prelaunch phase of the research life cycle include concept testing, product testing, name testing, package testing, and test marketing. We describe each of these activities in the following sections.

Concept testing.   **Concept tests** provide a system for shaping, defining, and formulating ideas to arrive at a basic concept for a product that has greater potential for market acceptance. Generally, concept tests are conducted to assess the relative appeal of ideas or alternative product positionings that aim the product at different target segments by highlighting particular product features that are most desired by given segments of the population.

CONCEPT TESTS
Tests conducted to assess the relative appeal of ideas or alternative product positionings that aim the product at different target segments.

Procedures for concept testing vary greatly. For example, at the outset of the prelaunch phase, concept testing can be used to screen new product ideas to identify the most promising concepts. In this type of concept test, respondents are

EXHIBIT 3—1

Interface between Product and Research Life Cycles

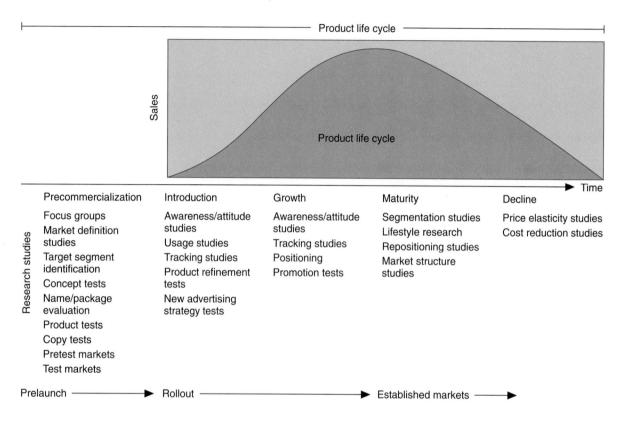

exposed to a core idea concept. The core idea concept focuses directly on the product's primary end benefit with little, if any, emphasis on secondary features. It is relatively straightforward and emotionless, and its objective is not to persuade the consumer to buy the product. Exhibit 3–2 presents a core idea concept.

Concept tests can also be used later in the prelaunch phase to estimate ultimate consumer demand for the basic product concept before introduction. A concept test at this stage would expose respondents to a positioning concept statement, which lists all the product's end benefits as well as various secondary features. A statement of this sort is much longer than a core idea concept, generally several paragraphs long. A positioning concept statement normally includes a photograph or illustration, and it makes an attempt to persuade. Exhibit 3–3 presents a positioning concept statement.

Two elements are critical in the concept statement. First, the copy must describe how the product works and its end benefits. Second, some type of illustration, most often a simple line drawing, showing either the product or the product package should be used.

Concept tests can also be used after rollout of a product in established markets for *product line extensions* of an existing brand. In this setting, the concept test should also indicate areas where the established brand is particu-

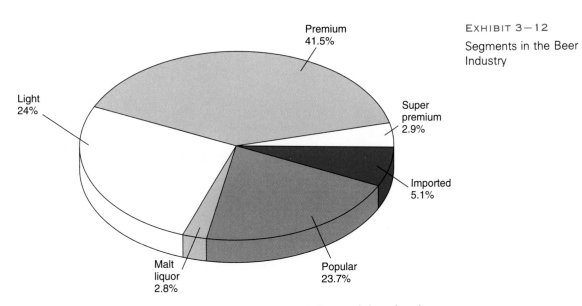

EXHIBIT 3—12

Segments in the Beer
Industry

Source: Adapted from "Beer Trends: Market Breakdown by Product," in *Beverage Industry Annual Manual 1989* (Cleveland: Edge, 1989), pp. 38–47.

a limited set of national-brand soft drinks. We call these *hierarchical structures* because the brands are partitioned into several nested subsets. Part A of the exhibit divides the soft-drink market according to the brand name (that is, a *brand-primary* market). Part B structures the market by attribute, whether the product is regular/diet, sugar/sugar-free, caffeine/caffeine-free (that is, a *form-primary* market). These structures have different implications. Consumers in one case first decide on which brand name to buy (Part A), while in the other case consumers first decide on the type of soft drink to buy and then choose the brand (Part B).

Consider now the competitive environment as it affects Dr. Pepper. If Part A of Exhibit 3–11 accurately reflects the market structure, then the lack of a diet, caffeine-free product does not hurt Dr. Pepper's share of the market; in fact, the implication is that introduction of such a product offering would have cannibalistic effects. The situation is different if Part B accurately reflects the market structure. If consumers follow a form-primary strategy, then Dr. Pepper could potentially increase its market share by introducing a caffeine-free product, whether regular or diet.

Market segmentation studies.   The term *market segment* simply refers to subgroups of consumers that respond to a given marketing mix strategy in a similar manner. More specifically, segments consist of subgroups of consumers who exhibit differing sensitivities to some marketing mix element.[3]

The beer market is a good example of a market that over time has become increasingly segmented. As Exhibit 3–12 reveals, the beer market is now made up of super premiums, premiums, low-price populars, imports, lights/low calorie, and malts. More recent entries include dry beer and low-alcohol and nonalcohol brands. Brand proliferation is presumably a direct result of

BOX 3–1

FROM THE USER'S PERSPECTIVE

HITTING THE BULL'S-EYE

Brand	Heavy User Profile	Life-Style and Media Profile	Top Three Stores
Peter Pan Peanut Butter	Households with kids headed by 18- to 54-year-olds, in suburban and rural areas	— Heavy video renters — Go to theme parks — Below-average TV viewers — Above-average radio listeners	Foodtown Super Market 3350 Hempstead Turnpike Levittown, NY Pathmark Supermarket 3635 Hempstead Turnpike Levittown, NY King Kullen Market 598 Stewart Ave. Bethpage, NY
Stouffers Red Box Frozen Entrees	Households headed by people 55 and older, and upscale suburban households headed by 35- to 54-year-olds	— Go to gambling casinos — Give parties — Involved in public activities — Travel frequently — Heavy newspaper readers — Above-average TV viewers	Dan's Supreme Super Market 69–62 188th St. Flushing, NY Food Emporium Madison Ave. & 74th St. NYC Waldbaum Super Market 196–35 Horace Harding Blvd. Flushing, NY
Coors Light Beer	Head of household, 21–34, middle to upper income, suburban and urban	— Belong to a health club — Buy rock music — Travel by plane — Give parties, cookouts — Rent videos — Heavy TV sports viewers	Food Emporium 1498 York Ave. NYC Food Emporium First Ave. & 72nd St. NYC Gristedes Supermarket 350 E. 86th St. NYC

Sources: Reprinted by permission of *The Wall Street Journal,* March 18, 1991. Dow Jones & Company, Inc. All Rights Reserved Worldwide.

recognizing the distinctive desires of beer customers with respect to taste and lifestyle.

MARKET SEGMENTATION STUDIES
Studies that provide guidelines for a firm's resource allocations among markets and products.

Market segmentation studies provide guidelines for a firm's marketing strategy and resource allocation among markets and products and, consequently, influence all marketing tactical plans and programs. By recognizing consumer heterogeneity, a firm can increase its profitability by segmenting its market.

Initially the contribution of segmentation analysis to marketing planning was to provide a framework for the analysis of existing data. Today its role has expanded to provide a basis for identifying the data needed for strategy development and implementation. Segmentation research is used to answer a wide variety of questions concerning market response to a firm's marketing strategies, including product or price changes, new product offerings, and the selection of target markets. Typical management questions that guide market segmentation studies include:

1. How do the evaluations of a set of new product concepts vary by different respondent groups—men versus women, users versus non-users of the company's brand, light versus heavy users, and so on?

2. Are there different promotion-sensitive segments for a new product concept? If so, how do they differ with respect to product use, concept evaluations, attitudes, and demographic and psychographic profiles?

3. How do the target markets for a new product concept differ regarding the end benefits sought, product use characteristics, and other background characteristics?

From these management questions we see that there is an intimate relationship between product positioning and segmentation analysis. Effectively positioning a product for a specific target—consumers who share certain characteristics such as similar reactions to price, promotion, and the like—presumes that these subgroups of consumers have actually been identified, that is, that the market has been segmented. In fact, it is reasonable to suggest that in order to develop effective marketing strategies, managers should apply the concept of segmentation in all activities.

Marketers are using segmentation analysis rather effectively. In particular, marketers can now target a product's best customers and the stores where they're most likely to shop. The accompanying box presents an analysis of three products' best targets in the New York area.

SUMMARY

This chapter described the concept of a research life cycle and specifically the notion that the research needs of a product or service change over time. The discussion centered on different types of marketing research studies undertaken in the prelaunch, rollout, and established markets phases of the research life cycle. Specifically, the discussion considered concept testing, product testing, name testing, package testing, market tracking, positioning, market structuring, and segmentation research.

KEY CONCEPTS

Research Life Cycle

Concept Tests

Name Tests

Market Tracking

Market Structuring

Product Life Cycle

Product Tests

Package Tests

Positioning

Segmentation

REVIEW QUESTIONS

1. Define the interface between the product life cycle and the research life cycle.

2. Describe the essence of concept testing.

3. What are the primary approaches to product testing?

4. Describe the reasons for conducting name and package testing.

5. Distinguish between positioning, market structuring, and market segmentation.

ENDNOTES

1. A thorough discussion of market tracking can be found in James F. Donius, *Marketplace Measurement: Tracking and Testing Advertising and Other Marketing Effects* (New York: Association of National Advertisers, Inc., 1986).

2. A. Koutsouiannis, *Modern Microeconomics,* 2nd ed. (London: Macmillan, 1979), p. 8.

3. A comprehensive critical review of the theory, research, and practice of market segmentation can be found in Yoram Wind, "Issues and Advances in Segmentation Research," *Journal of Marketing Research,* August 1978, pp. 317–37.

CASE 1: NBC DROPS SHOWS OLDER AUDIENCES FAVOR

By Kevin Goldman

The NBC network, after two years of double-digit declines in ratings and a troublesome trend toward an older audience, is embarking on major changes to attract the younger viewers advertisers seek most.

NBC, which lost its No. 1 position to CBS this season after six consecutive years on top, has unceremoniously jettisoned two of its reliable one-hour dramas, "In the Heat of the Night," starring ol' Archie Bunker-actor Carroll O'Connor, and "Matlock," starring silver-haired Andy Griffith. Both shows continue to perform respectably, running No. 2 in their time slots. Both do especially well among adults over age 55: "Matlock" ranks No. 3, and "Heat" is No. 5 when compared with all prime-time programs.

That, it turns out, is the problem. The two series perform far worse among the under-50 crowd that is the most coveted target for sponsors: "Heat" runs 65th and "Matlock" ranks 83rd among all prime-time shows this season. In their place, NBC is likely to try new shows with younger appeal.

"NBC is conforming to the preferences of the advertising community instead of trying to change the world," says Jerome Dominus, senior vice president at ad agency J. Walter Thompson. News Corp.'s Fox network "has made a fortune saying they aren't interested in people 50-plus. NBC is learning from this."

In some ways NBC is a victim of its own success. Instead of developing new hits, it stayed with some programs perhaps longer than it should have. That let it continue to win the household ratings race, but NBC also began losing the more important, younger demographic race as its audience aged with its shows.

Now the median age of the NBC viewer is 42 years old—up from age 39 just two TV seasons ago. At ABC, by contrast, the median viewer age is 36 years old, and at Fox it's only 28. Only CBS's median age is older—44 years old. Overall, 44% of all NBC viewers have passed age 50, up by one percentage point in three years.

The NBC network, owned by General Electric Co., acknowledges it is in a period of transition and must shed some veteran shows. The two cancellations are only part of the major restructuring of NBC's once potent prime-time line-up. In September, NBC will lose "The Cosby Show," whose final episode will be taped this evening in the Astoria, Queens, section of New York. NBC also is losing the once-popular "Night Court." And "The Golden Girls" will return with a new format and without co-star Bea Arthur.

Further, its Thursday schedule is besieged by unprecedented competition from its three major rivals. "Cheers" has shown signs of erosion and "L.A. Law" is having creative difficulties, recently dismissing its executive producer and bringing back co-creator Steven Bochco.

NBC originally had added the two older-skewing series to offer up the audience to those sponsors that wanted to reach the over-50 set. The two canceled shows were quickly snatched up by rivals, with Capital Cities/ABC Inc.'s ABC network acquiring "Matlock" and CBS Inc.'s CBS network buying "In the Heat of the Night," for much the same reason.

"We realize the strategic importance to attract an older audience at least one night of the week," says Larry Hyams, ABC's director of audience research.

Ultimately, NBC told the producers of "In the Heat of the Night" that it needed to move "onward and upward and thanks for the four years," says Edward B. Gradinger, president of MGM Worldwide Television Group, a unit of MGM-Pathe Communications Co. "They're going to try to be more like Fox and ABC."

Source: *The Wall Street Journal*, March 6, 1992, p. B4. Reprinted with permission.

"I would call this a rather dramatic move on their part," says David F. Poltrack, a CBS senior vice president. "Older viewers are a very important part of the prime-time audience and it's one we'll continue to appeal to."

NBC executives say they aren't looking to make a dramatic right-turn in the schedule. Rather, "we're trying to gradually transition an increasingly older-skewing schedule into one that features younger shows with overall younger demographics, which is more consistent to what advertisers are buying," says Perry Simon, NBC's No. 2 programming executive.

"We have no intention of turning into a kiddie network," he adds, citing "I'll Fly Away" and "Reasonable Doubts," two dramas that premiered last September, as "serious" shows that have broad appeal.

NBC's hopes to snare a younger audience rests on its still unfolding development season. Top candidates include a spinoff of Bill Cosby's show starring his wise cracking but earnest TV son, Malcolm Jamal-Warner. New versions of "Route 66" and "Journey to the Center of the Earth" are due, as are "Rise and Shine," a situation comedy from the off-center creators of "Northern Exposure," and comedies from Marcy Carsey and Tom Werner, the producers of "The Cosby Show" starring Robert Townsend, as well as a new show from the "Cheers" team.

Bill Croasdale, president of national broadcasting at Western International Media, characterizes NBC's move as "smart," but adds ominously, "The mystery is how good the replacement shows will be."

Case Questions

1. Define the research problem NBC is facing.
2. Develop the research objective(s) and set of research questions that should guide the research conducted by NBC.
3. Discuss the kinds of research studies that are consistent with the research objectives and research questions identified in question 2.

CASE 2: REDESIGN BOOSTS ROLD GOLD SALES

Frito Lay assigned Apple Designsource, a New York City-based marketing design firm, to create packaging for Rold Gold Pretzels that would help position it as a new and re-vitalized product in the East. This is where approximately 50% of all pretzels are consumed.

"Having recently re-formulated and improved the product, we now needed our packaging to communicate to the shopper that this was the best pretzel on the market today," explains Walt Root, senior product manager for new business development at Frito Lay.

"We wanted an exciting look that would be both eye-catching to the purchaser and appealing to the ultimate user."

Without a real need to retain brand equity, since Rold Gold's market share in the nation's pretzel belt was small, the design firm overhauled the graphics, changed the colors and greatly expanded the size of the window.

It is the window, according to the company's market research, which helps generate appetite appeal and plays a huge role within the pretzel category.

Source: *Snack Food,* May 1991, p. 22. Reprinted with permission.

"You usually can't go this far (with a packaging redesign), but we had no recognition in this area and so were pretty much given a license to start a new brand," adds Lee Peterson, senior creative service manager at Frito Lay. "Our previous packaging was very simple and offered little shelf impact. With the new packaging, however, the pretzels flew off the shelf."

The new packaging displays the brand name, in bold yellow letters, on a black diamond background. The product designator lies at the base of the diamond (a band of red for Thins, purple for Sticks, light blue for Tiny Twists, dark blue for Rods and green for Bavarian). The top and the bottom of the package are in light blue.

"We gave the package greater shelf impact and made it more masculine by adding a shape—a diamond—and a color—black—that males generally respond to," says Barry Seelig, president of Apple Designsource. "To emphasize the product's healthy, wholesome image, wheat stalks curl around the logo and a burst, with the trademark, 'Low Fat Snack, Baked and Crispy,' appears near the bottom of the package," he adds.

The new packaging scored an immediate hit. *Several months after its introduction, and without any increased advertising spending, Rold Gold has shown a sales increase in the heartland of well over 50%.*

Case Questions

1. Newly redesigned Rold Gold pretzels has been reintroduced and is apparently doing well. What problems and/or opportunities will Rold Gold likely face in the near future? Develop a list of research questions that will guide future research efforts.

2. On the basis of the research questions identified in question 1 determine what research studies Frito Lay should consider doing for Rold Gold pretzels.

CASE 3: FOOD GIANTS HOPE NEW 'HEALTHY' SOUPS WILL BE INGREDIENTS OF FINANCIAL SUCCESS

By Kathleen Deveny and Richard Gibson

On a shelf above the desk of Robert Bernstock, vice president of **Campbell Soup Co.**, sits a symbol of one of the most pressing challenges now facing the nation's largest soup maker. It is a can of Healthy Choice soup, made by archrival **ConAgra Inc.**

Mr. Bernstock will attempt to squash that challenge when Campbell soon announces a new line of more healthful soups—the company's most important product launch in recent years. Called Healthy Request, the soups promise to be lower in fat, sodium and cholesterol than Campbell's regular fare.

The Healthy Request launch, coming later this week, takes place at a time when Campbell is feeling the heat. David W. Johnson, who became Campbell's chief executive last year, has cut costs and pumped up earnings. But Campbell still counts on soup for half its profits, and U.S. per capita soup consumption has stalled at about 43 bowls a year. While the company still controls two-thirds of the $2.6 billion soup market, competitors have nibbled away at its dominance. Worse yet, for all of Campbell's efforts to convince consumers that "soup is good food," increasing numbers are shunning canned soup because of its high sodium content.

Source: *The Wall Street Journal,* September 4, 1991, p. B1. Reprinted with permission.

"We're very much trying to retain the loyalty of our customers," says Anthony Adams, Campbell's vice president of marketing research. "Healthy Request gets us out in front of their needs and out in front of the competition."

But Campbell's lead in healthy soups could be fleeting. ConAgra is about to roll out 10 low-sodium soups under its powerful Healthy Choice brand. Other brands, including Progresso, Lipton and Weight Watchers, are also cooking up healthier recipes of their own.

The contest between Campbell and ConAgra, however, promises to be the most bitter. Although it has no experience selling soup, ConAgra is nearly three times Campbell's size, with $19.5 billion in revenues. The two companies have long been rivals in the supermarket freezer case, where ConAgra's Banquet and Healthy Choice entrees compete with Campbell's Swanson and Le Menu lines. ConAgra has fared especially well recently: Since their introduction two years ago, Healthy Choice frozen dinners have scorched competitors, including Campbell.

Now ConAgra has similar aspirations in soup. "We breathe life into the markets we enter," boasts Charles D. Weil, president of ConAgra Frozen Foods, the unit launching Healthy Choice soup. "If we didn't think we could do a sizable [soup] business over time, we wouldn't be entering the market."

Critics have already begun sniping about just how wholesome the new soups are. And it's uncertain whether consumers will find them as pleasing to their taste buds as the salt-laden stuff they grew up on. Campbell's has had a very low-sodium line on the market for years, but consumers have been unmoved.

For the company that prevails, the prize is potentially large. The wholesome varieties may eventually account for 30% of the total soup market, by Campbell's estimate. Though consumers have largely ignored low-salt soups up to now, many would devour them if they tasted better, says Mona Doyle, president of Consumer Network Inc., which polls consumers nationally. To ballyhoo their shaped-up soups, the two marketers together are expected to pour as much as $20 million in print and television advertising.

The fight between the two food giants has already gotten nasty. They tangled in court last year when ConAgra tried to block Campbell's use of the word "healthy" on its label. In March, Campbell won the right to keep the word on its new soups but can't use the Healthy Request brand on other food products without ConAgra's consent.

Case Questions

1. On the basis of the material provided, what would you say were the research objectives and set of research questions facing the Campbell Soup Co. prior to introducing the Healthy Request product line?

2. Discuss what research projects should have been undertaken by the Campbell Soup Co. prior to the introduction of the Healthy Request products and relate each of these projects to the research objectives and research questions developed in question 1.

3. Discuss the product and research life cycles that Healthy Request will likely face.

ACQUIRING DATA: AN OVERVIEW

ROBERT A. SCHMITZ
DIRECTOR, MARKET RESEARCH
LEVER BROTHERS COMPANY

Dramatic changes in marketing information have occurred during the past decade, changes in the nature of the data used by manufacturers to monitor and analyze their businesses. At the heart of this information revolution is the point-of-sale scanner, tied to retail computer systems, that permits the explicit individual identification of virtually all consumer transactions that take place in the American marketplace.

Robert A. Schmitz has seen the effects of this revolution firsthand at Lever Brothers. In the past, researchers could only draw inferences for large areas over rather long time intervals. "They could tell whether sales were rising or falling, but, at best, they could only do so on a month-to-month basis," says Schmitz. Thus, sales changes could be related only inferentially to marketing actions such as price reductions, displays, or coupon offers.

"In the 1980s, new scanning technology—originally a system for managing inventory—was linked to merchandising, pricing, and promotional events occurring in stores to create an entirely new basis for assessing marketing programs."

As a result, marketing and sales management can now draw remarkably clear relationships between marketing actions (causal factors) and resulting consumer behavior. "We can, in fact, know which particular households made specific purchases and how those households were influenced by the incentives presented to them."

This is the good news. The bad news, says Schmitz, is that these databases are huge—exponentially larger masses of information than ever before encountered in the business world. "Lever Brothers is but a small part of Unilever, the world's largest packaged goods marketer. Yet the raw quantity of marketplace data that we alone are required to cope with day-to-day has grown enormously. Measured in computer memory, we must deal with something on the order of 200 times

more data today than we did only five years ago. In layman's terms, Lever Brothers receives marketplace data equivalent to 10,000 pages of single-spaced English text each and every day."

Although this volume of data places enormous stress on a company's computing capacity, computer technology has managed to keep pace of the growth. Today, says Schmitz, "It is people— particularly market researchers— who are paying the price.

"Traditionally, market researchers came from fields related to the social sciences. They were trained to look to survey research as the almost exclusive basis for dialogue with the consumer. Market researchers are now challenged not only to be proficient in the direct contact with consumers through survey research, but also to become quantitatively oriented marketing scientists developing and using skills focused on communicating the rather complex insights that causally linked marketplace data can provide.

"The truth is that, in the 1990s, those seeking to be successful in market research will need to develop functional skills in both of these fundamental disciplines—traditional survey research and complex quantitative analysis.

"The successful market researcher— and marketing practitioner—will find ways to reconcile these two complementary elements of consumer understanding within their career plans."

Robert A. Schmitz, a graduate of Syracuse University, has served in strategic and market research positions with Primerica Corporation, Majers Corporation, and Summa Group (Nielsen Marketing Research) before joining Lever Brothers. He is an active speaker and writer on market research topics, in particular the evaluation of promotion and advertising. He is a trustee of the Advertising Research Foundation and of the Marketing Science Institute.

Secondary Information: The Major Access Tools

READY TO ZERO IN ON CENSUS DATA

The U.S. Census Bureau has started to release the first wave of data from its 1990 head count, an outpouring that ultimately will be massaged into information usable to all marketers.

***

But over the next 24 months, the Census Bureau will release more refined data from the 90 million questionnaires it mailed last year. Although those data will be available to anyone who wants them, many marketers, agencies, and media will instead wait until geodemographic marketing services companies, which provide a geographic context for demographic data, work the information into a more meaningful form.

These companies can provide data so that Ralston Purina Co., for example, could learn what markets have a large number of pets, said Eric Cohen, director of marketing for CACI Marketing Systems, a geodemographic information marketer.

"Anyone with a market in which he's trying to sell something can use these data," Mr. Cohen said. "And this year, the Census Bureau is using Tiger [Topologically Integrated Geographic Encoding & Referencing]. . . .

"Before Tiger, the smallest unit we could look at was a block, but Tiger will go down to the immediate household, so a marketer can find out on a per-household basis such information as race, income, marital status, whether the house is rented or owned, etc."

"Campbell soup might use it to decide whether it wants more shelf space in a particular store if there are a lot of children in the neighborhood who would eat soup," Mr. Cohen said.

The growing trend among women toward giving birth later in life should be further verified by the census, he said, and that information would be important to marketers.

"A lot of [parents'] discretionary income is spent on that child," he said.

The expected rush of Hispanic, Asian, and other minority data from the census has caught the fancy of a number of marketers and ad agencies that want to keep up with these rapidly growing segments of the population.

"We are interested in getting basic information to bring us up to speed with the Asian population," said Doug Allgood, VP–special markets for BBDO Worldwide, New York. "That has been the greatest disparity because everything [now] is based on the 1980 census."

Gary McBride, senior VP–marketing and sales for Telemundo Group, the second-largest Spanish-language TV network, said he expects census numbers to show that the Hispanic population has grown by nearly 50 percent to about 48 million since the last census.

CHAPTER
OBJECTIVES

—

UNDERSTAND
the distinction between
primary and secondary
sources of marketing
information.

EXPLAIN
how to evaluate secondary
information.

INTRODUCE
traditional sources of
secondary market data.

DESCRIBE
a large number of reference
source materials.

Census results showed overall slowed growth, with explosive gains among minority groups, especially Asians and Hispanics. The Asian population grew 61.6 percent from 1980; the Hispanic segment was up 53 percent. Total growth was 9.8 percent.

"Projections show [minorities] will be the majority of all growth for the foreseeable future, accounting for as much as 80 percent," [publisher of *American Demographics* Peter] Francese said.

An increasingly fragmented society "makes advertising effectiveness more difficult; it means there must be more, different kinds of advertising messages. And it makes advertising research that much trickier to do," he said.

Source: Betsy Spethmann, "Census Data Base Adds Up to Success," *Advertising Age,* April 15, 1991, p. 6.

"That can only be positive for our business," [McBride] said. "It will help bring new advertisers to the market" as well as boost ad rates on Hispanic media and increase the market value of Spanish-language TV stations and other media properties.

Suzanne Kaufman, senior VP–associate media director, N W Ayer, ex-

pressed some skepticism about the census's final tabulation in the wake of reports of incomplete counts in several markets.

But Carl Knock, financial services division product manager at Claritas Corp., one of the information services companies that feeds census figures into databases, said people missed by census takers "are not exactly key marketing targets — they're the homeless and people who simply don't want to be found. And banks aren't exactly looking to those kinds of people to open up checking accounts."

David Poltrack, CBS senior VP–planning and research, said he hopes publication of census data, particularly those showing the "graying" of the population, will precipitate changes in the buying habits of advertisers and their agencies.

"Media buying has not taken into account the aging of the population," Mr.

Poltrack said. "The marketer is aware of it with new products developed toward an older population. The creative executions are aimed at an older target with older casts. But buying parameters have not changed."

Such a shift in buying would be particularly appealing to CBS, whose audience has skewed older than its network competitors.

"I think there will have to be a greater orientation to programming to the older audience on network TV," he said. "By that I mean ages 35 and above, not 65 and older. Another aspect is that adults in their 40s, who I believe will be the primary target market of the 1990s, watch more news and information programs than adults in their 30s and below.

"We've already seen a trend toward news, information, and reality-based programming, and that will be accelerated once advertisers recognize that age group is the middle of the market."

Census data hold "enormous potential" for marketers that can incorporate the data into their marketing strategies, said Howard Hunter, senior VP–general manager at Donnelley Marketing Information Services.

The Census Bureau's Tiger file, combined with the census's population figures, will allow marketers to develop an unprecedented profile of consumers, he said.

Retailers could "understand the mechanics of a trading area," from where customers live to where new stores might be situated, Mr. Hunter said.

But not everyone sees the census report as essential, particularly with the research data already available.

"Media people on a yearly basis restate demographic profiles of the population based on surveys done between the censuses," said Bob Warrens, senior VP–media research and resources, J. Walter Thompson USA, Chicago. "We have updates on key demographics like age or family-head status, and we feel we have a pretty fair and accurate ongoing tracking.

"But it's always good to check those projections against real numbers."

Similarly, W. B. Doner & Co., Southfield, Michigan, doesn't "expect to see any real surprises" from the census data, said Steve Levine, senior VP–executive media director. "We look at the census as a reaffirmation of what we've been projecting since the last census came out. If our projections based on the 1980 census were correct, the 1990 data should be more of a confirmation than anything else.

"We have to be mindful of the nature of any shift and how those shifts might impact our clients' businesses, but these are evolutionary, not revolutionary."

Source: Steven W. Colford, *Advertising Age,* April 15, 1991, pp. 16, 36. Used with permission.

INTRODUCTION

From how much shelf space Campbell Soup Co. uses in a particular neighborhood store to what the "graying" of the population means in media buying time, the 1990 U.S. census will give marketing researchers access to information that should allow them to develop an unprecedented profile of customers. This could increase the likelihood of choosing the best course of action. Applications could include (1) basic trending and forecasting, (2) target marketing, and (3) pricing strategy, as well as a variety of other business–related decisions. Consider the example in the accompanying box.

USING CENSUS BUREAU INFORMATION FOR PROBLEM SOLVING

BOX 4—1
—
FROM THE USER'S PERSPECTIVE
—

The Census Bureau is a virtual reservoir of information. Information from the Census Bureau, as well as other sources of secondary information, can be used to solve a variety of marketing-related problems. Consider the problem facing BUILD-A-LIKE, INC., a midsized manufacturing company located in Massachusetts. BUILD-A-LIKE is contemplating relocating operations to one of five southeastern states: Virginia (VA), North Carolina (NC), South Carolina (SC), Georgia (GA), and Florida (FL).

The first step in deciding on which state to relocate in was to evaluate each state on a number of general demographic and economic factors. Realizing that the *Statistical Abstract of the United States*, published by the Bureau of the Census, would provide the necessary data, BUILD-A-LIKE management compiled the following summary table.

	Business Failures per 10,000 Concerns, 1988		Unemployment, 1988		State Population Projections, 2000		Change in Crime Rate, 1987–1988		Hazardous Waste Sites, 1989	
	Rate	Rank	Rate	Rank	Total ($000)	Rank	Percent	Rank	Number	Rank
VA	78	30	3.9	38	6,877	12	5.5	3	20	19
NC	50	41	3.6	42	7,483	11	4.6	7	22	17
SC	59	37	4.5	32	3,906	24	4.9	6	23	16
GA	100	18	5.8	19	7,957	10	9.2	1	13	26
FL	103	17	5.0	28	15,415	4	5.1	5	51	6

	State/Local Government Direct General Expenditures per Capita, 1987		Unionized Manufacturing Employment, 1988		Motor Vehicle Accident Deaths per 100,000 Population, 1987		Retail Sales per Household, 1982–1988		Disposable Income per Capita, 1988	
	Dollars	Rank	Percent	Rank	Rate	Rank	Percentage Increase	Rank	Dollars	Rank
VA	2,400	33	12.2	31	18.2	34	54.0	7	15,050	10
NC	2,078	45	4.6	47	24.6	12	44.9	14	12,259	34
SC	2,121	42	3.1	49	31.7	2	43.5	18	11,101	41
GA	2,397	34	11.9	33	26.0	11	47.5	12	12,886	28
FL	2,351	35	8.9	40	23.3	17	42.0	21	14,338	16

Sources of existing market data are more widespread than you might expect; these are the sources researchers should consider first. Before spending time, money, and effort to collect new data, the researcher needs to determine whether useful information already exists and if it does, how to access it. This chapter discusses sources of already existing market research information, with particular emphasis on library and other traditional sources of secondary data. We begin by discussing two basic information sources, primary and secondary. Next we focus on how to evaluate

Filling out a census form

existing sources of market data, establishing criteria upon which to make the evaluation. The remainder of the chapter discusses traditional sources of existing domestic and international market data, and provides details on how these sources can be accessed.

INFORMATION SOURCES: PRIMARY VERSUS SECONDARY DATA

At the broadest level, information sources available to the marketing researcher can be classified as primary or secondary. Primary data are collected to meet specific research needs; in this sense they are customized and tend to require specialized data collection procedures. In Chapters 6 through 8 we discuss various ways to collect primary data.

Secondary data, which we discuss here, involve already published data collected for purposes other than the specific research need at hand. It is possible to distinguish between two types of secondary data: internal and external. **Internal secondary data** are available within an organization — accounting records, management decision support systems, sales records, and so on. **External secondary data** are available outside the organization from two main sources: (1) libraries and other public sources, and (2) syndicated services that collect data under standardized procedures intended to serve the needs of an array of clients. Syndicated services are discussed in detail in Chapter 5.

Some examples may clarify the different types of data. If firm A conducts a survey to determine a demographic or psychographic profile of purchasers of solar heating equipment, it is collecting primary data. Firm B might get this same consumer information from sales records, rather than approach people directly in a survey; in this case, the information is considered internal secondary data. It is secondary because it was not collected for the specific purpose, and it is internal because the data are

INTERNAL SECONDARY DATA

Data routinely collected by the organization or firm such as accounting records or sales records, etc.

EXTERNAL SECONDARY DATA

Data available outside the organization or firm supplied by libraries and/or syndicated data service companies.

derived from information that exists within firm B. A third firm might conduct a search for external secondary data with regard to these same consumers. That is, firm C might turn up a consumer market study conducted by the U.S. Department of Energy on the extent to which government policy has influenced the use of an alternative energy source. Such a study would be considered external secondary data, because the data were gathered for another purpose by an agency external to the firm.

EVALUATING SECONDARY INFORMATION

Determining the quality of information that is used in solving a marketing-related problem is essential, however the data are obtained. This is especially true in the case of external secondary information, because the data have been collected for a purpose that may be different from a firm's purposes and, moreover, collected by someone outside the organization. Information obtained from secondary sources is not necessarily equally reliable or valid. Secondary information can be misleading, and the data must be evaluated carefully in terms of recency and credibility.

To evaluate secondary information, you need to consider the source of the data, the measures used to get it, the time period in which the data were collected, and the appropriateness of the assumptions and conclusions. The user of secondary information should routinely ask the following general questions:[1]

1. *What is the purpose of the study?* A fundamental question concerns why the information was collected in the first place. Rarely are data collected without some intent, and the intent of the study ultimately determines the degree of precision, the types of measures used, and the method of data collection. Consider the consumer price index (CPI), which is calculated monthly by the U.S. Bureau of Labor Statistics. The CPI measures price movements in the United States; it is based specifically on 400 consumer items, with the index for each item based on the average price paid by a sample of wage earners and clerical workers during some key year. Specifically, the index represents an average for a family of four, living in an urban area, including a father, 38 years of age; a mother, 37, not employed outside the home; a boy, 13; and an 8-year-old girl. An index based on these assumptions clearly is not representative of the expenditures of most families. If you use the CPI, you must ask whether expenditure patterns for the group of respondents you are interested in are different from those used to define the index. Furthermore, because the index is only a rough barometer of purchasing power, you must question its usefulness as background for specific decisions that may require a high degree of precision.

2. *Who collected the information?* Because secondary information is collected by someone outside the organization, a natural question concerns the expertise and credibility of the source. Organizations that provide secondary information vary with respect to their technical competence, resources, and overall quality. First, you can learn about the reputations of various sources of secondary information by contacting clients and others

who have used the information provided by the source. Second, you can investigate how the data were obtained and assess the training and expertise present in the organization supplying the information.

3. *What information was collected?* You should always identify what information was actually collected by the organization supplying the data. In particular, it is important to identify

— What was measured. For example, were fares or riders counted in a study on mass transit use?
— In what context the data were collected. Were all the leading brands included in the taste study?
— What the relationship was between what was measured and the event of interest. Were self-report data used to infer actual behavior?
— How the data were classified. Were the data broken down by uses and markets, or were they simply aggregated?

4. *When was the information collected?* The time period over which secondary information was collected plays an integral role in how the data should be interpreted. Conditions specific to the time the data were collected may influence the results. If you want to interpret tracking data on U.S. sales of and consumer attitudes toward imported products such as Stolichnaya vodka, you will need to consider information on world affairs and, specifically, attitudes toward the exporting country at the time the data were collected. The passage of time may influence the definitions used, change the measurement instrument, or render the information obsolete.

5. *How was the information obtained?* An essential ingredient to consider in evaluating the quality of secondary information is the methodology employed to collect the data. Specific elements to examine include (1) the size and nature of the target sample, (2) the response rate obtained, (3) the questionnaire used, (4) the experimental procedures employed (if any), (5) the interview procedure followed, and (6) the analytical method used. The critical issue in evaluating the procedure employed in collecting data is one of bias; that is, was there anything in the collection procedures that could potentially lead to a particular result, that could produce results that are not generalizable to the target population, or that could invalidate the results?

6. *Is the information consistent with other information?* In principle, two or more independent sources of secondary information should agree. When you are evaluating secondary information, a good strategy is to attempt to find multiple sources of the data and then to compare their conclusions. When differences exist, you should try to find the reasons for them, and then eventually determine which source is more reliable. This may be difficult or even impossible to do, depending on the amount of disclosure concerning the collection procedure.

Exhibit 4–1 presents a flowchart indicating the various decisions that need to be made when using secondary data. The flowchart is divided into two main sections: one examines the applicability of secondary data to the objectives of the research project; the other examines the accuracy of the data.

Exhibit 4—1
Evaluating Secondary Data

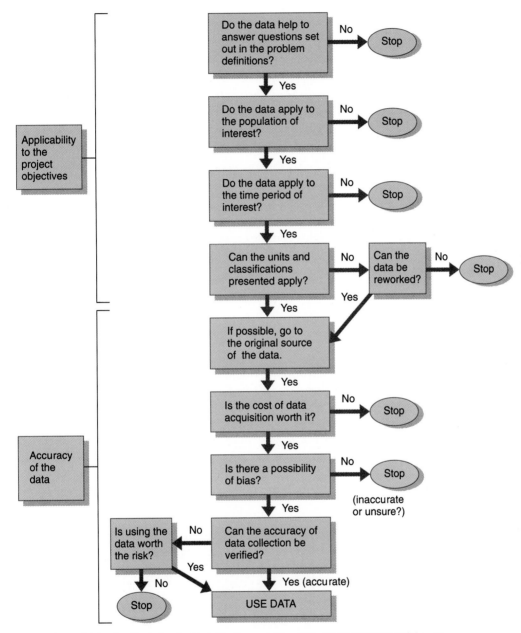

Source: Robert W. Joselyn, *Designing the Marketing Research (New York: Petrocelli/Charter, 1977), p. 15.*

TRADITIONAL SOURCES OF SECONDARY MARKET DATA

Secondary market data are produced by many organizations, including federal, state, and local governments; quasi-governmental organizations; trade associations; not-for-profit enterprises (such as research institutes and universities); commercial publishers; investment brokerage houses; and professional market research firms. The U.S. Bureau of the Census, the National Sporting Goods Manufacturers Association, Sales and Marketing Management, Smith-Barney, and Frost & Sullivan are examples of secondary market data producers. Because the data-producing organizations turn out millions of data elements per year, it frequently becomes difficult to see the forest for the trees.

The number of potentially useful print sources is considerable, so we concentrate here on an important group of reference works that can lead the researcher to other appropriate secondary source materials. These tools consist primarily of handbooks, directories, indexes, and compilations that guide the novice researcher through a complex maze of secondary source documents. It is important to be familiar with these reference works, most of which you can find in large research libraries or specialized business libraries.

Industrial Classification

One prerequisite for the researcher to become familiar with is the hierarchical structure that is used for organizing product and industry data. Presentation of secondary market data in many standard reference works follows the Standard Industrial Classification (SIC) scheme.[2] Every industry is assigned an SIC number by the federal government, and all the firms in an industry report activity according to industry number.

The SIC was developed for use in the classification of establishments by type of activity in which they are engaged. The purpose of the classification is to facilitate collection, tabulation, presentation, and analysis of var-

A library reference room

ious sorts of data. It also promotes the uniformity and comparability of data collected not only by federal and state governments but also by private organizations.

The SIC makes it possible for researchers to collect and disseminate industry data on a two-digit, three-digit, or four-digit level. The more digits there are in a level, the more specific the information. The following list includes examples of two-, three-, and four-digit codes and their respective descriptions.

Major group 20 — Food and Kindred Products
Industry group 202 — Dairy Products
Industry number 2022 — Cheese

The two-digit major group 20 includes all establishments engaged in the manufacture or processing of foods and beverages. The three-digit industry group 202 includes only firms that manufacture or process dairy products, and the four-digit industry number 2022 represents only establishments engaged in the processing of cheese. The four-digit level, which is usually the most descriptive, is as detailed as the *SIC Manual* gets. Other reference works extend the classification to as many as seven digits in order to identify and classify product-level information more precisely—if you want information on cheese dips, for example.

Locating the appropriate SIC numbers in the *SIC Manual* is a prerequisite to locating secondary information in many standard business directories, periodical indexes, and statistical compilations.

Guides to Business Information Sources

A guide to business information sources is one of the best places to begin searching for secondary source information. The vast array of business reference sources is more than we can cover in a single chapter, but descriptive guides explain the reference capability of the various sources. A guide can help the researcher identify the important standard source or recurring information sources on a specific subject. To locate information about a specific industry, for example, you use a guide to identify the major statistical information sources, the pertinent trade associations, and the trade journals or directories. Some useful business information guides are listed in Appendix 4A at the end of this chapter.

Directories

Because the pursuit of secondary market research frequently involves the identification of individuals or organizations that gather pertinent information, directories are useful sources. An indispensable tool that serves as an index to over 10,000 published directories is

The Directory of Directories, 5th ed.
Cecilia Ann Marlow, editor
Detroit: Gale Research Company, 1987

Trade associations frequently are the most accurate and up-to-date source of information regarding specific industries. Two directories that receive heavy use and can assist you in the identification of over 20,000 trade associations are

Encyclopedia of Associations, 23rd ed.
Karin Koek et al., editors
Detroit: Gale Research Company, 1988

National Trade and Professional Associations of the United States, 23rd ed.
John J. Russell, et al., editors
Washington, D.C.: Columbia Books, Inc., 1988

Data on the most specialized of products (e.g., tempered glass) are frequently collected by trade associations. Data of this nature may not be widely disseminated, so a researcher may need to contact an association directly for information.

Indexes to Business Literature

Marketing information must be as current as possible in order to be useful to the researcher. Significant shifts can and do occur in the marketplace, and these swings must be accurately reflected in marketing research. For these reasons, the business periodical literature is a critical current information resource. To access this literature, indexes identify articles on a specific subject in hundreds of different periodical publications. A researcher might use an index, for example, to locate survey data on supermarket shoppers appearing in a trade journal.

The major business indexes, which differ in scope, length of coverage, frequency of update, and format, are presented in Appendix 4B.

Indexes to Newspapers

Newspapers, like business periodicals, are important sources of business/market information, but many local newspapers are not included in traditional indexes. Appendix 4C provides information on three major newspaper indexes.

Developments in the information technologies have enhanced access to information in important city newspapers. Vu/Text, for one, is a database vendor that provides on-line search and access to the contents of many major-market newspapers such as the *Philadelphia Inquirer.* Other technology has made possible the introduction of *Newspaper Abstracts Ondisc,* produced by UMI. This database, available in many research libraries, contains abstracts and indexing from 1987 to the present for the *New York Times, The Wall Street Journal,* the *Christian Science Monitor,* the *Los Angeles Times,* the *Chicago Tribune,* the *Boston Globe,* and the *Atlanta Constitution.*

Indexes to Statistical Information

Indexes to statistical information are extremely important tools for marketing researchers. They provide regularly updated and detailed subject indexing of statistical contents of thousands of publications produced by government, trade, and commercial organizations. Appendix 4D lists the indexes to statistical information.

Indexes to Specialized Business Information Services

Beyond the marketing information you can glean from trade associations, business periodicals, government documents, and assorted other publishers of statistical information, commercial market research reports and investment brokerage house reports represent two additional important bodies of literature that are now indexed by subject. Firms such as Frost & Sullivan, Business Communications Company, and Predicasts regularly publish market surveys on various products and industries. Although these reports can be expensive, they may represent a low-cost alternative to primary research.

One source that provides subject indexing of published marketing research is

Findex, The Directory of Market Research Reports, Studies, and Surveys
Bethesda, Md.: NSA Directories, 1979 to present

Other important sources of marketing information are the reports of investment brokerage houses such as Bear Stearns, Inc., and Kidder Peabody & Company, Inc. The company and industry reports that expert professionals prepare for these firms can reveal information on market share or industry trends and forecasts. One index to these reports is

CIRR/Corporate and Industry Research Reports Index
Eastchester, N.Y.: J.A. Micropublishing, Inc., 1982 to present

Statistical Compilations

Statistical indexes direct the researcher to specific statistical publications. Statistical compilations actually reprint the data extracted from numerous secondary source documents. You can save considerable research time if you can find the data you need in one of the sourcebooks listed in Appendix 4E.

Census-Based Statistical Extrapolations

The various censuses conducted by the U.S. Bureau of the Census form the statistical foundation for much of the extrapolation done on U.S. population trends and economic activity. The various major components of the census series are detailed in Appendix 4F.

Two of the most useful compendiums of consumer market data that extrapolate from U.S. census figures are the *Sourcebook of Demographics and Buying Power* and the *Survey of Buying Power.*

Sourcebook of demographics and buying power. This publication measures the likelihood that households—by zip code area—will exhibit certain purchasing patterns when compared to the U.S. average. It is unique because of

TABLE 4–1

Example of Zip Code Area Analysis

NORTH CAROLINA   SOCIOECONOMIC PROFILE

C   CACI's 1988 Sourcebook of Demographics and Buying Power for Every Zip Code in the USA

ZIP CODE		MEDIAN HOUSEHOLD INCOME						AVG. HSHLD. INCOME 1988	AVG. HSHLD. SIZE 1988	AVG. FAMILY INCOME 1988	AVG. FAMILY SIZE 1988	# FAM- ILIES 1988	PER CAPITA INCOME 1988	% POP. IN POVERTY 1980	% POP. IN GROUP QTRS. 1980	EDUCATION		EMPLOYMENT PROFILE				
#	POST OFFICE NAME	1980	1988	1993	% ANNUAL GROWTH RATE 80-88	NAT'L CENTILE 1988	CENTILE WITHIN STATE 1988									MEDIAN YEARS OF EDUC. 1980	% COLLEGE GRADS 1980	% WHITE COLLAR 1980	% WOMEN IN LABOR FORCE 1980	AVG. TRAVEL MINS. TO WORK 1980	% UNEM- PLOYED 1980	EMPLOY- MENT/ POP. RATIO (%) 1980
28396	WAGRAM	12458	18611	20771	5.1	24	28	22107	3.0	24098	3.5	654	7096	24.0	2.7	11.5	8.8	33.9	55.1	23.4	12.0	53.1
28397	WAKULLA	11875	19583	23333	6.5	30	35	21444	3.6	22440	3.9	41	5949	24.8	0.0	10.6	6.2	14.9	52.2	32.3	9.8	51.1
28398	WARSAW	10926	18119	18132	6.5	21	23	22447	2.8	25213	3.4	1721	7875	23.0	0.5	12.1	12.6	35.5	48.8	22.1	4.7	59.9
28399	WHITE OAK	10101	15177	16809	5.2	9	5	16956	2.9	19017	3.4	374	5746	21.6	0.0	10.7	6.4	19.1	43.2	30.1	4.8	48.6
28401	WILMINGTON	8847	13704	15290	5.6	4	1	18339	2.4	21282	3.0	6380	7540	28.9	2.2	11.5	8.7	39.2	47.8	21.6	9.1	49.6
28402	WILMINGTON	0	0	0	0.0	0	0	0	32.0	0	32.0	1	165	0.0	98.4	14.4	28.0	0.0	0.0	11.4	0.0	86.0
28403	WILMINGTON	17163	26543	29159	5.6	72	87	30236	2.5	34472	3.0	14715	11724	9.7	1.9	12.7	22.1	56.9	51.1	21.5	6.0	59.8
28404	WILMINGTON	15000	23226	27500	5.6	55	65	25402	2.9	27394	3.3	117	8728	17.8	0.0	11.3	3.2	30.8	46.4	27.7	8.6	56.0
28405	WILMINGTON	18148	27725	30227	5.4	76	90	29862	2.9	31991	3.2	8291	10243	12.1	1.9	12.4	12.5	50.9	51.7	23.7	7.7	60.1
28420	ASH	11524	19035	22145	6.5	27	31	22633	2.8	25116	3.2	1059	8090	24.5	0.0	11.3	5.8	32.9	40.7	30.5	8.9	47.3
28421	ATKINSON	10921	16458	18453	5.3	13	11	19926	2.7	21595	3.3	374	7381	18.8	0.0	12.0	6.1	23.6	47.0	37.3	4.9	52.6
28422	BOLIVIA	14089	23029	26541	6.3	54	64	25307	2.8	27926	3.2	1174	9150	18.5	0.4	12.0	7.9	36.6	40.9	28.5	8.1	49.4
28423	BOLTON	12311	20093	22218	6.3	34	38	24306	3.2	26591	3.6	626	7640	28.5	0.7	11.0	4.0	20.9	40.1	33.7	7.2	53.2
28424	BRUNSWICK	12438	20204	21809	6.3	34	39	24593	2.6	27866	3.1	157	9151	18.6	3.1	12.1	11.3	50.6	52.5	20.7	8.0	55.8
28425	BURGAW	12981	18840	20808	4.8	25	30	22188	2.7	25430	3.2	1794	7825	20.7	3.9	11.6	8.4	40.5	47.8	27.3	7.4	52.3
28428	CAROLINA BEACH	13161	19935	21396	5.3	32	37	23409	2.4	26243	2.8	857	9371	10.7	3.1	12.3	9.0	45.6	46.3	23.3	6.4	54.7
28429	CASTLE HAYNE	17613	26888	29206	5.4	73	88	28138	2.8	30684	3.2	1686	9913	11.7	1.1	12.1	5.1	42.7	57.7	23.5	6.0	60.0
28430	CERRO GORDO	9462	14915	16486	5.9	8	5	19750	2.8	21755	3.3	507	6963	30.1	0.0	10.9	5.0	33.6	52.0	27.0	4.4	53.6
28431	CHADBOURN	9602	15226	16843	5.9	9	6	19282	2.7	22165	3.2	2045	7049	30.4	0.0	10.7	6.7	33.1	45.0	24.6	7.5	52.4
28432	CLARENDON	9703	15430	16929	6.0	10	7	19569	2.8	21752	3.2	460	7078	27.5	0.0	9.9	3.4	28.7	41.7	27.7	4.3	55.2

ZIP CODE		County FIPS CODE (SEE APPDX.)	1988 POP.	1988 AGE DISTRIBUTION (%)										MEDIAN AGE			RACE (%)					
#	POST OFFICE NAME			0-4	5-11	12-17	18-24	25-34	35-44	45-54	55-64	65-74	75+	1980	1988	1993	WHITE			BLACK		
																	1980	1988	1993	1980	1988	1993
28396	WAGRAM	165	2536	9.2	12.3	11.4	11.7	16.2	14.8	7.7	7.1	5.5	4.2	26.3	28.5	29.3	44.9	42.1	39.4	45.1	47.6	50.0
28397	WAKULLA	155	167	11.4	14.4	12.0	13.8	16.2	12.6	8.4	6.0	4.2	1.8	22.9	24.3	25.2	5.7	5.4	4.9	3.5	3.6	3.8
28398	WARSAW	061	6379	9.6	11.6	9.9	11.5	15.4	12.8	8.7	8.5	6.9	5.0	28.7	29.5	30.3	51.3	48.4	45.5	48.3	51.3	54.2
28399	WHITE OAK	017	1395	9.2	11.2	10.8	12.9	14.8	13.6	9.0	6.6	6.9	5.2	28.1	29.0	29.5	53.2	50.3	47.4	46.7	49.6	52.5
28401	WILMINGTON	129	23857	7.7	9.9	8.5	11.4	16.5	13.1	7.8	8.8	9.2	7.0	30.5	33.1	33.9	48.8	49.4	49.2	50.7	50.1	50.1
28402	WILMINGTON	129	185	0.0	0.0	0.0	56.8	28.6	10.8	1.6	0.5	0.0	0.0	22.9	24.7	25.3	89.0	89.2	89.8	7.1	7.6	7.5
28403	WILMINGTON	129	51649	6.4	8.8	8.6	11.9	16.9	15.1	11.0	9.7	7.2	4.4	30.6	33.7	35.2	89.7	89.2	88.4	9.9	10.0	10.7
28404	WILMINGTON	019	416	8.7	12.0	10.3	12.5	16.8	14.2	10.1	7.2	4.3	3.1	26.4	28.6	29.6	70.1	67.8	65.1	28.9	31.3	33.7
28405	WILMINGTON	129	29249	7.1	10.4	10.6	11.9	16.0	17.0	10.7	7.7	5.2	3.3	28.6	31.1	32.5	78.3	77.4	76.2	21.0	21.8	23.0
28420	ASH	019	3626	8.2	10.9	9.7	11.3	15.4	12.6	9.5	9.5	8.0	4.9	30.1	31.3	32.1	69.7	67.5	65.1	29.4	31.6	34.1
28421	ATKINSON	141	1369	9.5	11.8	10.6	10.4	13.7	11.9	9.0	8.4	8.4	6.4	31.0	30.1	30.3	51.4	48.4	45.4	48.5	51.6	54.5
28422	BOLIVIA	019	4063	8.0	11.1	10.2	11.0	14.9	13.3	9.7	9.0	8.0	4.7	30.2	31.5	32.1	74.1	72.3	70.2	25.3	27.1	29.1
28423	BOLTON	047	2390	9.5	11.8	11.0	12.6	14.8	12.6	9.5	7.4	6.7	4.4	27.4	28.5	28.9	32.2	30.0	27.9	46.3	48.1	49.9
28424	BRUNSWICK	047	563	7.6	9.9	9.2	10.8	15.5	14.2	10.5	8.9	7.3	5.9	30.9	33.1	34.1	68.5	66.3	63.7	30.9	33.2	35.8
28425	BURGAW	141	6579	7.5	9.9	9.8	10.7	15.1	13.5	9.8	9.3	8.0	6.4	31.4	33.0	33.7	59.3	56.4	53.6	40.5	43.3	46.2
28428	CAROLINA BEACH	129	2858	5.8	8.0	7.8	10.5	15.6	14.5	10.9	9.8	10.0	7.0	33.9	36.9	37.9	97.6	97.4	97.2	1.2	1.3	1.5
28429	CASTLE HAYNE	129	5812	7.3	10.2	10.2	11.2	16.3	16.3	11.0	8.8	5.7	3.1	29.1	31.7	33.3	78.9	76.5	74.1	20.3	22.7	25.1
28430	CERRO GORDO	047	1792	9.1	11.3	9.6	11.2	14.6	13.3	10.4	9.0	7.0	4.5	30.4	30.7	31.4	78.6	76.7	74.7	21.3	23.1	25.1
28431	CHADBOURN	047	7179	9.6	11.7	9.2	10.9	15.8	12.2	9.5	8.6	7.4	5.1	29.3	30.1	31.1	69.6	67.1	64.5	29.4	31.9	34.4
28432	CLARENDON	047	1568	8.6	10.7	9.3	11.7	14.6	13.4	12.1	8.3	7.0	4.3	30.4	31.3	32.3	88.7	87.4	66.1	11.0	12.2	13.5

the work in developing zip code demographic data. Besides supplying a population and socioeconomic profile for each zip code, the *Sourcebook* calculates buying power, which it calls the *purchasing potential index.*

The purchasing potential index in the *Sourcebook* is based on a national score of 100. An index score of 105 for apparel, for example, means that consumers in that zip code area have a 5 percent greater capacity to purchase apparel than the average U.S. consumer; a score of 85 would indicate 15 percent less potential to purchase apparel.[3]

Table 4–1 provides an example of the variety of zip code area analyses that are available for Wilmington, North Carolina.

Survey of buying power.   The *Survey of Buying Power* is published annually in two parts, in July and in October. It is most valuable for its current population and income analysis of metropolitan statistical areas, counties, and states, as well as population and income projections for these same geographic areas. Specifically, it includes, for each geographical area, population and other characteristics, total retail sales, effective buying income, and the buying power index (BPI). Table 4–2 illustrates these reports for several New York cities.[4]

The buying power index (BPI) is a weighted index that converts three basic elements—population, effective buying income (EBI equals gross income available after taxes to purchase goods and services), and retail sales—into a measurement of a market's ability to buy, and is expressed as a percentage of the U.S. potential. It is calculated by giving weights of 0.5 to the particular market's percent of U.S. EBI, 0.3 to its percent of U.S. retail sales, and 0.2 to its percent of U.S. population.

$$\text{BPI} = \underset{\text{(EBI \%)}}{0.5} + \underset{\text{(U.S. retail sales \%)}}{0.3} + \underset{\text{(Population \%)}}{0.2}$$

The BPI is probably one of the *Survey of Buying Power*'s most widely used single market measures. Because it is broadly based, it is most useful in estimating the potential for mass products sold at popular prices. The less a product's mass-market appeal, the greater the need for a BPI that is refined by more defining or discriminating factors, such as social class, income, age, or gender.

International Sources

Continuing globalization and searches for opportunities in new markets will require marketing researchers and managers to develop information on relevant overseas economies. There are a fairly large number of sources on international activity. Appendix 4G provides details on a relatively large number of available sources.

Other Sources

Three other basic sources of standardized market research information provide standardized data covering either product usage, media habits, and social trends, or consumer values and lifestyles.

— *The Study of Media and Markets* (New York: Simmons Market Research Bureau, Inc.). Simmons Market Research (SMRB) is one of the most widely used sources of product usage and media audience data. SMRB produces a wealth of market information; data are available for 750 product/service categories, 3,500 brands, and numerous media audiences (print and broadcast). SMRB data can prove useful in developing category and brand target segments and identifying the media that reach them. Many reference libraries have made SMRB volumes available, and SMRB data can be accessed through vendors that provide time-sharing services.

TABLE 4—2

Example of Reports in the *Survey of Buying Power*

New York

POPULATION*

METRO AREA County City	Total Population (thousands)	% of U.S.	Median Age of Pop.	% of Population by Age Group				Households (thousands)
				18–24 Years	25–34 Years	35–49 Years	50 & Over	
ALBANY-SCHENECTADY-TROY	879.9	.3510	34.1	11.5	16.6	21.2	27.2	338.0
Albany	293.1	.1169	34.0	13.3	16.7	20.8	27.6	116.0
— Albany	101.3	.0404	31.4	20.1	18.4	17.3	26.1	42.2
Greene	45.1	.0180	35.7	9.6	16.1	20.8	30.1	16.7
Montgomery	51.9	.0207	36.8	8.3	14.3	19.4	33.1	20.2
Rennselaer	154.6	.0617	32.9	12.7	16.6	20.5	26.1	57.7
— Troy	54.3	.0216	29.8	19.9	17.9	15.7	25.0	20.8
Saratoga	185.9	.0742	32.8	10.3	17.6	23.4	22.8	68.2
Schenectady	149.3	.0595	35.7	9.8	16.1	20.7	30.4	59.2
— Schenectady	65.6	.0262	32.9	12.7	18.9	17.3	28.7	27.8
SUBURBAN TOTAL	658.7	.2628	35.1	9.3	16.0	22.7	27.5	247.2
BINGHAMTON	264.4	.1054	34.0	11.0	16.5	20.1	28.2	100.6
Broome	211.8	.0844	34.2	11.7	16.5	19.7	29.0	81.7
— Binghamton	52.9	.0211	34.5	13.7	16.9	17.4	31.7	22.6
Tioga	52.2	.0210	33.0	8.2	16.7	21.5	25.1	18.9
SUBURBAN TOTAL	211.5	.0843	33.8	10.3	16.6	20.7	27.3	78.0
BUFFALO	966.3	.3852	34.8	10.5	16.3	20.1	29.7	376.1
Erie	966.3	.3852	34.8	10.5	16.3	20.1	29.7	376.1
— Buffalo	327.4	.1305	32.2	12.5	18.2	17.6	27.2	136.1
SUBURBAN TOTAL	638.9	.2547	36.5	9.5	15.3	21.4	30.8	240.0

* All data is based on *Sales & Marketing Management* estimates, December 31, 1990.
Reprinted by permission of Sales & Marketing Management. Copyright: Survey of Buying Power. August 19, 1991.

> — *Yankelovich Monitor* (New York: Yankelovich, Skelly, and White),
> 1970 to present, annual. The *Yankelovich Monitor* is a research service
> that tracks over 40 social trends and provides information about their
> shifts in size and direction and the resulting market implications.
> Social trend information as reported by the *Yankelovich Monitor* has
> proven useful in identifying likely shifts in demand for various
> product categories. One example is the U.S. shift to "white"
> liquors (e.g., vodka and gin) from "brown" (e.g., Scotch or
> blended whiskies).

EFFECTIVE BUYING INCOME

RETAIL SALES BY STORE GROUP

Total EBI ($000)	Median Hsld. EBI	Buying Power Index	Total Retail Sales ($000)	Food ($000)	Eating, Drinking Places ($000)	General Mdse. ($000)	Furniture/ Furnish. Appliance ($000)	Automotive ($000)	Drug ($000)
13,612,194	30,420	.3816	7,045,006	1,539,547	663,119	842,591	372,380	1,577,469	251,632
4,875,168	31,029	.1451	3,136,897	565,279	317,651	481,435	209,586	750,590	100,707
1,484,343	23,181	.0482	1,141,631	167,060	129,477	197,257	56,343	302,906	37,968
547,441	24,074	.0165	303,378	88,449	22,738	23,063	9,567	61,049	12,211
669,613	25,062	.0188	311,405	93,803	21,413	31,959	7,145	46,619	18,130
2,201,583	29,079	.0579	849,624	249,174	81,321	60,559	28,147	170,664	41,771
676,229	22,053	.0198	349,284	103,314	47,677	24,887	19,199	43,878	25,390
2,921,803	34,136	.0782	1,299,958	274,885	135,461	113,225	52,127	338,321	32,873
2,396,586	30,466	.0651	1,143,744	267,957	84,535	132,350	65,808	210,226	47,940
922,293	23,985	.0265	486,243	133,804	44,334	32,316	28,738	121,231	24,526
10,529,329	33,286	.2871	1,968,059	402,534	184,343	263,497	96,456	418,051	89,198
4,041,791	30,046	.1116	1,732,885	342,163	170,359	254,937	93,362	333,087	80,620
3,222,537	29,378	.0918	541,436	116,166	55,006	66,833	41,829	102,731	28,043
748,263	22,201	.0239	235,174	60,371	13,984	8,560	3,094	84,964	8,578
819,254	33,371	.0198	1,426,623	286,368	129,337	196,664	54,627	315,320	61,155
3,293,528	32,531	.0877	6,781,443	1,611,814	710,071	758,104	369,250	1,406,349	336,787
13,697,931	28,022	.3854	6,781,443	1,611,814	710,071	758,104	369,250	1,406,349	336,787
13,697,931	19,227	.3854	1,554,462	499,801	222,825	97,446	69,604	203,234	107,205
3,867,145	19,227	.1072	1,554,462	499,801	222,825	97,446	69,604	203,234	107,205
9,830,786	32,845	.2782	5,226,981	1,112,013	487,246	660,658	299,646	1,203,115	229,582

— SRI Values and Lifestyles (VALS) (Menlo Park, Calif.: SRI International). VALS is a research service that tracks marketing-relevant shifts in the beliefs, values, and lifestyles of a sample of the U.S. population. The VALS system divides the population into segments consisting of three major groups of consumers, which in turn are divided into nine specific segments. Tracking the shifts in the values and behavior of these segments can help researchers understand a target segment.

Box 4—2
▬
From the
User's
Perspective
▬

How to Construct a Custom BPI

The Buying Power Index, or BPI, was patented by *Sales & Marketing Management* and has been a part of the *Survey of Buying Power* for more than 30 years, providing marketers with a standardized measurement of the relative buying power of states, metros, counties, and cities. The BPI listed in the *Survey's* data sections is a general indicator constructed from data on total population, total effective buying income (EBI), and total retail sales—the three basic categories of statistics covered by the *Survey.*

For those who need to define their markets more specifically, however, it is possible to construct a customized version of the BPI, using any of the subclassifications of statistics in the *Survey's* three basic data fields. By selecting a demographic component (population), an economic component (income), and a distribution component (retail sales), you can use the formula outlined below to convert data from individual markets into a custom BPI for your product or service.

For our purposes, we will label these three BPI components as follows: Demographic = A; Economic = B; and Distribution = C. Looking at each of these areas individually, here's how you might go about selecting them:

A: Demographic. First of all, you'll need to isolate the population or household-related factor that best describes your "ideal" consumer. For example, if you're selling video games, the 18-and-under age segment is a better indicator of market potential than total population. On the other hand, if your product is media-oriented (magazines, mail-order catalogs, etc.), you may want to use household counts as your demographic component.

B: Economic. The next step involves selecting the income group(s) best suited to your product. Here, the *Survey* offers you five basic ranges of household incomes, and you can easily combine two or more groups to achieve a broader spectrum of potential. For example, if you're selling a premium-priced product, you might select households with incomes of $35,000 and above.

C: Distribution. Isolating a particular store group that parallels your preferred channel of distribution is the final step in the preliminary selection process. If you're selling beer, for example, you may want to combine Eating & Drinking Place sales and Food Store sales, since these are the two largest markets for your product. On the other hand, if you're selling shampoo, Drugstores and General Merchandise stores (which includes department stores and discount stores) would be a better distribution-related indicator.

Once these three factors have been selected, you can then compute your custom BPI by following this simple four-step process:

Step 1. For each market (region, state, metro, county, etc.), you'll first need to compare local activity to that for the United States as a whole, producing a ratio for each of the three BPI factors (A-B-C). In this example, the demographic component (A) would be calculated as follows:

$$\frac{\text{Market's Pop. under 18}}{\text{U.S. Pop. under 18}} = \text{A\%}$$

Next, using households with EBIs of \$35,000 and above as the economic factor (B), we compare the market with the appropriate U.S. total:

$$\frac{\text{Market's Hshlds. w/EBIs \$35,000+}}{\text{U.S. Hshlds. w/EBIs \$35,000+}} = \text{B\%}$$

And finally, we calculate the distribution component (C) by constructing a ratio of local Food Store sales to U.S. Food Store sales:

$$\frac{\text{Market's Food Store Sales}}{\text{U.S. Food Store Sales}} = \text{C\%}$$

Step 2. Armed with these percentages (A-B-C), we are now ready to assign weights to the demographic, economic, and distribution-related components, according to their perceived importance in the selling process. In all cases, the assigned weights should be expressed in decimals (50% = .5, 30% = .3, etc.).

Since income is often cited as the most important indicator of potential purchasing power, your weighting of these factors might look something like this:

Factor A (demographic) — .2 (20%)

Factor B (economic) — .5 (50%)

Factor C (distribution) — .3 (30%)

Step 3. Multiplying each component ratio (A-B-C) by its appropriate weight and adding the resulting totals will then give you the BPI for a particular market:

$$(.2 \times \text{A\%}) + (.5 \times \text{B\%}) + (.3 \times \text{C\%}) = \text{BPI}$$

The fractional figure you arrive at can then be used as a relative indicator to compare the potential buying power of this market to that for the United States as a whole (U.S. = 100.0000.)*

Step 4. Repeat this same procedure for each targeted market, compiling a list of markets ranked according to their BPIs. If your particular product warrants the construction of a BPI with only two factors (or possibly four or five), remember that the same principles apply in terms of weighting the various components. In other words, the percentages should still total 100 percent, regardless of the number of BPI components.

*Note: If you're selling your product in a limited number of markets, you may want to substitute the combined total of these markets for the U.S. totals in your calculations. In such a case, your BPI of 100.0000 would represent the total of these markets only.

Source: Reprinted by permission of *Sales & Marketing Management,* Copyright: Survey of Buying Power August 19, 1991.

SUMMARY

In this chapter we presented traditional sources of secondary marketing research information. We began our discussion by considering the differences between primary and secondary sources of information and then discussed how to evaluate secondary data. The majority of the chapter was devoted to discussing various sources of secondary data of different varieties. Those readers who will have to conduct their own research can use the appendixes at the end of this chapter, which present information about a large number of reference source materials.

KEY CONCEPTS

Primary Data

Secondary Data

Evaluating Secondary Data

Buying Power Index

Customized Buying Power Index

Directories

Indexes to Business

Indexes to Statistical Information

Statistical Compilations

International Sources

REVIEW QUESTIONS

1. Discuss the role that secondary information plays in the research process.

2. Describe a situation where it could be useful to employ both primary and secondary research. Are primary data preferred?

3. Visit your library, and examine the *SIC Manual.* Select an SIC number that represents an industry of interest to you, and identify three standard business reference works that use SIC numbers to organize their information.

4. Develop a customized BPI for the Columbia, South Carolina, metro area for a premium-priced video game product distributed through General Merchandise Stores.

ENDNOTES

1. This material is adapted from David W. Stewart, *Secondary Research: Information Sources and Methods* (Beverly Hills, Calif.: Sage Publications, 1984), pp. 23–33.

2. U.S. Office of Management and Budget, *Standard Industrial Classification Manual,* rev. ed. (Washington, D.C.: Government Printing Office, 1989).

3. This definition comes from the *Sourcebook of Demographics and Buying Power for Every Zip Code in the USA* (Arlington, VA.: CACI, 1986).

4. The definitions were taken from *Sales and Marketing Management's Survey of Buying Power,* July 27, 1987, pp. C-3, A-5, A-6.

Guides to Business Information Sources

Business Information, How to Find It, How to Use It
Michael R. Lavin
Phoenix, Ariz.: Oryx Press, 1987

Business Information Sources, rev. ed.
Loran M. Daniels
Berkeley, Calif.: University of California Press, 1984

Encyclopedia of Business Information Sources, 6th ed.
James Way, editor
Detroit: Gale Research Company, 1986

Information Sourcebook for Marketing and Strategic Planners
Van Mayros and D. Michael Werner
Radnor, Pa.: Chilton Book Company, 1983

Indexes to Business Literature

Business Index
Menlo Park, Calif.: Information Access Company, 1979 to present

Business Periodical Index
New York: H. W. Wilson Company, 1958 to present

F & S Index: Europe
Cleveland: Predicasts, Inc., 1980 to present

F & S Index: International
Cleveland: Predicasts, Inc., 1964 to present

Journal of Marketing (Every issue contains the section "Marketing Abstracts".) Chicago: American Marketing Association, 1936 to present

Topicator: Classified Article Guide to the Advertising/Communications/Marketing Periodical Press Florissant, Colo.: Topicator.

Indexes to Newspapers

National Newspaper Index
Menlo Park, Calif.: Information Access Company, 1979 to present
(Indexes of five newspapers: the *New York Times, The Wall Street Journal,*
the *Christian Science Monitor,* the *Los Angeles Times,* and the *Washington
Post*)

The New York Times Index
New York: The New York Times Company, 1981 to present

The Wall Street Journal Index
New York: Dow Jones & Company, Inc., 1958 to present

4D

Indexes to Statistical Information

American Statistics Index: A Comprehensive Guide to the Statistical Publications of the U.S. Government Bethesda, Md.: Congressional Information Service, 1983 to present

Indexes to International Statistics: A Guide to the Statistical Publications of International Intergovernmental Organizations Bethesda, Md.: Congressional Information Service, 1983 to present

Statistical Reference Index: A Selective Guide to American Statistical Publications from Private Organizations and State Government Sources Bethesda, Md.: Congressional Information Service, 1980 to present

Statistical Compilations

County and City Data Book
U.S. Bureau of the Census
Washington, D.C.: Government Printing Office, irregular
(Repackages census data relating to counties and cities)

Predicasts Basebook
Cleveland: Predicasts, 1974 to present
(Time series statistics on the U.S. economy, industries, products, and services)

Predicasts Forecasts
Cleveland: Predicasts, 1960 to present
(Statistical forecasts on products, industries, services, and the U.S. economy)

Standard & Poor's Statistical Service
New York: Standard & Poor's Corporation, monthly
(A current source for basic statistics on the U.S. economy, financial markets, and basic industries)

State and Metropolitan Area Data Book
U.S. Bureau of the Census
Washington, D.C.: Government Printing Office, irregular
(Repackages census data relating to states and metropolitan statistical areas)

Statistical Abstracts of the United States
U.S. Bureau of the Census
Washington, D.C.: Government Printing Office, annual
(An essential compilation of social, political, and economic data from a variety of public and private sources)

Census-Based Statistical Extrapolations

U.S. Bureau of the Census

Census of Housing (published every 10 years)

Census of Population (published every 10 years)

Census of Agriculture (published every 5 years)

Census of Construction Industries (published every 5 years)

Census of Manufacturers (published every 5 years)

Census of Retail Trade (published every 5 years)

Census of Service Industries (published every 5 years)

Census of Transportation (published every 5 years)

Census of Wholesale Trade (published every 5 years)

Census of Business Patterns (published annually)

County Business Patterns (published annually)

Sources of Secondary Data for International Marketing Research

1. Information available from international agencies
   a. The United Nations. United Nations publications can be obtained from:
   United Nations Publications
   Room CD2-853
   New York, NY 10017
   - *i.* United Nations Bibliographic Information System (UNBIS)
     (This database consists of the *United Nations Documents Index* for coverage of the organization's own documentation network and the current bibliographical information for books produced by specialized agencies, commercial publishers, governments, or other institutions.)
   - *ii.* *Bibliography on Transnational Corporations*
     (A computer-produced listing of 4,200 bibliographic items, with subject index.)
   - *iii.* *World Economic Survey*
     (A comprehensive survey of world economic conditions with emphasis on international trade, payments, and production.)
   - *iv.* *Handbook of International Trade and Development Statistics*
     (A major source of world economic data. Includes information on population, manpower, agriculture, manufacturing, mining, construction, trade, transport, communications, balance of payments, consumption, wages, prices, health, and education.)
   - *v.* *Economic Survey of Europe*
     (Annual survey analyzing the development of the European economy and world economic changes having an important bearing upon economic policies in Eastern and Western Europe.)
   - *vi.* *Economic Bulletin for Asia and the Pacific*
     (Review concerning agriculture, industry, transportation, trade, and balance of payments.)
   - *vii.* *Economic Survey of Latin America and the Caribbean*
     (Information about regional and internal economic developments in Latin America.)

   b. Organization for Economic Cooperation and Development. OECD publications can be obtained from:
OECD Publications Office, Suite 1305
1750 Pennsylvania Avenue, N.W.
Washington, D.C. 20006

      i. OECD Economic Surveys
(Each title in this series of economic studies is a booklet published annually. Each booklet has information concerning recent trends of demand and output, prices and wages, foreign trade and payments, economic policy, and prospects and conclusions in an individual member country.)

      ii. OECD Economic Outlook
(Semiannual survey of economic trends and prospects in the 21 member countries given in two volumes, imports and exports. The survey gives the quantity and value of international trade for 272 commodity categories and examines the current situation and prospects regarding demand and output, employment, costs and prices, and foreign trade for the OECD as a whole.)

      iii. Monthly Statistics of Foreign Trade
(This bulletin is intended to serve as a timely source of statistical data on the foreign trade by OECD member countries. The data cover not only overall trade by countries, but also a number of seasonally adjusted series, volume and average value indices, and trade by SITC sections.)

   c. International Monetary Fund (IMF). IMF publications can be obtained from:
International Monetary Fund
Washington, D.C. 20431

      i. International Financial Statistics
(Monthly publication that provides data for 104 countries on exchange rates, balance of payments, international reserves, money supply, price, interest rates, and other financial information.)

   d. The World Bank. World Bank publications can be obtained from:
The World Bank
1818 H Street, N.W.
Washington, D.C. 20433

      i. World Bank Atlas
(Annual publication that includes information such as population, gross domestic product, and average growth rates for every country in the world.)

      ii. World Bank: Annual Report
(Report containing information on developing countries around the world.)

2. Information available from U.S. government sources

   a. U.S. Department of Commerce. The following publications can be obtained through either:
U.S. Department of Commerce
Publications Sales Branch
Room 1617
Washington, D.C. 20230

or from a state's International Trade Administration Office, which is run by the Department of Commerce.

    i. *Commerce Information Management System (CIMS)*
(This database includes all information previously found in such publications as *Global Market Surveys, Country Market Surveys, Trade Lists,* and *Market Share Reports.* The database permits search for information on particular countries, industries, and products, and can provide a listing of potential buyers, distributors, and agents for different industries in selected countries.)

    ii. *Foreign Trade Reports, FT-410*
(Monthly publication that provides a statistical record of all U.S. exports by product and country of destination.)

    iii. *Business America*
(Monthly magazine that covers domestic and international news.)

    iv. *Overseas Business Report*
(Report compiled for a particular country that includes information on the best markets, industry trends, local regulations, investment alternatives, labor, and taxation.)

    v. *Export Promotion Calendar*
(Calendar prepared quarterly that lists all upcoming trade shows overseas by product category, country, and date.)

3. Information available from commercial publishers
  a. Reference material
    i. *International Market Information System*
(A computer bank containing import data on more than 1,900 products from 133 countries; prepared at Georgia State University in Atlanta.)

    ii. Inter-Trade Center File of Information Services
(A computer data bank of sources of information related to international trade from the World Trade Center in New York.)

    iii. *Sources of European Economic Information*
(A publication that describes nearly 2,000 statistical bulletins, yearbooks, directories, and reports for 17 European countries.)

    iv. *Business International Weekly Report*
(Weekly publication that reports on events and topics of interest to managers of worldwide operations. It is published by Business International Corporation of New York.)

    v. *Doing Business in . . .* Series
(A series of books published by Business International Corporation that explores doing business in particular countries.)

    vi. *Encyclopedia of Geographic Information Sources*
(Published by Gale Research of Detroit.)

    vii. *European Markets: A Guide to Company and Industry Information Sources*
(Guide available from Washington Researchers of Washington, D.C.)

   viii. *Exporter's Encyclopedia*
     (Published annually by Dun & Bradstreet International in New York. It is supplemented by twice-monthly bulletins and newsletters.)

   ix. *Reference Book for World Traders*
     (Covers information necessary for planning exports to and imports from all foreign countries. It is available from Croner Publications, Inc., of New York.)

   x. *World Advertising Expenditures*
     (Published by Starch INRA Hooper Group of Companies of New York.)

   xi. *Business Publications Rates and Data USA and International*
     (Listings of domestic and international publications and their rates in order to help potential exporters find marketing and advertising representation.)

  b. Magazines and newspapers

   i. *The Wall Street Journal*

   ii. The *Asian Wall Street Journal*

   iii. The *New York Times*

   iv. *European Marketing and Research,* the Netherlands

   v. *Financial Times,* England

   vi. *Nihom Keizai Shimbun,* Japan

   vii. *Frankfurter Algemeine,* Germany

   viii. *Business Week*

   ix. *Advertising Age*

   x. *Marketing News*

   xi. *Fortune*

   xii. *Forbes*

On-Line Data Sources and Other Syndicated Sources of Purchase Behavior and Media Exposure Information

VIDEOCART SHOPPING CART WITH COMPUTER SCREEN CREATES NEW AD MEDIUM THAT ALSO GATHERS DATA

VideOcart, an electronic point-of-purchase ad medium, may make Information Resources, Inc.—already a heavyweight in the $2 billion marketing research industry—a contender in the $57 billion ad and promotion industry.

IRI cofounder and chairman John Malec, who got the idea for VideOcart two years ago, called the shopping cart with a laptop computer screen on its handle "the most important new ad and promotion medium since television" and "the most profitable new product ever introduced by IRI." Debuted April 27 at New York and Chicago press conferences, VideOcart will be going into three test markets in September.

Although he said VideOcart was designed not as a marketing research tool but mainly as an ad medium and will make money from ad sales, the carts will gather data as shoppers push them down the aisles. The data will be "dumped" at the checkouts through an FM transmitter.

Among data gathered will be the VideOcarts' own paths through the store, the time spent in various parts of the store, and shoppers' opinions, Malec said. For some applications, shoppers will be able to interact with VideOcart to select information of interest through its touch-screen capability.

Data obtained from "interrogating" each cart will enable the grocer to analyze shopping patterns and the time spent shopping in each product category for optimal product placement and traffic management, according to IRI.

By January 1991, IRI aims to have 10,000 U.S. supermarkets outfitted with the computer-equipped shopping carts and linked with a satellite and nonaudible FM network. A personal computer in each store will direct a low-power FM transmitter to send ads to each cart's memory.

The ads will be shown at breaks in an information and entertainment program for consumers and won't interrupt the program, IRI said. The sequence of the ads shown will be determined by the route of the cart through the store.

As a shopper pushes a VideOcart down the aisles, the manufacturer ads for brands on the shelves being passed at that moment will be "triggered" at a rate of about two per aisle (about 32 per store) and appear on the flat, 6-by-8-inch liquid-crystal display mounted on the handles of the cart. Tie-in promotion ads also will be able to be used — for instance, a hot-dog bun ad when the cart is near the hot dogs.

But only about 15 percent of VideOcart's display time will be devoted to ads, Malec said. The rest of what he called "a friendly medium in which to display ads" includes a continually changing "video newsmagazine," "news to create a new shopping experience," store specials and maps, trivia questions, and videogames to play while waiting to check out.

"Now marketers can use the power of video to promote a brand at its point of purchase, where at least two thirds of buying decisions are made." Malec said.

The video isn't TV but attention-getting animated graphics created on personal computers and sent by modems between advertisers, ad agencies,

VideOCart was recently introduced by Information Resources, Inc., as "the first interactive, in-store, targetable video ad medium that will deliver specific product messages to individual shoppers."

and IRI, which will transmit the ads to the targeted stores on a "wide-area network" by satellite.

IRI already owns 19 percent of Media-link, Inc., which operates the Food Broker

Network (FBN), the food industry's satellite communications network.

Malec said the firm has talked with some manufacturers about participating in the three-store, three-city test market. Chicago, where IRI is based, will be one of the cities, he said. The other two cities—one West Coast and one East Coast, but not New York City—will be announced in a few weeks, he said.

Besides gathering sales data, the test markets will be used to perfect consumer programming and fine-tune the technology, he said. IRI also will be checking on factors such as the ideal length of ads, shopper interest in games and information, the way the shopper interacts with the unit, and opportunities for the grocers to contribute programming.

Malec said VideOcart's computer capabilities also will offer supermarkets some advantages, including sounding an alarm if a cart is taken too far from the store, as in an attempt to steal it. The stores also could use VideOcart to transmit information such as the shortest checkout line, the next number up at the deli counter, and that a red Ford in the parking lot has its lights on.

Malec said the carts could be equipped for "under $500 per cart." He said the average supermarket has about 100 carts and IRI would turn about 75 of them into VideOcarts, which he expects "shoppers will seek out" because they'll make shopping "efficient and fun."

Malec said about half of the cost of VideOcart, a $200 million capital project for the firm, will be funded through the project's own cash flow from the ad sales. About $50 million will be from new equity, possibly the sale of stock in IRI, and $50 million from additional debt.

Source: *Marketing News,* September 26, 1991, pp. 1–2. Reprinted with permission.

INTRODUCTION

Little voices in your head. Little images on your shopping cart. With the technology of the future such as the VideOcart, the latter could replace the former—thereby increasing the information shoppers receive at points of purchase, and thus increasing the availability of and access to information sources.

Today, more and more secondary sources of information can be accessed from on-line databases. The major access to these databases is a library, but the increased penetration of personal computers and the development of optical disc technology gives marketing executives information availability right in their offices. Many on-line suppliers sell data and reports on specialized topics directly to client companies. The data are collected on a regular basis by researchers who use standardized procedures. Information is then "syndicated" to various users, and common pools of data and reports are sold to different client companies.

In this chapter we discuss on-line databases and syndicated sources of purchase and media exposure information. The discussion begins with a description of the new age of information availability. We discuss a variety of on-line databases and how to access them. Attention then focuses on syndicated sources of purchase behavior and media exposure information. In the course of the discussion we consider the advantages and disadvantages of three basic sources of such information: diary panels, conventional store audits, and single-source services.

THE NEW AGE OF INFORMATION

With the rapid development of on-line information databases, the researcher can frequently monitor developments without ever leaving the office. Gathering secondary data, which once required trips to a large research library and countless telephone calls to potential information sources, may now be accomplished with a fraction of that effort. Indeed, thousands of new documents are becoming available every day; the data that could not be located one month ago may suddenly appear in the public domain.

Millions of pieces of potentially useful information are floating about the information environment. To get some notion of the magnitude and development of on-line databases, consider the following: In 1968 there were fewer than 250,000 items in bibliographic databases (one category of on-line databases). By 1980 this number was estimated to have grown to 75 million items in over 600 databases. Another source indicates that through 1987 the on-line database industry had grown to 3,699 databases compiled by 1,685 different producers. Assuming a constant rate of growth, we could estimate that we now have on-line access to approximately 450 million discrete pieces of information available for problem solving.

A number of factors have contributed to this explosive growth in on-line information systems:

1. Publishers and other data compilers are now using computers as their primary production technology—witness the almost-extinct practice of manual typesetting in the newspaper industry. Thus, editing and publishing tomorrow's edition of the *New York Times* automatically adds hundreds of new stories to the on-line *New York Times* database.

2. Companies referred to as *on-line vendors* serve as information supermarkets and provide easy access to hundreds of databases. These vendors greatly simplify the search process because they generally provide uniform search commands and protocols for each of the databases mounted on their computer. Thus, you could gain access to the on-line *New York Times* or the on-line version of *Business Week* and numerous other publications through Mead Data Central's Nexis services.

3. Telecommunications networks now provide low-cost access to remote databases with send or receive speeds of typically up to 2,400 characters per second.

4. Perhaps the most important element in on-line database expansion has been the market penetration of personal computers. Until a significant number of potential users were able to interact with remote databases, the market for on-line services was quite limited, mainly to research institutions and corporate libraries. The personal computer outfitted for communications and in the possession of thousands of information seekers has radically expanded the potential market. A current marketing strategy for database producers and on-line vendors is to reach the end-user market, the information consumer, rather than relying solely on intermediaries such as librarians and information specialists.

Fundamentals of accessing on-line databases are illustrated in Appendix 5A.

ON-LINE DATABASE SERVICES

We should be aware of a number of aspects concerning on-line database services. These include database varieties, directories, and vendors.

Database Varieties

The information represented in the hundreds of databases varies from discipline to discipline. Beyond subject matter, databases may differ in scope, geographic and chronological coverage, and the frequency with which they are updated. Databases also differ according to the type of information that they contain. These varieties may be categorized into several types.

— Bibliographic databases contain citations to journal articles, government documents, technical reports, market research studies, newspaper articles, dissertations, patents, and so on. Frequently, they provide summaries or abstracts of the cited material.

— Numeric databases contain original survey information such as time-series data. An example would be the sales data of sporting goods during the past 20 years.

— Directory databases are made up of information about individuals, organizations, and services. Using a directory database you could, for example, generate a list of business establishments in a given geographic area that have incorporated within the last two years.

— Full-text databases are perhaps the variety of on-line databases that will experience the most rapid growth during the next decade. As the name implies, such databases contain the complete text of the source documents that make up the database. An example of a full-text database is the New York Times Information Bank, which provides the complete text of each issue of the *New York Times*.

Directories of Databases

Among the numerous on-line database source listings are three directories that are particularly useful because they are updated periodically:

1. *Directory of On-Line Databases* (Santa Monica, Calif.: Cuadra Associates, Inc., 1979 to present).
2. *North American Online Director,* 2nd ed. (New York: R. R. Bowker, 1987).
3. Amy Lucas and Annette Novallo, ed., *Encyclopedia of Information Systems and Services,* 8th ed. (Detroit: Gale Research Company, 1988).

Information specialists who work with on-line services in large libraries or corporate information centers are good sources of direction in the use of directories.

Vendors

On-line vendors or gateways are intermediaries that generally mount numerous databases produced by many different organizations. They can supply descriptive and cost information on many of these databases. The advantages of accessing a database through an on-line vendor rather than directly through the producer are

1. One contract with a vendor can usually provide access to many different databases.
2. A vendor's on-line database index may help the researcher pinpoint the database(s) most appropriate for a specific search.
3. Search protocol is generally standardized across all of the databases on the vendor's system, which simplifies the research process.
4. One contract simplifies billing for the use of various databases with one periodic invoice.

There are hundreds of on-line vendors. The larger ones are described in Exhibit 5–1 with respect to the market served and growth rates in the 1980s.

Before selecting a vendor as a database supplier, you should examine the descriptions of the databases distributed, understand the charges or fee structures, verify that the vendor's system will support communications with your terminal or personal computer, inquire about the availability of database documentation (a detailed description of database content and record structure), and determine the level of user support that the vendor is willing to provide (on-site system training, for example).

The cost of an on-line search varies according to the database selected, the amount of on-line time used, and the volume of information retrieved. For example, a 10-minute search of ABI/Inform, a bibliographic database, retrieving 20 abstracted journal citations, would cost approximately $30.

CD-ROM DATA FILES

Up to now, we have discussed on-line information retrieval systems that are accessed using a telecommunications link between the user and a mainframe computer. Yet, local microcomputer-driven databases are proliferating with developments in optical disc technology. A 5-inch disc read by a laser beam, known as CD-ROM (compact-disc-read-only memory), is having a profound impact on the information industry. A number of on-line, mainframe databases are now being converted to this microcomputer-based technology, which preserves many of the useful search features of the

EXHIBIT 5—1

Growth of Online Services

Company	Service	Market	1988—89	1985—89
Prodigy Information Service	Prodigy (households)	General Interest	700.0%	—
Accu-Weather	Accu-Data	News	47.1%	—
Business Wire	Business Wire	News	40.4%	150.0%
Comtex Scientific	Newsgrid/OTC NewsAlert	News	38.9%	212.5%
TWA/Northwest Airlines	PARS	Airline	37.2%	133.7%
TRW	Credit Data Service	Credit	36.7%	167.8%
Information America	Information America	Sci/Tech/Prof	35.5%	
Data Transmission Network	Agricultural Service	Business/Financial	33.9%	874.8%
General Electric	GEnie	General Interest	32.7%	8788.9%
OCLC	OCLC	Sci/Tech/Prof	30.5%	61.9%
American Airlines	SABRE	Airline	28.2%	100.4%
Western Union	Easylink	General Interest	25.0%	96.5%
Maxwell Communications	Maxwell Online	Sci/Tech/Prof	23.9%	—
Dow Jones	Capital Markets Report	Business/Financial	22.2%	307.4%
Telerate	Telerate	Business/Financial	20.5%	148.7%
Reuters/Real-time	Monitor	Business/Financial	19.6%	227.4%
Quantum Computer Services	Quantum Link/PC Link, etc.	General Interest	19.0%	
Knight-Ridder	Dialog Info Services	Sci/Tech/Prof	18.6%	64.3%
PRC Realty	Mult. Listing Service	Sci/Tech/Prof	17.9%	79.2%
Knight-Ridder	K-R Financial Info	Business/Financial	16.8%	167.4%
Knight-Ridder	VU/TEXT	Sci/Tech/Prof	16.7%	197.9%
Datatek	Datatimes	Sci/Tech/Prof	14.7%	290.9%
British Telecom	Dialcom	General Interest	14.3%	113.3%
CompuServe	CompuServe Info Service	General Interest	12.7%	112.7%
Dow Jones	Prof. Investor's Report	Business/Financial	12.6%	—
Info Globe	Info Globe	Sci/Tech/Prof	9.9%	94.2%
Mead Data Central	LEXIS, NEXIS, MEDIS	Sci/Tech/Prof	9.7%	28.0%
NewsNet	NewsNet	News	8.8%	68.2%
Equifax	Credit Bureau Inc.	Credit	7.0%	44.6%
ADP	Financial Info Service/FS Partner	Business/Financial	6.9%	12.7%
General Videotex	Delphi	General Interest	6.7%	236.8%
Dow Jones	Dow Jones News/Retrieval	Business/Financial	6.5%	40.4%
FastFinder	FastFinder	Sci/Tech/Prof	5.3%	—
Delta	Datas Link	Airline	4.8%	—
Dun & Bradstreet	DunSprint	Credit	4.0%	119.8%
Texas Air	System 1 Direct Access	Airline	3.3%	—
United Airlines	Apollo	Airline	1.9%	66.7%
BusinessWire	Sports Wire	News	1.2%	—
BusinessWire	Entertainment Wire	News	0.0%	—
BusinessWire	Analyst Wire	News	0.0%	—

Source: Digital Information Group, Stamford, Conn. © 1991, Digital Information Group. Used with permission.

on-line versions, such as the use of differentiating or grouping commands (see the appendix at the end of the chapter for further explanation). As research libraries acquire these products, they are able to eliminate the fees previously associated with on-line database research. Once the CD-ROM is purchased, it can be used on an unlimited number of databases without incurring additional access fees.

Assessing market size with
CD-ROM data

					Growth	
Market	1990	1989	1988	1987	1989–90	1987–90
Industry-specific	141	54	35	19	161.1%	642.1%
Health care	101	40	26	16	152.5%	531.3%
Reference*	98	40	28	11	145.0%	790.9%
Professional	95	43	33	26	120.9%	265.4%
Science/technical	66	33	27	14	100.0%	371.4%
Business/financial	47	15	11	3	213.3%	1466.7%
Marketing	31	16	10	4	93.8%	675.0%
Government	21	11	9	4	90.9%	425.0%
Total	600	252	179	97	138.1%	518.6%

EXHIBIT 5–2

Number of North
American CD-ROM Titles
by Market

*Reference is a new classification made up primarily of titles classified last year as general interest and
library oriented professional titles. Some general interest titles were reclassified as noninformation and
don't appear in these statistics.
Source: Julie B. Schwerin, *Optical Publishing Industry Assessment 1990 Edition,* produced by InfoTech,
based in Pittsfield, Vermont, and published by the Optical Publishing Association in Dublin, Ohio.

A number of CD-ROM products currently available are useful in marketing research. Exhibit 5–2 displays the number of CD-ROM titles by various markets. Notice that marketing-oriented CD-ROM titles have grown from 4 in 1987 to 31 in 1990, a 675 percent increase. Exhibit 5–3 provides the average price for a CD-ROM for the same time period as Exhibit 5–2.

To illustrate the potential of CD-ROM databases, consider the plight of a group of financial advisers who are considering starting their own financial services business. It occurs to them that there may be different

Market	1990	1989	1988	1987	Change	
					1989–90	1987–90
Business/financial	$5,172	$4,599	$3,605	$2,382	12.5%	117.2%
Government	3,724	5,041	3,441	5,432	−26.1%	−31.4%
Marketing	2,576	2,110	2,177	3,025	22.1%	−14.8%
Science/technical	1,941	1,425	1,735	1,473	36.2%	31.8%
Professional	1,849	1,645	1,518	1,188	12.4%	55.7%
Health care	1,142	1,159	1,552	2,487	−1.5%	−54.1%
Industry-specific	1,075	2,118	2,128	3,123	−49.3%	−65.6%
Reference	815	783	1,062	1,081	4.1%	−24.6%
Average price	1,708	1,736	1,829	2,067	−1.6%	−17.4%

segments of customers who need financial advice. As a preliminary step in their investigation, they decide to check the business periodical literature for articles that may have been written on segmenting the financial services market. They use the bibliographic database, ABI/Inform Ondisc Availability from University Microfilms International (UMI). This CD-ROM database accesses periodicals from a variety of databases from January 1988 to February 1992. Exhibit 5–4 presents the search procedures and sample results of this exercise.

SYNDICATED DATA SOURCES

Exhibit 5–5 provides the framework for our discussion of syndicated data sources. Notice that the sources are categorized into three major headings: diary panels, audit services, and scanner-based data services.

A **diary panel** is a sample of various households that have agreed to record, in a diary, their purchases or media viewing for a specified period of time. For example, MRCA's SGIS consumer panel is comprised of 12,000 households containing over 30,000 individuals. MRCA receives diaries from the same panelists every month on its soft-good purchasing, which results in over 550,000 purchases being recorded every year. Nielsen's media panel is made up of a selected number of households that record their media viewing habits. These data are used to produce the famous TV ratings.

Audit services are used to record the sales of product at the retail level. Audit service companies get permission from supermarkets, drug stores, major discount houses, and other independent retailers to inventory the products in their stores for a specified period of time. You may have noticed people in a supermarket, especially later in the day or in the evening, with a hand-held scanner recording the amount of product on a shelf. Usually these are people working for an audit company.

DIARY PANEL

Sample of households that record, on a regular basis, their purchases or media habits in a diary.

AUDIT SERVICES

Record sales of product at the retail level.

EXHIBIT 5—4

Sample Result of a Search
Procedure

```
ProQuest      ABI/Inform              Jan 1988--Feb 1992

          Search Terms                    Item Count

(01):  segmentation → SEGMENTATION           794
(02):  financial → FINANCIAL               34888
(03):  (01) pre/1 (02)                         3
Search results in 3 item(s).


92-02724
Title:     Positioning Professional Services:
           Segmenting the Financial Services Market
Authors:   McAlexander, James H.; Schouten, John W.;
           Scammon, Debra L.
Journal:   Journal of Professional Services
           Marketing Vol: 7 Iss: 2 Date: 1991 pp:
           149+166 Jrnl Code: JPF ISSN: 0748-4623
Terms:     Market segmentation; Financial services;
           Market positioning; Target markets;
           Surveys; Characteristics; US
Codes:     8100 (Financial services industry); 7100
           (Market research); 9190 (United States)
```

Abstract: Market segmentation and positioning allow
marketers to differentiate themselves from competitors in
a way that is valued by customers and that results in
competitive advantage. Through an analysis of the
financial services market, a segmentation and positioning
strategy is developed based on the proposition that
consumers employ many kinds of professional service
providers to compensate for an inability or unwillingness
to perform certain tasks. The selection and use of
financial advisers varies considerably from segment to
segment. Knowledgeable, intrinsically motivated consumers
appear to have little interest in comprehensive services
from a financial planner. The selection and use of
financial advisers varies considerably from segment to
segment. Knowledgeable, intrinsically motivated consumers
appear to have little interest in comprehensive services
from a financial planner. Knowledgeable consumers who are
not intrinsically motivated are a potential target for
comprehensive financial services. Less knowledgeable but
intrinsically motivated consumers also represent a viable
target, but they will respond to different appeals. Such
consumers are good candidates for comprehensive financial
planning services as well. References. Charts.

```
92-02607
Title:     Applying Latent Trait Analysis in the
           Evaluation of Prospects for Cross-Selling
           of Financial Services
Authors:   Kamakura, Wagner A.; Ramaswami,
           Sridhar N.; Srivastava, Rajendra K.
Journal:   International Journal of Research in
           Marketing Vol: 8 Iss: 4 Date: Nov 1991
           pp: 329-349 Jrnl Code: IJR ISSN:
           0167-8116
Terms:     Market research; Studies; Financial
           services; Cross selling; Consumer
           behavior; Mathematical models
Codes:     7100 (Market research); 8100 (Financial
           services industry); 9130

Use + and - for Next and Previous Items.
                    F4=Output    F1=Help    F2=Commands
```

EXHIBIT 5—5

Typology of Syndicated
Sources of Purchase
Behavior and Media
Exposure Data

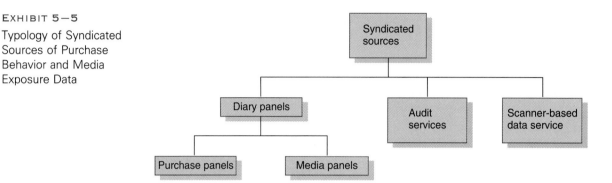

Audits typically are constructed in three stages. Initially, field representatives scan or count brands on the retail shelves to establish a beginning inventory. After a specified period of time (say 28 days) the field representatives return to the retail outlets and record what is on the shelf to establish an ending inventory. All purchases and transfers are monitored for the time period. Hence, given these three measures they can determine sales and market share of a particular brand for the time period.

Scanner-based data services collect data at the checkout counter using electronic scanner systems that measure the Universal Product Code (UPC). Consequently, scanner-based data companies have the capability for providing both audit services and purchase panel services. These companies are revolutionizing the marketing research industry and have proven to be formidable competitors for traditional audit services and diary panels.

SCANNER-BASED DATA
SERVICES

Collect data at checkout
counter using electronic scanning equipment.

Several factors may influence the choice of a particular syndicated service. Aside from the characteristics and quality of the information supplied, the supplier's reputation, technical competence, experience, and personnel are important (see Chapter 1). Many marketing research suppliers provide information on purchase behavior and media exposure, and we cannot discuss all of them. The information presented in this chapter is not an endorsement or advertisement, but for the most part, it is taken from promotional material supplied to client companies by marketing research suppliers.

Diary Panels

General characteristics.   Diary panels are maintained by commercial marketing research suppliers. Respondents are asked to record specific consumption behaviors as they occur. The respondents are asked to complete the diaries, for a certain period of time (e.g., every two weeks or every month, etc.) and return them to the marketing research supplier. The research supplier compiles the data and makes it available to marketing managers.

Data collected in diary panels can be useful for studying trends. Consider Box 5–1, which discusses Kentucky Fried Chicken's introduction of its "Lite'n Crispy" line of chicken. How might a food marketer gain insight

SKIN-FREE CHICKEN FROM KFC

BOX 5—1

—

FROM THE USER'S
PERSPECTIVE

—

Diet-conscious people with a craving for fried chicken are being targeted as Kentucky Fried Chicken introduces its skin-free chicken line.

Kyle Craig, president of Kentucky Fried Chicken USA, said he hopes Lite'n Crispy will fill the huge demand from "people who grew up with fried chicken but don't eat it or don't eat it as frequently because of nutritional concerns."

The line debuted in late January at about 700 Kentucky Fried Chicken restaurants in the Northeast.

But the leading chicken chain promised that the new product is still made with Colonel Harland Sanders' secret blend of 11 herbs and spices.

The product should be available at all 5,000 of the fast-food chain's restaurants in the U.S. later this year.

The Louisville-based restaurant company said it also was introducing salads and multigrain rolls in outlets that serve the Lite'n Crispy product.

Compared with Kentucky Fried's Extra Tasty Crispy chicken, the new lighter version has an average of 39% fewer calories, 45% less fat, 44% less sodium, and 37% less cholesterol, Kentucky Fried Chicken said in a statement.

It said the product is an average of 20% lower in fat and calories, and 32% lower in cholesterol than Kentucky Fried Chicken's Original Recipe.

The announcement comes against a background of growing sensitivities to health by leading fast-food purveyors. McDonald's Corp., for example, has offered prepackaged salads at its outlets for years, and other competitors offer salad bars.

In addition, many fast-food restaurants have switched to vegetable oil for deep-frying, dumping animal lard because of its links to heart disease.

"We knew consumers wanted 'better-for-you' products, but we also knew they were unwilling to compromise on taste or quality," Craig said.

"Removing the skin was relatively simple. Our greatest challenge was to develop a skin-free chicken which would retain flavor and moisture and still taste great."

Craig said that goal was accomplished during more than a year of development that led to the new recipe, which the company billed as the "biggest breakthrough since Colonel Sanders developed his secret blend."

After preparation with the traditional secret blend of herbs and spices, the lighter chicken is lightly covered with a new breading specially developed to absorb less oil during cooking in 100% vegetable oil, the company said.

Kentucky Fried isn't the first to tinker with skin-free chicken on the bone. Al Copeland Enterprises Inc., for example, parent of the Popeyes and Church's chicken chains, recently introduced a skinless fried chicken cooked in vegetable oil, on a test basis in some Popeyes outlets.

Hardee's Food Systems, parent of the Roy Rogers chain, cooks its fried chicken in vegetable oil and was the first to debut a grilled chicken sandwich, which is advertised as low in calories and fat.

John Merritt, Hardee's senior vice president of public affairs, said the company was watching closely how Kentucky Fried's new product sells. He didn't rule out copying it.

"Any time you got a good idea, plagiarism is the highest form of flattery," he said. "We've already analyzed this product, and it's not particularly hard to make. It's really not brain surgery here."

Source: *Marketing News*, March 18, 1991, p. 6. Reprinted with permission.

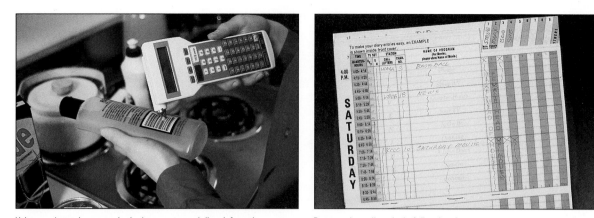

Using an electronic scanner in the home to recored diary information.   Papter and pencil method of diary keeping.

into the current consumption and trends of food consumption? One option would be to use the services of a panel such as MRCA's Menu Census. Participants in the Menu Census panel record information on meals eaten in or away from home for a 14-day period. They record such information as day of week, meal occasion, main meal versus snack, and whether the meal was consumed in the home, away from home, or skipped. In addition, they respond to such food item information as the method of preparation (baked, fried, boiled, etc), dish portion (main versus side dish), source (homemade, frozen, commercial, etc.), appliances used, and a variety of other factors. From this information, clear trends in food consumption can be spotted.

Diary panels can be classified by the type of information that is recorded. Diary purchase panels record purchase behavior, while diary media panels record what media members of the household have been exposed to in a specified period of time. For example, during a certain week, what people in the household watched which television programs? Probably the most famous diary media panel is run by Nielsen, which produces the popular and frequently cited television ratings. For most traditional diary panels, respondents are asked to use a self-administered questionnaire called a diary. These diaries are filled out for a specified period of time (see Exhibit 5–6). Recently, two electronic devices have been used in lieu of the traditional paper and pencil diary. Purchase panels provide members with a wand that can be used to scan the items purchased using the Universal Product Code. Some media panels have supplied participants with a device that resembles a television remote control. When the television is turned on, a prompt flashes at the top of the screen to remind the viewers to register who in the household is watching.

Two factors can affect the quality of panel data. The first is whether or not the panel members are representative of the target population. For example, many of the panels underrepresent minority groups and people of low education levels. The other is the potential for response bias. Some people, knowing that their purchases are being studied, may behave differently from the way they would otherwise. If panel data are used, the manager should be aware of three potential problems associated with these data: (1) Is the panel

EXHIBIT 5—6

Unique NPD Diary Features

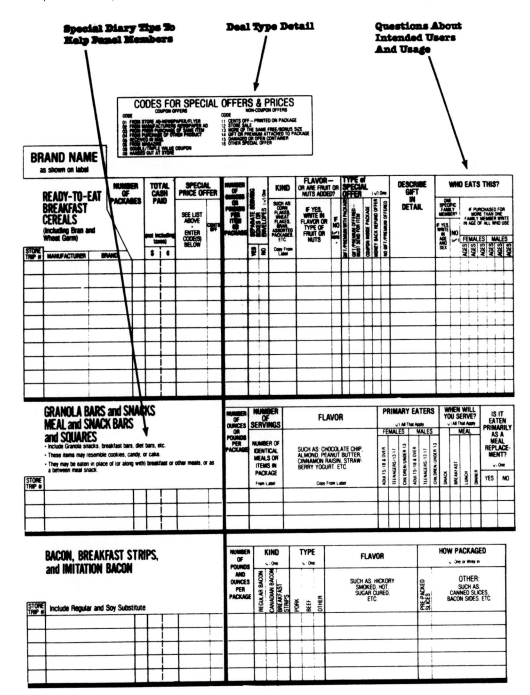

EXHIBIT 5—7

Using Diary Panel Data to Solve Marketing-Related Problems

How loyal are my brand's buyers vis-a-vis my main competitor?

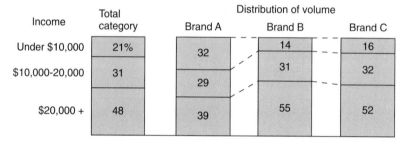

Of next 3 purchases same brand was bought

	My brand	Competitor
0 of 3 times	25%	17%
1 of 3 times	33	24
		24
2 of 3 times	21	35
All 3 times	21	

The competitor has much higher loyalty among his buyers than my brand does.

Marketing implication:
Efforts directed toward extending usage among existing buyers should increase loyalty. Options include in/on pack coupons, in-pack contests, premiums available for several proofs-of-purchase, etc.

How does my brand's demographic profile compare to other brands? Am I reaching my target audience?

		Distribution of volume		
Income	Total category	Brand A	Brand B	Brand C
Under $10,000	21%	32	14	16
$10,000-20,000	31	29	31	32
$20,000 +	48	39	55	52

Relative to both the category and competition, Brand A is not doing well among upper income households.

Marketing implication:
Advertising should be retargeted or revamped to reach the proper audience.

Should I promote my brand using a coupon or free sample?

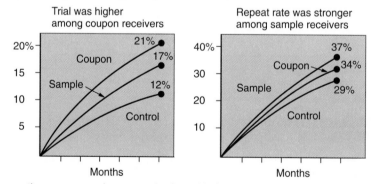

Trial was higher among coupon receivers

Repeat rate was stronger among sample receivers

Both promotions encouraged more purchasing, with the stronger trial/weaker repeat for coupon receivers resulting in as much sales as the free sample.

Marketing implication:
Since the sample cost three times as much, the coupon was chosen.

Source: National Purchase Diary Panel, used with permission.

representative of the desired target market? (2) Are there any problems of maturation; that is, has the average age of the panel members changed over time? (3) Are there response biases, such as not recording certain purchases because the panel members know their purchases are being recorded?

Uses. Diary media panels are used primarily for establishing network advertising rates, for selecting the appropriate media program or time to air a commercial, and for establishing demographic profiles of viewer or listener subgroups. Diary purchase panels traditionally have been used to forecast the sales level or market share of new products, to identify trends and establish demographic profiles of specific user groups, to evaluate test markets and controlled store tests, to test different advertising campaigns, and to estimate brand switching and trier-repeat purchases.

Exhibit 5–7 illustrates several ways diary panel data can be used to address marketing problems.

Audit Services

General characteristics. Suppose you were faced with the task of determining the level of retail sales of a particular brand and the gain or loss of market share given the introduction of a new brand into the market. One source to turn to would be syndicated suppliers offering audit services. Audits indicate what is happening in the marketplace not only for a given marketer, but for the competition.

The largest retail audit service for consumer packaged goods is the Nielsen Retail Index. It provides sales and market share data on products within the food, drug/health and beauty-aid, and alcoholic beverage industries at the actual point of sale on a bimonthly basis. Over 76,000 audits are conducted in over 11,000 separate retail outlets. The retail outlets are randomly chosen to represent population density, geographical location, and different store types.

Exhibit 5–8 displays a sample of data from the Nielsen Retail Index for brands of blueberry muffin mix. The data provide information on market share for two leading brands plus all other brands for the bimonthly periods.

In some cases a firm may wish to contract with a supplier to monitor the sales of a limited number of brands for a specified period of time. This is called a customized audit—that is, an audit that is conducted only for a particular client. One type of customized audit that still primarily rests on field representatives for the collection of the data is called a controlled store test. Here, changes in the marketing mix can be executed and evaluated by changes in sales against a control condition. Controlled store tests can be used to answer such questions as: What is the optimal price for my new brand? Does the new package design increase sales? Will the new brand draw from my competition or from my own brands?

There are two potential drawbacks concerning the use of audit data. The first is incomplete coverage. Audit services rely on the cooperation of retail outlets. Consequently it is possible that not all areas or retailers in an area are included in the audit. Another weakness of audits is the timeliness of the data.

EXHIBIT 5—8

Nielsen Retail Index Data for Brands of Muffin Mix

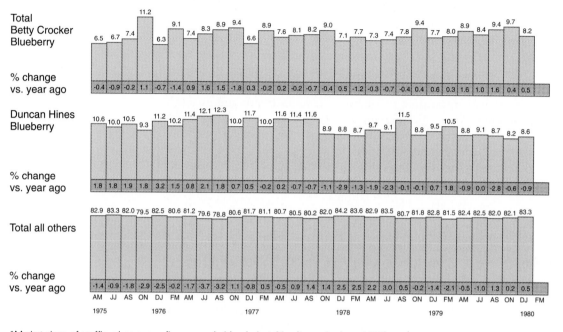

*Market share of muffin mixes over a five-year period (equivalent 24-unit-case basis × 1,000).

Source: A. C. Nielsen, used with permission.

There is typically a two-month gap between an audit's completion and the publication of the basic findings.

Stores equipped with scanners are changing the audit industry. Physical audits conducted by field representatives are most prominent for (1) brands that sell in small convenience stores that are not scanner-equipped; (2) categories where scanner penetration is still low (for example, some drug store chains have almost all stores scanner equipped, whereas other chains may have as little as 30 percent of the outlets scanner equipped); and (3) products that do not carry a Universal Product Code.

Uses.   Among the many uses of audit services are

1. Measuring consumer sales relative to competition.
2. Monitoring the full range of competitive activities.
3. Identifying where new products are appearing and the volume of sales in each geographical location.
4. Measuring the competitive impact of private brands.
5. Analyzing and correcting distribution problems, if they exist.
6. Developing advertising allocation schedules based on actual sales volume in a market.

Auditing merchandise in a grocery store aisle

7. Developing sales potentials for specific markets (category and brand development indexes). The varied sales data make audit services particularly valuable for researchers developing marketing strategies.

Scanner-Based Data Services

General characteristics.   The advent of the Universal Product Code (UPC) has made it possible to electronically record purchases as opposed to recording them in a diary for personal consumption data or taking an audit for general sales and market share data. Hence scanner-based data sources provide services that compete against both traditional panels and traditional audits.

Single-source services integrate information on both purchase behavior and media exposure for a panel of households, and in addition monitor sales and marketing activity at the retail level. Exhibit 5–9 summarizes Infoscan, a single-source syndicated database supplied by Information Resources Inc.

SINGLE-SOURCE SERVICES

Integrate information on peoples' purchase behavior and media exposure along with activity at the retail level.

EXHIBIT 5—9

InfoScan Data Collection

| UPCs for each grocery item are scanned at checkout. Information is sent from store to chain and on to IRI via telecommunication systems. | Household panel members present an identification card at checkout, which identifies and assigns items purchased to that household. Coupons are collected and matched to the appropriate UPC. Information is electronically communicated to IRI computers. | IRI field personnel visually survey stores and all print media to record retailers' merchandising efforts, displays, and ad features. Field personnel also survey retail stores for a variety of custom applications (e.g., average number of units per display, space allocated to specific sections, and number of facings). Results are electronically communicated to IRI computers. | Household panel members are selected for television monitoring and equipped with meters that automatically record the set's status every five seconds. Information is relayed back to IRI's computers. |

These databases are revolutionizing the syndicated data industry because of their flexibility and versatility.

Compared to instore audits, electronic scanner services tend to be more accurate, less costly, and provide shorter turnaround time for results. When the scanner services are integrated with a panel, as in single-source services, the suppliers provide experimental control to marketing researchers, because advertising copy can be targeted to specific households; and the purchases of these households can be monitored electronically. Hence, causal analysis of marketing mix variables can be assessed, such as: What is the effect of a coupon or an ad featuring a celebrity?

Scanner-based data sources have two potential problems. The first is the representativeness of the data. Not all retail outlets have scanners. However, this is quickly becoming less of a problem than in the 70s and 80s when scanner-based data services were founded. Another potential problem is the quality of the data. Volume tracking via electronic scanner systems is highly dependent upon the ability of checkout personnel to use the equipment properly. Errors in recording can occur if clerks do not properly scan all purchases. For example, a clerk may use the register to ring up a heavy item to avoid lifting it. In the case of scanning multiple purchases of the same product, but in different flavors or colors, the clerk may simply scan only one package and then ring in the number of purchases, which incorrectly records the transaction as consisting of several packages of one flavor or color.

Uses.   Among the primary uses of electronic scanner systems are sales, market share, retail price distribution, and modeling. Because of the quantity of data available about purchase behavior and panel characteristics and the highly controlled and monitored nature of the environment, single-source facilities in test markets have been used in a variety of marketing research projects. For example, they have been used in (1) new-product test markets, (2) product-repositioning studies, (3) copy-execution studies, (4) advertising-expenditure–level analysis, (5) advertising/promotion mix analysis, and (6) resizing inves-

Electronic scanning device

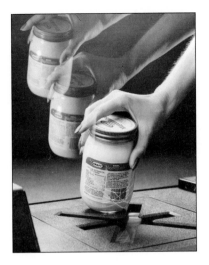

tigations. Single-source services provide a rich source of data that can be used when researchers develop marketing strategies.

SUMMARY

This chapter builds on our discussion of secondary sources for marketing and consumer-behavior–related information. We explained on-line databases and have provided an appendix (at the end of this chapter) that illustrates how such databases can be accessed. Atten-

tion then focused on syndicated sources of purchase behavior and media exposure information. Finally, we discussed advantages and disadvantages of three basic sources of such information: diary panels, conventional store audits, and scanner-based data.

KEY CONCEPTS

On-Line Databases   *Diary Media Panels*   *Scanner-Based Data Services*
CD-ROM Databases   *Audit Services*   *Single-Source Services*
Diary Purchase Panels

REVIEW QUESTIONS

1. A major manufacturer of medicinal preparations for veterinary use is considering the introduction of a line of mass-marketed health and beauty aids for the domestic pet market (e.g., dogs and cats). As an initial stage in the project, the firm was interested in discovering whether any articles on this industry have appeared in the business periodical literature.

   a. Use a bibliographic CD-ROM database to determine what articles have been written on this industry.
   b. What are the advantages of using a bibliographic database as compared to a traditional periodical index such as the *Business Periodicals Index?*

c. What other on-line databases might be useful in finding out more about this industry?

2. Should scanner services replace diary panels?

3. The representativeness of sample data is a prime concern of the user of market research information.

Evaluate the representation (or lack of representation) of

a. Diary panels.

b. Diary media panels.

c. Store audits.

d. Scanner services.

Accessing On-Line Databases: The Mechanics

To understand how to use on-line databases, you need to be familiar with the system that is required as well as the fundamentals of on-line searching.

Required System

To use an on-line database, you first need a device that will support data communications. Thus, the prerequisite is access to a "dumb" terminal equipped for communication (with an acoustical coupler) or a personal computer that includes a modem and appropriate communications software.

The second requirement is a telephone through which the data stream flows from the host computer to your local terminal. The host computer may be hundreds or thousands of miles away. Significant economies can be achieved by using a telecommunications network that provides local nodes in cities throughout the world (e.g., Telenet or Tymnet). In this way a marketing researcher in New York is able to dial the local number of a telecommunications network and thereby log on to a computer in California relatively inexpensively.

Once the researcher has established the capability to transmit and receive information, the next task is to identify the host computer(s) containing the database(s) and the information that is needed for the market research problem at hand.

Fundamentals of On-Line Searching

Although there are variations in search procedure from system to system or from vendor to vendor, one common theme in most of these systems is the use of the Boolean operators: *And, Or,* and *Not.* These system commands help the researcher link ideas together in different relationships.

The "And" search command requires that each term in the search statement exist in a record before it is retrieved. A simple field search performed in one bibliographic database using the "And" operator might be described as a *search for documents relating to market data (and) personal computers.* This command would retrieve a set of references in which both personal computers and market data are discussed.

The "Or" search command requires that any of the terms used in a search statement exists in a document before it is retrieved. For example, the search for *documents dealing with personal computers (or) microcomputers* would result in a set of documents dealing with either personal computers or microcomputers.

The "Not" command makes it possible to eliminate an idea or concept represented by a word or phrase from the search result set. For example, a search for *documents dealing with personal computers (not) minicomputers* would eliminate from the set of documents those personal computer references that discuss minicomputers.

These Boolean commands are best illustrated with the use of a diagram. Exhibit 5A–1 illustrates the search for *all documents containing market data that are related to personal computers or home computers, but not minicomputers.* The result is the shaded area, which represents all of the documents dealing

Diagram Showing Combination of Home Computers or Personal Computers (not minicomputers)

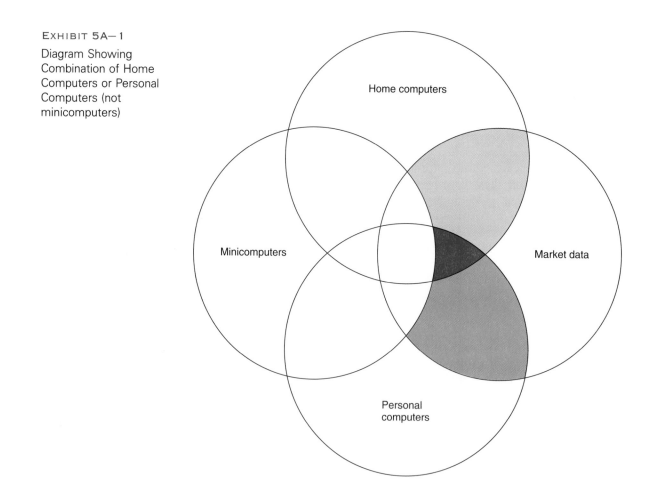

Home computers

Minicomputers

Market data

Personal computers

with market data and personal or home computers, but eliminates those that deal also with minicomputers.

Note that although these three Boolean operators are basic search commands in most on-line systems, they represent a small percentage of the search options that are available to the researcher.[1] Understanding and using these basic search commands, however, allows us to examine more closely a few considerations of the application of on-line databases to the market research function.

The example illustrates the effective use of secondary market information that is available on the Dialog system. In the interactive on-line environment, numerous vendors offer hundreds of databases that may be used in the search for relevant secondary market research information.

Consumer Demographics An automobile leasing company that specializes in exotic foreign cars is considering a local media advertising campaign in the tri-state region—New York, New Jersey, and Connecticut. Past company records indicate that the target markets are communities with median household incomes in excess of $50,000, median education of at least one year in college, and high socioeconomic status.

EXAMPLE

Database	Donnelley Demographics
Availability	Dialog Information Retrieval Service
Type	Numeric
Description	Donnelley Marketing Information Services produces a database of selected demographic information from the 1980 census that is enhanced with current and five-year projections for some data series. Arranged by a variety of geographic subdivisions, the database contains information on demographic characteristics and is reloaded annually.

Exhibit 5A–2 presents the search procedure that would be executed on the Dialog system.

EXHIBIT 5A—2

Consumer Demographic Analysis Prepared for an Automobile Leasing Company

---

```
File 575:D&B-Donnelley Demographics-11+91 (Copr. 1990 DMIS)
**FILE575: 1991 Estimates and 1996 projections now available
```

Set	Items	Description
?s ALO50000_99999		[The searcher(s) asks for communities with a median household income (AL =) between $50,000 and $99,999.]
S1 2648 AL=50000:99999		[The system responds with set 1. There are 2,648 communities in the United States that meet this requirement.]
?s VN=13.0:16.1		[The searcher(s) asks for communities that have a median educational level between 13 and 16 years (VN =).]
S2 4523 VN=13.0:16.1		[The system responds with set 2. There are 4,523 communities that meet this requirement.]
?s LA=75:99		[The searcher(s) ask for communities with a socioeconomic status indicator (SESI) between 75 and 99 (the average for the U.S. is 53).]
S3 4152 LA=75:99		[The system responds with set 3. There are 4,152 communities that meet this requirement.]
?ss st=ny or st=nj or st=ct		[The searcher(s) ask for all communities in New York (NY), New Jersey (NJ), and Connecticut (CT) (ST =).]
S4 2939 ST=NY (NEW YORK) S5 1111 ST=NJ (NEW JERSEY) S6 432 ST=CT (CONNECTICUT) S7 4482 ST=NY OR ST=NJ OR ST=CT		[The system responds with set 7, which is the resultant combination of sets 5, 6, and 7. There are 4,482 communities in this tri-state region.]

?ss s1 and s2 and s3 and s7
            2648 S1
            4523 S2
            4152 S3
            4482 S7
		[The searcher(s) now asks that all of the above demographic requirements be applied simultaneously.]

S8 501 S1 and S2 and S3 and S7 ?t 8/5/1		[The system responds with set 8. There are 501 communities in the database that meet all of the above requirements.]

Note: This database utilizes codes to represent search concepts. Thus, the searcher uses the code AL when specifying household incomes; GA for population in managerial positions; GB for population in professional positions; and so on.

ENDNOTE

1. The database vendors (such as Dialog) generally provide manuals and training for the use of system commands. There are also a number of books on this subject, such as C. C. Chen and S. Schweizer, *Online Bibliographic Searching: A Learning Manual* (New York: Neal-Schumen Publishers, 1981), or C. L. Borgman et al., *Effective Online Searching* (New York: Marcel Dekker, 1984).

Qualitative Interviewing and Research Methods

FOCUS GROUPS: A USEFUL CRYSTAL BALL FOR HELPING TO SPOT TRENDS

Rap music in commercials for string cheese, families spending more time together, the whole environmental thing— all old hat for trend spotters.

They could have told you about that stuff ages ago.

Using a mix of focus groups—where many trends are first discovered—open-ended surveys, and sometimes just hitting the streets, trend spotters have been able to help marketers tap into the next craze before it's even a blip in the world of quantitative research.

Trends just don't come out of the blue. They're "rooted in the way people live their lives," said Jane FitzGibbon, senior vice president/group director, consumer trends and insights at Ogilvy & Mather Advertising (O&M), New York.

And to see how people live their lives, O&M sends people to hang out in major cities, checking out what people buy, wear, eat, and talk about. They've even been known to collect a few menus. How the heck else would they have noticed that trend toward ethnic combinations in food?

Trend spotters have to be careful of fads. Just because they see a purple teapot in every store doesn't mean purple teapots are a trend. But if the researcher sees a lot of bright, metallic colors on other products, he or she may be on to something.

The behavioral approach is a "lot more disorderly, but you pick up a lot more," FitzGibbon said.

"I personally believe for trend forecasting that qualitative is better than pencil and paper surveys," she said. Surveys get people's guards up because they know their comments are being taken down verbatim.

Trend spotter Irma Zandl claims she knew about the whole vogueing thing "well before Madonna ever started talking about it." As president of Xtreme, a youth marketing firm in New York, Zandl makes it her job to keep up on these things.

Zandl said she relies "very, very heavily" on open-ended questionnaires sent to a panel of 1,600 youths around the country.

She also uses observational research to "see our target market in their natural surroundings." It really comes down to "shades and nuances" she said. The kid carrying the bottle of Evian is probably going to look a lot different from the one carrying a can of Pepsi.

Focus groups are helpful, but because

CHAPTER
OBJECTIVES

—

DESCRIBE
what is meant by qualitative
research.

DISCUSS
the primary methods of
observational study.

EXPLAIN
the major uses of focus
groups and depth interviews.

DESCRIBE AND
ILLUSTRATE
projective techniques.

they usually only cover the very specific needs of the client, there are ''other things that might be helpful to learn that are never touched on.''

Qualitative research reveals trends anywhere from three to four years before they show up in quantitative studies, said Zandl. There are things researchers can't get at with quantitative because people can't talk about things that are totally new.

Marketers have to pick up on the ''sensibility'' behind trends. The trend toward women being disenchanted with work doesn't mean they're all going to stay at home, but marketers should be aware that they don't want to be ''80s career women,'' either.

Nor should marketers dismiss fads,

Zandl said. Some of them can be around for three years and might be worth looking into.

And what's a trend in one market usually will rub off on another. Kids fueled the environmental movement among adults, and trends in the adult market have an impact on kids.

Marketers still overlook qualitative research as a way to spot trends, said Judith Langer, president of Judith Langer Associates, Inc., New York.

Qualitative is viewed as ''small scale'' and ''touchy-feely,'' she said, but an individual researcher can talk to as many as 2,000 consumers a year. That forms a cumulative picture of changing lifestyles and values.

''People will tell you what's going on before it's in a survey or shows up in a set of numbers,'' she said.

''If your antenna is up, you can pick up trends early,'' she said, but ''you have to be willing to make some leaps.''

Langer said she listens for the ''telling comment.'' Recently, a working mother was talking about ''stressed-out kids.'' It seems kiddies are feeling strained by their mother's hectic schedules. Feeling guilty, moms are compensating by buying treats for the tykes

131

If stressed-out kids turn out to be a trend, Langer said, the implications for food and beverage manufacturers, restaurants, and other "guilt-assuaging treats" are enormous.

Researchers also should explore consumers' lifestyles—what's happening in their lives, and how their attitudes and behaviors relate to the product. In a study for the Home Furnishings Council, for example, participants talked about what their homes meant to them.

From that, Langer discovered the trend was for consumers to view their homes as a "sanctuary."

Source: Cyndee Miller, *Marketing News,* May 27, 1991, p. 2.

INTRODUCTION

Trend spotters with a keen eye can often help marketers ferret out what is a flash-in-the-pan fad and what will be the next national craze. The previous two chapters (Chapters 4 and 5) discussed secondary sources of marketing research data. But when secondary data and syndicated sources of marketing research information are not enough, the researcher generally will gather the information from potential consumers in the relevant target market—otherwise known as collecting **primary data.**

PRIMARY DATA

Data collected from potential customers in relevant target markets in cases where secondary and syndicated sources are not sufficient to solve the marketing research problem at hand.

This chapter presents interviewing and research procedures frequently referred to as *qualitative data-collection methods* and begins our discussion of primary sources of marketing research data. Referring to Exhibit 6–1, we can see that qualitative research methods consist of direct inquiry, where the primary focus is on the researcher asking the respondent(s) questions, and observational techniques, where the primary focus rests on the researcher observing respondents' behavior. Sometimes qualitative techniques have been referred to as *"touchy-feely"* research techniques. However, in some circumstances, for example, trend spotting, the more intimate inquiry methods and/or the unobtrusive observational methods may be the only way to gather the data.

In this chapter four types of qualitative interviewing techniques will be discussed: focus groups, depth interviews, projective techniques, and observational methods.

Each of the interviewing and research data collection methods shown in Exhibit 6–1 has its own distinguishing set of characteristics. Before discussing each of these procedures in more detail, let us define several terms and characteristics that are often used to delineate the different types of interviewing and research data collection methods to be discussed.

Interviewing and Research Approaches

There are a number of different characteristics that can be used to distinguish between different types of interviewing and research method data collection procedures. As we discuss below, the following terms are not necessarily mutually exclusive, and a particular interviewing or research data collection method can possess more than one characteristic.[1] We will begin with the terms inquiry versus observation, two terms used to classify the various interviewing and research data collection methods discussed in

EXHIBIT 6—1

Qualitative Data-Collection Methods

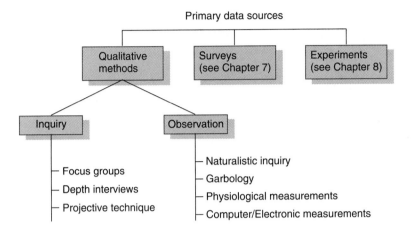

this chapter and then discuss three additional characteristics: (1) human versus mechanical, (2) disguised versus undisguised, and (3) structured versus unstructured. Since many of these terms are used to characterize what is referred to as qualitative research techniques we conclude with a discussion of this general approach to collecting data and contrast it to what is called quantitative research.

Inquiry versus observation.   These terms refer to whether an individual is specifically asked a question—**inquiry,** or whether the researcher observes an individual's behavior or reactions—**observation.** Focus groups, depth interviews, and projective techniques, since they usually involve asking questions, are inquiry interviewing techniques; whereas the methods of naturalistic inquiry, garbology, and physiological, computer, and electronic measurement techniques are observational in that they collect information on an individual's reactions and behavior. The method of observation can be direct or indirect and recorded via human or mechanical devices.

Direct versus indirect.   The term **direct** refers to observational interviewing methods where the behavior under investigation is observed directly. Following a shopper around in a supermarket and recording what is put in the shopping basket and eventually paid for at the checkout represents direct observational measurement of the shopper's grocery purchases. The term **indirect** is used to characterize those data collection methods that infer the behavior under study from something that is observed. For example, inferring a household's consumption behavior by examining items that are found in the household's garbage is an indirect method of observation.

Human versus mechanical.   These terms refer to who is collecting the information. It may be more practical and cheaper to record a shopper's pur-

INQUIRY
Interview in which a person responds to a set of questions.

OBSERVATION
Interviewing research method which involves observing an individual's behavior.

DIRECT OBSERVATION
Observational interviewing method where the behavior under investigation is observed directly, either by human or mechanical methods.

INDIRECT OBSERVATION
Observational interview method where the behavior is inferred, not directly observed.

chases at the checkout via electronic scanner devices than to have human recorders—interviewers—following shoppers around. In many instances, mechanical observation is more accurate and cheaper than human recording. Human and mechanical recording can also be used with inquiry interviewing methods. Having computer work stations equipped with a program that administers and records an individual's responses to a set of questions represents mechanical recording, as opposed to having an interviewer present.

Disguised versus undisguised.   The term **disguised** refers to interviewing and research data collection procedures where the individual being observed has no knowledge that he or she is being observed or no knowledge of the purpose of the study. Shoppers selecting a variety of microwavable soup may not have knowledge that their choices and selection process are being observed if a movie or video camera is innocuously positioned close to the microwavable soup display. In contrast, the term **undisguised** refers to interviewing and research data collection procedures where the individual being observed knows that he or she is being observed. Having an observer standing next to the microwavable soup display and recording shoppers' choices and comparison shopping behavior could alert the shopper that his or her behavior is being monitored. The risk with undisguised interviewing is that if individuals know they are being observed they may behave differently—the presence of an observer may influence the behavior being observed. With inquiry interviewing methods, the researcher will sometimes make an attempt to disguise the questioning so that the respondent cannot guess the purpose of the study.

Structured versus unstructured.   The term structured refers to interviewing procedures where the questions and possible responses to the questions asked are pre-specified and fixed. Most of us have received a questionnaire in the mail. This type of interviewing procedure is structured in that the questions you are asked to respond to have all been pre-determined and there is no possibility of changing a question, say, in light of one of your responses. "Pencil and paper" questionnaires exemplify structured interviewing formats. On the other hand, the term unstructured refers to interviewing procedures where there is no predetermined set of questions to be asked. This kind of free-flowing interviewing is best exemplified by focus groups and depth interviews.

Qualitative research methods, which are the subject of this chapter, can be described by several of the terms discussed above. Focus groups and depth interviews, for example, represent human inquiry, methods that, generally speaking, involve unstructured and undisguised question formats. Physiological measurement represents direct mechanical observation that is often structured and disguised. It is important to again reiterate that the terms defined above are not mutually exclusive and do not provide a clearly delineated taxonomy for all of the varied kinds of interviewing and research data collection methods.

Qualitative interviewing and research data collection techniques differ from **quantitative research methods** procedures in the extent to which the study results can be projected to a wider population of interest. Tech-

---

DISGUISED INTERVIEW.
Interviews and other data collection procedure where the individual being observed has no knowledge that he or she is being observed or knowledge of the purpose of the study.

UNDISGUISED INTERVIEW.
Interview in which the respondent knows he or she is being observed or has knowledge of the purpose of the study.

STRUCTURED INTERVIEW
Method of interviewing where the questions are completely predetermined.

UNSTRUCTURED INTERVIEW
Method of interviewing where questions are not completely predetermined and the interviewer is free to probe for all details and underlying feelings.

QUALITATIVE RESEARCH METHODS
Techniques involving small numbers of respondents who provide descriptive information about their thoughts and feelings that are not easily projected to the whole population.

QUANTITATIVE RESEARCH METHODS
Techniques involving relatively large numbers of respondents, which are designed to generate information that can be projected to the whole population.

niques that are most closely associated with qualitative research, for example, focus groups or depth interviews, involve analyzing responses of a relatively small number of individuals—for example, as we discuss below most focus groups range from 6 to 12 individuals. Quantitative research projects generally involve large numbers of individuals and quite often the aim of the study is to project the results to a wider population. For example, the objectives of a quantitative study might be to make definitive statements (i.e., inferences) about the population of low-fat product users and the reasons why certain individuals are heavy users. In contrast, a focus group of heavy users of low-fat products could identify the feelings and motivations of these consumers, but the objective would not be to generalize these results, based on six to twelve individuals, to the entire population of heavy product category users.

FOCUS GROUPS

The **focus group interview,** a time-honored data-collection method in marketing research, is used by every *Forbes* 500 company including General Motors, AT&T, and Xerox.[2] Box 6–1 presents a case study of the use of focus groups by the Buick division of General Motors in developing the Regal two-door, six-passenger coupe introduced in 1987.

Focus groups provide a good opportunity for marketers to experience firsthand how consumers think and feel about a product. They frequently provide information that would be difficult if not impossible to obtain through traditional interviewing methods.

FOCUS GROUP INTERVIEW Interviews in which the interviewer, in this case called the moderator, listens to a group of consumers talk about a brand, product/service, or consumption experience.

Procedure[3]

Focus groups usually involve anywhere from 6 to 12 people, recruited to meet defined characteristics—age, gender, use of certain products, frequency of product use—who meet with a moderator to discuss a subject for anywhere from one to two hours.

In other words, if you are recruited to participate in a focus group, you will have been selected because you meet a certain demographic profile and use a particular product or service. An example might be a male between the ages of 18 and 35 who uses disposable razors and is a past-30-day user of aerosol shaving cream.

The research firm conducting the focus group interview invites participants to come to their interviewing facility. They are told ahead of time how long a session will last, what the general topic of discussion will be, and the payment for participating. They are usually conducted in commercial research facilities. The focus group room should provide a relaxed and comfortable setting—typically the room looks like a boardroom, although it can also look like an ordinary living room. Usually, one wall of the room is a one-way mirror into an observation room for members of the sponsoring firm who wish to observe the focus group. The observation room contains audiovisual equipment to tape the sessions for future analysis.

Exhibit 6–2 presents a typical focus group setting.

BOX 6—1

FROM THE USER'S PERSPECTIVE

AN EXAMPLE OF A USEFUL FOCUS GROUP

The Buick division of General Motors used focus groups to help develop the Regal two-door, six-passenger coupe introduced in 1987. The effort began more than three years prior to introducing the car, when Buick held about 20 focus groups across the country and asked what features customers wanted in a new car. The target customers were those wealthy enough to afford a $14,000 price tag, which meant annual incomes of $40,000 or above; the price at the time was about $1,000 to $2,000 more than the average new car. All participants, gathered in every major geographical region of the country, had purchased new cars within the past four years.

What these groups indicated was that the customers wanted a legitimate back seat, at least 20 miles per gallon gas consumption, and 0-to-60-miles-per-hour acceleration in 11 seconds or less. They also wanted a stylish car, but they didn't want it to look like it just landed from outer space.

After Buick engineers created clay models of the car and mock-ups of the interior, the company went back to yet another focus group of target buyers. The customers didn't like the oversized bumper and the severe slope of the hood. They did like the four-wheel independent suspension.

Focus groups also helped to refine the advertising campaign for the Regal. Participants were asked first which competing cars most resembled the Buick in terms of image and features. The answer was Oldsmobile, a sister General Motors Division. GM's response was to reposition Buick above Oldsmobile by focusing on comfort and luxury features such as full six-passenger seating, wood-grain instrument panels, velour-type fabrics, and special stereo systems.

Source: Reprinted by permission of FORBES magazine. (c) Forbes Inc., 1987.

A given focus group session should be limited to participants who have similar backgrounds and experiences. When a group includes people of quite diverse backgrounds, some respondents may feel inhibited and may not participate or may express guarded responses, what they consider to be responses acceptable to the other participants. To ensure complete coverage of target segments, the firm may want to commission more than one focus group on any given topic. Hence, people participating in a given focus group will have similar backgrounds and experiences with the other people in that group but will have different backgrounds and experiences to people participating in the other focus groups being conducted. In general, the more diverse the markets and customers, the more groups will be needed.

Focus group participants are recruited; that is, usually they are chosen by a field service that also provides the physical facility. Participants generally are paid anywhere from $30 to as much as $150 for a session. Identifying and recruiting appropriate participants for focus groups is perhaps the most important task because it greatly influences the quality of the response; disastrous results can occur if the wrong people are recruited. The researcher must provide the field service with clear and specific profiles on the types of people that should be recruited. Exhibit 6–3 outlines seven important rules for recruiting focus group participants.

Focus groups are led by a moderator. The role of the moderator is not to lead or direct the group discussion, but rather to keep it focused on the topic of interest. The moderator wants members of the group to discuss a certain set of topics within a certain time, although not in any particular order. It is the moderator's responsibility to ensure that every member of the focus group participates in the discussion, without allowing one or two strong personalities to dominate the discussion. Ideally, the moderator should do this while saying as little as possible.

EXHIBIT 6—3

Seven Rules in Recruiting
Focus Group Participants

1. Specifically define the characteristics of people who will be included in the groups.
2. If you are conducting an industrial focus group, develop screening questions that probe into all aspects of the respondents' job functions. Do not depend on titles or other ambiguous definitions of responsibilities.
3. If you are conducting an industrial focus group, provide the research company with the names of specific companies and employees, when possible. If specific categories of companies are needed, a list of qualified companies is critical.
4. Ask multiple questions about a single variable to validate the accuracy of answers. Therefore, if you want to recruit personal computer users, do not simply ask for the brand and model of personal computers they use. In addition, ask them to describe the machine and its function; this will ensure that they are referring to the appropriate equipment.
5. Require that recruiters provide completed screener questionnaires at the end of each day. Check them carefully to ensure that appropriate people were recruited from appropriate companies. When in doubt, make a follow-up call to confirm the participant.
6. Do not accept respondents who have participated in a focus group during the previous year.
7. Have each participant arrive 15 minutes early to complete a prediscussion questionnaire. This will provide additional background information on each respondent, will reconfirm their suitability for the discussion, and will help the company collect useful factual information.

Source: Joe L. Welch, "Research Marketing Problems and Opportunities with Focus Groups," *Industrial Marketing Management* 14 (1985), p. 248.

The process of obtaining focus group members is facilitated by using a screening questionnaire, which clearly sets forth the qualifications that a person must possess in order to be in the focus group. A moderator controls the flow of discussion and usually attempts to move the group from a general discussion of the product category to a discussion of a specific product or specific characteristics of a product. A **discussion guide** establishes the plan of the focus group interview, including the topics that will be covered and sometimes the time allocated to each topic. The discussion guide is not a questionnaire, but provides an agenda that is flexible enough to be altered as the group discussion progresses.

DISCUSSION GUIDE
Agenda that establishes the plan of the focus group interview, including the topics to be covered and sometimes the time allocated to each topic.

After finishing the group sessions, the moderator turns over the interview tapes to the client. Frequently, the moderator is asked to prepare a written report that provides an interpretation of the group discussion.

Reasons for Conducting

The overriding reason for conducting focus groups is to collect more detailed, in-depth responses from individuals concerning their experiences with products or services. Focus groups provide a good opportunity for marketers to experience firsthand how consumers think and feel about a product or service. Because of the unstructured nature of the data collection exercise, they frequently provide information that would be difficult if not impossible to obtain through the use of more structured interviewing methods.

There are at least five pragmatic reasons for conducting focus groups.

1. *"Experiencing Consumers."* As we previously stated, the primary reason for conducting focus groups is to provide management with the opportunity to here consumers talk about their experiences with products and services.

2. *Timing.* Focus groups can be executed quickly. Completion of three or four geographically dispersed focus groups, along with final reports, can usually be accomplished in no more than four weeks. Typically, information from a focus group is available one week after the study has been authorized.

3. *Cost.* As research projects go, focus groups are relatively inexpensive. A one-group study costs approximately $3,000 to $4,000, two groups $5,000 to $6,000, and four groups $10,000 to $12,000. Costs will vary according to the length of the interview and the target population—how difficult it is to locate qualified participants and the amount that has to be paid for their cooperation.

4. *Flexibility.* Because focus groups use an unstructured interviewing format they allow the researcher or marketing manager to change aspects of the study design in response to information gleaned from the group discussion. Thus tentative ideas and hypotheses can be modified as the focus group is in progress.

5. *Security.* Focus groups allow highly sensitive concept and product prototypes to be exposed to a limited, preselected group of individuals in a tightly controlled environment. In addition, the moderator is keenly aware of the client's security needs and knows what information to provide to the focus group participants.

Uses

Focus group interviews are typically the first step in the research process for many types of marketing problems. Because they are used in the early, exploratory stages of the research process, their primary usefulness is not in providing precise quantitative information but rather in providing qualitative, descriptive information that bridges the gap between the firm (and its products) and the consumer. The following applications and examples briefly describe a number of uses, from generating ideas for advertising to seeking explanation of survey results.[4]

— *New products screening.* Products in concept or prototype stage are presented to potential user groups. Group technique is preferred due to need for depth of response, need to view prototype or imagine concept, and confidentiality. Works best when design personnel are present.

  Example: The reduction of the number of electric telephone concepts from 6 to 3 for a quantitative test.

— *Identification of attitudes underlying purchase of established products.* Focus group interviews conducted to explore reasons for purchase/nonpurchase among users/nonusers in effort to tailor marketing strategy.

  Example: The study conducted to identify the reasons for the falling sales of a firm's pre-fab houses.

— *Evaluation of advertising concepts.* Ad concepts at idea, storyboard, or animatic stage are presented to consumer groups for evaluation. Works best with presence of creative personnel.

Example: Evaluation of potentially humorous animatics for commercial development.

— *Pre-quantitative issue and language identification.* Prior to conducting a quantitative study, salient issues and the language of the consumer are explored through groups.

Example: The identification of language used by teenagers to describe shopping for fashionable clothing.

— *Packaging and/or name screening.* Responses to package and/or name alternatives probed, with emphasis on emotional reactions to packages and connotations of names.

Example: The selection of a new name for a home test kit from six alternatives.

— *Acquisition of general background information on a product or service.* Used by ad agencies when pursuing an account or searching for creative ideas.

Example: An ad agency that needed to know something about spackling products in a hurry.

— *Idea generation.* Groups conducted among consumers or management personnel to generate new product ideas.

Example: The determination of a list of banking services to be presented to a consumer group.

Though focus groups have many valid uses, they can be used in an unethical manner. Focus groups should not be used to serve a client's hidden agenda. Exhibit 6–4 presents several illustrations of unethical focus groups.

EXHIBIT 6–4

Ethical Standards for the Use of Focus Groups

Focus groups have many valid uses, but they can be used in an unethical manner to serve a client's hidden agenda. The following types of focus groups are considered unethical.

Sell groups: Focus groups that attempt to get a set of people together (doctors, lawyers, engineers, etc.) to make a sales pitch.

Prayer groups: These are usually political and designed to get consumers to say what the client wants to hear.

Tour groups: Focus groups that are commissioned for the sole purpose of getting the client and/or marketing researcher to visit an attractive location.

T-groups: Here the client wants to generalize from a percentage of the respondents liking the product to national market share.

Right-to-life groups: Here the clients keep changing moderators and groups of people until they find a group that is in favor of the idea.

Ethnic groups: Here the client limits the type of people eligible for the focus group so that they will fit specific notions of product users.

Source: Adapted from Alexa Smith, "Focus Groups Being Subverted by Clients," *Marketing News,* June 8, 1984, p. 7.

DEPTH INTERVIEWS

The depth interview, often referred to as a *one-on-one,* attempts to uncover people's underlying motivations, prejudices, attitudes toward sensitive issues, and so on. Exhibit 6–5 discusses the factors affecting the choice of focus groups versus one-on-one interviews.

Depth interviews can prove most useful if the marketing research issue under study deals with (1) personal, emotionally charged, or embarrassing matters; (2) behaviors where socially acceptable norms exist and where pressures to conform in group discussions would influence responses; (3) a complex behavioral or decision-making process that requires a detailed, situation-specific, step-by-step description; and (4) when group interviews are difficult to schedule for the target population (doctors and other professionals, for example). One example of the use of depth interviewing is a technique called *laddering,* which is based on means end theory.[5] Depth interviews, with frequent probing, are used to determine linkages between attributes (A), consequences, (C), and values (V). Exhibit 6–6 provides an example of a laddering interview with the resulting ladder.[6] When analyzed across respondents, these laddering techniques can provide valuable information for the development of advertising strategy by identifying the linkages between attributes and consequences on the one hand and the values that a person (or group of people) wishes to achieve.

DEPTH INTERVIEW ("ONE-ON-ONE")

Sessions in which free association and hidden sources of feelings are discussed, generally through a very loose, unstructured question guide, administered by a highly skilled interviewer. It attempts to uncover underlying motivations, prejudices, attitudes toward sensitive issues, etc.

EXHIBIT 6–5

Focus Groups versus One-on-One Interviews

Factor	Focus Groups	One-On-One Interviews
Value of interaction	Use when interactions of participants will spark new thought (Example: physicians discussing treatment procedures)	Use when interactions are limited or appear to be nonproductive (Example: preschool children discussing new cereal product)
Sensitivity of subject matter	Use when subject matter is such that participants will not withhold information or temper remarks (Example: do-it-yourself mechanics discussing auto parts)	Use when subject matter is so sensitive that few respondents would speak openly in group setting (Example: research on selling strategies of competitive insurance agents)
Cost and timing	Use when turnaround critical and need to economize present	Use when turnaround not critical and budget will permit high costs of execution and reporting
Depth of information per respondent	Assumes most respondents can say all that they know in 8–12 minutes (Example: group conducted among women on use of prepared cake mixes)	Permits greater depth of response per individual; use when subject matter complex and participants very knowledgeable (Example: interviewing CPAs on tax preparation)
Logistics	Assumes that an acceptable number of respondents can be assembled in one location	Use when respondents are geographically dispersed and travel costs prohibitive

Source: The Burke Institute.

Interviewer: You indicated that you would be more likely to drink a wine cooler at a party on the weekend with friends. Why is that?

Respondent: Well, wine coolers have *less alcohol* than a mixed drink and because they are so *filling* I tend to drink fewer and more slowly.

Interviewer: What is the benefit of having less alcohol when you are around your friends?

Respondent: I never really have thought about it. I don't know.

Interviewer: Try to think about it in relation to the party situation. When was the last time you had a wine cooler in this party-with-friends situation?

Respondent: Last weekend.

Interviewer: Okay, why coolers last weekend?

Respondent: Well, I knew I would be drinking a long time and I *didn't want to get wasted.*

Interviewer: Why was it important to not get wasted at the party last weekend?

Respondent: When I'm at a party I like to *socialize,* talk to my friends, and hopefully make some new friends. If I get wasted, I'm afraid I'd make an ass of myself and people won't invite me next time. It's important for me to be *part of the group.*

The summary ladder is

V   sense of belonging
    (part of the group)

C   socialize

C   avoid getting drunk
    (wasted)

A   less alcohol/filling

Depth interviews also are useful for studying routine or ritualistic behaviors. They have been used in brand-name research to understand consumers' perceptions and responses to names.[7] Other commercial applications have included copy and concept evaluations, where respondents are queried concerning what they recall or what they feel after listening to an advertisement.

Basically, depth interviews attempt to uncover the content and intensity of respondents' feelings and motivations beyond straightforward or simplistic responses to structured questions. Given that they follow psychoanalytical methods, they can be expensive. It takes a long time to conduct depth interviews, transcribe the tapes, and read the transcriptions; interviews should be analyzed by an experienced practitioner who knows the technique and the product category under study.

PROJECTIVE TECHNIQUES
A class of techniques which presume that respondents cannot or will not communicate their feelings and beliefs directly; provides a structured question format in which respondents can respond indirectly by projecting their own feelings and beliefs into the situation while they interpret the behavior of others.

PROJECTIVE TECHNIQUES

In certain situations it may be beneficial for researchers to obtain information on respondents' feelings and beliefs indirectly. **Projective techniques** presume respondents cannot or will not communicate their feelings and beliefs directly. Instead, respondents are allowed to respond indirectly by projecting their own feelings and beliefs into a situation as they interpret the behavior of others.

The shopping list study conducted by Maison Haire in the late 1940s typifies a classic use of projective techniques.[8] Remember that the world

Conducting a depth interview

was a little different in the 1940s. First of all, in the typical household the wife (the shopper) did not usually work outside the home. Second, frozen or instant foods were not readily accepted, and the microwave was years away. Haire was interested in assessing the lack of acceptance of Nescafé's instant coffee. He believed that buyers were either unable to articulate and/or were unwilling to provide the true motivation for not buying instant coffee.

The study exposed two groups of homemakers to a typical shopping list. One group looked at shopping list I and the other group at shopping list II, both shown in Exhibit 6–7. Note that the lists are identical except for the type of coffee to be purchased; one list specifies instant coffee, the other the traditional ground coffee. The women panelists were asked to describe the homemaker who made up the list they were looking at.

A summary of the responses is provided in Exhibit 6–8. The image of the instant coffee user is certainly unflattering. It is unlikely that this kind of information could have been obtained from traditional structured interviews.

Among the more frequently used projective techniques are

1. *Word association.* You are probably familiar with word association tests, where respondents are presented with a list of words, one at a time, and asked to indicate the word that comes immediately to

WORD ASSOCIATION
Projective technique whereby respondents are presented with a list of words, one at a time, and asked to indicate what word comes immediately to mind.

Shopping List I	Shopping List II
pound and a half of hamburger	pound and a half of hamburger
2 loaves Wonder bread	2 loaves Wonder bread
bunch of carrots	bunch of carrots
1 can Rumford's baking powder	1 can Rumford's baking powder
Nescafé instant coffee	1 lb. Maxwell House coffee (drip ground)
2 cans Del Monte peaches	2 cans Del Monte peaches
5 lbs. potatoes	5 lbs. potatoes

*Fifty people responded to each shopping list.

EXHIBIT 6–7
Maison Haire Shopping Lists*

EXHIBIT 6—8

Summary of Responses to Shopping Lists Shown in Exhibit 6-7

1. 48 percent of the people described the woman who bought Nescafé as lazy; 4 percent described the woman who bought Maxwell House as lazy.

2. 48 percent of the people described the woman who bought Nescafé as failing to plan household purchases and schedules well; 12 percent described the woman who bought Maxwell House this way.

3. 4 percent described the Nescafé woman as thrifty; 16 percent described the Maxwell House woman this way.

4. 16 percent described the Nescafé woman as not a good wife; 0 percent described the Maxwell House woman this way. 4 percent described the Nescafé woman as a good wife; 16 percent described the Maxwell House woman as a good wife.

SENTENCE COMPLETION

Projective technique whereby respondents are asked to complete a number of incomplete sentences with the first word or phrase that comes to mind.

UNFINISHED-SCENARIO STORY COMPLETION

Projective technique whereby respondents complete the end of a story or supply the motive for why one or more actors in a story behaved as they did.

THIRD-PERSON ROLE PLAYING

Projective technique that presents respondents with a verbal or visual situation and asks them to relate the feelings and beliefs of a third person to the situation, rather than to directly express their own feelings and beliefs about the situation.

CARTOON COMPLETION TEST

Projective technique that presents respondents with a cartoon of a particular situation and asks them to suggest the dialogue that one cartoon character might make in response to the comment(s) of another cartoon character.

mind. The respondent's response and the time it takes to respond are recorded and analyzed according to the frequency with which a response is given, the amount of time elapsed, and the number of respondents unable to respond within the time allowed. Elapsed time is important because hesitation could indicate that respondents are searching for a "socially acceptable" response.

2. *Sentence completion.* Sentence completion tests ae based upon free association similar to word association. The respondent is asked to complete a number of incomplete sentences with the first word or phrase that comes to mind. Responses are then analyzed for content.

3. *Unfinished-scenario story completion.* The unfinished-scenario story-completion technique requires respondents to complete the end of a story, or supply the motive for why one or more characters in a story behaved as they did.

4. *Third-person role playing.* The third-person role-playing technique presents respondents with a verbal or visual situation and asks them to describe the reactions of a third person—a friend, a neighbor, or a "typical" person—to the situation, rather than to express their own reactions directly. The idea is that the respondent will reveal personal feelings and beliefs while describing the reactions of a third party. A popular version of the third-person technique presents the respondent with a description of a shopping list and asks for a characterization of the purchaser, which is what Maison Haire did in the instant coffee research.

5. *Cartoon completion.* A cartoon completion test presents respondents with a cartoon of a particular situation and asks them to suggest the dialogue that one cartoon character might make in response to comments of another character.

Exhibit 6–9 illustrates several of these projective techniques. Projective techniques require a highly skilled interviewer; for successful results, completed interviews must be analyzed and interpreted by experienced professionals. Not surprisingly, the cost per interview is high compared with other types of survey interviewing methods. As a result, projective techniques are not used extensively in commercial marketing research, except for word association, which is frequently used in brand-name studies.

EXHIBIT 6—9

Examples of Projective Techniques

Word Association

Subjects are asked to respond to a list of words, read to them one at a time, with the first word that comes to mind. The words of interest (in this case, methods of conducting banking transactions) are dispersed throughout the list to try to disguise the purpose of the study.

Stimulus Word	Response
Mechanic	_____
Bank teller	_____
Dry cleaner	_____
House	_____
Automatic teller machine	_____
Automobile	_____
Waiter	_____
Bank by phone	_____

Sentence Completion

Subjects are asked to complete a sentence with the first thought that comes to mind.

1. What I like most about automatic teller machines is _____
2. People who use automatic teller machines are _____
3. Automatic teller machines may be convenient, but they _____

Unfinished-Scenario Technique:

Subjects are asked to complete an unfinished scenario with what they think is happening.

Bill has just received a large commission check. He is out of town and intends to deposit it in an automatic teller machine because_____

A friend tells him he should_____
because_____

Cartoon Completion

Subjects are asked to fill in the response of a character in a cartoon setting.

OBSERVATIONAL METHODS

OBSERVATIONAL
METHODS
Data collection techniques
that observe behavior either
directly or indirectly by mechanical methods or human
observer.

We have distinguished methods of data collection at the broadest level: according to whether they involve asking the respondent to report on some behavior retrospectively or whether they directly or indirectly, by human or mechanical methods, observe the behavior under study.

Observational methods, as distinguished from interviews, can be particularly important primary-data research tools, especially where respondents are either unable or unwilling to report past behavior, and in cross-cultural research, where it is likely that respondents from different cultures may be asked imperfectly translated questions about concepts that may not exist in their cultures. There are a number of ways marketing researchers apply observational techniques. These include the use of naturalistic inquiry, "garbology," physiological measurement, and computerized or electronic measurement.

Naturalistic Inquiry

NATURALISTIC INQUIRY
Research methods used for
the study of culture.

Naturalistic inquiry methods are conducted in natural settings. As such, the data collected are inevitably time- and context-dependent. The assumption here is that it is not possible to understand a behavior without knowing its relationship to the time and context that produced, harbored, and supported it.[9]

ETHNOGRAPHY
The study of culture.

Academic researchers have applied naturalistic inquiry in the study of various consumption behaviors.[10] In the commercial arena, advertising agencies have used a special form of naturalistic inquiry called **ethnography** (the study of cultures) for some time. Young & Rubicam (Y&R), for example, has used ethnography to observe people's lives in order to create ads that are consistent with reality; it has helped them to come up with new-product ideas.[11] Y&R observes right in people's homes such things as how parents and children interact, which brand-name products are in the refrigerator, and how a home is decorated. One of Y&R's ethnography projects deals with what they label as the "new traditional woman." They found that new traditional women are not what you might think of as the stereotypical executive. In fact, new traditional women typically have left the work force to care for their families, planning to return to the work force eventually.

"Garbology"

GARBOLOGY
Indirect observational research technique for the
study of product
consumption.

Checking the garbage cans of households and recording the goods consumed, as evidenced by the discarded cans, bottles, and wrappers, is an indirect observational research method for the study of product consumption. It is an indirect method because the researcher does not actually observe the consumption taking place, but rather takes the discarded container as implicit evidence of the consumption. The notion of using samples of garbage as indicators of consumption is not new. Charles Parlin used it in the early 1900s to prove to the Campbell Soup Company that, contrary to their assumption, wealthy people who usually had household help did not use canned soup, whereas blue-collar families did.[12]

Garbage analysis begins with the collection of a household's garbage, which is usually done by the local sanitation department at periodic intervals, for example, twice a week.[13] Each household's garbage is placed in specially marked plastic bags and then transported to a central facility where sorting takes place. The contents of each bag are weighed and recorded by experienced sorters who note the respondent code, the census location of the household, the date, and the name of the sorter. Sorters record brand, price, and other product/consumption information.

Physiological Measurement

Methods that monitor a respondent's nonvoluntary responses to stimuli fall under the umbrella of physiological measurement. These methods involve mechanical observation, and they are typically obtrusive in nature. Two physiological measurement instruments that have had limited use in studies of shopping behavior and reactions to advertising are the pupilometer and the galvanometer. A pupilometer attaches to a person's head and measures interest and attention by the degree of dilation in the pupil of the eye. The galvanometer measures excitement levels according to the electrical activity level in the person's skin.

PHYSIOLOGICAL
MEASUREMENT
Methods that involve mechanical observation

There are two drawbacks in using physiological measures: their obvious unnatural and obtrusive nature, and the fact that the measurements lack a clear affective (i.e., like/dislike) component. For example: What can we conclude about someone's reaction if their pupils dilate or if the electrical activity level in their skin increases? Is the response favorable or unfavorable?

Computerized or Electronic Measurement

Several variants of observational research involve computerized or electronic measurement of behaviors.

Scanners. Optical scanning via Universal Product Codes (UPC) represents a form of mechanical observational measurement. Scanner services that permit extensive data on product category, brand, store type, price, quantity, and customer to be recorded automatically were discussed in more detail in Chapter 5.

Eye tracking. Eye movement research has been used in advertising and package research for many years. Technological developments in fiber optics, digital processing, and advanced electronics, however, have advanced beyond the old days of "eye cameras" and heavy equipment with bite bars and forehead restraints. Today, lightweight equipment is available. Typically, a mini-computer paces the stimulus material for the respondent and records and displays eye movement automatically through a dual disk–driven system. Current eye-tracking methods have considerable advantages over early electronic measurement devices, such as the tachistoscope, which varied the

Tracking the eye movements of a subject watching a TV commercial

The individual views a screen onto which 35 mm slides are projected (e.g., store scenes, actual ads). Each person is provided with a remote control switch. The switch lets respondents control viewing time.

The Perception Research Services, Inc. (PRS), eye tracker records each participant's visual experience. The tracker simultaneously pinpoints where the respondent is looking and superimposes that point directly onto the material being viewed. PRS is able to determine not only where respondents look, but how long they stay on a particular point.

Eye-tracking information is recorded directly onto computer tape for data processing. This allows for a continuous record of visual response as it takes place. PRS has the capability of recording eye movements per second. (It can also be placed on videotape for client viewing.)

A software program depicts the test item in terms of individual components that can be modified at any time for additional analysis. For shelf-display work, each package on a shelf may become a component. For ad testing, headline, subhead, main illustration, subillustration, logo, product shot, and individual copy lines can be differentiated.

The movement of the eye is charted from the time the test item is first viewed until the time the viewing is terminated. The results are a record of the viewing sequence, the time given to each item, copy readership, and, most important, those areas that are bypassed quickly or overlooked totally. Eye tracking shows stopping power.

length of time (e.g., $\frac{1}{10}$ of a second, $\frac{3}{10}$ of a second) that a subject was exposed to a visual image, such as a consumer's exposure to a package as part of a mass display.

Exhibit 6–10 provides details on the eye-tracking procedure used by Perception Research Services, and Exhibit 6–11 depicts a classic example of using eye tracking to pretest advertising.

RESPONSE LATENCY

Physiological measure of the time interval between the asking of a question and the response to that question

Response latency. Response latency measures the interval between the asking of a question and the response to that question. The length of deliberation before answering a question is taken to indicate the respondent's confidence or certainty in the answer—or lack of certainty. The most common way to measure response latency is with a computer that displays one question at a time; the lapses in time between the display and the participant's response are measured.

Response latencies are most useful when people are asked to choose between two options. For example, consider the following question:

Please check which brand of coffee you prefer.   Folgers   ☐
                                                   Yuban   ☐

EXHIBIT 6—11

Example of the Use of Eye-Tracking Technology

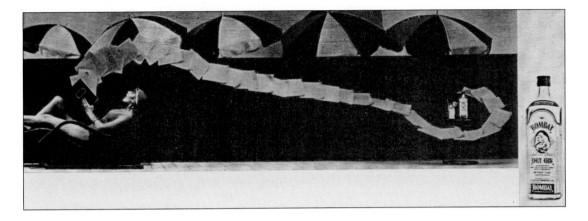

An original *Bombay* gin ad looked like the one shown above.

However, when the ad was pretested, eye tracking showed that readership of the copy below the visual was virtually nonexistent, and the Bombay bottle on the far right was being ignored by 9 out of 10 readers. As you might imagine, this translated to recall levels that could only be classified as disappointing.

When followed up with verbal questioning to uncover gin drinkers' attitudes toward the advertising and their perception of the product, we found the ad was confusing; it failed to convey an upscale image for Bombay and for the types of drinkers who were likely to buy Bombay. Most important, it required a copy link between the visual and the message because many readers failed to understand the relevance of the artwork.

Based upon the pretest findings, the agency (TBWA) instituted a number of major, though subtle, revisions. You'll note that in the ad below the size of the Bombay bottle on the far right has been increased. But, most important, the line, "Nothing attracts like the imported taste of Bombay Gin," provides the explanation for the visual and the imported heritage of the product, which justifies premium pricing and positions Bombay as a quality gin.

NOTHING ATTRACTS LIKE THE IMPORTED TASTE OF BOMBAY GIN.

This revised execution was attention-getting, memorable, meaningful, and motivating. In fact, the unaided recall level for this ad was almost 100 percent higher than the level for the original execution.

Source: Perception Research Services, Inc. Reprinted with permission.

From your answer, we can tell which brand of coffee you prefer, but we cannot tell by how much. Here, response latency would help to determine how much you prefer one of the brands over the other. The longer it takes you to respond, the more similar the options are. If immediately after you are presented with this choice you check Folgers, we would conclude that you strongly prefer Folgers to Yuban because you required almost no deliberation time. If you spend a considerable amount of time deliberating though, we would conclude that the two brands are similar to you and that you have no strong preference for one brand over the other.

An advantage of response latency is that it is unobtrusive; that is, the respondent does not know that the measure is being recorded. It is also relatively easy and inexpensive to implement, assuming of course that the necessary equipment is available.

SUMMARY

In this chapter we have described what is meant by qualitative research techniques to collect primary data. Qualitative research methods generally meet one or more of these criteria: (1) small sample sizes; (2) unstructured question format; (3) indirect measurement of respondent's feelings and beliefs; and (4) direct observation. Popular qualitative research techniques are focus groups and depth interviews, each with relevant implementation considerations. A variety of projective techniques used in marketing research are based on the assumption that respondents for whatever reason do not communicate their feelings directly; these techniques allow respondents to project their own reactions into a situation when they interpret them as the behavior of others. Finally, beyond these methods, there are various human and mechanical procedures for direct or indirect observation of behavior.

KEY CONCEPTS

Focus Group Interview

Depth Interviews

Projective Techniques

Naturalistic Inquiry

Observational Techniques

Physiological Measurement

REVIEW QUESTIONS

1. Discuss the primary observational methods of interviewing. What, if any, are the advantages of using them compared to using quantitative research methods?

2. What are factors that might affect the number of focus groups that should be conducted?

3. Under what circumstances would you suggest that a depth interview be conducted, rather than a focus group?

4. What role does the moderator play in focus group interviews? In what way might the moderator affect the quality of the data?

5. Describe the distinguishing features of naturalistic inquiry studies, and illustrate the major types of projective interviewing techniques.

One business already subject to questions because of the rising research refusal rate is the Nielsen television rating system. The ratings are used by the television networks as a measure of which shows viewers like and by consumer-products companies to place more than $12 billion worth of advertising annually.

In the first three months of this year, Nielsen reported an unexpectedly sharp drop from the year before in the number of households watching television. In daytime last February, for example, about 2.2 million people of the more than 27 million who had watched the year before turned off their sets—a drop of 8 percent.

"Everyone is fearful of self-selection and worried that the generalizations you make are based on cooperators only," said Verne B. Churchill, the chairman and chief executive of Market Facts, one of the nation's largest designers of custom market research surveys.

He said that rising refusal rates on telephone surveys had moved his company to depend more on mail surveys using large, fixed groups of people. "We get a high completion rate because they know we're legitimate questioners and we're not out to sell anything," Mr. Churchill said. "But there's still fear that this panel is different from the rest of the population."

Source: Randell Rothenberg, Copyright (c) 1990 by The *New York Times,* October 5, 1990, pp. A1, D4. Reprinted by permission.

styles, a rise of eight percentage points since 1985.

The lack of participation was also felt this year by the Census Bureau, whose findings determine each state's representation in Congress and some amounts of federal aid to states and cities. In 1980, three quarters of all households initially mailed back their census forms, said John J. Connolly, the assistant to Barbara Everitt Bryan, the director of the Census. This year, the bureau's experts expected 70 percent to do so, but so far, only 63 percent have.

INTRODUCTION

Surveys generally involve reaching a large number of people to answer a set of questions. A survey could consist of an interviewer asking questions of respondents and then writing down their answers, as in a telephone interview, or asking respondents to complete a written questionnaire themselves, as in a mail survey. Just getting people to respond to surveys is becoming increasingly difficult these days.

This chapter discusses four general types of survey interviewing methods: mail, telephone, in-home personal, and mall-intercept surveys. Each method has its own advantages and drawbacks; each is best suited for certain types of surveys. We discuss these special qualities that you will want to consider when you are choosing a survey interviewing method.

SURVEY METHODS

Researchers' choices of survey techniques can change over the years. A survey asking 140 corporate marketing research directors to name the two or three data-collection methods used most often in a past year indicates that the two most popular data-collection methods were central WATS (i.e., telephone surveys) and mall-intercept surveys.[1] Exhibit 7–1 shows the complete results. Compared to the results of a similar survey taken in

EXHIBIT 7–1

Survey Research Techniques

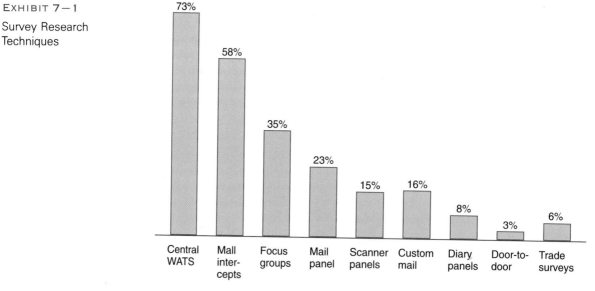

Total sample

Question 3a: Which two or three survey methods have accounted for the greatest proportion of your outside, custom dollar expenditures in the past year or so?

Source: Market Facts, Inc., *Practices, Trends, and Expectations for the Market Research Industry, 1988–1989* (Chicago: Market Facts, Inc., October 1988), pp. 88–89.

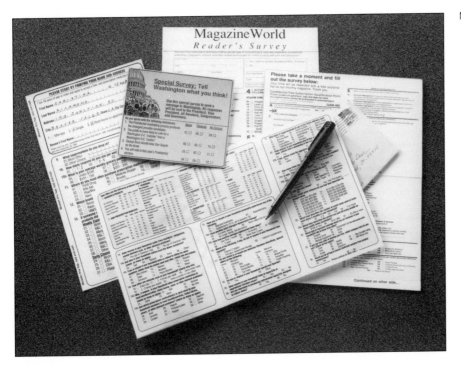

Magazine insert mail survey

1987, the 1991 survey found an increase in the use of mail panels, direct ("cold") mail, focus groups, and central telephone (WATS) surveys; it found decreases in the use of purchase diaries and in-home interview surveys.

Mail surveys involve mailing a questionnaire directly to a sample of respondents, with the completed questionnaire returned by mail to the firm conducting the study. An alternative method is to hand-deliver the questionnaire to the respondent and make arrangements to pick up the completed questionnaire.[2] Mail surveys can also be attached to products, as is standard practice with warranty cards, or distributed as inserts in magazines and newspapers.[3] Exhibit 7–2 presents an example of a survey using a warranty card.

There are two types of mail surveys: **direct (cold) mail surveys** and **mail panels.** Cold mail surveys involve mailing questionnaires to individuals who have not agreed in advance to participate in the study. If you were to purchase a mailing list and then use this list for your sample, this would represent a cold mailing.

Mail panels maintained by commercial marketing researchers consist of large and nationally representative samples of households that have agreed to participate periodically in mail questionnaires.[4] They represent an important resource in a pool of respondents who are agreeable to participating in research projects and ready to answer questions whenever they are asked to do so. Households that agree to participate in a mail panel are often compensated with a variety of incentives—direct (cash) payments, redeem

MAIL SURVEYS

Data-collection method that involves sending out a questionnaire to a sample of respondents.

DIRECT "COLD" MAIL SURVEYS

Surveys in which questionnaires are sent to a "cold" group of individuals who have not previously agreed to participate in the study.

MAIL PANELS

Representative samples of households that have agreed to participate periodically in mail questionnaires.

EXHIBIT 7—2

Example of Warranty Card
Questionnaire

Product Registration Card

Thank you for purchasing this Black & Decker product. Please register your name and address right away to help us contact you in the unlikely event of a product recall. This information will also help us design new products and better understand our customers.

Return this card for a chance to win the Black & Decker small appliance of your choice!

A quarterly drawing will be held from the Product Registration Cards received during the preceding 3 months. We will send the winner a Black & Decker small appliance of their choice. In order to participate, simply complete and return this registration card at once. Offer void in Canada and other countries where restricted or prohibited by law. The odds of winning depend upon the number of participants.

1. ☐ Mr.   **2.** ☐ Mrs.   **3.** ☐ Ms.   **4.** ☐ Miss   83D01-01

First Name   Initial   Last Name

Street   Apt. No.

City   State   ZIP

❷ Home Telephone:
(Area code)

❸ Date of Purchase
Month   Day   Year

❹ **Now that you have purchased this Black & Decker product, how has your opinion of Black & Decker changed?**
1. Much more positive than before
2. Somewhat more positive than before
3. About the same as before
4. Somewhat more negative than before
5. Much more negative than before

❺ **Do you or anyone else in your household own or plan to purchase any of the following in the next 6 months?**

	Own	Plan to Buy
1. Toaster Oven		1.
2. Food Processor		2.
3. Electric Can Opener		3.
4. Popcorn Popper		4.
5. Coffee Grinder		5.
6. Electric Juicer		6.
7. Slow Cooker		7.
8. Electric Food Steamer		8.
9. Electric Wok		9.
10. Microwave Oven		10.
11. Drip Coffeemaker		11.
12. Blender		12.
13. Appliance Mounted Under-The-Cabinet		13.
14. Mixer		14.
15. Food Chopper		15.
16. Sandwich Grill		16.
17. Crepe Maker		17.
18. Pasta Maker		18.
19. Espresso Maker		19.
20. Cordless Hand Held Vac		20.
21. Corded Hand Held Vac		21.
22. Auto-Off Iron		22.
23. Smoke Alarm		23.
24. Rechargeable Light		24.

❻ **Date of birth of person whose name appears above:**
Month   Year   1 9

❼ **Excluding yourself, what is the SEX and AGE (in years) of children and other adults living in your household?**
1. No one else in household

Male	Female	Age	Male	Female	Age
1.	2.	years	1.	2.	years
1.	2.	years	1.	2.	years

❽ **Marital status:**
1. Married   3. Widowed
2. Divorced/Separated   4. Never Married (Single)

❾ **Occupation:**   You   Spouse
Homemaker .... 1.
Professional/Technical .... 2.
Upper Management/Executive .... 3.
Middle Management .... 4.
Sales/Marketing .... 5.
Clerical or Service Worker .... 6.
Tradesman/Machine Oper./Laborer ... 7.
Retired .... 8.
Student .... 9.

Self Employed/Business Owner .... 10.

❿ **Which group describes your annual family income?**
1. Under $15,000   7. $40,000-$44,999
2. $15,000-$19,999   8. $45,000-$49,999
3. $20,000-$24,999   9. $50,000-$59,999
4. $25,000-$29,999   10. $60,000-$74,999
5. $30,000-$34,999   11. $75,000-$99,999
6. $35,000-$39,999   12. $100,000 & over

⓫ **Education: (Please check those which apply) You   Spouse**
Some High School or less .... 1.
Completed High School .... 2.
Vocational/Technical School .... 3.
Some College .... 4.
Completed College .... 5.
Some Graduate School .... 6.
Completed Graduate School .... 7.

⓬ **Which credit cards do you use regularly?**
1. American Express, Diners Club
2. MasterCard, Visa, Discover
3. Department Store, Oil Company, etc.
4. Do not use credit cards.

⓭ **For your primary residence, do you:**
1. Own a House?
2. Own a Townhouse or Condominium?
3. Rent a House?
4. Rent an Apartment, Townhouse or Condominium?

Conducting an on-site interview

Mall intercept interview

A WATS interviewing room

able stamps, gifts, and letters, for example. We should also mention that some universities and private agencies maintain panels on a smaller basis.

Telephone surveys involve calling a sample of respondents with a series of questions. Telephone surveys are usually conducted from a central location, which allows for the monitoring of the interviewers. The use and percentage of dollars budgeted for WATS (Wide Area Telephone Service) telephone interviewing continues to increase, and it is still the most frequently used data-collection method.

The **personal in-home survey** involves asking questions of a sample of respondents face-to-face in their homes. In-home personal surveys were very popular in the 1950s and 60s, but changing demographics and family lifestyles have caused a marked decrease both in the use and the percentage

TELEPHONE SURVEYS

Surveys that involve phoning a sample of respondents drawn from an eligible population and asking them a series of questions.

PERSONAL IN-HOME SURVEY

Survey that involves asking questions of a sample of respondents face-to-face in their homes.

of dollars budgeted for in-home personal surveys in the last 20 years. Dual career families and single-parent families have reduced the likelihood of finding someone at home.

Mall intercept surveys interview respondents at a central-location, usually a shopping mall. Respondents are intercepted while shopping and asked to participate in a survey. Underlying this popular interviewing method is the rationale that it's more efficient to have respondents come to the interviewer than to have the interviewer go to the respondents. This method has been used for more than 20 years, dating back to the first enclosed shopping mall.

MALL INTERCEPT PERSONAL SURVEY

Survey method using a central-location test facility at a shopping mall; respondents are intercepted while they are shopping.

FACTORS AFFECTING THE CHOICE OF A SURVEY METHOD

There are a number of factors to consider in deciding which type of survey method will work best in a given research project. If your objective is to maximize a single survey characteristic—lowest cost, for example—the choice would not be that difficult. The problem is that frequently the researcher must select a method that satisfies multiple criteria. You might want to choose a survey method that (1) permits the use of visual stimuli, (2) can be completed within two weeks with at least a 50 percent response rate, and (3) costs no more than $6.00 per respondent. Because of the multiple criteria, the decision is more difficult. The factors you need to consider in selecting a survey method include

1. *Versatility.* The extent to which the survey method can handle different question formats and scenarios.
2. *Quantity of data.* The amount of information that can be collected.
3. *Sample control.* The ease or difficulty of ensuring that desired respondents are contacted.
4. *Quality of data.* The accuracy of the data collected using a particular data-collection method.
5. *Response rate.* The number of completed interviews divided by the number of attempted interviews.
6. *Speed.* The total time it takes to complete the study by using a particular data-collection method.
7. *Cost.* The cost per completed interview.
8. *Uses.* How the collected data will be used.

Versatility

Methods allowing the greatest versatility are in-home personal surveys and mall-intercept surveys. In both cases the interviewer interacts directly with the respondent, so visual cues such as concept illustrations, product packages, or sample advertisements can be used, which is one of the most attractive features of these methods. Face-to-face interaction between the interviewer and the respondent also means that in-home and mall-intercept methods afford the greatest freedom in questionnaire format and length.

Mail surveys and mail panels are the least versatile. Because surveys that are delivered by the mail must be self-administered, questionnaires must be straightforward and simple; there are no interviewers to explain directions or answer questions. Hence, there is no opportunity to follow up incomplete responses, confirm unclear responses, or provide assistance in the case of complicated directions to questions.

Telephone surveys fall in between. They have the advantage of an interviewer, so the questionnaire can be more complex than one sent by mail, but not as complex as in-home or mall-intercept surveys. One drawback to telephone interviewing is that you cannot show a respondent anything. One method that increases the versatility of the telephone uses both the telephone and mail and therefore allows for the use of visual cues. Respondents are contacted first by telephone and told that they will receive a package by mail; then they are called again after the package has arrived and the interview is conducted by telephone.

Quantity of Data

The factor that contributes the most to the quantity of data that can be collected is the length of the interview. Without question the best method to use for long interviews is the personal in-home survey. While mall-intercept surveys also have the advantage of having an interviewer present, mall-intercept interview time is more limited than in the case of in-home surveys because respondents typically are in a hurry. General Foods, a heavy user of mall-intercept surveys, typically limits the interview to 25 minutes or less.[5]

Telephone interviews typically last about 15 minutes, thus the shortest of any method, although interviews of up to one hour have been successful.[6] Also, as Box 7–1 reveals, how long a person will stay on the telephone answering research questions varies from individual to individual. Mail surveys typically can generate more data than telephone interviews but less than in-home interviews.[7]

Sample Control

Mail surveys require an explicit list of individuals or households that are to be surveyed. Frequently, you can purchase these lists from suppliers that specialize in generating mailing lists, or from companies that sell member or subscriber lists (credit card companies, magazine publishers, and so on). Catalogs of mailing lists describe thousands of lists available for purchase.[8]

In many instances, however, mailing lists are unavailable, and when they are available they may be incomplete or dated. One supplier estimates that in its national database of U.S. households, which consists of 74 million names and addresses, 12 to 15 percent of the names listed will change because of normal population mobility. Moreover, 5 to 10 percent of its records nationwide are rural, with addresses consisting of only two lines, and these can be treated as undeliverable by local post offices.[9] Even

Box 7—1

■

FROM THE
USER'S
PERSPECTIVE

■

STUDY REVEALS WHO INTERVIEW "TERMINATORS" ARE

If an interviewer can get a survey respondent to talk for 20 to 25 minutes, he might as well keep him on the telephone for 45 minutes, a study of survey "terminators" revealed.

The study, presented to the Newspaper Research Council at its recent fall conference in Cincinnati by C. Harry Murphy, research director for Landmark Communications, set out to uncover who quits an interview, why he terminates the survey, and when he stops participating.

The 1988 Hampton Roads Study, from which this data was collected, found that the median termination time was 11.7 minutes, and of the total who stopped the survey questioning, 83 percent did so within 23 minutes.

In addition, questions requiring decision-making answers, such as why a respondent shops a certain store, resulted in more terminations.

Since few terminators refused to answer the first six questions on the survey, which were basic demographic information, Murphy noted that it was possible to draw a basic portrait of who they are.

For example, age was the biggest factor identifying a terminator, Murphy said, adding that older respondents have a tendency to end more interviews and to end them faster. There was little difference between men and women in the tendency to end survey interviews and, although two thirds of the terminators quit the interview before occupation questions, the largest group of terminators was not in the labor force, with professional/managerial/sales workers being the least prone to stop the questioning.

Studying the terminators helped discover that long lists of places, items, and so on often lead to ending an interview, as do thought-provoking questions, Murphy reported.

The base for interviews usually begins with an introduction, daily and Sunday questions, and demographics—which takes about six minutes—followed by another six minutes for basic questions.

At this point, Murphy noted, the survey has already lost about half of those it would lose if the interview lasted 45 minutes, yet a 45-minute increase can yield more than four times the data at a cost of 20 percent more.

Source: Debra Gersh, *Editor & Publisher*, October 29, 1991, p. 16. Reprinted with permission.

if a complete and accurate mailing list is available, researchers have little control over who actually fills out the questionnaire once it has arrived at the intended address.

Like mail surveys, telephone surveys are highly dependent on available and accurate lists, in this case lists of telephone numbers. You may say that there is always the telephone directory—but then there are unlisted numbers, which can create a serious source of bias. Nationally, about 30 percent of all households have unlisted telephones, with the number increasing by about 1.5 percent a year.[10]

The map shown in Exhibit 7–3 was constructed by Survey Sampling, Inc. The map consists of the nine census divisions and presents the high-

EXHIBIT 7–3

A Survey Researcher's View of the United States

Unlisted rate	17.6%
Contact rate	59.4%
Cooperation rate	50.3%
Surveyed rate	24.4%

1

Unlisted rate	29.1%
Contact rate	57.1%
Cooperation rate	47.8%
Surveyed rate	26.7%

2

Unlisted rate	26.4%
Contact rate	57.4%
Cooperation rate	54.9%
Surveyed rate	25.9%

5

Unlisted rate	30.6%
Contact rate	57.8%
Cooperation rate	57.1%
Surveyed rate	24.2%

3

Unlisted rate	26.0%
Contact rate	59.7%
Cooperation rate	60.8%
Surveyed rate	27.0%

6

Unlisted rate	21.8%
Contact rate	56.0%
Cooperation rate	59.3%
Surveyed rate	25.8%

4

Unlisted rate	31.3%
Contact rate	53.5%
Cooperation rate	53.5%
Surveyed rate	20.9%

7

Unlisted rate	33.7%
Contact rate	55.1%
Cooperation rate	55.7%
Surveyed rate	31.3%

8

Unlisted rate	49.1%
Contact rate	53.1%
Cooperation rate	46.1%
Surveyed rate	29.4%

9

Total United States

Unlisted rate	31.1%
Contact rate	56.4%
Cooperation rate	53.2%
Surveyed rate	26.0%

Source: Survey Sampling, Inc., 1990.

Metro Area	Total Households	Households with Telephones (%)	Estimated Telephone Households Unlisted (%)
Oakland	790,900	95.6	59.6
Los Angeles–Long Beach	3,025,800	93.4	59.5
Las Vegas	299,600	90.8	59.5
San Jose	525,700	97.0	59.3
Fresno	226,200	93.0	59.0
Sacramento	572,800	94.6	55.8
Riverside-San Bernardino	913,700	93.6	55.3
San Diego	911,800	95.0	54.8
Anaheim-Santa Ana	841,200	96.6	54.3
Oxnard-Ventura	221,200	95.8	53.2
San Francisco	645,600	95.6	52.6
Bakersfield	186,800	91.8	51.6
Jersey City	207,900	88.8	49.1
Detroit	1,621,000	96.1	38.4
Portland	491,800	94.6	37.5
Tacoma	217,900	93.8	37.5
Chicago	2,224,300	94.2	36.6
Miami-Hialeah	701,800	90.8	36.5
Tucson	266,200	91.2	35.7
Newark	651,400	94.2	34.9
San Antonio	458,800	92.2	34.5
Phoenix	826,000	91.8	34.0
Philadelphia	1,788,400	95.7	33.2
Honolulu	267,300	95.4	32.4
Albuquerque	189,800	92.2	32.3

Note: The unlisted rate is determined by comparing the estimated number of telephone households with the actual number of households found in telephone directories. Estimated telephone households are computed by taking projected household estimates at the county level calculated by Market Statistics for *Sales & Marketing Management* magazine and applying a figure from the U.S. Census that indicates the percent of households with a telephone.

Source: *Fact Sheets* (New York: Survey Sampling, Inc., 1991). © Copyright Survey Sampling, Inc., 1991. All rights reserved.

lights for these geographical areas: the unlisted rates (the number of homes with unlisted numbers), the contact rate (the proportion of calls resulting in contact with an English-speaking person), the cooperation rate (how likely people in these regions are willing to cooperate), and the survey frequency (how often surveys are conducted in that region). Note that the unlisted rate can range from as high as 49.1 percent for the Pacific region to 17.6 percent for the New England region. Table 7–1 highlights the 25 metropolitan areas with the highest unlisted rates.

As an attempt to include people with unlisted telephone numbers as potential respondents, some researchers have used a method called **ran-**

dom digit dialing. This method starts with the known prefixes (the first three numbers) and then randomly generates the last four digits.[11] Alternatively, a number might be selected from the telephone book, but instead of dialing this number, a constant (e.g., 4) is added to the last digit and that number is called.[12] In Chapter 9, random digit dialing techniques are illustrated in the course of discussing sampling theory and practices.

RANDOM DIGIT DIALING DESIGNS
Samples of numbers drawn from the directory, usually by a systematic procedure. Selected numbers are modified to allow all unlisted numbers a chance for inclusion.

In-home surveys provide strong sample control. For example, the researcher has control over which households are interviewed, the number of call-backs, and the degree to which other members of the household participate in the survey. At the same time, although the potential exists for a high level of sample control, today there are problems with the use of in-home personal interviews that did not exist 20 to 30 years ago. First, nearly half of all women are employed outside the home, and it has become increasingly difficult to find respondents home during the day. Interviewers must visit the household either on weekends or at night, and they are likely to have to make several call-backs to respondents who are not at home or who are unavailable. Second, interviewers are increasingly reluctant to venture into inner-city neighborhoods. Moreover, increasing crime rates make many people cautious about letting strangers into their homes or even opening the door to strangers.

Two sample-control problems exist with respect to mall intercepts. Usually the interviewer chooses which respondents will be intercepted, and the choice of respondents of course is limited to mall shoppers. Frequent mall shoppers have a greater chance of being included in the sample; in fact, this problem is compounded further because interviewing is often limited to Thursday, Friday, and Saturday. Also, a potential respondent can either intentionally avoid or initiate contact with the interviewer. Furthermore, the demographics of shoppers can vary drastically from mall to mall. On the positive side, however, easy access to respondents is a clear benefit of mall intercepts. The limitations of night work involved with in-home personal surveys don't apply. And weather is not a problem.

Quality of Data

The quality of the data collected by any survey method depends in large part on measures taken to decrease response errors, which occur whenever respondents do not provide an accurate answer to a question, for whatever reason. Response errors may occur because of:

1. *Intentional factors.* Respondents may provide an answer that they think will help the researcher. Some people just tend to agree or disagree with most questions, a tendency called **acquiescence bias.** In new-product tests respondents may give all favorable ratings regardless of their true feelings about the new product because they want to help the researcher.

2. *Unintentional factors.* In some cases respondents cannot give accurate answers because of illiteracy. In other cases, respondents may *want* to give an accurate answer but do not, simply because their memory is incorrect. Another source of unintentional response errors can be

ACQUIESCENCE BIAS
Tendency of some people to agree or disagree with most questions.

the questionnaire itself. The question format or the instructions for completing the questions may lead respondents to give certain answers. (Guidelines for proper questionnaire construction are discussed in Chapter 12.)

3. *Interviewer effects and biases.* The mere presence of an interviewer can affect how respondents answer questions. Generally speaking, the interviewer is likely to get better cooperation and potentially more accurate answers if the interviewer and the respondent have similar backgrounds, especially with respect to observable characteristics such as age, gender, and race. Put simply, the interaction between the interviewer and the respondent can lead to biases. If the interviewer gives some indication of approval or disapproval of a response, this action may influence the response to subsequent questions. Also, interviewers can simply misreport responses, or even cheat by falsifying answers to questions.

4. *Societal factors.* In some cases, respondents may give what they perceive as the socially acceptable response. Responses to questions such as: "How often in the last four weeks have you consumed enough alcohol to become intoxicated?" or "How often do you donate blood?" may be guided by what respondents think is socially acceptable behavior rather than their actual behavior. These kinds of errors are referred to as **social desirability effects.**

SOCIAL DESIRABILITY
EFFECTS

Tendency of some people to give what they believe is a socially acceptable response to a question.

Because of face-to-face contact with the interviewer, in-home personal and mall-intercept surveys can yield more–in-depth responses and more-complete data than telephone or mail interviews.[13] On the other hand, the presence of an interviewer can have profound effects on the quality of the data collected, particularly in the case of embarrassing or sensitive questions.[14] Interviewers can alter questions or give intentional or unintentional cues by their tone of voice or vocabulary.[15] In effect, each respondent personally interviewed could receive a different survey. Some evidence suggests that, depending on the survey topic, the interviewer's age, gender, race, social class, authority, or opinions can affect the respondent's answers to the questions, especially with face-to-face contact.[16] Finally, interviewers can cheat; that is, they can intentionally falsify all or part of the interview.

All these potential drawbacks can be minimized through proper survey control and design.[17] In the case of in-home personal surveys, the standard practice to safeguard against interviewer cheating or creating bias is to validate the interviewer's work by re-interviewing a sample of the respondents and asking several of the original questions again.

Interviewer effects are less troublesome for mall intercepts than for in-home surveys, because there is opportunity to monitor the interviewing process. Conducting telephone interviewing at a central telephone facility allows someone to monitor a portion of each interviewer's work to ensure that the questionnaire is being administered properly and that no cheating is taking place.

The absence of an interviewer for cold mail and mail panel surveys eliminates interviewer bias caused by the potential for altering questions, their appearance or speech, the projection of cues to respondents, or cheating. Also, because a mail survey does not involve any social interaction between an interviewer and a respondent, evidence suggests that for sensitive or embarrassing questions, mail surveys yield better-quality data than either personal or telephone interviews.[18] Finally, because the instrument is self-administered, respondents can work through the questions as quickly or slowly as they want.

On the negative side, however, the respondent cannot seek clarification without an interviewer; thus, the quality of data may be suspect because of inaccuracies caused by confusing questions. Pretesting the questionnaire can, however, eliminate or at least reduce the chance of respondent confusion. Finally, because respondents are able to scan the entire questionnaire before answering any of the questions, a bias can be created if respondents try to maintain consistency among their responses.

Response Rate

Response rate refers to the percentage of the sample who cooperate and complete the questionnaire. Suppose your survey consists of a mailing of 1,000 questionnaires to a random sample of households across the nation. And 50 of the questionnaires are returned because of incorrect addresses or the families had moved. Two hundred completed questionnaires are returned. The response rate for this mailing would be 21 percent (200/950)—the number of households that cooperated (200) divided by the total number of eligible (1,000 − 50) households:

$$\text{Response rate} = \frac{\text{Number of households that cooperated}}{\text{Total number of eligible households}}$$

RESPONSE RATE
The total number of respondents sent questionnaires who complete and return them, expressed as a percentage.

Low response rates, caused by factors such as not-at-homes and refusals, present the potential for **nonresponse error,** which is a particularly nagging problem in survey research. One problem with low response rates is that the usable sample (i.e., the number of returned questionnaires) may be too small. This of course could easily be corrected by doubling or tripling the initial contacts. The basic problem is: Would the results change if those people who did not return the questionnaire had returned the questionnaire?

NONRESPONSE ERROR
Survey error due to low response rates caused by not-at-homes or refusal to complete the survey.

To see this, assume that one question of interest in a mailing of 1,000 is whether a family intends to take a vacation more than 500 miles from their home. Let's say that of the 200 returned questionnaires 50 families respond yes. You would therefore conclude that 25 percent (50/200) of the households intend to vacation at least 500 miles from home. But what about the 800 households that did not return the questionnaire? If these nonrespondents are similar to the people who did respond, then the nonresponse presents no problem other than a small sample size. If they are different, however, your conclusions may be misleading.

Consider the two extremes, where all the 800 nonrespondents would have responded either yes or no. In that case, the percentage of households that intend to vacation more than 500 miles from home could now vary from as low as 5 percent (50/1000), if all 800 households responded no, to as high as 85 percent (850/1000), if all households responded yes. Because you do not have any information from the nonrespondents, you can only make assumptions as to how similar or different their responses would be from those who responded. The major question that needs to be answered is: How similar (dissimilar) are the respondents from the nonrespondents?

Nonresponse has several causes. Exhibit 7–4 presents possible outcomes from a telephone interview, only one of which results in a completed interview. Thus, there are many factors that can add to the nonresponse rate. There are some recommended methods you can use for reducing nonresponse errors for survey methods that use an interviewer and those that don't.

Survey methods using interviewers

Not-at-homes.   Low response rates caused by not-at-homes can be a serious problem with personal in-home interviews and telephone surveys. However, employing a series of call-backs can drastically reduce the percentage of not-at-homes. Most consumer surveys use three to four call-backs. Notice from Exhibit 7–3 there are only slight differences in contact rates across the 9 census divisions.

Available data clearly indicate that (1) people are generally not home as much as they once were, and (2) the best time to reach an individual is in the evening. Societal and lifestyle changes and two wage-earner families can explain why it is becoming increasingly more difficult to contact respondents.

Surveys should have prescribed plans for and control over call-backs. In the case of telephone surveys, a control sheet is commonly used to record the outcome of each attempted contact. Typically, the first call yields the most responses, but the second and third calls have higher responses per call.[19] The ultimate issue in call-backs involves weighing the benefits of reducing nonresponse bias against the cost of additional call-backs. As call-backs are completed, the difference in responses between the call-back respondents and the respondents already in the sample should be evaluated. If the differences in response are slight, fewer call-backs or no further call-backs may be warranted.

Refusals.   The second factor contributing to low response rates is refusals. Some respondents either cannot or will not answer the questions. Notice from Exhibit 7–3 that the cooperation rate can range from a high of 60.8 percent in the east south central region to a low of 46.1 percent in the Pacific region. Procedures for reducing refusals vary depending on the method of data collection.

Procedures that are recommended for reducing refusals for interviewer-based surveys are prior notification, motivating the respondent, and proper writing and administration of the questions.

1. **Prior notification** involves sending potential respondents an advance letter to notify them of the impending telephone or personal contact. Advance letters appear to have a positive effect on response rates for samples of the general public.[20] The rationale behind this procedure is that respondents often react with caution when reached by an unexpected telephone caller or contacted by an interviewer in their home. The advance letter tries to relieve wariness while at the same time create some predisposition toward cooperation.

2. Aside from offering incentives, an interviewer can try to motivate the respondent by increasing the respondents' interest or involvement and thereby gain their cooperation. One type of procedure, called the **foot-in-the-door technique,** involves first getting re-

EXHIBIT 7—4

Telephone Contacts: Possible Outcomes

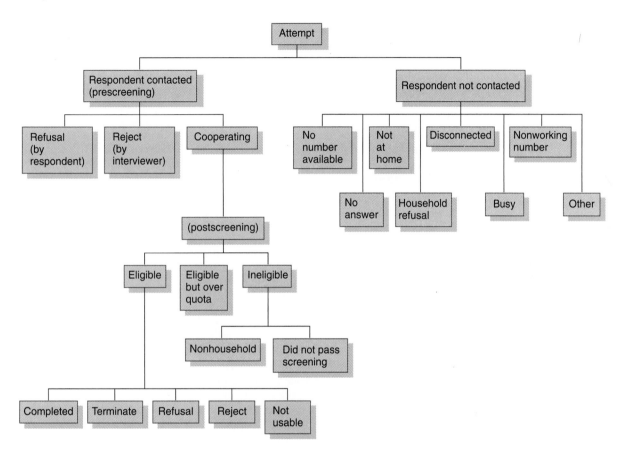

Source: Frederick Wiseman and Philip McDonald, *Toward the Development of Industry Standards for Response and Nonresponse Rates* (Cambridge, Mass.: Marketing Science Institute, 1980), p. 29.

spondents to complete a relatively short, simple questionnaire, and then, at some later time, asking them to complete a longer questionnaire on the same general topic. Although the evidence indicates that this procedure generally increases response rates, the increase may not be significant in view of the substantial added expense.[21]

3. Proper writing and administration of the questions relates to the skills and expertise of both the person putting together the questionnaire and the interviewer who administers it. Skilled interviewers can reduce the proportion of refusals by not accepting an answer of no to a request for cooperation without making an additional plea. This procedure, called *refusal conversion* (or *persuasion*), has been found to decrease refusal on the average by about 7 percent.[22]

Survey methods without interviewers.   A number of ways have been investigated to reduce refusals in the case of mail surveys. Among these are prior

REFUSAL CONVERSION (PERSUASION)

Method of reducing nonresponse; skilled interviewers reduce the proportion of refusals by not accepting a refusal to a request for cooperation without making an additional plea.

notification, characteristics of the cover letter, follow-up procedures, and characteristics of the questionnaire.

1. Prior notification has successfully increased response rates.[23] It can also accelerate the rate of return. An advance letter or telephone call informs respondents that they will be receiving a questionnaire shortly and requests their cooperation.

2. Characteristics of the questionnaire's cover letter that could be useful in reducing refusals have been extensively investigated. The cover letter is integral to the mail survey and may be the most logical and efficient vehicle for persuading individuals to respond. The cover letter is the first part of the mail-out package that respondents are likely to read. It introduces the survey and tries to motivate the respondent to fill it out and return it as quickly as possible. Specific elements that should be included in the cover letter are discussed in Chapter 12.

3. Follow-up involves contacting the respondent periodically after the initial mailing. Follow-ups, or reminders, are almost universally successful in reducing refusals and usually are less costly than prior notification procedures. Follow-up procedures involve a sequence of mailings. Exhibit 7–5 describes a typical sequence.

4. Specific aspects of the questionnaire have been investigated for their potential to reduce refusals. Two of the obvious and possibly important aspects affecting response rates are questionnaire length and the absence or presence of an incentive. A comprehensive literature review of the techniques used to increase response rates has concluded that questionnaire length is nearly unrelated to response rates.[24] Monetary incentives, whether prepaid or promised, increase response rates.[25] Prepaid monetary incentives increase response rates over promised incentives. The amount of incentive paid also has a strong positive relation to response rate, but the use of large monetary incentives may well exceed the value of the additional information obtained. Nonmonetary incentives, that is, premiums and rewards (for example, pens, pencils, or books), increase response rates over not offering any nonmonetary incentive, although this finding is based upon only a few studies. Charitable donations have also been employed.

Cold mail surveys typically yield the lowest response rates of any of the methods. A mail survey sent to a list of randomly selected respondents, without any prenotification or follow-up, typically will yield no more than 10 percent response. If multiple premailings and postmailings are made, it is possible to generate response rates of 80 percent. Mail panels, because of the assured respondent cooperation, generally have response rates in the 70 to 80 percent range.[26] In-home personal surveys generally have response rates in excess of 80 percent, which makes them preferred. The refusal rate for mall-intercept interviews is typically in the range of 10 to 30 percent. The proportion of completed interviews for telephone surveys is frequently in the 60 to 80 percent range.

Speed

The fastest survey method is the telephone survey. Using a central telephone facility, enough interviewers can be assigned to a study to ensure

One Week:	A postcard reminder sent to everyone. It serves as both a thank you for those who have responded and as a friendly and courteous reminder for those who have not.	EXHIBIT 7—5
Three Weeks:	A letter and replacement questionnaire sent only to nonrespondents. Nearly the same in appearance as the original mailing, it has a shorter cover letter that informs nonrespondents that their questionnaire has not been received and appeals for its return.	Sequence of Follow-Ups in Mail Survey
Seven Weeks:	This final mailing is similar to the one that preceded it, except that it is sent by certified mail to emphasize its importance. Another replacement questionnaire is enclosed.	

Source: D. A. Dillman, J. G. Gallegos, and J. H. Frey, "Reduce Refusal Rates for Telephone Interviews," *Public Opinion Quarterly*, 1976, pp. 66–78. Published by The University of Chicago Press.

that several hundred telephone interviews can be scheduled and completed each day. Next to telephone surveys, mall-intercept studies are the fastest. When surveying several central mall facilities, even moderately large studies (say 500 respondents) can be completed in a few days.

Mail surveys tend to be the slowest of the methods. It usually takes several weeks for completed questionnaires to be returned, and the elapsed time for a mail survey will be even longer if follow-up mailings are required. Once questionnaires have been sent out, a marketing research firm has little control over the time it takes for them to be returned. Mail panels usually do not need follow-up procedures and are therefore faster than cold mail surveys, but they are still slower than the other survey methods.

The time to conduct in-home personal surveys depends on the number of interviewers available in each of the market areas of the study. When interviews can be conducted in each market simultaneously, you can complete a large study relatively quickly. In general, in-home personal surveys are faster than mail surveys, but slower than mall-intercept or telephone surveys.

Cost

The relatively low cost of mail surveys is one of their most attractive features. The data-collection cost, excluding analysis and report generation, can be as low as $2.50 per completed interview. If response rates are low, however, the cost, including follow-up mailings, can be higher than other methods.

Mail panels generally offer the lowest cost per respondent of any research medium. Access to a mail panel is often sold on a shared-cost basis, which allows a limited number of firms to have access to a proportion of the general panel sample for a specific dollar cost. Participating firms agree to a minimum number of mailings and a specific amount of information to be asked for. One mail panel service specifies the minimum number of mailings as 1,000, increasing in increments of 1,000, with survey information limited to a single two-sided card called a Data Gage. Exhibit 7–6 illustrates a Data Gage.

Economies of scale can reduce the cost of shared-cost computer card mailing to as little as 30 cents per household. Another reason mail panels

EXHIBIT 7—6

Data Gage

ANSWER THIS SIDE FIRST   Job No. 1346

Please answer the following questions on this side <u>and</u> the other side of this card.

1. How frequently, if at all, do you purchase the following snack items? ("X" ONE FOR EACH ITEM)

	Once a Month or More	Every 2-3 Months	Less Often	Never
Regular potato chips	1 [ ]	2 [ ]	3 [ ]	4 [ ] (9)
Flavored potato chips (Bar B-Q, Sour cream & onion, etc.)	[ ]	[ ]	[ ]	[ ]
Processed Potato Chips (Pringles, Munchos, etc.)	[ ]	[ ]	[ ]	[ ]
"Home style" Potato chips	[ ]	[ ]	[ ]	[ ]
Cheese Puffs (Cheeto's etc.)	1 [ ]	2 [ ]	3 [ ]	4 [ ] (13)
Corn chips (Frito's etc.)	[ ]	[ ]	[ ]	[ ]
Tortilla chips (Doritos, etc.)	[ ]	[ ]	[ ]	[ ]
Pretzels	[ ]	[ ]	[ ]	[ ]
Peanuts/other nuts	[ ]	[ ]	[ ]	[ ]
Flavored Crackers (<u>Not</u> Saltines)	[ ]	[ ]	[ ]	[ ] (18)
Dips (Canned or refrigerated)	1 [ ]	2 [ ]	3 [ ]	4 [ ] (19)
Dried fruit snacks (Fruit Roll-Ups, Fun Fruits, etc.)	[ ]	[ ]	[ ]	[ ]
Sweet baked goods (Hostess Snack Cakes Twinkies, Dunkin' Sticks, etc.)	[ ]	[ ]	[ ]	[ ]
Frozen potato products (French fries, Tator Tots, etc.)	[ ]	[ ]	[ ]	[ ]
Frozen dessert snacks (Pudding Pops, Eskimo Pies, Dole Fruits Bars, etc.)	[ ]	[ ]	[ ]	[ ] (23)

ANSWER <u>OTHER</u> SIDE FIRST   Job No. 1346

2a. Within the past year, to which, if any, of the following charities have you contributed money? (RECORD UNDER 2a)

2b. To which of the following have you volunteered your time? (RECORD UNDER 2b)

	2a. Contributed Money	2b. Volunteered Your Time
American Cancer Society	[ ]1	[ ]1
American Heart Association	[ ]2	[ ]2
American Lung Association	[ ]3	[ ]3
Arthritis Foundation	[ ]4	[ ]4
Easter Seals	[ ]5	[ ]5
March of Dimes	[ ]6	[ ]6
Multiple Sclerosis (MS) Society	[ ]7	[ ]7
Muscular Dystrophy Assn. (MDA)	[ ]8	[ ]8
National Kidney Foundation	[ ]9	[ ]9
United Way	[ ]0	[ ]0
Other	[ ]-0	[ ]-0
None	[ ]-X	[ ]-X
	(24-25)	(26-27)

3. Do you own

	Yes	No
A programmable calculator?	[ ]1	[ ]2 (28)
A calculator with a tape print out?	[ ]1	[ ]2 (29)

4. Are you, or is someone in your household, a member of the American Automobile Association (AAA)?

Yes   [ ]1   No   [ ]2   (30)

5. Does anyone in your household normally pack a lunch to school or work?

School [ ]1   Work [ ]2   Neither [ ]3   (31)

6a. Which of the stores listed below have you <u>heard</u> of?

6b. Which, if any, have you visited <u>within the past year</u>?

Stores	Heard of? Yes	Heard of? No	Visited in past year? Yes	Visited in past year? No	
Pier 1 Imports	[ ]1	[ ]2	[ ]1	[ ]2	(32-33)
Color Tile	[ ]1	[ ]2	[ ]1	[ ]2	(34-35)
Eckerd Drugs	[ ]1	[ ]2	[ ]1	[ ]2	(36-37)

(38-78 open)

79 [0] [1] 80

Source: Market Facts, Inc. Used with permission.

are cost-efficient is that detailed demographic information on every household is already on file, and no additional data collection is necessary. No interviewing expenditures are necessary. The availability of demographic data permits identification of specific targets at a reasonable cost.

Mail panel services also produce customized mailings where all aspects of a mailing are tailored to the specific needs of a single firm. Essentially, for the right price, these mail panel services can facilitate almost any type of customized research project. Mail panel firms also utilize special subgroups of the total panel sample—for example, a baby panel or a student panel—and offer certain syndicated products such as beverage consumer mail panels.

In-home personal surveys are generally the most expensive of all survey methods. As the need for call-backs increases, the cost of a personal survey can skyrocket because the interviewer may have to make repeated visits to a given neighborhood just to complete a single interview. The cost of data collection per completed interview, excluding analysis and report generation, can be as low as $5 to $10, but the cost per completed interview can be hundreds or even thousands of dollars.

The cost of mall intercepts and telephone surveys falls in between mail and in-home personal surveys. Cost in this case is a function of incidence rate and length of interview. Incidence rates refer to the proportion of respondents meeting some criteria on a set of screening variables. They are discussed in greater detail in Chapter 9. If you are conducting a survey on a new type of dry cat food, presumably you'll want to require that eligible respondents at least own a cat. You might even specify further that eligible respondents must purchase dry cat food at least twice a month, own their own home, and have a family income in excess of $50,000. Clearly, the more restrictions imposed, the lower the incidence rate of such respondents in the population, and, consequently, the more expensive the survey cost per respondent. Table 7–2 provides prototypical cost information per respondent for mall intercepts, and Table 7–3 provides the same information for telephone surveys for different incidence rate and length of interview situations.

Uses

Cold mail surveys are often used in executive, industrial, or medical studies. Respondents selected typically share considerable interest in the survey topic, and the sample is small and geographically dispersed. The cold mail survey is rarely used in attitude and usage studies of consumer products and services because of the potential of low response rates.

Mail panels provide a vehicle for collecting meaningful data in virtually all areas of marketing research. Panels provide an effective way to handle in-home product testing because specific ultimate users can be identified and targeted to receive the product. Another important application of mail panels is in cost-efficient surveys of low-incidence groups. In this case the entire panel is used to identify users of a low-incidence product, who are then either reached with a mail or telephone survey. This two-step procedure can greatly reduce the cost of surveying low-incidence groups.

TABLE 7—2

Cost Per Interview—
Central Location
Interviewing

Interview Length (minutes)	Incidence	
	80%	10%
10	11.20	24.50
15	15.20	28.50
20	18.70	32.00
25	22.20	35.50

TABLE 7—3

Cost Per Interview—
Central Location
Interviewing by Phone

Interview Length (minutes)	Incidence	
	80%	10%
10	8.50	28.00
15	11.90	31.40
20	15.30	34.80
25	18.70	38.20

Mail panels have been used in successful and innovative ways to gather national and/or regional information. Panel members have been used, for example, as a national consumer field force to audit and report on a variety of products and services. They have been asked to visit department stores and request catalogs, to visit fast food restaurants and record prices, and to buy products and report satisfaction.

Telephone surveys are typically used in studies that require national samples. In fact, when you face a small and geographically dispersed group of respondents, telephone interviewing may be the only practical way of reaching them. Telephone surveys have replaced door-to-door personal interviews for many attitude and usage studies, particularly in market tracking studies that periodically assess customer awareness, attitudes, and usage behavior in a product category. Telephone surveys are also used in product tests to obtain opinions after respondents have used the test product. Finally, telephone surveys are increasingly used as an efficient way to conduct call-back interviews with respondents who were previously contacted through a mail survey or by a personal interview.

Historically, in-home personal interviews were used frequently before the telephone became ubiquitous and the shopping mall sprung up. They were useful when visual cues or exhibits needed to be shown and in complex attitude and opinion studies. Today, however, the trend is to use mall intercept interviewing.

Mall intercept personal surveys are regularly used in concept tests, name tests, package tests, product tests, copy tests, and in some simulated test-market studies. In general, the requirements of visual cues and exhibits will dictate whether a mall intercept personal survey should be used.

By way of summary, Exhibit 7—7 compares the various survey methods along the dimensions we have discussed.

EXHIBIT 7—7

Summary Comparison of Major Data-Collection Methods

Criteria	Direct/Cold Mailing	Mail Panels	Telephone	Personal In-Home	Mall Intercept
Complexity and versatility	Not much	Not much	Substantial but complex or lengthy scales difficult to use	Highly flexible	Most flexible
Quantity of data	Substantial	Substantial	Short, lasting typically between 15 and 30 minutes	Greatest quantity	Limited 25 minutes or less
Sample control	Little	Substantial, but representativeness may be a question	Good, but nonlisted households can be a problem	In theory, provides greatest control	Can be problematic; sample representativeness may be questionable
Quality of data	Better for sensitive or embarrassing questions; however, no interviewer present to clarify what is being asked	Better for sensitive or embarrassing questions; however, no interviewer present to clarify what is being asked	Positive side, interview can clear up any ambiguities; negative side, may lead to socially accepted answers	Chance of cheating is greater	Unnatural testing environment can lead to bias
Response rate	In general, low; as low as 10%	70–80%	60–80%	Greater than 80%	As high as 80%
Speed	Several weeks; completion time will increase with follow-up mailings	Several weeks with no follow-up mailings, longer with follow-up mailings	Large studies can be completed in 3 to 4 weeks	Faster than mail but typically slower than telephone surveys	Large studies can be completed in a few days
Cost	Inexpensive; as low as $2.50 per completed interview	Lowest	Not as low as mail; depends on incidence rate and length of questionnaire	Can be relatively expensive, but considerable variability	Less expensive than in-home, but higher than telephone; again, length and incidence rate will determine cost
Uses	Executive, industrial, medical, and readership studies	All areas of marketing research; particularly useful in low-incidence categories	Particularly effective in studies that require national samples	Still prevalent in product testing and other studies that require visual cues or product prototypes	Name tests, package tests, copy tests

NEWER TECHNOLOGICAL APPROACHES

COMPUTER-ASSISTED
TELEPHONE
INTERVIEWING (CATI)
Survey systems involving a
computerized survey instrument. The survey questionnaire is entered into the
memory of a large mainframe
computer, into a small microprocessor, or even into a personal computer. The interviewer reads the questions
from the CRT screen and
records the respondent's answers directly into the computer memory banks by using
the terminal keyboard or special touch- or light-sensitive
screens.

SELF-ADMINISTERED CRT
INTERVIEW
An interviewing method
where the respondent sits at
a computer terminal and answers the questionnaire by
using a keyboard and a
screen.

Computer-assisted telephone interviewing (CATI) is a new technology-based survey method that is fast becoming a dominant force in
collecting data from respondents. It involves a computerized survey instrument entered into the memory of a large mainframe computer, into a
smaller microprocessor or minicomputer, or even into a personal computer.

The interviewer conducts the interview in front of a CRT terminal,
which has a televisionlike screen and a typewriterlike terminal keyboard.
The interviewer reads the questions from the screen and records the respondent's answers directly in the computer memory banks by using the
terminal keyboard or special touch- or light-sensitive screens. CATI systems can provide labor-saving functions such as automatic dialing as well.

CATI systems allow questionnaires with many complex skip patterns
(e.g., if the answer to question 5 is yes, go to question 15; if no, continue)
to be programmed into the computer—in these cases the computer and not
the interviewer quickly selects the next question. Because the data are
entered directly into the computer as the questions are answered, these
systems are faster and generally less expensive than telephone surveys
using paper-and-pencil questionnaires.

Another innovation in data-collection methods is the on-site, **self-
administered CRT interview.** In principle, a CRT self-administered interviewing station can be set up anywhere electrical and telephone service
is available. Typically, self-administered CRT interviews have been used to
collect data at trade shows, professional conferences, product clinics, central interviewing locations, and shopping malls.[27] The computer configuration of the on-site location can vary. The site can be computerized by the
use of personal computers, and each PC can support three or four CRTs.
CRTs can be hard-wired directly to a microcomputer or minicomputer, or
the CRTs can be linked directly through telecommunications equipment to
a centrally located mainframe computer.

Because the interview is self-administered, no interviewer is needed, and
interviewer bias is not a problem. Such methods may induce respondents

Using a computer to record
interview responses

to answer sensitive or socially embarrassing questions if they feel less threatened by a machine. As with CATI systems, self-administered CRT interviews solve such problems as skipping over questions, misunderstanding instructions, ignoring skip patterns, or giving contradictory responses to two or more questions. The computer will not allow a respondent to make these kinds of errors.

As with CATI systems, data are entered into computer memory immediately. Data analysis can proceed quickly, and interim reports can be generated daily. A reasonable estimate of data-collection costs for 300 to 600 respondents, excluding data analysis and report generation, ranges from $6 to $10 per interview for a syndicated study or $18 to $23 per interview for a customized, exclusive study.[28]

SUMMARY

In this chapter we have discussed different types of survey interviewing methods, comparing the distinctive nature of mail, telephone, personal in-home, and mall intercept interviews. Each interviewing method has pluses and minuses in terms of its versatility, quantity and quality of data collected, sample control, response rate, nonresponse bias, speed of completion, cost, and potential use, all of which affect the ultimate choice of a particular interviewing method. Selecting the appropriate survey method is never a forgone conclusion, because no one survey method is superior to all others in all situations. We ended our discussion by describing how sophisticated computer technology can improve interviewing.

KEY CONCEPTS

Cold Mail Survey

Mail Panel Survey

Telephone Survey

In-Home Personal Survey

Mall Intercept Survey

Response Rate

Nonresponse Error

Methods for Reducing
   Nonresponses

Computer-Assisted Telephone
   Interviewing (CATI)

REVIEW QUESTIONS

1. What factors would you consider when choosing among mail, telephone, personal, and mall intercept interviews?

2. For each of the following research problems, recommend a survey method. Provide justification for your choice.

   a. Determine the attitudes and opinions of urban females with an income between $35,000 and 60,000 toward a new antitheft device.

   b. Assess the general voting public's attitude toward increasing the speed limit from 55 to 65 miles an hour.

   c. Conduct a taste test of a new muffin formula.

3. Discuss the issues involved in dealing with nonresponse errors. What approaches are available for handling this potentially serious problem?

4. Consider that you wish to interview commercial purchasers of facsimile machines with respect to the

brands and features they considered when making a purchase.

  a. What type of survey interviewing method would be most appropriate? Justify your choice.
  b. What special problems face researchers who wish to interview respondents in the workplace?

5. Develop the following:

  a. Two research problems that would be appropriate for the use of CATI and CRT interviewing methods.
  b. An exhibit similar to Exhibit 7–7 for the above two new computer approaches to interviewing.

ENDNOTES

1. Market Facts, Inc., *Practices, Trends, and Expectations for the Market Research Industry* (Chicago: Market Facts, Inc., April 1987).

2. C. H. Lovelock, R. Stiff, D. Cullwick, and I. M. Kaufman, "An Evaluation of the Effectiveness of Drop-Off Questionnaire Delivery," *Journal of Marketing Research,* November 1976, pp. 358–64.

3. J. K. Klompmaker, J. D. Lindley, and R. L. Page, "Using Free Papers for Customer Surveys," *Journal of Marketing Research,* November 1976, pp. 358–64.

4. This material follows the presentation found in Market Facts, Inc., *Why Consumer Mail Panels Are the Superior Option* (Chicago: Market Facts, Inc., 1986).

5. Al Ossip, "Mall Intercept Interviews," Second Annual Advertising Research Foundation Research Quality Workshop (New York: Advertising Research Foundation, 1984), p. 24.

6. S. Sudman, "Sample Surveys," in *Annual Review of Sociology,* vol. 2. eds. A. Inkeles et al. (Palo Alto, Calif.: Annual Reviews Inc., 1976), pp. 107–20.

7. See L. Kanuk and C. Berenson, "Mail Surveys and Response Rates: A Literature Review," *Journal of Marketing Research,* November 1975, pp. 440–53; and Julie Yu and Harris Cooper, "Quantitative Review of Research Design Effects on Response Rates to Questionnaires," *Journal of Marketing Research,* February 1983, pp. 36–44.

8. For example, see *1973–74 Catalog of Mailing Lists* (New York: Fritz S. Hotheimer, Inc., 1972).

9. *Fact Sheets* (New York: Survey Sampling, Inc., 1988).

10. Data and findings reported in this section have been taken from *Fact Sheets* (New York: Survey Sampling, Inc., 1988).

11. For example, see "A National Probability Sample of Telephone Households Using Computerized Sampling Techniques" (Radnor, Pa: Chilton Research Services 1976); "Random Sampling by Telephone—An Improved Method," *Journal of Marketing Research,* November 1964, pp. 45–48; J. O. Eastlack, Jr., and Henry Assael, "Random Digit Dialing as a Method of Telephone Sampling," *Journal of Marketing Research,* February 1972, pp. 59–64; Gerald J. Glasser and Dale D. Metzger, "Random Digit Dialing as an Efficient Method for Political Polling," *Georgia Political Science Association Journal,* Spring 1974, pp. 133–51; and E. Laird London, Jr., and Sharon K. Banks, "Boulder Shopping Survey: Shopping Habits and Attitudes of Boulder Residents" (Boulder, Colo.: Department of Community Development, March 1976).

12. E. L. Landon, Jr., and S. K. Banks, "Relative Efficiency and Bias of Plus-One Telephone Sampling," *Journal of Marketing Research,* August 1977, pp. 294–99. For more details, see *Fact Sheets* (New York: Survey Sampling, Inc., 1988); C. L. Rich "Is Random Digit Dialing Really Necessary," *Journal of Marketing Research,* August 1977, pp. 300–301; A. B. Blankenship, "Listed versus Unlisted Numbers in Telephone Survey Samples," *Opinion Quarterly,* February 1977, pp. 39–42; G. J. Glasser and G. D. Metzger, "National Estimates of Nonlisted Telephone Households and Their Characteristics," *Journal of Marketing Research,* August 1975, pp. 359–61; and J. Honomichl, "Arbitron Updates Unlisted Phone Numbers," *Advertising Age,* January 15, 1979, p. 40.

13. See, for example, E. Telser, "Data Exercises Bias in Phone vs. Personal Interview Debate, But If You Can't Do It Right, Don't Do It at All," *Marketing News,* September 10, 1976, p. 6; and T. F. Rogers, "Interviews by Telephone and In-Person Quality of Response and Field Performance," *Public Opinion Quarterly,* Spring 1976, pp. 51–65.

14. J. Colombotos, "Personal vs. Telephone Interviews Effect Responses," *Public Health Reports,* September 1969, pp. 773–820; and T. T. Tyebjee, "Telephone

Survey Methods: The State of the Art," *Journal of Marketing,* Summer 1979, pp. 68–78.

15. See M. Collins, "Interviewer Variability," *Journal of Marketing Research Society* 2 (1980), pp. 77–95.

16. See P. B. Case, "How to Catch Interviewer Errors," *Journal of Advertising Research,* April 1971, pp. 39–41; Spring 1976, pp. 84–85; and B. Bailar, L. Bailey, and J. Stevens, "Measures of Interviewer Bias and Variance," *Journal of Marketing Research,* August 1977, pp. 337–43.

17. For details, see D. S. Tull and L. E. Richard, "What Can Be Done about Interviewer Bias," in *Research in Marketing,* 3rd ed., ed. J. Sheth (Greenwich, Conn.: JAI Press, 1980), pp. 143–62.

18. B. Dunning and D. Calahan, "Mail versus Field Self-Administered Questionnaires: An Armed Forces Survey," *Public Opinion Quarterly,* Spring 1972, pp. 105–8.

19. Leslie Kish, *Survey Sampling* (New York: John Wiley & Sons, 1965), p. 552.

20. D. A. Dillman, J. G. Gallegos, and J. H. Frey, "Reduce Refusal Rates for Telephone Interviews," *Public Opinion Quarterly,* Fall 1976, pp. 66–78.

21. R. M. Graves and L. J. Magilavy, "Increasing Response Rates to Telephone Surveys: A Door in the Face for Foot-in-the-Door," *Public Opinion Quarterly,* Fall 1981, pp. 346–58.

22. Ibid, p. 357.

23. See, for example, B. J. Walker and R. B. Burdick, "Advance Correspondence and Error in Mail Surveys," *Journal of Marketing Research,* August 1977, pp. 379–83.

24. Yu and Cooper, "Quantitative Review of Research Design Effects on Response Rules to Questionnaires," *Journal of Marketing Research* 20 (February 1983), pp. 36–44.

25. See, for example, Del I. Hawkins, Kenneth A. Coney, and Donald W. Jackson, Jr., "The Impact of Monetary Inducement on Uninformed Response Error," *Journal of the Academy of Marketing Science,* 16, no. 2 (Summer 1988), pp. 30–35.

26. We should note that, although mail panels have a high response rate, the response rate for recruitment into the panels is not necessarily high.

27. For typical applications, see B. Whalen, "On-Site Interviewing Yields Search Data Instantly," *Marketing News,* November 9, 1984, pp. 1, 17.

28. Bush and Haire, "An Assessment of the Mall Intercept As a Data Collection Method," *Journal of Marketing Research,* May 1985, p. 165.

Experimental Research Methods

POINT-OF-PURCHASE DISPLAYS: INTERACTIVE MERCHANDISING SYSTEMS

Supermarket executives have been unhappy with manufacturer-provided displays for some time now. Surveys indicate that the majority of supermarket executives are at most marginally satisfied with their current racks.

Reasons for dissatisfaction include such things as the racks are ineffective for inventory control, they do not use space effectively, and they do not effectively help consumers shop. Another criticism is that current racks are too often unattractive and clash with the store's decor.

One clear winner in point-of-purchase merchandising is the L'eggs rack. Evaluations of L'eggs racks indicate that the racks have "consistent presentation and appearance," and are continually supported and maintained.

A growing trend in point-of-purchase merchandising is the use of interactive merchandising systems (IMS). IMS attempt to aid consumers in shopping by providing informative material that potentially can help the consumer make the right selection. Estimates are that over

45 percent of retailers today use at least one IMS, and these displays are used in a variety of departments, including generic grocery, meat and seafood, spices, health and beauty aids, and electric and hardware.

For example, Raid, the popular insecticide, has developed an Insect-A-Guide to help people learn about the pests they're trying to kill. The in-store display features various Raid products arranged under a color code to help consumers pick the right spray for the right bug. A flip chart gives information on the habits of insects and suggests ways to knock'em dead. The unit can be arranged in three configurations to accommodate various store sizes.

Source: Adopted from "Retailers Unhappy with Displays from Manufacturers," *Marketing News,* October 10, 1988, p. 21.

INTRODUCTION

An important issue not covered in the discussion of interactive merchandising systems (IMS), and particularly Raid's Insect-A-Guide, concerns how to evaluate whether this new merchandising tool increases the sales of Raid. You may think that this is a rather simple problem: Monitor the sales of Raid for, say, a four-week period under current merchandising practices, then introduce the new IMS display and monitor sales for another four weeks. Comparing sales over these two four-week periods should answer the question of whether the new display works!

As we will come to understand, this approach is not totally satisfactory, since any differences in sales across the two periods could be a result of the new display, or equally the result of any number of other factors that have not been controlled for. Weather factors, for example, might cause an increase in insects, which would translate into more sales of Raid. The problem here is that the researcher cannot be sure whether the difference in sales has to do with the new display or with some other factor.

Marketing researchers use experimental data-collection methods when they want to determine the effect of changes in one or more variables (e.g., the introduction of a new merchandising display), on some other variable (e.g., sales), controlling for other extraneous influences (e.g., the weather). Extraneous influences are factors outside of the experiment that if left uncontrolled could result in an erroneous conclusion about whether the change in one variable actually caused the change in the other variable.

In this chapter we discuss a variety of experimental data-collection methods that marketing researchers use. We explain each experimental design with a typical marketing research project proposal. We begin by discussing the key elements in experimentation. Next, we consider several conditions that should be in place when investigating *causal* relationships. This is followed by a discussion explaining the differences between *laboratory* and *field* experiments, two basic types of experimental environments. We then turn our attention to the issue of validity, specifically threats to *internal* and *external* validity. Finally, we discuss and illustrate specific types of experimental designs that are used in marketing research.

RESEARCH ENVIRONMENTS

LABORATORY
EXPERIMENTAL
ENVIRONMENT

Research environment constructed solely for the experiment. The experimenter has *direct control* over most, if not all, of the crucial factors that might possibly affect the experimental outcome.

There are two basic types of experimental environments: laboratory and field. A **laboratory experimental environment** allows the researcher to have direct control over most of, if not all, the crucial factors that might affect the experimental outcome. The setting is specified and controlled to the degree necessary to assess the relationships under study. Laboratory experiments have been used in concept testing, taste testing, package testing, advertising effectiveness studies, and simulated test markets. For example, in advertising research studies, individuals are recruited to a testing facility where eyetracking equipment is used to measure their physical reactions to various test commercials. The testing environment is unnat-

A laboratory experiment

ural, as individuals do not watch the commercials in their living rooms, subject to the normal kinds of distractions; however, the potential for a viewer to be distracted while viewing a commercial is the very reason why this experimenter decided to use an environment in which such distractions can be minimized.

A **field experimental environment,** on the other hand, is more of a natural setting—an environment where the behavior under study would likely occur. Many marketing research studies are conducted in natural settings. In such settings, the researcher should exercise as much control as possible over factors that could influence the experimental outcome. For example, consider again an advertising research study, this time one that uses an on-air testing approach. On-air tests evaluate the effectiveness of advertisements under actual conditions, in-market.

Field experiments in the form of on-air tests are available through BehaviorScan. Recall that BehaviorScan, discussed in Chapter 5, involves a network of markets equipped for advertising transmission and controlled store testing. In each market, UPC scanners installed in supermarkets allow for the tracking of individual purchases by over 2,500 households.

FIELD EXPERIMENTAL ENVIRONMENTS

Natural settings; experiments undertaken in the environment in which the behavior under study would likely occur.

Is a movie theater a laboratory or a field experimental environment?

Special technology in these markets allows the researcher to target alternative advertising to custom-matched panels of households. If an advertiser wants to determine which of two possible campaigns produces the desired results, the technology allows exposure of one set of households to one campaign, with a demographically matched set of households exposed to the other campaign. The effects of the two campaigns would be determined by tracking sales with the UPC scanners. Thus, the commercial is tested in a natural environment.

Laboratory and field experiments have different strengths and weaknesses, which will become clearer after explaining some basic concepts in experimentation. Note, finally, that marketing researchers frequently combine laboratory and field experiments. The four-color communication effectiveness study described in Box 8–1 (pages 184–85) describes such a situation.

EXPERIMENTATION

An experiment can be described in terms of four key elements. Each element will be illustrated in the context of an in-store experiment designed to evaluate Raid's new IMS display.

1. Control over and manipulation of the variable considered to be a cause; this variable is usually called the **independent variable** and presumably can "explain" why changes in some other variable occurred. In the case of Raid, its new IMS display represents the independent variable—because it provides consumers with helpful information, it can possibly explain why sales increase in stores in which it is used.

2. Measurement of the variable considered to be the effect; this variable is usually called the **dependent** (or criterion) **variable.** This is the variable that the researcher wishes to "explain." Because one purpose of the new IMS

INDEPENDENT VARIABLE

A factor in an experiment over which the experimenter has some control; if the experimenter manipulates its value, this is expected to have some effect upon the dependent variable.

display is to aid consumers in shopping, unit sales is the dependent or criterion variable.

3. Two, or more, groups of subjects (individuals, stores, etc.) are used—at least one group that is exposed to the manipulation and at least one group that is *not* exposed to the manipulation. The group exposed to the manipulation is called the **experimental group,** and the other is called the **control group.** The stores in which the new IMS display is used are the experimental group, and the stores that continue to use current Raid racks are the control group. Results in the experimental group are compared to those obtained in the control group.

4. Random assignment of subjects to the experimental and control groups. **Random assignment** is a procedure that can potentially control for extraneous factors having nothing to do with the independent variable that might influence the dependent variable and thereby confound the experiment. If extraneous factors are not controlled, the risk is that the experimenter may conclude that the independent variable can explain changes in the dependent variable, when in fact it does not. For example, suppose the new Raid IMS displays are to be tested in a number of stores for a four-week period beginning the first week in May. Suppose further that retail outlets in Florida are selected to receive the new IMS display. Each test store is matched in terms of store size and sales with a store in the Midwest, and these stores serve as the control group. A potential problem with this approach is that weather/climate differences that exist between these two regions may play a very important role in influencing how many pest control products are purchased. Rather than having the new IMS display used only by Florida retailers, a better approach would be to randomly assign Florida and Midwest stores to the test and control groups. In this way, weather conditions, as well as other store-related factors, influence both the test and control groups in the same way. Random assignment of subjects to test and control groups attempts to spread the influence of extraneous factors "equally" across these groups and thereby control for their effects.

CAUSAL RELATIONSHIPS

At the heart of experimentation is the desire to make a **causal inference;** that is, whether a change in one variable produces a change in another variable. To conclude that a causal relationship exists between two variables, at least three conditions must be satisfied: (1) concomitant variation, (2) time order of occurrence of variables, and (3) control over other possible causal factors.

Concomitant Variation

Concomitant variation is the degree to which two variables are related. For one variable to be considered to be the cause of another, it must be shown that changes in one variable (the presumed cause) are associated with changes in the other variable (the presumed effect). Increases in price, for example, are associated with decreases in sales, and decreases in price

DEPENDENT (OR CRITERION) VARIABLE
The response measure under study in an experiment whose value is determined by the independent variable.

EXPERIMENTAL GROUP
The group of respondents that is exposed to the manipulation.

CONTROL GROUP
The group of respondents that is *not* exposed to the manipulation.

RANDOM ASSIGNMENT
Process by which respondents are randomly assigned to treatment conditions for the purpose of controlling extraneous factors in an experimental setting.

CAUSAL INFERENCE
Relationship where a change in one variable produces a change in another variable. One variable affects, influences, or determines some other variable.

CONCOMITANT VARIATION
The degree to which a variable (X) thought to be a cause covaries with a variable (Y) thought to be an effect.

BOX 8—1

—

FROM THE
USER'S
PERSPECTIVE

—

STUDY: COLOR MAKES ANY MESSAGE MORE EFFECTIVE

Four-color communication materials will enhance the effectiveness of any printed message, according to a recent study.

The study, by Maritz Motivation Co. and Southern Illinois University, Edwardsville, consisted of three experiments and was conducted in a natural setting and a controlled laboratory environment. Attitudinal, cognitive, and physiological measures were used to assess the impact of three factors: color, shape, and size.

In the first experiment, subjects evaluated the effectiveness of one-color, two-color, and four-color mailers. The three mailers were identical with the exception of color and company names. One mailer was produced in four-color and had a major airline company name, while the other two mailers were two-color and one-color with major telecommunications and computer company names, respectively. The different names were needed to assess recall in a later portion of the experiment.

The company names were the same length (three letters) and color to control potential bias in the recall portion of the experiment. No significant differences were found when subjects rated their familiarity with the three company names.

The natural setting portion of the experiment was designed to examine the attention-gaining power of the mailers. First, subjects sat at a desk for one minute with three identical mailers positioned in front of them, unaware that they were being filmed. They were then told to relax until they were called into the room where the experiment was taking place.

Over half of the subjects (55.2%) initially picked up the four-color mailer. Nearly one fifth (17.2%) chose the two-color, followed by 13.8 percent who only chose the one-color mailer, and 13.8 percent of the subjects did not pick up any of the mailers.

These preliminary results suggest that most people will be attracted to four-color communication materials when given a choice. Keep in mind, people receive a huge amount of information everyday. Using four-color communication increases the chances that the information the organization wants to convey will be read.

The next portion of the experiment explored which color of mailer was most appealing, rather than attention-getting, on a wide variety of dimensions. Subjects were asked to rate each of the mailers on a series of 16 semantic differential questions using bipolar adjectives.

These results supplied even more evidence to support the use of four-color communications. In almost all cases, the four-color mailer had a greater impact than the two-color followed by the one-color.

Four-color mailers appeared more exciting, lively, complex, fun, sophisticated, original, strong, and enlightening than either two-color or one-color mailers. In addi-

are associated with increases in sales. That is, there is concomitant variation between price and sales.

Another way of stating this is that price changes and sales changes are associated or correlated. Association between two variables makes the hypothesis that the variables are causally related more probable. For example, if we find that in the stores in which the new Raid IMS display is used, sales for Raid products are much larger than the sales in stores using current racks—that is, IMS display retailers are associated with higher sales levels of Raid products—then we are more comfortable with entertaining the hypothesis that the IMS display leads to (causes) increased sales.

tion, the four-color mailer was rated as more expensive looking, superior, and better overall. One exception to this trend was that one-color mailers were rated to be "more tasteful" than two-color or four-color.

Although the three mailers were identical except for color, the four-color mailer was perceived to be more complex, lively, and original. In other words, using four-color communications does more than simply add color to the presentation, it adds personality.

This alone has important implications in the rationale for choosing four-color mailers.

Another interesting question was whether the type of color would affect how well people remember certain aspects of the communication. To test this, subjects were contacted about 24 hours after the experiment. They were asked to recall everything they could about the mailers they had seen.

More than two thirds (69%) of the subjects remembered the airline company name located on the four-color mailer, compared to 45 percent for the two-color (telecommunications company) and 41 percent for the one-color (computer company).

Thus, four-color communication also facilitates memory.

Heart rates of participants were recorded to determine any physiological effect of color on arousal and attention. No major differences were found in subjects' heart rates across the three mailers.

The research also included two other experiments designed to investigate the size and shape of communication pieces. Using the same methodology as the previous color experiment, the results of the size study provided some support for the use of larger mailers.

The larger mailer (8½-by-11½) was more attention-getting and memorable than medium (5½-by-8½) and smaller (3-by-5) mailers. In most cases, the largest mailer had the greater appeal. The medium-size mailer, however, was thought to be more lively and complex, while the small mailer was considered more sophisticated and original.

Another question in the study was whether shape (horizontal, square, or vertical) would influence participants' perceptions of the communication pieces, but no significant differences were found among the three shapes.

Source: Matthew D. Shank and Raymond LaGarce, *Marketing News,* August 6, 1990, p. 12. Reprinted with permission.

Temporal Ordering of Variables

In order to infer cause-and-effect relationships, the researcher should have knowledge of when the time changes in the variables under study took place. Simply put, if you want to say that changes in some variable X cause changes in some variable Y, the changes in X should have occurred prior to observing any change in Y. **Temporal ordering** of variables refers to the condition that in order to conclude that one variable is the cause of another variable, it must be demonstrated that the cause occurred before the purported effect. In the context of the IMS display effectiveness test, for

TEMPORAL ORDERING
The cause of an event should precede its occurrence in time.

example, we must be careful to monitor the sales of Raid products *after* the new displays have been installed.

Elimination of or Control over Extraneous Factors

In thinking about how to manage the various aspects surrounding an experiment it might be useful from a managerial perspective to distinguish between the various types of factors that enter into an experimental setting. We have already discussed several of these factors. Independent variables are factors that are manipulated and thought to explain changes in one or more dependent variables, which are the factors that are measured. Other factors have no bearing on the experimental results; and these factors, since they are irrelevant, can be safely ignored; for example, in the case of the Raid IMS display effectiveness study, we probably do not have to concern ourselves with whether an individual owns an automobile. Other factors are relevant in the sense that they can influence the dependent variable; for example, weather conditions in the regions in which the test and control stores are located in the case of the Raid IMS display effectiveness study. Such factors are referred to as **extraneous factors,** and their effects on the dependent variable must be controlled for.

EXTRANEOUS FACTORS
Variables that can possibly affect the dependent variable and, therefore, must be controlled.

Researchers must be sure that the observed relationship between the cause and effect variables is not attributable to, say, a third variable that, for whatever reasons, is related to both the cause and the effect. To give another example, consider the possible causal relationship between the sales of antifreeze and the amount of snowfall. Most likely there is an association between the sales of antifreeze and the amount of snowfall. Furthermore, sales of antifreeze probably occur before it snows. Hence, the first two criteria for inferring a causal relationship are satisfied. Yet, sales of antifreeze do not cause it to snow. You can purchase all the antifreeze you want and it will not cause it to snow, or you can stop buying antifreeze and it will not cause it to stop snowing. Both the sale of antifreeze and snowfall are related to a third variable—the temperature. Satisfaction of this criterion of causality, elimination of or control over extraneous factors, is the primary aim of experimental designs. Only with an experimental design can you control for possible third variables or extraneous factors.

VALIDITY

There are two principal goals in conducting an experiment: (1) to draw valid conclusions about the effects of an independent variable on the dependent variable, and (2) to make valid generalizations from specific results to a larger population or setting of interest. If the first goal is satisfied, then we say that the design has *internal validity*. Satisfying the second means that the design has *external validity*.[1]

Internal Validity

INTERNAL VALIDITY
Examines whether experimental manipulation actually is the cause of the changes observed in the dependent variable.

Internal validity examines whether the experimental manipulation (i.e., the change in the independent variable) actually is the cause of the changes observed in the dependent variable. Consider again the Raid IMS merchandising display we have been discussing. Assume that the average sales for the four weeks after introduction of the new display are $550, while the average sales for the four weeks prior to introduction of the new display were $500. Suppose we subtract the average sales figures after introduction of the new display (which we will denote as O_2) from the average sales prior to introduction of the new display (which we will denote as O_1):

$$O_2 - O_1 = \$550 - \$500 = \$50$$

(Note that we use the letter O to denote an observation/measurement and the subscript 1 or 2 to denote time ordering.) We would like to conclude that the "true effect" of the new merchandising display (the manipulation) is an average increase of sales of $50 or 10 percent. Remember that the design has not controlled for other factors that could also affect sales levels such as weather or competitors' actions. We use T to denote the true effect of the independent variable, often called the **treatment** or **experimental effect,** and E to denote these other possible extraneous factors. Recognizing the existence of extraneous factors, the difference between the sales levels before and after the display change actually is

$$O_2 - O_1 = T + E$$

Thus, the problem that we now face is to determine how much of the $50 increase comes about because of the new merchandising display (T) and how much is attributable to extraneous factors (E) that have nothing to do with the new display. One solution to the problem is to add a control group and use random assignment.

To see how this works, assume that the researcher picks out 20 stores that are as similar as possible with respect to size and competitive environment. Ten stores are randomly selected to get the new display, and the other 10 stores will keep the old display. Now there are two groups, an *experimental group* (those receiving the manipulation—the new IMS display) and a *control group* (those stores using the current racks). As before, we express average sales for the stores in the experimental group as

$$O_2 - O_1 = T + E$$

For the stores in the control group, we denote average sales for the first four weeks as O_3 and average sales for the second four weeks as O_4. In theory, control groups and random assignments allow us to control for extraneous factors by "spreading" the effects of such factors across the experimental and control groups. Specifically, consider the cause of any differences observed in average sales in the two time periods for stores in the control group. Stores in the control group did not receive the manipulation, the new merchandising display, and consequently any difference in average sales levels across the first four weeks and the second four weeks must be attributable to factors other than the new display. Thus,

$$O_4 - O_3 = E$$

In other words, any change in sales must be due to extraneous factors alone. Because control group stores and experimental group stores are

TREATMENT (OR EXPERIMENTAL) EFFECT
Impact of the treatment conditions on the dependent variable. Each treatment condition's effect indicates the influence of that condition on the dependent variable.

identical, we can also safely conclude that extraneous factors should effect those stores roughly in the same manner. For this reason, we can use the estimate of the effect of extraneous factors in the control group as our best estimate of the affects of extraneous factors in the experimental group. By comparing the two groups, we are able to determine the effect of the new merchandising display on changes in average sales levels:

$$(O_2 - O_1) - (O_4 - O_3) = (T + E) - E = T$$

In other words, through the use of a control group and random assignment, the effects of extraneous factors may "cancel out." Note, however, that this does not *eliminate* extraneous factors that may affect sales, but it does *control* for them, which allows the researcher to determine the effect of the manipulation on the dependent variable.

Threats to internal validity.   The internal validity of an experiment is threatened whenever extraneous factors exist and are left uncontrolled. In comparing the different types of research environments, experiments conducted in laboratory settings are, all else the same, more likely to be internally valid than field experiments. Because laboratory experiments are conducted in a rigidly specified setting, it affords the researcher tighter control over possible confounds (i.e., extraneous factors). Regardless of the setting in which the experiment takes place, the researcher must try to rule out all rival explanations that might produce differences in the dependent variable, otherwise results of an experiment can be compromised.

There are several confounding circumstances affecting internal validity. The most common threats have to do with the following.[2]

HISTORY

Threat to internal validity; refers to those specific events that occur simultaneously with the experiment, but that have not been controlled for.

History.   **History** refers to those specific events that occur simultaneously with the experiment, but that have not been controlled for. Because these events occur at the same time as the experiment, they can affect the dependent variable and, thus, are confounded with the experimental conditions. For example, consider a "heavy-up" advertising program, in which a greater-than-average amount of advertising money is allocated to a mature brand (e.g., Bromo Seltzer) that is currently not being supported. The advertising program is launched in one or two test markets and sales are monitored before and after the program launch. The difference between before-and-after sales levels is the assumed change due to the manipulated variable, that is, the increased advertising expenditures. However, other factors related to competitor's attempts to "jam" the test (e.g., trade promotions, couponing) that occur at the same time as the heavy-up advertising experiment could have produced (or nullified) the observed change in sales levels.

MATURATION

Threat to internal validity; refers to changes in biology or psychology of the respondent that occur over time and can affect the dependent variable irrespective of the treatment conditions.

Maturation.   **Maturation** refers to changes in the biology (growing older, more experienced) or psychology (changes in beliefs, perceptions) of the respondent that occur over time and can affect the dependent variable irrespective of the treatment conditions. During the experiment respondents may become tired, bored, or hungry—influencing the response to the treatment condition. In general, tracking and market studies that span several months or years are particularly vulnerable to maturation factors because there is no way to know how respondents might be changing over time. Also, maturation can be prevalent in experiments dealing with physiological responses, such as taste-testing studies.

Testing.   **Testing** refers to the consequences of taking before-and-after exposure measurements on respondents. It occurs when the first measurement, taken before exposure to the treatment condition, affects the second measurement, taken after exposure to the treatment condition. Thus, the postexposure measurement on the dependent variable is not due to the experimental treatment conditions alone but is a direct result of the respondent's preexposure measurement. For example, consider an advertising testing service in which respondents are prerecruited and asked to appear at a central testing location. These respondents are given a pretreatment exposure questionnaire covering, among other things, attitudes and intentions to buy a certain brand, which the respondent is aware of but has never tried. After viewing an advertisement for the test brand, they are again asked to fill out the questionnaire. Suppose that the experimenter finds no change when comparing pre- and postexposure attitudes or intention-to-buy scores. The researcher might conclude that the advertising execution has had no effect. An alternative explanation is that respondents have sought to maintain consistency in their pre- and postexposure measurement responses. Thus, what drove postexposure measurement was not the experimental treatment condition but simply the respondent's preexposure responses. In general, testing effects occur because: (1) the respondent becomes expert at completing the measurement instrument, (2) becomes annoyed at being asked to complete the same questionnaire twice, or (3) becomes "frozen" in the sense of giving a consistent answer based on the initial questioning, and so on. If the respondent is unaware of being measured, testing effects are unlikely to surface.

Instrumentation.   **Instrumentation** refers to changes in the calibration of the measurement instrument or in the observers or scorers themselves. Instrumentation is most likely to occur when interviewers are used in a before-and-after exposure study. In such settings, interviewers may, with practice, acquire additional skills that make the second reading more precise. On the other hand, interviewers may become bored or tired, and by the time of the second measurement, their performance may have diminished and the recordings may have become less precise.

Selection bias.   **Selection bias** refers to the improper assignment of respondents to treatment conditions. It occurs when selection assignment results in treatment groups that differ on the dependent variable before their exposure to the treatment condition. In general, selection bias can occur if respondents are allowed to self-select their own treatment condition or if treatment conditions are assigned to groups. Consider a pricing study in which two price conditions are assigned to various retail outlets (high, low) based on store volume. Because of size differences the experiment can become confounded. The problem is one of nonequivalence of groups. That is, store size affects sales levels irrespective of which price condition was assigned to a store.

TESTING
Threat to internal validity; refers to the consequences of taking before-and-after exposure measurements on respondents.

INSTRUMENTATION
Threat to internal validity; refers to changes in the calibration of the measurement instrument or in the observers or scorers themselves.

SELECTION BIAS
Threat to internal validity; refers to the improper assignments of respondents to treatment conditions.

MORTALITY

Threat to internal validity; refers to the differential loss (refusal to continue in the experiment) of respondents from the treatment condition groups.

Mortality.   **Mortality** refers to the differential loss (that is, refusal to continue in the experiment) of respondents from the groups thus rendering the control and experimental groups nonequivalent. In general, experimental studies spanning a year or more, even several months, are particularly vulnerable to mortality effects. This is a serious problem in purchase diary panel studies. In addition, mortality effects can surface in experiments where one (or more) of the treatment conditions is relatively undesirable. For example, the recent trend toward irregular-sized, shorter umbrellas has made it difficult to product-test normal-sized, new-product versions because of their greater inconvenience. Over time, the treatment group with regular-sized umbrellas experiences some loss of respondents, and the respondents who do remain may be different from the other respondents participating in the experiment.

The threats to internal validity are not mutually exclusive. They can occur simultaneously and in certain instances can also interact with one another. For example, *selection-maturation-interaction* refers to the case where, perhaps because of self-selection, the treatment groups change with respect to the dependent variable at different rates over time.

External Validity

EXTERNAL VALIDITY

Determination of whether the research findings of a study (cause-and-effect relationships) can be generalized to and across populations of persons, settings, and times.

By **external validity** we mean whether the findings of an experiment remain the same if the manipulation were to be introduced to a larger population—that is, whether the results are generalizable. For example, the researcher investigating Raid's Insect-A-Guide is most likely not concerned merely with the change in Raid's sales for the test supermarkets, but rather what will happen if the displays are introduced nationally.

Threats to external validity.   The external validity of an experiment is threatened whenever the experiment is conducted in such a way so as to make the results of the experiment nongeneralizable. Because field experiments are conducted in realistic environments, they are, all else the same, more externally valid than laboratory experiments. The following are the most common threats to external validity.[3]

REACTIVE OR INTERACTIVE EFFECTS OF TESTING

Threat to external validity that occurs when a preexposure measurement increases or decreases the respondent's sensitivity or responsiveness to the experimental treatment conditions and thus leads to unrepresentative results.

Reactive or interactive effects of testing.   The **reactive or interactive testing effect** occurs when a preexposure measurement increases or decreases the respondent's sensitivity or responsiveness to the experimental treatment conditions and, thus, leads to unrepresentative results. In contrast to other testing effects with reactive or interactive testing effects, the preexposure measurement does not directly affect the postexposure measurement; rather, the experimental treatment condition gains more notice and reactions than it would have if the preexposure measurement had not been taken. For example, in the advertising testing study the pretreatment exposure questionnaire could heighten respondents' interest, thus making them particularly sensitive to the advertising that they see. Reactive or interactive testing effects occur when the preexposure measurement and the treatment conditions interact to produce a joint effect on the dependent variable.

Interactive effects of selection bias.   **Interactive effects of selection bias** is a situation that occurs when the improper selection of respondents interacts with experimental treatment conditions to produce misleading and unrepresentative results. Because of improper assignment of respondents to treatment conditions, some of the groups have a differential sensitivity or responsiveness to the experimental treatment conditions that cannot be generalized to the wider population.

Surrogate situations.   This threat to external validity occurs because of the use of experimental settings, test units, and/or treatment conditions that differ from those encountered in the actual setting that the researcher is interested in. **Surrogate situations** produce ungeneralizable results. Consider a case in which we are interested in measuring subjects' reactions to various advertisements. The subjects view the ads in a controlled environment and their attention to the ad is more or less forced as a result of the experimental procedure. We must ask ourselves if the ads will capture the same attention and subsequent information processing when viewed in a naturalistic setting. Recall scores could be lower or higher for all five treatment conditions simply due to the way people process the ad when it is aired outside the controlled laboratory setting.

Demand Artifacts

Demand artifacts are those aspects of the experiment that cause respondents to perceive, interpret, and act upon what is believed to be the expected or desired behavior.[4] Demand artifacts occur because human respondents do not respond passively to experimental situations. Suspicion about the purpose of the experiment, the respondent's prior experimental experience, and obtrusive premeasurements and postmeasurements are just a few of the possible extraneous factors that can produce demand bias if these artifacts either increase the possibility that the respondent knows the true purpose of the experiment or if the artifacts influence the respondent's perceptions of appropriate behavior.[5]

Demand artifacts may have affected experimental studies investigating the quality connotations of price.[6] Early price-quality studies typically presented respondents with brands differentiated only by some letter identification and the relative price (the brands were exactly the same) and found that respondents usually would choose the high-priced brand.[7] Respondents may have correctly guessed the purpose of the study and hypothesized that the experimenter expected them to choose higher priced brands primarily for products that differ in quality.

Demand artifacts pose serious threats to both internal and external validity. They can confound the internal validity of an experiment when they interact with the experimental treatment conditions to produce misleading results. They also affect generalization of the findings because it is very unlikely that the same set of demand characteristics operating in a laboratory setting will characterize a real-life situation.

EXPERIMENTAL DESIGNS

There are so many different experimental designs that it is unrealistic to cover them all in one chapter. Instead, we explain specific experimental designs that marketing researchers frequently use, and provide examples of how they are used. Before we discuss specific experimental designs, however, some notation needs to be introduced. The notation described below will be useful in describing the various designs.

Notation

The use of symbols is an effective way of explaining how experimental designs work.

- RR indicates that respondents have been randomly assigned to one of the experimental groups and receives one of the treatment conditions.
- EG refers to the experimental group, that is, one of the treatment conditions.
- CG refers to the control group—the group that is not exposed to the experimental treatment.
- X represents the exposure of a group of respondents to one of the experimental treatment conditions.
- O refers to the observation or measurement of the dependent variable for each respondent.

After-Only Design

AFTER-ONLY DESIGN

Experiment that exposes respondents to a single treatment condition followed by a post-exposure measurement.

Exhibit 8–1 presents a marketing research proposal for an **after-only design** involving an advertising recall study. The design calls for telephoning 200 respondents in any of 34 cities who say they watched a particular TV show the night before in any of the 34 cities. Respondents are asked both **unaided recall**—no "clues" (prompts) are given to the respondents—and aided recall questions—respondents are given specific details concerning what they might have seen the night before.

	X	O_1
Respondents who claim to have watched a specific TV show the night before	Test-market advertisement	Unaided and aided recall of specific copy points

The problem with this general type of design is a lack of internal validity; that is, you notice there is no control group and no random assignment of respondents. Thus, because there is no prior/before measurement, the only threats to internal validity that are controlled for relate to testing, instrumentation, and interactive testing effects. With respect to the specific design described in Exhibit 8–1, notice that the action standard, however,

EXHIBIT 8—1

Marketing Research
Proposal: After-Only
Design

Brand:	Brand Z hair conditioner
Project:	Recall (R) study
Background and Objectives:	The brand group has developed a TV advertisement introducing Brand Z. The objective of this research is to evaluate this copy in a real-life setting.
Research Method:	A minimum of 200 respondents who claim to have watched a particular TV show the night before will be contacted by telephone in any of 34 cities.
Information to Be Obtained:	This study will provide information on the incidence of unaided and aided recall along with specific information on which copy execution points were remembered.
Action Standard:	In order to be judged successful, the percentage of unaided and aided recall scores must be significantly above category norms at the 80 percent confidence level.

calls for the results to be compared to category norms. A norm is the average score, either aided or unaided, for all commercials tested in this product category aired in a similar setting—prime-time television, for example. In effect, these norms act as a control and give the researcher standards of comparison for judging the results of the experiment.

Before-After Design

Exhibit 8–2 presents a marketing research proposal that describes a **before-after design** for a new advertising campaign. In this design, a measurement is taken from respondents both before and after they are exposed to the manipulation. The treatment effect (T) is computed by taking $O_2 - O_1$, the difference between the before and after measurements:

$$T = O_2 - O_1$$

BEFORE-AFTER DESIGN
Experiment where a measurement is taken from respondents before they receive the experimental treatment condition; the experimental treatment is then introduced, and post-treatment measure is taken.

O_1	X	O_2
Recruited respondents are given a questionnaire covering attitude, images, and intention measures	Test advertisement	Respondents are given a questionnaire covering attitude, images, and intention measures as well as overall reaction to the test advertisement

This design again lacks internal validity because there is no control group, a shortcoming somewhat compensated for by the category norms compiled by the supplier.

Before-After with Control Design

This design adds a control group to the basic before-after design just discussed. Random assignment is an important characteristic of this design—respondents are assigned randomly to one of the treatment groups

Project:	Branded women's hair shampoo
Background and Objectives:	The brand group has developed a new advertising campaign for branded women's hair shampoo. The objective of this research is to evaluate the effectiveness of a TV advertisement that portrays the brand's new image.
Research Method:	A minimum of 150 respondents will be recruited to central theater locations in four test cities. At the central testing location respondents are first given a personal interview. Next, they view a TV show in which the test advertisement is embedded twice. After viewing, they are again given a personal interview.
Information to Be Obtained:	This study will provide information on brand attitude, image, and purchase intent change scores as well as overall reaction to the test commercial and recall scores.
Action Standard:	All results are compared to category norms at the 80 percent confidence level.

or to the control group. The test and control groups therefore are considered to be equivalent with respect to all other variables that could possibly affect the dependent variable. To once again see why this is important, let's say that individuals with high IQs also tend to have better recall. If this is so, in an advertising recall study you would not want any IQ differences in the people who are exposed to the manipulation and those in the control group. With random assignment, there is no reason to believe that one group will differ significantly from the other with respect to, say, IQ levels.

Exhibit 8–3 presents a marketing research proposal that describes this type of design for a dollar-off promotional program for a brand not now supported by promotional dollars.

By adjusting the standard before-after treatment effect $(O_2 - O_1)$ by the effect that would have been obtained without the experimental treatment $(O_4 - O_3)$, the difference $(O_2 - O_1) - (O_4 - O_3)$ reflects the "true" experimental effect:

$$T = (O_2 - O_1) - (O_4 - O_3)$$

	EG		
RR	O_1	X	O_2
15 outlets randomly assigned	Share of market, week ending 11/17	Dollar-off promotion, week of 11/18	Share of market, week ending 11/24
		CG	
RR	O_3		O_4
15 outlets randomly assigned	Share of market, week ending 11/17		Share of market, week ending 11/24

Brand:	Brand A mouthwash
Project:	Dollar-off promotional study
Background and Objectives:	The marketing management team has proposed a dollar-off promotional study for brand A, a brand that is not currently supported. The object of this research is to assess the likely impact that such a program will have.
Research Method:	The Buffalo, New York, area is selected as the test market. A total of 30 retail outlets will participate in the study. Stores will be randomly assigned to an experimental treatment group (dollar-off promotion) and to the control group (no promotion).
Information to Be Obtained:	This study will provide information on before and after shares of market.
Action Standard:	To be judged successful the promotional campaign should produce at least a 1.0 percent change in share of market.

EXHIBIT 8—3

Marketing Research Proposal: Before-After with Control

To illustrate how results from before-after with control experiments are interpreted, let us consider the (hypothetical) market share results from the dollar-off promotional study described in Exhibit 8–3.

— Before week ending 11/17: 5.3 (experimental); 5.4 (control).
— After week ending 11/24: 6.8 (experimental); 5.6 (control).

Note that the before-after design by itself would indicate the estimated effect of the dollar-off promotional program to be 1.5 share points $(6.8 - 5.3)$. Use of a control group makes it possible to adjust this effect by what is gained without the dollar-off promotional program. Hence, the true treatment effect is calculated to be

$$T = (6.8 - 5.3) - (5.6 - 5.4)$$

or 1.3 share of market points, which exceeds the action standard requirement expressed in the proposal.

With the exception of mortality, this design controls for all remaining threats to internal validity. With respect to threats to external validity, however, this design does poorly because of the pre-exposure measurement.

After-Only with Control Design

A control group can be added to the standard after-only design with respondents randomly assigned to the experimental and control groups. In such designs, the treatment effect is simply the difference between O_1 and O_2:

$$T = O_2 - O_1$$

One problem with **the after-only with control design** is that without a pretest there is no way to guarantee equivalence of respondents in the control and experimental groups. To make respondents in the experimental

AFTER-ONLY WITH CONTROL DESIGN
Experiment where a control group is added to the standard after-only design to control for extraneous sources of bias.

EXHIBIT 8—4

Marketing Research
Proposal: After-Only with
Control Group

Project:	New Raid IMS display
Background and Objectives:	Marketing analysts for the Raid product line want to determine whether a new IMS display increases sales.
Research Method:	The design calls for a sample of 20 stores, matched according to store sales volume and size and sales of bug spray and related products, to be randomly assigned to either the experimental or control group. Stores assigned to the experimental group will receive the new IMS display. Control group stores will continue to use current Raid racks.
Information to Be Obtained:	Sales of Raid products for the four-week period covering 5/1 to 5/31.
Action Standard:	To be judged superior, the experimental stores must achieve a 10% increase in Raid product sales over their market control store counterparts.

and control groups more similar in real-life applications, respondents are typically matched on one or a set of background characteristics, as the following example illustrates.

Exhibit 8–4 presents a marketing research proposal describing an after-only with control group design that might be used to test the superiority of the new Raid IMS display.

	EG	
RR	X	O_1
After matching, stores are randomly assigned	New Raid IMS display	Sales covering four-week period, 5/1–5/31
	CG	
RR	X	O_2
After matching, stores are randomly assigned	Current Raid display rack	Sales covering four-week period, 5/1–5/31

Time-Series Design

TIME-SERIES DESIGN
Experiment that involves periodic measurements on some group or individual, introduction of an experimental manipulation, and subsequent periodic measurement.

LONGITUDINAL SURVEYS
Questioning of the same or different respondent at different points in time.

Time-series designs involve periodic measurements of some group or individual reaction, introduction of an experimental manipulation, and subsequent periodic measurements. This is also called a **longitudinal study (or survey),** since it involves questioning (the same or different respondents) over time. Generally, this design does not involve randomization, and the timing of treatment presentation as well as the selection of respondents exposed to the treatment is usually not under the researcher's direct control. As we demonstrate below, this design bears a basic similarity to the before-after design, but because you take many preexposure and postexposure measurements, the time-series design provides more control over extraneous factors. However, it still only provides direct control over maturation, testing, and instrumentation effects.

EXHIBIT 8—5

Marketing Research
Proposal: Time-Series
Design

Brand:	Chewing gum
Project:	National tracking study
Background and Objectives:	The chewing gum brand group has requested that a national tracking study be conducted next year. The objective of the study will be to track changes in awareness, consumer perceptions, and use resulting from any proprietary or competitive changes in the chewing gum market.
Research Method:	The study will be conducted over the next year in monthly waves beginning in February. Interviewing will be conducted by long distance from a central location. Strict probability methods will be used to select telephone numbers from all working exchanges and numbers in the continental United States. Respondents will be randomly selected within a household. Two hundred (200) past-30-day chewing gum users will be interviewed for 11 months, February through December, yielding a total sample of 2,220.
Information to Be Obtained:	The study will provide information on changes in brand awareness, consumer perceptions, and use patterns.

Exhibit 8–5 presents a marketing research proposal requested by a chewing gum brand group for a national tracking study to be conducted next year.[8] Exhibit 8–6 summarizes this design.

To demonstrate the effects of the new competitive entry on the market, we have plotted possible trends for share of last purchase data for the established brand in Exhibit 8–7. The X, in the figure, denotes the approximate market entry time of the new diet chewing gum. In market A the new competitive product entry has had both a short-run and a long-run negative effect on share of last purchase for the established brand. In market B, the new product has had only a temporary short-run negative effect on share of last purchase, as our share of market has bounced back to preentry levels by the end of the year. In markets C and D, the new product has not had a real effect, for the changes that have occurred since its introduction are consistent with the preentry purchase history. You will note that if we had examined only the change between June and July,

EXHIBIT 8—6

Time-Series Quasi-Design

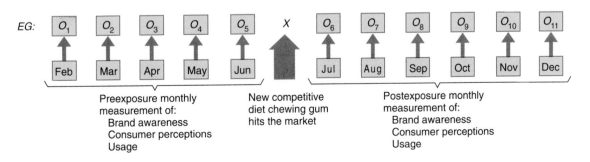

EG: O₁ Feb O₂ Mar O₃ Apr O₄ May O₅ Jun X O₆ Jul O₇ Aug O₈ Sep O₉ Oct O₁₀ Nov O₁₁ Dec

Preexposure monthly measurement of: Brand awareness, Consumer perceptions, Usage

New competitive diet chewing gum hits the market

Postexposure monthly measurement of: Brand awareness, Consumer perceptions, Usage

EXHIBIT 8—7

Share of Last Purchase for Established Brand

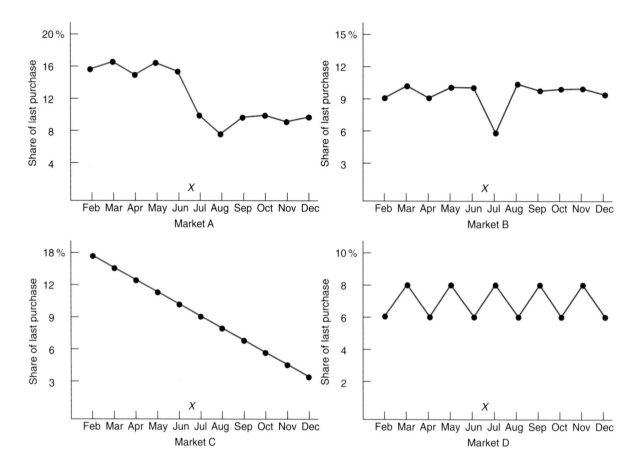

as would be the case in a one-group after-only design, it would be easy to conclude that the diet chewing gum had a detrimental effect on our share of last purchase in all four markets; moreover, we could not have understood the nature of the effects in markets A and B.

SELECTION OF A DESIGN

Table 8–1 summarizes the potential threats to validity in each of the designs that we have discussed. Note that we have used the phrase *potential errors* in discussing threats to validity. In fact, the potential for errors does not mean there will be actual errors; and although in principle a design might not control for a potential source of error, the marketing researcher can build in specific controls when designing the experiment.

The challenge facing marketing researchers is that the experimental designs providing the tightest controls over internal validity may be the most

TABLE 8—1

Experimental Designs and Potential Errors

Source of Potential Error	Experimental Design				
	After-Only	Before-After	Before-After with Control	After-Only with Control	Time-Series
History	X	X	√	√	X
Maturation	X	X	√	√	√
Testing	√	X	√	√	√
Instrumentation	√	X	√	√	√
Selection Bias	X	X	√	√	X
Mortality	X	√	X	X	X
Interactive Testing Effects	√	√	X	√	X
Interactive Effects of Selection Bias	X	X	X	√*	X
Surrogate Situations	X	X	X	X	X
Demand Artifacts	X	X	X	X	X

Note: √ indicates a method of controlling for the error is provided by the design; X indicates no method of controlling is incorporated in the design.

*Assumes matching prior to random assignment.

artificial, which may compromise the ability to generalize research findings. Yet the value of marketing research is that sample results can be projected to represent larger untested populations. Hence, the issue of internal versus external validity is not a trivial one. The dilemma has led many researchers to suggest that designs that are tight in internal validity be used in early stages of marketing research projects to identify treatment conditions known to have specific effects under controlled conditions. Then, depending on the costs and risks involved, these conditions can be subjected to further testing in more natural settings.[9] Such designs, if properly developed and controlled, can provide the marketing researcher with a valid way to extend experimentation into real-life market settings.

SUMMARY

This chapter discusses experimentation. Experimental designs are useful when the researcher wants to infer cause-and-effect relationships between independent and dependent variables. Experimental designs control for other possible causes of the dependent variable. A significant portion of the chapter is devoted to the concepts of internal and external validity of experiments and factors that affect validity. The chapter also explains the distinction between laboratory and field experiments, especially in regard to their ability to provide control of those crucial factors that might affect the experimental outcome. The chapter concludes with a presentation of the five most commonly used experimental designs in marketing research and a comparison of the designs with respect to their internal and external validity.

KEY CONCEPTS

Causality

Experimentation

Manipulation

Control of Extraneous Factors

Internal Validity

External Validity

Laboratory Experiment

Field Experiment

After-Only Design

Before-After Design

Before-After with Control Design

After-Only with Control Design

Time-Series Design

REVIEW QUESTIONS

1. Discuss the advantages and disadvantages of laboratory and field experiments.

2. Discuss the various methods for controlling extraneous sources of variation.

3. Discuss the differences between internal and external validity.

4. Compare the before-after with the before-after with control experimental design with respect to controlling for threats to internal validity.

5. a. A manufacturer of products sold in food stores wishes to find out whether a 10-cents-off coupon could be effective in winning new customers. Develop an appropriate experimental design to address this issue.

   b. A manufacturer of women's shoes located in the Northeast is interested in ascertaining the effects of instituting a 25 percent across-the-board increase in price. The company, a differentiated marketer catering to professional and nonprofessional women, distributes its shoe line to leading retailers nationwide. Determine an appropriate experimental design to investigate the effects of the price increase.

ENDNOTES

1. Definitions of internal and external validity (and our ensuing discussion) are based on the work of P. T. Campbell and S. T. Stanley, *Experimental and Quasi Experimental Design for Research* (Chicago: Rand Mc-Nally, 1963); and T. D. Cook and P. T. Campbell, *Experimentation: Design Analysis Issues for Field Settings* (Chicago: Rand McNally, 1979), Chapter 2.

2. Campbell and Stanley, *Experimental and Quasi Experimental Design,* pp. 5–6; and Cook and Campbell, *Experimentation: Design Analysis Issues,* Chapter 2.

3. Ibid.

4. A. G. Sawyer, "Demand Artifacts in Laboratory Experiments in Consumer Research," *Journal of Consumer Research,* March 1975, pp. 20–30.

5. See, for example, R. Rosenthal and R. L. Rosnow, *Artifacts in Behavioral Research* (New York: Academic Press, 1969); R. L. Rosnow and L. S. Aiken, "Mediation of Artifacts in Behavioral Research," *Journal of Experimental Social Psychology,* May 1973, pp. 181–201.

6. Sawyer, "Demand Artifacts," p. 31.

7. See J. D. McConnell, "The Price-Quality Relationship in an Experimental Setting," *Journal of Marketing Research,* August 5, 1968, pp. 300–303.

8. Commercial marketing research studies using this type of design would schedule respondents so that there would be 200 different respondents each month.

9. See A. G. Sawyer, P. M. Worthing, and P. E. Sendak, "The Role of Laboratory Experiments to Test Marketing Strategies," *Journal of Marketing,* Summer 1979, pp. 60–67.

Case 1: Consumers' Attitudes and Perceptions toward Seafood When Eating Out: Preliminary Phase

The lack of acceptance by the consumer of squid, mackerel, pollock, whiting, hake, and other underutilized species impedes the fishing industry from developing and using these existing fisheries despite the abundance of the available product. The specific problems being encountered are in the marketplace. Although problems of quality and handling techniques also exist, solutions to these problems are to little or no avail unless consumers will accept the product.

All sectors of the fishing industry that are concerned with these species, from harvesting to processing to distribution, are affected by the problem of consumer nonacceptance. Even popular species are underused at certain times of the year. In this area of scarce resources, the result is to deny use of abundant resources to all sectors of the fishing industry. Such denial affects the costs of other processing and distribution resources and capabilities, contributes to greater cyclical fluctuations within the industry, denies greater employment opportunities, and inhibits commercial food-service establishments from providing lower cost seafood menu items, which would benefit the consumer and increase consumption of all species.

A major market for fish is the food-service industry. As viable as this industry is, however, it selects only certain seafood products and sells them with a minimum of marketing effort and much ignorance about the consumer who eats seafood away from home.

Marketing research has explored the attitudes, perceptions, and behavior of the food-market seafood buyer and resultant home-consumption patterns. The away-from-home seafood buyer, however, consumes twice as much seafood as the at-home eater and provides a vital link not only in total consumption, but also in the exploration of new uses and species. Yet he or she orders seafood or fish only about 7 percent of the time in all restaurants.

This research is directed at understanding the marketing process that is most effective for expanding consumption of both traditional and nontraditional fish in commercial food-service establishments. This knowledge is essential to the stabilization, maintenance, and growth of the fishing industry, and it is advanced by empirical identification of consumers' beliefs, attitudes, intentions, and behaviors toward seafood products and their promotion. Specifically, the broad objective of the full research project is threefold:

1. To provide an analysis of consumer beliefs, attitudes, intentions, and behavior toward product characteristics of fish eaten in commercial food-service establishments, especially underutilized species, both fresh and frozen.
2. To develop an effective foundation for generating marketing tactics and strategies for food-service operators in preparing, serving, merchandising, advertising, promoting, menu listing, naming, and pricing of fish products, especially underutilized species.
3. To provide an analysis of delineated market segments that will orient the food-service operator toward optimal marketing effectiveness for fish and fish products, especially underutilized species.

The research was confined to Massachusetts for funding and resource-limitation reasons. As such, it pays particular attention to fish species of the northeastern

Source: Material for this case was supplied by Dr. Robert C. Lewis, Department of Hotel Administration, University of Massachusetts.

seaboard and to the attributes of Massachusetts consumers. Generalizations beyond Massachusetts should be made with caution, but it is believed that the findings have nationwide implications.

Part I of the Research

The purpose of this part of the research project was to provide a foundation and qualitative basis for the more extensive quantitative research that would follow. As the first phase of a comprehensive study, it examines

— General attitudes and perceptions toward seafood.
— Factors affecting those attitudes and perceptions.
— Attitudes, feelings, and beliefs that influence consumers' behavior patterns toward eating fish when dining out.

Specific objectives were to explore

— Tastes and preferences.
— Familiarity with the product.
— Knowledge of nutritional attributes.
— Previous consumption.
— Present consumption.
— Home versus away-from-home usage.
— Associations.
— Awareness, knowledge, familiarity, consumption, and attitudes toward nontraditional species.

Focus group research was undertaken to collect data. Four focus group interviews of 8 to 10 persons each were held in geographically different areas, including both inland and coastal markets. This enabled us to examine any differences that might exist between consumers who have immediate access to a wide variety of fresh fish and those who are farther removed from it.

Sample

Two focus groups, one male and one female, were held in the Boston and Springfield, Massachusetts, areas. Participants for the interviews were prescreened on several factors so that they would represent a cross-section of the restaurant-eating public. These factors included age, income, education, marital status, frequency of eating in restaurants, type of restaurant visited, and frequency of selecting seafood when eating out.

Virtually all participants had attended high school and most had completed college. The groups were about evenly divided between married and single or divorced participants. Representative job descriptions included clerk, secretary, homemaker, bookkeeper, supervisor, draftsperson, teacher, and contractor. About 75 percent were Massachusetts natives.

All participants had eaten dinner at least twice in a table-service restaurant during the previous month. Approximately one-third claim they eat out at least eight times a month; some claim they eat out as often as five times a week.

All participants order finfish for their main course at least occasionally when dining out. Over half reported they eat fish frequently when at restaurants. Half of these say they always eat fish at restaurants.

Method

Each focus group session began with an introduction to what a focus group is and how one is conducted. The moderator emphasized that there were no right or wrong answers and strongly encouraged participants to express their own opinions. Discussion was free-flowing and generally exploratory, but it also was probing and directed toward certain topic areas. (The full moderator's guide for conducting the sessions is shown in Exhibit 1.)

Case Question

Critique and evaluate the approach taken in the focus-group phase of this study.

EXHIBIT 1

Moderator's Guide

Introduction
A. Moderator.
B. Focus-group technique, taping, etc.
C. Participant introductions (name, where live, where born, how often eat out [non-fast-food])

Background Information
A. Favorite restaurant/why?
B. What influences our choices of food?
   1. Things in childhood—As a child did you try new foods?
   2. Peer group.
   3. Religion.
   4. Geographical preferences (where).
   5. Parental pressure.

Seafood Consumption
(Not shellfish such as crab, lobster, shrimp; talk about fish such as sole, halibut, cod.)
A. How frequently eat seafood when eat out?
   1. What kinds?
   2. Why? (benefits).
     a. Health.
     b. Taste.
     c. Price.
     d. Nutrition.
   3. More or less than in the past?
   4. Eating habits change as you get older.
   5. Why not others?
B. Present consumption habits.
   1. Home.
   2. Away from home.
     a. Why at restaurant and not at home?
     b. Is restaurant an experience or just a place?
C. Favorite seafood
   1. Why/what makes it a favorite?
     a. Fish itself.
     b. Sauce.
     c. Texture.
     d. Manner in which it is prepared.
   2. Elements that appeal the most.
   3. How important familiarity?
D. Describe a typical dining out experience—in terms of menu selection.
E. Influencers/preconceived ideas.
   1. Waiter/waitress.
   2. Menu.
   3. People you are with.
   4. Specials of the day.
   5. Table tents on tables.
   6. Any particular tastes or names that may have an influence.

EXHIBIT 1
(*concluded*)

F. Do you try new dishes?
   1. Why?
   2. Why not?
G. What catches your attention?
   1. Description.
   2. Name.
   3. Price.
   4. Others.
H. Expectations.
   1. What will it taste like?
   2. What kinds/names?

I. Types of restaurants.
   1. More likely to trust a particular type of restaurant.
   2. More likely to try something new in a restaurant you trust.
   3. How does type of restaurant influence choice?

Menu Evaluation (hand-cut menus)
A. What catches your eye first?
   1. Price.
   2. Descriptions of fish.
   3. Benefits seen in eating fish.
B. Probe for specifics of factors making favorite/underutilized species.
   1. Would you eat this kind? (Try new terms).
   2. Why?
   3. Why not?
   4. Would you try it?
   5. How familiar are you with these species? (Some on menu, others like monkfish, dog fish.)
C. Fresh fish versus frozen.
   1. Likes/dislikes.
   2. Do you trust the menu?
   3. Trust the waiter/waitress?
D. Methods of preparation.
   1. Broiled.
   2. Baked.
   3. Fried.
   4. Steamed.
   5. Sautéed.
   6. In chowders.

Marketing Influence/Strategy
A. Restaurant's role in educating the consumer.
   1. Waiter/waitress.
   2. Special promotions.
   3. Descriptions.
B. Other media used to influence.
   1. TV.
   2. Articles.
   3. Commentaries.
   4. News item.
   5. Julia Child-type program.

CASE 2: COKE TARGETS YOUTH MARKET WITH CD, TAPE PROMOTION

ATLANTA — Opting for the sound of music rather than the dubious whiz-bang technology of last year, Coca-Cola Co. is planning a huge compact disc and cassette giveaway for its summer promotion.

Source: *Marketing News,* April 29, 1991, p. 5. Reprinted with permission.

The Atlanta-based soft-drink maker said it will place 5.6 million mini CDs and 100 million certificates for $1 cassettes inside multipacks of Coca-Cola Classic, Diet Coke, and Sprite beginning in May. The CDs and tapes will feature youth-oriented artists from Sony Music's Columbia and Epic labels.

The promotion is aimed squarely at the youth market, with the featured artists heavy on the dance and rock side.

"We feel strongly we have the right music at the right time," said Ted Host, senior vice president at Coca-Cola USA. "The music is top of the chart artists."

The new promotion follows last summer's "MagiCans," which offered cash prizes stuffed into ejector-equipped cans. That promotion, billed as one of Coke's largest, was killed early amid complaints of malfunctioning prize mechanisms and reports that the chlorinated water used to make the winning cans feel like the real thing would leak.

Host rejected the suggestion that the company was trying to play it safe with the music giveaway after the widespread publicity over the problems with MagiCan. While it was in progress, the 1990 promotion gave Coke sales increases, he said.

"We thought the MagiCan was extremely successful," Host said. "We just see this as another Coke promotion."

For most consumers, the MagiCan probably is long forgotten, said AMA Chairman Kenneth L. Bernhardt, head of the marketing department at Georgia State University, Atlanta.

"I think people have fairly short memories on promotions, unless you remind them enough of it," he said. If they [Coke] came out with something similar to last year's, people probably would remember."

Summer promotions are important to the industry, with hot weather and added leisure time making it a prime season for soft-drink consumption.

Under the new "Coca-Cola Pop Music" promotion, one in 19 multi-packs will contain one of four 3-inch CDs with at least four songs each. All other packages will contain a certificate that can be redeemed with $1 for a six-song cassette.

Case Question

Coke management was quite certain that the ultimate consumer, the soda drinking market, would react favorably to the promotion. However, Coke was less certain of the feelings of its other customers, the trade — that is, distributors, wholesalers, retailers, and so forth. Coke wanted to conduct focus group interviews with members of the trade.

What recommendation would you provide for this audience as compared to the typical consumer focus group? Prepare a moderator's guide for the focus group sessions.

CASE 3: SODA POP CONCERN IS UNDER SCRUTINY FOR ALCOHOL IMAGE

BY LAURA BIRD

NEW YORK — A tiny soda company with its sights on expansion is poised to exploit the cult status of its burgundy-colored soda with a new ad campaign aimed at teens. But the product's name — Cheerwine — is attracting scrutiny from federal regulators and criticism from anti-alcohol activists.

Source: *The Wall Street Journal*, April 20, 1992, p. B8. Reprinted with permission.

Critics contend Cheerwine, from closely held Carolina Beverage Corp., Salisbury, N.C., improperly encourages teen-agers to drink alcohol, just as candy cigarettes may encourage children to smoke. A spokesman for the U.S. Bureau of Alcohol, Tobacco and Firearms said the agency may start an inquiry into the brand.

"We want to find out what's in it and why they use the term wine if it's soda," the spokesman said.

A new Cheerwine commercial, created by Long, Haymes & Carr, a Winston-Salem, N.C., unit of Interpublic Group, targets 12-year-olds through 17-year-olds with a song about the soda's "Diff'rent Kinda Cool." The spot shows a couple of stick-figure teens surfing, dancing, and driving a car, all the while drinking Cheerwine.

"We get a funky little feelin' while we're cruisin' around," the characters sing in the spot. "When we hit this cool party, they were throwin' it down."

Some activists contend the commercial, and the soda pop's name, send a mixed message to teens about drinking. "It's almost like they're developing drinkers for tomorrow's generation," said Andy Briscoe, national public affairs director of Mothers Against Drunk Driving. "They could have come up with a catchy name without a link to alcohol," said Patricia Taylor, director of the alcohol policies project for the Washington, D.C., group Center for Science in the Public Interest.

But Lee Peeler, associate director of advertising for the Federal Trade Commission, said the label may be no more insidious than those for root beer or ginger ale. He added, "We'd be concerned about how the product is portrayed in the ads," and declined to speculate on the new spot, which he hadn't seen.

Mark Ritchie, president of Carolina Beverage, said the Cheerwine name and recipe were invented 75 years ago, by his great-grandfather, Louis D. Peeler (no relation to Mr. Peeler of the FTC). The Peeler family still owns the majority of the company stock.

Although Mr. Ritchie wouldn't disclose company sales, he said Cheerwine is sold in 11 states and is among the top three brands in its strongest markets in the western North Carolina area. "We don't want to anger any parents with misinformation," he said, adding that the new commercial is entirely appropriate.

Case Question

Mr. Ritchie was afraid of potential trouble with the FTC because of pressure from the activists groups. He called his advertising agency, Long, Haymes & Carr, and asked his account executive what he could do to protect his brand name in the event of litigation. His account executive said that it would be nice to have a study demonstrating that the name "Cheerwine" did not cause the soda to have an alcohol image. Mr. Ritchie gave his permission to hire an independent research firm to conduct the study.

Prepare a research project proposal to submit to Mr. Ritchie and his advertising agency.

CASE 4: MCDONALD'S TESTS CATFISH SANDWICH

NASHVILLE, TENNESSEE—McDonald's Corp. is trying to hook customers in southern test markets, including one in Kentucky, on a new catfish sandwich.

The chain is serving its newest sandwich in Bowling Green, Ky.; Memphis, Chattanooga, and Jackson, Tenn.; Huntsville, Ala.; Jonesboro, Ark.; and Columbus, Tu-

Source: *Marketing News,* March 18, 1992, p. 10. Reprinted with permission.

pelo, Greenville, and Greenwood, Miss., said Jane Basten, a marketing specialist for McDonald's in Nashville.

The sandwich consists of a 2.3-ounce catfish patty, lettuce, and tangy sauce served on a homestyle bun.

The company will evaluate the sandwich based on sales and supply availability after a six-week ad campaign ends in mid-April.

"The advertising will be similar to what we're doing right now with the grilled steak sandwich," Basten said. "We will promote it to the fullest and see what happens."

She said the catfish is being supplied by The Catfish Institute, an industry promotion association based in Belzoni, Miss.

Catfish Institute director Bill Allen said catfish farmers, processors, and marketers are "very excited about this prospect for our industry. This is super good news.

"But we don't want to get our hopes up too much and start thinking this is going to be our salvation, because we already have a viable industry."

Allen said that catfish firms that remember earlier tie-ups with major restaurant chains such as Church's Fried Chicken are cautiously optimistic about the McDonald's deal.

Case Question

The management team for new product development was interested in assessing the relevancy of the chosen test markets to the three states designated for rollout if the test market was satisfactory. If successful, the product was designed to be introduced into Tennessee, Alabama, and Georgia.

What are your conclusions about the representativeness of the test cities to the designated rollout states? Present secondary data to support your conclusions.

CASE 5: RESEARCHER: TEST ADS FIRST TO "ZAP-PROOF" THEM

BY JOE AGNEW

Consumers' potential for zapping, skipping, and ignoring ads should be measured before the ads are placed on the air and in print, according to Lee Weinblatt, president of the Pretesting Co., Englewood, N.J.

Although exceptionally strong media campaigns might eventually reach the eyes and ears of audiences, he said, it is more efficient to design commercials and ads that gain and hold the audience's attention and deliver a message that is relevant and believable.

"Our data clearly show that it is exceptionally difficult to force communication on an audience," Weinblatt said. "Communication and pretesting efforts must reflect this fact."

In most studies conducted in forced-exposure situations, Weinblatt said, "executions strong on hard facts and product comparisons usually had the highest levels of communication and 'convinceability.' "

He said, however, that studies using "real world" simulations have found that few of these executions were ever listened to or read.

Source: *Marketing News*, February 29, 1988, p. 18. Reprinted with permission.

"Besides entertainment, care must also be taken to leave behind a strong, relevant, and believable message to reach nonusers," Weinblatt said. "While a number of 30-second commercials which achieve both goals have been tested, this has not been found among many 15-second executions."

He said data strongly suggest that simply increasing broadcast budgets will not solve the problem of a commercial or ad that does not gain and hold the attention of people who don't use the products and services.

To measure the impact of zapping over a wide variety of product categories, Weinblatt said his company conducted five tests, each using the same controlled test design.

Each test consisted of at least 100 respondents who went through the Pretesting Company's two patented methodologies, the Simulated Network and PeopleReader.

For testing TV commercials, respondents were seated individually before a color TV, were given a remote control, and were told to choose from three different popular programs for the next half hour.

Respondents could view each show for as long as they wished, and they could switch back and forth among the three networks, Weinblatt said. Respondents selected the one show they liked best, and then they described that program's strengths and weaknesses.

The programs came from three videotape recorders synchronized with each other. At exactly the same time on all three networks, a commercial pod appeared consisting of five commercials: three 30-second and two 15-second spots.

Three of the five commercials were different on all three stations, while two of the commercials—a 15-second and a 30-second spot—appeared at the same moment on all three networks.

If respondents zapped a commercial, Weinblatt said, they would find different commercials on each of the other programs. However, if either two of the same test commercials were zapped, the exact commercial would be found on all three channels.

Toward the end of the half-hour program, there was another commercial pod and the same two test commercials were repeated, synchronized on all three channels.

Case Questions

1. Comment on the research design utilized by the Pretesting Co. to assess the amount of zapping.

2. A brand manager was trying to decide between two advertising campaigns for the introduction of a new brand. One advertising campaign used a humorous approach, while the other utilized a celebrity endorsement. Both campaigns communicated the same end-benefit information and only varied by the executional technique. The brand manager was interested in the three criteria: Would the ads attract the attention of the viewers? Would the ads hold the viewers' attention long enough to communicate the prime end-benefit of the brand? And would the ads' ability to attract and hold attention wear out (i.e., would they lose effectiveness over time)?

   Use the basic format of the Pretesting Company to design an experiment that will provide the information necessary to recommend to the brand manager which of the two advertising campaigns he/she should use for the introduction of the brand.

SAMPLING THEORY AND PRACTICES

TERRENCE COEN
VICE PRESIDENT AND DIRECTOR OF SALES AND MARKETING
SURVEY SAMPLING

We are a busier population today. Household needs for multiple incomes are increasing. And, as the U.S.A. becomes a service-oriented rather than manufacture-oriented economy, nontraditional work hours continue to increase. The net result is a decline in response to survey research.

So says Terrence Coen, vice president and director of sales and marketing at Connecticut-based Survey Sampling, a widely recognized source of samples for survey research.

"We're not likely to see a change in cooperation rates," he believes, referring to the increasing unwillingness of consumers to answer questions. "To top it all off, there is a concern for privacy, which is inviting legislation, which may allow people to self-exclude from research surveys."

Marketing research that relies on the practice of sampling has had to undergo a shift in strategy because of these recent trends. Traditionally, sampling involves probability versus nonprobability. Probability represents sampling a portion of a given population to project the tendencies of that larger population.

Nonprobability sampling is targeting a small segment of consumers, ". . . even though they might not be representative of the entire universe," Coen says. For example, while something like one third of all households may cook with charcoal on at least an occasional basis, only three to four percent may use a mesquite-based product. The cost of screening to identify that small percentage may not be cost effective. Alternatively, an available list of purchasers of such a product may serve as the basis for obtaining a general feel or attitude; but it could not be reliably projected to the entire universe of mesquite-based charcoal users.

CHAPTER 9
The Sampling Process

CHAPTER 10
Sample Size Determination

The problem associated with the probability approach is the expense and difficulty of the project coupled with consumers' increasing unwillingness to cooperate—either directly or through the use of unlisted phone numbers, which Coen indicates is approaching 30 percent of all telephone households.

According to Coen, there are about 93 million households in the United States. In that universe, just under 85 million have telephones, 63 million of which have directory listings. "That creates a problem of representation when doing telephone surveys, unless random digit samples are utilized," Coen says.

On the brighter side, new technology is helping market researchers to improve the efficiency of random digit sampling. There are now databases of business telephone numbers that can be eliminated from random digit samples before calls are made. Also, hardware and software have been developed to help detect non-working phone numbers. "All of this results in a more efficient random sampling and less wasted unproductive phoning time," Coen says.

Terrence Coen has served as vice president and director of sales and marketing for Survey Sampling, Inc., a leading provider of statistical samples for consumers and business to business research, since 1988. Under his direction, SSI has pioneered a series of new sampling methodologies and related services designed to help reduce field costs, better define study estimates, and expand research opportunities. Previously, Mr. Coen served in similar positions for Dun & Bradstreet's Dun's Marketing Services and for Market Data Retrieval.

The Sampling Process

WASHINGTON—The Federal Government's most important food consumption survey, which is instrumental in setting such Government policies as the school lunch program and calculating the tolerance level for pesticide residues in food, is so flawed it is probably useless, according to a scientific panel and the General Accounting Office.

That agency, an investigative arm of Congress, faults both the Department of Agriculture, which conducts the National Food Consumption Survey once a decade, and the company that did the work, National Analysts, a marketing concern, for mishandling the 1987–88 survey, which cost $7.6 million.

The Agriculture Department's Food and Nutrition Service uses the food and nutrient data to evaluate billion-dollar assistance programs like food stamp allotments and the school breakfast and lunch programs. The Environmental Protection Agency uses it to set pesticide tolerance levels in food. The Food and Drug Administration uses it to calculate nutrient-consumption levels and determine public exposure to pesticides and toxic metals. The Government also uses it to track food trends.

The problem with the survey "really complicates any statement about dietary changes in the population," said Catherine Woteki, director of the Food and Nutrition Board at the National Academy of Sciences.

The worst problem is the survey's low response rate of 34 percent, making it questionable whether the data are representative of the population, the G.A.O. said. Such surveys also require follow-up studies of those who do not respond. National Analysts, which conducted the survey, told both the Agriculture Department and the General Accounting Office that its follow-up data had been lost, but finally acknowledged that no follow-ups were conducted, the report said.

The G.A.O. undertook the investigation at the request of Representative George E. Brown Jr., Democrat of California. It notified the Agriculture Department of the problems and the department asked the Federation of American Societies for Experimental Biology to review the data. The clinical research organization's report said it "does not recommend use of the data" and if the Agriculture Department chose to publish the data, it "should include a strongly worded cautionary statement concerning the potential for nonresponse bias."

Agencies that rely on the department's data have two other choices: use data collected by the Department of Health and Human Services in its Health and Nutrition Examination Survey, or Hanes, or keep using the 1977–78 survey. "Within the scientific community there has always been some question about the validity of that survey," Dr. Woteki said.

CHAPTER
OBJECTIVES

EXPLAIN
the purpose of sampling.

DESCRIBE
the steps in the sampling
process.

DEFINE
the population and the
sampling frame.

DESCRIBE
various probability and
nonprobability sampling
designs.

DISCUSS
approaches to determining
sample size.

DESCRIBE
considerations in selecting
the sampling units.

DISCUSS
the estimation of population
characteristics.

reported that women 19 to 50 years of age were consuming 41 percent of their calories from fat; the Hanes 1976–80 study found the same group consuming 36 percent from fat.

"We have a big nationwide campaign going on about reduction of fat," Dr. Woteki said. "If the 77–78 survey is not reliable, how can we assess the change?"

Some Government agencies like the E.P.A. have decided to ignore the latest Agriculture Department survey. This May, the G.A.O. warned the E.P.A. of serious problems with the data. "The sample was so small for some subgroups that they may not be useful to extrapolate to the entire population," said Kevin Donohue, assistant director of the G.A.O.'s resources, community and economic development division. "The tolerance levels may not be set at levels that will protect all these subgroups," which include nursing infants and pregnant women.

Linda Fisher, Assistant Administrator in the E.P.A.'s office of pesticides and toxic substances, said the agency had decided to continue to use the 1977–78 data to determine consumption rates despite its flaws because the data were more reliable. "It is out of date," she said, "because eating patterns have changed. People are eating more fruits and vegetables."

Source: Marian Burros, Copyright (c) 1991 by The *New York Times Company,* September 11, 1991, pp. C1, C4. Reprinted by permission.

The response rate was 62 percent in the earlier survey, "a very low response rate compared to other surveys at the time," Dr. Woteki said. The nonrespondents in that survey were not followed up.

The Hanes studies have a response rate of 77 percent to 86 percent, and health professionals have always considered them more reliable gauges of food consumption patterns than the U.S.D.A. survey. But it does not collect some of the statistics that the Agriculture Department does.

The differences are often serious. The 1977–78 food consumption researchers

INTRODUCTION

Survey results are important and sometimes even used to set national policies. Sampling involves selecting a relatively small number of elements from a large population to make definitive statements about the population at large. The purpose of sampling is to obtain a representative **sample.** If a sample is representative, then the survey results can be extrapolated to the entire population.

Sampling mistakes can be costly. In the case of the latest Agriculture Department survey of food and nutrition, costing $7.6 million, it appears to be doubtful whether its results are sufficiently reliable to be of use in setting national policies. This lack of reliability is due to nonresponse bias and underrepresentation of specific subgroups, problems that can plague any survey. Such potential problems, however, must be considered when planning the sampling design. After the survey is completed, there is little that can be done to correct these problems.

In this chapter we discuss the steps involved in designing a sampling plan. First, we explain the objectives of sampling. Next, we describe each step in the sampling process, including a discussion of the various types of sampling designs and the principal factors governing their use.

THE OBJECTIVES OF SAMPLING

Sampling procedures allow marketing researchers to make informed decisions on the basis of limited information or, stated somewhat differently, in the absence of perfect knowledge. The researcher lacks perfect knowledge because in most realistic situations it is impossible or impractical to conduct a **census.** A census takes place when the researcher obtains data from or about every member of the population. The cost and time required to take a census usually precludes its use in marketing research studies.

Sampling is a basic human activity. Although you might not realize it or call it by name, in the course of our daily routines we all "take samples." You are sampling, for example, when

1. Browsing in a bookstore, you pick up several different books and look at a few pages of each before deciding which to buy.
2. Cooking spaghetti, you stir the pot and then fish out one or two pieces to taste whether the spaghetti is done.
3. Deciding which required course to take, you ask students who have taken the courses before about the grading practices of various instructors.

In all of these situations, the purpose of your sampling is to help you make a better informed decision. The objective of sampling is to support the most precise conclusion about a variable of interest in the entire population (e.g., the doneness of all of the spaghetti in the pot) based upon results obtained in a sample of the population (e.g., the doneness of one or two pieces). We are exposed to the power of sampling every November in election years. Turning on the television set or radio as early as 7 P.M., when many of the polling places are still open, and hearing who the "projected" winner is, seems, to many of us, quite amazing. Sampling is not magic, however.

Sampling involves the consideration of two basic issues, selection and estimation:

1. The selection of items from a population so that the items selected are representative of the population.
2. The estimation of a characteristic of interest (that is, a variable) in a population, based upon what is observed in the sample.

THE SAMPLING PROCESS

You sample when you want to measure a characteristic of some target population, but it is impractical and unrealistic to collect information on every member of the population. The sampling process begins with a precise definition of the target population and ends with computing a sample-based estimate of the characteristic of the population that you wish to measure.

To provide an accurate estimate of the population characteristic of interest involves a number of decisions and activities. Exhibit 9–1 lists the various steps involved in designing a sampling plan. Each of these steps will be discussed in more detail.

Define the Population

A **population** (also called the **universe**) is that set of people, products, firms, markets, and so on, that is of interest to the researcher. It is the responsibility of the researcher or manager to provide a precise definition of the population of interest. To be precise, a population must be defined in terms of *elements, units,* and *time.* The population for a new "tuna-in-a-jar" concept test, for example, was defined as females between the ages of 18 and 54 who purchased at least one 6.5-ounce can of tuna in the past 30 days and shopped in supermarkets during the period September 15–30.

POPULATION/UNIVERSE
Set of people, products, firms, markets, etc., that contains the information that is of interest to the researcher.

Elements:	Females between the ages of 18 and 54 who purchased at least one 6.5-ounce can of tuna in the past 30 days and shopped in
Units:	Supermarkets
Time:	During the period September 15–30

Once the population of interest has been defined, it is commonly referred to as the *target population.* The elements that make up that population are called **sampling units.** In the new tuna-in-a-jar concept test study, supermarkets are designated as the sampling units. That is, although females between the ages of 18 and 54 who purchased a 6.5-ounce can of tuna in the past 30 days might be sampled directly, it is easier to select supermarkets, the place at which canned tuna is purchased, as the sampling unit

SAMPLING UNITS
Elements making up the population.

EXHIBIT 9—1

The Sampling Process

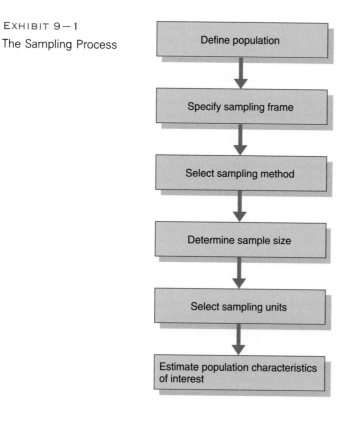

and interview all females who qualify as elements of the population. In some situations the population element and sampling unit will be the same; in others they will be different.

Let's consider another illustration. Suppose the brand manager of a new safety door lock system is interested in determining the awareness of and attitudes toward the locking system. The target population is single women between the ages of 25 and 54 who rent apartments in high-rise apartment buildings in Dallas, Texas, as of January 1992.

Elements:	Single women between the ages of 25 and 54 who rent apartments in
Units:	High-rise apartment buildings in Dallas, Texas, as of
Time:	January 1992

It is the responsibility of the marketing research supplier to provide explicit instructions to the field service concerning the qualifications of the target population. This is accomplished by providing a list of *screening* questions that are used to qualify respondents. A set of screening questions for a burger image study is provided in Exhibit 9–2. To be eligible to be included in this study, an individual must be between the ages of 18 and 34 (see Question B) and must have eaten a hamburger at a fast food chain in the past month (see Question C).

EXHIBIT 9—2
Screening Questions

APPROACH MALE OR FEMALE ADULTS WHO APPEAR TO BE BETWEEN 18 AND 34 YEARS OF AGE. CHECK INTERVIEWER INSTRUCTIONS FOR SEX QUOTAS.

Hello, I'm _____ from _____, a marketing research firm. We are conducting a study in this area and would like to include your opinions.

IF RESPONDENT'S ANSWER TO ANY QUESTION IS MARKED, "TERMINATE", CIRCLE THE NEXT AVAILABLE NUMBER IN THE TERMINATION BOX FOR THAT ANSWER. THEN, ERASE AND RE-USE SCREENER. NEVER ERASE CIRCLED TERMINATION BOX NUMBERS!

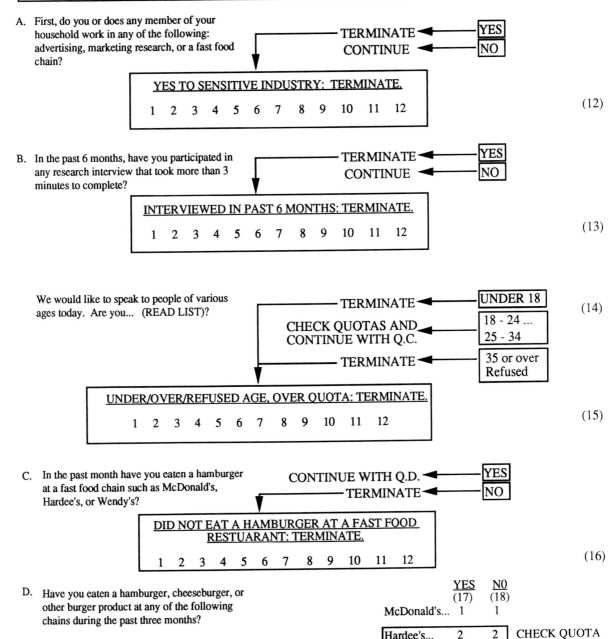

A. First, do you or does any member of your household work in any of the following: advertising, marketing research, or a fast food chain?

TERMINATE ← YES
CONTINUE ← NO

YES TO SENSITIVE INDUSTRY: TERMINATE.
1 2 3 4 5 6 7 8 9 10 11 12

(12)

B. In the past 6 months, have you participated in any research interview that took more than 3 minutes to complete?

TERMINATE ← YES
CONTINUE ← NO

INTERVIEWED IN PAST 6 MONTHS: TERMINATE.
1 2 3 4 5 6 7 8 9 10 11 12

(13)

We would like to speak to people of various ages today. Are you... (READ LIST)?

TERMINATE ← UNDER 18   (14)
CHECK QUOTAS AND CONTINUE WITH Q.C. ← 18 - 24 ... / 25 - 34
TERMINATE ← 35 or over / Refused

UNDER/OVER/REFUSED AGE, OVER QUOTA: TERMINATE.
1 2 3 4 5 6 7 8 9 10 11 12

(15)

C. In the past month have you eaten a hamburger at a fast food chain such as McDonald's, Hardee's, or Wendy's?

CONTINUE WITH Q.D. ← YES
TERMINATE ← NO

DID NOT EAT A HAMBURGER AT A FAST FOOD RESTUARANT: TERMINATE.
1 2 3 4 5 6 7 8 9 10 11 12

(16)

D. Have you eaten a hamburger, cheeseburger, or other burger product at any of the following chains during the past three months?

	YES (17)	NO (18)	
McDonald's...	1	1	
Hardee's...	2	2	CHECK QUOTA
Wendy's...	3	3	
Burger King...	4	4	

Screening questions explicitly define who should be included in the sample and who should be excluded. Most marketing research surveys exclude certain individuals for a variety of reasons. For example, in the burger image study, the first question on the questionnaire asks whether the individual or any household member works in advertising, marketing research, or for a fast food chain. Typically, this is the first question asked, and the interview is terminated at this point if the individual indicates that he or she or someone else in their household works in one of these industries, or in the product or service area dealt with in the survey. These individuals are excluded for so-called security reasons—they may be competitors or work for competitors, and the researchers would not want to alert them to what the study is about.

Specify the Sampling Frame

SAMPLING FRAME

A list or set of directions that identifies the target population.

The sampling frame is the vehicle the researcher uses to assemble eligible sampling units. Put simply, a **sampling frame** is a list of the sampling units. A sampling frame can be a list of telephone numbers as in a telephone survey, a list of names and addresses as in a mail survey, or any other type of list that allows the researcher to identify eligible sampling units. Lists typically are organized by geographic area; for example, by state, city, and county. If no list or organized breakdown of the target population exists, then location sampling (as in mall-intercept surveys) or random-digit dialing (as in telephone surveys) is probably the only alternative. Exhibit 9–3 describes how telephone numbers can be randomly generated using a variety of approaches.

Lists of sampling units are available from a variety of sources. Local community utility companies have a fairly complete list of households. Area telephone branches frequently cooperate and give out a list of working exchanges. Magazine publishers, organizations, credit card companies, and professional associations are well-known sources of lists. Many companies are in the business of selling lists. Exhibit 9–4 shows examples of the types of mailing lists that can be purchased. Though costs vary, a list can usually be purchased for between $50 and $120 per 1,000 names.

A list rarely matches the target population exactly. A list of residents of a given community, for example, usually does not include new arrivals or households living in dwellings built since the list was created. In addition, lists often contain duplicate entries—households with multiple telephone numbers, for example. To gain a better representation of the target population, lists are often combined. This can also lead to duplicate entries, for example, households whose names and addresses appear on more than one list. Thus a list can overrepresent or underrepresent a target population.

OPERATIONAL POPULATION

The sampling frame that is used.

The sampling frame defines what is called the **operational population.** When a sampling frame contains the sampling units of interest plus additional sampling units, then it suffers from **overregistration.** For example, assume the target population is all consumers taking at least five airline trips who exercise the automatic flight insurance option offered by a major credit card company. To conduct the survey you buy a mailing list from

OVERREGISTRATION

Condition that occurs when a sampling frame consists of sampling units in the target population plus additional units as well.

EXHIBIT 9—3

Random-Digit Dialing Procedures

The only solution to the problem of unlisted telephone numbers is to generate phone numbers by some random process. This practice, referred to as *random-digit dialing* (RDD), is simple in theory—phone numbers are generated at random. However, practical considerations complicate the picture greatly. The first and foremost of these is the relatively small proportion of working numbers among all possible 10-digit telephone numbers. Only about 1 in 170 of all possible telephone numbers (9,999,999,999 possible) are actually in use (60,000,000 residential numbers). The proportion of working residential numbers in RDD samples can be increased dramatically by selecting from only the 103 working area codes (first three digits). This approach yields approximately 1 working residential number for every 17 randomly generated. From a cost standpoint this rate is still too low, entailing too many unproductive dialings. The question at this point is, what type of RDD system will simultaneously cut the proportion of unproductive dialings while including a proportionate number of unlisted phone homes in the sample? There are three alternative approaches that meet these two objectives to varying degrees: the four-digit approach, three-digit approach, and approaches built around the use of a telephone book.

Four-Digit Approach

Taking the four-digit approach the researcher must, in addition to restricting the sample to the 103 working area codes, select numbers only from working central offices or exchanges. The last four digits of the number are generated via some process that approaches randomness. There are approximately 30,000 working exchanges in the continental United States or about 300 million possible numbers. This approach will, therefore, yield approximately one working number for every five generated randomly. Problems with this approach relate to the fact that all exchanges have an equal probability of being selected while some have a high proportion of all possible numbers in service and others have only a small proportion in service.

Three-Digit Approach

The next logical progression in RDD technology is the three-digit approach. The three-digit method increases the proportion of working numbers to better than one in three. This is possible because the phone company does not assign numbers from a particular exchange at random but from within working banks of 1,000 numbers. Consulting the section of a criss-cross directory where phone numbers are listed numerically will show that within a particular exchange certain sequences of 1,000 numbers (000–999) are totally unused while other groups of 1,000 are, for example, 70 percent in use. Employing the three-digit option, the user must specify area codes, exchanges, and "working banks" (fourth digit) of numbers within exchanges. Working banks may be identified from a criss-cross directory or selected via a probability sample from the telephone book. A bank with no working listed numbers has no chance of being selected, while a bank with 60 percent of its numbers listed has twice as much chance of being selected as one with only 30 percent listed. The final step of the three-digit approach is to generate the last three digits of each working area code/exchange/bank by means of some random process.

The three-digit method is more efficient in eliminating nonworking numbers, but increases bias due to missing (from the directory) new working banks that have been activated. The four-digit method is safer from the standpoint of avoiding bias, but more expensive due to the greater number of calls that must be made. It is suggested that the three-digit method is most appropriate when the directory or directories for the area of interest are relatively current or when there has been little growth in the area since the publication of the most recent directory. In other cases the four-digit method should be given serious consideration.

Using Telephone Books

RDD samples can also be generated from the telephone book. In general, this is accomplished by selecting numbers at random from the book and adding a random number as the sixth or seventh digits. Somewhere between one in two and one in three of the numbers generated will be working residential numbers. This is a viable approach because all exchanges and banks are proportionately represented in the book. Generally, the phone book is recommended as an RDD sample source only in those cases where the appropriate computer hardware and software are not available. There are two major reasons for making this recommendation. First, the construction of a sample by this approach is fairly time consuming and expensive whether it is done for or by the interviewers. Second, if the interviewers are given directions and left to generate the numbers themselves, the researcher loses all control over the validity of the sample.

Computer programs can incorporate three- or four-digit approaches and generate RDD samples at very low cost. In addition, the printout can be set up to capture additional data and to help the researcher control field costs and proper execution of the sampling plan.

Source: Roger Gates and Bob Brobst, "RANDIAL: A Program for Generating Random Telephone Numbers," *Journal of Marketing Research* 14 (May 1977), p. 240.

EXHIBIT 9—4

Example of a Mailing List

QUANTITY		PRICE
3,400	Moose Lodges	$40/M
3,400	Mortgage Banking Companies	$40/M
11,350	Mortgage Banking Executives	$40/M
19,300	Mortgage Companies	$40/M
21,900	Morticians	$40/M
41,000	Motels	$40/M
57,000	Motels & Hotels	$40/M
545	Motel & Hotel Chains	$75
3,900	Motion Picture Producers	$40/M
12,100	Motion Picture Theaters	$40/M
8,550	Motorcycle Dealers	$40/M
3,500,000	Motorcycle Owners	Inquire
12,000	Moving & Storage Companies	$40/M
9,600	Muffler Shops	$40/M
38,200	Municipal Government Officials	$40/M
5,770	Museums	$40/M
790	Museums, Art	$75
18,600	Museum Officials	$40/M
2,400	Music Department Chairmen, Colleges	$60/M
22,000	Music Professors, College	$60/M
15,000	Music Teachers, High School	$45/M
3,950	Music Instruction, Private	$40/M
7,600	Musical Instrument Dealers	$40/M
21,000	Music, Records, Tapes, Musical Instruments Dealers	$40/M
65,000	Musicians (Select Instrument)	$50/M
425	Mutual Funds	$75
1,750	Mutual Fund Executives	$75
465	Mutual Savings Banks HQ	$75

N

QUANTITY		PRICE
15,700	Nail Salons	$40/M
18,000	National Advertisers	$40/M
69,000	National Advertisers Executives	$40/M
340	National Parks	$75
2,100	Naturalists	$40/M
5,900	Naval Engineers	$40/M
235,000	Navy Officers, Retired & Reserved	Inquire
3,950	Narcotics & Drug Abuse Centers	$40/M
40,630	Navigators (Air), Flight Engineers	$40/M
10,900	Needlework & Yarn Shops	$40/M
16,350	Neon Sign Dealers	$40/M
2,500	Neurologists	$40/M
5,260	Neuroscientists	$40/M
160	News Features Syndicates	$75
2,400	Newsdealers & Newsstands	$40/M
3,175	Newsdealers, Wholesalers & Distributors	$40/M
11,200	Newsletter Publishers	$40/M
22,130	Newspaper Executives	$40/M
3,500	Newspapers, College	$40/M
1,710	Newspapers, Daily	$75
520	Newspapers, Daily with circulation of 25,000 or more	$75
1,040	Newspapers, Daily with circulation of 10,000 or more	$75
115	Newspapers, Daily, Canadian	$75
6,900	Newspapers, Weekly	$40/M

QUANTITY		PRICE
675	Newspapers, Weekly, with circulation of 10,000 or more	$75
9,200	Night Clubs, Discos	$40/M
220,000	Non-Profit Tax Exempt Organizations	$40/M
8,600	Notaries, Public	$40/M
8,275	Novelties (Advertising) Jobbers	$40/M
1,900	Novelty & Souvenir Shops	$40/M
22,500	Nuclear Industry Executives	$40/M
1,200	Nuclear Medicine Specialists	$75
1,900	Nuclear Physicists	$40/M
150	Nudist Clubs	$75
13,750	Nurseries & Greenhouses	$40/M
53,000	Nursery Schools & Kindergartens	$40/M
8,000	Nurses, Directors of	$55/M
205,000	Nurses, Hospital	Inquire
4,600	Nurses, Private Duty	$55/M
2,000,000	Nurses, Registered	Inquire
9,400	Nurses, Registries	$40/M
21,200	Nursing Homes	$40/M
12,800	Nursing Homes, 50 beds or more	$40/M
6,700	Nursing Homes, 100 beds or more	$40/M
14,800	Nursing Homes, Private	$40/M
1,300	Nursing Schools	$75
1,765	Nutritionists	$75

O

QUANTITY		PRICE
23,350	Obstetricians & Gynecologists	$40/M
30,000	Occupational Therapists	Inquire
15,500	Oceanographers	$40/M
3,400	Odd Fellows Lodges	$40/M
5,500	Office Building Management Companies	$40/M
31,300	Office & Building Cleaners	$40/M
14,200	Office Equipment & Supplies Dealers	$40/M
9,300	Office Machine Dealers	$40/M
1,200	Office Machine Manufacturers	$75
10,050	Office (Commercial) Stationers	$40/M
389	Office Parks	$75
2,000,000	Office Workers, Home Address	Inquire
115,000	Offices, Government, All Levels	Inquire
19,000	Oil Burner & Furnace Dealers & Distributors	$40/M
17,400	Oil (Fuel) Dealers	$40/M
52,000	Oil Industry Executives	$40/M
15,500	Oil (Petroleum) Bulk Stations	$40/M
18,000	Oil (Petroleum) Wholesalers	$40/M
8,100	Oil (Petroleum) Producers & Refiners	$40/M
935	Oil Pipeline Companies	$75
3,650	Oilwell Drilling Contractors	$40/M
6,200	Oilwell Supply Companies	$40/M
735	Opera Companies	$75
300,000	Opinion Leaders	$40/M
310,000	Opportunity Seekers (Male/Female)	$40/M
12,200	Ophthalmologists	$40/M
2,100	Optical Equipment & Supplies, Wholesale	$40/M
15,300	Opticians	$40/M
23,200	Optometrists	$40/M
4,400	Oral Surgeons	$40/M

Source: Alvin B. Zeller, Inc., 37 East 28th Street, New York, NY 10016.

one of the major credit card companies. This list is the sampling frame, and it most likely suffers from overregistration because it will include consumers who (1) do not travel five times a year and/or (2) do not use the automatic flight insurance.

If, on the other hand, the sampling frame does not include all of the sampling units, then it suffers from **underregistration.** Use of a telephone book as a sampling frame for a telephone survey is an example of underregistration; all people who have unlisted numbers are omitted. As we saw in Chapter 7, unlisted numbers vary by region and pose a formidable problem in using telephone directories. The difference between the operational population and the target population is called the **sampling gap.** In selecting a sampling frame, the objective is to minimize the sampling gap—the larger the sampling gap, the greater is the chance for misleading and inaccurate results.

> **UNDERREGISTRATION**
> Condition that occurs when a sampling frame contains fewer sampling units than the target population.

> **SAMPLING GAP**
> Difference between the operational population and the target population.

Select a Sampling Method

An important issue in designing the sampling plan concerns the method of drawing the sample. There are two general sample categories: *probability samples* and *nonprobability samples.* Exhibit 9–5 presents a taxonomy of the various types of sampling designs that we will consider.

The choice between using a probability or a nonprobability sampling design depends on the objectives of the study. Generally speaking, if the study calls for projectable totals, (that is, survey results need to be extrapolated to the entire population with a prespecified margin of error), then probability sampling designs will be needed.

Probability sampling designs. In a **probability sampling design,** each sampling unit has a known probability of being selected. The ability of a sample to estimate population characteristics depends on how representative the sample is with respect to the population of interest. With probability samples the researcher can determine the survey's **margin of error.** The **margin of error** in a survey refers to how confident the researcher is that if all of the target population were surveyed, the findings for the total population would differ from the findings based on the sample by no more than a specified number of percentage points in either direction. In opinion polling, for example, researchers often make the following type of claim:

> **PROBABILITY SAMPLING DESIGNS**
> Sampling procedures for which each sampling unit has a known probability of being selected.

> **MARGIN OF ERROR**
> Reflects how confident the researcher is that if all of the target population were surveyed, the findings for the total population would differ from the findings based on the sample by no more than a specified number of percentage points in either direction.

> Chances are 19 of 20 that if all registered voters in the United States had been surveyed using the same questionnaire, the finding would differ from these poll results by no more than 2.6 percentage points in either direction.

The margin of error establishes a region in which we expect the population value to lie. This region is in more formal terms called a **confidence interval.** Thus, instead of relying solely on a single estimated value (e.g., the percentage of people agreeing with the statement "The U.S. Congress is ineffective," is 63%), we can establish an interval in which the true population value is thought to lie. Confidence intervals will be discussed in greater detail.

> **CONFIDENCE INTERVAL**
> A range or interval established by the sample results in which the true population value is thought to lie.

EXHIBIT 9—5

Taxonomy of Sampling Designs

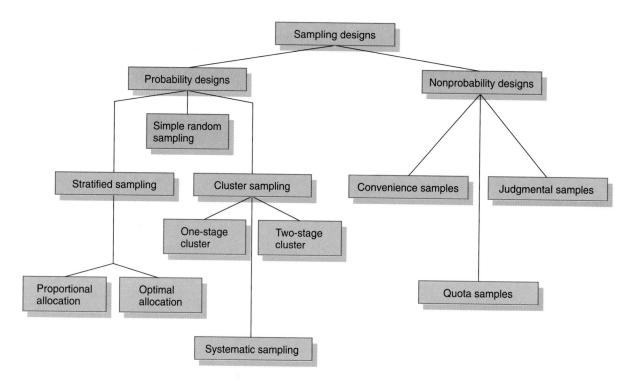

Probability sampling procedures, whatever the design, share two fundamental features:

1. Before the sampling takes place, it is possible to specify every potential sample of a given size that could be drawn from the population and the corresponding probability of selecting each sample.
2. Every sampling unit has a known, nonzero chance of being selected.

The importance of these two characteristics cannot be overstated. It is these two fundamental characteristics of probability designs that allow pollsters to predict voting behavior and accurately measure consumer opinions. And because of these characteristics, the sampling distribution of the estimate can be determined and confidence intervals constructed.

Simple random sampling.   The simplest method of drawing a probability sample is to do it randomly. The method is equivalent to a lottery system in which names are placed in an urn and drawn out randomly. **Simple random sampling** (SRS) guarantees that every sample of a given size, as well as every individual in the target population, has an equal chance of being selected.

Procedure.   Simple random sampling involves the following steps:

1. Number each sampling unit in the sampling frame from 1 to *N*.

SIMPLE RANDOM
SAMPLING

Design guaranteeing that every sample of a given size as well as every individual in the target population has an equal chance of being selected.

2. Select a sample of *n* units from the sampling frame using a table of random numbers and measure each sampling unit on the variable of interest.

3. Compute a confidence interval estimate for the variable of interest.

To draw a simple random sample, a sampling frame will be needed. Population elements (or sampling units) in the list are selected randomly with use of tables of random numbers. A table of random numbers is simply what the name implies; it is a table containing a list of numbers, where the numbers have been generated at random. A random-number table is presented in Appendix I at the end of the book. Many interviewing facilities have the capability of generating random numbers by computer. This is extremely useful in telephone surveys using the method of random-digit dialing or other methods that involve randomly generating some portion of the seven-digit number to be dialed (see Exhibit 9–3).

Uses.   Simple random samples have many desirable features. They are easily understood and used, and they allow one to project sample results to the entire target population. Nevertheless, simple random samples are, with the exception of random-digit dialing telephone surveys, rarely used in commercial marketing research studies. There are a number of reasons for this.

First, simple random sampling may be infeasible—it requires that all elements in the population be identified and labeled (numbered) prior to sampling. Prior identification is often impossible. Second, simple random sampling can be expensive because in order to adequately represent a population, large samples may be needed, and it can result in samples spread out over a large geographical area, making data collection time-consuming and costly. This occurs because under simple random sampling each element in the population has an equal chance of being included in the sample. Consider drawing a simple random sample of various brand-user groups in a specific target population. Under simple random sampling the expected representation of a brand-user group is its population proportion, or market share. To illustrate, suppose a brand has a 1 percent market share. A 1 percent share means that we can expect to find only one brand user for every 100 category users interviewed. Thus, if we require, say, 100 brand users, we would need to interview, in principle, 10,000 category users.

Finally, simple random sampling does not guarantee that the sample drawn will be representative of the target population—it may not include specific subgroups of the population. A simple random sample of past-30-day facial-moisturizer users, for example, could result in a sample in which specific brands of the category are underrepresented or overrepresented in relation to their actual market shares, leading to distorted results. Although simple random samples will represent a population well on average, a given sample (and particularly a small one) may not represent the target population well at all. For this reason, some sampling procedures attempt to guarantee that the correct proportion of subpopulation elements will find their way into the ultimate sample.

Stratified random sampling.   **Stratified random sampling** involves subdividing the population into a number of groups, called *strata*, the Latin plural for *stratum*. Stratified sampling involves the following procedures:

STRATIFIED SAMPLING
Design that involves partitioning the entire population of elements into subpopulations, called strata, and then selecting elements separately from each subpopulation.

(1) a sample is drawn from each group (*stratum*); (2) a mean or proportion is calculated for each stratum; and (3) the individual stratum means or proportions are then combined to obtain an estimate of the population mean or the population proportion.

The purpose of dividing the population into strata is to take advantage of the fact that sampling units belonging to the same stratum should be homogeneous, or more similar to each other than to sampling units belonging to different strata. If sampling units belonging to the same stratum are homogeneous with respect to what is being measured, then the within-stratum variances should be small, compared to those of the population as a whole. In other words, proper representation across the strata results in more efficient sampling in the sense that when the individual stratum means and variances are combined and confidence intervals constructed, the range of the confidence interval will be smaller than the confidence interval computed from a sample taken from the entire population. Put simply, stratified random samples in principle can result in more precise estimates than simple random sampling.

Procedure.   The steps for estimating a population characteristic from a stratified random sample are

1. Decide on a stratification variable and how many strata to use.
2. Obtain a sampling frame for the population that allows all sampling units in the population to be placed into one, and only one, stratum.
3. Decide how many sampling units are to be selected from each stratum; that is, what percentage of the overall sample size will come from each stratum.
4. Draw a probabilistic sample (e.g., a simple random sample, or SRS) from each stratum based on the sample size determined in step 3.
5. For each stratum compute an estimate of the mean or proportion and its appropriate standard deviation.
6. Based on the information obtained from each stratum, prepare a confidence interval estimate for the overall population.

There are two common methods for determining the number of sampling units to select from each of the available strata. These methods are called *proportional allocation* and *optimal allocation*.

1. *Proportional allocation.* The rationale underlying **proportional allocation** is that the size of each stratum should dictate the number of sampling units selected. Larger strata should be sampled more heavily. Thus, the total sample to be selected is "allocated" across the strata in direct proportion to the size of each stratum compared to the overall population.

2. *Optimal allocation.* The rationale underlying **optimal allocation** is that the within-stratum variability as well as the size of the stratum should dictate how many sampling units to select. Specifically, if the within-stratum variance is large, then sampling units making up this stratum are more heterogeneous. If a stratum has considerable vari-

PROPORTIONAL ALLOCATION

Sampling design guaranteeing that stratified random sampling will be at least as efficient as SRS. The number of elements selected from a stratum is directly proportional to the size of the stratum.

OPTIMAL ALLOCATION

Double weighting scheme where the number of sample elements taken from a given stratum is proportional to the relative size of the stratum and the standard deviation of the distribution of the characteristic under consideration among all elements in the stratum.

ance, this means that, all else the same, you will have to select more sampling units in order to estimate the mean or proportion accurately than would be the case for a stratum where the sampling units are nearly identical.

To use optimal allocation, you need to know not only the strata sizes but also the within-stratum variability. Of course, in practical applications the researcher will not have knowledge of the population within-stratum variances, so some estimate has to be used. Unfortunately, not much can be said concerning how to best go about doing this. One approach is to rely on estimates of variance within each stratum obtained from previous studies; however, in many applications there is no such information available. Put simply, to use the optimal allocation method, the researcher must make some intelligent guess about the variability within each stratum.

Uses.   Stratified random sampling is a popular sampling procedure because it combines the conceptual simplicity of simple random sampling with potentially significant gains in precision. An increasing trend today is the use of stratified sampling designs in telephone interviewing. Survey Sampling, Inc., a supplier specializing in survey sampling methods, combines stratified sampling with systematic sample selection to gain efficiency for nondirectory telephone interviewing. (See Box 9–1.)

The increased precision (or smaller sampling error) afforded by stratified random sampling is related directly to the ability to divide the population into homogeneous strata. The characteristic used to form the strata (i.e., on what basis the population is divided into groups) is called the *stratification variable,* and this variable must bear some relationship to the variable being measured.

For example, assume you are interested in estimating the yearly expenditures on windshield de-icer for all U.S. households (HHs). It is reasonable to suspect that HH expenditures on windshield de-icer vary dramatically by region; people living in Minnesota use more de-icer than people living in Louisiana. And if the density of U.S. HH population is less in those parts of the country where weather conditions are harsh, a simple random sample of U.S. HHs without regard to region might well yield an unrepresentative sample with respect to yearly expenditures on windshield de-icer. In this case, a reasonable stratification variable to use would be geographical region, and you could divide the country into strata based on, for example, average temperature. The point here is that HHs in the same part of the country are probably more similar to each other with respect to their expenditures on windshield de-icer than they are to HHs in other parts of the country, especially areas where the average temperatures are markedly different. Using geographic region as a stratification variable can reduce sampling fluctuations.

Cluster sampling.   In the sampling designs discussed so far, each sampling unit is selected separately. In **cluster sampling** the sampling units are selected in groups. For example, rather than sampling each household

CLUSTER SAMPLING
Design whereby a sample of clusters is first selected and then a decision on which sampling units to include in the sample is made.

BOX 9—1

—

FROM THE
USER'S
PERSPECTIVE

—

DESCRIPTION OF SAMPLING PROCEDURE FOR TELEPHONE INTERVIEWING

Stratification to counties

To equalize the probability of telephone household selection from anywhere in the area sampled, samples are first systematically stratified to all counties in proportion to each county's share of telephone households in the survey area. After a geographical area has been defined as a combination of counties, the sum of estimated telephone households is calculated and divided by the desired sample size to produce a sampling interval:

Total estimated telephone households ÷ Desired sample size = Interval
                    750,000   ÷   6,000   =   125

A random number is drawn between 0 and the interval (125) to establish a starting point. Assuming the starting point is 86, then the 86th, 211th, 336th, 461st, . . ., records would be selected for the sample, each time stepping through the database by a factor of 125. This is a systematic random sample because the sample is selected in a systematic "*n*th" fashion from a random starting point. Any county whose population of estimated telephone households equals or exceeds the sampling interval is automatically included in the sample, while smaller counties are included with a probability proportionate to their size.

Using our example, where the sample size is 6,000, let us also assume that the geographical area selected covers three counties. The sampling interval allows the proportionate distribution of the sample over three counties.

Selection of numbers within counties

For each county included in the sample, one (or more) unique telephone number is selected by systematic sampling from among all working blocks of numbers in all telephone exchanges assigned to the county. A working block is defined as 100 contiguous numbers that contain three or more residential telephone listings:

the phone number 266/7558

exchange/block

In this example, for the exchange 266, the entire block comprises the numbers 7500 to 7599. Exchanges are assigned to a single county on the basis of where listed residents live. For those overlapping county lines, the exchanges are assigned to the county with the highest number of listed residents.

Selection among exchanges

Once the sample has been allocated, a second sampling interval is calculated for each county by dividing the number of listed-telephone households for the county by the portion of the sample allocated to that county. Each exchange and each working block within an exchange are weighted by their share of listed-telephone households. For example, assuming a desired sample size of 6,000 and assuming that 28 percent of the sample is to be drawn from a certain county, if the total number of listed-telephone households in the database for this county is 159,600, that number is divided by 1,680, which gives us an interval of 95.

Next, from a random start between 1 and 95, the exchanges and working blocks that fall within the interval are sampled on a systematic basis. Next, two more digits are randomly chosen from the range 00–99 and added to each of the selected blocks. The result is a complete number made up of the exchange, the block, and the two random digits (for example, 266 + 75 + 59).

Source: Survey Sampling, Inc. Used with permission.

separately, a cluster sampling design might call for city blocks to be selected first, and then sampling each household on each selected block.

Procedure.   Cluster sampling procedures can be described broadly by three features:

1. The entire population of sampling units is divided according to some classification variable or natural grouping into mutually exclusive and exhaustive subsets, called clusters.
2. Clusters are then selected based on a specified probability design such as simple random sampling.
3. Elements are either probabilistically drawn from each selected cluster, or, for each selected cluster, all the elements are included in the sample.

There are many different types of cluster sampling designs. At the most general level, cluster sampling can involve either a *single stage* or *multiple stages*. By a *stage* we mean simply a step in the sampling process. For example, if stores that participate in a test-market study are the clusters, and calendar weeks are the sampling units, there could be two steps involved in selecting the sample upon which to base an estimate of volume sold for the test brand under study. The first step might involve selecting a sample of stores, and the second step could be selecting a sample of calendar weeks for each of the stores selected at the first step.

A single-stage cluster sample entails one step because once the sample of clusters is selected, every sampling unit within each of the selected clusters is included in the sample. In the test-market study, for example, all of the sales data for the test brand from each selected store would be included in the sample. If the clusters are chosen by simple random sampling, and within each cluster all sampling units are selected, we refer to this design as **simple one-stage cluster sampling.**

Multistage cluster sampling designs entail two or more steps. For example, in a telephone survey we might first take a sample of states. Second, we might take a sample of counties within each sample cluster (states). Third, we might take a sample of working telephone exchanges within each of the counties selected in the second stage. And finally, we might take every telephone number within each working exchange selected in the third stage. Note that in multistage cluster sampling more than one sampling frame is likely to be used in drawing the sample. After each stage, however, the sampling frame for the next stage involves only those clusters chosen at the preceding stage.

Uses.   There are two primary advantages of cluster sampling: feasibility and economy. For these reasons, cluster sampling is frequently used in practice, especially in area sampling, that is, surveys covering geographical areas. The practical feasibility of cluster sampling comes about because in many settings the only sampling frame readily available for the target population is one that lists clusters. Lists of geographical regions, blocks, telephone exchanges, and the like can usually be easily compiled, and the researcher can thus avoid compiling a list of all individual elements for the

SIMPLE ONE-STAGE CLUSTER SAMPLING

One-step design in which first stage clusters are selected by SRS, and within each selected cluster all sampling units are chosen.

MULTISTAGE CLUSTER SAMPLING

A cluster sampling design involving two (or more) steps.

Using a city block map to draw a sample

target population, a process almost never feasible in terms of time and resources for populations of any reasonable size.

Cluster sampling is generally the most cost-effective means of sampling. Cost efficiencies come about because of the relative ease with which sampling frames can be assembled and the reduced costs associated with traveling. Consider in-home personal surveys, for example. If a geographical area such as a census tract defines the clusters, then once the sample of census tract clusters is selected and households are selected from within the sample census tract, the cost of traveling from household to household will usually be low. Cost economies arise from selecting a relatively small number of census tract clusters and sampling many households from the selected census tracts, as opposed to taking a simple random sample of households spread across many census tracts. Traveling costs for visiting households that are in different census tracts are usually higher than the traveling costs for visiting households in the same census tract.

Although practical and economical, cluster sampling is not without disadvantages. First, and perhaps most serious, for a given sample size, the estimates obtained from cluster sampling designs are frequently not as precise as those obtained with other sampling designs. The reliability of cluster samples may be poor, depending on the extent to which sampling units within a cluster are homogeneous. Sampling from few different clusters in order to minimize traveling costs can lead to unrepresentative samples if the sampling units selected from a given cluster are very homogeneous. If clusters are homogeneous, then, to obtain a good estimate of the characteristic of interest, many clusters will have to be selected. Of course, this procedure negates the cost efficiencies of using a clustering design. In practice, clusters do tend to be fairly homogeneous. Households who live on the same block, for example, are frequently similar with respect to demographic and socioeconomic factors and often exhibit similar shopping behavior. Thus, in cluster sampling the within-cluster sampling units should be somewhat heterogeneous with respect to the variable of interest.

The second principal disadvantage of cluster sampling is its complexity. The most complex cluster designs occur when each cluster in the population does not have the same number of sampling units. The complexity of cluster designs leads to several difficulties. The procedure for drawing the sample becomes more difficult and estimation formulas become much more involved. If the first-stage clusters are selected randomly, however, then estimation formulas are greatly simplified, and closely resemble those used with simple random sampling.

Nonprobability sampling designs. All **nonprobability sampling designs** share a common characteristic: There is no way of determining exactly what the chance is of selecting any particular element in the sample. Consequently, estimates are not statistically projectable to the entire population, and the survey's margin of error cannot be determined. This is not to say that nonprobability samples are necessarily inaccurate and always inferior to probability samples. Nonprobability samples can be good (representative) or bad (unrepresentative), depending on the approach and controls used in selecting the sample. Certain nonprobability designs produce what are called *purposive samples* because certain "important" segments of the target population are intentionally overrepresented in the sample. Some of the major nonprobability sampling approaches are *convenience sampling, judgmental samples,* and *quota samples.*

1. *Convenience samples.* **Convenience samples** involve selecting sampling units on the basis of where and when the study is being conducted. For this reason convenience samples are also referred to as *accidental samples,* since sampling units are selected by "accident." Convenience samples provide very little or no control over who is included in the sample. If respondent participation is voluntary or if the interviewer, as opposed to the researcher, selects sampling units, then convenience samples are produced. For example, 100 women might be intercepted in a shopping mall and interviewed without any directions as to who should be intercepted. There is no way to assess the representativeness of the sample. Mail surveys often produce convenience samples. Because of the self-selection and voluntary participation that accompany this data-collection method, the issue of nonresponse is extremely important.

2. *Judgmental samples.* **Judgmental samples** involve selecting certain respondents for participation in the study, presumably because they are representative of the population of interest and/or meet the specific needs of the research study.

Judgmental samples are frequently used in commercial marketing research studies. To be included in a concept testing study, for example, respondents are typically required to be category users, that is, to have used the product within, say, the last 30 days. The presumption here is that category users define the relevant target population.

Test markets exemplify judgmental samples; that is, the assumption in such studies is that the specific community, neighborhood, or metropolitan area is representative of the entire market. Another example is scanner databases, since the presumption is that the cities included have been

NONPROBABILITY SAMPLES
Form of sampling where there is no way of determining exactly what the chance is of selecting any particular element or sampling unit into the sample.

CONVENIENCE SAMPLING
Sampling method in which respondent participation is voluntary or which leaves the selection of sampling units primarily up to the interviewer.

JUDGMENTAL SAMPLING
Sampling method in which respondents are selected because it is expected that they are representative of the population of interest and/or meet the specific needs of the research study.

selected because they are representative of the entire U.S. population. There is some debate about whether the judgmentally selected samples of cities represent only those specific cities or the entire country.

Another special kind of judgmental sampling is called the *snowball design.* **Snowball designs** involve first locating respondents who have the necessary qualifications to be included in the sample and then using these respondents as informants to identify still others with the desired qualifications—that is, who belong to the target population. Snowball designs are typically used when it is necessary to reach a small, specialized target population.

3. *Quota samples.* **Quota samples** involve selecting specific numbers of respondents who have certain characteristics, such as gender or specific product use, known or presumed to affect the subject of the research study. In the burger image study previously introduced (see Exhibit 9–2), quotas are established for age (Question B) and for Hardee's customers (Question D). The quota for Hardee's customers was established to ensure that a sufficient number of Hardee's customers would be included in the sample.

Quota samples are designed to ensure that the proportion of the sample elements with a certain characteristic is approximately the same as the proportion with this characteristic in the population of interest. In other words, quota samples are used to ensure that the sample is representative of the entire population. Commercial marketing research studies commonly set quotas on interviews based on age, gender, and income. In many instances, the quotas are based on *volume contribution.* For example, if a particular age category represents 30 percent of a company's business, then this age category should make up 30 percent of the sample.

Whether quota samples actually produce representative samples can be hard to assess.[1] If researchers overlook an important characteristic that indeed affects the subject of the research study, then the quota samples will not be representative. Moreover, because quota samples are frequently used in mall intercept surveys, there is potential for overrepresenting the kinds of people who frequent high-traffic shopping malls.

Determine Sample Size

One of the first questions asked is how large the sample should be. The responsibility of the researcher is to decide exactly how many sampling units are to be drawn from the population. A number of factors can influence the size of the sample, including (1) cost and/or time limitations, (2) industry standards, and (3) statistical precision.

1. *Cost and/or time limitations.* This factor, often referred to as *all-you-can-afford,* determines sample size on the basis of the project's budget.

2. *Industry standards.* Industry standards refer to those rules of thumb, developed from experience, that have become standard industry guidelines for determining how large a sample to draw. Industry standards for determining sample size are used with nonprobability designs. Conventional guidelines on sample size vary with the type of research study being undertaken. In concept and product testing studies, for example, it is conventional practice to have 200 to 300 respondents per concept/product being tested.

3. *Statistical precision.* Statistical precision is a basis for determining sample size when probability sampling designs are used. Statistical precision refers to the difference between the results obtained from the sample information and the results that would be obtained if the entire target population were surveyed. With probability sampling designs the researcher can specify a desired precision, that is, a margin of error, and then, using the normal approximation rule (described below), determine the required sample size needed.

The discussion of these approaches to determining sample size has been intentionally brief. In the next chapter we return to the issue of sample size determination and provide additional details on each of the approaches described above.

Select the Sampling Units

Once the appropriate sampling design has been selected and the required sample size determined, the next step is to use the sampling frame available to select (or draw) the required number of sampling units in the appropriate manner. How sampling units are selected will vary with the sampling design. Explicit instructions are needed as to how the sampling units should be selected. Operational procedures to be used in the selection of sampling units in the data-collection phase of a study are specified in the instructions to the field service. Exhibit 9–6 presents an example of an operational sampling plan.

Estimate the Characteristic of Interest

Once the necessary data have been collected from the sampling units selected, the next step is to compute an estimate of the population characteristic of interest on the basis of the sample information. In other words, you use the sample information to make inferences (i.e., projections) about the target population. Depending on the nature of the variable of interest, the researcher will compute either a mean or a proportion. The mean or proportion calculated from the sample information will on average be on target if the sample size is large. A mean or proportion obtained from a given sample, however, will not be precisely equal to the population value. Thus, it is prudent to provide a confidence interval instead of relying on a specific sample-based estimate when making inferences about the value of the variable in the entire population.

Confidence intervals are ranges (i.e., lower and upper bounds) in which the "true" population characteristic is assumed to lie. A confidence interval for a mean is of the form

$$\mu = \overline{X} \pm \text{Sampling error} \tag{9-1}$$

where $\overline{X}$ denotes the sample mean, μ the population value, and $\overline{X} \pm$ Sampling error defines the length of the interval.[2] We see that the difference between any specific sample mean $\overline{X}$ and the population mean μ is attributable to sampling error.

EXHIBIT 9–6

Operational Sampling Plan

A. Block diagram

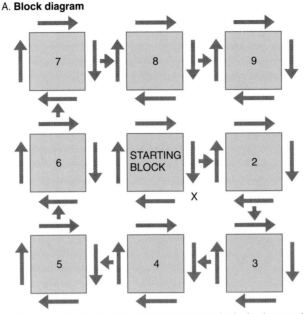

If for any reason this map does not adequately depict the area indicated by the intersections we have outlined above, please draw a map of the area, as it actually looks, on the back of this sheet. Once you have done so, follow the normal instructions for interviewing as detailed below.

B. Where to start interviewing

Starting at the corner indicated by the X, go around the entire block in a clockwise manner until you have reached your quota. If you have not reached your quota, follow the arrow to the next block; again start at the corner and follow the same procedure as before. Start interviewing at the _____ dwelling unit you come to.

C. How to select subsequent households for interviewing

When you encounter a dwelling where (1) no one is at home, (2) the respondent refuses to be interviewed, or (3) no qualified respondent is available, go to the very next dwelling unit. Follow this procedure until an interview is obtained. After each completed interview, skip _____ households and continue interviewing until you have completed your quota of _____ interviews.

Sampling error can be decomposed in terms of two components.

$$\text{Sampling error} = Z_{CI} \times \text{SE} \qquad (9\text{-}3)$$

$$= Z_{CI}\frac{\sigma}{\sqrt{n}}$$

The first component, Z_{CI}, has to do with how confident you wish to be that the interval actually brackets μ. If you set a confidence level of 95 percent, you are saying that following this approach in the long run will result in a correct interval 19 times out of 20, or a 5 percent chance of error (i.e., 1 out of 20). To find the value for Z_{CI}, we can take two approaches. The first uses the Z-table in the statistical appendix at the end of this book,

TABLE 9–1

Values of the Normal
Distribution

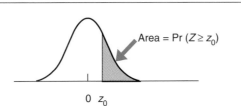

Next Decimal Place of Z_0

Z_0	0	1	2	3	4	5	6	7	8	9
1.0	.159	.156	.154	.152	.149	.147	.145	.142	.140	.138
1.1	.136	.133	.131	.129	.127	.125	.123	.121	.119	.117
1.2	.115	.113	.111	.109	.107	.106	.104	.102	.100	.099
1.3	.097	.095	.093	.092	.090	.089	.087	.085	.084	.082
1.4	.081	.079	.078	.076	.075	.074	.072	.071	.069	.068
1.5	.067	.066	.064	.063	.062	.061	.059	.058	.057	.056
1.6	.055	.054	.053	.052	.051	.049	.048	.047	.046	.046
1.7	.045	.044	.043	.042	.041	.040	.039	.039	.038	.037
1.8	.036	.035	.034	.034	.033	.032	.031	.031	.030	.029
1.9	.029	.028	.027	.027	.026	.026	.025	.024	.024	.023
2.0	.023	.022	.022	.021	.021	.020	.020	.019	.019	.018
2.1	.018	.017	.017	.017	.016	.016	.015	.015	.015	.014
2.2	.014	.014	.013	.013	.013	.012	.012	.012	.011	.011
2.3	.011	.010	.010	.010	.010	.009	.009	.009	.009	.008
2.4	.008	.008	.008	.008	.007	.007	.007	.007	.007	.006
2.5	.006	.006	.006	.006	.006	.005	.005	.005	.005	.005
2.6	.005	.005	.004	.004	.004	.004	.004	.004	.004	.004
2.7	.003	.003	.003	.003	.003	.003	.003	.003	.003	.003
2.8	.003	.002	.002	.002	.002	.002	.002	.002	.002	.002
2.9	.002	.002	.002	.002	.002	.002	.002	.001	.001	.001

while the second approach uses the Z-table shown in Table 9–1. Both will give us the same answer; they are simply different methods for finding the appropriate value for Z_{CI}. We will explain both methods and allow you to choose the one you feel most comfortable using. To use the Z-table in the statistical appendix, the first step is to specify the desired confidence, then subtract this from 1 to get the error rate. For example, with a 95 percent confidence we have a 5 percent error rate. Because the normal curve is symmetric, we divide the error rate in half. In this case we would allow .05/2, or a .025 percent error in each tail. The appropriate Z_{CI} is found by looking up the value for $1 - .025$, or .975, in the Z-table. From the statistical appendix, we can see that the value of Z_{CI} is 1.96.

To use the type of Z-table shown in Table 9–1, we simply take the error rate in each tail (.05/2 or .025) and find this value in the table. Notice that the value for Z_{CI} is the same as the table in the statistical appendix $Z_{CI} = 1.96$.

The second component of sampling error has to do with how much $\overline{X}$ fluctuates. The variability of $\overline{X}$ is directly measured by the standard error:[3]

$$SE = \frac{\sigma}{\sqrt{n}}$$

where σ denotes the standard deviation and n is the sample size. You can see that the length of the confidence interval will decrease as sample size (n) increases, because increasing n has the effect of reducing the standard error of $\overline{X}$. Thus, for a given level of confidence you can increase the precision by increasing the sample size. The length of the confidence interval is also affected by the confidence level. If you must be more certain that confidence intervals are correct, that is, that they bracket μ, then you would increase the confidence level to, say, 99 percent, which increases the range of the interval. This result is based on the fact that, all else the same, a larger interval is needed to be sure that μ has been bracketed.

We are now in a position to write a formal expression for a confidence interval:

$$Pr(\overline{X} - 1.96\ SE < \mu > \overline{X} + 1.96\ SE) = 95\% \tag{9-4}$$

This expression states that there is a 95 percent probability that the random interval $\overline{X} - 1.96\ SE$ to $\overline{X} + 1.96\ SE$ brackets μ. Stated somewhat differently, if you sampled repeatedly and constructed intervals like the one above, then 95 times out of 100 the interval you constructed would indeed bracket μ.

To illustrate, consider once again a type of claim made in opinion polling:

Chances are 19 of 20 that if all registered voters in the U.S. had been surveyed using the same questionnaire, the finding would differ from these poll results by no more than 2.6 percentage points in either direction.

The procedure followed in this poll lets the pollsters say that any reported percentage estimate differs from its population value by no more than 2.6 percentage points in either direction. Furthermore, this statement can be made with 95 (19/20) percent confidence. Given that 46 percent of the sample agree that the national economy will get better next year, pollsters could say, for example, on the basis of this poll we are 95 percent confident that the percentage of U.S. voters who thought as of March 1991 that the national economy will get better next year is between 43.4 and 48.6 percent.

$$(0.46 - 0.026,\ 0.46 + 0.026)$$

The range of the confidence interval will depend on the survey's margin of error.

SUMMARY

In this chapter we have described the sampling process—a method for making informed decisions on the basis of limited information. The objective of sam-

pling is to make the most precise conclusions about a variable of interest in the entire population based upon results obtained using a relatively small sample of that population. You have seen that sampling involves determining (1) how to select items from a population, so that the items selected are representative of the population, and (2) how to provide an estimate of a population characteristic (i.e., a variable) of interest, based upon what is observed in the sample.

Certain steps are basic to every sampling process. We described each of the steps in designing a sampling plan in some detail. Specific types of probability and nonprobability designs were discussed as well as the conditions favoring one approach over another. Sample size is a crucial aspect of sampling that we did not discuss in great detail. Chapter 10 demonstrates methods for sample size determination.

KEY CONCEPTS

Sampling	*Random Samples*	*Nonprobability Sampling Designs*
Population	*Simple Random Samples*	*Convenience Samples*
Element	*Stratified Random Sampling*	*Judgmental Samples*
Sampling Unit	*Sampling Interval*	*Quota Sample*
Sampling Frame	*Stratification Variable*	*Confidence Interval*
Probability Sampling Designs	*Cluster Sampling*	

REVIEW QUESTIONS

1. Identify the target population and a likely sampling frame for the following scenarios.

   a. A café in downtown New York City develops a new blend of coffee and would like to conduct a taste test with their patrons.

   b. A private Minneapolis country club debates offering a discount program to those wanting joint use of the golf course and the tennis courts.

   c. The United States Army conducts a national search for eligible recruits.

   d. A professional golfer begins a national campaign to sell his latest instructional video.

   e. The mayor of Atlanta wants to increase small business development in the city in order to increase productivity and decrease unemployment.

   f. A local fitness club would like to double its current membership by promoting greater awareness of its facilities as well as the long-term benefits to its consumers.

   g. Over 10,000 assembly-line employees are sponsoring a national push for better working conditions at all U.S. assembly plants.

2. A handful of the PAY-LO grocery stores in a southeastern city noticed diminishing store traffic during the previously busy 5 P.M.–8 P.M. time period. The area manager found that other chain stores had not seen such a decrease in store traffic during the same time slot. Store management commissioned a survey to study changing shopping patterns. In order to encourage participation, the research department offered each participant $5.00 worth of groceries. The written survey took only five minutes, and most participants were able to complete the survey instrument while waiting in the checkout line.

   a. What type of sampling method was used?

   b. Outline the advantages and disadvantages of the method used.

3. A southwestern company that manufactured and distributed a newly patented sunglass lens decided it was time to expand. Potential test areas in four southeastern states were reviewed and analyzed in terms of demographics, purchase patterns, and so on. Finally, Miami, Florida, and Savannah, Georgia, were selected.

   a. What type of sampling method was used?

   b. Outline the advantages and disadvantages of the method used.

4. Weight-Loss Center of America wanted to assess its spring advertising campaign. The company's re-

search department decided upon the use of a number of focus groups. They selected 8 to 12 overweight individuals who were walking around a local mall.

a. What type of sampling method was used?
b. Outline the advantages and disadvantages of the method used.

5. For each of the situations described in Question 1, discuss whether a probability or a nonprobability design is more appropriate, and which particular design you would select.

ENDNOTES

1. See Leslie Kish, *Survey Sampling* (New York: John Wiley & Sons, 1965), pp. 562–66, for a discussion of the problems in quota samples.

2. For a proportion, denoted by P, with population value, π, the length of the confidence interval is
$$\pi = P \pm \text{Sampling error} \qquad (9\text{-}2)$$

3. The standard error of a proportion is:
$$\sqrt{\frac{P(1 - P)}{n}}$$

Sample Size Determination

AMERICANS, MORE OPTIMISTIC ABOUT THE ECONOMY, HAVE BECOME LESS EAGER FOR FEDERAL REMEDIES

WASHINGTON — When it comes to what the government should be doing to get the country out of the recession, most Americans seem ready to heed the advice of former Carter administration economist Charles Schultze: "Don't just do something — stand there."

A new nationwide *Wall Street Journal/ NBC News* poll shows that, for the first time since the end of World War II, voters aren't clamoring for any of the traditional government tools to pull the country out of an economic downturn. (See Table 1.)

Moreover, there is a growing feeling that the worst of the recession is already over — an attitude fueled by the outcome of the Persian Gulf war. In the survey,

TABLE 1

"During the next year, do you think the national economy will get better, get worse or stay about the same?"

Economy	March 1991	January 1991
Better	46%	25%
Worse	20	40
About same	27	28

"Would this action be extremely effective, quite effective, just somewhat effective or not that effective in ending the recession?"

Action	Extremely/ Quite Effective	Just Somewhat/ Not That Effective
Lowering interest rates	42%	55%
Lowering taxes	40	57
Loosening regulations to make it easier for banks to make loans to individuals and businesses	38	55
Increasing government spending to help the unemployed	31	64

Source: *The Wall Street Journal/NBC NEWS POLL.*

nearly half of the voters — 46% — expect the national economy to get better in the next year. In a poll just a month ago, only 25% thought so. That striking change in attitude could give a major boost to the economy by spurring consumer and business spending.

"The poll shows a sharp turnaround in people's attitude toward the economy," say pollsters Peter Hart, a Democrat, and Robert Teeter, a Republican, who conducted the survey for the Journal and NBC. "The first peace dividend is a psychological sense that we're going to come out of the economic doldrums. This isn't to say that everything is terrific, but that we've turned a corner" toward recovery.

To be sure, voters say the Bush administration, Congress, and the Federal Reserve aren't doing enough to combat the recession. But majorities say that tax cuts, interest-rate reductions and increased government spending, the traditional solutions, won't do much good.

Further, they clearly believe that the economy is getting better on its own. Nearly seven out of 10 voters now believe that the recession will be a mild one; in December, only 45% thought it would be mild.

How Poll Was Conducted

The Wall Street Journal/NBC News poll was based on nationwide telephone interviews of 1,505 registered voters conducted Friday through Tuesday by the polling organizations of Peter Hart and Robert Teeter.

The sample was drawn from 315 randomly selected geographic points in the continental U.S. Each region of the country was represented in proportion to its population. Households were selected by a method that gave all telephone numbers, listed and unlisted, an equal chance of being included. One registered voter, 18 years or older, was selected from each household by a procedure to provide the correct number of male and female respondents. The results of the survey were minimally weighted by gender, race and income to assure that the poll accurately reflects registered voters nationwide.

Chances are 19 of 20 that if all registered voters in the U.S. had been surveyed using the same questionnaire, the findings would differ from these poll results by no more than 2.6 percentage points in either direction. The margin of error for subgroups would be larger.

INTRODUCTION

Opinion polling is an activity that relies heavily on sampling. Because the objective in opinion polling is to project sample results to the entire population with an acceptable margin of error, an important question concerns the number of people to survey so that the sampling error associated with survey results is within desirable limits. In the recent opinion poll conducted by *The Wall Street Journal* and NBC News, for example, the opinions of only 1,505 registered voters were used to make inferences concerning the entire population of voters with a ±2.6 percent margin of error.

> Chances are 19 of 20 that if all registered voters in the U.S. had been surveyed using the same questionnaire, the finding would differ from these poll results by no more than 2.6 percentage points in either direction.

How large a sample is needed in order for the estimates obtained from the sample to be reliable enough to meet the objectives of the survey is a fundamental concern in designing and implementing a research study. Researchers, when responding to requests for proposals (RFPs), are usually required to designate an appropriate sample size and the survey's margin of error.

In this chapter we describe procedures for determining how large a sample to select. We begin our treatment by discussing the sampling distribution and its relationship to sampling theory. Next we present a discussion of reliability, precision, and confidence levels, and their influence on the size of the sample selected. We then demonstrate how to determine the required sample size for a given level of precision and confidence using simple random samples. Other approaches to sample size determination in cases where nonprobability designs are being used are considered next. Finally, we discuss other issues that together with the required sample size determine how many people must be contacted in order to ensure that the desired number of interviews is completed.

THE SAMPLING DISTRIBUTION

Understanding a *sampling distribution* is fundamental to understanding why sampling theory works. Knowledge of what a sampling distribution is and how it is used removes much of the mystery from sampling theory.

The Random Sample

The random sample is a fundamental concept of sampling. We have drawn up Table 10–1, which presents sales data on a population of 100 stores, to illustrate this concept. If you were to take a random observation from the population of stores, what is the probability that the sales of that store would be $35,000, for example? The table indicates a probability of 6 in 100, or 0.06. The third column of the table, $p(X)$, gives the relative frequencies. These relative frequencies can be viewed as the **probability distribution of the population.**

PROBABILITY
DISTRIBUTION OF THE
POPULATION

A frequency distribution of all elements of a population.

Sales ($000) X	Frequency	Relative Frequency $p(X)$	Mean μ $Xp(X)$	Variance σ^2 $(X - \mu)^2 p(X)$
20	1	.01	.20	.81
23	6	.06	1.38	2.16
26	24	.24	6.24	2.16
29	38	.38	11.02	0
32	24	.24	7.68	2.16
35	6	.06	2.10	2.16
38	1	.01	.38	.81
	$N = 100$	1.00	29.00	$\sigma^2 = 10.26$
				$\sigma = 3.20$

TABLE 10–1

Sales, Mean, and Variance for a Population of 100 Stores

From the population probability distribution, we can calculate the population mean, μ, and the standard deviation, σ.[1] The calculated mean and standard deviation can be used to characterize any individual observation in a random sample. In other words, if you were to select a store at random from this population, you might find that its sales were $20,000 (although this in fact has a low probability of occurrence). You could say, nevertheless, that this store comes from a population with average sales of $29,000, with a standard deviation of $3,200. In Exhibit 10–1 we graph the population probability distribution and sketch it as a smooth curve. The figure shows that the distribution of store sales about the mean sales of $29,000 is symmetrical. It also shows that the probability of finding a store with sales of $20,000 or, for that matter, $38,000 is extremely low.

How many would constitute a good sample?

EXHIBIT 10—1

Sales for a Population of 100 Stores: Bar Graph of Distribution in Table 10–1

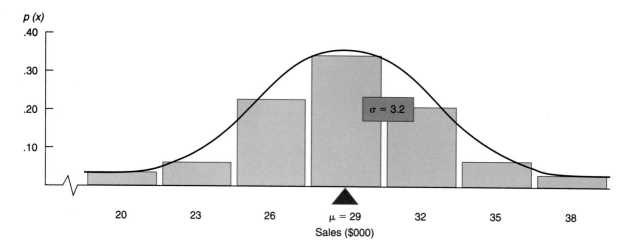

Drawing a Random Sample

Let us now suppose that four stores have been randomly selected from this population. We use *n* to denote the size of the sample to be selected. Selecting a simple random sample can be accomplished through the use of a table of random numbers. The first step is to number the stores from 1 to 100. Because numbering the population elements requires three digits (001 to 100), you must select three-digit random numbers from a table of random numbers in order for every element in the population to have a chance of being selected into the sample. (A table of random numbers is included in the Appendix at the end of the book and also in Table 10–2.)

TABLE 10—2

Abridged Set of Random Numbers

Line	(1)	(2)	(3)	(4)	(5)	(6)	(7)	(8)	(9)	(10)
1	10480	15011	015 36	02011	81647	91646	69179	14194	62590	36207
2	22368	46573	25595	85393	30995	89198	27982	53402	93965	34095
3	24130	48390	22527	97265	76393	64809	15179	24830	49340	32081
4	42167	93093	062 43	61680	07856	16376	39440	53537	71341	57004
5	37570	39975	81837	16656	06121	91782	60468	81305	49684	60072
6	77921	069 07	11008	42751	27756	53498	18602	70659	90655	15053
7	99562	72905	56420	69994	98872	31016	71194	18738	44013	48840
8	96301	91977	05463	07972	18876	20922	94595	56869	69014	60045
9	89579	14342	63661	10281	17453	18103	57740	84378	253 31	12568
10	85475	36857	53342	53988	53060	59533	38867	62300	081 58	17983

EXHIBIT 10—2

A Typical Random Sample of Stores' Sales Drawn from a Population of 100 Stores: Shaded Dots Correspond to Stores Sampled

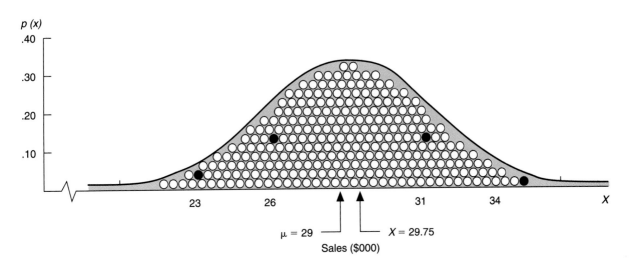

Next you would choose a random starting point in the random number table and select elements according to the random numbers selected. Starting at line 9 in Table 10–2, in the ninth block and using the first three columns, for example, you find that the number 253 is in the first three positions. Each entry in the blocks has 5 random digits. The number of digits used is determined by the size of the population. In this case any three digits from the set of five can be used. The number selected, 253, is greater than 100 and does not correspond to any store in the population. Moving down the column (in using the random number table you are permitted to move in any and all directions), the next three-digit number is 081, and, therefore, the 81st store in the population would be selected into the sample. Following this approach would lead to selecting stores corresponding to the numbers 81, 69, 15, and 62 —note after exhausting the numbers in column 9, you moved to line 1, column 10, and then back to line 1 column 1.

Because the sample is chosen in a random fashion, the odds are that the sample will be representative of the population from which it is drawn. While it may happen that a sampling unit with an extreme value is selected—a store with sales of $38,000, for example—this value is likely to be offset by sampling units that have values closer to the population mean or sampling units whose values are at the other end—a store with sales of $20,000, for example. Exhibit 10–2 illustrates this result. The shaded dots correspond to the $n = 4$ stores selected, which have sales of $23,000, $26,000, $32,000, and $38,000. Although none of the stores selected has sales equal to the population average, the sample mean of $29,750 is fairly close to it. Because of averaging, the sample mean is less extreme than the individual sampling units in the population, whichever units are selected. A **sample distribution** is a frequency distribution of the elements of a single sample.

SAMPLE DISTRIBUTION
A frequency distribution of all the elements of a single sample.

The Reliability of the Sample

On the average, the sample mean $(\overline{X})$ will equal the population mean (μ). At the same time, because of sampling fluctuations, an individual sample mean will not exactly equal μ. For example, in the random sample of $n = 4$ stores, $\overline{X} = \$29,750$, which is slightly more than $\mu = \$29,000$. Whenever you take a random sample, the crucial question should be: How *much* above or below the population mean is the sample mean?

To answer this question you need to calculate the **sampling distribution of the sample mean $\overline{X}$**. This can be accomplished empirically by taking all possible samples of a given size and computing $\overline{X}$ each time. By recording how each $\overline{X}$ varies from sample to sample, the sampling distribution of $\overline{X}$ can be built up. The standard deviation of $\overline{X}$ is called the **standard error,** and it includes the reliability of the sample.

The larger n is, the smaller the standard error becomes. This result is consistent with the intuitive notion that as we take larger samples, the sample mean $\overline{X}$ should be a more accurate estimate of the population mean μ. Thus, the difference between any particular $\overline{X}$ and μ decreases as the sample size n increases.

The Normal Approximation Rule

To calculate a survey's margin of error you need to know the shape of the sampling distribution of $\overline{X}$. Exhibit 10–3 shows a most useful result in this regard. The figure presents three different populations and shows how the sampling distribution of $\overline{X}$ changes shape as n increases. Notice that if the population is *normal,* or the sample size is large (a safe rule is 30 or more), then no matter what shape the population probability distribution assumes, the sampling distribution of $\overline{X}$ has an approximately normal shape. An important implication of this result is that, even when dealing with proportions, the normal approximation concept applies.

Exhibit 10–4 summarizes the **normal approximation rule,** also known as the *central limit theorem,* for means and proportions. When estimating a proportion, we substitute P for $\overline{X}$ and π for μ.

The normal approximation rule is important because we can now use the familiar normal distribution tables to determine how closely a sample mean $\overline{X}$ (or sample proportion P) is to μ (or to π). To illustrate, suppose that a random sample of $n = 10$ stores is selected from the population of 100 stores described in Table 10–1, and you want to know the chance that the sample mean will be within $2,000 of the population mean μ. According to the normal approximation rule, $\overline{X}$ is distributed normally with

$$\mu = \$29,000$$

and standard error

$$\frac{\sigma}{\sqrt{n}} = \frac{3,200}{\sqrt{10}}$$

Finding the probability that $\overline{X}$ is within $2,000 of μ is equivalent to finding the probability that $\overline{X}$ is between $27,000 and $31,000. Let us first consider

SAMPLING DISTRIBUTION OF THE MEAN
A frequency distribution of the means obtained from all possible samples of a given size.

STANDARD ERROR (S_y)
Indication of the reliability of an estimate of a population parameter; it is computed by dividing the standard deviation of the sample estimate by the square root of the sample size.

NORMAL APPROXIMATION RULE
No matter what shape a probability distribution assumes, the sampling distribution of $\overline{X}$ has an approximately normal distribution as the sample size increases.

Exhibit 10–3

A Sampling Distribution of $\overline{X}$ for Different Populations

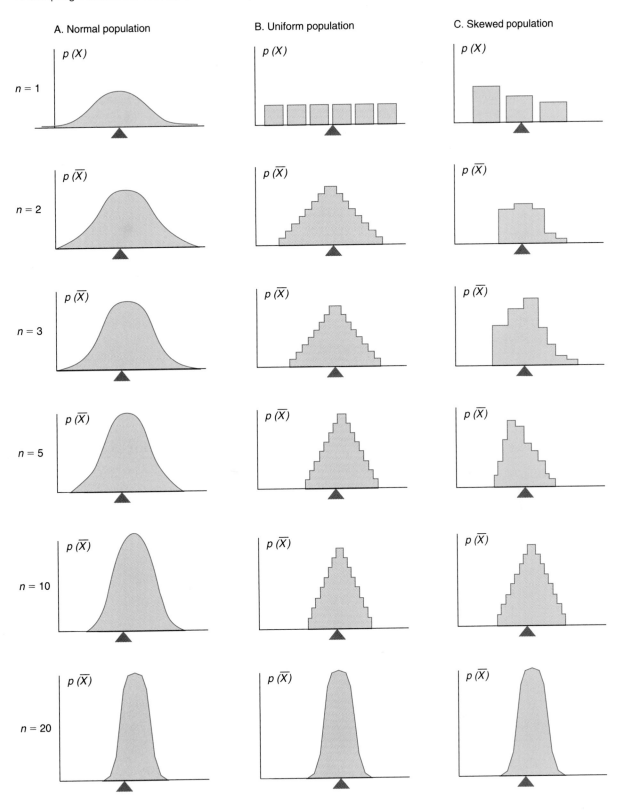

EXHIBIT 1O—4

The Normal Approximation
Rule

The Normal Approximation Rule for Means

In simple random samples (SRS) of size n, the sample mean $\overline{X}$ fluctuates around the population mean μ with a standard error of $\sigma/\sqrt{n}$ (where σ is the population standard deviation).

Therefore, as n increases, the sampling distribution of $\overline{X}$ concentrates more and more around its target μ. It also gets P closer and closer to a normal (bell-shaped) distribution.

The Normal Approximation Rule for Proportions

In simple random samples (SRS) of size n, the sample proportion P fluctuates around the population proportion π with a standard error of $\sqrt{\pi(1 - \pi)/n}$.

Therefore, as n increases, the sampling distribution of P concentrates more and more around its target π. It also gets closer and closer to a normal (bell-shaped) distribution.

the probability that $\overline{X}$ is above \$31,000. To evaluate this probability we calculate the *standardized Z-value* that reflects the number of standard errors an estimated value is away from the mean:

$$Z = \frac{\overline{X} - \mu}{\dfrac{\sigma}{\sqrt{n}}} \tag{10-1}$$

$$= \frac{31,000 - 29,000}{\dfrac{3,200}{\sqrt{10}}}$$

$$= 1.976$$

EXHIBIT 1O—5

Sample Distribution of $\overline{X}$

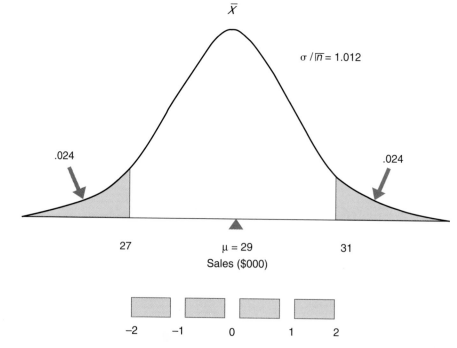

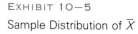

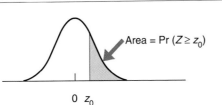

TABLE 10—3

Values of the Normal
Distribution

Next Decimal Place of Z_0

Z_0	0	1	2	3	4	5	6	7	8	9
1.0	.159	.156	.154	.152	.149	.147	.145	.142	.140	.138
1.1	.136	.133	.131	.129	.127	.125	.123	.121	.119	.117
1.2	.115	.113	.111	.109	.107	.106	.104	.102	.100	.099
1.3	.097	.095	.093	.092	.090	.089	.087	.085	.084	.082
1.4	.081	.079	.078	.076	.075	.074	.072	.071	.069	.068
1.5	.067	.066	.064	.063	.062	.061	.059	.058	.057	.056
1.6	.055	.054	.053	.052	.051	.049	.048	.047	.046	.045
1.7	.045	.044	.043	.042	.041	.040	.039	.038	.038	.037
1.8	.036	.035	.034	.034	.033	.032	.031	.031	.030	.029
1.9	.029	.028	.027	.027	.026	.026	.025	.024	.024	.023
2.0	.023	.022	.022	.021	.021	.020	.020	.019	.019	.018
2.1	.018	.017	.017	.017	.016	.016	.015	.015	.015	.014
2.2	.014	.014	.013	.013	.013	.012	.012	.012	.011	.011
2.3	.011	.010	.010	.010	.010	.009	.009	.009	.009	.008
2.4	.008	.008	.008	.008	.007	.007	.007	.007	.007	.006
2.5	.006	.006	.006	.006	.006	.005	.005	.005	.005	.005
2.6	.005	.005	.004	.004	.004	.004	.004	.004	.004	.004
2.7	.003	.003	.003	.003	.003	.003	.003	.003	.003	.003
2.8	.003	.002	.002	.002	.002	.002	.002	.002	.002	.002
2.9	.002	.002	.002	.002	.002	.002	.002	.001	.001	.001

This means that the critical value of $31,000 for the sample mean is nearly 2 standard errors above its population value of $29,000. Exhibit 10–5 depicts this situation.

From the standard normal table given in Appendix I (see also Table 10–3), the probability that Z will exceed ± 1.976 is only .024. (The format of Table 10–3 is different from the Z-table shown in the appendix. As we discussed in Chapter 9, both tables, however, yield the same results. For example, $\Pr(Z > \pm 1.976) = (1.000 - .9756 = .024.)$ This is shown by the shaded area in Exhibit 10–5. Because the normal distribution is symmetric we need not explicitly calculate the probability below $27,000. It too is equal to .024. Thus the probability that the sample mean is between $29,000 and $31,000 is equal to .952:

$$.952 = 1.000 - .024 - .024$$

which means that there is a 95.2 percent chance that the sample mean will be within $2,000 of the population mean. Or you could say that the

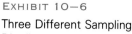

Three Different Sampling
Distributions

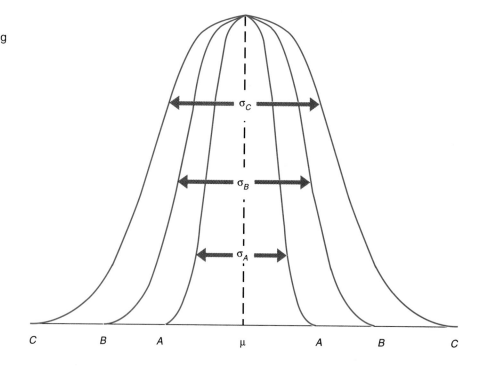

chances are a little greater than 19 of 20 that if all 100 stores were sampled,
the findings would differ from the sample results by no more than $2,000
in either direction.

RELIABILITY, PRECISION, CONFIDENCE LEVELS, AND THE SIZE OF THE SAMPLE

The degree to which $\overline{X}$ is above or below μ is determined by the sampling
distribution of $\overline{X}$, or, alternatively, by the variance of $\overline{X}$. In other words,
the variance or standard error of an estimate is a measure of the sampling
variability of the estimate over all possible samples. And assuming that our
measurement device is fairly free of error, the **reliability** of an estimate can
be judged by the size of its standard error; the smaller the standard error,
the higher the reliability of the estimate.

RELIABILITY

Refers to the sampling variability of an estimate and is
directly related to the size of
the standard error.

Exhibit 10–6 shows three different sampling distributions, A, B, and C.
Notice that all three distributions have identical mean values equal to μ. Yet
distribution A has a much smaller variance, σ_A^2, than either of the other
distributions, and, hence, any particular sample drawn from this distribution will yield a $\overline{X}$ that is more likely to be closer to μ. Another way to say
this is that estimates from distribution A are more reliable, in the sense that
if you take repeated samples, the estimates obtained will be more like each
other and, in this case, closer to μ than the estimates obtained from the
other two distributions.

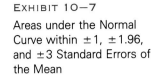

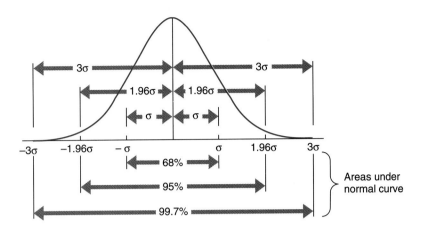

When we speak of **precision,** we refer to the difference between the estimate and the corresponding population value. And, as we concluded in the previous chapter, this difference is attributable to sampling error:

$$\mu = \overline{X} \pm \text{Sampling error}$$

PRECISION

The difference between the estimate and the corresponding population value.

Precision can be defined in terms of the magnitude of the sampling error, or, equivalently, in terms of the range of the confidence interval around μ. Recall that the width of the confidence interval is given by

$$\overline{X} \pm Z_{CI} \frac{\sigma}{\sqrt{n}}$$

where Z_{CI} corresponds to the critical value of the normal curve associated with the degree of confidence that has been set. For example, if you want to be 95 percent confident that on repeated sampling the confidence interval brackets μ, you find the Z-value such that .025 (.05/2) percent of the area is in each tail of the distribution. Consulting the values of the normal curve found in Appendix I, we find that in this case $Z = 1.96$. Thus, 95 percent of the area under the normal curve is within ± 1.96 standard errors of the mean. Areas under the normal curve for ± 1, ± 1.96, and ± 3 standard errors of the mean are shown in Exhibit 10–7.

To determine the required sample size, we must specify the degree of precision wanted, as well as the desired level of confidence. In terms of the opinion survey taken by *The Wall Street Journal* and NBC News, the poll was conducted such that the

Chances are 19 of 20 that if all registered voters in the U.S. had been surveyed using the same questionnaire, the findings would differ from these poll results by no more than 2.6 percentage points in either direction.

That is, the researchers conducting this poll decided that (1) with regard to precision, the percentage estimates reported should differ from the population values by no more than ± 2.6 percentage points; and (2) with regard to confidence levels, results should be able to be relied on with 95 percent

(19/20) confidence. (Confidence levels are, by convention, usually set at 90 percent, 95 percent, or 99 percent.)

From the discussion above, there are some basic relationships that we should be aware of.

1. All else the same, with larger samples the range of the confidence interval will narrow because the standard error of the estimate decreases.
2. All else the same, in order to be more certain that a given confidence interval will bracket the population mean, the range of the interval must increase.

Let H denote the desired precision level, that is, the allowable permitted difference between the estimate and the population value. An accepted formula for determining sample size is

$$n = \frac{Z_{CI}^2}{H^2} \sigma^2 \tag{10-2}$$

In all sample size calculations the resulting value of n is rounded up to the nearest integer. The actual form of (10-2) will vary depending on the sampling design being used and whether we are estimating means or proportions. Because rarely in practice is the population variance σ^2 known, you need to substitute an appropriate sample-based estimate when determining n. Finally, when more than one population characteristic is being estimated, a somewhat modified approach must be followed. All of these issues will be taken up shortly.

From formula (10-2) it should be clear that to increase either the precision or the confidence level the required sample size must also increase. Increased precision or confidence has the effect of reducing the survey's margin of error.

Suppose you would like your estimate to be twice as precise; that is, you want to narrow the range of the confidence interval by one half, or, equivalently, you want to reduce the sampling error by one half. Letting c denote the amount of increase in precision desired, it follows from the relationships shown above that

$$n_{New} = c^2 \times n_{Old} \tag{10-3}$$

Thus doubling the precision (halving the range of the confidence interval) increases the required sample size by a factor of four. Similarly, if you want your estimate to be three times as precise (reducing the range of the confidence interval by one third), the required sample size must increase by a factor of nine. In general, whenever precision is increased by a factor of c, the required sample size will increase by a factor of c^2.

The same result holds for an increase in the confidence level. Suppose that you want to increase the confidence level from 95 percent to 99 percent. In this case define c by

$$c = \frac{Z_{.99}}{Z_{.95}} \tag{10-4}$$

$$= \frac{2.575}{1.96} = 1.31$$

According to formula (10-4), the required sample size would increase by a factor of approximately c^2, *or* 1.72.

SAMPLE SIZE DETERMINATION

There are four factors that influence sample size determination:

1. The desired degree of precision (H). This is the maximum difference between $\overline{X}$ and μ or P and π that you are willing to tolerate. One approach to specifying the degree of precision is simply to take one half of the length of the desired confidence interval.
2. The critical value of Z for the stated level of confidence.
3. The estimate of the population standard deviation. This can be based on prior studies or on a small-scale pilot study.
4. The projected resources, especially time and money.

To illustrate how to determine the required sample size consider Exhibit 10–8, which shows four questions from an opinion poll concerning a number of social issues. Researchers are interested in estimating the following population characteristics:[2]

Question 1: The mean level of approval toward legalized abortion.
Question 2: The proportion of Democrats versus members of other political parties.
Question 3: The mean age.
Question 4: The population of females versus males.

Question 1

Question 1 is used to estimate a mean—the mean level of approval toward legalized abortion. Formula (10-2) provides an accepted formula for this estimate

$$n = \frac{Z^2_{CI}}{H^2}\sigma^2$$

Suppose the researcher wants a 95 percent confidence level and a tolerance of $\pm$ .1. The estimate of the standard deviation in the population is also required. As we indicated above, this estimate is based on experience, a pilot study, or some other estimate. Based on normal approximation theory, an acceptable procedure to follow is to estimate the standard deviation by taking one sixth of the range, that is, the difference between the largest and the smallest values

$$\hat{\sigma} = \frac{\text{Maximum value} - \text{Minimum value}}{6} \qquad (10\text{-}5)$$

$$= \frac{7 - 1}{6} = 1$$

EXHIBIT 10—8

Four Sample Questions

---

1. In general, rate how you feel about legalized abortion.
   (Show the card, say "Just pick the number that best represents your feeling.")

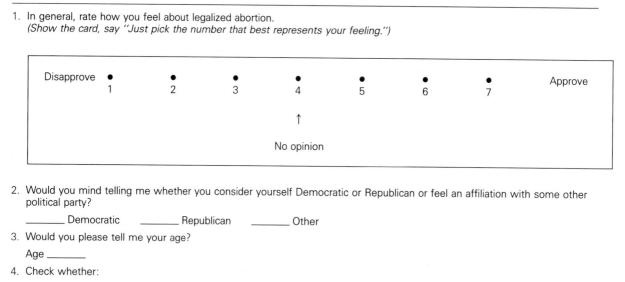

2. Would you mind telling me whether you consider yourself Democratic or Republican or feel an affiliation with some other political party?

   _____ Democratic   _____ Republican   _____ Other

3. Would you please tell me your age?

   Age _____

4. Check whether:

   _____ Female   _____ Male

The required sample size for question 1 is

$$n = \frac{(1.96)^2(1)^2}{(.1)^2} = 384.16 \text{ or } 385$$

A sample size of $n = 385$ individuals should be selected to ensure that the desired confidence and tolerance levels are achieved.

Question 2

Question 2 is used to estimate a proportion—the proportion of Democrats versus members of other political parties in the population. An accepted formula for determining sample size in the case of proportions is

$$n = \frac{Z^2_{CI}}{H^2} \hat{P}\hat{Q} \qquad (10\text{-}6)$$

where $\hat{P}$ is an initial approximation of the population of interest, and $\hat{Q} = 1 - \hat{P}$.

For a 95 percent confidence level, a tolerance of $\pm.025$, and an initial approximation of $\hat{P} = .42$ (based on the 1988 presidential election), the sample size required is

$$n = \frac{(1.96)^2(.58)(.42)}{(.025)^2} = 1,497.30 \text{ or } 1,498$$

Question 3

Similar to question 1, question 3 is used to estimate a mean—the mean age of the respondents. Thus, you can follow the same procedure as in question 1 to determine the appropriate sample size. For an approximate estimate of the standard deviation you can apply formula (10-3), setting the maximum value equal to 100 and the minimum value equal to 18, the legal voting age.

$$\hat{\sigma} = \frac{\text{Maximum value} - \text{Minimum value}}{6}$$

$$= \frac{100 - 18}{6} = 13.67$$

For a 95 percent confidence level, a tolerance level of ± 3, and an approximate standard deviation of 13.67, the required sample size is

$$n = \frac{(1.96)^2(13.67)^2}{3^2} = 79.76 \text{ or } 80$$

Question 4

Question 4, like question 2, is used to estimate a proportion—the proportion of females versus males in the population. For a 95 percent confidence level, a tolerance level of $\pm .02$, and an initial approximation of $\hat{P} = .5$, the required sample size is

$$n = \frac{(1.96)^2(.5)(.5)}{(.02)^2} = 2,401$$

Notice that by assuming an equal proportion of each gender, we have produced the most conservative estimate of the standard deviation in the population. For a proportion, the standard deviation will assume its maximum value when $\hat{P} = .5$.

Having determined a minimum sample size for each question, the researcher must now determine the minimum sample size for the study. In other words, which of the calculated sample sizes is the "correct" one for this study? The recommended approach is to use the largest sample size. This will ensure that the desired confidence levels and tolerance levels will be achieved for all estimates. In the present case, the researcher would set the required sample size at $n = 2,401$ respondents.

If resources are limited, however, the researcher may choose a compromise sample size, say, $n = 1,498$. It should be recognized that for a 95 percent confidence level reducing the sample size to 1,498 has the effect of increasing the tolerance level from $\pm .02$ to $\pm .025$ for gender (question 4).

$$H = \sqrt{\frac{Z^2_{CI}\hat{P}\hat{Q}}{n}} \tag{10-7}$$

$$= \sqrt{\frac{(1.96)^2(.5)(.5)}{1,498}} = .025$$

If, on the other hand, the sample size is reduced to 1,498 and the tolerance level is held at $\pm .02$, the reliability coefficient for question 4 becomes $Z = 1.548$, which results in a confidence level of approximately 88 percent, instead of 95 percent.

$$Z = \sqrt{\frac{nH^2}{\hat{P}\hat{Q}}} \qquad (10\text{-}8)$$

$$= \sqrt{\frac{(1,498)(.02)^2}{(.5)(.5)}} = 1.548$$

Thus, choosing a smaller than required sample size has its consequences. Each time a smaller sample size value is chosen, the researcher must realize that the confidence level, the tolerance level, or both will be compromised for those estimates requiring a larger sample size.

OTHER APPROACHES

The basic approach to sample size determination assumes the use of probability samples. When studies use nonprobability samples, however, the approach to sample size determination does not rely on precision or statistical properties of the estimates. In other words, when using nonprobability samples, there are no statistical formulas for determining the appropriate sample size. There are, nevertheless, some general approaches to take.

Cost Limitations

The cost limitation method, or "all-you-can-afford," determines sample size on the basis of the budget allocated to the project. This approach involves

1. Subtracting from the available budget all non–sampling-related costs (for example, fixed costs of designing the survey, questionnaire preparation, data analysis, and report generation).
2. Dividing the result from step 1 by an estimated cost per sampling unit to arrive at the desired sample size.

To illustrate, suppose that the research budget established for a mall intercept concept test is $58,000. The concept is for a new brand of women's facial moisturizer, and interviews are scheduled to last 25 minutes. Studies have shown that the likelihood of intercepting in a shopping mall a woman who has used a facial moisturizer in the last 30 days is 80 percent.

Estimated nonsampling costs are as follows:

Design of survey = $3,000
Questionnaire preparation = $1,000
Coding and tabulation = $10,000
Analysis = $3,000
Report generation and presentation = $5,000

The total of all nonsampling costs comes to $22,000.

The research firm estimates that the cost per sampling unit for a 25-minute interview at an incidence of 80 percent is equal to $20.25.

Before calculating the maximum sample size possible, the firm applies a standard profit margin (covering overhead and profit) of 60 percent to both nonsampling and sampling costs.

$$(.60 \times \$22,000) + 22,000 = \$35,200$$
$$(.60 \times \$20.25) + 20.25 = \$32.40$$

Subtracting nonsampling costs from the total budget yields

$$\$58,000 - 35,200 = \$22,800$$

The maximum sample size possible is

$$n = \frac{\$22,800}{\$32.40}$$
$$= 703.7 \text{ or } 704$$

This means that approximately 700 respondents can be sampled.

Industry Standards

Industry standards are rules of thumb developed from experience that have become accepted guidelines for determining the size of a sample to draw. Conventional guidelines on sample size vary according to the type of marketing research study as well as the number of cells included in the study. Typically, *cells* refer to different manipulations of the marketing mix elements. Testing different concepts, different names, or different products, or testing the same product at different prices, all constitute multiple-cell designs.

Table 10–4 gives minimum and typical sample sizes for different sorts of marketing research studies. These guidelines are applied most often when some form of quota sampling is used, although they apply to other types of nonprobability designs as well.

INDUSTRY STANDARDS Those rules of thumb developed from experience, that have become standard industry guidelines for determining how large a sample to draw.

Type of Study	Minimum Size	Typical Size Range
Market study	500	1,000–1,500
Strategic study	200	400–500
Test-market penetration study	200	300–500
Concept/product test	200	200–300/cell
Name tests	100/name variant	200–300/cell
Package tests	100/package variant	200–300/cell
TV commercial test	150/commercial	200–300/commercial
Radio commercial test	150/commercial	200–300/commercial
Print ad tests	150/advertisement	200–300/advertisement
Focus group	6/region	8–12/region

INCIDENCE RATES AND CONTACTS NEEDED

Incidence Rate Calculation

In most commercial marketing research studies a criterion for inclusion in the survey is past use of the brand or product/category under study. Product/category use incidence is ordinarily known and supplied by the client (the firm commissioning the research). This defines the **gross incidence**—the percentage of the entire population who are product-category users. **Net incidence** is the factored-down gross incidence, which includes *all* target population qualifications. It is also called the *effective* or *overall* incidence. To illustrate, we consider a survey in which a qualified respondent must meet the following requirements:

— 18–55 (no specific age breakouts).
— Used any OTC cold remedy in the past month.
— No known health restrictions, drug allergies.
— No one in household employed by advertising agency, marketing research company, or drug manufacturer.
— Has not participated in a marketing research study in the past three months.

The product/category use incidence was quoted at 60 percent. This was confirmed to be the gross incidence level—that of "past one-month OTC cold-remedy usage." The next step is to calculate the net incidence level. This involves taking the gross incidence of 60 percent and reducing it for all other qualifications. Note that the screening/data-collection method affects the qualification percentages. Let us assume an in-person mall intercept screening method was used. Calculating the net incidence is a

GROSS INCIDENCE

Product/category use incidence for the entire population.

NET INCIDENCE

The factored-down gross incidence that includes all target population qualifications.

multiplication process. As shown below, the gross incidence is multiplied by the qualification percentages for all inclusion components.

$$\text{Net incidence} = \text{Gross incidence} \times \text{Qualification percentages}$$

$$\text{Qualification percentages} = \begin{aligned} &92\% \text{ age } 18-55 \\ &88\% \text{ no health restrictions/drug allergies} \\ &97\% \text{ no household employment} \\ &96\% \text{ no past research participation} \end{aligned}$$

$$\text{Qualification percentage} = 92\% \times 88\% \times 97\% \times 96\%$$
$$= 75.4\%$$

$$\text{Net incidence} = 60\% \times 75.4\% = 45.2\%$$

The net incidence will determine the number of contacts required for a given sample size or quota.

Determining the Number of Contacts Needed

So far we have concentrated for the most part on determining the required sample size needed to ensure reliable results, that is, survey results that are generalizable. To get this required sample size, the researcher must consider a number of other factors as well. These factors along with the required sample size will determine the number of contacts (i.e., telephone calls, mailings, or whatever) that will be necessary, and ultimately the cost and time of fielding the study.

Among the most important factors influencing the number of contacts needed are

1. The **reachable rate,** which measures the quality of the sampling frame.
2. The **net incidence rate,** which measures the percentage of contacts who will qualify for the interview.
3. The **completion rate,** which is the percentage of those people from the target population who agree to participate and actually complete the questionnaire.

The reachable rate (R) reflects how good the sampling frame is. In the case of a telephone study, for instance, the list may include nonworking numbers, and the percentage of working numbers in the list is used to determine the reachable rate. Similarly, mailing lists may be dated, with some addresses no longer active because people have moved. For mail surveys the percentage of active addresses in the list is used to determine the reachable rate.

The net incidence rate (I) simply refers to the percentage of population who qualify for inclusion in a survey. If the target population consists of

REACHABLE RATE

An objective measure reflecting the quality of the sampling frame.

NET INCIDENCE RATE

The percentage of contacts who qualify for the interviews.

COMPLETION RATE

The percentage of those people from the target population who agree to participate in and complete the interview.

EXHIBIT 10—9

Cat Food Study—
Incidence Rate Calculation

Let's say that you are conducting a national study on cat food purchasing habits. Obviously, you need to talk to people who buy cat food. But what is the incidence of people who buy cat food? There are many sources for this type of data. Past experience has shown that a client's own product and brand managers usually have the best information on incidence rates. Studies show that cat food is purchased by about 30 percent of the country's households.

Accurate incidence data are critical to determining the proper size of your sample because an incidence figure that is too high will probably leave you short of sampling units once your study is in the field. So, even if any adult who answers the phone will qualify instead of 100 percent for your interview, we recommend you use an incidence rate of 90 percent to cover those instances where an adult answers the phone, but there is a language or other communication problem.

Now let's look at how we establish the completion rate, which is the percentage of people who, once they qualify for a study, will agree to participate by completing the interview. In our cat food study, assume that we're planning a 10-minute interview and one that's not terribly sensitive. The study will be conducted in the field for four days in August. During that time, we'll make one initial attempt and up to three call-backs in our effort to reach a qualified respondent at each telephone number selected.

Because the interview is relatively short and not sensitive, we might start by recommending a 50 percent completion rate. But conducting a study during August, when many people tend to be on vacation, may mean it will be harder to reach people. So, it would be wise to drop the completion rate to 45 percent. If we had a longer interview (15 minutes or more), we would subtract another 5 to 10 percent from the completion rate. The same would be true in the case of a sensitive topic (e.g., political issues, personal finance, hygiene). Finally, if we were to reduce the number of call-backs, we would also reduce the completion rate by 5 to 10 percent for each attempt that we eliminate.

Because this is going to be a telephone interview, we also know that some numbers selected will be nonworking. We'll assume that Survey Sampling, Inc.'s (SSI) random-digit super sample will be used, which yields a working telephone rate of at least 55 percent.

Adding the final element to the decision sequence, let's say that we want to be 99 percent certain that the estimate based on the sample differs from the true population value by no more than 5.0 percentage points in either direction.

people who buy cat food, for example, those people who do not buy cat food do not qualify for inclusion. Accurate incidence data are crucial to determining the number of contacts that will be necessary, which is necessary for accurate estimation of the cost of collecting the data. Per unit interviewing costs have to do with the length of the interview as well as the incidence rate. Low incidence rate categories mean that, all else the same, many more contacts will have to be initiated.

The completion rate (C) measures the percentage of people who, once they qualify for inclusion in the survey, agree to cooperate and complete the questionnaire. Completion rates vary depending on (1) the length of the interview; (2) the sensitivity of the topic; (3) the time of the year; (4) the number of attempts made to reach a respondent; and (5) the length of time the study is in the field.

Once the researcher estimates the reachable rate, the incidence rate, and the completion rate, the necessary number of contacts to ensure that the proper sample size will be obtained can be calculated as follows:

$$\text{Contacts} = \frac{n}{R \times I \times C} \qquad (10\text{-}9)$$

To illustrate, consider the study described in Exhibit 10–9. To calculate the number of contacts needed for this cat food study, the first step is to compute the required sample size. The objective is to report survey find-ings that differ from the results based upon the entire population of ca food purchasers by no more than ±5.0 percentage points in either direction at the 99 percent level of confidence. Thus

$$H = .050$$
$$Z = 2.575$$

Now you need to establish a standard of approval for this cat food product. Assume that in order for the new concept to be judged successful 25 percent of the respondents must rate it as superior to their current brand. Thus we set $\hat{P} = .25$ and calculate n as

$$
\begin{aligned}
n &= \frac{Z^2{}_{CI}\hat{P}\hat{Q}}{H^2} \\
&= \frac{(2.575)^2(.25)(.75)}{(.050)^2} \\
&= 497.30 \text{ or } 498
\end{aligned}
$$

To ensure that the required sample size of 498 will be obtained, you adjust this number by the reachable, incidence, and completion rates (see Exhibit 10–9) to establish the number of contacts to initiate.

$$
\begin{aligned}
\text{Reachable rate } (R) &= .55 \\
\text{Net Incidence rate } (I) &= .30 \\
\text{Completion rate } (C) &= .45
\end{aligned}
$$

$$
\begin{aligned}
\text{Contacts} &= \frac{n}{R \times I \times C} \\
&= \frac{498}{.55 \times .30 \times .45} \\
&= 6{,}707.07 \text{ or } 6{,}708
\end{aligned}
$$

This means that over 6,700 contacts will be necessary in order to ensure that a required sample of 498 respondents is obtained.

SUMMARY

In this chapter we have discussed procedures for deter-mining the size of a sample. We began by emphasizing how reliability, precision, and confidence levels all in-fluence the size of the sample to be selected. We then demonstrated how to determine the required sample size for a given level of precision and confidence using simple random samples. Next, we considered the way to approach sample size determination in the case of nonprobability designs. Finally, we explained the issues other than the required sample size that determine the number of people to contact in order to ensure that the desired number of interviews is completed.

KEY CONCEPTS

Sampling Distribution   *Precision*   *Net Incidence Rate*

Random Sample   *Required Sample Size*   *Completion Rate*

Normal Approximation Rule   *Reachable Rate*

Reliability   *Gross Incidence Rate*

REVIEW QUESTIONS

1. The average tee shot for golfers on the PGA tour is 262 yards (μ). Suppose a random sample of $n = 20$ is selected from the total of 200 players. What are the chances (the probability) that the sample mean ($\overline{X}$) will fall within 5 yards of the population mean (μ), assuming that the normal approximation rule is in effect with $\overline{X}$ normally distributed and $\sigma = 10.2$?

2. The president of a large Florida resort area, called Mickey World, has decided to hire your services in order to estimate the number of non-Floridians entering Mickey World each day. The president figures that "about 15,000 ($\overline{X}$) non-Floridians enter the park daily, give or take 2,000 (σ^2)." You will need to compute a 99 percent confidence interval based upon your results from sampling 250 tourists.

3. Your marketing professor wants you to determine the sample size necessary to estimate the number of students that will make the Dean's List this year with 99 percent certainty, within ± 10 students. The average number receiving the honor from previous years in the overall student body (population) is 35. You know that $\sigma^2 = 9.82$.

   a. Compute the required sample size.
   b. Last year's records show a variance of 22.34. Recompute the necessary sample size. Discuss why the necessary sample size has increased or decreased.
   c. How would the sample size change if the only information your professor shared with you was that former students making the Dean's List ranged from 25 to 48?

4. A large computer company estimates the variance for the number of defective computers coming off the production line to be 10.0. A sample of 27 computers are needed from the population in order to be 90 percent sure that the average number of defects differs by no more than ± 2 units from the true mean.

   a. If this computer company then decides it wants to be twice as precise, what is the new required sample size?
   b. How would your results differ if the computer company decided to increase the confidence interval from 95 percent to 99 percent?

5. A local newspaper decided to call 2,000 of their subscribers and inquire about satisfaction with delivery. The newspaper company wanted findings that would differ from the true results of the population by no more than ± 2.5 percentage points in either direction at the 99 percent level of confidence. Was the sample size selected large enough to meet the newspaper's requirements? If not, how large a sample was needed?

6. A state university athletic department has $85,000 to hire a research firm in order to contact as many alumni as possible at any collegiate game to determine if a new concept for "one price gets you a season ticket to all home sporting events" is in the best interest of their alumni. Past studies show that three in four attendees of any school event are alumni and are willing to be interviewed. You know that a 50 percent profit margin is required by the research firm. If the nonsampling costs total $44,500 and the sampling cost per unit is $17.75, how many alumni can the university expect to be included in the study?

ENDNOTES

1. Following convention, we use Greek letters to denote population values.

2. The following discussion is adapted from Joe K. Ballenger and Sandra K. McCune, "A Procedure for Determining Sample Size for Multiple Population Parameter Studies," *The Marketing Educator,* Fall 1990, pp. 30–33.

CASE 1: A HEAD & SHOULDERS STUDY

A market researcher calls with the following specs:

Three hundred interviews with females 18 years old or older who shampoo their hair at home. One hundred will be with Head & Shoulders users, the rest with users of any other shampoos. The effective telephone incidence for Head & Shoulders users is 20 percent; all-other-brand users is 75 percent. The interview length is 15 minutes.

In response to these specifications, the junior research analyst estimates that 767 contacts will be needed, 500 for the Head & Shoulders quota and 267 for all-other-users quota ($100 \div .20 = 500; 200 \div .75 = 267$). With 767 contacts required and assuming a 30 percent productive dialing ratio (finding a respondent home), the number of dialings needed was estimated at 2,557 ($767 \div .30 = 2,557$). The total hours required for interviewing was estimated as

$$
\begin{array}{lll}
2{,}557 \text{ dialings} \times 1.5 \text{ minutes} = & 3{,}835.5 \text{ minutes} \\
767 \text{ contacts} \times 3 \text{ minutes} = & 2{,}301 \\
300 \text{ completes} \times 15 \text{ minutes} = & \underline{4{,}500} \\
& 10{,}636.5 \text{ minutes} = & 177.28 \text{ hours}
\end{array}
$$

The junior research analyst also included time spent on qualified refusals and break-offs, estimated at 10 percent. Thus, the estimate of total hours of interviewing was 195 hours. At $20 an hour, the bid submitted was $3,900.

Case Questions

1. Comment on the incidence-rate projections.
2. Develop a probabilistic sampling design for this study. What potential problems do you anticipate?

CASE 2: CHANGING COMPLEXION OF RESTAURANT INDUSTRY

In response to the dramatic changes that have taken place in the restaurant industry, the Restaurant Association of America recently commissioned a survey of restaurant owners. The study called for a national probabilistic sample; its objectives were to estimate the incidence of the following types of eating establishments:

1. Fast-food.
2. Casual.
3. Dinner.
4. Fine dining.

Another objective was to collect various data on menu offerings and price structures. Subgroup analysis will be undertaken by restaurant type and geographical region. Assume that you have been retained to evaluate the procedures used. The necessary details follow.

Sampling Plan

Selection of firms to conduct the sampling.   Various firms specializing in drawing probabilistic telephone samples were solicited and asked to supply a national probability sample of restaurant establishments; in addition, several county samples also were requested. These samples were judged for accuracy and completeness in relation to census and county data. A single firm was selected.

Selection of sampling frame. The chosen sample was based on a frame of all restaurant establishments located in the contiguous United States.

Sample selection procedures. The chosen design was that of a probability-replicated sample, comprising 70 randomly selected, stratified, and matched samples of 50 restaurants, each from a frame of all eligible restaurants in the United States and each having a known chance of selection.

The total database was filtered to create a population consisting only of telephone numbers falling into the *Yellow Pages* categories of restaurants. The filtering process resulted in a population of 302,247 restaurants. The file was then geographically sorted by area codes and exchange, and a systematic selection was made to produce the final sample. A sample of 10,000 restaurants was first sampled from this list and was verified; then 5,000 restaurants were selected into the final target sample.

Sample size considerations. The objective was to estimate the incidence (proportion) of each of the five categories of eating establishments with ± 5 percent. After some discussion it was felt that a sample of 1,000 establishments would be sufficient.

Response rates. Great care was given to achieve high response rates by completing five call-backs. The total number of calls made exceeded 3,000, which represented about a 30 percent response rate.

Survey instrument (questionnaire construction and administration). The following procedures were undertaken:

1. Questionnaire was subjected to rigorous pretests, and the instrument was constructed according to acceptable standards.
2. Questionnaire was administered by executive interviewers, especially those trained in the food-service industry, to ensure objective and accurate responses.
3. Computer-driven CRT interviewing center was employed.
4. Twenty-five percent of the interviews were verified.

Case Question

Prepare in memo format an evaluation of the sampling design and procedures used.

CASE 3: BIGGER TV GUIDE TUNED TO READERS

BY GEORGE LAZARUS

Is bigger better for TV Guide?

So far, it's thumbs up for a larger format of the digest-sized weekly under test in three markets, Pittsburgh, Nashville and Rochester, N.Y., for the last two months.

Source: *Chicago Tribune,* May 17, 1991, p. 3–2. Reprinted with permission.

With positive newsstand response for the 7½-by-10-inch format, exactly twice the current digest size, TV Guide boss Joseph Cece is encouraged enough to expand the test shortly to "a bigger market," likely in the western part of the country.

Cece, the Radnor, Pa.-based president-publisher of Rupert Murdoch-owned TV Guide, in Chicago this week to meet with the advertising community, declined to identify the fourth test market. Sources suggest it might be San Diego.

Beyond reporting that sales have increased in initial test areas — the bigger size is being distributed exclusively in Nashville and Rochester, with both the bigger and digest sizes available in Pittsburgh — Cece is understandably keeping open the publication's options.

A larger format for the digest-sized weekly, which made its debut in 1953, has been rumored for some time, more so since Murdoch's $3 billion buyout in 1989 of Triangle Communications, most of the money going for TV Guide. Murdoch since has said he overpaid for TV Guide, sources saying by as much as $400 million to $500 million.

Readers and advertisers, attracted by a more inviting layout, will prefer a larger format, but a bigger size will present additional production costs, including paper, of course.

Observers believe the 15.8 million-circulation TV Guide eventually will go to the larger format, best indications being by mid-1992. The format change is a much safer bet than TV Guide ever returning to the 20 million-circulation peak enjoyed in 1978.

Under Murdoch, Cece contends the weekly is much more profitable, $20 million to $30 million extra annually from a publication that already was a good bottom-line producer. Total profitability probably tops $100 million annually, but TV Guide won't divulge a figure.

Even in a weak-advertising environment that has affected all media, TV Guide has pockets big enough to splurge for the larger size, which will finally match the format of TV weekly publications of many newspapers.

Case Question

Assume that the new 7½-by-10 inch format was introduced 16 months ago and now Mr. Cece is interested in conducting a telephone interview of 3,000 people nationally to assess their opinions of the new format.

Choose from among simple random sampling, stratified sampling, or cluster sampling and design a sampling plan to interview 3,000 people.

CASE 4: BAR CODE TECHNOLOGY HELPS TRACK FLORIDA TOURISTS

BY W. LYNN SELDON JR.

When it comes to tourism, it's tough finding out exactly who's going where and why.

In an industry where marketing is so important, tracking tourists is a game many tourism officials must play. But there's never been an efficient and convenient way to track tourists until now.

Florida is at the forefront of tracking tourists with technology. The force behind this development is SouthEast Advantage (SEA) and its CEO and chairman, John L. Welday.

Source: *Marketing News,* November 12, 1990, pp. 8–9. Reprinted with permission.

SEA took grocery store technology and brought it to tourism.

SEA is a discount travel club that recently devised a coupon book for Florida attractions that allows marketing officials to track tourists.

The company developed a proprietary Tourist Tracking Systems (STTS) bar code that identifies each merchant discount coupon, as well as the individual or company redeeming it, Welday said.

"It offers a detailed audit of all coupons redeemed and by whom, as well as mailing lists and disks," he said.

This system is arranged by selling or giving coupon books to incoming Florida tourists, distributed through direct mail to more than 1.4 million Florida-bound vacationers two or three months before they arrive.

They also are distributed through 32,000 travel agents, who issue more than 11 million Florida airline tickets each year, meeting planners, thousands of major corporations, and to TV viewers.

Alamo Rent A Car's promotion alone promises to distribute more than 132 million merchant's discount cheques.

The coupons provide consumers with a merchant's best discount. Participants include Universal Studios Florida, Rivership Grand Romance, Mardi Gras, the Miami MetroZoo, PGA Passport (200 PGA golf courses) and many more.

According to the Florida Division of Tourism, the average family spends more than $3,500 on its Florida vacation. Visitors who come by auto have an annual family income of about $25,000, while visitors who fly in top $60,000. Knowing where and how the money is spent obviously is important.

When travelers receive the coupon book, they give the issuer vital information about themselves and receive a set of bar code labels they must affix to each coupon they redeem.

Each tourist has his or her own bar code, and, when used, their names, addresses, and phone numbers are known and traced by STTS users. The coupons and the bar codes are nontransferable.

Official Airline Guides, publishers of many magazines for travel agents and frequent travelers, said of SEA's efforts: "An exciting breakthrough is taking place in Florida, which is sure to have a dramatic effect on the way the state is promoted."

This comes at a crucial time for state officials, when their tourism budget was just cut by more than $500,000 and visitor figures are down.

When coupons are redeemed, the bar codes and SEA do the rest. SEA already knows who "owns" each bar code. It uses the information to give merchants a monthly computer printout and diskette listing SEA discount users and distributors of the merchant's coupons. Merchants then can use the lists for marketing efforts.

The Florida Retail Federation is seeking to promote SEA's program to its more than 7,000 major and local retail members.

These simple bar codes can lead to user printouts, mailing labels, and statistical tracking. For a fee, SEA can provide tourist figures generated by the bar codes.

The net result of this program is the development of Florida's largest computer data base of tourist profile information.

Sixty-eight percent of the state's visitors come back within about a year, according to the Florida Division of Tourism. The coupon books are good for 18 months, and return visitors can still use them on the next trip.

The benefits of tracking tourists this way, according to SEA, can help merchants do the following:

— Plan advertising by reviewing user printouts of tourist origins by area code, city, Zip code, state, or country.

— Know which travel agents and tour operators have done the best job promoting the merchant's business.

- — Track foreign visitors who have received coupons from airlines or foreign travel consultants.
- — Discover which auto rental agencies recommend a merchant's business to their customers.
- — Establish a relationship with major corporations that have used coupons for incentive travel.
- — Align marketing promotions with cruise lines offering both land and sea packages.
- — Support the local chamber of commerce's or tourist development council's worldwide marketing activities.
- — Review referrals from hotel and motel corporations, franchises, and local establishments.
- — Encourage return of associations, colleges, and universities for annual meetings and reunions.
- — Expose and test performance of new products and services by issuing different coupons.

Case Question

Comment on the sampling plan used by SouthEast Advantage to distribute its coupon books.

MEASUREMENT, SCALING, AND QUESTIONNAIRE DESIGN

RICH JOHNSON
CHAIRMAN
SAWTOOTH SOFTWARE, INC.

The wave of the future for questionnaires can be seen in the growth of CATI and CAPI, which incorporate computer technology to improve the efficiency and quality of interviewing.

"CATI (computer-assisted telephone interviewing) is already used very widely," says Rich Johnson, chairman of Idaho-based Sawtooth Software, Inc., a ten-year-old company that produces PC-based software for the marketing research industry.

"CAPI (computer-assisted personal interviewing) should experience explosive growth in the next ten years, as personal computers become familiar objects in most households," he believes. "Everybody will have access to them, and it will be easy for any interview to be computer-assisted."

Sawtooth designed Ci2, a system used for telephone and self-administered PC interviewing. Interviewers or respondents view the questions on the screen and respond using the keyboard. According to Johnson, by the late 1980s Ci2 was widely used by market researchers, who suggested additional features that the ideal interviewing system might have. "We therefore began development of the next generation of a computer interviewing system, to be called Ci3," he says.

Johnson called it unusual for small companies like his to invest in marketing research, but detailed information was needed from users of Ci2 about the features desired in the new product. Since Sawtooth's own product could be used to research the market for this new product, they tried what was a novel approach at that time — disk-by-mail (DBM) interviews.

With a letter explaining the survey's

purpose, a computer-assisted interview was put on diskette and mailed to Sawtooth's current customers—market research organizations, end-user companies, and government agencies. The respondent put the disk into a nearby PC and typed "RUN." The interview was administered automatically. After the last question was answered, the respondent was thanked and asked to return the diskette in a postpaid envelope.

"The computer-assisted method permits a high degree of control over what happens in the interview, as well as effortless randomization to overcome order bias and elaborate branching capabilities to maximize efficiency," according to Johnson.

Another benefit is that respondents are often more interested in DBM interviews than interviewer-administered, telephone, or paper-and-pencil interviews because the computer can be perceived as responsive and visually compelling.

"Electronic interviews generally result in higher levels of respondent interest and attention, and DBM surveys often have response rates exceeding 40 percent. The data are of higher quality, and that means anything you do with the data will work better, including measurement and scaling," Johnson says.

Rich Johnson earned a Ph.D. in psychometrics from the University of Washington in 1959. After a tenure in Personnel Administration at Procter & Gamble, he shifted his efforts to marketing research. His experiences as a consultant led him to cofound the John Morton Company, where he became involved in the use of small computers for survey interviewing. In 1982 he founded Sawtooth Software, a leading supplier of interviewing software throughout the world.

Concepts of Measurement and Measurement Scales

THE BEST PLACES TO LIVE NOW

It's a case of places changing places. In our four previous annual surveys of the 300 largest U.S. metropolitan areas, the most livable locales tended to be on the West or East coast. This time, top honors go largely to cities located in the Rockies, Texas, and the Midwest. Our No. 1 place to live this year: Provo/Orem, Utah, the sister cities (pop. 263,600) where the living is easy, taxes are moderate, and the economic engine is running on all cylinders. "People tell me they would take a 50% pay cut to live here, just for the quality of life," says Utah County commissioner Gary Herbert.

Middle America's excellent showing in this year's rankings reflects the shifting fortunes of the nation's regional economies. "In the 1980s, the U.S. had a bicoastal economy," says David Shulman, managing director of real estate research at Salomon Bros. "In the 1990s we're going to see strength in the middle of the country, especially among low-cost, medium-size cities with affordable housing. These are the types of places that match the needs of employers and employees," Shulman explains.

To set the criteria for this year's rankings, we asked a representative sample of 252 MONEY subscribers (median age: 46; median household income: $61,000) what they valued in a place to live. Specifically, they rated the importance of 43 factors, such as a low crime rate and low local taxes, on a scale from 1 up to 10. Our readers' top priorities were clean water, low crime, clean air, abundant medical care, and strong local government.

Next, we collected the most timely data available on each of the 300 largest U.S. metropolitan areas. Then, with the help of Fast Forward, a Portland, Ore. computer consulting firm, we awarded points to each metro area based on how well it delivered on the attributes that MONEY subscribers said they wanted. Finally, to discover local attractions or drawbacks that our data might have missed, MONEY reporters visited the top five and bottom five places plus Terre Haute, Ind., the spot that this year moved up the most notches on our list—to No. 70 from 288 in 1990.

In our continuing effort to improve the rankings, we added more comprehensive data to the equation this year. The new facts enabled us to grade the 300 metro areas more accurately when measuring five regional characteristics:

— *Housing affordability.* Century 21, the real estate brokerage, provided an exclusive list of the prices and property taxes for a typical three-bedroom home in each area as well as housing appreciation from a year ago. The least expensive homes in the U.S. today are in Texarkana, Texas ($57,000); Williamsport, Pa. ($60,000); and Bryan, Texas ($62,000).

— *Strength of municipal finances.* This year, we factored in each metropolitan area's Standard & Poor's municipal bond rating. The cities with AAAs as of December 1990: Charlotte, N.C.; Charlottesville, Va.; Dallas; Grand Rapids; Greensboro, N.C.; Lincoln, Neb.;

Pueblo, Colo.; Raleigh, N.C.; and Stamford, Conn.

— *Job prospects.* We obtained rates of employment growth for the past year from the Economic Outlook Center at Arizona State University. After Provo/Orem, the biggest job incubators were Las Vegas; Lafayette, La.; and Santa Rosa, Calif.

— *Environmental quality.* Analyst Benjamin Goldman, who spent five years researching such things as air pollution and hazardous waste for his forthcoming book, *The Truth About Where You Live* (Times Books), provided figures on those subjects.

— *Quality of libraries.* The Public Library Data Service, an arm of the American Library Association, supplied us with new figures on how much libraries across the U.S. spend, per capita, on books.

Source: Roberta Kirwan, *Money,* September 1991, pp. 130, 132, 137. Used with permission.

INTRODUCTION

It's easy to dance to. Give the song a 10. Cities are not the only things subjected to ratings. From the simple to the complex, assigning scores is how we find out who or what is the best in any given field. *Consumer Reports,* for instance, has made a reputation for accurately rating a wide variety of nondurable and durable products. Developing accurate and reliable rating systems is what measurement is all about. Simply put, *measurement* is the process by which scores or numbers are assigned to the attributes of people or objects. As in the case of ratings of cities, the rank assigned should convey accurate information about what is being investigated, in this case the quality of life in various metropolitan areas.

The type of information being sought strongly influences how scores or numbers will be assigned. If you want precise information on cigarette consumption, for example, you might ask individuals to report how many packs of cigarettes they smoke in a day, or in an average week. On the other hand, if you want to collect information on perceptions of cigarette smoking, you might ask individuals to classify themselves as either heavy or light smokers. These two questions yield very different types of measurements. In the former case, responses are given in packs per day (or packs per week), whereas in the latter case, responses are classificatory, producing two categories of smokers.

Measurement involves the use of some sort of scale: feet, inches, centimeters, yards, dollars, and so on. There are many different types of measurement scaling techniques. Various scaling techniques have different properties, and you must understand the proper way to use them because the way in which a characteristic or trait is measured has important implications for the interpretation and analysis of the data collected.

This chapter illustrates a variety of frequently used measurement scales. We start by introducing basic concepts of measurement and scaling. Then we distinguish between two general types of measurement scales: *noncomparative* and *comparative.* We describe the particular ways many of the commonly used comparative and noncomparative scales are used. We compare single-item and multiple-item scales and present illustrations of the more commonly used multiple-item scales. The final two sections of the chapter discuss issues related to the concepts of measurement validity and reliability.

MEASUREMENT DEFINED

MEASUREMENT
Process of assigning numbers to objects to represent quantities or attributes.

Measurement involves "rules for assigning numbers to objects to represent quantities or attributes."[1] Stated somewhat differently, **measurement** relates to the procedure (the rules) used to assign numbers that reflect the degree or amount of a characteristic of an object, a person, an institution, a state, or an event. An example would be rating a movie on a scale of 1 to 10. Note that measurement (i.e., the number you give the movie) reflects the extent to which the movie has certain characteristics—in this case, its entertainment value or how likable it is. We take measurements on an object or a person with respect to the level of an attribute they have. It is not consumers who are measured—only their age, income, social status, perceptions of brand benefits, purchase intentions, or some other relevant characteristic.

The most critical element in measurement is specifying the rules for assigning numbers to the characteristics to be measured. Characteristics of objects or persons take on meaning only in the context of the numbers assigned; if you don't know the rule being applied, you cannot accurately understand the characteristic in question. Consider, for instance, the characteristic of consumer *brand loyalty* and a pattern of purchases for two hypothetical consumers during a given period:

Consumer 1: A B C A B B
Consumer 2: A C B C C C

Brand loyalty could be measured, on the one hand, by computing the proportion of the six purchases devoted to the most frequently purchased brand. In that case, consumer 1, who purchased brand B three times out of six, has a brand-loyalty score of 0.50 (3/6); consumer 2, who purchased brand C four times out of six, scores 0.67 (4/6). If brand loyalty is measured by counting the number of different brands purchased, on the other hand, then both consumers get the same brand-loyalty score; they each bought three brands in the period. Conclusions about the brand loyalty of these two consumers depend upon which measurement rule the researcher adopts.

A logical question is: Which of these two measurement rules is more correct? The answer is far from clear. Many characteristics that we investigate in marketing research studies can be measured in a variety of ways. You choose measurement rules according to the objectives of the study, the precise definition of the characteristic to be measured, and the correspondence between the measurement rule and the characteristic.

Level of Measurement

The end result of measurement is to assign to each individual, household, or object a number that reflects the amount of a characteristic possessed; in this way, the researcher can differentiate individuals, households, or objects according to how much of the basic characteristic they possess. Depending on the characteristics being measured, however, the numbers assigned have different properties.

Nominal measurement.   Michael Jordan of the Chicago Bulls wears number 23 on his jersey; Patrick Ewing is number 33 on the New York Knicks. These jersey numbers provide a means of identifying these superstars and represent nominal measurement. With **nominal measurement** the numbers or letters assigned to objects serve merely as labels for identification and classification. Nominal data allow us to put an object in one and only one of a set of mutually exclusive categories or classes with no implied ordering. Your telephone number and social security number are further examples of nominally scaled data. The numbers assigned have no specific properties other than to identify the person assigned the number.

NOMINAL MEASUREMENT
Measurement in which the numbers assigned allow us to place an object in one and only one of a set of mutually exclusive and collectively exhaustive classes with no implied ordering.

Nominal-scaled variables are frequently referred to as *nonmetric* or *qualitative*. Sometimes nominal-scaled variables are referred to as *categorical*. Variables such as gender, religious denomination, and political affiliation, for example, are generally viewed as qualitative because the numbers assigned actually do not reflect the amount of the attribute possessed by an individual.[2] In fact, any ordering of the numbers assigned to the characteristic (say, reversing the numbers assigned) would have no effect on the numbering system because the numbers are not measuring anything in the first place. Because nominal data do not possess order, distance, or origin, only a limited number of statistics are permissible. To be more specific, with nominal-scaled data it is not meaningful to compute the mean because "average gender" or "average political affiliation," for example, have no meaning. Nominal-scaled data can be counted—it is legitimate to say that 55 percent of the sample is female. The appropriate measure of central tendency of nominal-scaled data is the *mode,* the value that appears most frequently. The appropriate measure of dispersion is the frequency (see Exhibit 11–1).

Ordinal measurement.   Ordinal-scaled data are ranked data. Use of rank-order data lets us say that one object has more, or less, or the same amount of an attribute as some other object. A ranking of metropolitan areas, for instance, allows you to determine which area came in first, which area came in second, and so on; however, the ranking does not convey any information about the degree of distance or interval between the first- and second-ranked cities. **Ordinal measurement** results in a sequence in which the object occupying the first position in the list is more (less) preferred than the second, the second more (less) than the third, and so forth. Similar to nominal measurement, the numbers assigned do not reflect the magnitude of a characteristic possessed by an object. In contrast to nominal measurement, however, the numbers assigned arrange the objects or alternatives according to their magnitude in an ordered relationship.

Suppose, a person rank-orders four brands according to overall preference as

A(2) B(1) C(4) D(3)

where the number in parentheses is the respective brand's rank order. Thus brand B is most preferred, followed by brands A, D, and C, respectively. You can tell from this response only the order of preference, with no further information on the difference in overall preference among the brands.

Does the difference in overall preference between the first- and second-ranked brands equal the difference in overall preference between the second- and third-ranked brands? A little thought will show that this assumption cannot be made. Even though the difference between the rank-order numbers 1 and 2 does equal the difference between the rank-order numbers 2 and 3, there is no way to draw conclusions about differences in (the degree of) preference from these data because the numbers assigned as ranks reveal nothing about the extent of the person's preferences. We know that B is preferred to A, but not by how much.

ORDINAL MEASUREMENT
Measurement in which the response alternatives define an ordered sequence so that the choice listed first is less (greater) than the second, the second less (greater) than the third, and so forth. The numbers assigned do not reflect the magnitude of an attribute possessed by an object.

Scalar Nature of Data	Range	Central Tendency	Dispersion
Nominal	Number of categories	Mode	Frequency in each category
Ordinal	Number of scalar positions	Median	Percentile or interquartile range
Interval and ratio	Top score minus bottom score plus 1	Mean	Standard deviation

*All statistics appropriate for lower-order scales (nominal is the lowest) are appropriate for higher-order scales (interval and ratio are the highest).
Source: Adapted from William J. Gephart, "Statistics, Educational," with the permission of the publisher from *Encyclopedia of Education,* Volume 8, Lee C. Deighton, Editor in Chief. Copyright © 1971 by Crowell Collier and Macmillan Inc.

EXHIBIT 11—1

Appropriate Statistics for Nominal, Ordinal, Interval, and Ratio Data*

Read the list of packaged ice cream brands on the card I just gave you.

A. Breyers   D. Frusen Glädjé

B. Sealtest   E. Hood

C. Häagen-Dazs   F. Borden

Tell me which packaged ice cream brand you prefer most. Now, excluding that brand, mention the brand of packaged ice cream that you next most prefer. (*Continue until all brands have been considered.*)

(1) __C__   (3) __F__   (5) __B__
(2) __D__   (4) __A__   (6) __E__

EXHIBIT 11—2

Ordinal Measurement of Preference Data

Ordinal data allow any transformation in numbering as long as the basic ordering of the objects is maintained. That is, we could have assigned the numbers 40 to brand C, 35 to brand D, 30 to brand A, and 10 to brand B, and we would have preserved the preference rank ordering of the four brands. Because ordinal-scaled data imply only order, the appropriate measures of central tendency are the *mode* and the *median,* the latter giving the value below which 50 percent of the observations lie. The percentile or interquartile range are the most frequently used measures of dispersion (see Exhibit 11–1).

Ordinal measurements are used frequently in commercial marketing research studies. Preference data typically are collected with ordinal measures, as demonstrated in Exhibit 11–2.

Interval measurement. Interval-scaled data allow us to say how much more one object has of an attribute than another object has. **Interval measurement** indicates how far apart two or more objects are with respect to the attribute in question, allowing us to compare the different measurements. That is, on an interval scale, the difference in the amount of an attribute between a measurement of 2 and a measurement of 3 is equal to the difference in the amount between a measurement of 3 and one of 4; furthermore, the difference between a measurement of 1 and one of 2 is one

INTERVAL MEASUREMENT

Measurement that allows us to tell how far apart two or more objects are with respect to the attribute and consequently to compare the difference between the numbers assigned. Because the interval data lack a natural or absolute origin, the absolute magnitude of the numbers cannot be compared.

EXHIBIT 11–3

Interval Measurement:
Two Typical Question
Formats

A. Please indicate your degree of agreement or disagreement with each of the following statements by selecting the appropriate response.

Breyers Ice Cream Is:	Strongly Agree	Agree	Neither Agree nor Disagree	Disagree	Strongly Disagree
Wholesome	_____	_____	_____	_____	_____
Healthy	_____	_____	_____	_____	_____
Premium-priced	_____	_____	_____	_____	_____
Unique	_____	_____	_____	_____	_____
Good value	_____	_____	_____	_____	_____

B. I would like you to rate the six brands of packaged ice cream on an overall basis. [*Hand respondent the card.*] Using the phrases on this card, please tell me how you would rate [*Brand checked following "x".*] overall? [*Record in appropriate place below.*] And how would you rate [*Insert next brand.*]? [*Record in appropriate place below. Continue for each checked brand.*]

	Excellent	Very Good	Good	Fair	Poor
( ) Häagen-Dazs	5	4	3	2	1
(x) Breyers	5	4	3	2	1
(√) Hood	5	4	3	2	1
(√) Frusen Glädjé	5	4	3	2	1
(√) Sealtest	5	4	3	2	1
(√) Borden	5	4	3	2	1

half the difference between a measurement of 2 and one of 4. For interval measurement the arithmetic *mean* is the most frequently used measure of central tendency, and the standard deviation is the most frequently used measure of dispersion (see Exhibit 11–1).

This is not to say, however, that interval data allow comparison of the absolute magnitude of the measurements across objects. To state it differently, there is no way to say that the object assigned the number 4 on an interval scale has twice or double the characteristic being measured as the object assigned the number 2. More specifically, consider the Fahrenheit temperature scale, which is interval in nature. When the temperature reads 40°, you can not say that it is twice as hot as if it was 20°. The reason is that interval scales such as the Fahrenheit temperature scale do not possess a natural or absolute origin (zero point). 0° temperature is a relative point on the Fahrenheit temperature scale and does not indicate the absence or lack of temperature.

Interval measurements are frequently used in commercial marketing research studies, especially for gathering attitudinal and overall brand-rating information. Exhibit 11–3 demonstrates two typical question formats.

Ratio measurement.   Ratio-scaled data have the same properties as interval-scaled data—with one important difference. **Ratio measurement** yields a natural or absolute origin. Thus, we can legitimately say that the object assigned the number 4 has twice the characteristic being measured as the object assigned the number 2 on a ratio scale. Ratio data are frequently associated with directly observable physical events or entities. Directly observable relevant marketing constructs that have ratio data properties include market share, sales, income, and number of sales persons per territory, for example. For ratio measurement, the most frequently used measures of central tendency and dispersion are the mean and standard deviation, respectively (see Exhibit 11–1).

SCALE TYPES

The various types of measurement scales fall into two broad categories: *noncomparative* and *comparative scales.*

Noncomparative Scaling

Noncomparative scaling requires the respondent to evaluate each object on the scale provided independently of the other objects being investigated. Noncomparative rating scales do not ask the respondent to compare the object being rated against either another object or some specified standard. For example, in rating a specific brand, the respondent assigns a rating based upon whatever standard is appropriate for him or her; the design of the study provides no comparison baseline such as "your ideal brand." This is not to say that respondents use no standard, just that the researcher has not provided it. Because each object is rated independently, noncomparative scaling is frequently referred to as *monadic* scaling. Monadic scales are the most widely used scaling technique in commercial marketing research studies.

Line marking/continuous rating scales.   The **line marking/continuous rating scale** instructs the respondent to assign a rating by placing a mark on a line at the position that best describes the object under study. Note that no explicit standard for comparison is given. Exhibit 11–4 shows two versions of a continuous rating scale.

In one case (Type A), the use of numbers and descriptions along the continuum helps the respondent locate the rating. In the other case (Type B), however, the respondent is free to check anywhere on the line without the aid of numbers; a score is usually determined by dividing a five-inch line into as many categories as desired and assigning a score based on the category into which the respondent's mark falls. Scores also can be determined by measuring the distance, in millimeters or inches, from the left- or right-hand end of the scale and coding the distance from 0 to 127 (millimeters) or 0 to 100 (1/20 inch).

Itemized rating scales.   An **itemized rating scale** provides a scale that has numbers and/or brief descriptions associated with each category and

RATIO MEASUREMENT
Measurement that has the same properties as interval scales, but which also have a natural or absolute origin.

NONCOMPARATIVE SCALING
Scaling method whereby the respondent is asked to evaluate each object on a scale independently of the other objects being investigated.

LINE MARKING/ CONTINUOUS RATING SCALE
Procedure that instructs the respondent to assign a rating by placing a marker at the appropriate position on a line that best describes the object under study.

ITEMIZED RATING SCALE
The respondent is provided with a scale having numbers and/or brief descriptions associated with each category and asked to select one of the limited number of categories, ordered in terms of scale position, that best describes the object under study.

EXHIBIT 11—4
Continuous Rating Scale

Please indicate your overall opinion of Mike Tyson by placing a mark (x) at the appropriate location on the line shown below.

Type A

```
0  10  20  30  40  50  60  70  80  90  100
Unfavorable          Neutral              Favorable
```

Type B

```
Unfavorable                              Favorable
```

EXHIBIT 11—5
Itemized Rating Scales

Please indicate your overall opinion of Mike Tyson by placing a mark (x) in one of the categories shown below.

Type A
Favorable   Unfavorable

| _____ : _____ : _____ : _____ : _____ : _____ : _____ |
| Extremely | Quite | Slightly | Neither | Slightly | Quite | Extremely |

Type B
Favorable   Unfavorable

_____ : _____ : _____ : _____ : _____ : _____ : _____

Type C
Favorable   Unfavorable

| _____ : _____ : _____ : _____ : _____ : _____ : _____ |
| 7 | 6 | 5 | 4 | 3 | 2 | 1 |

Type D
Favorable   Unfavorable

| 7 | 6 | 5 | 4 | 3 | 2 | 1 |

asks the respondent to select one of the limited number of categories, ordered in terms of scale position, that best describes the object under study. Several different types of itemized rating scales are illustrated in Exhibit 11–5.

Itemized rating scales are frequently used to measure purchase intentions. Purchase intention scales represent an attempt to measure a respondent's interest in a brand or product. More specifically, they provide information to get at the key issue: How likely is a respondent to purchase a given brand, product, or concept? Two types of purchase intent scales are frequently used: a 5-point itemized rating scale and an 11-point purchase probability scale. Exhibit 11–6 presents each type of scale.

The 5-point itemized rating scale is the more commonly used purchase intent scale, at least in commercial marketing research. Interest typically focuses on top-box purchase intent scores. **Top-box** refers to the percentage of respondents rating a brand, product, or concept in the most favorable category on the rating scale, that is, those checking the first choice, (e.g., the "definitely would buy" category on the 5-point scale). Top-box percentages are routinely used as a criterion of performance in marketing research, and the item achieving the highest top-box score is deemed the strongest or most acceptable.

TOP BOX
Percentage of respondents rating a brand, product, or concept in the most favorable category on the rating scale.

EXHIBIT 11—6

Purchase Intent Scales

If this new product were available at an outlet where you usually shop, how likely would it be that you would purchase it?

Five-Point Scale

___ Definitely would buy.

___ Probably would buy.

___ Might or might not buy.

___ Probably would not buy.

___ Definitely would not buy.

Eleven-Point Scale

10 — Certain, (99 in 100).

9 — Almost sure (9 in 10).

8 — Very probably (8 in 10).

7 — Probably (7 in 10).

6 — Good possibility (6 in 10).

5 — Fairly good possibility (5 in 10).

4 — Fair possibility (4 in 10).

3 — Some possibility (3 in 10).

2 — Very slight possibility (2 in 10).

1 — Almost no chance (1 in 10).

0 — No chance (0 in 100).

Itemized rating scales can take on a variety of formats depending upon the number of categories, the nature and degree of verbal description, the number of favorable and unfavorable categories, the specification of a neutral position, and the forced or unforced nature of the scale.

Number of categories.   Theoretically, itemized rating scales can include any number of response categories. The basic issue concerns the respondent's ability to discriminate among categories. To be more specific, researchers who favor using a large number of scale categories argue that respondents are capable of making fine distinctions, while those who favor using only a limited, and usually small, number of scale categories claim that respondents have trouble drawing fine distinctions and forcing them to do so results in ambiguous data at best. Is there an optimal number of categories to choose in all situations? Probably not. In most marketing research applications, rating scales typically include between five and nine response categories; this is simply an observation, however, and not generalizable to all circumstances.[3]

Nature and degree of verbal description.   Various types of verbal descriptions and numeric formats can be used. Verbal category descriptors help to ensure that each respondent is operating from the same base; it is worth noting at the same time that the presence and nature of verbal category descriptors can affect responses.[4] Pictures and other types of graphic illustrations can also be used, especially if the respondents are children. Two graphic itemized rating scales are shown in Exhibit 11–7.

Number of favorable and unfavorable categories.   If an equal number of favorable and unfavorable scale categories are specified, the scale is called **balanced**; if an unequal number are specified, the scale is said to be **unbalanced.** An unbalanced itemized rating scale might look like this:

Excellent ___

Very good ___

Good ___

Fair ___

Poor ___

BALANCED SCALE

Scale using an equal number of favorable and unfavorable categories.

UNBALANCED SCALE

Scale using an unequal number of favorable and unfavorable scale categories.

EXHIBIT 11—7

Graphic Itemized Rating
Scales

A. Please mark (X) on the face that best describes how you feel about the Bill Cosby Show.

B. Now I would like to know how you would expect these new cough drops to taste *just* based on what I read to you. Picture a thermometer scale that goes from zero to 100, where 100 is the very best, and 0 is the very worst. As a cough drop for your own use, what number from 0 to 100 would best describe your expectation of the *overall taste qualities* of the cough drops I read about? (DO *NOT* READ LIST. RECORD ONE ANSWER.)

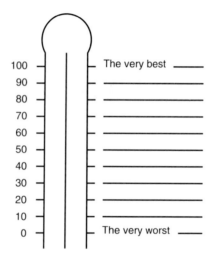

When are unbalanced rating scales useful? It seems reasonable that when you expect the distribution of responses to be skewed, either positive or negative, you would use an unbalanced scale that has more categories in the direction of the skewness. For example, unbalanced scales are frequently used when asking socially threatening questions. Studies of heavy users of a product or service represent another justified use of an unbalanced scale because most of the respondents are presumed to have favorable reactions to product features and imagery.

Specification of a neutral position.   If a balanced rating scale is used, the researcher must decide whether to employ an *even* or an *odd* number of scale items. Using an odd number of scale items, the middle scale position generally becomes the neutral point. A balanced, odd-numbered itemized rating scale is shown in Exhibit 11–5, Type A. Some researchers argue against including a neutral position because they say respondents really are not neutral and should be forced to indicate a nonneutral response. Proponents of scales offering neutral positions have decided that it is possible for a respondent to be neutral and that respondents who can indeed be neutral regarding the object under study should be able to express their neutrality.

Scale Type	Measurement	Properties	Advantages/Disadvantages
Continuous rating	Interval	Order distance	Information on intensity is obtained. Easy to administer. Not very cognitively taxing. Differences between objects may not surface. Requires template for coding.
Itemized rating	Interval	Order distance	Information on intensity is obtained. Easy to administer. Not very cognitively taxing. Highly flexible with the use of verbal descriptors and different numbers of response-item categories. Differences between objects may not surface.

EXHIBIT 11—8

Summary of Noncomparative/Monadic Scales

Forced or unforced nature of a scale. In a **forced itemized rating scale** respondents must indicate answers even though in fact they may have no opinion on or no knowledge about a subject. While respondents with no opinion may mark the midpoint of the scale, enough of such responses will distort measures of central tendency and variance. A scale with a "no opinion" or "no knowledge" category avoids the forcing problem.

Exhibit 11–8 presents a comparison of the two monadic scales we have discussed.

FORCED ITEMIZED RATING SCALE

Procedure in which a respondent indicates a response on a scale, even though he or she may have "no opinion" or "no knowledge" about the question.

Comparative Scaling

Comparative scaling means that the subject compares one set of objects directly with another. For example, a respondent may be asked to make a direct comparison in terms of the flavor of his or her current brand of toothpaste against competing brands. Comparative scaling requires results to be interpreted in relative terms according to ordinal or rank-order properties; that is, the scores obtained indicate that one brand is preferred to another, but not by how much. An attractive feature of comparative scales is that they make it possible to detect relatively small differences among the

COMPARATIVE SCALING

Scaling process in which the subject is asked to compare a set of stimulus objects directly against one another.

Using a funny face item (face scale) with children as respondents

objects being compared. Also, comparative scales are easily understood by people answering questionnaires. Note, however, that because the instructions direct the respondent to compare objects, differences that a respondent may never have considered can surface as an artifact of the instructions.

Paired comparisons.   Probably the most widely used comparative scaling technique is paired comparisons. The **paired comparison scale** presents two objects at a time and asks the respondent to select one of the two according to some specified criterion. Paired comparisons yield ordinal-scaled data; for example, brand A is preferred to brand B; brand A tastes better than brand B, and so on. Marketing researchers frequently use paired comparisons, especially when the objects are physical products.

To illustrate the use of paired comparisons, consider a mall-intercept package design study in which 100 consumers are exposed to four new package designs. After qualifying the respondents, the interviewer presents each respondent with an 8-inch-by-8-inch poster showing a color picture of two different package designs, asking which of the two designs is most preferred. With a total of four package designs, the respondent views six posters, one at a time, in random order. Labeling the four package designs by the letters A, B, C, and D, the six paired comparisons are

(A,B) (A,C) (A,D) (B,C) (B,D) (C,D).

To tabulate the paired comparison data you simply form a table whose elements indicate the percentage of people who chose each package design when paired with the other three package designs. The first portion of Table 11-1 presents such a table. The numbers in this table give the proportion of times the package design listed in a column was chosen over the package design listed in a row. For example, package A was chosen by 80 percent of the respondents (or 80 percent of the time) when paired with

TABLE 11-1

Paired Comparison Data

Proportion of Times Column Package Design Chosen over Row Package Design			
	A	B	C	D
A	—	.20	.75	.40
B	.80	—	.90	.70
C	.25	.10	—	.35
D	.60	.30	.65	—

Calculation of Rank-Order Values			
	A	B	C	D
A	—	0	1	0
B	1	—	1	1
C	0	0	—	0
D	1	0	1	—
Sum	2	0	3	1

package B; consequently, as shown in the table, package B was chosen 20 percent of the time when paired with package A. When paired with package C, package A was chosen 25 percent of the time, and so forth.

It is often desirable to form a rank ordering of the objects used in the paired comparisons. In the context of the package design study just described, notice that package C was preferred to all other packages (all of the proportions appearing in the package C column are greater than 0.50), and package B was not preferred to any of the other packages (all of the proportions appearing in the package B column are less than 0.50). Thus, the paired comparisons indicate that package C is the "winner," that is, most preferred, whereas package B is the "loser," that is, least preferred.

To obtain the full rank ordering, it is convenient to form another table, which is shown in the second portion of Table 11–1. If the package design listed in a given column is preferred (that is, it has a proportion > 0.50) to the package design listed in a row, a 1 is placed in the corresponding row and column position in the table. If the package design listed in a given column is not preferred (that is, it has a proportion < 0.50), a 0 is placed in the corresponding row and column position in the table.[5] Thus, the table is filled with 1s and 0s, indicating which of the column elements were preferred or not preferred, respectively. The rank order of the package designs is calculated by simply summing the column elements. The order of preference for the four package designs is: C is preferred to A, D, and B; A is preferred to D and B; and D is preferred to B. It is often convenient to write the rank ordering in the following way

$$C > A > D > B.$$

Paired comparisons are relatively easy to administer and to analyze. However, with even moderate numbers of objects (that is, products or attributes), the number of paired comparisons can become extremely large. In general, with n brands there are

$$n(n - 1)/2$$

paired comparisons. With only six brands, for example, there are 15 paired comparisons. As the number of paired comparisons increases, so does respondent fatigue and possibly frustration.

Rank-order scales. Following paired comparison scales, the most widely used comparative scaling technique is simple rank ordering. **Rank-order scales** require respondents to be simultaneously presented with several objects that they order or rank.

To illustrate the use of simple rank order, assume that 10 people are ranking four brands according to their preference for each. Each person is shown a list of four brands and instructed to place a 1 beside the brand he or she most prefers, a 2 beside his or her second choice, and so forth. The first portion of Table 11–2 presents data for a sample of 10 individuals. According to the table, the first individual ranks brand B first, brand A

RANK-ORDER SCALE
Scale in which respondents are presented with several objects simultaneously and requested to "order" or "rank" them.

TABLE 11–2
Rank-Order Data

Simple Rank-Order Data

Respondent	A	B	C	D
1	2	1	3	4
2	1	2	4	3
3	2	1	3	4
4	4	2	1	3
5	3	1	2	4
6	2	1	3	4
7	1	3	2	4
8	4	2	1	3
9	2	1	4	3
10	3	1	4	2

Tabulated Rank-Ordered Data

Brand	Ranking			
	1st	2nd	3rd	4th
A	2	4	2	2
B	6	3	1	0
C	2	2	3	3
D	0	1	4	5

second, brand C third, and brand D fourth; the second individual ranks brand A first, brand B second, brand D third, and brand C fourth, and so on.

The second portion of Table 11–2 presents summary information. Here the numbers in the table give the number of times each brand was ranked either first, second, third, or fourth. For example, brand A was ranked first twice, while brand B was ranked first six times. One way to use the rank-ordered data to scale the brands according to preference is to multiply the frequency of times a brand was ranked first, second, third, and fourth by the ranking. For the rank-ordered data of Table 11–2

Brand A: $(2 \times 1) + (4 \times 2) + (2 \times 3) + (2 \times 4) = 24$
Brand B: $(6 \times 1) + (3 \times 2) + (1 \times 3) + (0 \times 4) = 15$
Brand C: $(2 \times 1) + (2 \times 2) + (3 \times 3) + (3 \times 4) = 27$
Brand D: $(0 \times 1) + (1 \times 2) + (4 \times 3) + (5 \times 4) = 34$

The scaling procedure uses an ordinal scale with low numbers indicating higher preference; for example, brand B is preferred to brands A, C, and D; brand A is preferred to brands C and D; and brand C is preferred to brand D:

$$B > A > C > D$$

CONSTANT SUM SCALE
Procedure whereby respondents are instructed to allocate a number of points or chips among alternatives according to some criterion—for example, preference, importance, and so on.

Constant sum scales. The **constant sum scale** is a popular device that marketing researchers use to deal with the problem of having respondents evaluate objects two at a time. Here respondents allocate a number of

Below are five characteristics that you might consider in purchasing an automobile. Please allocate 100 points among the characteristics so that your allocation represents the importance of each characteristic to you. The more points a characteristic receives, the more important the characteristic is to you. If the characteristic is not at all important, you can assign zero points. If a characteristic is twice as important as some other characteristic, you should give it twice as many points. The number of points must sum to 100.

Characteristics	Number of Points
1. Styling	50
2. Ride	10
3. Gas mileage	35
4. Warranty	5
5. Closeness to dealer	0
	100

EXHIBIT 11—9

Constant Sum Scale

points or chips (say, for example, 100) among alternatives according to some criterion (for example, preference or importance). Instructions are for respondents to allocate the points or chips in such a way that if they like brand A twice as much as brand B, they should assign brand A twice as many points or chips.

Implementation of the constant sum scale differs depending on the type of interview. For example, in a personal interview you can actually give respondents 100 *chips* and have them allocate the chips among a set of alternatives with respect to some criterion that you specify. This method has the advantage of allowing visual inspection of the actual height or number of chips allocated, and respondents are free to move the chips around to represent their reactions. In a mall interview you probably would ask the respondent to allocate 100 *points* among the alternatives. The respondent is still free to change the allocation, but because chips are not actually being distributed, the inspection is more difficult. Exhibit 11–9

Using poker chips for constant sum scale

presents a typical application of the constant sum method used to describe automobile characteristics. Notice the allocations have been filled in to illustrate how a typical respondent might have reacted.

To scale the characteristics, you simply count the points assigned to each characteristic by each person. Note that the scale, using 100 points, ranges from 0 to 100 for each object, where *n* equals the number of respondents (the sample size).

One problem with using a constant sum scale in mail surveys is that the respondent may allocate more or less of the points or chips available. That is, if the respondent is instructed to allocate 100 points but instead allocates 112 points or 95 points, the researcher must adjust the data in some way

---

EXHIBIT 11−10

Constant Sum Scale Used in Concept and Product Testing Study

Now I'd like you to think about the last 10 times you bought shampoo or asked someone to buy it for you. Please divide 10 points to indicate how many of each brand you bought (or requested) the last 10 times. Please give us your best estimates, even if you can't remember exactly what you bought. You may assign the points any way you wish, as long as the points add up to 10. [*Hand questionnaire with pencil to respondent.*] [*After respondent has finished, take back questionnaire. Total must add up to 10.*]

Brand	Code	Points
Agree II	(6)	
Alberto VO-5	(7)	5
Body on Tap	(8)	
Breck	(9)	3
Fabergé Organic	(10)	
Finesse	(11)	
Flex	(12)	
Halo	(13)	
Halsa	(14)	
Head and Shoulders	(15)	1
Ivory	(16)	
Jhirmack	(17)	
Johnson's Baby Shampoo	(18)	1
L'Oreal	(19)	
Mink Difference	(20)	
Pert	(21)	
Sesame Street	(22)	
Silkience	(23)	
Suave	(24)	
Tame	(25)	
Timotei	(26)	
Vidal Sassoon	(27)	
Other brand(s):_____	(28)	

SPECIFY

Total must equal   10

EXHIBIT 11—11

Line Marking Scale

[*Have the respondent read the instructions along with you.*]

You have previously indicated the set of carbonated soft drinks that you considered when making your last purchase. Now, I'm going to present you with pairs of carbonated soft drinks, and I would like you to indicate how similar the brands are to each other. We are going to make this easy for you by having you mark a line anchored by the phrases "exactly the same" and "completely different." For example, if you think that Diet Pepsi is quite similar to Diet Coke, your response might look like this.

Diet Pepsi versus Diet Coke

Exactly the   Completely
same — X ——————————————————————————————— different

[*Hand respondent first pair.*]

7UP versus Coca-Cola Classic

Exactly the   Completely
same ——————————————————————————————— X —— different

[*Hand respondent second pair.*]
Sprite versus 7UP

Exactly the   Completely
same — X ——————————————————————————————— different

Note: The judgments as measured from the left-hand end of the scale indicate dissimilarity, that is, the longer the measurement, the more dissimilar is the pair. Judgments can be coded from 0 to 127 (millimeters) or 0 to 100 (1/20 inch).

(say, by proportionately increasing or decreasing the points allocated) or delete this respondent's data.

Another problem relates to the cognitive effort that is required of respondents. In the automobile example, for instance, respondents might find it complicated to allocate points in a manner consistent with the way they actually value each characteristic.

Constant sum scales are used in commercial concept and product testing studies. In these types of studies constant sum scales are used to collect purchase history data. Exhibit 11–10 illustrates the use of a constant sum scale in collecting information on shampoo purchase behavior. Notice the respondent is asked to allocate 10 points according to how many of each brand was bought over the 10 last shopping occasions. The illustrative data presented indicate that Alberto VO-5 accounts for about 50 percent of this person's shampoo consumption.

Line marking/continuous rating comparative scale.   Line marking/continuous rating scales can also assume a comparative format when collecting information on similarity judgments. Typically, the respondent is presented with object pairs and asked to judge their similarity by marking a five-inch line anchored at one end by the phrase "Exactly the same" and at the other end by "Completely different."

Exhibit 11–11 shows the typical instructions provided to respondents and an example of how the line marking scale would be used in assessing the perceived similarities and dissimilarities among a set of carbonated soft drinks.

EXHIBIT 11—12

Summary of Comparative Scales

Scale Type	Measurement	Properties	Advantages/ Disadvantages
Paired comparison	Ordinal	Order interval with transformation	Easy to administer. Easy to analyze. May force differences to be expressed when none exist. Large number of comparisons may cause respondent fatigue.
Rank order	Ordinal	Order	Easy to administer. Can be used to handle large number of alternatives. Respondents may have difficulty in ranking a large number of alternatives. May force differences to be expressed when none exist.
Constant sum	Interval	Order distance	Information on intensity is obtained. Easy to administer. Can be cognitively taxing. Respondents may allocate more points or fewer points than the specified number.
Line marking	Interval	Order distance	Information on intensity is obtained. Easy to administer. Requires template for coding. Large number of comparisons may cause respondent fatigue.

Each sort of comparative scale has its own pluses and minuses for marketing research projects. By way of summary, Exhibit 11–12 presents a comparison of the various comparative scales just described.

SINGLE-ITEM VERSUS MULTIPLE-ITEM SCALES

A multiple-item scale usually consists of a number of statements that the respondent must react to, for example, indicate how favorable or unfavorable each statement is. An overall score is then determined by combining the reactions to each of the statements.

Multiple-item scales are frequently used in attitude measurement. Attitudes represent a person's likes and dislikes of an object or a situation, based upon the person's beliefs; to some degree, attitudes determine how a person will *respond* to that object in the future.

> For our purposes we agree that: Attitude is a learned predisposition to respond in a consistently favorable or unfavorable manner with respect to a given object.[6]

This description specifies three fundamental characteristics about attitudes: They are learned; they affect behavior; and they are consistent with regard to an object.

Though attitudes can be measured with a single-item rating scale, multiple-item scales provide at least two principal advantages. First, because attitudes are complex, reflecting much of a person's learned beliefs and experiences, a single-item scale may provide only a crude measure of an individual's overall feelings about an attitude object. Attitudes are likely to be multifaceted; many different factors influence how a person feels about an object or issue. Single-item scales provide no information about the possible reasons for why the specific attitude has taken shape. Second, including multiple items in a scale and then combining the ratings on the various statements to form a combined score permits an assessment of two important measurement properties: validity and reliability. We discuss these after describing several multiple-item scales that are frequently used in marketing research.

MULTIPLE-ITEM SCALES

Semantic Differential Scale

Charles Osgood, George Suci, and Percy Tannenbaum are credited for the development of the semantic differential scale.[7] Their scale was originally used in psychological and personality research to measure the perceived meanings of words and concepts. They found that the perceived meaning of a variety of words and concepts could be decomposed in terms of three components: *potency, activity,* and *evaluation.* In marketing research studies, the semantic differential scale is frequently used to measure attitudes toward and imagery surrounding products and services. Generally, only the evaluative (e.g., good/bad) component is measured.

The **semantic differential scale** consists of a number of bipolar (opposite) adjective phrases or statements that could be used to describe the objects being evaluated. In the original scale development work of Osgood, Suci, and Tannenbaum, only single-word bi-polar adjectives, not phrases, were used. However, common practice in marketing research applications is to use adjective phrases as well.

The semantic differential scale in Exhibit 11–13 consists of bipolar adjective phrases and statements that pertain to Kmart. Each bipolar adjective rating scale consists of seven categories, with neither numerical labels nor category descriptions other than for the anchor categories. To remove any position bias, favorable and unfavorable adjective phrases are randomly distributed to the left-hand and right-hand anchor positions. The respondent is asked to check one of the seven categories that best describes his or her views about the object (Kmart) along the continuum implied by the bipolar adjective pair. An overall attitude score is computed by summing the responses on each adjective pair. Before computing the overall score, the response categories must be coded. Usually the categories are assigned values from 1 to 7, where a 1 is assigned to the unfavorable adjective phrase and a 7 is assigned to the favorable adjective phrase. Thus, before assigning codes and summing, the researcher must be careful to reverse the individual scale items where necessary so that each attitude continuum ranges from unfavorable to favorable, or vice versa.

Ratings on each of the bipolar adjective pairs are frequently used to provide a profile or image of the objects being investigated. This is accomplished by plotting the mean ratings on each bipolar adjective pair for each of the objects.

SEMANTIC DIFFERENTIAL
Scaling technique where a measure of the person's attitude is obtained by rating the object or behavior in question on a set of bipolar adjective scales.

EXHIBIT 11–13

Semantic Differential Scale

We would like you to tell us what you think about (Kmart). Below are a number of statements that could be used to describe (Kmart). For each pair of adjective phrases, please check the category that best describes your feelings about (Kmart).

Modern	_____ : _____ : _____ : _____ : _____ : _____ : _____	Old-fashioned
Low prices	_____ : _____ : _____ : _____ : _____ : _____ : _____	High prices
Unfriendly employees	_____ : _____ : _____ : _____ : _____ : _____ : _____	Friendly employees
Knowledgeable employees	_____ : _____ : _____ : _____ : _____ : _____ : _____	Unknowledgeable employees
Limited product assortment	_____ : _____ : _____ : _____ : _____ : _____ : _____	Wide product assortment
Sophisticated customers	_____ : _____ : _____ : _____ : _____ : _____ : _____	Unsophisticated customers
Quick service	_____ : _____ : _____ : _____ : _____ : _____ : _____	Slow service
Inviting atmosphere	_____ : _____ : _____ : _____ : _____ : _____ : _____	Cold atmosphere
Attractive interior	_____ : _____ : _____ : _____ : _____ : _____ : _____	Unattractive interior
Inconvenient store hours	_____ : _____ : _____ : _____ : _____ : _____ : _____	Convenient store hours

Exhibit 11–14 presents illustrative pictorial profiles for Kmart and J. C. Penney. Notice that to facilitate interpretation of the profiles, all of the favorable adjective phrases are positioned on the same side. From this "snake plot" it appears that, among other things, J. C. Penney has an edge over Kmart when it comes to attractiveness of interiors, friendly and knowledgeable employees, wide product assortment, sophisticated customers, and inviting atmosphere. Kmart has an edge over J. C. Penney when it comes to low prices, quick service, and convenient store hours. Overall it appears that J. C. Penney is more favorably perceived than Kmart since the profile of J. C. Penney is in general closer to the more favorable end (the left end) of the scales.

Stapel Scale

STAPEL SCALE

Procedure using a single criterion or key word and instructing the respondent to rate the object on a scale.

A modification of the semantic differential scale, the **stapel scale** uses a single criterion or key word and instructs the respondent to rate the object on a scale from, for example, "does not describe" to "describes completely." Typically, each scale item has 10 response categories with no neutral or indifference category. The scale is generally presented with numerical labels, but no verbal labels. Exhibit 11–15 presents an example using four of the adjective phrases used in the previously described semantic differential scale.

Ratings given in response to a stapel scale can be analyzed by using procedures similar to those used for analyzing responses to the semantic differential scale. An overall evaluative score can be computed for each respondent by summing the ratings given to each scale item. Similarly,

EXHIBIT 11—14

Semantic Differential Profiles for Kmart and J. C. Penney

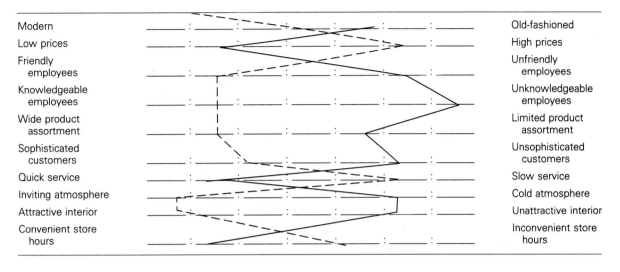

Modern		Old-fashioned
Low prices		High prices
Friendly employees		Unfriendly employees
Knowledgeable employees		Unknowledgeable employees
Wide product assortment		Limited product assortment
Sophisticated customers		Unsophisticated customers
Quick service		Slow service
Inviting atmosphere		Cold atmosphere
Attractive interior		Unattractive interior
Convenient store hours		Inconvenient store hours

Key:Kmart _____ ;   J. C. Penney _ _ _ .

EXHIBIT 11—15

Stapel Scale

Please select a plus + number for words or phrases that you think describe (Kmart) accurately. The stronger you feel the word or phrase describes the store, the larger the plus number you should choose. Select a minus − number for words or phrases that you think do not describe (Kmart) accurately. The less you feel the word or phrase describes the store, the larger the minus number you should choose. You can therefore select any number from + 5 for words or phrases you think are very accurate, to − 5 for words or phrases you think are very inaccurate.

+ 5	+ 5	+ 5	+ 5
+ 4	+ 4	+ 4	+ 4
+ 3	+ 3	+ 3	+ 3
+ 2	+ 2	+ 2	+ 2
+ 1	+ 1	+ 1	+ 1
Low prices	Friendly employees	Cold atmosphere	Slow service
− 1	− 1	− 1	− 1
− 2	− 2	− 2	− 2
− 3	− 3	− 3	− 3
− 4	− 4	− 4	− 4
− 5	− 5	− 5	− 5

snakelike profile plots can also be constructed from the mean rating on each scale item.

Compared to the semantic differential scale, the stapel scale is easy to construct since the researcher can avoid the difficult task of developing bipolar adjective phrases or statements. The stapel scale, however, has not enjoyed much popularity in commercial marketing research. There are perhaps two reasons for this. First, compared to the semantic differential scale, the instructions and format of the stapel scale appear to be more complex. Second, the descriptor adjectives can be phrased in a positive, neutral, or negative vein. There is some evidence suggesting that the use of different phrasings can have an affect on scale results and on a respondent's ability to respond.[8] The choice between using a semantic differential scale or a stapel scale will probably have to be decided on the basis of the particular research setting at hand, since very little evidence has appeared favoring the superiority of one scale over the other. In fact, two studies have found no significant differences between these two scale types.[9]

Likert Scale

The Likert scale bears the name of its originator, Renis Likert.[10] A **Likert scale** consists of a number of evaluative statements concerning an attitude object. The number of statements used will depend on the number of salient characteristics associated with the attitude object and, therefore, will vary from study to study. Usually, a Likert scale will have 20 to 30 statements. An even number of favorable and unfavorable statements should be used so that the scale is balanced. A balance of unfavorable and favorable statements reduces the likelihood of acquiescence bias, (the tendency to agree or disagree with a set of questions), which is more likely if all of the statements are in the same direction.

Exhibit 11–16 presents an illustrative Likert scale that a store like Kmart could use to measure customer attitudes toward itself and a competitor like J. C. Penney. As shown in the exhibit, the response categories of a Likert scale usually will not have numerical labels, just verbal labels.

For analysis purposes, numerical codes are assigned to each response category in order to compute an overall evaluative score that reflects the respondent's attitude toward each attitude object, in this case, Kmart and J. C. Penney. The most typical way to code response categories is to assign the numbers 1 through 5, although in some cases other codes have been used, for example, $+2$, $+1$, 0, -1, -2. When assigning the numbers, care must be taken to ensure that response categories are coded in a consistent fashion. The "strongly agree" category for a favorable statement should receive a value of 5; similarly, the "strongly disagree" category for an unfavorable statement should also receive a value of 5. A respondent's overall evaluative score is computed by summing his or her numerical ratings on all of the statements making up the scale.

The success of using a Likert scale will in large measure be determined by the quality of the scale items used. The scale items selected should possess three qualities: (1) they should capture all relevant aspects of the attitude object; (2) they should be unambiguous; and (3) they should be sensitive enough to discriminate among respondents with respect to the attitude object under investigation. The recommended practice is to first generate a relatively large pool of statements and then prune the number of statements according to how well each statement discriminates between respondents holding favorable and unfavorable attitudes. Various procedures have been suggested for generating an initial pool of statements and narrowing it.[11]

EXHIBIT 11—16

Likert Scale

Please indicate by checking (X) the appropriate category the extent to which you agree with the following statements about (Kmart).

	Strongly Disagree	Disagree	Neither Agree nor Disagree	Agree	Strongly Agree
1. The store has an inviting atmosphere.	_____	_____	_____	_____	_____
2. The clerks are knowledgeable.	_____	_____	_____	_____	_____
3. The store's checkout lines move slowly.	_____	_____	_____	_____	_____
4. The store offers a wide product assortment.	_____	_____	_____	_____	_____
5. The store has an unattractive interior.	_____	_____	_____	_____	_____
6. The clerks are unfriendly.	_____	_____	_____	_____	_____

VALIDITY

Validity asks the question: Are we measuring what we want to measure? When measuring physical properties, such as using a doctor's scale to measure the weight of an individual, we feel comfortable knowing that the measuring device is measuring the desired characteristic. That is, the number read from the scale is the actual weight of the individual. However, when the characteristic to be measured is not immediately visible (attitudes, opinions, beliefs, etc.) the validity of the measurement comes into question. We are sure that at one time or another we have all said, "That test was not a true reflection of my ability." If this is true, then the test was not a valid measure of the ability it was designed to measure.

To be valid, a scale must fully capture all of the aspects of the characteristic or trait to be measured. For example, if we wanted to measure your mathematical skills and asked questions on geometry but not topics such as algebra, trigonometry, and reasoning, we would not be validly measuring your mathematical skills. For this reason, if we want to measure such traits as attitudes or opinions, we want a measurement scale with multiple items to ensure that domain of the characteristic to be measured is appropriately covered.

VALIDITY
The extent to which the measuring device measures what it was designed to measure.

RELIABILITY

Undoubtedly, we have all heard someone refer to a person or a product as reliable. Used in this way, the term *reliable* means that the person consistently does what he or she promises, or that the product performs in a consistent fashion each time it is used. Used in a measurement context, reliability means much the same. **Reliability** means that events are *reproducible*. If a measurement scale is reliable, then repeated measurements of the same characteristic will yield similar scores over time and

RELIABILITY
The extent to which measures are reproducible.

across situations. Reliability implies consistent and stable measurement from one use of the scale to the next.

What can cause a measurement scale to be unreliable? If respondents misunderstand a question, for instance, then a source of error is introduced that will result in imperfections in the measurement process. Because of confusion, responses to such a question will be highly variable, governed by such transitory factors as whim, mood, or by the respondent's answers to previous questions. In such cases, the measurements taken will not be stable over time. The cause of low reliability is random error. **Random error** refers to transient factors, both personal and situational, that affect the measurement scale in different ways each time it is administered.

Methods for assessing the reliability of a measurement scale focus on the two dimensions of reliability. The first dimension focuses on the *stability* of the scale items. **Test-retest reliability** measures the stability of a set of scale items by administering the measurement scale to the same group of individuals at two different times. If the two sets of measurements correlate highly, then the measurement scale is viewed as consistent and reliable. The time interval between administering the measurement scale can be problematic. On the one hand, the interval should be long enough that responses given at the time of the second administration are not influenced by the responses given at the time of the first administration. On the other hand, the interval should be not so long that the respondent's attitude or position on the issue being investigated has changed. Though there are no general guidelines to give, an interval of about two to four weeks seems reasonable.

The second dimension of reliability concerns the *equivalency or internal consistency* of the scale items. Equivalency or internal consistency of a set of scale items refers to the degree to which scores obtained from the various individual scale items are consistent. There are several methods available for measuring internal consistency. With the **split-half method,** the scale items are randomly split into two sets, with an equal number of items in each, and then the scores obtained in each split-half are correlated. The stronger the association, the more internally consistent are the items.[12]

All else the same, we would expect single-item scales to be much more susceptible to random error and therefore less reliable than multiple-item scales. Summing the ratings across the items of a multiple-item measurement scale to form a composite score has the effect of neutralizing random fluctuations, that is, by summing, negative and positive errors in responses tend to cancel.

VALIDITY VERSUS RELIABILITY

A measurement scale can be reliable, yielding consistent and stable results over time and situations, yet not valid. In contrast, however, a measurement scale that is unreliable cannot be valid. Reliability, then, is a *necessary* but not *sufficient* condition for validity.

Exhibit 11–17 illustrates the concepts of reliability and validity in the context of a dartboard game involving three players. The first situation

RANDOM ERROR
Transient factors that affect the measurement scale in different ways each time it is administered.

TEST-RETEST RELIABILITY
Method for calculating reliability; respondents are administered identical sets of scale items at two different times under similar conditions. The reliability coefficient is computed by correlating the scores obtained from the two administrations.

SPLIT-HALF METHOD
Split-half reliability scale items randomly split into two sets. The scores from each set are correlated.

EXHIBIT 11—17

Illustrations of Possible Reliability and Validity Situations in Measurement

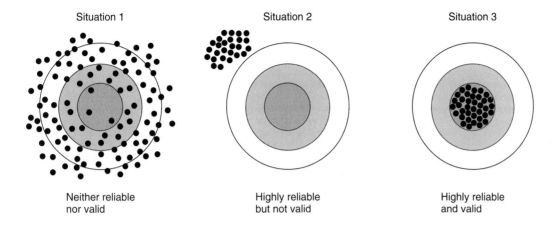

Situation 1	Situation 2	Situation 3
Neither reliable nor valid	Highly reliable but not valid	Highly reliable and valid

shows holes all over the target. This dart thrower is neither consistent nor very accurate. This illustrates a lack of reliability and validity. The second dart thrower is much more consistent. This illustrates reliability, but the holes in the target are far from the center, which means that he or she is off the mark. The final dart thrower is highly reliable and valid. This dart thrower has a steady eye that is on target.

SUMMARY

This chapter has explained measurement concepts and illustrated a variety of measurement scales. An understanding of complex measurement issues is essential in understanding the way to analyze the numeric scores that are assigned to respondents' answers. Two varieties of single-item measurement scales, noncomparative and comparative, were discussed and illustrated. The discussion then focused on the advantages of using multiple-item scales as opposed to single-item scales, followed by a description of three multiple-item scale types: semantic differential scales, stapel scales, and Likert scales. The chapter concluded by discussing issues related to the concepts of measurement validity and reliability.

KEY CONCEPTS

Noncomparative/Monadic Scaling

Continuous Rating/Line Marking Scale

Itemized Rating Scale

Graphic Rating Scale

Comparative Scaling

Paired Comparison

Rank-Order Scale

Constant Sum Scale

Semantic Differential Scale

Stapel Scale

Likert Scale

Validity

Reliability

REVIEW QUESTIONS

1. From the following questions, name the type of scale (nominal, ordinal, interval, or ratio) being used. Justify your answers.

   a. Which of the three major networks do you watch most frequently?
   _____ NBC   _____ CBS   _____ ABC

   b. The temperature today will reach a high of?
   _____ 0°F–25°F   _____ 51°F–75°F
   _____ 26°F–50°F   _____ 76°F–100°F

   c. How much do you typically spend at the grocery?
   _____ Under $20.00   _____ $40.01–$60.00
   _____ $20.00–$40.00   _____ Over $60.00

   d. How would you rank the following items where 1 is is most preferred and 5 is least preferred?
   _____ Milky Way   _____ Baby Ruth
   _____ Almond Joy
   _____ Snickers   _____ Reeses

   e. How many animals do you have?_____

   f. How close are you in pounds to your ideal weight?
   _____ Within 10 lbs.   _____ Within 20 lbs.
   _____ Within 30 lbs.

   g. Your best SAT score falls in which of the following groups?
   _____ Below 800   _____ 1101–1250
   _____ 801–950   _____ 1251–1400
   _____ 951–1100   _____ 1401 and above

2. Think about your university's cafeteria. Suppose that the university is interested in measuring the image it has with its student body. Develop a set of 10 scale items to measure the perceived image of the cafeteria, using each of the three multiple-item formats discussed in this chapter.

3. Consider the set of instructions and measurement scale shown in Exhibit 1 below.

   a. What type of measurement scale is being used?
   b. Is this scale monadic or comparative? Explain.

EXHIBIT 1

Q. Which brand(s) of medicine(s) for allergies listed below have you used in the past year? (CHECK AS MANY AS APPLY.) Now, for each brand of medicine for allergies that you indicated you have used in Q17, please rate that brand on a scale of "Excellent" to "Poor" for each characteristic listed below.

   To do this, think about the brand and write the number on the line under the remedy and next to the characteristic that best expresses your opinion of its rating regarding that characteristic.

   Please use the following scale:

Excellent = 1	Very Good = 2	Good = 3	Fair = 4	Poor = 5

Used past year (CHECK AS MANY AS APPLY.)	Allerest [ ] 1	Chlortri-meton [ ] 2	Benadryl [ ] 3	Dimetapp [ ] 4	Drixoral [ ] 5	Sudafed [ ] 6	Dimetane [ ] 7	Contac [ ] 8 (66)

67–78 OPEN

18. Characteristic Ratings

	Allerest	Chlortri-meton	Benadryl	Dimetapp	Drixoral	Sudafed	Dimetane	Contac
Treats more than one symptom at a time ...	___(13)	___(13)	___(13)	___(13)	___(13)	___(13)	___(13)	___(13)
Doesn't make you drowsy	___(14)	___(14)	___(14)	___(14)	___(14)	___(14)	___(14)	___(14)
Relieves nasal congestion/stuffiness	___(15)	___(15)	___(15)	___(15)	___(15)	___(15)	___(15)	___(15)
Is specifically for children under 12	___(16)	___(16)	___(16)	___(16)	___(16)	___(16)	___(16)	___(16)
Gives relief for four hours or less	___(17)	___(17)	___(17)	___(17)	___(17)	___(17)	___(17)	___(17)
Can use as frequently as needed	___(18)	___(18)	___(18)	___(18)	___(18)	___(18)	___(18)	___(18)
Helps you breathe easier	___(19)	___(19)	___(19)	___(19)	___(19)	___(19)	___(19)	___(19)
Is a product that was previously available only by doctor's prescription	___(20)	___(20)	___(20)	___(20)	___(20)	___(20)	___(20)	___(20)
Relieves itchy skin	___(21)	___(21)	___(21)	___(21)	___(21)	___(21)	___(21)	___(21)
Provides fast relief	___(22)	___(22)	___(22)	___(22)	___(22)	___(22)	___(22)	___(22)
Relieves a headache	___(23)	___(23)	___(23)	___(23)	___(23)	___(23)	___(23)	___(23)
Contains just enough medication	___(24)	___(24)	___(24)	___(24)	___(24)	___(24)	___(24)	___(24)

4. The following question appeared on a survey for potential television buyers and received the following response shown in the table.

   Five characteristics of televisions are listed below. Please allocate 100 points among the characteristics so that your allocation represents the importance of each characteristic to you when making a purchase decision.

Characteristics	Number of Points
1. Clear picture	40
2. Price	20
3. Warranty	15
4. Year of make	10
5. Name of brand	15

a. What type of measure scale was used?
b. What can you conclude from these data?

ENDNOTES

1. J. C. Nunnally, *Psychometric Theory* (New York: McGraw-Hill, 1967), p. 2.

2. For this reason some have argued that nominally scaled variables do not actually represent measurement.

3. For additional evidence, see E. P. Cox, II, "The Optimal Number of Response Alternatives for a Scale: A Review," *Journal of Marketing Research,* November 1980, pp. 407–22; A. M. Givon and Z. Shapira, "Response to Rating Scales: A Theoretical Model and Its Application to the Number of Categories Problem," *Journal of Marketing Research,* November 1984, pp. 410–19.

4. A. R. Wildt and M. B. Mazis, "Determinations of Scale Response: Label Versus Position," *Journal of Marketing Research,* May 1978, pp. 261–67; R. I. Haley and P. B. Case, "Testing Thirteen Attitude Scales for Agreement and Brand Discrimination," *Journal of Marketing,* Fall 1979, p. 31; and H. H. Friedman and J. R. Leefer, "Label Versus Position in Rating Scales," *Journal of the Academy of Marketing Science,* Spring 1981, pp. 88–92.

5. Proportions equal to 0.50 are randomly assigned a value of 1 or 0.

6. M. Fishbein and I. Ajzen, *Belief, Attitude, Intention and Behavior* (Reading, Mass.: Addison-Wesley, 1975), p. 6.

7. Charles Osgood, George Suci, and Percy Tannenbaum, *The Measurement of Meaning* (Urbana, University of Illinois Press, 1957).

8. Michael J. Etzel, Terrell G. Williams, John G. Rogers, and Douglas J. Lincoln, "The Comparability of Three Staple Forms in a Marketing Setting," in *Marketing Theory: Philosophy of Science Perspectives,* ed.

Ronald F. Bush and Shelby D. Hunt (Chicago: American Marketing Association, 1982), pp. 303–6.

9. See Del I. Hawkins, Gerald Albaum, and Roger Best, "Staple Scale or Semantic Differential in Marketing Research," *Journal of Marketing Research* 11 (August 1974), pp. 318–22; and Dennis Menezes and Norbert F. Elbert, "Alternative Semantic Scaling Formats for Measuring Store Image: An Evaluation," *Journal of Marketing Research* 16 (February 1979), pp. 80–87.

10. Renis Likert, "A Technique for the Measurement of Attitudes," in *Attitude Measurement,* ed. Gene F. Summers (Chicago: Rand McNally, 1970), pp. 149–58.

11. See Gil Churchill, "A Paradigm for Developing Better Measures of Marketing Constructs," *Journal of Marketing Research* 16 (February 1979), pp. 64–73; or William J. Lundstrom and Lawrence M. Lamont, "The Development of a Scale to Measure Consumer Discontent," *Journal of Marketing Research* 8 (November 1976), pp. 373–81.

12. One problem in using the split-half method concerns how to split the items. How the items are split will affect the degree of association obtained across the split-halves. For this reason, a number of other approaches to assessing internal consistency have been developed. One popular approach is to compute *Cronbach's alpha,* which forms all possible split-half partitions of a measurement scale and computes what is, essentially, the mean association across all possible subsets. For further details see L. J. Cronbach, "Coefficient Alpha and the Internal Structure of Tests," *Psychometrika* 16 (1951), pp. 297–334.

Questionnaire Design: Including International Considerations

Scenario One: Big City, USA. April 1, 1990. Jonathon Doe, an account executive for a Black Enterprise 100s company, is in his study preparing next week's work schedule, when there's a knock at his door. He hesitates, not expecting any visitors, but then answers. The visitor, a "census enumerator," asks for about 10 minutes of Doe's time. Doe declining, closes the door, and returns to his work. He mutters to no one in particular, "Who cares about the census. What does it have to do with me?"

Scenario Two: Again, it's April 1. Earlier in the week, Jane Doe, a freelance writer, received a census form in the mail. After taking a brief look at it, she put it aside saying she would get back to it later; she was busy on a story. Now it's later, and the census form remains unopened. "Why worry about the census?" she wonders, "what does it have to do with me?"

While the two scenarios are fictitious, they illustrate the decisions all Americans faced two years ago when the Census Bureau of the Department of Commerce conducted a national decennial census of the U.S. population, which is done every 10 years, in accordance with the U.S. Constitution.

Many people were expected to ask those questions: "Why bother with the census? What does it have to do with me?"

Well, the reasons are many, and the ways in which most citizens responded, particularly blacks and other minorities, impacts on our communities throughout the 1990s and into the 21st century.

"The type of political representation that African-Americans and other minorities are to realize in the 1990s," said Billy Tidwell, director of research at the National Urban League, "is dependent on the census count."

Understanding the Census. Many Americans, especially minorities, are unaware of the significance of the census except, for some, as an infringement on their privacy. The census, however, has a direct impact on the political, social, and economic interests of all citizens, especially blacks and other minorities who have lacked political empowerment, or whose communities have been underfunded or underserved. Census data are used to reapportion seats in the U.S. House of Representatives and state, county and municipal legislatures.

chapter 12

CHAPTER
OBJECTIVES
—

EXPLAIN
the importance of
questionnaire design.

DISCUSS
how questions should be
worded.

DISCUSS
how questionnaires should be
constructed and organized.

EXPLAIN
the importance of pretesting
the questionnaire.

DISCUSS
particular design issues to
consider when conducting
international marketing
research projects.

Moreover, census data are used by policy makers, civic groups, researchers, and others to determine where to locate hospitals, schools, senior citizen centers, transportation services, and other services and facilities. In addition, the social and economic data from the census are used by businesses to conduct marketing studies and to assess the adequacy of local labor pools. Said Rudolph Brewington, deputy chief of information services for the Census Bureau: "The census gives a complete picture of a community — income, race, density, et cetera — information that's important to all businesses. McDonalds, for example, does not open a restaurant in America without first reviewing census demographic data."

Census data are also used to enforce fair lending practices, assess the need for the development or the expansion of lower-income housing, and to identify areas requiring the establishment of affirmative action programs. In other words, the statistical and demographic data that resulted from the 1990 census will help determine the social, political, and economic well-being of blacks over the next decade.

The Census Questionnaire. By April 1, 1990, designated "Census Day," millions of Americans completed 1990 Census questionnaires. Appointment counts of the population, based on the census, were then delivered to the President by December 31 of 1990; and redistricting counts to all states by April 1, 1991.

The census was conducted primarily through mailed questionnaires, although some citizens, including the homeless, were visited by census enumerators. Both short and long forms were used. Both contained questions pertaining to the respondent's race, age, marital status, whether or not they rent or own their own residence, and the number of rooms in that residence. The short form had 17 questions, and in general took about 10 to 15 minutes to complete. The long form had 61 questions and could be completed in about 45 minutes. Additional questions on the long form included ancestry, birthplace, educational level, ethnicity, migration status and the language spoken in the respondent's household. Also included were questions about disabilities, employment status, fertility, and the respondent's workplace.

Population Changes Based on Projected Census Estimates

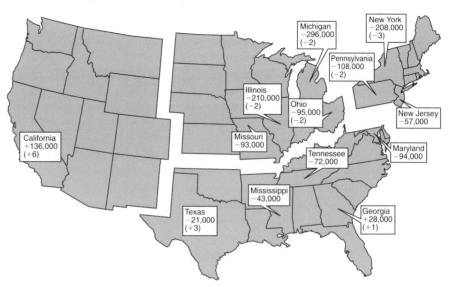

The numbers shown are population changes in congressional districts represented by blacks based on projected 1990 census estimates. More than enough constituents live in four California districts and one in Georgia, eliminating a need to redraw boundaries. Elsewhere, it's a different story. Various state legislatures are expected to change district borders in Illinois, Maryland, Michigan, Mississippi, Missouri, New Jersey, New York, Ohio, Pennsylvania, Tennessee, and Texas because of huge population losses. A district will range in size from 540,000 to 583,000 people, with the average being 560,000. The figure in parentheses shows the projected gain or loss of congressional districts in the state.

The data collected by the census affects communities in many tangible ways. Said the Rev. Marshall Sheppard of the Mount Olive Tabernacle Baptist Church in Philadelphia: "The census is important for the black church for reasons which are economic, political, and social. It will enable us to better articulate our concerns through the use of the data provided." [Sheppard is a former president of the Progressive National Baptist Convention, which represents 1,200 to 1,300 churches nationally.] And he argues that anyone concerned about the community's well-being must be counted. "It borders on foolhardiness for a person not to be concerned about his self-interest."

INTRODUCTION

Why bother with the census? What does it have to do with me?

Throughout the 1990s and into the 21st century, the answers to those questions will be answered in a myriad of ways—by legislators, policy makers, civic groups, researchers, and many others.

The information collected by the 1990 census questionnaire will undoubtedly become a benchmark for virtually all the statistics collected by the federal government and consumer information groups.

A questionnaire is a data collection instrument. It formally sets out the way in which the research questions of interest should be asked. On first

ASKING QUESTIONS

BOX 12—1

—

FROM THE USER'S
PERSPECTIVE

—

You may think that asking questions and designing a questionnaire are simple matters. Yet, faulty questionnaire design is a major contributor to nonsampling errors and specifically to response errors. Response errors occur because respondents do not give accurate answers to questions that have been asked, and many factors that lead a respondent to give inaccurate responses can be traced directly to improper questionnaire design and construction. As the examples below demonstrate, the format of a question, the content of a question, or the organization of the questions can induce a respondent to give an inaccurate response.

Format problem

What is your religious preference?

Jewish ___Catholic ___Protestant denomination ___Other ___Specify ___None

The blank lines may be confusing. The respondent may wonder whether the blank lines should be used for the response category before it or the one after it.

Content problem

Do you believe that IBM personal computers are the most compatible and the best buy for the money?

The question considers *two* aspects of IBM's product performance—compatibility and value. If a respondent feels that IBM personal computers are the most compatible *but* not necessarily the best buy for the money, how should the person respond?

Organization problem

Q1. Did you purchase a maintenance contract for your FAX machine?
Yes . . .
No . . .
Q2. Do you think that maintenance contracts are a good investment?
Yes . . .
No . . .
Q3. What is the anticipated cost of the maintenance contract?
Less than $50 per year
$50–$100 per year
$101–$200 per year
More than $200 per year

The confusion in the questions shown above relates to whether question Q3 should be answered by all respondents or only by those who have purchased a maintenance contract.

thought, it may seem that questionnaires should be simple to put together—all that is required is to know what questions you wish to ask.

However, even simple questions require proper wording and organization if the researcher wants accurate information. The format, the content, or the organization of the questions can induce a respondent to give an accurate or an inaccurate response, as the examples in Box 12–1 illustrate.

In this chapter we focus first on design issues such as how questions should be worded, given the specific objectives of the study, and the target group of respondents who will be questioned. We then turn our attention to how the questionnaire should be organized and pretested. The general principle and procedures we recommend apply to mail, telephone, personal, and computer-assisted telephone interviews (CATI). Finally, recognizing the opportunities of the opening of markets abroad, we discuss questionnaire design issues that should be considered in conducting marketing research studies in international markets.

QUESTIONNAIRE DESIGN

By the time the researcher arrives at the questionnaire design stage of a given study, the marketing problem has probably been expressed in a set of appropriate research questions. Now these questions must be translated into the language of the respondent and then arranged in a questionnaire in a valid, logical fashion that will produce meaningful results.[1] Hence, we can view questionnaire design in terms of four interrelated activities: (1) preliminary considerations, (2) asking questions, (3) constructing the questionnaire, and (4) pretesting the questionnaire.

Exhibit 12–1 provides a summary of these activities.

Preliminary Considerations

Before you even start to consider how questions should be asked, you must translate the marketing problem into a set of research questions that identify (1) exactly what information is required, (2) exactly who the appropriate target respondents are, and (3) what data-collection method will be used to survey these respondents. These questions were covered earlier in Chapters 2, 7, and 9. We repeat them here because there is no way to overstate their importance.

Asking Questions

All too often, formulation of the questionnaire is thought to be the easiest part of designing a survey. Yet question wording is a crucial element in maximizing the validity of survey data. Building good questions seems like a simple task. After all, we ask questions all the time. Often the responses we get, however, are based on how we word our questions. Seemingly small changes in wording can cause large differences in responses.

Consider a well-known example: Two priests, a Dominican and a Jesuit, are talking about whether it is a sin to smoke and pray at the same time. After failing to reach a conclusion, each goes off to consult his respective superior. The next week they meet again. The Dominican says, "Well, what did your superior say?" The Jesuit responds, "He said it was all right." "That's funny," the Dominican replies, "my superior said it was a sin." Jesuit: "What did you ask him?" Reply: "I asked him if it was all right to smoke while praying." "Oh," says the Jesuit, "I asked my superior if it was all right to pray while smoking."[2]

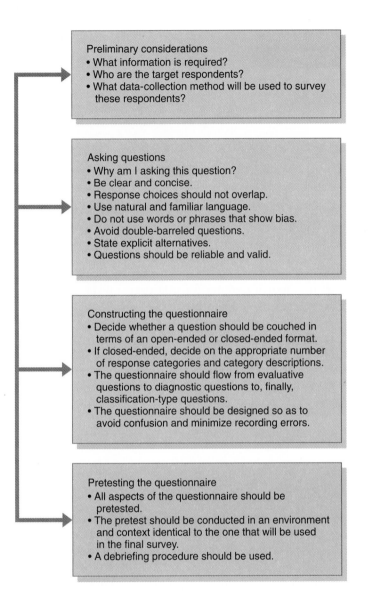

EXHIBIT 12—1

Questionnaire Design
Activities

General guidelines.   A general rule in constructing a questionnaire is always to ask yourself Why am I asking this question? You must be able to explain how each survey question relates to the research question that underlies management's problem.

Three general guidelines help in devising a good questionnaire.

1. Write specific questions only after you have thoroughly thought through your research questions. Write the research questions down.
2. When you are working on the questionnaire, constantly refer to your research questions.
3. For each question you write, consider how the information obtained from responses will help in answering your research questions.

Conducting an in-home personal
interview

Workable questions on generic issues may already exist. Before you create new questions, it is worth looking for questions on the same topic that other researchers may have asked in other studies. Most questionnaires include some questions that have been used before; in fact, even some "new" questions have probably been adapted from questions used in the past. The point is that the reuse of questions is not only permitted but is also encouraged in survey research and in social science in general.[3] Reusing questions that have demonstrated acceptable levels of reliability and validity can allow you to (1) reduce the time needed for testing, (2) compare results across a number of studies, and (3) establish response reliabilities for the study at hand.

Basic principles. There are a number of specific considerations to keep in mind in developing questions. The basic principles that follow from what could be called the "art" of asking questions.

Principle 1: Be clear and precise. A question should be understandable to both researcher and respondent. In addition, it should allow responses consistent with the desired level of measurement and response options that will afford actionable results. For example, consider the following two questions, which are intended to identify volume of coffee consumption.

---

1. How many cups of coffee do you drink in a typical workday? [*Write in number.*]

2. How frequently do you drink coffee? [*Record choice below.*]

Extremely often	1
Very often	2
Not too often	3
Never	4

Notice that the first question is more precise than the second version with respect to the amount of coffee consumed as well as the time interval in which the consumption takes place. We can, therefore, obtain a more accurate estimate of the volume of coffee drunk during a typical workday from question 1. Question 2 lacks precision and specificity since neither the amount of coffee consumed nor the time interval in which consumption takes place is provided.

Principle 2: Response choices should not overlap and should be exhaustive. Along with clarity and precision goes the idea of **mutual exclusivity.** What this means is that response choices to a question should not overlap with one another and should cover the entire range of possibilities relevant to the target population. Consider the following question.

MUTUAL EXCLUSIVITY
Condition in which the response choices to a question do not overlap with one another.

Which of the following categories best describes your total household income before taxes in 1992? [*Circle one answer only.*]

Less than $10,000	1
$10,000–$15,000	2
$15,000–$25,000	3
$25,000 or higher	4

The responses allowed make it possible for people who live in households with incomes of exactly $15,000 or $25,000 to choose two response categories. Choices 2 and 3 should be written instead as $10,000–$14,999 and $15,000–$24,999. If responses are not mutually exclusive, it is difficult to say where the "true" response lies.

Principle 3: Use natural and familiar language. Consider who makes up your sample when constructing your questions. Phrase questions in the colloquial language of your respondent group. By this we don't mean that questions should be chatty but that the language should be appropriate to the target respondents. Not only do different ethnic and social groups express reactions differently, but so do people who live in different regions of the country. Think about a sandwich prepared on a long loaf of bread: This is variously referred to as a *grinder,* a *hoagie,* a *hero,* or a *submarine* in different parts of the country.

The familiarness of language has an effect on the willingness of respondents to give accurate responses to "threatening" questions.[4] Threatening questions are those that people ask to report on personal or contrary-to-norm behavior not generally discussed in public without discomfort. Response effects to such questions can result in the overstatement of desirable behavior (voting, for example) and the understatement of less socially acceptable behaviors (alcohol or drug abuse, for example). Response effects due to threatening questions are shown to be reduced if respondents are allowed to select their own words for describing the threatening behavior under study. An example (see the next page) shows how this has been done in a study of alcohol use.

EXAMPLE

The standard question for intoxication read:

During the past year, how often did you become intoxicated while drinking any kind of alcoholic beverage?

Respondents were handed a card containing the following response categories:

— Never.   — Every few weeks.
— Once a year or less.   — Once a week.
— Every few months.   — Several times a week.
— Once a month.   — Daily.

The alternative procedure allowed respondents to first provide their own word for intoxication through the following question:

Sometimes people drink a little too much beer, wine, or whiskey so that they act different from usual. What word do you think we should use to describe people when they get that way, so that you will know what we mean and feel comfortable talking about it?

The intoxication question then read:

Occasionally, people drink on an empty stomach or drink a little too much and become (respondent's word). In the past year, how often did you become (respondent's word) while drinking any kind of alcoholic beverage?

No response categories were offered for either item.

Other techniques can be used to improve response accuracy for threatening or sensitive questions. One way, as we indicated in Chapter 11, is to use *unbalanced scales* that include additional categories on the heavy end, which would be useful in collecting data on alcohol consumption.

Principle 4: Do not use words or phrases that show bias. Biased or leading words or phrases are those implying approval or disapproval. **Loaded questions,** as they are called, suggest by their wording what an answer should be or indicate the researcher's position on the issue under study. In both instances, respondents are not given a fair chance to express their own opinion, and a consistent measurement error is introduced that would not exist if neutral phrasings were used (see the next example).

LOADED QUESTIONS
Questions that suggest what the answer should be or indicate the researcher's position on the issue under study.

EXAMPLE

Leading questions can take a variety of forms. Consider the following question:

What did you dislike about the product you just tried?

The respondent is not given a "way out" if he or she found nothing to dislike. A more suitable way to ask this question would be to first ask:

Did you dislike any aspects of the product you just tried?
_____Yes   _____No

Certain words and phrases also can induce bias. For example:

Do you think Johnson & Johnson did everything possible in its handling of the Tylenol poisoning situation?

This is a leading question because the use of the phrase *everything possible* can produce biased responses. The issue is whether Johnson & Johnson acted *reasonably* in its handling of the Tylenol poisoning situation.

Another type of bias can occur when a respondent is required to rate a series of objects (such as brands of toothpaste) on the same set of characteristics. The potential problem here is that particular reactions, either favorable or unfavorable, to a specific question are elicited because one question comes before or after another. This type of bias is called **order bias** and can be particularly troublesome in concept and product testing. Research has shown that the rating of objects may be related to the order in which they are presented; in other words, brands receive different ratings depending on whether they are shown first, second, third, and so on. The following example presents an illustration.

ORDER BIAS
Condition whereby brands receive different ratings depending on whether they were shown first, second, third, etc.

EXAMPLE

Shown below are the mean brand ratings of 60 respondents who evaluated three brands of analgesics (Bufferin, Excedrin, and Tylenol) where the order of rating was varied. For each of the six possible combinations, each brand was evaluated monadically on a seven-point itemized scale.

Tylenol	1.0	Tylenol	1.5	Bufferin	3.0
Bufferin	6.0	Bufferin	5.5	Tylenol	1.0
Excedrin	3.0	Excedrin	3.0	Excedrin	6.0
Bufferin	3.5	Excedrin	2.5	Excedrin	3.5
Excedrin	3.0	Tylenol	1.5	Bufferin	3.5
Tylenol	3.5	Bufferin	6.5	Tylenol	3.0

It is clear from the preference ratings that the brand rated immediately following Tylenol received a relatively higher score. Thus the order in which the brands of analgesics were presented to the respondent may have affected the ratings given.

In order to control for order bias, the order of questions on attributes should be varied (rotated) across respondents. Rotating questions across respondents minimizes the chance of systematic order effects because any biases are now randomly (uniformly) distributed. Note that with self-administered interviews, the rotation of questions is extremely difficult to implement and often impractical.

Principle 5: Avoid double-barreled questions.   Questions in which two opinions are joined together are called **double-barreled.** These questions ask respondents to answer two questions at once even though their opinions about the two may be different. Consider, for example, the question:

DOUBLE-BARRELED QUESTIONS
Questions in which two opinions are joined together.

Do you believe that McDonald's has fast and courteous service?

Here, questions about two different attitudes, namely, speed and courteous service, are conjoined. A customer might agree with the claim of fast service but not with the claim that it is courteous.

Principle 6: State explicit alternatives.   The specification of an explicitly stated alternative can have dramatic effects on responses. Consider the two forms of a question asked in the "pasta-in-a-jar" concept test shown in the next example.

EXAMPLE

Version A: Would you only buy pasta-in-a-jar if it were available in a store where you normally shop?

Version B: If pasta-in-a-jar and the canned pasta product you are currently using were both available in the store where you normally shop, would you

a. Buy only the canned pasta product?

b. Buy only the pasta-in-a-jar product?

c. Buy both products?

The stated alternatives in version B give the researcher some context for interpreting the reaction to this new concept. For example, in version A, 42 percent of the respondents indicated that they would buy the new pasta-in-a-jar product. When specific alternatives were added in version B, the number of respondents indicating that they would buy only the new pasta-in-a-jar product was only 24 percent.

Principle 7: Questions should meet criteria of validity and reliability. The issues of whether questions measure what the researcher is attempting to measure and whether these responses can be replicated later are significant in question building. You should not assume that the same questioning approach works equally well for all product/service categories and all interviewing methods.   The validity and reliability of data can be severely compromised if respondents cannot answer the questions accurately. Two aspects of questions might make it impossible for a respondent to answer.

1. *Relevance.* Questionnaires can include questions on topics about which respondents are uninformed; in other words, the question is not relevant because the respondent has never been exposed to or lacks experience about the subject. An all-too-common example is to ask a respondent's opinion, in general or on specific performance characteristics, about a brand or a service that he or she has never heard of or used. Respondents in such situations typically do not indicate their lack of knowledge, thereby compromising validity. The problem of relevance can be minimized by selecting the proper target populations and allowing respondents to indicate lack of knowledge by direct questioning or by including a "don't know" category in the responses.

2. *Memory.* Respondents can be asked questions about events too far in the past that they cannot remember well. Forgetting can cause three types of response effects: omission, telescoping, and creation.[5] **Omission** occurs when the respondent cannot remember past events. **Telescoping** occurs when a respondent compresses time or remembers an event as occurring more recently than it actually did.

OMISSION

Interviewing condition that occurs when a respondent cannot recall that an event has occurred.

TELESCOPING

Condition that occurs when a respondent either compresses time or remembers an event as occurring more recently than it actually occurred.

For example, a respondent might indicate two visits to a particular store in the last week, although one of the visits occurred 10 days ago. **Creation** means that a respondent recalls an event that did not actually occur.

It is reasonable to expect that **unaided questions,** ones that do not provide any clues to the answer, can result in omission or understatement of specific events. **Aided questions,** on the other hand, ones that do provide clues that could help the respondent recall more accurately, can increase telescoping and creation. You can minimize response effects due to memory factors by (1) asking respondents questions only about *important* events that occurred within the last few days[6] and (2) informing respondents that the aided-recall questions may contain bogus items.[7]

Constructing the Questionnaire

After you draw up the substance of questions according to principles of good question design, you must arrange the questions in a format that yields meaningful results in a cost-efficient and timely manner. Two important issues that should be considered when constructing a questionnaire are response formats and the questionnaire's flow and layout.

Response formats.   There are two basic types of response formats: *open-ended* and *itemized* (closed-ended).

Open-ended questions.   The **open-ended question format** lets the respondent choose any response deemed appropriate, within the limits implied by the question. The next example shows a question series that allows respondents to choose their own words in describing their reactions to a commercial.

CREATION

Situation whereby a respondent recalls an event that did not actually occur.

UNAIDED QUESTIONS

Questions that do not provide any clues to the answer or help the respondent recall more accurately.

AIDED QUESTIONS

Questions that provide clues that will potentially help the respondent recall more accurately.

OPEN-ENDED QUESTION FORMAT

The respondent is allowed to choose any response deemed appropriate, within the limits implied by the question.

EXAMPLE

What did the commercial say?
_____
_____
_____

What did the commercial show?
_____
_____
_____

Did you like anything about the commercial you just saw?
_____
_____
_____

Not all studies include open-ended questions. When they are included, the primary purpose is to obtain the respondent's own verbalization of, comprehension of, and reaction to stimuli. The stimuli may represent ads, commercials, packages, products, concepts, and so on, so it is impractical to set rules for the processing of all open-ended questions. There are several good reasons for asking open-ended questions.

1. Open-ended questions are useful to check and/or corroborate the results of quantitative or closed-ended questions. Along these same lines, open-ended questions also may be used to develop a wider range of response than is possible using quantitative or structured questions.

2. Open-ended questions may be used to obtain direct comparisons and to specify particular causes for preference or rejection when two or more stimuli (e.g., products or concepts) are involved in a test.

3. Open-ended questions are useful in determining whether a particular communication vehicle (e.g., commercial or concept) conveys its intended objectives.

4. Open-ended questions elicit respondents' general reactions to or feelings on exposure to specific ads or packages (products or concepts) involved in a test.

There are several drawbacks to using open-ended questions. First, they are not well suited for self-administered questionnaires, simply because most respondents will not write elaborate answers. Second, answers to open-ended questions may be more of an indication of the respondent's ability to articulate a response than a measure of the respondent's knowledge about or interest in the issue being investigated. Third, interviewer bias can be a serious problem with the use of open-ended questions. Finally, open-ended questions must be coded or categorized for analysis, which can be a tedious task laden with ambiguities. (We discuss this issue in Chapter 13.)

ITEMIZED (CLOSED-ENDED) QUESTION FORMAT

The respondent is provided with numbers and/or predetermined descriptions and is asked to select the one that best describes his or her feelings.

Itemized (closed-ended) questions. An **itemized (closed-ended) question format** requires respondents to select from specified numbers or descriptions the one that best describes their feelings. Itemized questions can take on many different formats. Recall that in Chapter 11 we discussed in some detail several issues related to itemized question formats: namely, (1) the number of response alternatives (such as paired or multiple choice), (2) the nature and degree of verbal description, (3) the number of favorable and unfavorable categories, (4) the statement of a neutral position, and (5) the forced or nonforced nature of the scale. The next example presents several illustrations of an itemized question format. It shows structured response alternatives to a purchase intent question.

The obvious advantages of itemized question formats relate to (1) their ease of use in the field; (2) their ability to reduce interviewer bias; (3) their ability to reduce bias based on differences in how articulate respondents are; and (4) their relatively simple coding and tabulation requirements. To be effective, however, itemized question formats call for a substantial amount of effort, particularly with respect to pretesting. The application of itemized question formats presumes that the specified set of response categories is exhaustive, that is, that it adequately reflects all the possible and relevant responses at the appropriate level of precision, so that it will not produce distortions in the data.

Balanced with neutral position
    Definitely would buy
    Probably would buy
    Might or might not buy
    Probably would not buy
    Definitely would not buy

Balanced without neutral position
    Definitely would buy
    Probably would buy
    Probably would not buy
    Definitely would not buy

Balanced, nonforced
    Definitely would buy
    Probably would buy
    Don't know/no answer
    Probably would not buy
    Definitely would not buy

Balanced, graphic rating
    (Place an "X" in the position on the line that indicates your likelihood of buying Product X.)
    Would _____Would
    not buy   Might or   buy
                                  might not buy

    Dichotomous
    Would buy
    Would not buy

Unbalanced
    Definitely would buy
    Probably would buy
    Might or might not buy
    Would not buy

Logical flow.   In everyday life, if you want to know what someone did, you generally ask them about what they did and then about the details surrounding this event before you go on to talk about another unrelated situation. This is also the typical flow in marketing research surveys: There is a progression from evaluative to diagnostic questioning, or vice versa, and then to classification questions. To respondents, questionnaires should represent a logical flow of successive, carefully thought-out examinations. Exhibit 12–2 provides a sequence of question topics appearing in a product concept test that might be asked of a group of respondents after the interviewer has read a description of a new product idea to them. When designing the flow of the questionnaire, there are several specific issues to consider.[8]

EXHIBIT 12—2

Questionnaire
Organization

Evaluative
    Purchase intent
Diagnostic
    Reasons for expressed level of purchase intent
    Uniqueness (of idea)
    Believability (of idea)
    Importance of main benefit
    Expected frequency of usage
    Ratings of a series of product benefits
Classification
    Age
    Marital status
    Family size
    Education
    Occupation
    Income

Introducing the questionnaire.   Many respondents will have some initial suspicions or fears concerning why they are being interviewed. An
introduction must dispel these concerns. It need not be long and complicated, however. Just a few statements at the beginning of the interview can
describe the nature and purpose of the study in such a way as to make the
respondent feel more at ease.

In personal interviews interviewers should identify themselves and the organization they represent, and then immediately give a one- or two-sentence
description of the purpose of the study. In mail surveys the nature and purpose
of the study is given in the cover letter that accompanies the questionnaire.
The major points to cover in the introduction are listed in Exhibit 12–3.[9]
Note that these points should be covered in less than one page.

The first questions.   Avoid bad initial impressions at all costs. The opening questions should be easy and nonthreatening and, if possible, interesting
and significant to the respondent. Some survey researchers suggest opening
with a question that is of interest to the respondent even if it is not relevant to
the study at hand, for instance, a question about movie-going behavior.

In personal interviews it is common to begin with a fairly general open-
ended attitude question concerning the topic of the study. This forces the
respondent to focus on the relevant topic and gives the respondent the
opportunity to reveal those views that he or she feels are most salient. In
mail and other self-administered questionnaires the practice is to start with
a simple closed-ended question.

Demographic questions.   Many demographic questions are perceived
as personal and even threatening by at least some respondents, so they
generally are asked at the end of the questionnaire. Obviously, a refusal to
answer the income question will not affect responses to other questions if
the income question is the last question in the questionnaire.

What the study is about and its social usefulness (if applicable).

Why the respondent is important.

Promise of confidentiality.

Explanation of the identification number appearing on the questionnaire.

Reward for participation.

What to do if questions arise.

Thank you.

EXHIBIT 12—3

Major Points in a
Questionnaire Introduction

Funnel and inverted-funnel sequences. Typically a **funnel sequence** is followed when the respondent is assumed to have some ideas about a topic. *Funnel sequence* refers to the procedure of asking the most general (or unrestrictive) question about the topic under study first, followed by successively more restrictive questions. This approach minimizes the chance that early questions will condition or bias responses to questions that come later. The funnel sequence technique is also useful when the interviewer needs to ascertain something about the respondent's frame of reference. A funnel sequence used to determine first what a respondent thinks about a new-product concept in general and then his or her reactions to specific end-benefit claims is shown in the next example. If the ordering of the questioning is reversed, responses dealing with *aroma* might be emphasized when responding to the second question, simply because the respondent has been sensitized to this particular end benefit.

FUNNEL SEQUENCE

The procedure of asking the most general (or unrestricted) question about the topic under study first, followed by successively more restricted questions.

1. What is your overall reaction to the new-product concept?
2. Did you find anything hard to believe about the new-product concept?
3. Did you find the claims made about aroma hard to believe?

EXAMPLE

In other instances, an **inverted-funnel sequence** can be useful. This technique inverts the funnel sequence in the sense that questioning begins with specific questions and concludes with general ones. Such an approach compels respondents to consider certain specific points in reaching their evaluations. This approach is useful when the interviewer wishes to ensure that all respondents base their evaluations on similar specific factors. The inverted-funnel–sequence approach appears most useful for low-salience topics, that is, topics about which respondents are without strong feelings or about which they have not formulated a point of view.

Note that the funnel sequence approach is useful only in personal and telephone interviews. In mail and other self-administered questionnaires the respondent can circumvent the funnel design by looking over the entire questionnaire before starting to answer it. The inverted-funnel–sequence approach can be used in all types of interviews since no bias is introduced if the respondent examines all of the questions before beginning.

INVERTED-FUNNEL SEQUENCE

Sequence inverted in the sense that the questioning begins with specific questions and concludes with the respondent answering the general question.

Changing topics.   Questionnaires frequently include questions that deal with more than one topic. In such instances all the questions that deal with one topic should be listed together before a new topic begins. Transition phrases should be included between topics to direct attention to the next topic (e.g., We are now going to ask you about . . . .)

Filter questions.   A question that is asked to determine which branching question, if any, should be asked is referred to as a **filter question.** Such questions are included to ensure that all possible contingencies are covered and to reduce the chance of interviewer or respondent error; they are also used to encourage complete responses.

Skip patterns in a questionnaire can become quite complicated for an interviewer or respondent. In many instances the appropriate skip pattern is based on several questions. A simple procedure the researcher can use to account for all contingencies is to make a flow chart of the logical possibilities and then to prepare the filter question and instructions according to the flow chart.

The example on the next page provides an illustrative flow chart along with the corresponding filter questions. We see that a *yes* answer to question 4 qualifies the respondent as being aware of brand X. Questions 4*a* and 4*b* establish three distinct respondent groups and determine which questions will be asked next. For instance, respondents answering *no* to question 4*a* and *no* to question 4*b* constitute *aware nontriers* and are next asked about why they have not tried the brand in the last year.

Placement of filter questions is important, and two guidelines may be helpful. First, if only a single filter is used, it should be placed just before, or as close as possible to, its corresponding branching question. The interviewer wants to avoid having to flip back and forth in the questionnaire. Second, if multiple filter questions are required, they should all be asked before proceeding to more detailed questions. If all of the filter questions are not asked before the more detailed questions, respondents may discover that they can avoid answering detailed questions by giving certain answers to the filter questions.

Exhibit 12–4 provides a checklist of the major points that should be considered when planning the flow of the questionnaire.

Layout considerations[10]

Use of booklets.   There are at least three reasons to recommend the use of a booklet format in questionnaires: (1) Booklets prevent pages from being lost or misplaced; (2) booklets allow the interviewer or respondent to move from one page to another more easily; and (3) booklets look professional and are easy to follow when used in self-administered interviews.

Appearance of self-administered questionnaires.   Just the appearance of mail and other self-administered questionnaires can have a dramatic effect on the respondents' cooperation. As a general rule, a questionnaire should look as easy to read (and answer) as possible to the respondent and should have a professional appearance. The date, title of the study, and name of the organization conducting the study should appear on the first page of the questionnaire.

Use of blank space and typeface.   A tendency to guard against in questionnaire design is crowding questions together to try to make the question-

Q4. Have you heard of brand X?
    Yes [*Ask a.*]
    No [*Skip to Q8.*]
    Not sure [*Skip to Q8.*]

    If Yes,
    a. Have you used brand X in the last 30 days?
       Yes [*Skip to Q7.*]
       No [*Ask b.*]
    b. Have you used brand X in the last 6 months?
       Yes [*Skip to Q6.*]
       No [*Ask Q5.*]

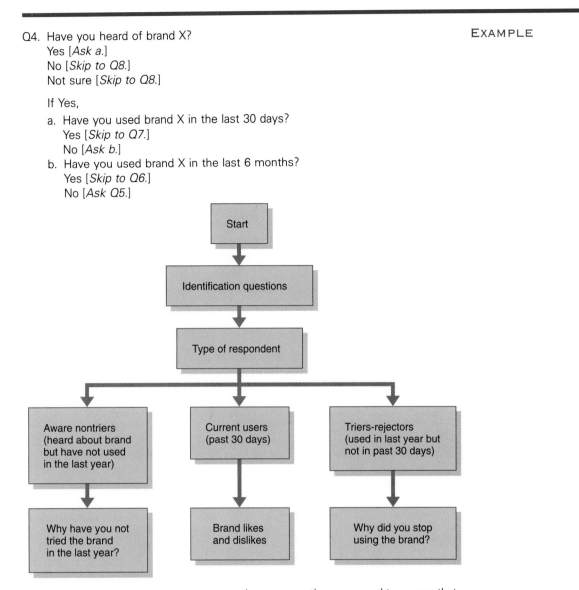

In this instance, answers to awareness and usage questions are used to ensure that all segments of the sample fall into one and only one question sequence.

naire look shorter. Crowded questions with little blank space between them can, in fact, give the impression of a complicated questionnaire. And the respondent's perception of the difficulty involved is extremely relevant to cooperation rates, especially in self-administered questionnaires. Less-crowded questions with ample blank space look easier and generally result in higher cooperation rates and fewer response errors by interviewers or respondents. Along these same lines, the type should be sufficiently large and clear so as to cause no strain in reading; avoid photoreducing questionnaires whenever possible.

1. Start with easy, salient, nonthreatening, but necessary questions. Put the more difficult or threatening questions near the end of the questionnaire. Never start a mail questionnaire with an open-ended question that requires a great deal of writing.

2. Since some demographic questions are threatening, put these questions at the end of the interview. If at all possible, avoid asking demographic questions first.

3. For personal interviews use funneling procedures to minimize order effects. Start with the general questions and move to specific questions. For low-salience topics, however, it may be necessary to ask questions about specific dimensions of the topic before asking for a summary view.

4. If questions deal with more than one topic, complete all questions on a single topic before moving to a new topic.

5. When switching topics, use a transitional phrase to make it easier for respondents to switch their trains of thought.

6. To ensure that all contingencies are covered, make a flow chart for filter questions. Filter questions should not require extensive page flipping by the interviewer or respondent or require remembering answers to earlier questions.

7. If multiple filter questions will be asked, try to ask all of them before asking the more detailed questions. Otherwise, respondents may learn how to avoid answering detailed questions.

Source: S. Sudman and N. M. Bradburn, *Asking Questions* (San Francisco: Jossey-Bass, 1983), pp. 207–8.

Color coding.   Although color does not influence response rates to questionnaires, or make them easier for interviewers to use, color coding can help in some respects. Printing a questionnaire designed for a certain group of respondents on one color of paper and a questionnaire designed for another respondent group on a different colored paper is useful. For example, one color could be used for respondents who have used a particular product in a test involving a number of products and a different color could be used for respondents who have not used the product.

Question numbering.   There are at least two good reasons for numbering questions in a questionnaire. First, numbering questions may help alert the interviewer or the respondent that a question has been skipped inadvertently. Second, numbering questions helps in developing interviewer instructions, especially with regard to appropriate skip patterns.

Fitting questions on a page.   Splitting questions, or response categories, between one page and the next is not recommended. Interviewers or respondents may assume that a question has ended at the end of a page, and this will result in misleading answers based upon incomplete questions. You should also generally avoid splitting a series of related questions.

Interviewer instructions.   Directions for individual questions should be placed as near as possible to the questions and usually just before or just after the question, depending on the nature of the directions. If the instructions deal with how the respondent should answer or how the question should be administered, they should be placed before the question. If, on the other hand, the instructions relate to how the answers should be recorded or how the interviewer should probe, they should be placed after the question. Distinctive type (e.g., capitals or italics) is commonly used to distinguish instructions from questions. The objective is to avoid having interviewers mistakenly read directions to respondents as part of the question.

Response category format. The example below presents unacceptable formats of commonly asked demographic questions. Beginning questionnaire designers often make mistakes like these. In the example notice that the page looks crowded and confusing. It is quite possible that respondents may be confused about whether the blank lines should be used with the response categories before or after them. This confusion can lead to response errors. Notice also that there is no space provided for responses to question Q29.

EXAMPLE

Q22. Your sex: _____ Male _____ Female

Q23. Your present marital status: _____ Never married _____ Married _____ Separated _____ Widowed

Q24. Number of children you have in each age group: _____ Under five years _____ 5–13 _____ 14–18 _____ 19–25 and over

Q25. Your present age: _____

Q26. Do you own (or are you buying) your own home? _____ No _____ Yes

Q27. Did you serve in the armed forces? _____ No _____ Yes (Year entered _____ Year discharged _____)

Q28. Are you presently: _____ Employed _____ Unemployed _____ Retired _____ Full-time homemaker

Q29. Please describe the usual occupation of the principal wage earner in your household, including title, kind of work, and kind of company or business. (If retired, describe the usual occupation before retirement.)

Q30. What was your approximate net family income, from all sources, before taxes, in 1992?

Less than $3,000 _____	10,000 to 12,999 _____	20,000 to 24,999 _____
3,000 to 4,999 _____	13,000 to 15,999 _____	25,000 to 30,000 _____
5,000 to 6,999 _____	16,000 to 19,999 _____	Over $30,000 _____
7,000 to 9,999 _____		

Another tendency of beginning questionnaire designers is to place category or column headings in a sideways format to conserve space, as the next example illustrates. Sideways formatting requires constant shifting of the page or head-twisting to read the category headings. A better presentation is to design a questionnaire with ample space for conventionally placed category headings.

The generally accepted standard is to use vertical answer formats for individual questions, which means that the interviewer or respondent will be reading down a single column.

Another formatting strategy is to use *grids,* which are appropriate when there are a number of simultaneous questions that use the same set of response categories (e.g., What brands of toothpaste have you ever heard of? Which brand or brands of toothpaste have you used in the past 30 days? Which *one* brand do you use most often?). A grid format requires instructing the interviewer or respondent to record the response in the appropriate column. (See the following example.)

EXAMPLE

Much has been said about the quality of life offered by various sizes of cities. We would like to know how you feel. First, please show which city size is best for each of the characteristics by putting an "X" in the appropriate column by each item. Second, please look back over the list and show which three of these characteristics would be most important to you if you were selecting a new community in which to live by ranking them from 1 (most important) to 3 (third most important).

	City below 10,000 People	City of 10,000 to 49,999 People	City of 50,000 to 149,999 People	City of 150,000 People or Over
Equality of opportunities for all residents, regardless of race				
Place in which to raise children				
Community spirit and pride				
General mental health of residents				
Adequacy of medical care				
Protection of individual freedom and privacy				
Friendliness of people to each other				
Adequacy of police protection				
General satisfaction of residents				
Respect for law and order				
Lowest costs for public services (like water, sewer, and police)				
Recreational and entertainment opportunities				

Source: From D. A. Dillman, *Mail and Telephone Surveys: The Total Method* (New York: John Wiley & Sons, 1978), p. 139.

Skip instructions.   Skip instructions are communicated to interviewers or respondents by two methods: verbal instructions and arrows that point to the next question. Both methods are acceptable.

Several guidelines should be followed with regard to skip instructions. First, the instruction should be placed immediately after the answer that generates the skip, not after the question. This format ensures that the interviewer or respondent will not forget or ignore the instructions. Second, skip instructions do not belong at the beginning of a subsequent question when there have been questions in between. For example, the instructions

[*If the respondent answered yes to Q10, ask Q15.*
Otherwise skip to Q12.]

Fragrances

5a. [*Hand respondent card* A.] Listed on this card are several brands of fragrances. Would you please tell me which of these brands you have personally used in the past three months? [*Circle all mentioned below in column 5a.*]

5b. Which brands, if any, have you personally used in the past month? [*Circle all mentioned below in column 5b.*]

5c. Now, which one of these brands would you say you personally use most often? [*Circle one below in column 5c.*]

	(5a) Past 3 Months	(5b) Past Month	(5c) Most Often
Arpège	1 (20)	1 (23)	1 (26)
Aviance	2	2	2
Avon (all)	3	3	3
Babe	4	4	4
Cachet	5	5	5
Chanel No. 5	6	6	6
Chantilly	7	7	7
Charlie	8	8	8
Emeraude	9	9	9
Estée	1 (21)	1 (24)	1 (27)
Farouche	2	2	2
Intimate	3	3	3
Jean Naté	4	4	4
Je Reviens	5	5	5
Jontue	6	6	6
Joy	7	7	7
L'Air du Temps	8	8	8
Masumi	9	9	9
My Sin	1 (22)	1 (25)	1 (28)
Norell	2	2	2
Nuance	3	3	3
Rive Gauche	4	4	4
Shalimar	5	5	5
Tabu	6	6	6
Tigress	7	7	7
White Shoulders	8	8	8
Wind Song	9	9	9
Youth Dew	0	0	0
Other (specify)			
_____	X	X	X
_____			
_____			
None		Y	

[*Take back card* A.]

placed at the beginning of question 15 would require the interviewer to turn back to locate the respondent's answer to question 10. In this case the skip instructions should be placed after the response to the filter question (that is, question 10), and the appropriate response categories should be placed before the follow-up question. Backward flow should be avoided.

Precoding.   It is important when constructing the questionnaire to consider how the data ultimately will be processed and analyzed. If processing and analysis decisions are reserved until after the interviewing is complete, uncorrectable problems are likely to surface. Experienced researchers generally do as much precoding preparation as possible. Precoding of closed-ended questions and precolumning of the entire questionnaire is completed before using the questionnaire in the field. As we discuss in some detail in Chapter 13, precoding involves assigning a numerical value to every possible response to a closed-ended question. Precolumning involves assigning each question and response category contained in the questionnaire to a specific location in the data file, which allows the information to be "read-in" properly by the computer.

Exhibit 12–5 provides a checklist of the major points that should be considered when designing the questionnaire layout.

Pretesting the Questionnaire

Pretests are indispensable to the development of good questionnaires. In fact, the effectiveness of the itemized question format is largely attributable to pretesting, which is necessary to determine the appropriate set of response categories. A thorough pretest exposes the potential for both respondent and interviewer error. There are at least five considerations involved in pretesting.[11]

1. *What items should be pretested?* All aspects of the questionnaire, including layout, question sequence, word meaning, question difficulty, branching instructions, and so on, should be part of the pretest.

2. *How should the pretest be conducted?* To whatever extent possible, the pretest should involve administering the questionnaire in an environment and context identical to the one to be used in the final survey. Essential features of a pretest are **debriefing** and/or **protocol analysis.** Debriefing, which takes place after a respondent has completed the questionnaire, involves asking respondents to explain their answers, to state the meaning of each question, and to describe any problems they had completing the questionnaire. Protocol analysis calls for the respondent to "think aloud" while completing the questionnaire.

3. *Who should conduct the pretest?* In the case of telephone and personal pretest interviews, a number of parties should participate. First, the project director and/or person responsible for developing the questionnaire should complete several pretest interviews. The majority of the pretest interviews should be conducted by regular staff interviewers. It is a good idea to assign both experienced and relatively new interviewers to do the pretest interviews.

4. *Who should be the respondents in the pretest?* Respondents involved in the pretest should resemble the target population as much as possible

DEBRIEFING
Procedure of asking respondents to explain their answers, to state the meaning of each question, and to describe any problems they had with answering or completing the questionnaire.

PROTOCOL ANALYSIS
Procedure in which the respondent "thinks aloud" while completing the questionnaire.

---

1. Use booklet format for ease in reading and turning pages and to prevent lost pages.

2. A mail or self-administered questionnaire should look easy to answer and should be professionally designed and printed. The date, the title of the study, and the name of the organization conducting the study should appear on the first page of the questionnaire.

3. Do not crowd questions. Be sure that sufficient space is left for open-ended questions since the answer will not be longer than the space provided.

4. Use sufficiently large and clear type so that there is no strain in reading.

5. Colored covers or sections of the questionnaire may be helpful to interviewers when multiple forms or complex skipping patterns are used.

6. Each question should be numbered, and subparts of a question should be lettered to prevent questions from being omitted in error and to facilitate the use of skip instructions. Indent subparts of questions.

7. Do not split a question between two pages because interviewers or respondents may think that the question is completed at the end of a page.

8. Provide directions and probes for specific questions at appropriate places in the questionnaire; identify these directions with distinctive type, such as capitals or italics.

9. Use vertical answer formats for individual questions.

10. Place skip instructions immediately after the answer to the filter question.

11. Precode all closed-ended questions to facilitate data processing and to ensure that all the data are in proper form for analysis.

12. Precolumn the questionnaire.

Source: S. Sudman and N. M. Bradburn, *Asking Questions* (San Francisco: Jossey-Bass, 1983), pp. 290–310.

EXHIBIT 12—5

Checklist of Major Points to Consider When Designing the Format of the Questionnaire

in terms of familiarity with the topic, attitudes and behaviors associated with the topic, general background characteristics, and so on. This is absolutely critical to administering a pretest.

5. *How large a sample is required for the pretest?* To a large degree, sample size depends on the variation of the target population. The more heterogeneous the target population, the larger the pretest sample required. Complex questionnaires also warrant a large pretest sample.

Pretesting questionnaires should be taken seriously: "No amount of intellectual exercise can substitute for testing an instrument designed to communicate with ordinary people."[12]

INTERNATIONAL CONSIDERATIONS

The success of a survey, whether international or domestic, rests on the ability of the researcher to ask the right questions in a manner that increases the likelihood that the respondent will provide the desired information. Beyond this challenge, there are additional considerations that are specific to conducting research in foreign markets. Many factors add to the complexity and diversity of conducting market research in international markets. These include the following:[13]

1. *Understanding the culture.* The first point to recognize is that consumers worldwide are a varied lot. For example, Table 12–1 presents an index of per capita spending in Europe by product and country. Notice that

TABLE 12–1
European Differences: An Index of Per Capita Spending

	Luxembourg	Denmark	West Germany*	France	Great Britain	Belgium	Italy	Netherlands	Spain	Ireland	Greece	Portugal
Total spending	116.4	114.6	111.8	109.8	105.8	105.7	104.2	101.5	74.4	59.9	59.7	52.1
Food	105.3	92.7	91.3	114.9	83.8	102.4	121.4	89.2	94.2	85.0	105.0	79.6
Drinks	111.5	126.0	155.9	115.6	79.8	74.6	75.2	105.7	66.2	200.8	61.4	64.2
Tobacco	258.8	124.4	98.2	101.8	100.0	125.8	103.8	112.5	89.9	96.0	154.1	0.6
Apparel and footwear	89.8	89.7	128.4	93.7	109.7	86.3	118.6	101.4	54.2	55.0	59.5	49.4
Housing	87.4	126.7	79.7	94.0	117.5	83.8	112.2	80.0	131.2	51.6	38.2	78.0
Heat and light	222.7	141.3	139.3	101.5	119.6	142.0	78.4	133.6	44.2	68.4	40.0	32.9
Furniture	180.2	110.6	171.8	120.7	72.4	100.7	87.9	112.1	50.7	30.9	23.6	35.0
Household textiles	82.7	119.7	128.8	111.5	73.7	93.5	98.3	71.8	100.1	60.5	105.5	63.3
Home appliances	168.2	101.7	128.5	100.3	132.7	117.3	93.9	81.4	54.0	39.1	48.9	28.7
Other household	98.6	79.7	108.9	117.7	74.5	174.1	118.9	101.5	73.2	50.1	76.1	62.8
Health and medical	88.4	83.3	130.8	146.8	93.4	128.4	83.7	114.7	45.6	53.2	36.4	31.7
Transportation, vehicles	244.1	133.6	150.4	100.4	113.1	132.4	96.6	99.6	39.3	37.5	17.6	17.2
Transportation, maintenance	190.0	109.3	130.3	123.9	97.6	99.1	84.3	62.3	88.8	50.2	30.7	63.5
Public transportation	25.9	104.9	75.4	88.9	139.2	46.0	105.4	68.8	93.7	41.8	264.6	34.8
Communications	246.3	155.6	124.7	114.5	81.1	52.6	100.8	185.0	45.0	35.8	178.6	15.1
Entertainment, education, and legal	87.9	152.3	116.7	99.5	112.0	107.5	112.8	114.8	51.5	74.6	42.9	56.3
Restaurants and hotels	83.7	52.4	68.1	100.7	138.4	89.8	105.1	63.7	139.7	8.7	76.8	31.5
Other	155.8	187.3	93.8	109.2	123.0	107.5	115.8	127.5	56.7	45.8	27.2	30.2

Note: 100 equals the average for Europe. Low indices, in some cases, reflect sales to foreign nationals.
*Prior to reunification.
Source: Donnés Sociales 1990, Institut National de la Statistique et des Éudes Économiques, Paris, France.

A product test in a Japanese market

there are substantial differences in all of the per capita spending indices. The second point to recognize is that a thorough understanding of the culture is necessary if the researcher is to obtain satisfactory response rates. Aside from the problems associated with high rates of illiteracy, in some cultures a woman will not consent to an interview by a stranger, let alone a man. In other cultures men will be reluctant to discuss topics such as personal hygiene or preferences in clothing because they feel this would be beneath their dignity—and they most definitely will not address these issues in the presence of a female interviewer. In addition, it is difficult, if not impossible, for respondents to answer questions concerning goods and services that have never been available or are not commonly used in the community, or whose use is not well understood.

2. *Lack of secondary data.* The usually voluminous amounts of secondary data available in U.S. markets are, in most cases, simply not available in every international market, especially in developing countries. Even when data are available, they may be of variable quality. For example, population censuses in some countries are frequently based on estimates made by nonprofessionals (e.g., village elders), and data on income and sales from tax returns can be grossly inaccurate in countries where such information is routinely undeclared or underreported. Table 12–2 presents census data from the last conducted censuses for European countries.

3. *Cost of collecting primary data.* A researcher faced with collecting market research information in international markets soon discovers that the costs of data collection can be considerably higher without a network of established marketing firms. Many foreign countries lack companies that are experienced in collecting information, which means that a sponsoring firm will have to invest in the development of sampling frames and other materials and in the training of interviewers and other necessary personnel.

TABLE 12−2

European Scorecard: Census Data

	Population (millions)	Last Census	Lowest Level of Geodemographic Data Available
EEC Nations:			
West Germany	62.168	May 25, 1987	Teil (3,000 to 7,000 people)
Italy	57.664	October 25, 1981	Sezione di Censimento (an average of 125 families)
United Kingdom	57.366	April 5, 1981	Ward (8,000 to 10,000 people)
France	56.358	March 4, 1982	Chef lieu (up to 20,000 people)
Spain	39.269	March 1, 1981	Municipality (an average of 4,000 people)
Netherlands*	14.936	February 28, 1971	Postal code (an average of 15 households)
Portugal	10.354	March 16, 1981	Seccao/quarteiras (an average of 151 people)
Greece	10.028	April 5, 1981	Commune (an average of 1,500 people)
Belgium	9.909	March 1, 1981	Quarterier (an average of 508 people)
Denmark†	5.131	November 9, 1970	Commune (an average of 300 people)
Ireland	3.500	April 13, 1986	Ward (3,000 to 15,000 people)
Luxembourg	0.384	March 31, 1981	Commune (an average of 3,254 people)
Eastern Europe:			
Poland	37.777	December 7, 1978	n.a.
Yugoslavia	23.842	March 31, 1981	n.a.
Romania	23.273	January 5, 1977	n.a.
East Germany	16.307	December 31, 1981	n.a.
Czechoslovakia	15.683	November 1, 1980	n.a.
Hungary	10.569	January 1, 1980	n.a.
Bulgaria	8.934	December 4, 1985	n.a.

*Last census supplemented by sample surveys and computerized population register.

†A computerized population register provides more up-to-date figures for 1976 and 1981.

Source: Midyear 1990 population projections and date of last census prepared by the Center for International Research; U.S. Bureau of the Census; CACI Limited in London; and embassy information offices.

Methodological Considerations

A number of methodological considerations influence the construction of questionnaires to be used in international research studies. These methodological problems essentially arise from two basic factors: (1) the complex cultural differences in the meaning of products and activities, and (2) the paucity of standardized data-collection instruments to measure marketing-related variables.

Functional equivalence.   The extent to which the same product is used for the same—or a similar—function in two or more countries is known as **func-**

tional equivalence. However, possessions tend to be used for different functions in different societies. In India, for example, the accumulation of jewelry represents less an interest in the display of social status than in security and accumulation of wealth. Refrigerators, used to store food in some countries, are used primarily for chilling water and soft drinks in other countries.[14] When General Mills entered the United Kingdom's breakfast-cereal market, a box featured a freckled, red-haired, crew-cut kid saying, "Gee kids, it's great." What General Mills failed to recognize was that the British family is not as child-oriented and permissive as the American family it was accustomed to, and that English parent-child relationships tend to be more authoritarian; consequently, the package had no appeal to the British housewife.[15]

A similar blunder was made by Binoca when it launched a talcum powder ad in newspapers in India. The ad showed an attractive, although apparently naked, woman dousing herself with talcum powder. The caption covering strategic portions of her body read: "Don't go wild—just enough is all you need of Binoca talc." The highly conservative Indian public found the advertisement distasteful and developed strong negative associations with the brand name.[16] To ask proper questions requires that researchers understand the functional equivalence, or lack thereof, of the activities being investigated.

Conceptual equivalence.   The extent to which the same concept (e.g., "family") has the same meaning in two or more countries is referred to as **conceptual equivalence.** However, concepts can have totally different meanings in different cultural environments. This requires the careful choice of the words used to convey the meaning of what the researcher is attempting to explore. The word *family,* for example, means something different in the United States, where it typically refers to only parents and children, than it does in many other cultures, where it may extend to grandparents, aunts, uncles, and other relatives.

Ethnic influences.   Researchers need to understand how the cultural values of a society will affect the approach to the research issue of interest. It may be possible to research problems in one culture but not in another because of cultural taboos and different levels of abstraction. For example, researching attitudes and behaviors concerning personal hygiene products may simply not be possible in certain cultures where the norms clearly proscribe public discussion of such issues.

Instrument equivalence.   It may not be possible to use the same measuring instrument in every culture. For this reason the researcher may choose to use what are called *emic instruments. Emic* refers to analysis in terms of a situation's internal or functional elements. An **emic instrument** is one that is constructed specifically for investigating an attitude in a specific culture. Closed-ended questions, for example, may work well in one culture, but because of cultural differences may be inappropriate in others; certain categories of response may have to be omitted, or additional categories may have to be added. Openended questions also may pose some problems, especially in markets where the level of literacy is low and where interviewer bias is prominent. Other types of interviewing methods, such as focus groups and consumer panels, may face

FUNCTIONAL EQUIVALENCE
Refers to the extent to which the same product in two or more countries is used for the same function.

CONCEPTUAL EQUIVALENCE
Refers to the extent to which the same concept has the same meaning in two or more countries.

EMIC INSTRUMENT
An instrument constructed for investigating a construct in a specific culture.

problems because of strong social-acquiescence tendencies that are the cultural norm in some countries.

ETIC INSTRUMENT

An instrument that can be used in different cultures to provide direct comparisons of the same variable across nations.

In some instances the researcher may attempt to construct **etic instruments,** which are transcultural in application, relating to the behavioral analysis of attitudes considered in isolation. This would permit direct comparison of the same variable across cultures. Attempts at developing etic instruments have employed nonverbal instruments such as picture completion, TAT instruments, and semantic differentials.[17]

Instrument translation.   It may seem obvious to suggest that a survey developed in one country be carefully translated into the language of the country where it is going to be administered and assessed; however, mistakes can happen even in the case of literal equivalence. Classic examples of this are the translation into Flemish of General Motor's "Body by Fisher" slogan that became "Corpse by Fisher," and a U.S. airline's advertisement of its Boeing 747 "rendezvous lounge" that translated into Portuguese as the "prostitution chamber."[18]

Several translation methods have been used in international research projects.[19]

1. *Direct translation.* The survey undergoes a single translation from one language into another by a bilingual translator. This method, however, exposes the instrument to all the problems discussed above.

2. *Back translation.* A variation of direct translation, this method requires that the translated survey be translated back into the original language by another bilingual translator. This lets the researcher correct any meaning problems between the original and retranslated instruments. Note that back translation requires that equivalent terms for words or phrases exist in the other language, which may not always be the case.

3. *Decentering.* A hybrid of back translation, this method involves a successive iteration process: translation and retranslation of an instrument, each time by a different translator. The back-translated versions in the original language are compared sequentially. If discrepancies occur, the original is modified, and the process is repeated until both show the same or similar wordings. Generally, each iteration should show more convergence.

There are several ways to evaluate the quality of translations.

1. Have a monolinguist evaluate the translated questionnaire for clarity and comprehensiveness.

2. Determine the extent of change in the meaning between two versions examined by bilingual evaluators.

3. Assess the respondent's ability to answer the translated questions correctly.

4. Pretest both the original and the translated questionnaire with a bilingual individual.

Sampling and fielding the survey.   In many countries telephone directories, census tract and block data, and detailed socioeconomic characteristics of the target population will not be available or are outdated. This adversely affects the ability to draw nonprobability as well as probability samples and to conduct personal interviews of any variety. For example, lacking age distributions for the target population, it is difficult for a marketing researcher to set representative age quotas. Moreover, in certain cultures, convenient samples are doomed to failure. In Saudi Arabia, for instance, because of the practice of purdah, the seclusion of women, shopping-mall interviews produce all-male samples.[20]

Inadequate mailing lists and rudimentary postal and telephone services can make marketing research in some countries extremely difficult. In many countries only a small percentage of the population has telephones, and an alarmingly large percentage of the telephone lines (over 50 percent) may be out of service at any one time.[21] Mail surveys suffer from similar problems. Delivery delays of weeks are common, and, in certain countries, expected response rates are lowered considerably because the questionnaire can be mailed back only at a post office.

The obstacles in conducting international marketing research studies are indeed formidable. Understanding the cultural environment in which the research is taking place is a necessary condition for success. The researcher must also avoid the tendency to blindly apply conventional research techniques and practices. Designing and implementing international research projects can be done effectively. It just takes effort and a sensitivity to asking the questions in a manner that increases the likelihood that respondents will provide the desired information.

SUMMARY

In this chapter we have considered issues in questionnaire design and construction. The four major activities involved in questionnaire design are: (1) preliminary considerations, (2) asking questions, (3) constructing the questionnaire, and (4) pretesting the questionnaire. Our discussion emphasized general guidelines and offered basic principles involved in asking questions. The

material on questionnaire construction focused on response formats, logical flow, and layout considerations. In our questionnaire pretest discussion we emphasized five decisions that the researcher must make. The remainder of the chapter considered the special case of conducting research in international markets, including methodological differences and concerns.

KEY CONCEPTS

Asking Questions

Loaded Questions

Double-Barreled Questions

Omission

Telescoping

Creation

Open-Ended Questions

Closed-Ended Questions

Questionnaire Flow

Funnel Sequence

Inverted-Funnel Sequence

Filter Questions

Skip Patterns

Skip Instructions

Pretesting

Functional Equivalence

Conceptual Equivalence

Ethnic Influences

Instrument Equivalence

Instrument Translation

Direct Translation

Back Translation

Decentering

REVIEW QUESTIONS

1. Analyze the following questions and make any corrections needed.

   a. How much do you make?_____

   b. Which sporting event do you attend most frequently?

_____ Baseball	_____ Hockey
_____ Football	_____ Tennis
_____ Basketball	_____ Golf

   c. Do you agree with the president's intentions to lower taxes?

   _____ Strongly agree

   _____ Agree

   _____ Neither agree nor disagree

   _____ Disagree

   d. Name the last 3 movies you rented.

   _____

   _____

   _____

   e. How many hours of television do you watch in a typical week?

_____ 0–10 hrs.	_____ 21–30 hrs.
_____ 11–20 hrs.	_____ 30 or more hrs.

   f. Don't you think MADD has saved many lives?

   _____ Yes   _____ No

   g. Check your favorite magazine.

_____ *Time*	_____ *People*
_____ *Newsweek*	_____ *Business Week*
_____ *Money*	_____ *Life*

2. Select from the following list of open-ended questions those that would be better posed as closed-ended questions. Of those selected, rewrite them to make them closed-ended.
   — Exactly how much money does that job offer?
   — What are your favorite lines of clothing?
   — From which high school did you graduate?
   — How satisfied are you with your hair stylist?
   — Most of the office work gets done on which day of the week?
   — Approximately how many jelly beans do you think there are in the jar?

3. Make up your own example to illustrate each of the following:
   a. loaded question
   b. double-barreled question
   c. an overlapping question

4. Distinguish among omission, telescoping, and creation. Discuss how aided and unaided questions influence each of these response effects.

5. Develop an appropriate introduction for a questionnaire dealing with students' attitudes toward the university cafeteria.

6. Evaluate the following questionnaire before the owners of a new bar and grill pass it out. How could you improve it?

   1. What sex are you?

   _____ Male   _____ Female

   2. Are you part of the 67% who recently replied they were dissatisfied with the bars/restaurants in town?

   _____ Yes   _____ No

   3. What kind of music do you like to hear?

_____ Rock	_____ Pop	_____ Jazz
_____ Traditional country	_____ Top 40	
_____ Other		

   4. Place an X on the line.

   The atmosphere is

   Good _____ Bad

   The managers are

   Good _____ Bad

   The service is

   Good _____ Bad

   5. About how much do you spend on a night out?

_____ $0–$20.00	_____ $40.00–$60.00
_____ $20.00–$40.00	_____ Above $60.00

   6. On a scale of 1 to 10, how would you rate your meal?_____

   7. Will you be coming back to see us soon?

   _____ Yes   _____ No

ENDNOTES

1. An excellent source for a detailed treatment of questionnaire design and construction issues is D. A. Dillman, *Mail and Telephone Surveys: The Total Method* (New York: John Wiley & Sons, 1978).

2. Adapted from Seymour Sudman and Norman M. Bradburn, *Asking Questions* (San Francisco: Jossey-Bass, 1983).

3. Normally permission from the originator of the question is neither required or expected, although you may want to communicate with the originator to find out whether there were difficulties with the question that were not reported in the published source. For questionnaires that have been copyrighted, permission from the publisher is required.

4. Ed Blair, Seymour Sudman, Norman M. Bradburn, and Carol Stocking, "How to Ask Questions about Drinking and Sex: Response Effects in Measuring Consumer Behavior," *Journal of Marketing Research,* August 1977, pp. 316–21.

5. Seymour Sudman and Norman M. Bradburn, "Effects of Time and Memory Factors on Response Surveys," *Journal of the American Statistical Association,* December 1973, pp. 805–15.

6. Yoram Wind and David Lerner, "On the Measurement of Purchase Data: Surveys Versus Purchase Diary," *Journal of Marketing Research,* May 1970, pp. 254–55.

7. Daniel Starch, *Measuring Advertising Readership and Results* (New York: McGraw-Hill, 1966), p. 20.

8. Parts of the following discussion are adapted from Sudman and Bradburn, *Asking Questions,* pp. 208–28.

9. A careful discussion of these points can be found in Dillman, *Mail and Telephone Surveys.*

10. Parts of the following discussion are adapted from Sudman and Bradburn, *Asking Questions,* pp. 208–28.

11. Our pretesting discussion is based on Shelby D. Hunt, Richard D. Sparkman, Jr., and James Wilcox, "The Pretest in Survey Research: Issues and Preliminary Findings," *Journal of Marketing Research,* May 1982, pp. 269–73.

12. Charles H. Backstom and G. D. Hursch, *Survey Research* (Evanston, Ill.: Northwestern University Press, 1963).

13. For further discussion, see S. P. Douglas and S. Craig, *International Marketing Research* (Englewood Cliffs, N.J.: Prentice Hall, 1983), chapter 1.

14. Y. A. Choudhry, "Pitfalls of International Marketing Research: Are You Speaking French Like a Spanish Cow," *ABER* 17, no. 4 (Winter 1986), pp. 18–28.

15. David A. Ricks, Y. C. Fu, and S. Arpan, *International Business Blunders* (Columbus, Ohio: Grid, 1974).

16. Ibid.

17. Choudhry, "Pitfalls of International Marketing Research," p. 23.

18. See Ricks et al., *International Business Blunders.*

19. Ibid, pp. 23–26.

20. David C. Pring, "American Firms Rely on Multinational Research Suppliers to Solve Marketing Problems Overseas," *Marketing News,* May 15, 1981, section 2, p. 2.

21. "Cairo's Telephone System Improves," *World Business Weekly,* February 16, 1981, p. 19.

Data-Collection Activities: Fielding the Questionnaire and Data Preparation

CENSUS ADJUSTMENT COULD BENEFIT CALIFORNIA AT NEW YORK'S EXPENSE

Tom Bradley ought to send David Dinkins a thank-you note. During the past decade, New York has spent millions of dollars in legal fees to force the Census Bureau to adjust its figures for an undercount. But a statistically adjusted census would probably benefit faster-growing states at the expense of slow-growth states. In other words, New York City Mayor David Dinkins is ordering his lawyers to pursue a claim that, if successful, would probably mean less federal aid for him and more for Los Angeles Mayor Tom Bradley.

Undercounted populations are a sore point in states such as New York, which stand to lose Congressional seats and federal aid to faster-growing areas of the country. An adjusted census would raise New York's official headcount, but it would also erode New York's share of the total U.S. population. Many allocations of federal aid are based on states' shares of the national population. For this reason, an adjusted census could mean a $10 million loss in federal aid to New York State each year, according to *American Demographics* calculations.

Los Angeles, Chicago, Miami, Houston, and New York City are currently suing the Department of Commerce and the Bureau of the Census to force an adjustment. One of their goals is obtaining a bigger share of federal aid that is decided, at least in part, based on population counts. This money totals about $40 billion a year, according to Census Bureau regional analyst Ron Prevost. It is used for transportation, construction, education, and health services, but the federal pie is not getting any larger.

California accounts for 11.97 percent of the total population of the United States, according to unadjusted figures from the 1990 census (see Table 1). If the figures are adjusted, California could grow to 12.15 percent of the total. This may not seem like much of a gain, but 0.1 percent of the $40 billion in federal grant money equals $40 million. Within the state, the share of money that different localities get would depend on how much each area gained from adjustment.

Florida would be the next largest gainer, increasing its share of the U.S. population by about 0.1 percent. Virginia ranks third among winners, picking up just 0.04 percent of the total population.

New York expects to be a big gainer from an adjusted census. The city has

CHAPTER 13

CHAPTER
OBJECTIVES

▬

DESCRIBE
activities and elements in
fielding a study.

DESCRIBE
the procedures for checking
and editing questionnaires.

EXPLAIN
coding practices for
closed-ended and open-ended
questions.

DESCRIBE
the processes involved in
transcribing raw data onto
magnetic tape or disk or
directly onto the computer.

spent "millions by now" in litigation, according to Evelyn Mann, director of the population division for New York City's planning department. If the census is adjusted, the state's population could increase by over half a million people. But

TABLE 1

Slim Gains: States with at least a 0.02 percentage point gain or loss in share of total U.S. population under a high series census adjustment

State	Percent of U.S. Total		State	Percent of U.S. Total	
	Before Adjustment	Gain after Adjustment		Before Adjustment	Loss After Adjustment
Winners			Losers		
California	11.97	0.18	Iowa	1.12	−0.02
Florida	5.20	0.10	Missouri	2.06	−0.02
Virginia	2.49	0.04	Kentucky	1.48	−0.02
North Carolina	2.67	0.04	Minnesota	1.76	−0.02
Georgia	2.60	0.03	New York	7.23	−0.02
Maryland	1.92	0.02	Massachusetts	2.42	−0.03
Texas	6.83	0.02	Wisconsin	1.97	−0.03
South Carolina	1.40	0.02	Indiana	2.23	−0.04
West Virginia	0.72	0.02	Michigan	3.74	−0.05
			Illinois	4.60	−0.06
			Pennsylvania	4.78	−0.06
			Ohio	4.36	−0.06

Note: Calculations are based on the Census Bureau's estimate of the highest possible undercount in each state and the District of Columbia.

it could also bring New York a net loss of revenue.

A census adjustment would have many other effects on politics in the 1990s. Census figures are used to determine the number of Americans who live in poverty, so an adjusted census might bring more welfare money to big cities. Congressional district lines are drawn on the basis of local population change, so an adjustment might mean greater representation in Congress for big cities. An adjustment would also imperil Congressional seats in Mississippi, Oklahoma, Pennsylvania, and Wisconsin, according to Election Data Services of Washington, D.C. It could give extra seats to California, Georgia, Montana, or New Jersey.

"The decennial population counts become significant when they describe the characteristics of the population," says David Kellerman, survey statistician with the governments division at the Census Bureau. "Most grant programs are created to target a need, and the numbers will identify issues that the Congress or the President feel need to be addressed."

Federal funds are distributed through complex formulas. These formulas make it difficult to measure the precise effect of population shifts on funding, says Kellerman. Some funds are protected from population loss through grandfather clauses; other funds actually increase if an area loses population. In some cases, an adjustment would benefit cities at the expense of neighboring nonmetropolitan areas. But federal funds are usually distributed to states and passed on to localities, he says. These grants are often based on the state's share of the national population.

Many states would be unaffected by a census adjustment. Twelve states, located primarily in the West, would gain or lose less than a million dollars a year in federal aid. The big losers would be northern industrial states such as Ohio, Pennsylvania, Illinois, Michigan, Indiana, and Wisconsin. Ohio, Pennsylvania, and Illinois could find up to $24 million a year missing from the federal check. Chicago lawyers should think twice about suing for an adjustment. If they win, their city may lose.

Source: Judith Waldrop and Susan Krafft, *American Demographics,* July, 1991, pp. 9–10. Reproduced with permission of the copyright owner.

INTRODUCTION

One of the most important aspects of the marketing research process is the data-collection phase. Certainly, the particular research design and data analyses are vital to the solution of a properly defined research problem. However, unforeseen difficulties such as those experienced by the Census Bureau in conducting the 1990 census can lead to questionable findings and perhaps even invalid conclusions.

This chapter describes the activities necessary in administering a survey and in preparing the raw data for data analysis. The research activities to be described affect both the quality of the data generated (its accuracy) and the validity (its generalizability) of the conclusions drawn from these data. The procedures and practices described serve two general purposes:

1. They establish, as far as possible, uniformity in fieldwork and in the processing of data.
2. They establish guidelines for the various steps in the processing of data.

FIELDING THE QUESTIONNAIRE

Fielding the questionnaire refers to the process of administering the data-collection instrument. We discuss how the data-collection (fieldwork) process actually works and describe procedures that are used to ensure that the information collected is, to the extent possible, free of errors caused by sloppy fieldwork.

Who Conducts Fieldwork?

You may recall from Chapter 1 our specification of three key players in the commercial marketing research business: corporations (manufacturers, the service industry, and the like), advertising agencies, and research suppliers. Corporations and ad agencies typically contract for a particular study, which the research supplier helps to design, execute, and analyze. The "execution" aspect includes data gathering.

At a research supplier, the data-collection function is the responsibility of the field department, a group normally headed by a director or vice president of field operations. Generally, the department is staffed by a number of field supervisors (who are responsible for day-to-day planning and control of specific studies), samplers (who purchase or establish samples firsthand), and people who provide clerical support for routing surveys to the interviewing sites and for checking the questionnaires in after data collection has been completed.

Depending upon the supplier's size and staffing ability, data may be collected by personnel either within or outside the organization. It is fairly typical for medium-sized and large research firms to have their own WATS telephone-interviewing capabilities. Some companies such as Market Facts and MARC also have the capability to conduct full-scale, mall intercept studies with their own personnel. In-house fieldwork operations give suppliers a competitive advantage because of cost efficiency and better quality control.

Suppliers that do not have their own means of data collection subcontract fieldwork to one or more of the thousands of independently owned and operated interviewing services. Many of these interviewing services are relatively small companies that conduct central-location personal interviews (mall intercept) and/or operate telephone interviewing facilities in one or more markets. An ever-decreasing number, however, conduct personal in-home (door-to-door) interviews.

Steps in Fielding a Study

The fielding of a study actually begins in the proposal stage of the research process (described in Chapter 2). At the time the supplier prepares its proposal, the project director and field director will discuss the research problem and a possible research method, including specification of the target audience, sampling, and interviewing methods. When all the study specifications have been determined, the field director prepares cost and timing estimates for conducting data collection. Activities in fielding a study follow this sequence:

1. Estimating costs.
2. "Alerting" the study.
3. Preparing field instructions.
4. Briefing.
5. Data collection.
6. Evaluation of fieldwork quality.

Estimating costs.   Estimating costs and time for conducting fieldwork is more an art than a science—no hard-and-fast rules. A sense of what it takes to collect the required number of interviews using a specific research approach comes from years of experience. Although there is no truly accurate estimation formula, there are a number of parameters you can consider in selecting specific sampling/interviewing methods.

In general, regardless of the method chosen, two factors determine the cost of the fieldwork: (1) incidence of qualified respondents and (2) questionnaire length.

Most studies require that respondents meet certain criteria in order to be interviewed. For example, a cola taste test may require a sample of people who have had at least two glasses of a carbonated cola beverage during the past week. Such individuals may account only for 35 percent of the population; that is, if you talk to 100 people, only 35 people will qualify (an incidence of 35 percent). As a general rule, the lower the incidence, the more people who must be screened for qualification, and the more the screening hours required.

The other key variable is questionnaire length. Interviewing hours are directly related to the amount of time it takes to administer a questionnaire to a qualified respondent. When questionnaire length goes beyond 15 to 20 minutes, other costs besides time can be incurred. With leisure time becoming more valuable, people tend to be less willing to participate in longer interviews. This results in lower cooperation rates for longer questionnaires; in this case, more screening may be needed, and incentives may need to be used to increase response rates (see Chapter 7).

The effects of incidence and questionnaire length are compounded by administrative costs. An interviewing supplier, whether inside or outside the company, employs supervisors and other staff who are responsible for training personnel and supervising the interviews. These supervisory costs are usually covered by adding a percentage (about 50 to 60 percent) to the cost of interviewing.

Different costs are incurred depending on the type of interviewing method used. Exhibit 13–1 details one procedure for estimating the field costs for a telephone interview. Factors such as the time of day of the interview, sample administration and control, and the need for trained interviewers can affect the cost of data collection for whatever type of survey method used.

"Alerting" the study.   With a "ballpark" cost estimate and expected study specifications at hand, the field director begins to subcontract the data collec-

---

EXHIBIT 13–1

Fielding a Telephone
Study

Assumptions

A. Required sample size: $n = 300$

B. 225 = Number of telephone numbers an interviewer can dial per 8-hour shift assuming
6 1/2 productive hours

C. 65% = Category incidence rate

D. 60% = Cooperation rate

E. 15 minutes = Questionnaire length

F. 3 minutes = Interviewer checking time

G. $215 = Cost per workday

Calculating Interviews per Workday

1. Contacts per day = B × C × D
      = 225 × .65 × .60
      = 87.75

2. Contacts per hour = Contacts per day/6.5
      = 87.75/6.5
      = 13.5

3. Time in minutes to reach qualified contact
      = 60/Contacts per hour
      = 60/13.5
      = 4.44

4. Time to interview = $\dfrac{\text{Time in minutes}}{\text{to reach qualified}} + \dfrac{\text{Interview}}{\text{time}} + \dfrac{\text{Interview}}{\text{checking}}_{\text{time}}$ respondent
      = 4.44 + 15 + 3
      = 22.44

5. Interviews completed per hour = 60/Time to complete interview
      = 60/22.44
      = 2.67

6. Interviews completed per workday = 6.5 × Interviews completed per hour
      = 6.5 × 2.67
      = 17.36

Calculating Field Costs

To determine field costs

1. Take completed interviews per workday (called *completes*):

    17.36

2. Divide required sample size by completes, which equals number of workdays needed to
complete interviews:

    300/17.36 = 17.28

3. Field costs are equal to cost per workday to complete interviews including overhead and
margin:

    17.28 × 215 = 3,715.2

    Hence, the field costs for the telephone survey are $3,715.20.

---

tion to one or more field services, whether they be internal or external to the
research supplier. This process sounds easier than it is. After the cost estimate
is constructed internally, the budgeted amount must be negotiated with the
various services, usually through an oral agreement arranged by telephone. It
is a real challenge for the field director to bring the study in under budget,
given the variation of data-collection costs from market to market.

INTERVIEWER INSTRUCTIONS—BE PRECISE!

Instructions to the interviewers should leave nothing to the imagination—they must be precise and unambiguous. A screener questionnaire for a carbonated soft drink study illustrates the degree of specificity that is required.

Carbonated Soft Drinks
(Screening Questionnaire)

Time Interview Begins:_____ | 1/5-1 |

Time Interview Ends:_____

Total Time: _____ | 1/6 | | 1/7 | _____

Hello, I'm _____from **Dimensions III,** a national market research company. We're conducting a study in your area, and I would like to ask you a few questions.

1. Are any members of your family or any of your close friends employed in any of the following occupations? [*Read list.*]

	Yes	No
Soft drink manufacturer or distributor	[ ]	[ ]
Selling soft drinks, vegetables, or fruit (wholesale or retail)	[ ]	[ ]
Advertising, sales promotion, public relations, or marketing research	[ ]	[ ]
Any form of radio or TV advertising	[ ]	[ ]
Editing or publishing	[ ]	[ ]

[*If "Yes" to any of the above occupations, terminate and record in "Col. 1" on Call Record Sheet. Erase and reuse Questionnaire.*]

[*Otherwise, continue with Q2.*]

2. Have you participated in any market research studies in the past 3 months?

Yes [ ] [*Terminate and record in "Col. 2" on Call Record Sheet. Erase and reuse Questionnaire.*]

No [ ] [*Ask Q3.*]

3. Which, if any, of the following products have *you, yourself,* consumed at home in the past month?

		Yes	No
Instant coffee	1/9	[ ]-1	[ ]-2
Frozen orange juice	1/10	[ ]-1	[ ]-2
Carbonated soft drink	1/11	[ ]-1	[ ]-2

[*Terminate and record in "Col. 3" on Call Record Sheet. Erase and reuse Questionnaire.*]

Once an agreement has been reached on the key parameters of the study in terms of sampling technique, questionnaire length, incidence, cost, and timing, an individual in the field department, usually called a *field supervisor,* prepares field instructions.

Preparing field instructions. The supplier formalizes the oral contract for services in its field instructions to the party (parties) conducting the fieldwork. Without mentioning the agreed-upon cost per interview, the instructions generally specify what are considered acceptable interviewing techniques, what

4. As you know, there are several brands of carbonated soft drinks. During the past three months, what specific brands of carbonated soft drinks have *you, yourself,* consumed at home? [*Do not read list.*]

1/12 [ ]-1 Dr Pepper
      [ ]-2 Coke
      [ ]-3 Classic Coca-Cola
      [ ]-4 7UP
      [ ]-5 Sprite
      [ ]-6 Slice
      [ ]-7 Pepsi
      [ ]-8 Cherry Coca-Cola
      [ ]-9 RC Cola
      [ ]-0 Mountain Dew
      [ ]-x Other Brand _____
      [ ]-y Diet Brand _____

[INTERVIEWER'S INSTRUCTIONS:

1. *If respondent mentioned any of the soft drink brands in Q4, (boxes 1–x) continue to* blue *questionnaire and count toward nondiet soft drink quota.*

2. *If respondent* did not mention *any soft drink brand in Q4 but mentioned some diet carbonated soft drink brand (box y) continue to* yellow *questionnaire and count toward diet soft drink quota.*

3. *If any of the quotas above have been filled, terminate and record in appropriate over quota "Col. 4" on Call Record Sheet.*]

Among other things, notice that the interviewer is *explicitly* instructed when to

1. Terminate the interview (see Question 1).
2. Ask the next question (see Question 2).
3. Read the set of appropriate answers (see Question 1).
4. Not read the set of appropriate answers (see Question 4).

The instructions given to the interviewers also clarify what to do after the screening questions have been asked. For example, the respondent receives a blue or yellow questionnaire, depending on his/her answer to Question 4. Finally, the screener questionnaire has been precoded—examine, for example, Questions 3 and 4.

can be expected from the field service operator or designated representative, and how interviewers are to conduct the specific interview at hand. Instructions are commonly divided into three parts: general, supervisor, and interviewer.

1. *General instructions.* The general instructions to interviewers reiterate what is acceptable in both a technical and an ethical sense. They may include direction on how to screen respondents by asking questions as they are stated, rather than in a manner that increases the chance of finding a qualified respondent, and how to ask open-ended questions using the proper "probing" method.

2. *Instructions to the interviewing supervisor.* The instructions to the interviewing supervisor provide the field operators with guidance in the planning, organization, and control of the fieldwork for which they are responsible. They itemize all materials shipped for interviewers to use, such as questionnaires, display materials, report forms, product, and so forth. A second section of the instructions describes the organization and control of the sample; for example, it answers such questions as

— Who is a qualified respondent?
— How should quota groups be filled?
— How is incidence of the groups recorded, and how and when should the key figures be reported to the supplier?
— When and where should the sample be selected?

A third section of the supervisor's instructions describes the interviewing procedure itself, as it will be conveyed to the interviewers at a briefing session. Finally, the agreed-upon work schedule is laid out, and billing instructions are provided.

3. *Interviewer instructions.* The interviewers' instructions are key to valid and reliable data generation. They specify detailed sample selection and questionnaire administration procedures on a question-by-question basis. Interviewer instructions provide direction so that fieldwork is conducted in a consistent manner by all who are involved. (See Box 13–1 on pp. 336–37.)

Briefing.   Having received the necessary materials and instructions from the supplier, the field operator holds a meeting of all interviewers taking part in the study. At the briefing session, which can be two to three hours in length, the field service supervisor establishes what is expected of each interviewer working on the study. The field instructions are reviewed, and each interviewer gets a chance to administer the questionnaire before actually meeting with respondents. The briefing is typically held on the day that interviewing begins so as to keep the instructions clear in the interviewers' minds.

Data collection.   Obviously, key to the quality of a study are the data. If quality data are not collected and provided in a timely manner, the marketing research effort is a waste of money.

The time needed for data collection can vary from a number of days to a number of months, depending upon the incidence and/or the difficulty in finding the group under study, the length of interview, the sample size, and the number of interviewers working on the study. Typical studies take less than two weeks to complete.

The quality of fieldwork is enhanced by good communication between the supplier's field department and its subcontractors, the field services. This process begins with the initial telephone contact, continues with good written instructions by the supplier and daily progress reporting by the service, and concludes with the suppliers' feedback in the form of an independent validation report, as we describe below.

Evaluation of fieldwork quality.   At the completion of the data-collection phase, the interviewer's work is scrutinized in at least two ways: *check-in* and *validation.* The completed work from a particular field service is usually collected by one of the supplier's field supervisors; this is called the *check-in process.* Questionnaires are counted to make sure that the necessary quotas (or cells) have been completed properly. For example, a quota for age might be $18-34 = 60\%$, $35-50 = 30\%$, and $51+ = 10\%$. Questionnaires usually are checked further in specific areas relating to complicated screening questions, skip patterns, open-ended question probing, and so on. Further details on check-in procedures are discussed in the following sections.

The second important quality check on fieldwork is making sure that the interview has actually taken place—the validation process. Some percentage, usually between 10 and 20 percent, of all respondents reported to have been interviewed are called again and asked a few questions to verify that the interview did take place. These questions may involve qualifying criteria (e.g., specific product usage) and/or questions generally related to the study (e.g., "Do you remember trying two cola soft drinks?"). When respondents cannot answer these questions satisfactorily, their interviews are often declared invalid and not processed. If more than one invalid questionnaire is traced to a given interviewer, it is often the practice to perform a 100 percent validation of that interviewer. If the interviewer was cheating, then all of his/her interviews would be discarded and the interviewer would not be paid.

STEPS IN PROCESSING THE DATA

Several functions must be performed in preparing the data for analysis. The major steps in processing the data are

1. Check-in.
2. Editing.
3. Coding.
4. Transferring the data.
5. Table specifications.

Check-In

The **check-in procedure** involves checking a job in from the field. Activities involved in the check-in procedure are

1. A check of all questionnaires for completeness and interviewing quality.
2. A count of usable questionnaires by required quota and/or cell groups.

Checking for acceptable questionnaires.   A questionnaire received from the field must be inspected to determine whether it is acceptable for use in the study. Several problems relating to completeness and interviewing quality can cause rejection of a questionnaire:

1. Portions of the questionnaire, or key questions, are unanswered.
2. There is evidence that the respondent did not understand the instructions for filling out the questionnaire and/or did not take the task

CHECK-IN PROCEDURE
Initial step in data processing; involves a check of all questionnaires for completeness and interviewing quality and a count of usable questionnaires by required quota and/or use groups as per study design.

seriously. In the former instance, it may be obvious that skip directions were not followed properly; in the latter instance, answers to the questions may show very little variance, say, all 1s or all 7s on a seven-point rating scale.

3. The returned questionnaire is physically incomplete, with one or more pages missing.
4. The questionnaire has been filled out by someone who should have been screened out of the sample, that is, a respondent who does not qualify for the target population.
5. The questionnaire has been completed properly but returned after a preestablished cutoff date.

Check-in personnel should keep notes on the quality of the fieldwork throughout the process, as well as during subsequent processing functions, for feedback to local supervisors.

Counting the questionnaires.   A count of usable questionnaires by required quota and/or cell groups must be maintained to detect any problems in adhering to the sampling requirements and acceptable attention levels specified in the study design. Shortages must be identified and any corrective action determined while the study is still in the field. The local supervisor should forward returned questionnaires on schedule to the research firm so that check-in, editing, and code building can start as soon as possible, as opposed to holding questionnaires until all fieldwork is completed.

Editing

EDITING PROCESS
Review of the questionnaires for maximum accuracy and precision.

Editing involves reviewing the questionnaires for maximum accuracy and precision. Editing instructions are written to include as complete a check as possible to evaluate the consistency and accuracy of responses. When two answers are inconsistent—for example, the respondent indicates no familiarity with the test brand, but also indicates that the brand was purchased on the last shopping trip—it may be possible to determine which, if either, of the two responses is correct. When this is not possible, both answers should be discarded. With respect to accuracy, the person responsible for editing concentrates on signs of interviewer bias or cheating; for example, common patterns of responses across different questionnaires for the same interviewer can signal potential problems. Finally, in addition to accuracy and consistency, the person who conducts the editing function is also concerned with response legibility, response clarity, and response completeness.

In all cases, the editor follows the editing instructions in resolving any ambiguities and may consult with the interviewer or recorder.

Coding Procedures

CODING
Assignment of a numerical value (code) or alphanumerical symbol to represent a specific response to a specific question along with the column position that the designated code or symbol will occupy on a data record.

Put simply, **coding** involves assigning a numerical value (code) or alphanumeric symbol to represent (1) a specific response to a specific question and (2) the column position that the designated code or symbol will oc-

Instructions for post-coding

cupy on a data record. The coding process entails several different activities. For certain types of question formats (such as closed-ended questions), the coding specifications are designated before fieldwork begins (**precoding**). Coding specifications for open-ended questions are much more likely to be designated after the questionnaires have been returned from the field (**postcoding**), although in certain instances a coding scheme for such questions can be developed before completion of the fieldwork.

Coding language includes two special uses of terminology: case and record. **Case** refers to the unit of analysis for the study; in other words, a case is that thing, object, person, or whatever was interviewed or used to supply the answers to the survey questions. A respondent is the most common unit of analysis in commercial marketing research studies, so each respondent would constitute a case. The total number of cases equals the sample size.

Record refers to a string of coded data in machine-readable format. For historical reasons, it has become customary to view a record as consisting of 80 field positions where each field position contains the coded responses for a specific question. The early way of transferring raw data from questionnaire to computer was via a computer card with 80 vertical columns. Data were literally holes punched onto a card by a keypunch machine.

Today data are entered directly into computer memory via online CRT workstations. Tab houses normally use personal computers and programming that simulates a keypunch machine, with data first entered onto a floppy disk and then, in most cases, uploaded onto a mainframe computer. If the data take up more than 80 field positions (columns), another record is utilized; if the data exhaust the next 80 field positions (columns), yet another record is utilized, and so on until all of the data have been recorded. Thus, a case can consist of one or many records, depending on the number of questions asked; together the number of cases and the number of records per case define the data set.

PRECODING
Coding specifications designated prior to fieldwork.

POSTCODING
Coding specifications designated after the questionnaires have been returned from the field.

CASE
The unit of analysis for the study.

RECORD
A string of coded data in a machine-readable format.

EXHIBIT 13—2

Data Entry

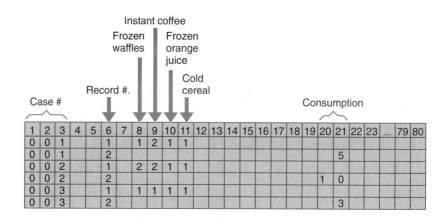

Issues of data processing and analysis are best addressed during questionnaire construction. If processing and analysis of the data are considered only after the interviewing is complete, uncorrectable problems are likely to surface. Experienced researchers generally do as much preparation as possible for data processing before the questionnaire is printed. Advance preparation undoubtedly saves substantial amounts of time and money and can eliminate questions that may not provide the needed information.

Coding close-ended questions.   Precoding and precolumning of the entire questionnaire are the two principal activities in preparing the data for processing. Precoding involves assigning a code number to every response to a closed-ended question; open-ended questions generally are not precodable. The precoding activity involves designating a coding scheme prior to undertaking fieldwork, and the actual codes as well as the field positions are printed on the questionnaire. The next example, which concerns breakfast foods and beverages (see next page), and Exhibit 13–2 show how this is done.

From Exhibit 13–2 we see that there are two records per case. The first respondent (case number 001) answered yes to consuming frozen waffles (a 1 in column 8 of record 1), frozen orange juice (a 1 in column 10 of record 1), and cold cereal (a 1 in column 11 of record 1), but answered no to consuming instant coffee (a 2 in column 9). Also, in a typical month 5 13 oz. boxes of natural cereal were consumed (a 5 in column 21 of record 2).

Responses of "don't know" and/or "not applicable" are also precoded with an assigned number such as 9 for a single-digit response, 99 for a two-digit response, and so on. If a response of 9 or 99 could be considered a legitimate response, then either more columns could be used or alphanumeric codes such as x or y could be used. For example, if an interviewee responded "I don't know" to the question of how many 13 oz. boxes of cereal are consumed in a typical month, then the response would be 99 in columns 20 and 21 of record 2.

Coding open-ended questions.   Open-ended questions are included in questionnaires to obtain a description of the respondent's reaction in the respondent's own words. The resulting variety of responses, however,

Consider the following question concerning breakfast foods and beverages:

	Yes	No
Frozen waffles	1/8[ ]-1	[ ]-2
Instant coffee	1/9[ ]-1	[ ]-2
Frozen orange juice	1/10[ ]-1	[ ]-2
Cold cereal	1/11[ ]-1	[ ]-2

The number to the left of the slash (/) denotes the record number (or card number); the number to the left of the box ([ ]) designates the field position that the response will appear in; the number to the right of the box ([ ]) gives the appropriate code; the box ([ ]) itself is used by the interviewer to record the elicited response. The same approach is used to code responses that do not fall into categories; for example, a respondent's consumption of natural and/or cold cereal brands might be requested and coded as follows:

How many 13 oz. boxes of natural and/or cold cereal does your family consume in a typical month? _____ 2/20–21

Here the number 2 to the left of the slash (/) indicates that this response will appear on the second record for each respondent; the numbers 20–21 to the right of the slash (/) indicate that the response to this question should be entered into the 20th and 21st field positions (or columns). Note two points: first, by reserving two spaces for the response, the largest response that can be recorded is 99; second, if the response is 9 or less only the 21st field position (or column) will be used. In other words, the entered response is right-justified. Exhibit 13–2 illustrates how the first three respondents' answers to these two questions would be entered into the computer.

   We see that the first three field positions (or columns) are dedicated to a case identification number, which indicates the respondent; field position (or column) number 6 indicates the record number; field positions (columns) 8 to 11 are reserved for responses to Question 5 where a 1 indicates that the product has been consumed in the past month and a 2 indicates that it has not; field positions (or columns) 20 and 21 on record 2 are reserved for the number of boxes of cold cereal consumed in a typical month.

makes coding open-ended responses difficult, and explicit instructions are necessary to ensure consistency among coders.

   The coding of open-ended questions usually involves

1. Taking a sample from all respondents, or from each cell in the case of quotas.
2. Writing down all responses from this sample, trying to group responses in terms of general overall categories (e.g., taste, texture, efficacy).
3. Creating codes from these responses (e.g., Taste = 1, Texture = 2, Efficacy = 3).

4. Writing down all responses that do not fit neatly into the established codes. If enough respondents mention one of these responses, establish a new code.

Most codes require what are called *nets,* that is, basic category headings. Using category headings allows one to group different ways of expressing the same basic idea under a common heading. Examples are

> *Efficacy*

Relieves headache pain.

Fast relief.

Long-lasting relief.

Extra strength relief.

> *Aroma*

Smells like an imported cigar.

Smells like an expensive cigar.

Smells good.

Category headings serve at least two purposes. First, they help to organize responses that relate to one idea. Second, and perhaps more important, category headings are used to determine how many *respondents* made comments related to the category as opposed to how many *responses* were made. For this purpose, it is necessary to net responses relating to the category. For example, if efficacy were an objective of an ad, you would want to know how many people expressed some reaction related to efficacy. We might have the following:

Efficacy	(86)
Relieves headache pain	50
Fast Relief	35
Long-lasting relief	12
Extra strength relief	26

There are, in fact, 123 separate references to efficacy (50 + 35 + 12 + 26). These 123 responses were made by 86 respondents (note the 86 in parentheses for the category heading); hence, some made more than one response relating to efficacy.

Transferring the Data

The next phase in data processing involves the physical transfer of the data from the questionnaires onto a magnetic tape or disk or directly into the computer via CRT entry. CATI and computer-assisted systems do not require the transfer of data because data are put into computer memory at the time of collection. As we indicated earlier, tab houses typically use a PC-based program, which simulates a keypunch machine, to produce a binary-coded or ASCII file on diskette. The diskette (i.e., file) is then uploaded to a mainframe computer. Two other methods are available for transferring the data. The first uses machine-readable **mark-sensed questionnaires,** which require answers to be recorded with a special pencil in an area coded specifically for that answer. The second is **optical scanning,** which involves direct machine reading of the numerical values or alphanumeric codes and transcription onto magnetic tape or disk.

Verification.   Data entry is relatively fast and inexpensive—an experienced operator can complete about 100 records per hour at a cost of 20 to 25 cents per record. Experienced operators do not make many errors. However, verification procedures are used to ensure that data from the original questionnaire have been transcribed accurately. Special verification programs are used for this purpose. These will increase the time and cost of data entry.

The automatic data entry in CATI or computer-assisted systems requires a different approach to verification. First, the system should allow a mistake to be corrected before it becomes part of the data file. Second, with CATI, it is often desirable to let the interviewer or respondent verify or contradict the response. If the answer is verified, the next question is repeated; if the answer is contradicted, the question is asked again.

Cleaning.   Data must be **cleaned** prior to the final tabulation, which entails a check of all internal inconsistencies, all possible codes, and all impossible punch codes.[1]

Frequency distribution. Typically, the initial step is to tabulate responses on a question-by-question basis. At the cleaning stage, these frequencies are sometimes called *marginals* because they give the number and percentage of respondents who chose each alternative. Consider, for example, the set of marginals shown in Exhibit 13–3, and, in particular, the 16th row, which gives information on the frequency distribution for 400 respondents who were asked the following question:

Last year what was your total taxable income?

Under $5,000	1/16	[ ]-1
$5,000–$9,999		[ ]-2
$10,000–$14,999		[ ]-3
$15,000–$19,999		[ ]-4
$20,000–$24,999		[ ]-5
$25,000–$34,999		[ ]-6
$35,000–$49,999		[ ]-7
$50,000 and over		[ ]-8
No answer		[ ]-9

The total column in Exhibit 13–3 gives the number of respondents who participated in the study (400). The next column is labeled N/A, which stands for not applicable; that is, not all respondents may have been asked all of the questions, given the skip patterns that apply (in this case, all responses were applicable). The T/R column gives the total respondent

MARK-SENSED QUESTIONNAIRE
Format that requires answers to be recorded with a special pencil in an area coded specifically for that answer and which can be read by a machine.

OPTICAL SCANNING
Direct machine reading of numerical values or alphanumeric codes and transcription onto magnetic tape, or disk.

CLEANING
A check of all internal consistencies, all possible codes, and all impossible punches.

EXHIBIT 13—3

Marginals for Income Categories

Project Number and Name

Column	Total	N/A	T/R	1	2	3	4	5	6	7	8	9	0	X	Y	
1	400	—	400	—	—	—	—	—	—	—	—	—	400	—	—	A01
	100.0	—	100.00	—	—	—	—	—	—	—	—	—	100.0	—	—	
2	400	—	400	100	100	99	1	—	—	—	—	—	100	—	—	A02
	100.0	—	100.0	25.0	25.0	24.8	.3	—	—	—	—	—	25.0	—	—	
3	400	—	400	40	40	40	39	41	40	41	40	39	40	—	—	A03
	100.0	—	100.0	10.0	10.0	10.0	9.8	10.3	10.0	10.3	10.0	9.8	10.0	—	—	
4	400	—	400	39	40	40	41	40	40	40	40	40	40	—	—	A04
	100.0	—	100.0	9.8	10.0	10.0	10.3	10.0	10.0	10.0	10.0	10.0	10.0	—	—	
5	400	400	—	—	—	—	—	—	—	—	—	—	—	—	—	A05
	100.0	100.0	—	—	—	—	—	—	—	—	—	—	—	—	—	
6	400	400	—	—	—	—	—	—	—	—	—	—	—	—	—	A06
	100.0	100.0	—	—	—	—	—	—	—	—	—	—	—	—	—	
7	400	—	400	154	172	59	14	1	—	—	—	—	—	—	—	A07
	100.0	—	100.0	38.5	43.0	14.8	3.5	.3	—	—	—	—	—	—	—	
8	400	—	400	94	216	65	22	3	—	—	—	—	—	—	—	A08
	100.0	—	100.0	23.5	54.0	16.3	5.5	.8	—	—	—	—	—	—	—	
9	400	—	400	51	176	136	36	1	—	—	—	—	—	—	—	A09
	100.0	—	100.0	12.8	44.0	34.0	9.0	.3	—	—	—	—	—	—	—	
10	400	198	202	13	52	58	77	2	—	—	—	—	—	—	—	A10
	100.0	49.5	50.5	3.3	13.0	14.5	19.3	.5	—	—	—	—	—	—	—	
11	400	200	200	2	19	13	154	12	—	—	—	—	—	—	—	A11
	100.0	50.0	50.0	.5	4.8	3.3	38.5	3.0	—	—	—	—	—	—	—	
12	400	202	198	6	47	52	87	6	—	—	—	—	—	—	—	A12
	100.0	50.5	49.5	1.5	11.8	13.0	21.8	1.5	—	—	—	—	—	—	—	
13	400	200	200	4	11	8	165	12	—	—	—	—	—	—	—	A13
	100.0	50.0	50.0	1.0	2.8	2.0	41.3	3.0	—	—	—	—	—	—	—	
14	400	400	—	—	—	—	—	—	—	—	—	—	—	—	—	A14
	100.0	100.0	—	—	—	—	—	—	—	—	—	—	—	—	—	
15	400	400	—	—	—	—	—	—	—	—	—	—	—	—	—	A15
	100.0	100.0	—	—	—	—	—	—	—	—	—	—	—	—	—	
16	400	—	400	25	40	60	70	90	40	25	10	40	—	—	—	A16
	100.0	—	100.0	6.3	10.0	15.0	17.5	22.5	10.0	6.3	2.5	10.0	—	—	—	
Column	Total	N/A	T/R	1	2	3	4	5	6	7	8	9	0	X	Y	

Note: Percentages may not add to 100 percent due to rounding.

Category Label	Code	Number	Percentage	Adjusted Percentage	Adjusted Cumulative Percentage
Under $5,000	1	25	6.3	6.9	6.9
$5,000–$9,999	2	40	10.0	11.1	18.0
$10,000–$14,999	3	60	15.0	16.7	34.7
$15,000–$19,999	4	70	17.5	19.4	54.1
$20,000–$24,999	5	90	22.5	25.0	79.1
$25,000–$34,999	6	40	10.0	11.1	90.2
$35,000–$49,999	7	25	6.3	6.9	97.1
$50,000 and over	8	10	2.5	2.8	99.9
No answer	9	40	10.0	—	
Total		400	100.0		

TABLE 13–1

Frequency Distribution for Income Categories

base for each question. Notice that Total minus N/A = T/R (400 − 0 = 400). The remaining columns give first the counts and then the percentages for each possible response. Notice that the base for the percentages is the total column.

After the rough marginals are examined and cleaned, a final (cleaned) set of frequency distributions is usually prepared. The result in this case would look like the frequency distribution in Table 13–1, which presents the income question data.

The first column (or stub) in Table 13–1 is the category label describing the levels of the variable. The next column identifies the number assigned to each level in the precoding process. The third column gives the number of respondents checking a particular category; for example, 25 people in the sample reported income less than $5,000. The next column reports the percent of the total sample represented by each category; for example, 60 people reported income in the category $10,000 to $14,999, which represents 15 percent of the 400 people. The adjusted percentage column provides the percentages responding to each level after adjusting for the people that did not answer the question. In this example, 40 people did not answer the question; therefore the denominator for the adjusted percentage column is 360 rather than 400. The last column presents the adjusted cumulative frequencies; for example, 34.7 percent of the sample reported income of $14,999 or less (125/360 = .347).

Missing responses. The final step in the cleaning process is consideration of missing responses. After isolating the questions for which missing responses have occurred, perhaps through frequency distributions or by obtaining a column-by-column count of the responses to each question, it is necessary to decide how to treat questions that some respondents did not answer. All of the popular statistical packages allow the user to designate which codes refer to missing values; for example, all missing values could be assigned the value 999. There are several possible strategies.

1. Preserving missing or blank responses is an acceptable practice for certain types of analyses. For example, blanks can be accommodated

in the case of simple tabulations simply by adjusting percentages and cumulative percentages for the percentage of missing responses, as in the final two columns of Table 13–1. For other types of analyses (such as regression analysis described in Chapter 17), blanks can be problematic.

a. **Casewise deletion** calls for discarding any case (respondent) with missing values for any variable. The obvious problem is that much of the available sample can disappear in this way.

b. **Pairwise deletion** preserves all the available nonmissing data for each calculation. For example, a respondent might have not answered the income question while providing complete answers to all other questions. This respondent's data would be included in all calculations except those involving the income variable. This approach works well for large samples where there are relatively few missing responses, and where there is no reason to believe that missing responses follow a systematic pattern across certain questions.

2. Assigning value to the missing data is also an acceptable strategy.

a. The **mean response** approach involves replacing a missing response with a constant—typically, the mean response to the question. Taking this approach lets the mean of the variable remain unchanged, and usually has very little effect on other statistics.

b. Under the **imputed response** approach, a respondent's answers to other questions are used to impute or deduce an appropriate response to the missing question. For example, if you have information on the educational level attained, you might fill in missing income data either by estimating the relationship between income and education for all respondents who have answered both questions or by substituting the mean income level of all respondents having the same educational level as the respondents who did not provide income data. This approach can be risky because it can introduce considerable research bias into the results.

Table Specifications

A table consists of a number of columns, called *banners,* and a number of rows, called *stubs.* The banners represent the various subgroups in the analysis. Results for various subgroups of respondents are of special interest to the marketing research manager, so a cross-tabulation singles them out for closer examination. Each particular subgroup (for example, light user, heavy user, male, female) is called a **banner point.** Typically, commercially available cross-tabulation programs allow up to 20 banner points per table, allowing simultaneous examination of a large number of subgroup interrelationships. The table **stub points** represent those questions in the questionnaire that the research analyst wishes to focus on. It is not uncommon to designate every question in an instrument as a stub, with the possible exception of the general variety of screener items used to qualify the respondent.

EXHIBIT 13—4

Table Specifications

Table Number	Table Title	Stub					Banner				
		Base	Question Number	Column Position	Description	(Code)	Banner Point	Question Number	Column Position	Description	(Code)
1	Overall rating of Carbonated Soft Drink— Coca Cola Classic	All	13	1/32	Excellent	(5)	A	14	1/15	Male	(1)
					Very good	(4)	B	14	1/15	Female	(2)
					Good	(3)	C	25	2/40, 41	Low income	(1–3)
					Fair	(2)	D	25	2/40, 41	Moderate income	(4–7)
					Poor	(1)	E	25	2/40, 41	High income	(8–10)

The research analyst generally provides tabulating specifications to the tab house, whose responsibility it is to form these tables. A typical tabulating specification form for a question rating Coca Cola Classic is shown in Exhibit 13–4. The specification form involves defining the following:

1. Table title.
2. Stub—The relevant base upon which the table will be formed (total respondents, brand X users, etc.), question number, column position(s), and the description and code for the stub.
3. Banner specifications—Question number, column position, and description and code for each banner point.

SUMMARY

This chapter has discussed data-collection activities, with particular emphasis on fielding the questionnaire and data preparation. We began our discussion by explaining fieldwork procedures and practices. In the course of that discussion, we described procedures for checking in questionnaires and the process of editing.

We then turned our attention to those functions that are necessary to transform the information collected into a form that allows the data to be analyzed. Among other issues, we discussed and illustrated coding procedures for closed-ended and open-ended questions. Finally, the chapter concluded by discussing how tables are specified.

KEY CONCEPTS

Estimating Costs

"Alerting the Study"

Field Instructions

Check-In

Editing

Coding

Transferring Data

Table Specifications

Banner

Stub

REVIEW QUESTIONS

1. What are some potential problems that might arise when coding open-ended questions?

2. After a job comes in from the field, list several reasons for rejecting a respondent's answers.

3. You are president of a company that analyzes and tabulates incoming data from mail surveys. One survey is causing you some trouble because a few of the questions deal with whether the respondent uses drugs on occasion. What could you do to ensure that a high percentage of respondents answer these sensitive questions truthfully? If you end up having received many surveys with these questions left unanswered, what might you recommend to your client company?

4. Discuss the different methods for handling missing data.

5. From the cross-tabulation shown on the next page, develop a frequency distribution (see Table 13–1) for (a) the total sample, (b) 1-line and 2-to-6-line businesses, and (c) the three regions.

6. You will have noticed that, for example, in the case of the "business customer" banner points shown in the cross-tabulation of question 5, the frequency counts do not add to the total number of respondents (826). Why?

ENDNOTES

1. We should note that many commercial tab houses still use multipunches (that is, assigning more than one number to a given column), which was a common procedure when data were transferred using computer cards and keypunch machines. If data have been multipunched, special spreading programs are needed.

Cross-Tabulation of Likelihood to Purchase Repeat-Dialing Service

Q8B. LIKELIHOOD TO PURCHASE REPEAT DIALING FOR YOUR BUSINESS AT COST OF $4.00 EACH MONTH

	TOTAL	REGION			BUSINESS CUSTOMER			NUMBER OF TELEPHONE LINES		PC 1+	MODEM 1+	FAX 1+	ANS MACH 1+
		METRO	STATE	OHIO	LESS THAN 3 YRS	3-10 YRS	MORE THAN 10 YRS	1	2-6				
TOTAL RESPONDENTS	836	214	343	279	146	241	439	527	253	117	104	131	333
NO ANSWER	70	16	36	18	10	12	46	47	14	6	5	9	22
TOTAL ANSWERING	766	198	307	261	136	229	393	480	239	111	99	122	313
REPEAT DIALING													
VERY LIKELY TO BUY													
5	69	13	25	31	6	27	34	34	29	15	18	18	30
	9.0	9.6	8.1	11.9	4.4	11.8	8.7	7.1	12.1	13.5	18.2	14.8	9.6
4	88	18	35	35	21	29	38	49	35	19	13	19	38
	11.5	9.1	11.4	13.4	15.4	12.7	9.7	10.2	14.6	17.1	13.1	15.6	12.1
3	148	41	52	55	36	39	73	90	46	20	18	25	83
	19.3	20.7	16.9	21.1	26.5	17.0	18.6	18.8	19.2	18.0	18.2	20.5	26.5
2	74	25	27	22	9	33	32	45	28	14	11	8	26
	9.7	12.6	8.8	8.4	6.6	14.4	8.1	9.4	11.7	12.6	11.1	6.6	8.3
1	387	101	168	118	64	101	216	262	101	43	39	52	136
	50.5	51.0	54.7	45.2	47.1	44.1	55.0	54.6	42.2	38.7	39.4	42.6	43.5
NOT VERY LIKELY TO BUY													
MEAN BASE	766	198	307	261	136	229	393	480	239	111	99	122	313
MEAN	2.19	2.08	2.09	2.38	2.24	2.34	2.09	2.06	2.43	2.54	2.60	2.53	2.36
STD DEV	1.39	1.29	1.38	1.46	1.31	1.44	1.38	1.33	1.46	1.48	1.55	1.52	1.39
STD ERR	.050	.092	.079	.090	.112	.095	.069	.061	.094	.141	.156	.138	0.78

351

BY PHIL FRAME

The foundering Oldsmobile Division will get the biggest makeover, moving to younger and more style-conscious buyers, as General Motors' new regime tries to focus the image of its car marketing divisions.

Marketing divisions would sacrifice models that blur their images and compete too closely with other GM vehicles, according to strategies for the mid-to-late 1990s under consideration by GM's North American Operations planners. While all product decisions are not final, conversations with many sources at the new North American Operations reveal general agreement on the focus each division will seek.

The plans under consideration include dropping Oldsmobile Cutlass Ciera and Bravada; Buick Roadmaster; Pontiac LeMans and the four-door Pontiac Grand Prix; and the 1997-model year remake of the Chevrolet Caprice, said sources at GM's new North American Operations.

Other product changes being considered:

— Replacing the Cadillac Allante with a domestic car.
— Dropping the Oldsmobile Ninety Eight.
— Dropping the Buick Skylark.

Spurred by angry investors and outside board members impatient with GM's $6.5 billion in losses over the past two years, planners are considering previously unthinkable options, NAO sources said. The sources also say the Buick Regal may be in jeopardy, but a division executive, who asked not to be named, strongly denied any plans to kill the model.

"It's totally untrue," the official said. "I don't know where that got started." He also said there is no plan now to eliminate the Skylark or Roadmaster.

"There's a danger in cutting too much — you can lose market share and volume forever," he said. "I'm not saying we won't have additions and deletions, though."

Among the five passenger-car marketing divisions plus Saturn Corp., Oldsmobile would have to shift the most dramatically from its current position on the GM perceptual map (see Exhibit 1, top right).

Oldsmobile. Outsiders commonly suggest eliminating the Oldsmobile division entirely. But GM executives steadfastly argue that they shouldn't discard a dedicated dealer body of 3,000 and decades of built-up brand equity.

Currently regarded internally as more conservative and nearly as pricey as Buick, Oldsmobile will get an image makeover by the late 1990s. It will embody the idea of cutting-edge expression for upscale customers between 30 and 45 years old.

Hard evidence of the change began two weeks ago when the division axed the slow-selling Custom Cruiser wagon and Toronado. Sources at NAO say the Bravada sport-utility could be dropped after the 1993 model year.

But Oldsmobile spokesman Guz Buenz said the Bravada is "very much a part of our product program going forward."

Another possible casualty is the Oldsmobile Ninety Eight, which may be dropped after the 1994 model year because it competes too closely with the Buick Park Avenue and is too conservative for Oldsmobile's intended new image, sources said.

Source: *Automotive News*, May 11, 1992, pp. 1, 42. Used with permission.

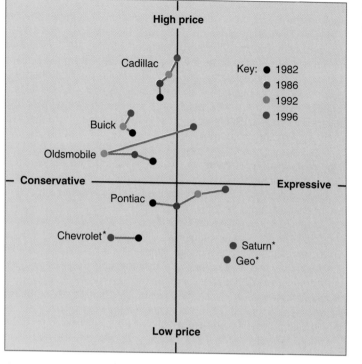

EXHIBIT 1

GM Car Markets

Note: Dots show how GM's car divisions perceive themselves in the marketplace.
*Chevrolet, Saturn, and GEO are not expected to change between now and 1996.
Source: GM and divisional sources.

Oldsmobile would continue selling the popular Achieva compact and mid-sized Eighty Eight.

The Toronado name is to be revived in the 1994 model year as a larger mid-sized four-door built on the all-new G-car platform. The 1996 model year would see a snazzy new Cutlass Supreme, based on the Anthem concept car displayed at several auto shows this year.

Oldsmobile will sell a version of the next-generation U-body minivan due in the 1996 model year. Oldsmobile currently sells the Silhouette minivan.

The conservative Cutlass Ciera may again be on the chopping block. Although the Ciera/Buick Century program was approved last December for the 1995 model year, the new Ciera may be cut if NAO planners decide it's too conservative for Oldsmobile or too much like the Century, built on the same platform, sources said.

Any plans to drop the Cutlass Ciera would be met with stiff opposition from Oldsmobile and its dealers. It was Oldsmobile's top seller in 1991 and remains so this year. The dilemma illustrates the difficulty in moving Oldsmobile so far away from its current position on the perception scale.

The transformation of Oldsmobile has been in the works since the late 1980s, but it has not yet happened. Since 1986, Oldsmobile believes it has become even more conservative. It will have to change faster because of a GM board mandate to accelerate plant closings, revamp North American operations and quickly return to profitability.

GM's other marketing divisions will make smaller moves to refine their images and further differentiate themselves from external competitors and internal allies.

Buick.   Buick will remain a division for conservative, wealthy, older people. Models such as the Regal, Skylark and Roadmaster are in danger, sources said.

Planners may consider dropping the Skylark after the 1996 model year, NAO sources said. The model was redesigned for the 1992 model year, but the car is selling horribly. Skylark sales are down 61 percent from the previous model year and 41 percent for the calendar year, compared with the first quarter of 1991. The car is built on the N-car platform with the Pontiac Grand Am and Oldsmobile Achieva.

Buick wants the wildly styled and high-priced compact so it can draw younger buyers into the fold. But NAO sources said GM can't afford that in a division that aims to cater to mature customers.

The B-body Roadmaster may die after the 1996 model year. Dwindling demand for large rear-wheel-drive cars has virtually killed off the B-body Chevrolet Caprice and did kill the Oldsmobile Custom Cruiser wagon. Although the Roadmaster is meeting its sales objectives, its life is tied to the Caprice, which is supposed to be the volume car on that platform.

Discussions about killing the Regal focus on whether it makes sense for Buick to have two mid-sized cars, NAO sources said. The sources said that if Buick keeps the Regal, it may be retained only as a coupe, while the Century would be sold only as a sedan.

When they are redesigned, the Century and Regal would be built off a single platform, instead of separate ones as they are now.

The Park Avenue would continue as Buick's flagship. A larger LeSabre, built off the G platform beginning in 1996, could help fill the void if Roadmaster dies. The LeSabre now is built on the H-platform, which will be consolidated with the G-cars. The new G platform debuts in the 1994 model year with the Buick Riviera and Oldsmobile Toronado.

Chevrolet.   Chevrolet is likely to lose the Caprice, which planners believe has become too expensive (base price nearly $18,000 including destination charge) for the division's value-conscious customers. But Chevrolet and GM don't want to abandon the police-taxi-utility fleet market that takes 50,000 Caprices per year, so they may continue building the current version.

The 1997 Caprice replacement has been cancelled or shelved indefinitely, sources said.

A Chevrolet source said the company will wait until 1995 or 1996 to decide whether to continue the current car and will save money in the interim because it isn't committing money for research, development and tooling.

Chevrolet spokesman Dave Hudgens declined comment on the division's future product plans.

Hudgens said earlier reports that the Caprice was killed caused concern at police agencies across the country because the car is the most popular pursuit vehicle.

"One police department went so far as to inquire about ordering more 1992s," Hudgens said.

The 1994-model W-body Lumina replacement, which will be larger than the current W-car, is expected to appeal to some Caprice buyers. A new all-aluminum small-block V-8 engine under development would be an option.

In the 1994 model year, Chevrolet also will debut a youthful, two-door, personal-luxury version of the Lumina called the Monte Carlo. It was not clear how such a vehicle would be reconciled with the value-conscious, conservative image other cars in the division are expected to carry.

The other Chevrolets are likely to remain, but the Cavalier and Corsica/Beretta will be combined onto one platform, and the Corvette and Camaro could share a platform in the future.

Chevrolet sources believe Geo has its own position in the market, nearly identical to Saturn's. It is not expected to change until perhaps 1997 when the Geo Prizm leaves the fold. Although Prizm is redesigned for 1993, it will leave at the expiration of GM's joint venture with Toyota Motor Corp. The joint venture — New United Motor Manufacturing Inc. — builds the Prizm and the Toyota Corolla.

Pontiac.   Pontiac's image will be more expressive and sporty.

It probably will lose the Korean-built LeMans, which will be sold through the 1993 model year and then probably be dropped, a Pontiac source said. The TransSport minivan may survive the platform trims, although some NAO sources suggest Pontiac will not get a version of the 1996 replacement vehicle. The four-door Grand Prix probably will be dropped, NAO sources say.

Cadillac.   Cadillac models will become slightly more upscale and more highly styled, sporty and sleeker — along the lines of the 1992 Seville and Eldorado. Only the Allante may depart, but not until a replacement, which will be similar to the Aurora concept car shown in 1989, is ready in the 1995 or 1996 model year.

Saturn.   Saturn will remain unchanged for now. Eventually, Saturn would like a mid-sized platform to compete against larger Japanese competitors such as the Honda Accord and Toyota Camry.

While Saturn officials have acknowledged the existence of such plans, they say they won't get the corporate go-ahead until they earn it by making a success of the compact car.

Suppose that GM is now interested in developing an "image" map for the sub-compact market. The procedure agreed upon for collecting subcompact brand images resulted in the survey shown in Exhibit 2. At most, four ratings would be collected from each respondent. To be eligible for inclusion in the study, a respondent had to (1) have purchased a subcompact automobile within the last three years, (2) have been under 45 years of age, and (3) belong to a household, no member of which, including the respondent, was employed within the last three years by either an advertising, public relations, manufacturer/dealer of automobiles, or marketing research firm. The ratings would be taken on the respondent's *ideal* subcompact automobile, the subcompact that the respondent *currently owned,* and the two sub-compacts that the respondent *considered* when making his or her last purchase of a subcompact. In other words, a respondent would be asked to rate, at most, four subcompact automobiles.

Each automobile would be rated on a set of 20 attributes. The attributes derived from focus-group interviews are listed below.

Sensible	Independent
Comfortable	Practical
Dependable	Down-to-earth
Luxurious	Youthful
Sporty	Contemporary
Family-oriented	Mature
High performance	Classic
Exciting	Affordable
Adventurous	Efficient
Fashionalbe	Economical

EXHIBIT 2
Survey of Subcompact
Owners

Screener
Respondent's full name: _____

Address: _____

City: _____ State: _____ Zip code: _____

Telephone number: (_____) _____

Interviewed by: _____ Date: _____

Hello, I'm _____ from _____

We're conducting a study of automobile purchases, and I'd like to ask [*name from listing*] a few questions about his/her selection of [*car make and model and year*].

1. Are you or any member of your household employed by . . .?

An advertising or public relations firm	A
A manufacturer or dealer of automobiles, or	B
A marketing research company	C

    [*If "yes" to any, terminate and circle next highest number: 01 02 03 04 05 06 07 08 09 10 11 12 13 14 15. Reuse screener.*]

2. Which of the following groups includes your age?

18–24	1
25–34	2
35–45	3
46 or above	4 [*If 4, terminate and circle next highest number: 01 02 03 04 05 06 07 08 09 10 11 12 13 14 15. Reuse screener.*]

3. Are you . . .? [*Read list.*]

Married	1
Single	2
Divorced	3
Separated	4
Widowed	5
[*Do not read.*] Refused	Y

4. What was the last grade of school you completed? [*Do not read list.*]

No formal schooling	1
Completed grammar school	2
Some high school	3
Graduated high school	4
Some college	5
Graduated college	6
[*Do not read.*] Refused	Y

5. Is your annual household income before taxes . . .? [*Read list.*]

Under $15,000	1
Between $15,000 and $24,999	2
Between $25,000 and $34,999	3
Between $35,000 and $49,999	4
$50,000 or more	5
[*Do not read.*] Refused	6

6. Could you tell me the make, model, and year of your last car?

    _____ _____ _____

7. Was your previous car new or used when you purchased it?

    New
    Used

8. Do you still own your previous car?

    Yes
    No

EXHIBIT 2

(*continued*)

9. Including yourself, how many persons are there in your household?

One	1
Two	2
Three	3
Four	4
Five	5
Six or more	6

10. How many are over the age of seventeen?
Number over 17_____

11. Are there any other cars currently owned by members of your household?

Yes
No

12. Could you tell me their makes, models, and years?

_____   _____   _____

_____   _____   _____

13. [If respondent still owns previous car or if other cars are owned by household members, ask:] Would you consider your [*name of car from listing*] your main or second car?

Main
Second

14. From the following list of options, would you tell me which ones you purchased?
[*For each "no," ask:*] Did you consider purchasing the option?

Air conditioning	Yes	Considered
Automatic transmission	Yes	Considered
Special radio or cassette	Yes	Considered
Sunroof	Yes	Considered
Special wheels	Yes	Considered
Turbocharger	Yes	Considered
Power steering	Yes	Considered
Dual mirrors	Yes	Considered
Tinted glass	Yes	Considered

15. Could you tell me which of the following features were major factors and which were minor factors in your choice of your [*car name from listing*]?

Economy

Easy to drive

High performance

Dependability

16. Which of the following words describe your ideal car? [On "A" forms, start at top of list; on "B" forms, start at bottom of list]

Sensible	_____
Comfortable	_____
Dependable	_____
Luxurious	_____
Exciting	_____
Adventurous	_____
Fashionable	_____
Independent	_____
Contemporary	_____

EXHIBIT 2
(*concluded*)

Generous	_____
Mature	_____
Classic	_____
Affordable	_____
Sporty	_____
Family-oriented	_____
Careful	_____
Performance	_____
Necessity	_____
Practical	_____
Down-to-earth	_____
Youthful	_____
Efficient	_____

The automobile manufacturer also was interested in understanding the tradeoffs subcompact car purchasers make with respect to attributes such as

Economy
High performance
Ease in driving
Dependability

Standard demographic data also would be collected.

Case Questions

1. Refer to Exhibit 2, the questionnaire developed by the marketing research group. Based on what you know about designing a questionnaire, discuss the following issues:

   — Is the questionnaire going to provide the necessary data?
   — Are there any problems with how the questions are asked?
   — Are there any problems with how the questions are constructed?

2. How can the questionnaire be improved? Develop a "better" questionnaire.
3. Prepare a set of interviewer instructions for your questionnaire.

CASE 2: BBQ PRODUCT CROSSES OVER THE LINES OF VARIED TASTES

Rich Products Corp. is hoping its frozen barbecue will appeal to the wide tastes in its narrow market, but it realizes consumers will need a nudge in that direction.

Enter Ruby Raylene Dodge, waitress down at the Pork-O-Rama and major figure in the company's marketing campaign for its new product, Rich's Southern Barbeque.

Source: *Marketing News*, September 12, 1988, p. 24.

Because barbecue is a regional delicacy—it varies in taste from county to county throughout the Southeast—Rich Products, Buffalo, N.Y., had to develop a tangy product to appeal to varied tastes and had to persuade consumers they'd like it, according to Joe Tindall, the company's product development manager of new products.

To cross over regional and local differences in the six-city market in the Southeast, Long, Haymes & Carr Advertising (LH&C), Winston-Salem, N.C., has launched a series of 30-second TV ads called "Please Don't Tell 'Em Ruby Sent You."

"The fictitious Ruby is supposed to give the product authenticity without trying to compete with barbecue restaurants or stands," said Don Van Erden, vice president/management supervisor, LH&C.

"Our research told us that no one has more rapport and credibility with the barbecue-eating public than the real-life barbecue waitress," Van Erden said. "In Ruby, we have a vivid persona who's believable because she's based on real barbecue waitresses we've observed."

Rich Products hopes Ruby will reach all consumers with her friendly Southern accent and down-home sincerity.

"I'm a loyal employee of the Pork-O-Rama, but my real true love is Rich's Frozen Barbecue," Ruby says in one spot. In another she's wearing a disguise. "I can't just go to my grocer's freezer for Rich's Barbeque," she says. "I've got a career at the Pork-O-Rama to consider."

She praises the product in all the spots, but fearful of losing her job, warns viewers, "Just please don't tell 'em Ruby sent you."

The microwavable barbecue entrees were test-marketed last year in Nashville, Tenn., Little Rock, Ark., and the Alabama cities of Birmingham, Huntsville, Montgomery, and Tuscaloosa. "That's the market now, but expansion into other areas is planned," Tindall said.

Case Questions

1. What measurement and scaling issues should be considered when developing a study to measure consumers' attitudes toward barbecue in general and specifically Rich's Barbeque?

2. Assume Rich's wanted to test people's preference for their barbecue versus the other leading brands (of which there are five). What would you recommend to measure these preferences?

CASE 3: CONSUMER ATTITUDES AND PERCEPTIONS TOWARD SEAFOOD WHEN EATING OUT: MEASUREMENT DEVELOPMENT

In Part II, Case Study 1, we introduced the preliminary phase of a study focusing on consumers' attitudes and perceptions toward seafood—in particular, nontraditional species—when eating out. The following describes the results from the focus-group interviews.

Eating Fish in Restaurants

Fish was seldom consumed at home. Participants objected to the residual odor after its preparation.

Source: Materials for this case were supplied by Dr. Robert C. Lewis of the Department of Hotel and Restaurant Administration, University of Massachusetts.

Those who do prepare fish at home emphasize the ease with which it can be prepared.

- "I like to eat foods I don't eat at home—my daughter is allergic to fish, so we don't eat it at home."
- "I like to eat fish when it's been cooked by someone else."
- "We never cook fish at home, but we love seafood, so we go out."
- "I don't like the smell of fish at home—when I go out that's my chance to have fish."
- "No one else in the house eats fish, so I get it when I go out."
- "I eat it more away from home because of the odor."
- "Fish out is a treat."
- "It's always a treat to have fish at home."
- "I don't think I've ever left home thinking about having a super fish meal. The only time I've done that is when I'm on vacation, down on the Cape or something."
- "Preparation of good fresh fish is quickly done at home—under the broiler— it's easy—so I order more difficult things when I go out."

Several participants established a link between trust in the knowledge of the restaurant staff and their willingness to try new dishes.

- "The better the restaurant—the more trust I have in the waiter and the more willing I am to try."
- "I'd have more trust in a more expensive restaurant—they pay their help better to be more informed."
- "If you've eaten in a restaurant before, you know how they cook."

Trust in the freshness of fish also was an issue.

- "I'll eat fish only in a restaurant that specializes—otherwise I feel it's not fresh—probably frozen."
- "I wouldn't ask them—they don't know."
- "If you're at the shore and you don't order seafood, you're foolish."

Some respondents were purists who preferred their fish broiled with butter and lemon, whereas others either had a favorite sauce or were willing to try new methods of preparation.

- "I don't like anything fried."
- "I like fish in a casserole."
- "Broiled or baked is always dry."
- "No bread crumbs—I like to see the fish."
- "It depends on the texture—is it flaky and moist or like rubber?"
- "If they're going to charge a big price I would hope they would do something to it."
- "I choose the fish first, then the method of preparation."

Some participants had tried a range of sauces and enjoyed them, while others had not.

Pro

- "Dill sauces."
- "Newburgh."
- "Ginger sauce."
- "Nothing too overpowering."
- "I had a good white cheese sauce—it was excellent."

Con

- "Never had any."
- "Don't like sauces—just butter."
- "Sauce could kill a good piece of fish—I like just lemon."
- "When I'm eating fish for health and weight, I stick to vegetables—no bread, no potatoes. I'd be defeating the purpose with a sauce."

Barriers to Fish Consumption

Some participants did not prepare fish at home because of the work involved in cleaning and deboning fish.

- "I don't like really strong fish."
- "I don't like the odor or a fishy taste."
- "I don't like bones—that's why I usually get scrod."
- "I don't like bones—I don't like to be surprised."
- "The skin is usually chewy and slimy."
- "I fish a lot—to get rid of bones it depends on the size of the fish and how you fillet it."

The discussion of odor led to some mention of freshness in several groups.

- "Fresh fish doesn't smell."
- "I get fish on the Cape—it has no odor."
- "Fresh-caught fish has no smell."
- "Supermarket fish smells when you cook it."
- "When you buy fish, you can see how fresh it is."
- "Oh, you can taste the difference."
- "In most big restaurants it's easy to get fresh fish."
- "If I'm in another part of the country, I won't order fish."

Reactions to Specific Fish

None of the fish named as favorites could be considered nontraditional. Scrod and swordfish were named most often.

- "I like scrod—there's an occasional bone, but it's not too bad."
- "I'd go for swordfish, if you want a meatier fish."
- "I go deep-sea fishing—I like flounder."

— "I like scrod—it's tender and moist."
— "Swordfish is my favorite—it's meatier, solid, chewy."
— "Swordfish has more flavor—almost sweet."
— "Salmon for one—I love the color—I was brought up on it."
— "Scrod—it's light, not oily, juicy."
— "I like scrod—the taste isn't fishy, it's flaky."
— "I like white fish that are sweet."
— "Fillet of sole, sometimes scrod."
— "I like swordfish or salmon, for the taste and texture."
— "Haddock—flavorful but mild."
— "Haddock—out of habit."
— "Haddock—a nice piece of fish, not too gamy."
— "I like salmon with hollandaise sauce."

Attitudes toward Nontraditional Fish

Of those people who were reluctant to try fish, the monetary risk was occasionally mentioned as a reason.

— "I don't want to pay $8 or $9 for something I might not like."
— "If you're going to spend $10 or $15, why try something you don't know you're going to like, when there are so many good things on the menu?"

For an overwhelming majority of participants, the name of the fish caused considerable reaction. Some reactions to specific fish are listed below.

Shark

— "I think it sounds unappetizing—*Jaws*—it bothers me to be deceived."
— "I suppose I would try it if I was in one of those moods to try something new."

Tilefish

— "Makes me think of Spanish or Italian tiles."

Monkfish

— "Doesn't sound tempting."

Skate

— "I think they ought to change the name—it sounds sharp."

In each of the groups there were participants who were eager to try new types of seafood or new methods of preparation and others who liked to play it safe.

— "I'll try something new if the ingredients look good."
— "I wouldn't order something I'd never had—a lot of fish is too strong."
— "I might taste someone else's."
— "If there is something in it that I know I like—otherwise, I wouldn't risk it."
— "I tried shark—it was really tasty—my dad came back from San Francisco and he was raving about it."

Participants were asked what they thought of specific seafoods named by the moderator. In some cases they reacted to the fish based on having tasted it, while in other cases they reacted to the name or its reputation. Some specific reactions are listed below.

Cod

— "Cod is a wormy fish."

Flounder

— "Flounder is a bottom feeder."

Pollock

— "I liked it; I've cooked it—it has a stronger flavor than scrod—it's a cheaper fish."

Whitefish

— "The only way I've had it was smoked—smoked was greasy."
— "It sounds like it's related to scrod or haddock."
— "Yes, sounds like scrod."

Mackerel

— "That's ok; it's a fish, not a predator."
— "You see them all the time in the grocery store."

Less well-known seafoods were greeted with a degree of suspicion. It may be inferred that the most common consumers' attitude is that if a species is underutilized, there must be a reason.

Shark

— "Most people have probably eaten shark and didn't realize it—it sometimes passes for swordfish or scallops."
— "Don't tell me its shark—I don't want to know."
— "I couldn't try shark—I don't know why—I just couldn't."

Butterfish

— "None would get my interest."
— "Maybe it's like sole or scrod."
— "It would be something I would ask about."
— "I would have to know what it tasted like."
— "I would try it if it were boneless, white."

Monkfish

— "They're the ugliest things in the world."

Skate

— "That doesn't sound good."
— "You know those perfectly round scallops, those are mostly skate, sometimes shark."

- "They look like rays."
- "If you saw one after you'd caught one, you'd probably never eat it."

Eel

- "I liked it."
- "No—I've caught one—they're slimy things."
- "No way I'd try it."
- "I've tried it—I didn't like the texture."
- "Definitely not—that's like a snake."
- "It tastes like salmon."
- "It's oily."
- "I've had it in a tomato and onion sauce—it's really not bad."

Squid

- "Definitely no."
- "I had it—didn't like it—nothing to do with the taste—it's the way they look."
- "My wife's family had it every Christmas—I've made it through all these years without trying it."
- "I think of those things as reptiles."
- "I would be more willing to try some of these exotic names if I was on vacation in a place where that might be the main food."

Case Questions

1. How can the results of the focus-group session help you to develop a questionnaire dealing with consumers' attitudes and perceptions toward nontraditional fish when eating out?
2. Prepare an outline of the questionnaire you would use to measure consumers' attitudes and perceptions toward nontraditional fish when eating out.
3. Based upon the information provided above and your answer to Question 2, develop a set of measurement scales to measure consumers' attitudes and perceptions toward nontraditional fish when eating out.

CASE 4: NATIONAL WINE TRACKING STUDY

The following case exercise is used as an interviewing tool at a New York-based supplier for junior research project directors. Included are:

1. A questionnaire (Exhibit 1).
2. A grid page (Exhibit 2).

The assignment is to prepare a set of data processing cleaning instructions for the grid page.

EXHIBIT 1

Questionnaire

National Wine Tracking Study
—Main Questionnaire—

[Interviewer: Do Not Read List for Q's 1–6.]

1. I'd like to ask you some questions about wine. Please tell me all the brands of wine you can think of. (Probe:) What others? [*Record all mentions on white grid page under Q.1, "Unaided aware."*]

2. What brands of wine do you recall having seen or heard advertised on TV, radio, or in magazines recently? (Probe:) What others? [*Record all mentions on white grid page under Q.2, "Unaided Advertising."*]

3. What brand of wine did you buy last? [*Record all mentions on white grid page under Q.3, "Bought last."*]
[*If no brand is mentioned anywhere in Q's 1, 2, or 3, skip to Q.7. Otherwise, continue.*]

4. And what brand did you buy the time before that? [*Record all mentions on white grid page under Q.4, "Bought time before last."*]

5. What brand are you most likely to buy next? [*Record all mentions on white grid page under Q.5, "Will buy next."*]

6. What brand would you consider buying next? [*Record all mentions on white grid page under Q.6, "Would consider buying."*]

7. Have you ever heard of (*brand*)? [*Record "yes" answers on white grid page under Q.7, "Aided aware."*]

   [*Ask Q.8 for each (*) brand mentioned in Q.1 or Q.7 but not Q.2.*]

8. Do you recall having recently seen or heard advertising for (*brand*)? [*Record "yes" answers on white grid page under Q.8, "Aided ad aware."*]

   [*Ask Q.9 for each (*) brand mentioned in Q's 1, 2, or 7 but not Q's 3–4.*]

9. Have you ever bought (*brand*)? [*Record "yes" answers on white grid page under Q.9, "Ever bought."*]

   [*Ask Q.10a for each (*) brand mentioned in Q's 3, 4, or 9.*]

10a. Have you bought (*brand*) in the *past two months?* [*Record "yes" answers on white grid page under Q.10a, "Bought past two months."*]

   [*Ask Q.10b for each (*) brand mentioned in Q.10a.*]

10b. How many bottles of (*brand*) did you buy in the past two months? [*Record number legibly on white grid page under Q.10b, "# of bottles."*]

EXHIBIT 2
Sample Grid Page

CARD 4 continued   DO NOT READ LIST

Start card 5

	Q.1 Un-aided aware (18)	Q.2 Un-aided advtg (24)	Q.3 Bought last (30)	Q.4 Bought time before last (36)	Q.5 Will buy next (42)	Q.6 Would consider buying (48)	Q.7 Aided aware (54)	Q.8 Aided ad aware (59)	Q.9 Ever bought (64)	Q.10a Bought past two months (69)	Q.10b # of bot.
3—•Almaden 1	1	1	1	1	1	1	1	1	1	1	6-
Almaden Light 2	2	2	2	2	2						
Almaden Golden 3	3	3	3	3	3						
•B&G...................4	4	4	4	4	4	4	4	4	4	4	8-
4—•Black Tower 5	5	5	5	5	5	5	5	5	5	5	10-
5—•Blue Nun 6	6	6	6	6	6	6	6	6	6	6	12-
•Bolla Or Soave Bolla 7	7	7	7	7	7	7	7	7	7	7	14-
Brolio..................8	8	8	8	8	8	8					
•Carlo Rossi 9	9	9	9	9	9	9	9	9	9	9	16-
•Cella 0	0	0	0	0	0	0	0	0	0	0	18-
	(19)	(25)	(31)	(37)	(43)	(49)	(55)	(60)	(65)	(70)	
The Christian Brothers....1	1	1	1	1	1	1					
2—•Folonari 2	2	2	2	2	2	2	2	2	2	2	20-
Fontana Candida 3	3	3	3	3	3	3					
Franzia 4	4	4	4	4	4	4					
6—•Gallo 5	5	5	5	5	5	5	5	5	5	5	22-
•Giacobazzi 6	6	6	6	6	6	6	6	6	6	6	24-
Gold Seal Catawba 7	7	7	7	7	7						
Great Western 8	8	8	8	8	8	8					
7—•Inglenook 9	9	9	9	9	9	9	9	9	9	9	26-
Italian Swiss Colony/											
Colony 0	0	0	0	0	0	0					
	(20)	(26)	(32)	(38)	(44)	(50)	(56)	(61)	(66)	(71)	
Krug 1	1	1	1	1	1	1					
8—•Lancers 2	2	2	2	2	2	2	2	2	2	2	28-
Los Hermanos 3	3	3	3	3	3	3					
9—•Mateus 4	4	4	4	4	4	4	4	4	4	4	30-
•Mondavi 5	5	5	5	5	5	5	5	5	5	5	32-
•Monterey Vineyards 6	6	6	6	6	6	6	6	6	6	6	34-
•Mouton Cadet (Moo-tawn											
ka-day)................7	7	7	7	7	7	7	7	7	7	7	36-
Nectarose................8	8	8	8	8	8	8					
1—•Partager (Par-ta-jhay) ..9	9	9	9	9	9	9	9	9	9	9	38-
10—•Paul Masson (Ma-sahn).....0	0	0	0	0	0	0	0	0	0	0	40-
	(21)	(27)	(33)	(39)	(45)	(51)	(57)	(62)	(67)	(72)	
•Masson Light.............1	1	1	1	1	1	1	1	1	1	1	42-
•Polo Brindisi............2	2	2	2	2	2	2	2	2	2	2	44-
•Prego 3	3	3	3	3	3	3	3	3	3	3	46-
	(21)	(27)	(33)	(39)	(45)	(51)	(57)	(62)	(67)	(72)	
11—•Riunite (Ree-u-nee-tee) ..4	4	4	4	4	4	4	4	4	4	4	48-
Ruffino 5	5	5	5	5	5	5					
•Sebastiani...............6	6	6	6	6	6	6	6	6	6	6	50-
•Sterling 7	7	7	7	7	7	7	7	7	7	7	52-
12—•Taylor California Cellars											
(Calif. Cellars) 8	8	8	8	8	8	8	8	8	8	8	54-
•Taylor California Cellars											
Light 9	9	9	9	9	9	9	9	9	9	9	56-
•Taylor Lake Country 0	0	0	0	0	0	0	0	0	0	0	58-
Taylor (Ask: "could (22)	(28)	(34)	(40)	(46)	(52)	(58)	(63)	(68)	(73)		
you be more specific"). 1	1	1	1	1	1	1					
•Valbon...................2	2	2	2	2	2	2	2	2	2	2	60-
•Vivante..................3	3	3	3	3	3	3	3	3	3	3	62-
Yago 4	4	4	4	4	4	4					
Other (specify)										80-4	80-5
_____0	0	0	0	0	0						
_____0	0	0	0	0	0						
_____0	0	0	0	0	0						
None x	x	x	x	x	x						
Don't Know ....y	y	y	y	y	y						
	23-	29-	35-	41-	47-	53-					

DATA ANALYSIS

WILLIAM D. NEAL
FOUNDER, SENIOR EXECUTIVE OFFICER
SOPHISTICATED DATA RESEARCH

Will data processing companies specializing in tabulation become outdated as more companies internalize the tabbing function?

No, says William Neal, founder and senior executive officer of Atlanta-based Sophisticated Data Research, a data processing services company specializing in the creation, management, and analysis of survey-generated databases.

Companies have been able to internalize that function because "the software packages are pretty good now," Neal says. "They can run on personal computers or microcomputers, so they say, 'Let's bring it in-house.' "

But the real cost of doing tabulation work is the people cost. "Research companies must have a reasonable amount of billable work that will keep two or more tabulation specialists working consistently," Neal says. "And you need to be invoicing at least three times [workers'] salaries to make an internal tabulation staff profitable."

However, the nature of research projects is that they are not consistent in terms of timing. "There is extreme variability in getting research projects processed, and you have to have sufficient staff to handle that variability," Neal warns. "And once you have four or five tabulation specialists, it becomes an operational issue, keeping that department properly supervised and busy enough to leverage its cost."

Neal believes that many of "the very large or particularly nasty, complicated projects will continue to be sent outside" even if a company chooses to do a portion of its own in-house tabulation. In addition, "projects requiring advanced statistical processing will often be subcontracted because of the special expertise and software required for that kind of analysis."

Companies are looking for two kinds of popular techniques from data processing services: cross-tabulation tables that include appropriate significance testing,

and mass graphical representations from tables such as bar charts and line charts "that summarize the data and provide a picture as opposed to numbers," Neal says.

In the area of statistical analysis, the more popular procedures remain market segmentation, product and service positioning, conjoint analysis for product optimization, and correspondence analysis for the examination of contingency tables.

But Neal sees some pitfalls in recent data analysis trends. "The software packages available today don't allow the analysts to really touch and feel the data. They get more removed from what the respondent level data is telling them. They dump the data into software packages and do wonderful, magical things.

"But they no longer have to get down to the point where they are examining individual response patterns. That can lead to very erroneous conclusions," adds Neal.

There is another pitfall brought about by the relatively easy-to-use software packages. "In both the tabulation packages—and especially in the statistical packages—you can violate many of the assumptions of a particular technique or statistic and not know about it," Neal says.

"We still see analysts who run a regression analysis and fail to consider issues of multicollinearity in the independent data set, and then they don't understand how to conduct a proper residual analysis."

William D. Neal received an M.S. in Industrial Management from Georgia Tech in 1973. While in graduate school, he founded SDR, Inc. In addition to his work with SDR, he gives lectures and teaches seminars, serves on the Editorial Review Board of *Marketing Research,* and is an ad hoc reviewer for several other publications.

Data Analysis: Exploring Basic Relationships

QUADRANT ANALYSIS DETECTS CONSUMER PROFILE CHANGES

Quadrant analysis, an accepted technique for determining the relative strength of a product in its category, can be used to confirm that the target consumer profile is correct, changing, or remaining the same.

Companies rely on focus groups, mail and telephone surveys, and panel information to gain an understanding of what their potential customer will look like. But is this profile a static entity?

Quadrant analysis discloses whether a brand is strong in a strong market for the category, weak in a strong market, strong in a weak market, or weak in a weak market.

It also can be used to identify which feature of the profile is the dominant one, relative to sales and share. This sort of analysis ought to be done annually, preferably every six months.

The data needed to develop the quadrants are BDI [brand development index] measures for the product and various demographic factors that might affect purchase: income, age, family size, education, and ethnicity.

The proportion that each of these demographic factors represents of the total population in each geographic sector would be calculated and indexed vs. the total U.S.

For example, if we were exploring the importance of the age factor, assuming that our consumer was apt to be in the 18–25 age group, we might do the following:

— Calculate the number of persons in the 18–25 group per 1,000 population in Area A.

— Calculate the number of persons in the group per 1,000 population in the total U.S.

— Divide Area A results by total U.S. results.

— Multiply the quotient by 100 to achieve the index.

— Repeat the same calculations for each geographic area.

CHAPTER
OBJECTIVES
—

DISCUSS AND ILLUSTRATE
data summary methods,
including measures of central
tendency and measures of
variability.

DISCUSS AND ILLUSTRATE
how cross-tabulations are
used.

DEMONSTRATE
how to graphically represent
data and explain the pitfalls to
avoid so that actual
relationships are not
distorted.

The chart above shows such data for a hypothetical product that is initially believed to appeal to the 18–25 age group. This demographic factor is considered to be the independent variable and appears on the x-axis.

The BDI is the dependent variable and appears on the y-axis. Slotted into the quadrants are 20 hypothetical sales districts; they are deliberately positioned in the quadrants to give a contradictory picture.

In the quadrants that reflect a heavy incidence of the 18–25 age group (1 and 2), the BDI is weak; in the quadrants where the group is not a significant portion of the population (3 and 4), the BDI is strong.

A product manager who sees this would want to try out other age groups or another demographic factor, such as income strata. Perhaps age is not the most important feature of the profile.

From a series of such quadrant analyses, a composite picture of the current user can be developed, a reaffirmation of the correctness of the product positioning can be made, and advertising and promotional campaigns can be retargeted where they seem appropriate.

Source: Grace Conlon, *Marketing News*, September 12, 1986, p. 42. Used with permission.

INTRODUCTION

You know the saying: A picture is worth a thousand words. In the context of data analysis, the *words* are the many responses that have been collected and the *picture* refers to procedures that succinctly capture the relationships of interest in the data. As we have seen, *quadrant analysis* is one particular way of graphically representing data to provide insights into the composition of current users and brands. We will discuss quadrant analysis again after becoming familiar with some other approaches for summarizing data.

This chapter focuses on methods used for inspecting data before testing the formal research hypotheses related to the specific study objectives. These methods help us understand the nature of the data collected and, consequently, give a preliminary glimpse of what relationships to expect. We begin by discussing various descriptive statistics, many of them familiar from your basic statistics training. We then return to cross-tabulations, which we introduced in Chapter 13. We conclude with a discussion of graphic methods for displaying data.

DATA SUMMARY METHODS: DESCRIPTIVE STATISTICS

It would be extremely tedious to examine each response to every question appearing in a particular questionnaire. A researcher can use a variety of statistics to summarize data. Descriptive statistics use a single number to summarize data. If a researcher wanted to know, for example, the most likely response to a question, he or she could compute a measure of *central tendency* such as the *mean* for interval or ratio data. If, in addition, the researcher wanted to know how responses are dispersed around the mean, a measure of *variability* such as the *variance* could be computed.

Mean level and dispersion represent two *informational components* of data. Measures of central tendency such as the mean tell you information about *elevation*—how high or how low the scores on a question tend to be. Measures of variability such as the variance tell you information about dispersion—how spread out are the responses to a question.

Measures of central tendency and variability are routinely reported when tabulating a study. Let's look at Table 14–1, for instance. The cross-tabulation comes from a product concept test for a new telecommunications redialing service. There are 13 banner points (including TOTAL) representing different subgroups of respondents. The table presents responses, labeled 1 through 5, to a likelihood-of-purchase question. Notice that the total number of respondents answering this question is 766. The 70 "no" answers appearing in the total column relates only to question Q8B. If you examine the business customer banner points and add these frequencies counts, the base is 826, which is 10 respondents less than the total respondent count appearing in the total column. This means that 10 respondents did not provide information that would allow a classification into one of the three business customer types. Mean levels, the *standard deviation* (σ, the square root of the variance), and the *standard error* ($\sigma/\sqrt{n}$) are reported at the bottom of the table.

TABLE 14–1

Cross-Tabulation of Likelihood to Purchase Repeat-Dialing Service

Q8B. LIKELIHOOD TO PURCHASE REPEAT DIALING FOR YOUR BUSINESS AT COST OF $4.00 EACH MONTH

	TOTAL	REGION			BUSINESS CUSTOMER			NUMBER OF TELEPHONE LINES		PC 1+	MODEM 1+	FAX 1+	ANS MACH 1+
		METRO	STATE	OHIO	LESS THAN 3 YRS	3–10 YRS	MORE THAN 10 YRS	1	2–6				
TOTAL RESPONDENTS	836	214	343	279	146	241	439	527	253	117	104	131	335
NO ANSWER	70	16	36	18	10	12	46	47	14	6	5	9	22
TOTAL ANSWERING	766	198	307	261	136	229	393	480	239	111	99	122	313
REPEAT DIALING													
VERY LIKELY TO BUY													
5	69 / 9.0	13 / 6.6	25 / 8.1	31 / 11.9	6 / 4.4	27 / 11.8	34 / 8.7	34 / 7.1	29 / 12.1	15 / 13.5	18 / 18.2	18 / 14.8	30 / 9.6
4	88 / 11.5	18 / 9.1	35 / 11.4	35 / 13.4	21 / 15.4	29 / 12.7	38 / 9.7	49 / 10.2	35 / 14.6	19 / 17.1	13 / 13.1	19 / 15.6	38 / 12.1
3	148 / 19.3	41 / 20.7	52 / 16.9	55 / 21.1	36 / 26.5	39 / 17.0	73 / 18.6	90 / 18.8	46 / 19.2	20 / 18.0	18 / 18.2	25 / 20.5	83 / 26.5
2	74 / 9.7	25 / 12.6	27 / 8.8	22 / 8.4	9 / 6.6	33 / 14.4	32 / 8.1	45 / 9.4	28 / 11.7	14 / 12.6	11 / 11.1	8 / 6.6	26 / 8.3
1	387 / 50.5	101 / 51.0	168 / 54.7	118 / 45.2	64 / 47.1	101 / 44.1	216 / 55.0	262 / 54.6	101 / 42.3	43 / 38.7	39 / 39.4	52 / 42.6	136 / 43.5
NOT VERY LIKELY TO BUY													
MEAN BASE	766	198	307	261	136	229	393	480	239	111	99	122	313
MEAN	2.19	2.08	2.09	2.38	2.24	2.34	2.09	2.06	2.43	2.54	2.60	2.59	2.36
STD DEV	1.39	1.29	1.38	1.46	1.31	1.44	1.38	1.33	1.46	1.48	1.55	1.52	1.39
STD ERR	.050	.092	.079	.090	.112	.095	.069	.061	.094	.141	.156	.138	.078

Measures of Central Tendency: The Mean

The **mean** is by far the most frequently used measure of central tendency. In standard notation we let X_i denote the values that a variable can assume, n the sample size (i.e., the number of respondents), and $\overline{X}$ the mean. Then

$$\overline{X} = \sum_{i=1}^{n} X_i/n \qquad (14\text{-}1)$$

where Σ is the summation operator, with the subscript letter indicating the observations over which to sum.

To compute the mean, you add all the values given by respondents to that question and divide by the sample size. In other words, the mean is simply the average value of a variable. As we indicated earlier, the mean provides information on elevation—how high or how low the scores are for a particular question. Examining Table 14–1, for instance, shows that the mean likelihood-to-purchase score for the new redialing concept is 2.19 across the entire sample, which is rather low compared to the highest value of 5. Notice that the mean level for this question can be obtained by the following operation:

$$X = \frac{69(5) + 88(4) + 148(3) + 74(2) + 387(1)}{766}$$

or equivalently by

$$\overline{X} = 5(0.09) + 4(0.115) + 3(0.193) + 2(0.097) + 1(0.505)$$

The first operation involves multiplying each response value by the number of respondents who gave that value and then, after summing, dividing by the total number of respondents. The second operation multiplies each response value by the percentage of respondents giving that response (for example, .09 = 69/766), and then sums these products.

Examination of mean levels also provides for a quick assessment of differences across subgroups as well. In Table 14–1, for example, respondents are classified with respect to region, whether they are a business customer, number of telephone lines, and ownership of four types of telecommunications equipment. Notice that mean purchase-likelihood scores range from a low of 2.06 for respondents having only one telephone line to a high of 2.60 for respondents owning one or more modems. In general, the mean purchase-likelihood scores for respondents owning telecommunication equipment is higher than the mean levels found in other subgroups, and, therefore, it appears that this type of respondent is, all else the same, more favorably disposed to the new redialing product concept.

There are other measures of central tendency that are applicable in the case of nominal or ordinal data. The **mode,** for instance, gives the most frequently occurring value. If you were to graph a distribution by counting up the number of times each unique response is given, the highest peak would be the mode. In Table 14–1 the mode is the fifth response category listed (the category labeled 1). The mode is best suited for categorical variables, or in cases where the responses to a variable have been categorized.

Another measure of central tendency is the **median.** The median is the value that is halfway between the highest and the lowest values. To determine the median you must first order the data either from high to low or from low to high and then record the number that is in the middle. When the sample has an even number of respondents, the median is calculated by adding the two numbers in the middle, and then dividing by two. For example, if you have a sample of 100, you add the responses for the 50th and the 51st observations in the arrayed data and divide by two.

MEDIAN

The value that is half way between the highest and lowest values.

Measures of Variability: The Variance

Measures of variability reflect the amount of dispersion or "spread" in the data. It is possible for two sets of data to differ in both central tendency and dispersion; another two sets of data may have the same central tendency but differ greatly in terms of dispersion. As we have indicated, the most commonly used measure of variability is the variance or standard deviation, although as demonstrated in Chapter 10, the range is also used as an approximation to the variance. The **range** is the difference between the largest and smallest observations in a data set. The range measures the total spread in any data set. It is simple and easily calculated, but does not take into account how the data are distributed between the largest and smallest values.

RANGE

The difference between the largest and smallest observations in a data set.

Recall that we discussed the variance and standard deviation in relation to sampling variability in Chapter 9. The **standard deviation** of a variable, X, denoted as s_x, is obtained by taking the square root of the variance:[1]

STANDARD DEVIATION

Used as a measure of variability when the data have interval or ratio scale properties—it is the square root of the variance.

$$s_x = \sqrt{\frac{\sum_{i=1}^{n} (X_i - \overline{X})^2}{n - 1}} \text{, or} \tag{14-2}$$

$$s_x = \sqrt{\frac{\sum_{i=1}^{n} X_i^2 - \frac{(\sum_{i=1}^{n} X_i)^2}{n}}{n - 1}} \tag{14-3}$$

where

n = Total sample size

X_i = Value of the ith observation

$\overline{X}$ = Mean of the variable of interest

Notice that the variance and standard deviation are calculated by taking the sum of squared deviations of X_i around its mean value $\overline{X}$. The more the individuals who participate in a study tend to give the same response to a particular question, the smaller will be the variance and standard deviation. When the standard deviation is small, you can conclude that the individuals are homogeneous (of like kind), and, consequently, the mean gives a good indication of the response of any particular individual. In contrast, if the variance or standard deviation is large, then individuals are heterogeneous and the mean may not be a very good indicator of the response of any particular individual.

Table 14–1 reports standard deviations for the entire sample as well as for each subgroup. Standard errors are also reported. Recall that we discussed standard errors in the context of sampling (Chapters 9 and 10) and used them in constructing confidence intervals. To compute the standard error of the mean, you divide the standard deviation by the square root of the sample size: $s_{\bar{x}} = \dfrac{s_x}{\sqrt{n}}$.

Notice that the standard deviations for the subgroups are not very different, ranging from a low of 1.29 to a high of 1.55. The standard errors show more disparity, which is accounted for by the differences in the base sizes of the various subgroups. We can use this information to construct 95 percent confidence intervals for the purchase likelihood of each subgroup by multiplying the standard error by 2 (actually 1.96, but let's use 2 for simplicity). It is interesting to note that none of the confidence intervals cover response category 3, a purchase-likelihood value that might indicate some indifference to the new redialing product concept. Take the modem 1+ subgroup, for example. The lower bound of the confidence interval is $2.60 - 2(.156) = 2.288$, and the upper bound is $2.60 + 2(.156) = 2.912$.

Another illustration will help explain the information conveyed by mean and variance. Table 14–2 presents means and variances for five adjective statements used in an automobile name study. Two hundred respondents were asked to rate three existing automobiles (the Celica, the Fiero, and the Pulsar) on five characteristics along a seven-point scale, where 1 indicates "does not describe at all" and 7 indicates "describes completely." The means and variances reported in the table were computed by summing across individuals and automobiles. That is, because each individual rated three automobiles, there are in effect 600 observations (200 × 3). What can you conclude from this information? From the mean levels it appears that individuals on the average rated the three automobiles as being consistent with the adjectives "powerful" and "sporty."

The variances provide some interesting insights as well. Notice that the variance of the ratings on "powerful" is relatively small, whereas the variance of the ratings on "dependable" is relatively large. What can account for a large or a small variance? In the context of this rating exercise, a small variance will be obtained if individuals are homogeneous in their perceptions—if most individuals rate each of the three automobiles similarly on "powerful." In the extreme case, if all individuals gave the same rating to each automobile on an adjective statement, the variance would be zero, indicating that these automobiles are on *parity* with respect to this adjective statement. Two situations can account for a relatively large variance for an adjective statement: Either individual respondents differ in terms of their automobile perceptions (the automobiles are perceived differently), or the automobiles may have similar mean ratings but individuals are different (each individual rates each of the three automobiles similarly on an adjective statement, but across individuals the ratings are different). The bottom portion of Table 14–2 illustrates these results.

Adjective	Mean	Variance
For men	4.61	2.13
Sporty	5.93	4.31
Dependable	4.27	5.92
Powerful	6.11	1.78
High quality	4.09	2.47

Individual	Celica	Fiero	Pulsar
Small Variance: Parity			
1	5	5	5
2	4	4	4
3	5	5	5
4	4	4	4
Large Variance: Automobile Differences			
1	4	6	1
2	3	7	1
3	4	6	1
4	3	7	1
Large Variance: Individual Differences			
1	1	1	1
2	7	7	7
3	1	1	1
4	7	7	7

TABLE 14—2

Automobile Names Rated on Five Characteristics

DATA TABULATION PROCEDURES

Descriptive statistics of central tendency and variability, although informative, are frequently not sufficient to let a researcher fully understand the relationships among a set of variables. For this reason we often turn to tabulation procedures, which can provide additional insights into the data before we consider what specific statistical analyses to perform.

Our discussion uses data collected from 100 respondents who participated in a banking study dealing with the use of and attitudes toward automatic teller machines (ATMs). A partial list of these questions is shown in Exhibit 14–1.

Frequency Distributions

Frequency distributions are useful for summarizing responses to specific questions as well as for data cleaning (discussed in Chapter 13). Table 14–3 presents the frequency distributions for two variables: having an ATM card and age. From the table you can see that 61 percent of the sample have an ATM card. With respect to age, 22 percent of the sample were between the ages of 18 and 34; 33 percent were between the ages of 35 and 54; and 45 percent were 55 years of age or older.

FREQUENCY DISTRIBUTIONS

Statistical procedures useful for summarizing responses to specific questions.

EXHIBIT 14—1

Some Bank Survey Questions Used in ATM Study

1. Do you have a checking account with the bank?

   Yes   [ ]

   No   [ ]   *[If no, terminate and record.]*

2. Which type of checking accounts do you have?

   Senior   Yes   [ ]-1   No   [ ]-0   (1/1)

   Now   Yes   [ ]-1   No   [ ]-0   (1/2)

   State   Yes   [ ]-1   No   [ ]-0   (1/3)

3. Do you have an automatic teller card with your account?

   Yes   [ ]-1   (1/4)

   No   [ ]-0   *[If no, go to question 5.]*

4. Do you use the ATM for (read list)

   Deposits   Yes   [ ]-1   No   [ ]-0   (1/5)

   Withdrawals   Yes   [ ]-1   No   [ ]-0   (1/6)

   Transfers   Yes   [ ]-1   No   [ ]-0   (1/7)

   [Show card demonstrating bank by phone service.]

5. If the bank offered this service would you

   Definitely use   [ ]-1   (1/8)

   Probably use   [ ]-2

   Might or might not use   [ ]-3

   Probably not use   [ ]-4

   Definitely not use   [ ]-5

6. Gender *[Record, don't ask.]*

   Female   [ ]-1   (1/9)

   Male   [ ]-2

7. Age group

   18–34   [ ]-1   (1/10)

   35–54   [ ]-2

   55+   [ ]-3

8. Household income

   Less than $15,000   [ ]-1   (1/11)

   $15,000 to $29,999   [ ]-2

   $30,000 to $49,999   [ ]-3

   $50,000 or more   [ ]-4

Cross-Tabulation

Given the distribution of the two variables in Table 14–3, you might want to conclude that older people are more likely to have an ATM card because the majority of the respondents were over the age of 54 (45 percent) and most of the people in the sample have an ATM card (61 percent). This conclusion is, however, speculative because neither of the two frequency distributions provide information on the joint distribution of the two variables—for example, the percentage of the sample who have an ATM card *and* who are over the age of 54. To examine the joint distribution of two variables, we use a procedure called *cross-tabulation,* which we introduced in Chapter 13.

TABLE 14—3

Frequency Distributions

ATM Value Label	Value	Frequency	Percent	Valid Percent	Cum Percent
NO	0	39	39.0	39.0	39.0
YES	1	61	61.0	61.0	100.0
	Total	100	100.0	100.0	

Valid cases   100   Missing cases   0

AGE Value Label	Value	Frequency	Percent	Valid Percent	Cum Percent
18-34	1	22	22.0	22.0	22.0
35-54	2	33	33.0	33.0	55.0
55+	3	45	45.0	45.0	100.0
	Total	100	100.0	100.0	

Valid cases   100   Missing cases   0

Source: Copyright (c) 1975 by SPSS, Inc. Reproduced with permission of SPSS Inc.

A **cross-tabulation,** an extension of the frequency distribution, is a common method of describing two or more variables at a time. A table cross-classifying the levels of one variable with the levels of some other variable provides the bivariate (two variables at one time) frequency distribution. These tables are also often referred to as *contingency tables*.

Table 14—4 presents the cross-tabulation table for ATM card ownership and age. The row and column totals (usually referred to as *marginals*) provide the same information as the frequency distribution where each is

CROSS TABULATION

Statistical procedure commonly used to describe the responses to two or more variables.

TABLE 14—4

Cross-Tabulation of ATM and Age

Count Row Pct Col Pct Tot Pct	Age 18-34 1	35-54 2	55+ 3	Row Total
ATM No 0	2 5.1 9.1 2.0	10 25.6 30.3 10.0	27 69.2 60.0 27.0	39 39.0
Yes 1	20 32.8 90.9 20.0	23 37.7 69.7 23.0	18 29.5 40.0 18.0	61 61.0
Column Total	22 22.0	33 33.0	45 45.0	100 100.0

Number of Missing Observations: 0

Source:Copyright (c) 1975 by SPSS Inc. Reproduced with permission of SPSS Inc.

EXHIBIT 14−2

Annotated Cell (1,1) of Cross-Tabulation in Table 14−4

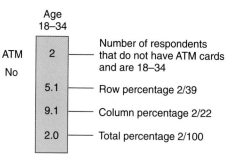

Age 18–34

ATM No

2 ——— Number of respondents that do not have ATM cards and are 18–34

5.1 ——— Row percentage 2/39

9.1 ——— Column percentage 2/22

2.0 ——— Total percentage 2/100

treated separately. The individual cells of the cross-tabulated table, though, provide additional information.

Note that there are four numbers in each cell of the cross-tabulated table. For ease of discussion, number the six cells or boxes of Table 14−4 from one to six beginning at the first row and continuing from left to right. Thus, cell 1 refers to individuals who do not have an ATM card and who are 18 to 34 years old, whereas cell 5 refers to individuals who have an ATM card and who are 35 to 54 years old. To understand the meaning of the four numbers appearing in each cell, look at the description of cell 1 in Exhibit 14−2. Only 5.1 percent (row percentage) of those respondents who do not have an ATM card are aged 18 to 34. Alternatively, if you look at the column percentage, you see that 9.1 percent of the people aged 18 to 34 do not have an ATM card. The conclusions drawn from cross-tabulating these two questions are distinctly different from the speculative conclusions we had reached by examining each variable separately. This is not always necessarily the case. Sometimes the conclusions drawn from examining separate frequency distributions are consistent with the conclusions obtained by cross-classifying two variables. This happens when the two variables in question are statistically independent, as we discuss further in Chapter 16.

Although cross-tabulations provide an efficient way to summarize data, keep in mind that they provide information only on bivariate (two variables at a time) relationships—no information is provided on relationships among three or more variables taken simultaneously. Also, while cross-tabulations can provide useful information in a condensed form, they are not an efficient way to search for results. For example, if you have 50 variables, there would be 1,225 possible two-way cross-tabulations to examine—clearly an unwieldy number. Thus, cross-tabulations are a useful tool in the initial examination of the nature of the data relationships, but they are not particularly well suited for searching for relationships among many variables.

The format of a cross-tabulation will depend on the software used. As indicated previously, in commercial marketing research the rows of the table are identified as stub points and the columns of the table are called banner points. *Banner points* represent subgroups of respondents who are of special interest for some reason and, consequently, are singled out for

TABLE 14–5

Banner

Your readership of news-related stories

	Total	Sex		Age			
		Male	Female	Under	35	35+44	45 & Over
	132	67	56	68		27	35
	100.0	100.0	100.0	100.0		100.0	100.0
No answer	5	3	–	1		3	1
	3.8	4.5	–	1.5		11.1	2.9
Read most	32	15	15	21		2	9
	24.2	22.4	26.8	30.9		7.4	25.7
Read part	53	28	23	26		14	12
	40.2	41.8	41.1	38.2		51.9	34.3
Skimmed or glanced at	40	21	18	20		8	11
	30.3	31.3	32.1	29.4		29.6	31.4
Read none, skipped	2	–	–	–		–	2
	1.5	–	–	–		–	5.7

Source: The example shown was developed using ACROSS, Strawberry Software, Inc.

closer examination. They might correspond to males and females, or different age groups, for example (see Table 14–5). The *stub points* represent the specific questions and the corresponding responses. In a readership study, for instance, the stub points might correspond to an individual's readership of news-related stories (as in Table 14–5). You might want to think of the banner points as explanatory variables and the stubs as either dependent or response variables. The elements of commercially prepared cross-tabulations give the column frequency and column percentage for each stub point. For example, Table 14–5 reveals that 18 females, representing 32.1 percent of all females surveyed, indicated that they skimmed or glanced at news-related stories.

GRAPHIC REPRESENTATION OF DATA

Graphs are a valuable means of summarizing and displaying data. Constructed in certain ways, however, they can be misleading. Improper graphing procedures can produce conclusions that are suspect.[2] Depending on their construction, graphs can hide differences or create them.

For example, consider Exhibit 14–3, which shows the number of public and private elementary schools for selected years between 1929 and 1970. According to the graph, we would conclude that the number of public schools has dropped substantially, but that the number of private schools has remained about the same for the period of study. Now certainly we would expect that the number of private schools is only a small percentage of the total number of elementary schools. By plotting the number of

EXHIBIT 14—3

Poorly Designed Bar
Graph of Number of
Public and Private
Elementary Schools,
1929–1970

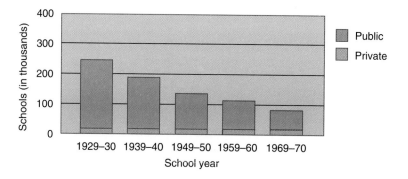

Note: The variation in the number of private schools is obscured by scale.
Source: From Howard Wainer, "How to Display Data Badly," *The American Statistician,* May 1984, p. 139.

private schools in thousands of schools from 0 to 400, any fluctuations in the number of schools are hidden by the scale. Exhibit 14–4, which also plots the number of private schools in thousands, but from 0 to 15, presents quite a different picture from that portrayed in Exhibit 14–3. The magnitude of a graph's scale is determined by the person who creates the graph. All observers should take care not to let the magnitude of a scale hide fluctuations when they exist, or create fluctuations when they don't exist.

Consider next Exhibit 14–5, which presents circulation data for two New York City daily newspapers. It appears that by early 1981 the *Post* had caught up to the *Daily News* in circulation. Yet notice the change in the scale at 800,000. Between 500,000 and 800,000 the scale intervals are 100,000, but now, at 800,000, the interval jumps to 700,000. This change of scale makes the difference in circulation appear smaller than it actually is. While it is true that the graph includes the circulation numbers, 1,491,000 for the *Daily News* and 732,000 for the *Post,* the crucial question is do readers of the graph rely on the numbers or the lines to make an interpretation?

Some of the more commonly used data graphics are bar charts and pie charts. Numerous graphic packages are available for both large mainframe computers and IBM (and IBM clones) and Macintosh personal computers. The graphs illustrated here were constructed using CHARTMASTER™ and SYSDAT™. Spreadsheet programs such as LOTUS 1-2-3® and EX-CEL 3.0 can also generate bar charts and pie charts.

Bar Charts

To illustrate the use of bar charts, let us consider an advertising study for a new suntan lotion. In this study, each respondent was assigned to one of three execution groups and, depending on the group to which the respondent was assigned, asked to evaluate one of three ads. After exposure to the particular advertising execution, each respondent rated the advertisement

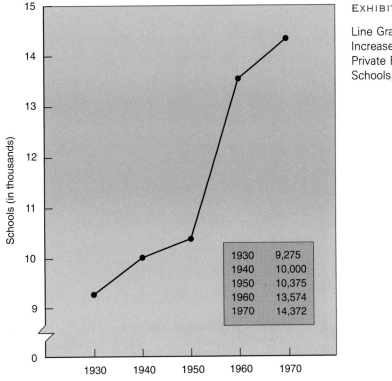

EXHIBIT 14—4

Line Graph Showing Increase in Number of Private Elementary Schools, 1930–1970

1930	9,275
1940	10,000
1950	10,375
1960	13,574
1970	14,372

Note: Unlike Exhibit 14–3, this graph shows a large increase.
Source: From Howard Wainer, ''How to Display Data Badly,'' *The American Statistician*, May 1984, p. 140.

on six semantic differential items. Table 14–6 shows the mean ratings. If the researcher wants to compare the advertisement rating evaluations on each semantic differential item for each of the advertising execution groups, constructing bar charts is one possibility.

A stacked bar chart, which stacks the three executions in columns for each semantic differential scale, is shown in Part A of Exhibit 14–6. A

	Group		
	1	2	3
High quality/low quality	4.32	4.00	2.68
Informative/uninformative	5.24	4.80	1.88
Good/bad	4.96	4.16	2.64
Persuasive/nonpersuasive	4.80	3.68	2.32
Artful/artless	3.76	3.04	2.92
Refined/vulgar	4.40	4.28	3.80

TABLE 14—6

Mean Ratings on Evaluative Dimensions

Group 1 = ''Fun in the Sun''
Group 2 = ''Serious Tanning''
Group 3 = ''At the Lake''

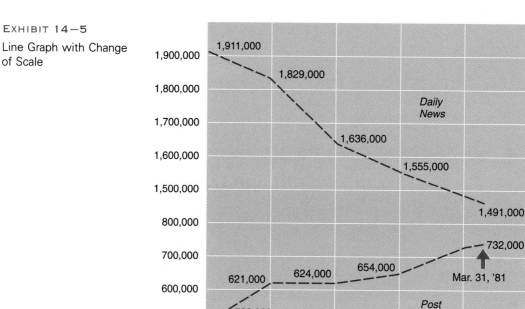

Source: From Howard Wainer, "How to Display Data Badly," *The American Statistician,* May 1984, p. 141.

clustered bar chart, which graphs execution groups side by side for each
semantic differential scale, is shown in Part B of Exhibit 14–6. For both bar
charts, the vertical axis gives the mean values and the six evaluative scales
are spread along the horizontal axis. Consequently, the higher the bar, the
greater the mean value for that characteristic of the advertisement.

From the clustered bar chart shown in Part B of Exhibit 14–6, we can
see that (1) execution group 1 is rated higher on each attribute than either
of the other two executions and (2) execution group 1 received its highest
rating on "informative/uninformative" and its lowest rating on "artful/
artless." The same conclusions can be drawn from the stacked bar chart;
however, in this form, across-group conclusions are sometimes more difficult to draw.

Pie Charts

Pie charts are an alternative method for presenting frequency distributions.
The larger the slice of the pie, the greater the frequency. The pie chart in
Exhibit 14–7 graphically depicts the overall attitude ratings of each advertising execution (group) for the new suntan lotion product. For translation
into pie chart form, variables were interpreted such that a response of 6 or
7 represents a favorable attitude (top-box score), a response of 3, 4, or 5
represents a neutral attitude, and a response of 1 or 2 represents an unfavorable attitude.

EXHIBIT 14—6

Bar Charts

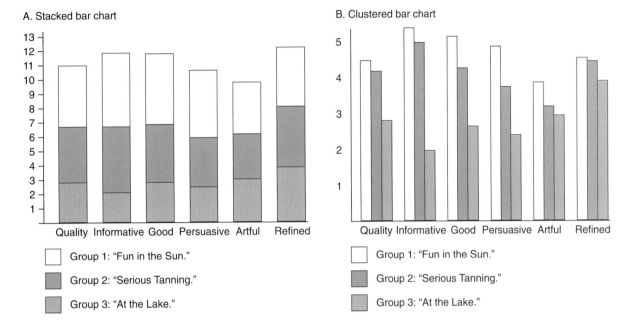

A. Stacked bar chart

Group 1: "Fun in the Sun."

Group 2: "Serious Tanning."

Group 3: "At the Lake."

B. Clustered bar chart

Group 1: "Fun in the Sun."

Group 2: "Serious Tanning."

Group 3: "At the Lake."

Quadrant Analysis

Quadrant analysis is a graphic technique that is typically used in commercial marketing research studies to analyze importance and attribute ratings. Many marketing research studies ask the respondent to indicate the importance that specific attributes play in his or her choice of one brand among various alternatives. The respondent is often asked to rate specified brands on their ability to deliver satisfactory amounts of the desired end benefits. Quadrant analysis produces a grid that shows which attributes are important and those attributes that a brand (or service) delivers. This type

Using graphics for data presentation

EXHIBIT 14—7

Pie Chart for Overall
Attitude Scores by
Execution

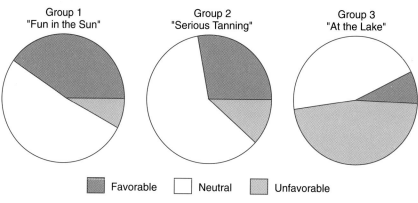

of analysis lets the researcher determine whether the attributes that a particular brand delivers are the attributes that respondents evaluate as being important.

An example can demonstrate how quadrant analysis works. In a study of the cold and cough remedy market category, respondents were asked to react to a list of characteristics that could be used to describe cold and cough remedy products and specifically to indicate how important each characteristic would be for the "ideal" cold and cough remedy product. Respondents were also asked to rate each brand that they had tried during the past 30 days on the same set of characteristics. Quadrant analysis was conducted on the top two box scores for both the importance (i.e., "extremely important" and "very important") and brand ratings (i.e., "describes completely" and "describes somewhat"). Table 14–7 presents the results of the first stage of the quadrant analysis for one of the brands, labeled simply brand L.

The second column of the table (labeled Y) gives the percentage of the sample who indicated that the characteristic in question is either extremely important or very important (i.e., top two boxes). The first column of the table (labeled X) gives the percentage of the sample who indicated that the characteristic in question is either extremely important or very important and who *also* agreed strongly or agreed somewhat (top-two-boxes for brand ratings) that brand L could be described by the respective characteristic. For example, the table indicates that 96.4 percent of the respondents felt that it is extremely important or very important that the "ideal" cold and cough remedy "provide fast relief" (characteristic 4); of those who rate this characteristic as top two box, 45.2 percent rated brand L as delivering this characteristic.

Exhibit 14–8 shows the quadrant map for this study. Characteristics are positioned in one of the four quadrants based on how their importance and delivery scores, shown in Table 14–7, compare to the median importance and delivery scores which are reported on the top of the page. Consider, for example, the characteristic "relieve body aches" (characteristic 1). Note that it is positioned in Quadrant 2 because its top two box importance score of 77.9 percent exceeds the median score of 73.5 percent, while its delivery score of 11.2 percent is below the median delivery score of 18.5 percent.

Y coordinate is percent top two box of importance.

X coordinate is percent of Y top two box and brand top two box.

TABLE 14–7

Quadrant Analysis

Attribute	Brand L	
	X	Y
1. Relieve body aches	11.2	77.9
2. Be gentle to the stomach	40.5	88.3
3. Provide relief that lasts six hours or longer	20.7	79.8
4. Provide fast relief	45.2	96.4
5. Provide extra strength relief	22.4	65.7
6. Be in a liquid form	46.7	56.9
7. Relieve watery, itchy eyes	8.1	51.9
8. Treat more than one symptom at a time	17.6	76.2
9. Be a good value for the money	32.9	81.2
10. Be a product for one specific symptom	11.9	23.1
11. Help you fall asleep	20.0	60.0
12. Be good for nighttime use	38.3	77.1
13. Be non-habit forming	51.0	92.4
14. Be convenient to use away from home	32.6	80.7
15. Relieve head cold symptoms	19.3	86.2
16. Help you to breathe easier	23.1	96.4
17. Loosen upper chest congestion	36.4	92.6
18. Relieve a cough	65.5	94.0
19. Relieve a headache	6.4	81.0
20. Prevent a cold from developing	6.9	76.9
21. Be appropriate for the whole family	31.0	49.8
22. Relieve sinus congestion	12.4	78.8
23. Relieve sneezing	8.8	75.7
24. Relieve a runny nose	14.8	90.5
25. Relieve nasal congestion/stuffiness	17.1	91.2
26. Have no side effects	37.1	96.2
27. Be in a tablet form	1.0	15.2
28. Be safe to use	52.1	97.9
29. Be a good tasting chewable tablet	2.9	51.9
30. Doesn't make you drowsy	22.9	64.8

EXHIBIT 14—8

Quadrant Map

The brand is brand L cough syrup.	
Median importance is 73.50 percent. Median delivery is 18.50 percent.	

Quadrant 2 High Importance Low Delivery	Quadrant 1 High Importance High Delivery
1. Relieve body aches	2. Be gentle to the stomach
8. Treat more than one symptom at a time	3. Provide relief that lasts six hours or longer
19. Relieve a headache	4. Provide fast relief
20. Prevent a cold from developing	9. Be a good value for the money
22. Relieve sinus congestion	12. Be good for nighttime use
23. Relieve sneezing	13. Be non-habit forming
24. Relieve a runny nose	14. Be convenient to use away from home
25. Relieve nasal congestion/stuffiness	15. Relieve head cold symptoms
	16. Help you to breathe easier
	17. Loosen upper chest congestion
	18. Relieve a cough
	26. Have no side effects
	28. Be safe to use.

Quadrant 3 Low Importance Low Delivery	Quadrant 4 Low Importance High Delivery
7. Relieve watery, itchy eyes	5. Provide extra strength relief
10. Be a product for one specific symptom	6. Be in a liquid form
27. Be in a tablet form	11. Help you fall asleep
29. Be a good tasting chewable tablet	21. Be appropriate for the whole family
	30. Doesn't make you drowsy

SUMMARY

In this chapter we have considered procedures for examining data before testing formal research hypotheses related to the specific objectives of the study at hand. These procedures allow researchers to better understand the nature of the data collected and give some initial insights into the relationships between and among the various variables. The procedures illustrated include the basic descriptive statistics of central tendency (mean, median, and mode) and measures of variability (variance, standard deviation, and range). We then discussed cross-tabulations and provided more complete illustrations of their uses. Finally, we considered graphic methods for displaying data that can be particularly effective in summarizing basic relationships.

KEY CONCEPTS

Mean	Standard Deviation	Bar Charts
Median	Range	Pie Charts
Mode	Frequency Distribution	Quadrant Analysis
Variance	Cross-Tabulation	

REVIEW QUESTIONS

1. Tables 1 and 2 (see the following pages) were obtained in a concept study for a new wine cooler. Based upon the means and standard deviations (and standard errors) shown in Table 1, what conclusions can you draw concerning the purchase intentions of the various subgroups (i.e., banner points)?

2. Interpret the cross-tabulation shown in Table 2.

3. Using the information given in Table 1, illustrate each of the graphic procedures discussed in this chapter.

ENDNOTES

1. From the definition of σ^2 and properties of the expected value, it can be shown that $E(s_x^2) = \dfrac{n-1}{n}\sigma^2$. Hence, s_x^2 is a biased estimator of σ^2 if we divide by n, but an unbiased estimator when we divide by $n - 1$. For a complete discussion of this relationship, see Paul G. Hoel, *Introduction to Mathematical Statistics*, 3rd ed. (New York: John Wiley & Sons, 1962), p. 229.

2. Howard Wainer, "How to Display Data Badly," *The American Statistician*, May 1984, pp. 137–47.

TABLE 1

Q.14A APPEAL OF PHRASE AS IT RELATES TO COUGAR: J — NOT SWEET LIKE WINE COOLERS, NOT FILLING LIKE BEER, AND MORE REFRESHING THAN WINE OR MIXED DRINKS

| | | GRND TOTL | GENDER | | AGE | | | ALCOHOL CONSUMPTION | | | |
			MALE	FE-MALE	21-24	25-34	35-49	3-5/WK	6-10/WK	11/WK	6+WK
TOTAL RESPONDENTS		300	150	150	101	123	76	131	91	78	169
TOTAL ANSWERING		300	150	150	101	123	76	131	91	78	169
SUBTOTAL:		242	119	123	84	102	56	108	68	66	134
TOP TWO BOX		80.7%	79.3%	82.0%	83.2%	82.9%	73.7%	82.4%	74.7%	84.6%	79.3%
EXTREMELY APPEALING	(5)	151	68	83	48	66	37	71	39	41	80
		50.3%	45.3%	55.3%	47.5%	53.7%	48.7%	54.2%	42.9%	52.6%	47.3%
	(4)	91	51	40	36	36	19	37	29	25	54
		30.3%	34.0%	26.7%	35.6%	29.3%	25.0%	28.2%	31.9%	32.1%	32.0%
	(3)	36	21	15	9	12	15	13	15	8	23
		12.0%	14.0%	10.0%	8.9%	9.8%	19.7%	9.9%	16.5%	10.3%	13.6%
	(2)	13	7	6	4	6	3	7	4	2	6
		4.3%	4.7%	4.0%	4.0%	4.9%	3.9%	5.3%	4.4%	2.6%	3.6%
NOT AT ALL APPEALING	(1)	9	3	6	4	3	2	3	4	2	6
		3.0%	2.0%	4.0%	4.0%	2.4%	2.6%	2.3%	4.4%	2.6%	3.6%
MEAN BASE		300	150	150	101	123	76	131	91	78	169
MEAN		4.21	4.16	4.25	4.19	4.27	4.13	4.27	4.04	4.29	4.16
STD. DEV.		1.01	.97	1.06	1.03	.99	1.04	1.00	1.08	.94	1.03
STD. ERR.		.059	.079	.086	.102	.089	.119	.087	.114	.107	.079

TABLE 2

Q.5 BEVERAGES CONSUMED AT LEAST OCCASIONALLY

VERSION A: POSITIVE PURCHASE INTENT

| | GRND TOTL | GENDER | | AGE | | | ALCOHOL CONSUMPTION | | | |
		MALE	FE-MALE	21-24	25-34	35-49	3-5/WK	6-10/WK	11+/WK	6+/WK
TOTAL RESPONDENTS	300	150	150	101	123	76	131	91	78	169
TOTAL ANSWERING	300	150	150	101	123	76	131	91	78	169
SOFT DRINKS	281	138	143	92	118	71	122	87	72	159
	93.7%	92.0%	95.3%	91.1%	95.9%	93.4%	93.1%	95.6%	92.3%	94.1%
JUICE	267	132	135	86	110	71	116	81	70	151
	89.0%	88.0%	90.0%	85.1%	89.4%	93.4%	88.5%	89.0%	89.7%	89.3%
BEER	261	143	118	88	112	61	103	83	75	158
	87.0%	95.3%	78.7%	87.1%	91.1%	80.3%	78.6%	91.2%	96.2%	93.5%
WINE	201	88	113	67	81	53	102	59	40	99
	67.0%	58.7%	75.3%	66.3%	65.9%	69.7%	77.9%	64.8%	51.3%	58.6%
ANY OTHER KIND OF BEVERAGE THAT INCLUDES ALCOHOL	236	109	127	78	99	59	109	71	56	127
	78.7%	72.7%	84.7%	77.2%	80.5%	77.6%	83.2%	78.0%	71.8%	75.1%

First table

CONSUMPTION BY GENDER				COMMITMENT			CONCEPT LIKEABIL.		PRODUCT TEST (EITHER)		
MALE		FEMALE			WINE OR				LIKE		
3-5 WK	6+ WK	3-5	6+ WK	BEER	WINE CLR	HARD ALC	VERY MUCH	SOME-WHAT	EXT/VERY	LIKE MOD	DIS-LIKE
42	108	89	61	158	108	101	130	170	127	86	11
42	108	89	61	158	108	101	130	170	127	86	11
31	88	77	46	126	87	89	109	133	107	65	6
73.8%	81.5%	86.5%	75.4%	79.7%	80.6%	88.1%	83.8%	78.2%	84.3%	75.6%	54.4%
20	48	51	32	81	61	59	76	75	78	31	5
47.6%	44.4%	57.3%	52.5%	51.3%	56.5%	58.4%	58.5%	44.1%	61.4%	36.0%	45.5%
11	40	26	14	45	26	30	33	58	29	34	1
26.2%	37.0%	29.2%	23.0%	28.5%	24.1%	29.7%	25.4%	34.1%	22.8%	39.5%	9.1%
7	14	6	9	22	12	6	16	20	11	13	4
16.7%	13.0%	6.7%	14.8%	13.9%	11.1%	5.9%	12.3%	11.8%	8.7%	15.1%	36.4%
3	4	4	2	6	6	3	5	8	5	6	1
3.7%	4.5%	3.3%	3.3%	5.6%	3.0%	3.8%	4.7%	3.9%	7.0%	9.1%	
1	2	2	4	4	3	3	0	9	4	2	0
2.4%	1.9%	2.2%	6.6%	2.5%	2.8%	3.0%	-%	5.3%	3.1%	2.3%	-%
42	108	89	61	158	108	101	130	170	127	86	11
4.10	4.19	4.35	4.11	4.22	4.26	4.38	4.38	4.07	4.35	4.00	3.91
1.08	.93	.95	1.18	.99	1.04	.95	.85	1.11	1.01	1.01	1.14
.166	.089	.101	152	.079	.101	.094	.074	.085	.090	.108	.343

Second table

CONSUMPTION BY GENDER				COMMITMENT			CONCEPT LIKEABIL.		PRODUCT TEST (EITHER)		
MALE		FEMALE			WINE OR				LIKE		
3-5/ WK	6+/ WK	3-5/ WK	6+/ WK	BEER	WINE CLR	HARD ALC	VERY MUCH	SOME-WHAT	EXT/VERY	LIKE MOD	DIS-LIKE
42	108	89	61	158	108	101	130	170	127	86	11
42	108	89	61	158	108	101	130	170	127	86	11
39	99	83	60	144	106	97	126	155	120	78	10
92.9%	91.7%	93.3%	98.4%	91.1%	98.1%	96.0%	96.9%	91.2%	94.5%	90.7%	90.9%
37	95	79	56	138	100	88	117	150	111	73	11
88.1%	88.0%	88.8%	91.8%	87.3%	92.6%	87.1%	90.0%	88.2%	87.4%	84.9%	100.%
40	103	63	55	158	90	87	112	149	110	74	11
95.2%	95.4%	70.8%	90.2%	100.%	83.3%	86.1%	86.2%	87.8%	86.6%	86.0%	100.%
31	57	71	42	98	91	75	95	106	91	50	8
73.8%	52.8%	79.8%	68.9%	62.0%	84.3%	74.3%	73.1%	62.4%	71.7%	58.1%	72.7%
29	80	80	47	124	94	95	112	124	102	65	7
69.0%	74.1%	89.9%	77.0%	78.5%	87.0%	94.1%	86.2%	72.9%	80.3%	75.6%	63.6%

Steps in Hypothesis Testing

WOMEN WALKING FOR HEALTH AND FITNESS: HOW MUCH IS ENOUGH?

Frequency, intensity, and duration of exercise provide the framework for developing an exercise prescription. The interaction of these factors has been thoroughly examined only with regard to the proper dose of exercise required to increase cardiorespiratory fitness. Because cardiorespiratory fitness and cardiovascular health have been considered synonymous, it is not surprising that the guidelines published in 1978 by the American College of Sports Medicine describing the quality and quantity of exercise necessary to increase fitness are often extrapolated to the prescription of exercise to prevent cardiovascular disease. However, attainment of a fit state may not be necessary to modify specific cardiovascular disease risk factors favorably.

The latter hypothesis is supported by recent epidemiologic data that demonstrate that persons who participate in physical activities that are less intense and, therefore, unlikely to have a profound impact on cardiorespiratory fitness, do, nonetheless, derive cardiovascular health benefits. However, it is difficult to quantify the amount of physical activity required to provide an apparent protective effect against the development of cardiovascular disease from epidemiologic data alone. While ample support shows low-level activity may lead to a less atherogenic lipid profile

among men, few studies have investigated this possibility among women.

Therefore, to explore separately and independently the relationship between cardiorespiratory fitness and cardiovascular health among women, we designed a 24-week, dose-response, randomized clinical trial among sedentary, premenopausal women, in which walking exercise intensity varied across three treatment groups (strollers, brisk walkers, and aerobic walkers) while keeping the distance and frequency constant. Statistical analyses focused on whether changes in clinical cardiovascular risk factors paralleled changes in cardiorespiratory fitness across the three walking groups and the control group.

Objective—We studied whether the quantity and quality of walking necessary to decrease the risk of cardiovascular disease among women differed substantially from that required to improve cardiorespiratory fitness.

Design—A randomized, controlled, dose-response clinical trial with a follow-up of 24 weeks.

Setting—A private, nonprofit biomedical research facility.

Participants—One hundred two sedentary premenopausal women, 20 to 40 years of age, were randomized to one of four treatment groups; 59 completed the

CHAPTER
OBJECTIVES

—

INTRODUCE
the notion of hypothesis
testing.

DEFINE
the steps in hypothesis
testing.

DISCUSS
type I and type II hypothesis
testing errors.

DISTINGUISH
between statistical
significance and practical
importance.

DISCUSS
the implications of performing
multiple hypothesis tests.

ΔV_{O_2} max mL/kg
per min

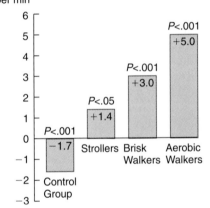

ΔHDL cholesterol
mmol/L (mg/dL)

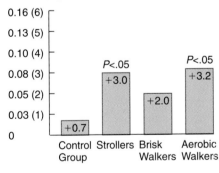

study (16 aerobic walkers [8.0-km/h group], 12 brisk walkers [6.4-km/h group], 18 strollers [4.8-km/h group], and 13 sedentary controls). Eighty-one percent were white, 17 percent black, and 2 percent Hispanic.

Intervention—Intervention groups walked 4.8 km per day, 5 days per week at 8.0 km/h, 6.4km/h, or 4.8 km/h on a tartan-surfaced, 1.6-km track for 24 weeks.

Main outcome measures—Fitness (determined by maximal oxygen uptake) and cardiovascular risk factors (determined by resting blood pressure and serum lipid and lipoprotein levels).

Results—As compared with controls, maximal oxygen uptake increased significantly ($P<.0001$) and in a dose-response manner (aerobic walkers>brisk walkers> strollers). In contrast, high-density lipoprotein cholesterol concentrations were not dose related and increased significantly ($P<.05$) and to the same extent among women who experienced considerable improvements in their physical fitness (8.0-km/h group, +0.08 mmol/L) and those who had only minimal improvements in fitness (4.8-km/h group, +0.08 mmol/L). High-density lipoprotein cholesterol also increased among the 6.4-km/h group, but did not attain statistical significance (+0.06 mmol/L; $P=.06$). Dietary patterns revealed no significant differences among groups.

Conclusion—Thus, we conclude that vigorous exercise is not necessary for women to obtain meaningful improvements in their lipoprotein profile. Walking at intensities that do not have a major impact on cardiorespiratory fitness may nonetheless produce equally favorable changes in the cardiovascular risk profile.

Source: John J. Duncan, Neil F. Gordon, and Chris B. Scott, *Journal of the American Medical Association* 266, no. 23 (December 18, 1991), pp. 3295, 3298. Used with permission.

INTRODUCTION

Hypothesis testing is used not only in medical clinical trials, but also extensively in marketing research. For example, if a manager of a company that produces an established brand of facial moisturizer for women is interested in testing package color changes, he or she might hypothesize that a change to a green package would produce greater visibility and recognition for the target population of 18- to 54-year-old women, who represent over 90 percent of this brand's franchise.

STATISTICAL HYPOTHESIS
A claim made about a population that can be subjected to testing by drawing a random sample from the population.

A **statistical hypothesis** is nothing more than a claim made about a population—a claim that can be subjected to testing by drawing a random sample from the population of interest. Hypotheses are expressed in terms of the population of interest—in this instance, the population of 18- to 54-year-old women. The researcher wants to substantiate or negate claims about this population with regard to the visibility and recognition of alternative package colors. It is not realistic, however, to test the green package color on all 18- to 54-year-old women. A sample of these women can be selected. Statistical hypothesis testing provides a formal procedure for assessing the claims about the population of interest based upon the information collected from a sample.

This chapter presents the framework for testing statistical hypotheses. Much of the discussion focuses on the steps that must be taken in conducting statistical hypothesis tests. We also discuss types of errors that hypothesis testing is subject to (type I and type II), comment on the issue of statistical versus practical significance, and discuss the implications of performing more than one hypothesis test on the same data set. A detailed discussion of conducting hypothesis tests under different measurement situations will be presented in Chapter 16.

STEPS IN HYPOTHESIS TESTING

There are a number of steps that should be followed in conducting statistical hypothesis testing. Exhibit 15–1 provides an outline of the steps that are discussed in this section.

In discussing the various steps in testing statistical hypotheses, we will utilize information collected from a package and pricing study of an established brand of facial moisturizer for women, described in Exhibit 15–2.

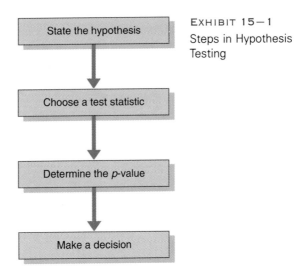

EXHIBIT 15—1

Steps in Hypothesis
Testing

Step 1: State the Hypothesis

Two hypotheses are stated to begin with: the **null hypothesis** (*HO*) and the **alternative hypothesis** (*HA*). The null hypothesis represents the claim about the population that we wish to test. The alternative hypothesis represents another claim about the population of interest that is in direct opposition with the null hypothesis. In the women's facial moisturizer package and pricing study described in Exhibit 15–2, for instance, interest centers on the (performance) relationships between the new package colors and the current cream-colored package. As you will see, the basic claim that will be subjected to testing is whether the new package colors are no different from the current package.

The essence of hypothesis testing is evaluating whether the difference between two or more treatments—say, different package colors or different prices—is large enough to conclude that the treatments are really different and is not simply attributable to sampling variation. To illustrate, consider Table 15–1, which presents visibility scores (percentage of respondents mentioning test brand) and purchase-intention scores (percentage of respondents checking top box—"definitely would buy"—on purchase intent question) for the six alternative package designs—three different colors and two price levels—tested in the facial moisturizing package and price study described in Exhibit 15–2. While the sample percentages and the bivariate plots (see Exhibit 15–3) make it appear that the new colors are superior to the current color, perhaps the observed differences are attributable simply to sampling fluctuations. In other words, is it possible that the new colors are really no better than the cream color currently being used—that we have, for whatever reason, drawn an unrepresentative sample? This is in essence the basic claim that will be subjected to testing.

To state the issue in formal statistical hypothesis testing terms, let us consider the green package color and whether it produces higher visibility

NULL HYPOTHESIS

The claim about the population that we wish to test.

ALTERNATIVE
HYPOTHESIS

Another claim about the population of interest that is in direct opposition with the null hypothesis.

EXHIBIT 15—2

Package and Pricing
Research Proposal

Package and pricing study for replacing an established brand of facial moisturizer for women.

Brand:	Women's facial moisturizer
Project:	Package and pricing study
Background and Objectives:	The beauty-aid group is considering replacing the current package design (cream-colored) and pursuing a premium price strategy, which would raise the current price of a 6-ounce container from $6.29 to $6.79. The objective of the study is to assess consumer reactions to three alternative package colors (green, yellow, and cream) and two alternative price levels ($6.79 and $6.29) in terms of visibility and purchase intentions.
Research Methods:	Three alternative packages (green, yellow, and cream) and two alternative prices ($6.29 and $6.79) will be evaluated monadically in central-location shopping centers in Des Moines, Iowa, and Minneapolis, Minnesota. Combinations of package and price alternatives will be viewed by 300 women aged 18 to 54 who use moisturizers. Fifty respondents will be assigned to each of the six cells according to age quotas. In order to determine consumers' reactions to each alternative package-price combination, respondents in each cell will be exposed to a slide showing the package and price variation and competitive leading brands. The test brand is to be shown in three positions within each cell to control order bias. Each slide will be shown for one second, and respondents will then be asked to recall the brands they have seen. After this questioning the test brand will be shown again for a prolonged period and respondents then questioned about purchase likelihood and product imagery.
Information to Be Obtained:	Information on visibility (percent of respondents mentioning test-brand name after one-second exposure) and purchase intentions will be collected.
Action Standard:	A recommendation to replace the current package with either of the two new designs (green or yellow) will be made if the following condition is met: One of the new designs must be found to be more visible (at the 80 percent confidence level or higher) than the current design; and a decision to change the price from $6.29 to $6.79 per 6-ounce container will be made if there are no significant differences (at the 80 percent confidence level or higher) between the respective top-box purchase-intent scores.
Supplier:	Burke Marketing Research.

levels than the collection of package designs that have been tested previously. Assume, for discussion purposes, that historical data indicate that visibility incidences for this age group have averaged about 25 percent with a variance of 0.1875 and top-box intention incidences have averaged about 48 percent with a variance of 0.2496. In expressing the null and alternative hypotheses, we use π to denote the percentage of the population of 18- to 54-year-old women who would recall seeing the facial moisturizing product if the green package design was used. $\pi^\star$ is used to denote the expected proportion based upon the collective testing experiences of the firm with respect to women's facial moisturizing package designs.[1]

The null hypothesis is that the green package color would produce visibility levels no different from what has been obtained in the past; that is,

HO: $\pi = \pi^\star = .25$

or equivalently

HO: $\pi - \pi^\star = 0$

Package Design	$6.29	$6.79	Color Averages
Visibility:			
Cream	26	26	26
Green	38	40	39
Yellow	30	30	30
Price averages	31	32	
Purchase Intention:			
Cream	54	40	47
Green	58	62	60
Yellow	56	42	49
Price averages	56	48	

TABLE 15-1

Visibility and Purchase Intentions

Note: This table provides summary results in terms of visibility (percentage of respondents mentioning test brand) and purchase intentions (percentage of respondents checking top-box—"definitely would buy"—on purchase-intent question). Also shown are column and row averages for colors and prices.

The alternative hypothesis represents the claim that the green package design is better in terms of visibility than the other package designs that have been tested previously; that is,

HA: $\pi > .25$

or alternatively

HA: $\pi - \pi^\star > 0$

EXHIBIT 15-3

Bivariate Plots*

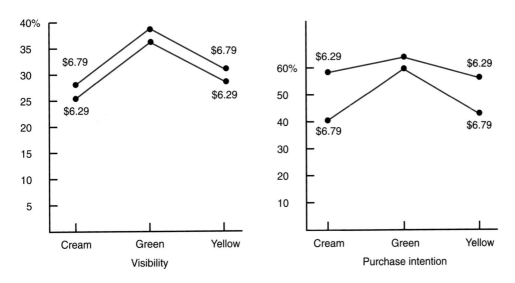

*These bivariate plots are based on the data from Table 15-1.

Notice that the null hypothesis is more restrictive than the alternative hypothesis. The approach to setting up the null hypothesis and the alternative hypothesis is to frame the null hypothesis in terms of a restrictive hypothesis that you hope to reject (e.g., the green package is no different from other package designs) in favor of an alternative, less restrictive hypothesis that is really the preferred outcome of the study (e.g., the green package is better than other package designs).

Because we would not suggest a change in the package color if the visibility level associated with the green package is less than 25 percent, we could also write the null hypothesis as

$$HO: \pi \leq \pi^\star \leq .25$$

The most difficult time we will have in testing the plausibility of the null hypothesis is when the visibility level is close to 25 percent. Thus, if we can reject the null and accept HA when the visibility level is around 25 percent, we will surely reject the plausibility of HO when the visibility level is much lower. In other words, rejecting

$$HO: \pi = .25$$

means that we are rejecting HO for all values less than or equal to 25 percent. In keeping with this perspective, we will use the equality sign when expressing the null hypothesis.

Step 2: Choose a Test Statistic

Each statistical hypothesis test requires the calculation of a test statistic, whose value is obtained from the sample data. The test statistic provides the vehicle for testing the plausibility of a statistical hypothesis. Its value is directly compared to the value specified under the null hypothesis. By applying laws of probability, we can assess the plausibility of the null hypothesis by determining the likelihood of obtaining a given value of the test statistic if the null hypothesis were indeed true. The choice of an appropriate test statistic is influenced by a number of factors: the sample size available, whether means or proportions are being tested, whether the population variance is known, whether one sample or two or more samples are being compared; and if two or more samples are involved, whether the samples are dependent or independent.

A variety of different test statistics will be discussed in Chapter 16. For now let us continue with the women's facial moisturizer package and pricing study and consider a test statistic appropriate for the null hypothesis defined in step 1 of the hypothesis testing process. The null hypothesis defined in step 1 states that there is no difference between visibility percentages for the green-colored package and those obtained with other package colors.

Specifically, let p denote the sample-based proportion of respondents exposed to the green-colored package who mentioned the test brand. The sampling distribution of a proportion follows a binomial distribution, but because the number of respondents exposed to the green-colored package is large ($n = 100$), the normal distribution provides a good approximation to the binomial distribution. In this case, the appropriate test statistic, Z, is

$$Z = \frac{p - \pi^\star}{\sqrt{\dfrac{\sigma^2}{n}}} \tag{15-1}$$

where p is the sample-based proportion, $\pi^\star$ is the population proportion under the null hypothesis, σ^2 is the population variance, and n is the number of respondents who have been exposed to the green-colored package.

This means the Z-test statistic is derived by taking the difference between the sample-based proportion and the population proportion specified under the null hypothesis divided by the standard error $\sqrt{\dfrac{\sigma^2}{n}}$. The Z-test statistic represents a standardizing transformation. p fluctuates around $\pi^\star$, but Z fluctuates around 0.

Inserting the population variance ($\sigma = 0.1875$) and the values given in Table 15–1 into equation 15–1, we find

$$Z = \frac{.39 - .25}{\sqrt{\dfrac{0.1875}{100}}}$$

$$= 3.23$$

Step 3: Determine the p-Value

Having calculated a test statistic, we now need to determine whether the value of the test statistic is so large (or so small) as to conclude that the null hypothesis is improbable. We do this by using the sampling distribution of the test statistic, under the assumption that HO is true, and the calculated p-value. The **p-value** is defined as

p-value $\equiv$ Pr [The sample value would be at least as large
(small) as the value actually observed,
if HO is true]

P-VALUE

Probability that the sample value would be at least as large (small) as the value actually observed, if HO is true.

The p-value is a measure of the agreement between what has been observed in the sample and the null hypothesis. It indicates the likelihood (probability) that we would have obtained the value of p that we actually observed if HO were indeed true. We will use the normal distribution to find the p-value by determining the area under the normal curve consistent with the shaded portion shown in Exhibit 15–4.

In step 2 we computed the value of the test statistic corresponding to the null hypothesis that the visibility level for the moisturizer's green-colored package is no different from the visibility level for other colors of packages. That value is 3.23. Table 15–2 shows an abridged version of the values of the normal distribution. This tabular form of the normal distribution shows the area under the curve from the mean to Z. To find the area associated with $Z \geq 3.23$, locate the row corresponding to $Z = 3.2$ and

EXHIBIT 15—4

p-Value: Probability p
Would Be at Least as
Large as the Value
Actually Observed, If HO
is True

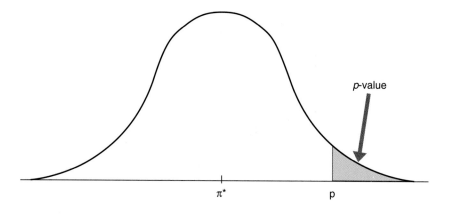

then go over to the column marked .03. The area under the normal curve
from 0 to 3.23 is .49938. Thus the area to the right of the normal curve is
equal to

$$0.5 - .49938 = .00064$$

(Remember the normal curve is symmetrical with half, .5, of the area lying
to each side of the mean.) Thus

$$\Pr(p \geq .39) = \Pr(Z \geq 3.23) = .00064$$

TABLE 15—2

Determining the Area under the Normal Distribution Associated with $Z \geq 3.23$

Entry represents area under the standardized normal distribution from the mean to Z.

Z	.00	.01	.02	.03	.04	.05	.06	.07	.08	.09
3.0	.49865	.49869	.49874	.49878	.49882	.49886	.49889	.49893	.49897	.49900
3.1	.49903	.49906	.49910	.49913	.49916	.49918	.49921	.49924	.49926	.49929
3.2	.49931	.49934	.49936	.49938	.49940	.49942	.49944	.49946	.49948	.49950
3.3	.49952	.49953	.49955	.49957	.49958	.49960	.49961	.49962	.49964	.49965
3.4	.49966	.49968	.49969	.49970	.49971	.49972	.49973	.49974	.49975	.49976
3.5	.49977	.49978	.49978	.49979	.49980	.49981	.49981	.49982	.49983	.49983
3.6	.49984	.49985	.49985	.49986	.49986	.49987	.49987	.49988	.49988	.49989
3.7	.49989	.49990	.49990	.49990	.49991	.49991	.49992	.49992	.49992	.49992
3.8	.49993	.49993	.49993	.49994	.49994	.49994	.49994	.49995	.49995	.49995
3.9	.49995	.49995	.49996	.49996	.49996	.49996	.49996	.49996	.49997	.49997

What can you conclude from this? If *HO* were indeed true, that is, if the green package is indeed no better than the average package, then the probability of observing a proportion at least as large as .39 (the percentage of people in the sample finding the green package better) is only .064 percent (.00064 × 100). Thus, it seems reasonable that the null hypothesis—that the green package produces visibility levels no different from those obtained in the past—is extremely implausible. This is illustrated in Exhibit 15–5.

Step 4: State the Decision Rule

Finally, to make a decision about the null hypothesis we must determine the **critical value** of the statistical distribution being used, which delineates the rejection region from the nonrejection region. If the alternative hypothesis is two-sided, then there will be a critical value for both the lower and upper tails of the distribution. The critical value comes from the values of the sampling distribution (for example, binomial, normal) being used for a given value of α.

CRITICAL VALUE

A value that delineates the rejection region from the non-rejection region.

To make a definitive statement about the plausibility of the null hypothesis, we must set a level of significance, which we denote as α. Recall that the level of significance determines how confident we are about the claims made in the null hypothesis. For example, if we set α = 0.05, then we are testing at the 95 percent level of confidence. This means that if you were to draw 100 samples in the same way, in 95 out of the 100 samples you would be led to the same conclusion as in the sample on which the particular test is being conducted.

The level of significance determines the **region of rejection,** which is expressed in terms of a range of values for the test statistic. If the test statistic falls within this range, then the null hypothesis is improbable. For the case we have been considering, the alternative hypothesis is directional; that is,

REGION OF REJECTION

A range of values that signals the rejection of the null hypothesis.

ONE-SIDED/ONE-TAILED TEST

A test for which the alternative hypothesis is directional, e.g., *HA*: π > .25.

$$HA: \pi > .25 \tag{15-2}$$

and the test is referred to as a **one-sided** or **one-tailed test.**

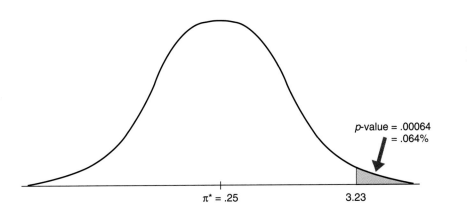

EXHIBIT 15–5

p-Value Corresponding to Z ≥ 3.23

p-value = .00064
= .064%

π* = .25   3.23

However, the alternative hypothesis can be nondirectional, which means the population value should be either greater than or less than .25:

$$HA:\ \pi \neq .25 \tag{15-3}$$

Notice here that the population value is hypothesized to be any value other than .25, hence we can use the "is not equal to" sign. In this case the region of rejection is divided into two equal portions, one corresponding to the lower tail of the distribution and one corresponding to the upper tail of the distribution. A nondirectional alternative hypothesis is called a **two-sided** or **two-tailed test.** Exhibit 15–6 illustrates one-sided and two-sided tests.

If the value of the test statistic falls in the rejection region delineated by the critical value at the predetermined α level, then you can conclude that the null hypothesis is improbable. In such cases you can say that the null hypothesis can be rejected at the predetermined level of confidence. Thus the decision rules are:

> Reject *HO* if test statistic *Z* falls in the region of rejection.
>
> Accept *HO* if test statistic *Z* falls in the region of nonrejection.[2]

TWO-SIDED/TWO-TAILED TEST

A test for which the alternative hypothesis is nondirectional, e.g., H_A: $\pi_A \neq .25$.

EXHIBIT 15–6
Region of Rejection

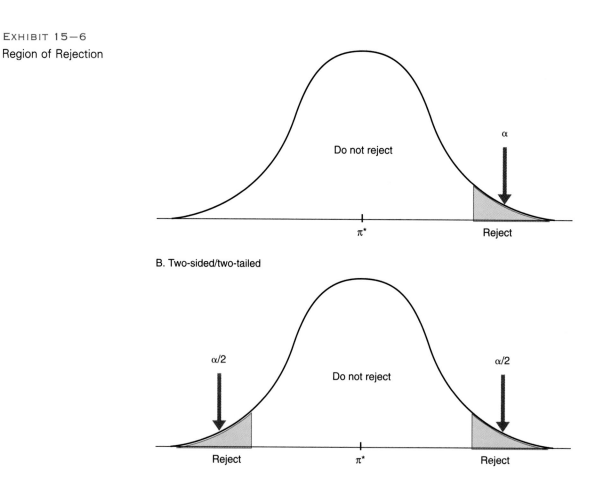

B. Two-sided/two-tailed

We can also state the decision rule in terms of the *p*-value.

Reject *HO* if its *p*-value $< \alpha$.

Accept *HO* if its *p*-value $\geq \alpha$.

For the women's facial moisturizer study let us set $\alpha = 0.05$ for the purpose of establishing a region of rejection. (In conventional hypothesis testing, α is generally set at .05; .10; or .01. We will have more to say about setting α levels later in this chapter.) The test under consideration is one-sided; consequently, from the values of the normal distribution found in Appendix I, locate the critical value of the standard normal distribution associated with a tail area of 5 percent. This value is between 1.64 and 1.65, so set the critical value equal to 1.645. The calculated value of the test statistic is 3.23 and falls in the region of rejection since it lies to the right of the critical value (see Exhibit 15–7). This finding causes us to reject the plausibility of the null hypothesis—that the green package is no different in terms of visibility than other package colors that have been tested in the past.

Value of test statistic > Critical value

3.23 > 1.645

As shown in Exhibit 15–8, in order not to reject *HO* at $\alpha = .05$, we would have to observe a sample-based proportion not exceeding

$$\frac{p - .25}{\sqrt{\dfrac{0.1875}{100}}} = 1.645$$

$$= 0.321$$

where again we have used the population variance ($\sigma^2 = 0.1875$).

To summarize, the observed value of *p* equals .39, which exceeds the value .321 and lets us safely conclude that the null hypothesis is not true.

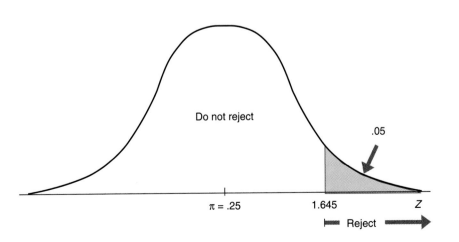

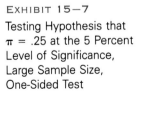

EXHIBIT 15–7

Testing Hypothesis that $\pi = .25$ at the 5 Percent Level of Significance, Large Sample Size, One-Sided Test

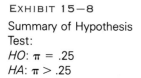

EXHIBIT 15—8

Summary of Hypothesis
Test:
HO: $\pi = .25$
HA: $\pi > .25$

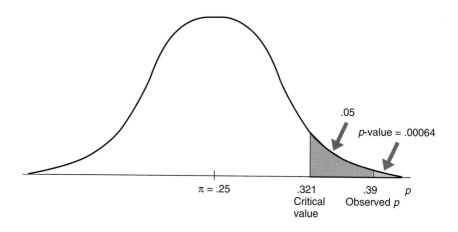

Therefore, we reject the null hypothesis. We can interpret this finding in two ways:

1. *HO* is true, but we have, for whatever reason, obtained an unrepresentative sample.
2. *HO* is not true at all, and visibility levels in excess of .25 are to be expected.

TYPE I AND TYPE II ERRORS

Hypothesis testing is subject to two types of error, customarily referred to as **type I error** and **type II error.** Type I error occurs when *HO* is in fact true but is nevertheless rejected on the basis of the sample data. Type II error occurs when, on the basis of the sample data, we fail to reject *HO* when in fact *HA* is true.

Exhibit 15–9 illustrates type I and type II errors in the context of the facial moisturizer study we have been discussing. Panel A of the exhibit depicts type I error—the situation when *HO*: $\pi = .25$ is true. Notice that because $\alpha = .05$, there is a 5 percent chance that a sample can yield a *p*-value that falls in the region of rejection, which leads us erroneously to reject the true *HO*. Thus the value of α indicates the likelihood of making a type I error.

Panel B of the exhibit illustrates type II error, the situation when *HA* is true. Here the true state of affairs is that the green package is actually superior to other colors in terms of visibility, generating visibility levels around 39 percent. The correct decision here is to reject *HO;* that is, the null hypothesis is false. The error is made when the sample-based value of *p* falls in the *HO* region of nonrejection. The probability of making such an error is called β, which is shown as the shaded region in Panel B. $1 - \beta$ is referred to as the **power of the test;** it indicates the probability of making a correct decision—rejecting *HA* when it is false.

The concept of type I and type II errors brings to light the basic dilemma of hypothesis testing: The researcher never knows whether *HO* is actually

TYPE I ERROR

Occurs when *HO* is in fact true but is nevertheless rejected on the basis of the sample data.

TYPE II ERROR

Occurs when, on the basis of the sample data *HO*, we fail to reject when in fact *HA* is true.

POWER OF THE TEST

Probability of making a correct decision—rejecting *HA* when it is false.

EXHIBIT 15−9

Type I and Type II Errors

A. *HO* is true

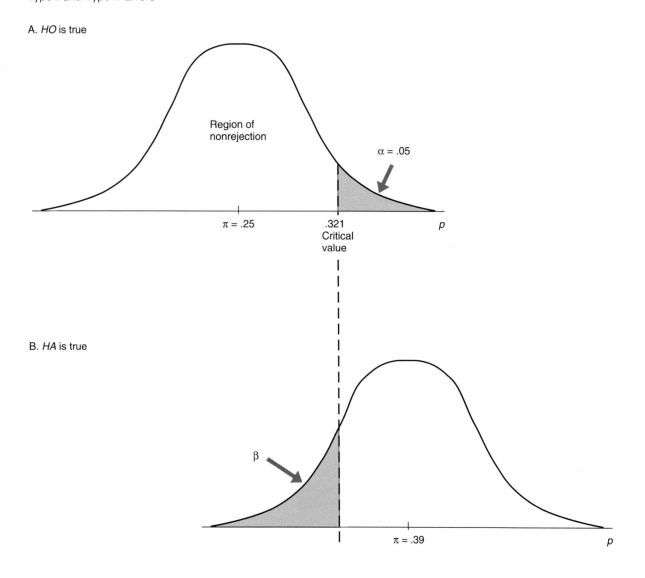

Region of
nonrejection

α = .05

π = .25

.321
Critical
value

p

B. *HA* is true

β

π = .39

p

true or false. Decisions concerning the truthfulness of *HO* are made under uncertainty. Hypothesis testing copes with this uncertainty by following rules of probability, the theory that has driven "smart" gamblers since the first wager was placed.

Table 15−3 sets out four possible results of a hypothesis test. You might understand these possibilities better if you think in terms of an analogy. Say that a jury is asked to decide whether a defendant is guilty as charged. Our legal system is founded on the presumption of innocence, so let *HO* be the hypothesis that the accused is indeed innocent, and *HA* the hypothesis that

TABLE 15—3

Four Possible Results of a
Hypothesis Test

	Decision	
State of the World	*HO Acceptable*	*HO Rejected*
If *HO* is true	Correct decision	Type I error
	Probability = 1 − α = Confidence level	Probability = α = Level of the test
If *HO* is false	Type II error	Correct decision
(*HA* true)	Probability = β	Probability = 1 − β = Power of the test

the person is guilty. A type I error occurs if an innocent person is judged
to be guilty, while a type II error occurs if a guilty person is set free.

Is it "better" or less of an error to convict an innocent person or to free
someone who is guilty? This dilemma is at the heart of the relationship
between type I and type II errors. There is a basic trade-off between these
two types of errors: If you try to minimize the chance of an innocent
person being convicted, this will inevitably lead to some guilty persons
going free. In more formal terms, reducing α will increase β. If, for example, we desire that no innocent person is ever convicted (α = 0), then
β = 1, which ostensibly means that every person, guilty or innocent,
must go free. In the case of marketing research, the only way to reduce β
without increasing α is to increase the sample size. This has the effect of
reducing sampling variability; that is, the sampling distribution of the
estimate is tighter. (In the case of litigation, increasing sample size is analogous to collecting additional evidence.)

As we mentioned earlier, in conventional hypothesis testing the general
approach is to set α at either .01, .05, or .10. Setting α at these levels says
something about the researcher's attitude toward type I error. The smaller
α is, the more the researcher wants to guard against the likelihood of
rejecting a null hypothesis that is true. The researcher is willing to live with
a greater likelihood of a type II error, accepting a false null hypothesis. An
exception to these conventional values of α frequently occurs in product
testing wherein α is sometimes set at .20. In product testing, the null
hypothesis is generally framed as "the new product will be successful
(when launched nationally)." Increasing the value of α to .20 is a recognition of the cost of product failure. In this case the researcher wants to
decrease the likelihood of introducing a new product that will ultimately
fail. In other words, the researcher is more sensitive to rejecting the null
hypothesis when it is false.

STATISTICAL VERSUS PRACTICAL SIGNIFICANCE

Rejecting the null hypothesis at a predetermined α level, or equivalently
obtaining a *p*-value less than α, indicates a statistically significant finding.
Essentially, to state that a finding is *statistically significant* means that our
hypotheses about a population are likely, given the sample evidence.

Remember that hypothesis tests deal with samples and not populations. With sampling comes the possibility of sampling error. And the difference between what you hypothesize and what you observe may be due to sampling error or because your hypothesis was incorrect. A statistically significant result indicates that the difference is not, at some specified α level, attributable to sampling error. The level of statistical significance, not surprisingly, is related to sample size.

The relevance of any research finding to managerial decision making is a totally separate issue from its statistical significance. "Statistical significance is a statement about the likelihood of the observed result, nothing else. It does not guarantee that something important, or even meaningful, has been found."[3]

An example will clarify this point. Assume you must decide between two vacation spots, say, Fort Lauderdale and Mexico City, for spring break. Assume further that an important factor in your decision is the average price for a hotel room. If we tell you, because we know the actual price, that the average price for a hotel room during spring break in Fort Lauderdale is $75.00 and the average price for a similar hotel room in Mexico City is $75.50, would this help you make your decision? That is, how relevant is this sort of difference, even if it is statistically significant. With large sample sizes, even small differences may be statistically significant.

Another example will illustrate the influence of sample size on statistical significance. Suppose an advertising manager is copy testing a print ad using day-after recall scores as the criterion. The norm for brand recognition for this type of ad is 30 percent; that is, 30 percent of the people who are questioned will report having seen the brand advertised. The results of the ad manager's survey indicate that 37 percent of the people questioned report having seen this particular ad. To test the hypothesis of no difference between the sample results and the norm, you could follow the approach described previously and use the Z-test statistic. The calculated values of the Z-test statistic for different sample sizes are

Sample Size	Z-Value
30	0.84
50	1.08
100	1.53
200	2.16
500	3.42

From our previous examples recall that at $\alpha = .05$ the value of the normal distribution is 1.645. With a sample size of 30, 50, or 100 you could not reject the null hypothesis, but if you had a sample size of 200 or more, you could reject the null hypothesis. The reason behind this result is that, with the smaller sample sizes, the difference observed (30 percent versus 37 percent recall) could very likely be due to sampling fluctuations. Sample sizes in excess of 200 provide more confidence that any difference observed is less likely to come from sampling fluctuations.

Hypothesis tests are performed to assess the plausibility of specific claims about a target population. Because of the distinction between statistical and practical significance it seems prudent to suggest that hypothesis testing not be performed blindly, but instead be used as yet another procedure for reducing the uncertainty inherent in decision making.

PERFORMING MULTIPLE HYPOTHESIS TESTS

Most commercial marketing research tabulation programs perform hypothesis testing. Recall that a table is defined by a banner and a stub. The researcher can specify any two banner points and test whether responses, that is, means or proportions, to the stub item are statistically significant. The null hypothesis is that there is no difference in responses between the two groups corresponding to the designated banner points with respect to the stub item.

There is, however, a caveat to performing multiple hypothesis tests on the same data set. The problem with this approach is that performing many hypothesis tests on the same data set increases the probability of detecting a statistically significant difference beyond the α level set by the researcher. The repeated use of hypothesis tests on the same data set alters the *simultaneous* level of significance and capitalizes on chance relationships.

We can illustrate the problem conceptually within the context of the women's facial moisturizer study that we have been discussing. Suppose you wish to consider whether the green- and cream-colored package designs differ significantly with respect to visibility *and* purchase intentions. Following the steps in hypothesis testing discussed above, you could test each of these hypotheses separately at some predetermined α level, say, $\alpha = 0.05$. Though you conduct the tests separately, the two tests are not independent since the same data set is being used; moreover, you actually are concerned with the correctness of both tests.

For a single hypothesis test the probability of being correct, that is, accepting HO when it is true, under repeated sampling, is $1 - \alpha$; in this case, 0.95. When two hypothesis tests are performed, the probability of both being correct would be 0.95×0.95 if the two tests are independent. Thus, even if the tests are independent, the probability of being correct is only 0.9025. If the tests are performed on the same data set, then, in a strict sense, the inferences that you make are not independent. Visibility and purchase-intent measures are not independent since they come from the same respondents. When the tests are not independent, the simultaneous level of significance cannot be determined exactly by the repeated use of separate hypothesis tests. Thus, when evaluating the results of performing multiple hypothesis tests, it is important to realize that the effective α level is greater than the level set by the researcher, and, consequently, a greater number of tests may be statistically significant. In such cases, the researcher is capitalizing on chance.

One informal way of averting this problem is to set what is referred to as the *familywide error rate* and to adjust the α levels of the individual hypothesis test in such a way as to perserve the familywide error rate across all of the hypothesis tests performed. To illustrate, suppose you wish to perform five hypothesis tests on the same data set at $\alpha = 0.05$. To ensure that the familywide error rate is 0.05, each individual hypothesis test would be performed at the $0.05/5 = 0.01$ α level. Thus, dividing the familywide error rate by the number of hypothesis tests performed gives the confidence level for each individual hypothesis test.

SUMMARY

Marketing research provides data that are intended to reduce the risk inherent in making the day-to-day decisions faced by marketing managers. While graphic displays of data and simple descriptive statistics can prove useful to the marketing manager, certain kinds of decisions require more formal statistical procedures to allow the manager to test specific claims about a population of interest on the basis of data collected from a sample. Essentially, statistical hypothesis testing allows the manager to assess the probability that the claims made about the population are true.

We began the discussion by outlining the steps that must be taken when conducting statistical hypothesis testing. First, the null and alternative hypotheses must be stated. Next, based on the specification of the null hypothesis, a test statistic is calculated from the sample data. Once the researcher or manager specifies the level of confidence, a region of rejection is established by consulting a table of values from the appropriate distribution of the test statistic. If the calculated test statistic falls in the region of rejection, then the sample evidence supports the rejection of the null hypothesis. We then introduced the notion of type I and type II errors. The remainder of the chapter was devoted to discussing statistical versus practical significance and the implications of performing multiple hypothesis tests on the same data set.

KEY CONCEPTS

Null and Alternative
  Hypotheses

Test Statistic

p-Value

Normal Distribution

Region of Rejection

Critical Value

Type I and Type II Errors

Statistical Significance versus
  Practical Importance

Familywide Error Rate

REVIEW QUESTIONS

1. Describe the steps in performing hypothesis tests. Discuss the difference between a null hypothesis and an alternative hypothesis.

2. What is the relationship between the p-value and the region of rejection?

3. In a test of the statistical significance of a proportion, the value of the test statistic is equal to 2.109. Would the hypothesis be rejected or accepted?

4. Let us assume the value of a population proportion is equal to 0.40 with a population variance of 0.21. If the plan is to collect a sample of 100 respondents, what value of p must be observed in order to reject the null hypothesis (i.e., $\pi = 0.40$) at $\alpha = 0.01$?

5. What will happen to the probability of committing a type II error when the significance level is increased from 0.01 to 0.05? Discuss the relationship between type I and type II errors.

ENDNOTES

1. It is conventional to use Greek letters to represent population parameters. That is, we express the null and alternative hypotheses in terms of π, which denotes population proportions.

2. In a strict sense we can never actually "accept" the null hypothesis. All the sample evidence can allow us to do is to "fail to reject" the null hypothesis.

3. William L. Hays, *Statistics for the Social Sciences,* 2nd ed. (New York: Holt, Rinehart, & Winston, 1973), p. 384.

Hypothesis Testing of Differences

AD CLAIMS STAND OR FALL AT NAD HEARING

Most of the claims you see advertised have been confirmed in some way by research findings, especially when the claims involved a competitive brand. But how far are companies willing to "stretch" their data?

Smart companies make sure that their tests support all of their claims. That's how Diet Pepsi notched a victory over Diet Coke in a postscript to one of the cola wars' major ad battles.

Coca-Cola Co. complained to the Council of Better Business Bureau's National Advertising Division (NAD) that the "Billy Crystal" and "Ray Charles" TV spots for Diet Pepsi continued to use unsubstantiated taste preference claims.

The complaint came after Pepsi modified the spots last spring following a February complaint to NAD by Coca-Cola. This time around, Coca-Cola argued statements that "Diet Pepsi is better-tasting than Diet Coke" and "Diet Pepsi beats Diet Coke" amounted to a revival of the disputed taste test claims.

When NAD first reviewed Coca-Cola's challenge in April, Pepsi elected not to submit substantiation because it said the claim, "Diet Pepsi—the taste that beats Diet Coke," had been discontinued.

After reviewing Coca-Cola's taste test data and consumer perception studies related to the original and modified ads, NAD ruled the modified spots "contained no unsubstantiated implied claim."

Other companies are not as careful as Pepsi—or as lucky.

McCain Foods challenged Nestle TV spots claiming, "National taste tests prove that Stouffer's makes the best-tasting frozen pizza." Stouffer submitted taste test results and said that in six geographically dispersed locations, Stouffer's frozen pizzas were preferred. Stouffer's

CHAPTER
OBJECTIVES
—

DISCUSS
those factors influencing the
selection of an appropriate
hypothesis testing procedure.

DESCRIBE
hypothesis tests for one
sample.

DESCRIBE
hypothesis tests for two or
more independent samples.

DESCRIBE
hypothesis tests for two or
more related samples.

Deluxe varieties and square pizzas weren't included.

NAD ruled the superiority claim was stated in universal terms but the testing was limited. Stouffer agreed to modify the ads.

Sometimes, even claims that do not directly name a competitor are considered too sweeping to be supported.

Sterling Drug, on behalf of its Thompson & Formby subsidiary, challenged Kop-Coat Inc.'s claim that its Wolman RainCoat water repellent is, ''America's favorite . . . outperforms all-purpose sealers on decks . . . The only way to be sure that your deck will have a beautiful life.''

After examining Kop-Coat's test data, NAD ruled the claims couldn't be substantiated. Kop-Coat agreed to modify the three claims.

The type of data used can also add to or detract from a claim's validity.

NutraSweet Co. challenged a Sugar Foods Corp. magazine ad claiming, ''30 million people prefer Sweet 'N Low. That's 40% more than Equal. . . . And that's why 86% of all foodservice operators choose (Sweet 'N Low) as their primary sugar substitute.'' NutraSweet said Sugar Foods based a taste preference claim solely on market share data. NAD concluded that market share data weren't directly relevant and recommended the claim be modified or discontinued. Sugar Foods said the campaign had run its course.

Source: Kate Fitzgerald and Janice Kelly, *Advertising Age* 61, no. 35 (August 27, 1990), p. 34. Used with permission.

INTRODUCTION

Claims such as "Diet Pepsi is better tasting than Diet Coke" need to be substantiated. Hypothesis testing can do that, that is, provide evidence that supports one brand's claim of superiority over another.

This chapter discusses and illustrates those hypothesis tests most frequently used in commercial marketing research. Exhibit 16–1 presents a roadmap for the ensuing discussion.

We begin by discussing those factors that influence the choice of a particular hypothesis testing procedure. Next, we present hypothesis tests for proportions (that is, nominal data) under a variety of situations. Then we focus on hypothesis testing in the case of means (that is, interval data) and again consider several different situations.

All of the hypothesis testing procedures discussed in this chapter will be illustrated with manual computations, which speed and enhance the learning process and reinforce concepts. As you might suspect, the computations required to perform hypothesis tests can be easily automated by using a computer program.

Most computer statistical software packages (for example, SPSSX, SAS, SYSTAT, MINITAB, and STATGRAPHICS) can perform a wide variety of hypothesis tests. Most of the popular spreadsheet programs, such as Lotus 1-2-3®, can also be used to perform hypothesis testing. To help you appreciate the ease of performing hypothesis testing with computer programs, many of the hypothesis tests discussed will also be illustrated with MARITZ STATS, a commercially available interactive software package.

FACTORS AFFECTING HYPOTHESIS TESTS

Each data analysis situation brings with it a set of factors that influence the choice of an appropriate test statistic. The choice of which particular hypothesis test to use depends on several factors, including (1) the level of measurement, (2) the sample size, (3) whether the population variance is known, (4) the number of samples available, and (5) whether the samples are related.

The level of measurement determines whether the focus of the hypothesis test is on proportions or on mean levels. If the data are nominal or ordinal scaled, then the researcher will in most cases be interested in testing for differences between proportions. If the data are interval or ratio scaled, then the focus will likely be on differences between means.

The size of the sample and whether the population variance is known are factors that influence the sampling distribution of the test statistic. You saw in Chapter 15 that the normal distribution can be used to test hypotheses about proportions when the sample size is reasonably large and the population variance is known. As you will see, when these conditions are not in place, other sampling distributions may have to be used.

EXHIBIT 16−1

Typology of Statistical Tests

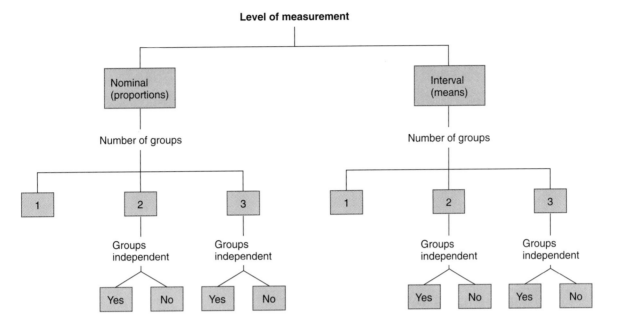

The number of samples available dictates the form of the test statistic. When a single sample is available, the researcher more often than not is interested in testing a sample-based result against a norm or standard. For example, in Chapter 15 we tested the visibility of the green-colored package against historical data. This constitutes a one-sample test.

When more than a single sample is available, the researcher must first distinguish between **independent** and **related** samples. We say that two or more samples are independent if the responses from individuals in one sample in no way influence the responses from individuals in the other samples. Obviously, if the same individual is present in each of the samples, say, in a longitudinal tracking study, then the samples cannot be independent. Related samples can also come about in studies employing a before-after design (see Chapter 8). Under this scenario, prior to exposure to a stimulus, say, a new advertisement for an established brand, respondents are asked their attitudes about a set of brands; they are then exposed to the stimulus, and then asked for their attitudes again. The preexposure ("before") and postexposure ("after") measurements constitute two samples, and interest centers on the change, if any, taking place between the preexposure and postexposure measurements. Any statistical test of the extent of change must, however, take into consideration the dependency of the measurements since both measurements come from the same individual. In other words, any test of change must in some way adjust for the fact that an individual's postexposure score is at least in part affected by his or her preexposure score.

INDEPENDENT AND RELATED SAMPLES

When the samples are independent, responses from individuals in one sample in no way influence the responses from individuals in another sample. When the samples are related, for example studies employing before and after designs, responses in one sample can have been influenced by responses in another sample.

TESTS OF PROPORTIONS

Many types of marketing research studies attempt to make inferences based upon the number of respondents who gave a particular response to a question. In those cases we are testing hypotheses about proportions. In this section we consider hypothesis tests concerning proportions in situations involving: (1) a single sample, (2) two samples, independent and related, and (3) more than two samples, independent and related.

One-Sample Tests

The null hypothesis for a one-sample statistical hypothesis test of a proportion would state that its population value is equal to some predetermined value:

HO: $\pi = \pi^{\star}$

The alternative hypothesis, HA, depends on whether the test is one-sided or two-sided:

One-sided: HA: $\pi < \pi^{\star}$ or HA: $\pi > \pi^{\star}$

Two-sided: HA: $\pi \neq \pi^{\star}$

The appropriate test statistic is

$$Z = \frac{p - \pi^{\star}}{\sqrt{\dfrac{\pi^{\star}(1 - \pi^{\star})}{n}}} \tag{16-1}$$

where

p = Value of the proportion based upon the sample data
$\pi^{\star}$ = Prespecified population value of the proportion
n = Sample size

Exhibit 16–2 shows an abridged typical marketing research proposal for brand Q mouthwash. Results of the survey indicate that 46 of the 200 people interviewed (23 percent) were able to recall the commercial without any prompting (unaided recall). The category norms for a TV commercial for this product class is 18 percent. We can now use a one-sample hypothesis test of proportions to determine whether the sample proportion of 23 percent is statistically significantly greater than the category norm of 18 percent.

First, we specify HO and HA:

$$HO: \pi = .18$$
$$HA: \pi > .18$$

Note again that we could specify the null hypothesis as

EXHIBIT 16—2

Marketing Research Proposal: Day-After Recall Study

Brand:	Brand Q mouthwash
Project:	Day-after recall
Background and Objectives:	The ad agency has developed a TV ad for the introduction of the mouthwash. The objective of the ad is to create awareness of the brand. The objective of this research is to evaluate the awareness generated by the ad measured by aided- and unaided-recall scores.
Research Methods:	A minimum of 200 respondents who claim to have watched the TV show in which the ad was aired the night before will be contacted by telephone in 20 cities.
Information to Be Obtained:	The study will provide information on the incidence of unaided and aided recall.
Action Standard:	For the ad to be judged successful, the percentage of aided and unaided recall must score significantly above category norms at the 90 percent confidence level.

$HO: \pi \leq .18$

There is little reason to do this, however, for if we accept HO for values around .18, we would surely accept it for values much less than .18.

Now we compute the value of the test statistic according to equation 16–1:

$$Z = \frac{.23 - .18}{\sqrt{\dfrac{(.18)(.82)}{200}}}$$
$$= 1.84$$

The action standard in the proposal states that ad recall standards must exceed the norm at the 90 percent confidence level, so we set $\alpha = .10$. From the normal distribution table you can find that the critical value corresponding to a one-sided test at the stated α level is equal to 1.28. The value of the test statistic is therefore in the region of rejection, $1.84 > 1.28$, so we reject the null hypothesis (see Exhibit 16–3). Notice also that

$$Pr(p \geq .23) = Pr(Z \geq 1.84)$$
$$= .5 - .467$$
$$= .033$$

which means that if the new commercial were no better than the category norm, there would be only a 3.3 percent probability of observing a recall incidence proportion as large as 23 percent. Thus the available evidence indicates that the new commercial does score better than the norm.

Statistical data analysis computer programs do not, as a general rule, perform one-sample hypothesis tests on proportions. The reason for this is that the test statistic is easily calculated from summary descriptive statistics—to perform this test you need to know only the observed proportion and its standard error.

EXHIBIT 16–3

Hypothesis Test:
HO: π = .18,
HA: π > .18

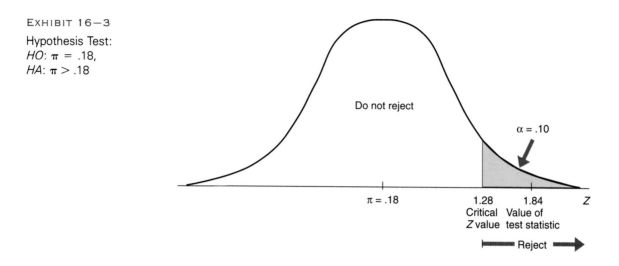

Two-Sample Tests

In some cases the statistical hypothesis to be tested involves equality, or the lack of it, between two sample groups. The two samples can be independent or related.

Independent samples. Where the groups under investigation are *independent,* respondents belong to one and only one of the groups. That is, we might want to test the equality of usage incidence of a particular product between men and women.

The appropriate null hypothesis for an independent sample test of proportions is that the population proportion in one group is equal to the population proportion in the other group. That is

$$HO: \pi_1 = \pi_2$$

The alternative hypothesis, *HA*, again depends on whether the test is one-sided or two-sided:

One-sided: $HA: \pi_1 < \pi_2$ *or* $HA: \pi_1 > \pi_2$

Two-sided: $HA: \pi_1 \neq \pi_2$

The appropriate test statistic is

$$Z = \frac{p_1 - p_2}{\sqrt{p^\star(1 - p^\star)\left(\dfrac{1}{n_1} + \dfrac{1}{n_2}\right)}}$$

(16-2)

EXHIBIT 16—4

Marketing Research
Proposal: Concept
Evaluation

Service:	Mid South Telephone Company
Project:	Concept evaluation
Background and Objectives:	Mid South Telephone, an independent telephone company, has developed a security service designed to appeal to both homeowners and renters. The purpose of this research is to evaluate the appeal of the service to the two groups: renters and owners.
Research Method:	Using census data, a minimum of 140 homeowners and 60 renters will be recruited to central locations at two locations in Mid South's market. At the central locations, respondents will view a TV pilot in which the test ad is embedded twice. After viewing the pilot, respondents will be given a personal interview.
Information to Be Obtained:	The study will provide information on attitudes and purchase-intent of the security services.
Action Standard:	Top-box purchase-intent scores will be compared between the two groups. If the groups differ on purchase intent at the 90 percent confidence level, management will consider a segmentation strategy.

The numerator of equation 16–2 is simply the difference between the observed proportions. The denominator of equation 16–2 is the standard error of the difference in the two observed proportions, where

$$p^\star = \frac{n_1 p_1 + n_2 p_2}{n_1 + n_2}$$

p_1 = Value of the proportion in group 1
p_2 = Value of the proportion in group 2
n_1 = Sample size of group 1
n_2 = Sample size of group 2

Consider the prototypical marketing research proposal shown in Exhibit 16–4. Managers of Mid South Telephone want to know whether the appeal of a new security system varies depending on whether a person is a homeowner or a renter.

Results of the study indicate that 17.9 percent of the homeowners (25 out of 140) definitely would buy (top-box) and 15 percent (9 out of 60) of the renters definitely would buy. The statistical hypothesis test to be performed will shed light on whether the observed difference in purchase intentions between these two groups (types of people) is statistically significant.

First we specify the null and alternative hypotheses:

HO: $\pi_O = \pi_r$
HA: $\pi_O \neq \pi_r$

where the subscripts o and r are used to denote the homeowner and renter groups, respectively. Notice that the alternative hypothesis is framed as a two-sided test. Without prior knowledge about homeowners and renters, this is a reasonable approach to take.

Hypothesis Test:
HO: $\pi_O = \pi_r$,
HA: $\pi_O \neq \pi_r$

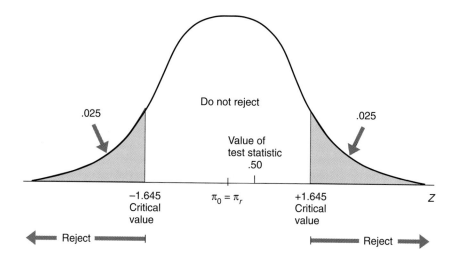

Next we calculate the test statistic. To accomplish this we need to first calculate $p\star$:

$$p\star = \frac{(.179)140 + .15(60)}{140 + 60} = .17$$

The estimate of the standard error of the difference in these two proportions is

$$\sqrt{(.17)(.83)\left(\frac{1}{140} + \frac{1}{60}\right)} = .058$$

Thus the test statistic is

$$Z = \frac{.179 - .15}{.058}$$
$$= .50$$

The action standard in the proposal states that the owner and renter groups must differ at the 90 percent confidence level before management would consider a segmentation strategy, that is, developing separate marketing programs. At $\alpha = .10$, the critical value from the normal distribution table is 1.645 (obtained by first dividing α by two before looking in the table because the alternative hypothesis is two-sided). As the value of the test statistic (.50) is less than the critical value (1.645), we cannot reject the null hypothesis (see Exhibit 16–5). We conclude, therefore, that there is no statistically significant difference between the owner group and the renter group with regard to their purchase intentions.

The manual computations for testing an independent two-sample hypothesis test on proportions can be automated by the use of computer programs. Exhibit 16–6 shows sample input and output from the MARITZ STATS interactive computer program for the two-sample hypothesis test just described.

Related samples.   Where the groups under investigation are not independent, the statistical hypothesis test concerns *related samples*. Say you are

EXHIBIT 16—6

Sample Input and Output for Independent Two-Sample Hypothesis Test on Proportions

---

T-TEST FOR INDEPENDENT GROUPS

This module computes the T-test statistic for every possible combination of groups within a category. You may test as many as 10 groups at a time. The program will indicate when a 'SIGNIFICANT DIFFERENCE' is found based on the critical value for the number of tests performed.

How many groups do you want to test? (2÷10, or Q to QUIT): 2*
What overall CONFIDENCE LEVEL do you want to use?
                    (choices are 80, 90, 95, and 99) : 90

For significance testing, classical statistical theory and CfMC use a POOLED estimate for the variance of a difference. Some statisticians and marketing researchers (like Randy) prefer a SEPARATE variances estimate.

Would you like to use a POOLED or SEPARATE variances estimate for this test? (P or S) p

```
** GROUP 1 **
PERCENTAGE     = .179
SAMPLE SIZE    = 140

** GROUP 2 **
PERCENTAGE     = .15
SAMPLE SIZE    = 60
```

	GROUP NUMBER	
	1	2
PCT (%)	0.18	0.15
FREQ	0	0
SAMPLE	140	60

Are all groups correct? (Y or N) y

GROUPS TESTED	Z-VALUE	SIGNIFICANT?	DEGREES OF FREEDOM
1 vs 2	0.046	No	198

2 GROUPS /   1 TESTS performed /   CRITICAL VALUE = 1.645

---

interested in whether usage incidences for a sample of respondents have increased after rolling out a new advertising campaign. Each time period during which you measure usage incidences represents one group; questioning the same respondents at another time period gives you a related-sample hypothesis test. The issue here is that the measurement collected in one time period is not independent of the measurement collected in the previous time period because it relates to the same individual.

In the case of related samples, the null and alternative hypotheses are the same as those specified in the case of independent samples. The test statistic is,

TABLE 16−1

Before and After Recall Scores

A.

After \ Before	Yes	No	Total
Yes	23	7	30
No	2	68	70
Total	25	75	100

B.

After \ Before	Yes	No	Total
Yes	a	b	
No	c	d	
Total			

in principle, also identical to the one in equation 16−2, but the denominator, that is, the standard error of the difference, needs to be adjusted to account for the fact that some or all of the respondents in one group are in the other group as well.

To illustrate, suppose a group of 100 customers are asked whether or not they remember seeing a particular advertisement. After a new campaign is launched, the same people are asked again if they recall seeing the ad. Consider Table 16−1, which provides a cross-classification of the possible outcomes. Panel A of the table provides the number of people falling in each of the possible outcome cells. In Panel B the cells are assigned letters (a, b, c, and d), which will be useful when describing how the standard error of the difference is manually computed. Before the new campaign was launched, 25 people (a + c) recalled seeing the ad, while after the new campaign 30 people (a + b) indicated that they had seen the advertisement. In testing the hypothesis of no change in recall, the proportions .25 (before) and .30 (after) are not independent because both include 23 people (cell a) who indicate that they recall seeing the ad both times.

Letting p_b and p_a denote before and after recall percentages, respectively, the null and alternative hypotheses can be stated as

$HO: \pi_a = \pi_b$

$HA: \pi_a > \pi_b$

Note we use a one-tailed alternative because it was expected that the new campaign would increase recall scores.

Using the notation of Table 16−1 Panel B, the appropriate test statistic for a related two-sample hypothesis test is[1]

$$Z = \frac{p_a - p_b}{\sqrt{\dfrac{b + c - [(b - c)^2/n]}{n(n - 1)}}} \qquad (16\text{−}3)$$

Manual computations show

$$\sqrt{\frac{7 + 2 - [(7 - 2)^2/100]}{100(99)}} = .030$$

and therefore

$$Z = \frac{.30 - .25}{.030}$$

$$= 1.67$$

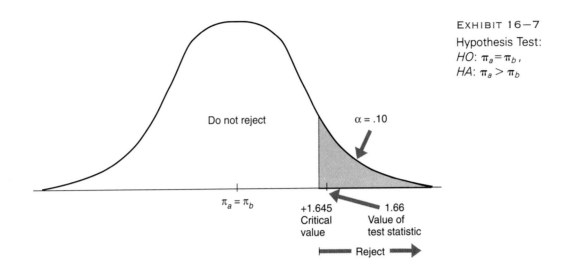

EXHIBIT 16-7
Hypothesis Test:
HO: $\pi_a = \pi_b$,
HA: $\pi_a > \pi_b$

At $\alpha = .05$, the critical value from the normal distribution table is 1.645. Because the value of the test statistic (1.67) is greater than the critical value (1.645), we can reject the null hypothesis of no change in before-after recall incidences (see Exhibit 16–7). In other words, the new campaign is significantly better, at least with respect to recall, than the campaign previously used.

The related two-sample hypothesis test just described is referred to as the *McNemar test*. This test is available in the MARITZ STATS interactive computer program. Exhibit 16–8 shows sample input and output.

Tests of More Than Two Samples

Perhaps data have been collected on more than two samples. The samples available may be independent or related. In either event, now we have more than two proportions to examine, and the question is whether there exist statistically significant differences among the groups.

Independent samples.   With G denoting the number of groups (i.e., proportions) that we wish to test, the null and alternative hypotheses can be stated as follows:

HO: $\pi_1 = \pi_2 = \ldots = \pi_G$
HA: Not all π's are equal

A chi-square test statistic is used to test this hypothesis. The logic behind the chi-square test is similar to that for the Z-statistic that we have been using—the proportions observed in the sample are compared to the proportions that we would expect to observe if the null hypothesis were indeed true. The chi-square test statistic, denoted by X^2, is

$$X^2 = \sum_{g=1}^{G} \frac{(O_g - E_g)^2}{E_g} \tag{16-4}$$

EXHIBIT 16—8

Sample Input and Output for Related One-Sample Hypothesis Test on Proportions

```
                            McNEMAR TEST
The McNemar Test is used to test for differences between two sets of answers
from the SAME sample when the data are nominal scale. An example is a YES=NO
measurement taken on the same respondents both before and after some event.
The data are arranged as follows, where the entries are frequency counts:
```

After Ad Campaign

Q: Have you, yourself, ever heard
   of MY-T-FINE lip balm?

		Yes	No
Before Ad Campaign	Yes	31	6
	No	57	34

```
The hypothesis to be tested for this example is
Is the proportion of respondents who have heard of MY-T-FINE lip balm
unchanged after the ad campaign?
Press <ENTER> to continue or Q to Quit . . .
Data format for McNemar test:
```

Condition 2

		Category 1	Category 2
Condition 1	Category 1	A	B
	Category 2	C	D

```
Now, please enter FREQUENCIES for variables B and C.
Enter FREQUENCY B: 7
Enter FREQUENCY C: 2
What CONFIDENCE LEVEL do you want to use?
    (choices are 80, 90, 95, and 99) : 90
Z =        1.667     SIGNIFICANTLY DIFFERENT        critical value = 1.645
```

where

O_g = Observed count in group g
E_g = Expected count in group g
G = Number of groups

To determine the region of rejection for the chi-square distribution, we need to specify the degrees of freedom, df, in addition to α, the significance level. The chi-square distribution is a skewed distribution whose shape varies with the number of degrees of freedom. As the degrees of freedom become larger, the shape of the chi-square distribution becomes more

TABLE 16–2

Determining the Area under the X^2 Distribution for a One-Tailed Test (α = .05, df = 5)

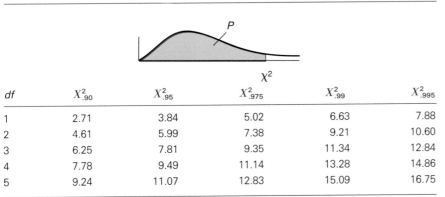

df	$X^2_{.90}$	$X^2_{.95}$	$X^2_{.975}$	$X^2_{.99}$	$X^2_{.995}$
1	2.71	3.84	5.02	6.63	7.88
2	4.61	5.99	7.38	9.21	10.60
3	6.25	7.81	9.35	11.34	12.84
4	7.78	9.49	11.14	13.28	14.86
5	9.24	11.07	12.83	15.09	16.75

symmetrical. The degrees of freedom in testing G proportions will be equal to

$$df = G - 1$$

An abridged version of the chi-square table is shown in Table 16–2. The chi-square distribution is not symmetrical and its shape varies with the degrees of freedom. To find the critical value, you locate the row corresponding to the appropriate degrees of freedom and move across to the column corresponding to the level of significance.

In Chapter 15 we introduced a package design study for a brand of women's facial moisturizer. Three different package designs of different colors were tested in terms of visibility and purchase intentions. Table 16–3 presents the observed counts for each package tested. Note that across the three package colors 156 of 300 respondents indicate a top-box purchase-intent score, which yields an overall top-box purchase incidence rate of 52 percent (156/300). Thus, in each cell (i.e., package design), we would expect around 52 people.

The null and alternative hypotheses can be stated as

HO: $\pi_c = \pi_g = \pi_y = .52$

HA: Not all three package designs are equal

The subscripts c, g, and y are used to denote the three package colors (cream, green, and yellow, respectively). If the various package colors do not produce different responses with respect to purchase intentions, we would expect that in each cell around 52 people would have checked the top-box as the null hypothesis states.

The test statistic is computed following equation 16–4.

$$X^2 = \frac{(47 - 52)^2}{52} + \frac{(60 - 52)^2}{52} + \frac{(49 - 52)^2}{52}$$

$$= 1.88$$

G = 3 groups, so df = 2. Setting α = .05 and consulting the chi-square distribution table, we find that the critical value for this test is 5.99. Therefore

TABLE 16—3

Top-Box Purchase Incidences for Three Package Designs

Package Design Color	Top-Box Incidences
Cream	47
Green	60
Yellow	49
	——
	156

we cannot reject the null hypothesis that all three colors result in the same level of purchase interest. This is shown in Exhibit 16–9.

The manual computations for testing a hypothesis test on proportions for three or more independent samples can be automated by use of computer programs. Exhibit 16–10 shows sample input and output from the MARITZ STATS interactive computer program for the three-sample hypothesis test just described.

Related samples.   In a hypothesis test of three or more related samples, the same individual is measured at more than two points in time. Because of the cost involved in attempting to contact the same people over time, these type of data occur infrequently in commercial marketing research. Though rarely conducted in the United States, longitudinal tracking of attitudes, usage, and opinions of the *same* customers would produce this kind of data.

Where the hypothesis test concerns the same people measured at three or more points in time, the appropriate test statistic is Cochran's Q test. The calculation of Cochran's Q is somewhat cumbersome, and, coupled with the fact that these type of data are not frequently encountered in commercial marketing research, we will not illustrate this type of hypothesis test. Interested readers can consult Siegel.[2]

TESTS OF MEANS

A slightly different approach to statistical hypothesis testing is appropriate when you want to make statements about population mean values rather than population proportions. In this section we consider hypothesis tests on means in situations involving: (1) a single sample, (2) two samples, independent and related, and (3) more than two samples, independent and related.

One-Sample Tests

The null hypothesis for a one-sample statistical hypothesis test of a mean states that its population value is equal to some predetermined value:

$$HO: \mu = \mu^\star$$

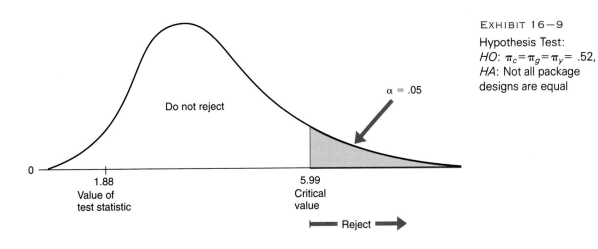

EXHIBIT 16—9

Hypothesis Test:
HO: $\pi_c = \pi_g = \pi_y = .52$,
HA: Not all package
designs are equal

The alternative hypothesis *HA* will depend on whether the test is one-sided or two-sided.

One-sided: *HA*: $\mu < \mu^\star$ or   *HA*: $\mu > \mu^\star$

Two-sided: *HA*: $\mu \neq \mu^\star$

The appropriate test statistic varies depending on whether the population variance is assumed to be known or must be estimated on the basis of the sample data. If the population variance is known, then the appropriate test statistic is

$$Z = \frac{\overline{X} - \mu^\star}{\sigma/\sqrt{n}} \qquad\qquad (16\text{-}5)$$

where $\overline{X}$ is the sample mean, which is our best estimate of μ, and σ is the population standard deviation. The critical value of the test statistic can be found by consulting the normal distribution table at the appropriate α level, in the same manner as in testing hypotheses about proportions.

If the population variance is not known, it must be estimated with the sample variance. In this case, the appropriate test statistic is

$$t = \frac{\overline{X} - \mu^\star}{s/\sqrt{n}} \qquad\qquad (16\text{-}6)$$

where *s* denotes the sample estimate of the population standard deviation. If *HO* is true, the test statistic is assumed to follow Student's *t*-distribution.

EXHIBIT 16—10

Sample Input and Output for Independent Three-Sample Hypothesis Test on Proportions

```
Do you want to perform a:
1) CHI-SQUARE GOODNESS-OF-FIT TEST, which measures the agreement between a
   given frequency distribution and a standard or norm
2) some other CHI-SQUARE TEST (HOMOGENEITY or INDEPENDENCE)
Please enter your choice (1, 2, or P to see the previous screen) 1
What overall CONFIDENCE LEVEL do you want to use?
How many categories are in the frequency distribution? 3
Do you want to enter FREQUENCY COUNTS or COLUMN PERCENTAGES? (F or P)
                      COL
                      1
                      _
ROW 1                 0
ROW 2                 0
ROW 3                 0
   FREQUENCY COUNT for row 1 column 1 = 47
   FREQUENCY COUNT for row 2 column 1 = 60
   FREQUENCY COUNT for row 3 column 1 = 49
                      TEST DIST.          STD. DIST.
                      (observed)          (expected)
ROW 1                 47                  0
                      30.1%               0.0%
ROW 2                 60                  0
                      38.5%               0.0%
ROW 3                 49                  0
                      31.4%               0.0%
COLUMN                156                 156
TOTALS                100.0%              100.0%
(standard distribution will be keyed in later)
Is this correct? (Y or N) y
Since you want to do a CHI-SQUARE GOODNESS-OF-FIT TEST, information about the
distribution you want to use for comparison is required. For the standard
(norm) frequency distribution you want to test agreement with:
The BASE (column total) is assumed to be 156
FREQUENCY COUNT for row 1 = 52
FREQUENCY COUNT for row 2 = 52
FREQUENCY COUNT for row 3 = 52
                      TEST DIST.          STD. DIST.
                      (observed)          (expected)
ROW 1                 47                  52
                      30.1%               33.3%
ROW 2                 60                  52
                      38.5%               33.3%
ROW 3                 49                  52
                      31.4%               33.3%
COLUMN                156                 156
TOTALS                100.0%              100.0%
Is the standard distribution data correct? (Y or N) y
                      TEST DIST.          STD. DIST.
                      (observed)          (expected)
ROW 1                 47                  52
                      30.1%               33.3%
ROW 2                 60                  52
                      38.5%               33.3%
ROW 3                 49                  52
                      31.4%               33.3%
COLUMN                156                 156
TOTALS                100.0%              100.0%
CHI-SQUARE            Significant?        DF           crit. value
1.885                 No                  2            5.991
Do another CHI-SQUARE TEST? (Y or N)
```

TABLE 16—4

Determining the Area under the *t*-Distribution for a Two-Tailed Test ($\alpha = .05$, df $= 30$)

df	$t_{.25}$	$t_{.10}$	$t_{.05}$	$t_{.025}$	$t_{.010}$	$t_{.005}$
20	.69	1.33	1.72	2.09	2.53	2.85
21	.69	1.32	1.72	2.08	2.52	2.83
22	.69	1.32	1.72	2.07	2.51	2.82
23	.69	1.32	1.71	2.07	2.50	2.81
24	.68	1.32	1.71	2.06	2.49	2.80
25	.68	1.32	1.71	2.06	2.49	2.79
26	.68	1.31	1.71	2.06	2.48	2.78
27	.68	1.31	1.70	2.05	2.47	2.77
28	.68	1.31	1.70	2.05	2.47	2.76
29	.68	1.31	1.70	2.05	2.46	2.76
30	.68	1.31	1.70	2.04	2.46	2.75
40	.68	1.30	1.68	2.02	2.42	2.70
60	.68	1.30	1.67	2.00	2.39	2.66
120	.68	1.29	1.66	1.98	2.36	2.62
∞	.67	1.28	1.64	1.96	2.33	2.58

Table 16–4 presents *t*-distribution values for a two-tailed test. To find the critical value of the test statistic, we need to set α and calculate the degrees of freedom that will equal $n - 1$, where n is the sample size. If you examine the *t*-distribution for larger degrees of freedom, that is, larger sample sizes, you will note that its values are less spread out. When df $= \infty$, the *t*- and *Z*-distributions give the same values, which reflects the fact that as $n \to \infty$, $s^2 = \sigma^2$.

To illustrate a one-sample test of means we use a potato chip package test, described in Exhibit 16–11. Package image was measured using a five-item semantic differential scale. Responses to the items are summed to form a composite score for each respondent, so the minimum score possible is 5 and the maximum score is 35. Across the 200 respondents participating in this test, the average image score equaled 27, with a standard deviation of 10.5. Years of package-testing experience with this scale have established a norm of 25 as the criterion to judge new package designs.

To test whether the new package design is superior to others that have been tested in the past, we first specify the null hypothesis:

HO: $\mu = 25$

or equivalently

HO: $\mu \leq 25$

EXHIBIT 16—11

Marketing Research
Proposal: Package Test

Brand:	Potato chips
Project:	Package test
Background and Objectives:	The brand group is considering changing the package design for its line of potato chips. The objective of the research is to determine the image portrayed from the recommended alternative package design.
Research Method:	A minimum of 200 respondents will be recruited at four major locations. Respondents will be exposed to the new package design through 35-mm slides of the recommended package and competing products. There will be 10 competing products, and, to minimize bias, three random layouts of each test will be used. Respondents will be exposed to the recommended package at four different intervals: ⅛ second, ¼ second, ½ second, and 1 second. Following exposure, respondents will be escorted to a different area and shown a storyboard of the product with its new package design.
Information to Be Obtained:	Data will be collected on visibility and image of the new package design.
Action Standard:	To be considered for further development, the new package design must score more than the norm, established from previous research with the current package design, at the 90 percent confidence level.

The alternative hypothesis is

HA: $\mu > 25$

The alternative hypothesis has been stated in terms of a one-sided test, because the expectation is that a new package design will outperform existing ones.

Next we compute the value of the test statistic according to equation 16–6, because we will use the estimate of the sample standard deviation.

$$t = \frac{27 - 25}{10.5 / \sqrt{200}}$$
$$= 2.69$$

The action standard in the proposal states that the new package design must score greater than the norm at the 90 percent confidence level; therefore, we set $\alpha = .10$ and compute df $= 200 - 1 = 199$. From the t-distribution table (Table 16–4), we find that the critical value corresponding to a one-sided test at the stated α level and df is equal to 1.28. The value of the test statistic is in the region of rejection, $(2.69 > 1.28)$, so we reject the null hypothesis (see Exhibit 16–12). Notice also that

$$\Pr(\overline{X} \geq 27) = \Pr(t_{.05;199} \geq 2.69) = \Pr(Z \geq 2.69)$$
$$= 1.0 - 0.9964$$
$$= .0036$$

which means that if the new package design were no better than the norm, there would be only a .36 percent probability of observing a mean response score as large as 27. Thus the available evidence indicates that the new package design does score better than the norm.

Statistical data analysis computer programs do not, as a general rule, perform one-sample hypothesis tests on means. The reason for this is that

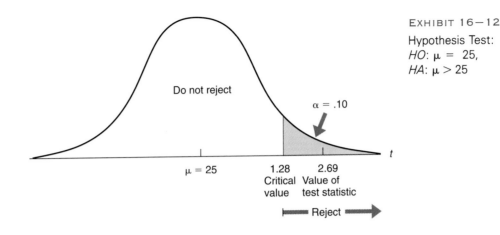

EXHIBIT 16—12

Hypothesis Test:
HO: μ = 25,
HA: μ > 25

the test statistic is easily calculated from summary descriptive statistics—to perform this test you only need to know the observed mean value and its standard error.

Two-Sample Tests

In some cases the statistical hypothesis to be tested involves equality, or the lack of it, between two sample groups. As is the case in tests of hypotheses about proportions, there are independent and related samples to consider. In the case of *independent* samples, respondents belong to one and only one of the groups. The standard example we gave is testing whether men and women have similar attitudes toward an established brand in a category. In the case of *related* samples, the groups under investigation are not independent—measurements are collected from the same individual at two or more times and are therefore related. For example, preexposure and postexposure attitudes differ from, say, exposure to a new advertising campaign.

Independent samples.   The appropriate null hypothesis for an independent sample test on means is that the population mean in one group is equal to the population mean in the other group. That is,

$$HO: \mu_1 = \mu_2$$

or equivalently

$$HO: \mu_1 - \mu_2 = 0$$

The alternative hypothesis *HA* is either one-sided or two-sided:

One-sided: $HA: \mu_1 < \mu_2$ or $HA: \mu_1 > \mu_2$

Two-sided: $HA: \mu_1 \neq \mu_2$

EXHIBIT 16–13

Marketing Research
Proposal: Corporate
Image Study

Service: Project:	Pirelli Cable Company Corporate image study
Background and Objectives:	Given the results of a previous image study, management at Pirelli commissioned a media campaign primarily designed to (1) increase awareness of the company and (2) create favorable perceptions of the company's technical support. The campaign was targeted to purchasing managers and technical managers at independent telephone companies with greater than 10,000 trunk lines. The objective of this study is to assess the level of awareness and perceptions of technical support provided by Pirelli by the target audiences.
Research Method:	A national probability telephone sample of 175 technical managers and 125 purchasing managers will be used to collect data on the perceptions of technical support and awareness levels.
Information to Be Obtained:	The study will provide information on awareness levels of the company and the perceptions of technical support provided by Pirelli.
Action Standard:	Media strategy will be assessed for change if there are any differences in perceptions or awareness levels between the two managerial groups at the 90 percent confidence level.

The appropriate test statistic is

$$t = \frac{\overline{X}_1 - \overline{X}_2}{\sqrt{s_1^2/n_1 + s_2^2/n_2}} \qquad (16\text{-}7)$$

The numerator of equation 16–7 is simply the difference between the observed means. The denominator of equation 16–7 is the standard error of the difference in the two observed means, where we have assumed that the variances in the two groups are not equal.[3] Critical values of the test statistic can be found by consulting the t-distribution table at the appropriate α level and df, where the degrees of freedom are equal to $n_1 + n_2 - 2$.

To illustrate statistical hypothesis testing on mean scores for two independent samples, we present the marketing research proposal shown in Exhibit 16–13. Managers of the Pirelli Cable Company want to find out whether perceptions of technical support services vary depending on the position of the respondent in the organization.

Perceptual ratings were measured on a nine-point agree-disagree scale. Results of the telephone survey reveal that the average perception score for technical managers is 7.3, and the average perception score for purchase managers is 8.2. The standard deviations of the scores in the technical and purchasing manager groups are 1.4 and 1.6, respectively.

First we specify the null and alternative hypotheses:

HO: $\mu_t = \mu_p$

HA: $\mu_t \neq \mu_p$

where the subscripts t and p are used to denote the technical and purchasing manager groups, respectively.

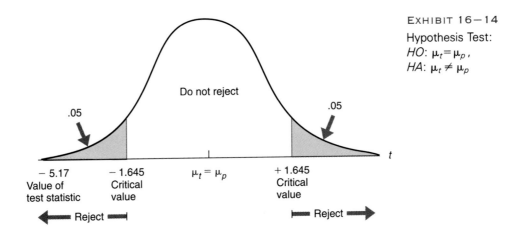

EXHIBIT 16—14

Hypothesis Test:
HO: $\mu_t = \mu_p$,
HA: $\mu_t \neq \mu_p$

Next we calculate the test statistic according to equation 16–10.

$$t = \frac{7.3 - 8.2}{\sqrt{[(1.4)^2/175] + [(1.6)^2/125]}}$$
$$= -5.06$$

The action standard in the proposal calls for the test to be performed at the 90 percent confidence level; thus we set $\alpha = .10$. As this is a two-tailed test, we divide α by two before consulting the t-distribution table. The critical value of the test statistic with

$$df = 125 + 175 - 2 = 298$$

is ± -1.645. The value of the test statistic (-5.06) is less than the critical value (-1.645), so we reject the null hypothesis and conclude that the purchasing managers have more favorable perceptions (see Exhibit 16–14).

The manual computations for testing a two-sample hypothesis test on mean scores for independent samples can be automated by use of computer programs. Exhibit 16–15 shows sample input and output from the MARITZ STATS interactive computer program for the two-sample hypothesis test just described.

Related samples. For statistical hypothesis testing of related samples, the null and alternative hypotheses are stated in a slightly different fashion from those for independent samples. It is useful to think in terms of a before-after design, which simplifies the discussion. In the case of means, the null and alternative hypotheses for related samples are stated in terms of difference scores, which reflects the fact that the same person is measured twice and appears in both samples. The appropriate null hypothesis is

$$HO: \delta = 0$$

The null hypothesis is one of no difference or, stated somewhat differently, no change in the before and after measurements.

Exhibit 16—15

Sample Input and Output for Independent Two-Sample Hypothesis Test on Mean Scores

---

T-TEST FOR INDEPENDENT GROUPS

This module computes the T-test statistic for every possible combination of groups within a category. You may test as many as 10 groups at a time. The program will indicate when a 'SIGNIFICANT DIFFERENCE' is found based on the critical value for the number of tests performed.

How many groups do you want to test? (2-10, or Q to QUIT): 2

** GROUP 1 **

```
MEAN                  = 7.3
STANDARD DEVIATION    = 1.4
SAMPLE SIZE           = 175
```

** GROUP 2 **

```
MEAN                  = 8.2
STANDARD DEVIATION    = 1.6
SAMPLE SIZE           = 125
```

	GROUP NUMBER	
	1	2
MEAN	7.30	8.20
STD	1.40	1.60
SAMPLE	175	125

Are all groups correct? (Y or N) y

What overall CONFIDENCE LEVEL do you want to use?
(choices are 80, 90, 95, and 99) : 90

For significance testing, classical statistical theory and CfMC use a POOLED estimate for the variance of a difference. Some statisticians and marketing researchers (like Randy) prefer a SEPARATE variances estimate.

Would you like to use a POOLED or SEPARATE variances estimate for this test? (p or S) S

GROUPS TESTED	T-VALUE	SIGNIFICANT?	DEGREES OF FREEDOM
1 vs 2	−5.06	Yes	298

2 GROUPS = 1 TESTS performed = CRITICAL VALUE = 1.645

The alternative hypothesis *HA* is either one-sided or two-sided:

One-sided: *HA*: δ < 0   or   *HA*: δ > 0

Two-sided: *HA*: δ ≠ 0

The test statistic has the usual form:

$$t = \frac{\bar{d}}{s_d / \sqrt{n}} \qquad (16\text{-}8)$$

In the numerator of equation 16–8 $\bar{d}$ denotes the mean value of the difference scores computed across each respondent, which is our best estimate of the extent to which change has occurred. s_d appearing in the denomi-

Subject	Preexposure Attitudes (A_1)	Postexposure Attitudes (A_2)	Attitude Change (d_i)
1	50	53	3
2	25	27	2
3	30	38	8
4	50	55	5
5	60	61	1
6	80	85	5
7	45	45	0
8	30	31	1
9	65	72	7
10	70	78	8

TABLE 16–5

Before-After Experimental Results

nator denotes the standard deviation of the difference scores, which is computed in the usual manner, that is

$$s_d = \sum_i \frac{(d_i - \bar{d})^2}{n - 1}$$

The test statistic is assumed to follow a t-distribution, if HO is indeed true, with df $= n - 1$.

Table 16–5 presents preexposure and postexposure attitude scores from a hypothetical advertising study involving 10 people. The table also gives the difference scores. The null and alternative hypotheses can be stated as

HO: $\delta = 0$

HA: $\delta > 0$

Note we have used a one-tailed alternative, because postexposure attitude shifts are expected to be favorable.

From the difference scores provided in Table 16–5, note that $\bar{d} = 4.0$ and $s_d = 3.02$. Following equation 16–8 we find

$$t = \frac{4.0}{3.02/\sqrt{10}}$$
$$= 4.19$$

At $\alpha = .05$, the critical value from the t-distribution table (see the Appendix at the end of this book) with df $= 9$ is 2.26. The value of the test statistic (4.19) is greater than the critical value (2.26), indicating that we can reject the null hypothesis of no change between preexposure and postexposure attitudes (see Exhibit 16–16).

Note that once the mean difference score is determined along with its associated standard error, the hypothesis test for a related-samples test of means is operationally analogous to a one-sample hypothesis test. Thus this test can be easily implemented by obtaining the necessary summary descriptive statistics for the difference scores, and no special computer software program is needed.

EXHIBIT 16–16

Hypothesis Test:
HO: $\delta = 0$,
HA: $\delta > 0$

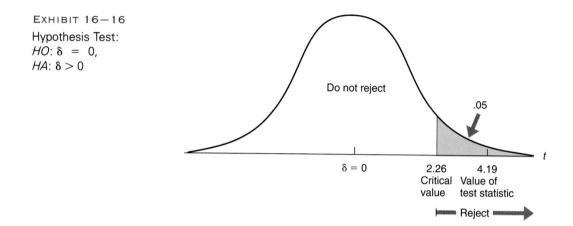

Tests of More Than Two Samples

A research design may require that data be collected from more than two samples. The samples available may be independent or related. In either event, the key question is the same as in the case of two means, namely, "Are the mean scores really different?" Once again the issue involves whether the sample means differ because of actual differences in the underlying population means, or whether the observed differences are primarily due to chance fluctuations. The statistical procedure used to test hypotheses on mean scores from more than two samples is called *analysis of variance* (ANOVA).

Independent samples.   Hypothesis tests on mean scores for three or more independent samples is best understood by way of example. Suppose a fleet manager is concerned with testing whether four brands of tires experience different amounts of tread loss after 25,000 miles of driving. Company policy is to replace a tire if the difference in thickness from its maximum tread thickness at the time the tire is mounted on the vehicle exceeds 13 mils (a mil equals 0.001 inch). The test question is complex because the tires cannot be tested in any abstract or theoretical way; they must be mounted on cars. Moreover, they can be mounted in various positions on the cars. Exhibit 16–17 shows two possible mounting schemes.

The positioning of the tires on the cars ultimately determines whether particular sources of variation can be analyzed. For example, it should be fairly obvious that design 1, which equips each car with a single brand of tire, will not allow you to distinguish between car performance and tire performance. Such a research design would totally confound tire brands and cars. In other words, there is no way to assess whether differences in tire performance are due to the tires or simply a result of the fact that the cars that are being used are different with respect to how they handle and drive.

In design 2 brands of tires have been randomly assigned to the cars. Here there is no confounding of tire and car performance variation because there is no systematic relationship between tires and cars. Table 16–6 presents differ-

	Design 1 Car				Design 2 Car			
	I	II	III	IV	I	II	III	IV
Brand Distribution:	A	B	C	D	C	A	D	A
	A	B	C	D	A	A	C	D
	A	B	C	D	D	B	B	B
	A	B	C	D	D	C	B	C

EXHIBIT 16—17

Two Possible Mounting Schemes

ences in tread loss (measured in mils) for 16 tires tested according to design 2. (There are some other calculations shown in the table that we will describe shortly). The car on which each tire was mounted is shown in parentheses. As expected, the mean tread loss for the four brands differs.

As usual, the null hypothesis is that there is no difference in the population means, or, equivalently, there is equality of population means. The null hypothesis is

$$HO: \mu_1 = \mu_2 = \mu_3 = \mu_4$$

The alternative hypothesis also assumes the usual form, namely, that at least one of the population means differs. For testing purposes, we will assume that all four populations are normally distributed, with a common variance of σ^2.[4]

Rejection or acceptance of the null hypothesis depends on the extent to which the sample means differ from one another. To measure the amount of variation in the sample means $\overline{X}_i$, we first compute the grand mean, $\overline{\overline{X}}$, and use it to calculate the variance. The variance formula assumes the same general form

$$s_{\overline{X}}^2 = \frac{1}{g} \sum (\overline{X}_i - \overline{\overline{X}})^2 \tag{16-9}$$

except that we substitute $\overline{X}_i$ for X_i, $\overline{\overline{X}}$ for $\overline{X}$, and g, which is the number of group means, for n.

Judging whether the $\overline{X}_i$ values are different requires that we assess whether such differences could conceivably come about because of chance fluctuations. For example, even if you could mount identical tires on identical cars and have each car driven by the same driver over the same terrain, you would still expect some differences in the sample means obtained. And such differences would be solely due to chance fluctuations. Thus the problem can be stated as judging whether the differences in Table 16–6 are of the same order of magnitude as those that result from chance fluctuations.

To measure these chance fluctuations, it seems reasonable to measure the variation in tread loss for each brand of tire separately. These individual brand variations can be computed by taking the sum of the squared deviations

$$\sum_{j=1}^{n} (X_{ji} - \overline{X}_i)^2 \tag{16-10}$$

TABLE 16–6

Tread Loss for Four
Brands of Tires: Design 2
(Random Assignment)

	Brand			
	A	B	C	D
	17 (I)	14 (II)	12 (I)	13 (I)
	14 (II)	14 (III)	12 (II)	11 (I)
	13 (II)	13 (III)	11 (III)	10 (III)
	13 (IV)	8 (IV)	9 (IV)	9 (IV)

$$\overline{X}_i = 14.25 \quad 12.25 \quad 11.0 \quad 10.75 \qquad \overline{\overline{X}} = 12.06$$
$$(\overline{X}_i - \overline{\overline{X}}) = 2.19 \quad 0.19 \quad -1.06 \quad -1.31 \qquad \Sigma(\overline{X}_i - \overline{\overline{X}}) = 0^*$$
$$(\overline{X}_i - \overline{\overline{X}})^2 = 4.80 \quad 0.04 \quad 1.12 \quad 1.72 \qquad \Sigma(\overline{X}_i - \overline{\overline{X}})^2 = 7.68$$

$^*\Sigma(\overline{X}_i - \overline{\overline{X}})$ does not equal 0 exactly because of rounding errors.
Adapted from Charles Hicks, *Fundamental Concepts in the Design of Experiments* (New York: Holt, Rinehart and Winston, 1982).

where X_{ji} is the jth observation on brand i. For ease of notation, let SS_i ($i = 1, 2, \ldots, G$) denote the G individual-brand–variation components.

After computing the sum of the squared deviations for each brand of tire, a pooled estimate s_p^2 of the within-brand variance can be obtained by summing and dividing by the total degrees of freedom. With n observations on each tire, there are, in general,

$$g(n - 1) \tag{16-11}$$

degrees of freedom, and the pooled variance is

$$s_p^2 = \frac{SS_1 + SS_2 + \cdots + SS_G}{g(n - 1)} \tag{16-12}$$

To illustrate let's calculate the between-brand variance, $s_{\overline{X}}^2$, and the within-brand variance, s_p^2, from the data provided in Table 16–6. First,

$$s_{\overline{X}}^2 = \frac{7.68}{4 - 1} = 2.56$$

For s_p^2 we begin by computing the sum of squared deviations for each brand:

$$\sum_{j=1}^{4} (X_{j1} - \overline{X}_1)^2 = (17 - 14.25)^2 + (14 - 14.25)^2 + (13 - 14.25)^2$$
$$+ (13 - 14.25)^2$$
$$= 10.75$$

$$\sum_{j=1}^{4} (X_{j2} - \overline{X}_2)^2 = (14 - 12.25)^2 + (14 - 12.25)^2 + (13 - 12.25)^2$$
$$+ (8 - 12.25)^2$$
$$= 24.75$$

$$\sum_{j=1}^{4} (X_{j3} - \overline{X}_3)^2 = (12 - 11)^2 + (12 - 11)^2 + (11 - 11)^2$$
$$+ (9 - 11)^2$$
$$= 6$$

$$\sum_{j=1}^{4} (X_{j4} - \overline{X}_4)^2 = (13 - 10.75)^2 + (11 - 10.75)^2 + (10 - 10.75)^2 \\ + (9 - 10.75)^2 \\ = 8.75$$

Summing and dividing by the appropriate degrees of freedom yields

$$s_p^2 = \frac{10.75 + 24.75 + 6 + 8.75}{4(4 - 1)} = \frac{50.25}{12} = 4.2$$

Computing the within- and between-brand variances provides a standard of comparison. In essence, the logic is that if the variance in the sample means (the between variance, $s_{\overline{x}}^2$) is large relative to the chance fluctuation (the within variance, s_p^2), then we should conclude that the means are different.

If all four samples actually come from the same population, both s_p^2 and $s_{\overline{x}}^2$ can be used to infer σ^2, the population variance. To decide whether $s_{\overline{X}}^2$ is large relative to s_p^2, we examine the ratio $s_{\overline{X}}^2/s_p^2$. Actually, the test statistic we use is a slight modification of this ratio:

$$F = \frac{n s_{\overline{X}}^2}{s_p^2} \tag{16-13}$$

It is called an F-ratio in honor of the famous English statistician Sir Ronald Fisher (1890–1962).

Because

$$\sigma_{\overline{X}}^2 = \frac{\sigma^2}{n}$$

we have the following expression for σ^2:

$$\sigma^2 = n\sigma_{\overline{X}}^2$$

Thus, by introducing n in the numerator of equation 16–13, the numerator and denominator should be equal if the samples come from the same population, and hence F should fluctuate around 1 if HO is indeed true. In other words, the larger F is, the less probable the null hypothesis of equal population means.

To find the p-value associated with a particular value of F, we use the F-distribution table. The F-distribution depends on the degrees of freedom in the numerator, which is equal to $g - 1$, and the degrees of freedom in the denominator, which is equal to $g(n - 1)$.

The F-distribution table is read in much the same way as the t-distribution table. Consider Table 16–7, which presents a portion of the complete F-distribution table that appears in the Appendix at the end of the book. Suppose you are testing at the 95 percent confidence level and the F-ratio has 4 degrees of freedom in the numerator and 20 degrees of freedom in the denominator. To find the correct critical value, you locate the row corresponding to 20 (the degrees of freedom in the denominator) and the column corresponding to 4 (the degrees of freedom in the numerator) for $F_{.05}$. The correct value is 2.87.

TABLE 16—7

Determining the Area under the F-Distribution (4 df in numerator, 20 df in denominator, $\alpha = .05$)

v_2†	v_1*								
	1	2	3	4	5	6	7	8	9
1	161.40	199.50	215.70	224.60	230.20	234.00	236.80	238.90	240.50
2	18.51	19.00	19.16	19.25	19.30	19.33	19.35	19.37	19.38
3	10.13	9.55	9.28	9.12	9.01	8.94	8.89	8.85	8.81
4	7.71	6.94	6.59	6.39	6.26	6.16	6.09	6.04	6.00
5	6.61	5.79	5.41	5.19	5.05	4.95	4.88	4.82	4.77
6	5.99	5.14	4.76	4.53	4.39	4.28	4.21	4.15	4.10
7	5.59	4.74	4.35	4.12	3.97	3.87	3.79	3.73	3.68
8	5.32	4.46	4.07	3.84	3.69	3.58	3.50	3.44	3.39
9	5.12	4.26	3.86	3.63	3.48	3.37	3.29	3.23	3.18
10	4.96	4.10	3.71	3.48	3.33	3.22	3.14	3.07	3.02
11	4.84	3.98	3.59	3.36	3.20	3.09	3.01	2.95	2.90
12	4.75	3.89	3.49	3.26	3.11	3.00	2.91	2.85	2.80
13	4.67	3.81	3.41	3.18	3.03	2.92	2.83	2.77	2.71
14	4.60	3.74	3.34	3.11	2.96	2.85	2.76	2.70	2.65
15	4.54	3.68	3.29	3.06	2.90	2.79	2.71	2.64	2.59
16	4.49	3.63	3.24	3.01	2.85	2.74	2.66	2.59	2.54
17	4.45	3.59	3.20	2.96	2.81	2.70	2.61	2.55	2.49
18	4.41	3.55	3.16	2.93	2.77	2.66	2.58	2.51	2.46
19	4.38	3.52	3.13	2.90	2.74	2.63	2.54	2.48	2.42
20	4.35	3.49	3.10	2.87	2.71	2.60	2.51	2.45	2.39
21	4.32	3.47	3.07	2.84	2.68	2.57	2.49	2.42	2.37
22	4.30	3.44	3.05	2.82	2.66	2.55	2.46	2.40	2.34
23	4.28	3.42	3.03	2.80	2.64	2.53	2.44	2.37	2.32
24	4.26	3.40	3.01	2.78	2.62	2.51	2.42	2.36	2.30
25	4.24	3.39	2.99	2.76	2.60	2.49	2.40	2.34	2.28
26	4.23	3.37	2.98	2.74	2.59	2.47	2.39	2.32	2.27
27	4.21	3.35	2.96	2.73	2.57	2.46	2.37	2.31	2.25
28	4.20	3.34	2.95	2.71	2.56	2.45	2.36	2.29	2.24
29	4.18	3.33	2.93	2.70	2.55	2.43	2.35	2.28	2.22
30	4.17	3.32	2.92	2.69	2.53	2.42	2.33	2.27	2.21
40	4.08	3.23	2.84	2.61	2.45	2.34	2.25	2.18	2.12
60	4.00	3.15	2.76	2.53	2.37	2.25	2.17	2.10	2.04
120	3.92	3.07	2.68	2.45	2.29	2.17	2.09	2.02	1.96
∞	3.84	3.00	2.60	2.37	2.21	2.10	2.01	1.94	1.88

*v_1 = Degrees of freedom for numerator.

† v_2 = Degrees for freedom for denominator.

We have already calculated how much variance there is among the four sample means:

$$s_{\overline{X}}^2 = 2.56$$

and how much variance there is within each of the four brands of tires:

$$s_p^2 = 4.2$$

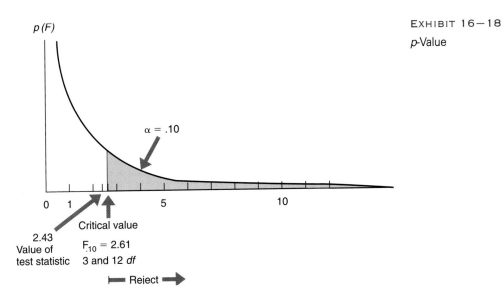

From equation 16–13 the F-ratio is

$$F = \frac{ns_{\bar{X}}^2}{s_p^2}$$

$$= \frac{4(2.56)}{4.2} = 2.43$$

The degrees of freedom for F are

$$df = (g - 1) \text{ and } g(n - 1)$$
$$= (4 - 1) \text{ and } 4(3 - 1)$$
$$= 3 \text{ and } 12$$

You must now examine the F-distribution table in the Appendix and locate the row corresponding to 12 and the column corresponding to 3 at the appropriate α level. Looking down the column, you locate the critical F-value that corresponds to the confidence level you are testing at. If you wish to test at the 90 percent confidence level, for instance, $\alpha = .10$, the critical F-value is $F_{.10} = 2.61$. Because the observed F-value of 2.43 is less than the critical value $F_{.10} = 2.61$, you conclude that

$$p\text{-value} > .10$$

and there is no reason to reject the null hypothesis of equal mean tread loss among the four brands. This result is graphed in Exhibit 16–18.

A convenient way to summarize the calculation of the F-ratio is to construct an ANOVA table, whose general form is shown in Table 16–8. The first row gives the calculations for the numerator of the F-ratio, and the second row the calculations for the denominator. The mean squares

TABLE 16–8

One-Way ANOVA Table with Equal Sample Sizes

Source of Variation	Sum of Squares, SS	df	Mean Squares, MS	F-Ratio
Factor G: differences between brand means $\bar{X}_i$	$SS_g = n \sum_{i=1}^{g} (\bar{X}_i - \bar{\bar{X}})^2$	$(g-1)$	$MS_G = SS_G/(g-1)$ $= ns_{\bar{X}}^2$	$F = \dfrac{MS_G}{MS_E}$ $= \dfrac{ns_{\bar{X}}^2}{s_p^2}$
Error E: differences between observations X_{ji} and means $\bar{X}_i$	$SS_E = \sum_{i=1}^{g}\sum_{j=1}^{n} (X_{ji} - \bar{X}_i)^2$	$g(n-1)$	$MS_E = SS_E/g(n-1)$ $= s_p^2$	
Total	$SS_T = \sum_{i=1}^{g}\sum_{j=1}^{n} (\bar{X}_{ji} - \bar{\bar{X}})^2$	$gn-1$		

(MS) column is obtained by taking the sum of squared deviations (SS) and dividing by the appropriate df, which gives the variances.

The ANOVA table is useful to express several fundamental relationships. The first column defines the sources of variation as the constituent components of the overall sum of squared deviations. The overall variation is obtained simply by computing the sum of squared deviations of each observation from the grand mean. A double summation sign is used to indicate that the summation is over both rows and columns, that is, over all elements in Table 16–8. The first component, labeled factor G, gives the between variation that is attributable to brands, and the second component, labeled error E, gives the within variation that is due to chance fluctuations or random error. From the table we see the important result that

$$SS_{\text{Total}} = SS_G + SS_E \qquad (16\text{-}14)$$

and a similar result holds for the respective degrees of freedom shown in the df column.

It is customary to refer to the variance between brands as the *explained variance,* because differences among the respective brands can be explained by the fact that the brands come from different populations. It is also customary to refer to the within-brand variance as the *unexplained variance,* because it is random and cannot be explained by differences due to brands. The *F*-ratio is sometimes referred to as the *variance ratio:*

$$F = \frac{\text{Explained variance}}{\text{Unexplained variance}} \qquad (16\text{-}15)$$

Table 16–9 presents the ANOVA table for the car and tire data we have been discussing. The between sums of squares (SS_G) appearing in the table can be derived from Table 16–6:

$$SS_G = n[(\bar{X}_1 - \bar{\bar{X}}) + (\bar{X}_2 - \bar{\bar{X}}) + (\bar{X}_3 - \bar{\bar{X}}) + (\bar{X}_4 - \bar{\bar{X}})]$$
$$= 4[4.80 + 0.04 + 1.12 + 1.72]$$
$$= 30.69$$

Source	SS	df	MS	F-Ratio	p-Value
Brands	30.69	3	10.2	$\frac{10.2}{4.2} = 2.43$	$p > .10$
Error	50.25	12	4.2		
Total	80.94	15			

The within sums of squares (SS_E) has been calculated in computing the pooled estimate of the within-brand variance. From previous computations note that

$$SS_E = \sum_{j=i}^{4} (X_{j1} - \overline{X}_1) + \sum_{j=1}^{4}(X_{j2} - \overline{X}_2) + \sum_{j=1}^{4}(X_{j3} - \overline{X}_3) + $$
$$\sum_{j=1}^{4}(X_{j4} - \overline{X}_4) \qquad (16\text{-}16)$$
$$= 10.75 + 24.75 + 6 + 8.75$$
$$= 50.25$$

The total sums of squares (SS_T) can also be derived from Table 16–6:

$$SS_T = \sum_{j}\sum_{i} (X_{ji} - \overline{\overline{X}})^2$$
$$= (17 - 12.06)^2 + (14 - 12.06)^2 + \cdots + (9 - 12.06)^2$$
$$= 80.94$$

Note that

$$SS_T = SS_G + SS_E$$
$$80.94 = 30.69 + 50.25$$

In reasonably sized problems, the manual computations necessary to construct the ANOVA table can become tedious. ANOVA is, however, relatively simple to perform if you use a computer program. All of the commercially available statistical packages such as SPSSX, SAS, BMDP, SYSTAT, and STATGRAPHICS provide ANOVA programs. Exhibit 16–19 presents sample input and output statements for the ANOVA problem we have been discussing. The ANOVA was performed with SAS.

Related samples.   In a hypothesis test of three or more related samples, the same individuals are measured at more than two points in time. As we indicated previously, this type of research design can be extremely costly. Consequently, with the exception of longitudinal tracking studies, this type of data occurs infrequently in commercial marketing research.

Where the hypothesis test concerns the differences in the mean scores for people who have been measured at three or more points in time, *repeated-measures* ANOVA is the appropriate statistic procedure to use. Repeated-measures ANOVA can become rather complex with issues far beyond the scope of our discussion. Most intermediate and advanced statistical textbooks contain some treatment of repeated-measures designs.[5]

EXHIBIT 16—19

Sample Input and Output for ANOVA Problem

```
1           SAS(R) LOG  CMS SAS 5.18              VM/CMS USER BATCH1
NOTE: COPYRIGHT (C) 1984, 1986 SAS INSTITUTE INC., CARY, N.C.  27512, U.S.A.
NOTE: BATCH1 RELEASE 5.18 AT UNIVERSITY OF SOUTH CAROLINA (01416004).
NOTE: CPUID   VERSION = FF  SERIAL = 011636  MODEL = 4381.
NOTE: SAS OPTIONS SPECIFIED ARE:
      LEAVE=OK LEAVE=64K MACRO
1 OPTIONS LS=72;
2
3 DATA ANOVA;
4 INPUT Z X1 X2 Y;
5 LABEL Z='ID' X1'CELL' X2='TIRE' Y='DEPENDENT';
NOTE: DATA SET WORK. ANOVA HAS 16 OBSERVATIONS AND 4 VARIABLES.
NOTE: THE DATA STATEMENT USED 0.11 SECONDS AND 60K.
23 ;
24 PROC ANOVA;
25 CLASSES X1;
26 MODEL Y=X1;
27 TITLE "ONE WAY ANOVA';
NOTE: THE PROCEDURE ANOVA USED 0.22 SECONDS AND 892K
      AND PRINTED PAGES 1 TO 2.
NOTE: SAS USED 892K MEMORY.
NOTE: SAS INSTITUTE INC.
      SAS CIRCLE
      PO BOX 8000
      CARY, N.C. 27512-8000
           ONE WAY ANOVA
                     14:17 WEDNESDAY, JANUARY 22, 1992
      ANALYSIS OF VARIANCE PROCEDURE
         CLASS LEVEL INFORMATION
      CLASS      LEVELS    VALUES
      X1           4        1 2 3 4
NUMBER OF OBSERVATIONS IN DATA SET = 16
 ONE WAY ANOVA
                              14:17 WEDNESDAY, JANUARY 22, 1992
ANALYSIS OF VARIANCE PROCEDURE
DEPENDENT            DEPENDENT
VARIABLE: Y
```

SOURCE	DF	SUM OF SQUARES	MEAN SQUARE
MODEL	3	30.68750000	10.22916667
ERROR	12	50.25000000	4.18750000
CORRECTED TOTAL	15	80.93750000	
MODEL F =	2.44		PR > F = 0.1145
R-SQUARE	C.V.	ROOT MSE	Y MEAN
0.379151	16.9645	2.04633819	12.06250000
SOURCE	DF	ANOVA SS	F VALUE PR > F
X1	3	30.68750000	0.1145

SUMMARY

Hypothesis testing procedures permit specific claims about a population of interest to be tested on the basis of data collected from a sample of customers. Essentially, statistical hypothesis testing allows the manager to assess the probability that the claims made about the population are true.

This chapter considered hypothesis testing procedures for proportions and mean scores under a variety of situations. We began by discussing those factors that influence the choice of a hypothesis testing procedure.

Next, attention was directed to hypothesis testing for proportions for one sample, two samples, and more than two samples. We discussed the appropriate testing procedure for independent and related samples when more than one sample is available. Hypothesis tests concerning mean scores were also treated. Again the discussion considered one-sample, two-sample, and more-than-two-sample hypothesis tests for independent and related samples.

KEY CONCEPTS

Independent versus Related Samples

Z-Test Statistic

Chi-Square Distribution

t-Test Statistic

t-Distribution

F-Test Statistic

F-Distribution

ANOVA Table

Explained and Unexplained Variation

REVIEW QUESTIONS

1. Discuss the difference between conducting an independent sample hypothesis test and a related sample test.

2. The brand group for a manufacturer of washing machines believed that at most 30 percent of the households owning a washing machine used liquid detergent. If the proportion was greater than the hypothesized value, management would consider adding a line of products specifically designed for the use of liquid detergent. A survey of 500 households indicated that 165 used liquid detergent. What do you conclude?

3. In a coupon test the action standard called for a difference between a test coupon and a control coupon at the 90 percent confidence level. That is, to be considered for use the test coupon must outscore the control coupon at the 90 percent confidence level. To this end, samples of 500 test coupons and 500 control coupons were randomly delivered. The results indicated that 7 percent of the control coupons and 10 percent of the test coupons were redeemed. What do you conclude and why?

4. Your college of business was interested in starting a program to prepare students for the GMAT exam. The program consisted of a three-week course designed to familiarize students with the content areas of the exam. To evaluate the program, the college randomly selected 10 students from among the 210 students in the senior class that had already taken the exam. These students participated in the three-week preparatory class. The average GMAT score for all 210 students was 570. The scores before and after the course are given in the table below.

a. What do you conclude about the course? Be sure to substantiate your conclusions.

b. Comment on the general procedure employed by the college.

Student	Before	After
1	550	555
2	580	590
3	560	555
4	570	575
5	565	580
6	585	590
7	560	570
8	570	565
9	575	585
10	585	595

ENDNOTES

1. W. J. Dixon and F. J. Massey, *Introduction to Statistical Analysis* (New York: McGraw-Hill), p. 250.

2. S. Siegel, *Nonparametric Statistics for the Behavioral Sciences* (New York: McGraw-Hill 1956) pp. 161–63.

3. If the variances of the two samples are equal, a pooled variance estimate should be used in the denominator of equation 16–7.

4. All that we say in this chapter holds approximately for nonnormal populations with equal or unequal variances as well, as long as the sample sizes are about equal.

5. A particularly thorough treatment of ANOVA and repeated-measures designs can be found in B. J. Winer, *Statistical Principles in Experimental Design* (New York: McGraw-Hill, 1971).

Correlation and Regression Analysis

THE GREAT CEO PAY SWEEPSTAKES

If you think American CEOs are overpaid, you'll find this latest news depressing: They're making more than ever, and the connection between their pay and performance is weakening.

These are among the results of Fortune's third annual survey of CEO compensation. The study examines CEO pay at 200 major companies drawn primarily from the largest enterprises on the Fortune Industrial 500 and Service 500 lists. As in previous studies, foreign-owned companies and companies at which the CEO has not served an entire fiscal year in that position have been excluded. Also as in the past, a standard computer program for performing the statistical technique known as multiple regression analysis has calculated how much each CEO would have received had he been paid

CEOs WHO MOST EXCEEDED THE COMPUTER MODEL'S PAY

	CEO	Company	Performance IQ*	Compensation (in thousands)		
				Actual	Model	Percent Higher
1	James Wood	A&P†	105	$28,160	$3,240	769%
2	Paul B. Fireman	Reebok International	100	$14,610	$1,770	725%
3	Martin S. Davis	Paramount	102	$17,160	$2,250	663%
4	Michael D. Eisner	Walt Disney	114	$35,410	$7,280	386%
5	Richard K. Eamer	Nat'l Medical Ent.	99	$13,840	$3,600	284%
6	Roberto C. Goizueta	Coca-Cola	108	$10,640	$3,220	230%
7	Alan C. Greenberg	Bear Stearns	99	$ 4,530	$1,540	194%
8	S. Parker Gilbert	Morgan Stanley	108	$ 7,170	$2,930	145%
9	Richard L. Gelb	Bristol-Myers Squibb	105	$ 6,590	$2,770	138%
10	Anthony J. O'Reilly	H. J. Heinz	106	$10,360	$4,420	134%

*Elements of Performance IQ: total return to investors during CEO's tenure, ten-year trend in total return, five-year average ratio of stock price to book value, five-year growth of sales and assets, five-year validity of sales and asset growth, five-year average return on equity, five-year trend in return one quity.
†For fiscal year ended 2/28/89.

according to the prevailing standards of the whole group. The program figures the average weights these companies as a group assign to such factors as company size, industry, long-term performance, business risk, and CEO tenure in determining the CEO's compensation. Then it assigns these average weights to each CEO individually in order to arrive at what is called the computer-model pay. In the select group of those seven CEOs who have crossed the $10 million mark, the lowest paid, if that term can be used at all, is Anthony O'Reilly of H. J. Heinz, who earned $10.4 million last year. The highest-paid, Michael Eisner of Walt Disney, earned $35.4 million.

The average pay of all 200 CEOs is an eye-popping $2.8 million, not counting perquisites and such fringe benefits as

AND THOSE WHO LAGGED FURTHEST BEHIND

	CEO	Company	Performance IQ	Compensation (in thousands)		Percent Lower
				Actual	Model	
191	Michael W. Wright	Super Valu Stores*	101	$1,160	$3,230	−64%
192	M. Anthony Burns	Ryder System	98	$1,410	$4,010	−65%
193	Leon Hess	Amerada Hess	94	$ 300	$ 930	−68%
194	George M.C. Fisher	Motorola	98	$1,180	$3,680	−68%
195	A. Dano Davis	Winn-Dixie Stores	102	$ 530	$1,660	−68%
196	James T. Lynn	Aetna Life & Casualty	98	$1,450	$4,590	−68%
197	James C. Cotting	Navistar International	94	$ 590	$1,900	−69%
198	Lew R. Wasserman	MCA	101	$ 560	$2,280	−75%
199	David D. Glass	Wal-Mart Stores†	109	$ 840	$3,490	−76%
200	Harold B. Finch Jr.	Nash-Finch	102	$ 380	$1,720	−78%

*For fiscal year ended 2/28/89.
†For fiscal year ended 1/31/89.

pensions and insurance. But talk of averages doesn't begin to reflect the status of the $10 million men, who are in a class by themselves. They collectively earned $104 million more last year than their computer-model pay—what they would have received if paid according to the prevailing standards of the group. If their pay had been excluded from the model, the average pay of the remaining 193 CEOs would have dropped by 20%—from $2.8 million to $2.3 million.

How to calculate CEO pay? We start with salary and bonus—that's the easy part. We then consider the value of any grants of restricted stock—shares the executive receives free but may not sell during a restriction period, typically five years—and payouts under other incentive plans. If a CEO receives stock options, we assign them a value at the time of grant. Why not wait until he exercises them and takes his gain, when the precise value can be determined? Because many CEOs don't realize option gains until after retirement, so the gains are never reported. To assign options a value, we use the highly regarded Black-Scholes option pricing model.

A CEO receives salary and bonus every year, but the other forms of compensation may occur less often, so counting their entire value in a single year could be unfair. We therefore spread their value over three years, including one-third in this year's pay figure, one-third next year, and one-third the year after that.

CEO pay is not entirely senseless. The computer program that calculates the prevailing compensation standards of the group also reveals which factors do and don't influence pay levels. For example, company size has an effect. A 10% increase in size—measured by a combination of sales, assets, and number of employees—brings an average 2% increase in pay.

Long-term company performance is another influence. This study summarizes it in a compound rating called Performance IQ, which comprises three stock-market-related measures and six accounting measures (see table footnote for details). The average Performance IQ for the group is 100, and a ten-point rise in Performance IQ earns a 24% increase in pay. Riskier companies pay more: When Beta, the widely used measure of stock price volatility, rises from 1 to 1.1, CEO pay tends to rise 4%.

All these influences—company size, performance, business risk, and the others—together account for 45% of the variation in CEO pay. What does that say about the remaining 55% of pay variation? It says, unhappily, that this remaining variation has nothing whatever to do with these many factors. In other words, it says that the market for CEO services is chaotic.

It may be getting even more so. Scarcely anyone would dispute that company performance ought to be a major factor, if not the major factor, in setting CEO pay. Yet the link between the two seems to be weakening. Two years ago in this study a ten-point increase in Performance IQ was good for a 31% rise in pay. Last year the percentage dropped to 26%, and this year, as noted, it is 24%. More unsettling, the primary reason for linking pay and performance—namely, that this will motivate the CEO to perform better—may be invalid. Even if it is, of course, there remains the secondary reason, which is that paying more for better performance is simply fair and just—as long as the company also lowers pay for poor performance.

Source: Graef S. Crystal, *Fortune,* June 18, 1991, pp. 94–95. Reprinted with permission.

INTRODUCTION

If CEO pay were based solely on performance, it would be a simple calculation. Instead, it is based on company size, industry, long-term performance, business risk, and CEO tenure. Using regression analysis to predict what CEO compensation should be shows how complex the process is.

Understanding the relationships that exist between sets of variables is extremely important in marketing research as well. In this chapter we discuss measures of correlation and regression analysis. Measures of correlation quantify the extent to which two variables are associated. Regression analysis is a model that attempts to understand the dependence of one variable, called the **dependent** or **criterion variable** (for example, CEO compensation), on one or more other variables, called the **explanatory** or **independent variables** (for example, performance). The point is to predict the mean or average value of the former on the basis of the known values of the latter.[1]

The chapter begins with a discussion of correlation and covariance, concepts that we introduced previously in Chapters 8 and 14. Next, the discussion turns to calculating correlation coefficients for different measurement scales, including nominal, ordinal, and interval. Because the two variables being correlated may have different measurement properties, we then demonstrate how correlation coefficients can be computed for variables having mixed scales. The remainder of the chapter is devoted to the regression model. First, simple regression, which considers the relationship between a dependent variable and a single explanatory variable, is discussed. Then we turn to multiple regression, which considers the relationship between two or more explanatory variables, and discuss several important conditions underlying the proper use of this procedure.

The statistical concepts discussed in this chapter will be illustrated with manual computations. As stated in Chapter 16, the reason for this is that such activities speed and enhance the learning process and reinforce the concepts being introduced. Where appropriate, we will also present sample input and output from SPSSX, a widely used statistical data analysis package.

CRITERION OR DEPENDENT VARIABLE
The variable to be predicted.

EXPLANATORY OR INDEPENDENT VARIABLE
The variable upon which the prediction is based.

CORRELATION

Before demonstrating how a correlation coefficient is computed under different measurement conditions, let us review the concept of correlation. To say that two variables correlate implies that there is a systematic relationship between them. Exhibit 17–1 presents a scatter diagram of the relationship between units sold of 20 varieties of a canned soup and the shelf space allocated to each variety. Notice that there is a systematic relationship between these two variables; the more shelf space allocated to a variety, the more units are sold. Thus, there seems to be an *association* between units sold and shelf space allocated—that is, knowledge of the amount of shelf space allocated to a variety implies something about how many units of that variety are likely to be sold. If you were told, for example, that a certain variety of canned soup has been allocated only a small proportion of the total shelf space available, then, based upon the relationship presented in the figure, you would most likely guess that the number of units sold of that variety will be correspondingly low.

EXHIBIT 17–1

Scatter Diagram for Units
Sold and Shelf Space

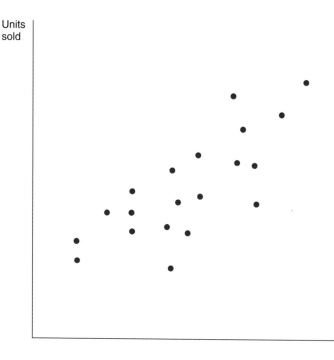

It is important to emphasize, however, that association does not imply causality. That is, you cannot conclude from the scatter diagram that the amount of shelf space allocated to a variety of canned soup determines (i.e., *causes*) how many units of that variety will be sold. As we discussed in Chapter 8, there are a number of conditions that must be in place, for example, controlling extraneous factors, before causality can be proven. In this example, it may be that the shelf space allocated to a variety of canned soup simply reflects how well that variety sells—managers give more shelf space to those varieties that are more popular.

Though we must be careful in making statements about causality, correlation analysis does allow us to make inferences about the relationship between two variables. Consider the two cross-tabulations shown in Table 17–1. The table cross-classifies the responses of 100 individuals according to their gender and purchase behavior. Consider first the cross-tabulation shown in Panel A. Suppose you are asked to guess the probability that a female would purchase. Looking at Panel A, your best guess is .50, because half of the females purchased (25/50) and half (25/50) did not. Knowledge of a person's gender does not help you very much in predicting purchase behavior. And, as we will see shortly, the correlation coefficient for these two variables is zero—gender and purchase behavior have no association.

Now consider Panel B of Table 17–1. Here, the marginals are the same—50 percent of the sample purchased, while 50 percent did not, and the sample is evenly divided between males and females. Faced with the same question as before, you would now conclude that the probability of

A.

Gender \ Purchase	Yes	No	Total
Male	25	25	50
Female	25	25	50
Total	50	50	100

B.

Gender \ Purchase	Yes	No	Total
Male	0	50	50
Female	50	0	50
Total	50	50	100

TABLE 17—1

Cross-Tabulation of Purchase and Gender

a female purchasing is 1.0—all of the 50 females surveyed initiated a purchase. In this case, there is a very strong association between gender and purchase behavior. In fact, the correlation coefficient for Panel B is 1.0, indicating that gender and purchase behavior are perfectly correlated.

Measures of correlation are symmetrical in nature. The correlation between variable X and variable Y is the same as that between variable Y and variable X. Two variables can be **positively correlated, negatively correlated,** or **uncorrelated.** Parts C, D, and G in Exhibit 17–2 depict these three conditions. In Exhibit 17–2C the two variables are positively correlated, $r > 0$. Notice that there is an upward trend to the data—when X is large, Y is also large. Exhibit 17–2D depicts negative correlation, $r < 0$. Notice that there is an inverse relationship between the two variables—when X is large, Y is small whereas when X is small, Y is large. Exhibit 17–2G depicts the situation when two variables are uncorrelated, $r = 0$. Notice that there is no systematic relationship between the two variables—when the values of X are large, some Y-values are large and some are small, and when the values of X are small some values of Y are small and some are large.

The correlation between two variables lies between the limits of -1 and $+1$. If the correlation between two variables is equal to $+1$, we say that the two variables exhibit *perfect positive correlation* (see Exhibit 17–2A). If the correlation between two variables is equal to -1, we say that the two variables exhibit *perfect negative correlation* (see Exhibit 17–2B). As shown in these two figures, perfect positive or negative correlation means that there is an exact linear relationship between the two variables. Correlation measures the *linear association* between two variables. Thus, as depicted in Exhibit 17–2H, $r = 0$ even though $Y = X^2$ (where X assumes both positive and negative values).

POSITIVE CORRELATION
Relationship where, as the value of one variable increases (decreases), there is a tendency for the value of the other variable to increase (decrease).

INVERSE OR NEGATIVE CORRELATION
Relationship where, as the value of one variable increases (decreases), the value of the other variable decreases (increases).

NO OR ZERO CORRELATION
A situation in which there is no systematic relationship between the level of one variable and the level of another variable.

EXHIBIT 17–2

Correlational Patterns

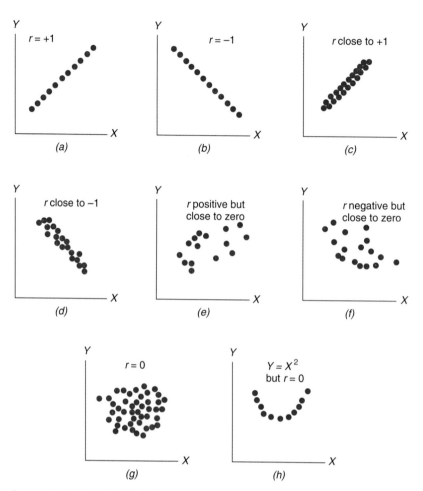

Source: Adapted from Henri Theil, *Introduction to Econometrics* (Englewood Cliffs, N.J.: Prentice Hall, 1978), p. 86.

MEASURES OF CORRELATION

To illustrate the computation of correlation coefficients under different measurement conditions, we will use the data presented in Table 17–2. The table provides data on a number of operating characteristics for 20 firms.

Interval or Ratio Variables

PEARSON PRODUCT MOMENT CORRELATION

Measure of the linear association between two interval or ratio-scaled variables.

Suppose you are asked to determine the relationship, if any, between the size of sales force and (1) market coverage, (2) items recorded out of stock, (3) the average dollar amount of a sale, and (4) the turnover ratio of the firm. Because all of these variables are measured on either an interval or a ratio scale, we use a measure of correlation called the **Pearson product moment correlation.** Developed in the early 1890s by Karl Pearson, this is one of the most commonly used measures of correlation.

TABLE 17–2

Operating Characteristics of 20 Firms

Firm	Size of Sales Force	Market Coverage (percent)	Out-of Stock Items	Average Sales($)	Turnover Ratio	Technical Assistance*	Service*	Delivery Time Performance	Computer-Assisted Ordering
1	100	10	30	30	30	1	3	1	0
2	100	20	22	50	40	8	9	1	0
3	200	20	17	40	35	15	14	0	0
4	400	20	16	35	25	6	7	1	0
5	300	30	14	40	20	12	12	1	0
6	400	40	19	25	30	3	2	0	1
7	400	30	15	35	25	5	6	0	0
8	500	30	14	30	20	11	10	1	1
9	600	50	13	45	15	14	11	0	0
10	500	60	10	35	10	10	13	0	0
11	600	60	11	40	20	4	4	0	1
12	700	40	9	30	15	9	8	−1	1
13	800	60	12	45	20	2	1	−1	1
14	800	70	6	35	25	7	5	0	0
15	900	70	2	45	30	13	15	−1	0
16	800	80	10	35	25	20	18	0	0
17	1,000	60	6	45	35	16	19	−1	1
18	900	80	2	40	30	19	20	−1	1
19	1,000	80	3	35	40	17	17	−1	0
20	1,000	90	5	50	45	18	16	−1	1

*Industry ranking.

Let us begin with the relationship between sales-force size and market coverage. Exhibit 17–3 provides a scatter diagram where the number enclosed in parentheses identifies the firm. You can see that these two variables exhibit a positive correlation—as sales-force size increases so does market coverage. Letting X_i denote sales-force size for the ith firm and Y_i denote market coverage for the ith firm, the Pearson product moment correlation between the two variables, which is denoted by r_{XY}, is

$$r_{XY} = \frac{\dfrac{\sum\limits_{i=1}^{n} (X_i - \overline{X})(Y_i - \overline{Y})}{n - 1}}{\sqrt{\dfrac{\sum\limits_{i=1}^{n} (X_i - \overline{X})^2}{n - 1}} \sqrt{\dfrac{\sum\limits_{i=1}^{n} (Y_i - \overline{Y})^2}{n - 1}}} \qquad (17\text{-}1)$$

The expressions in the denominator of this equation are the standard deviations of X and Y. The expression appearing in the numerator of this equation is the *covariance* between X and Y. Because the denominator must

EXHIBIT 17—3

Scatter Diagram of Market Coverage and Sales-Force Size

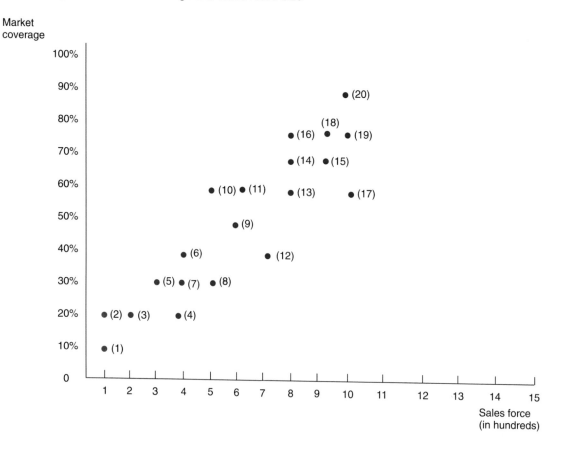

be nonnegative (variances and standard deviations can never be negative), the algebraic sign of the Pearson product moment correlation coefficient is determined by the covariance between X and Y. Positive covariation leads to positive correlation, and, similarly, negative covariation leads to negative correlation.

Table 17–3 presents manual computations for the numerator and denominator of equation 17–1. From this table we can compute the correlation coefficient between sales-force size and market coverage:

$$r_{XY} = \frac{\dfrac{124,000}{19}}{\sqrt{\dfrac{1,680,000}{19}} \sqrt{\dfrac{11,200}{19}}}$$

$$= \frac{6526.32}{(297.36)(24.28)}$$

$$= 0.904$$

TABLE 17−3

Summary Calculations for Computing Correlation Coefficients between Sales-Force Size and Market Coverage

Size of Sales-Force X_i	$(X_i - \overline{X})$	$(X_i - \overline{X})^2$	$(X_i - \overline{X})(Y_i - \overline{Y})$	$(Y_i - \overline{Y})^2$	$(Y_i - \overline{Y})$	Market Coverage (%) Y_i
100	−500	250,000	20,000	1,600	−40	10
100	−500	250,000	15,000	900	−30	20
200	−400	160,000	12,000	900	−30	20
400	−200	40,000	6,000	900	−30	20
300	−300	90,000	6,000	400	−20	30
400	−200	40,000	2,000	100	−10	40
400	−200	40,000	4,000	400	−20	30
500	−100	10,000	2,000	400	−20	30
600	0	0	0	0	0	50
500	−100	10,000	−1,000	100	10	60
600	0	0	0	100	10	60
700	100	10,000	−1,000	100	−10	40
800	200	40,000	2,000	100	10	60
800	200	40,000	4,000	400	20	70
900	300	90,000	6,000	400	20	70
800	200	40,000	6,000	900	30	80
1,000	400	160,000	4,000	100	10	60
900	300	90,000	9,000	900	30	80
1,000	400	160,000	12,000	900	30	80
1,000	400	160,000	16,000	1,600	40	90
Total 12,000	0	1,680,000	124,000	11,200	0	1,000

$$\overline{X} = \frac{12,000}{20} = 600 \qquad\qquad \overline{Y} = \frac{1,000}{20} = 50$$

We conclude, therefore, that sales-force size and market coverage are highly correlated, which verifies our initial conclusion drawn from visual inspection of the scatter diagram of Exhibit 17−3.

The correlation between sales-force size and the other firm characteristics listed in Table 17−2 can be computed in a similar manner. When many variables are being considered, statistical data analysis programs can prove useful. Exhibit 17−4 presents sample output from the SPSSX correlation program. Notice that the correlation coefficients are displayed in matrix format. Because the correlation of a variable with itself is unity, the correlation coefficients appearing on the main diagonal of the matrix are all equal to one. The correlation coefficients for different pairs of variables correspond to the off-diagonal elements and appear in the upper and lower triangles of the correlation matrix. Because correlation is symmetric, $r_{XY} = r_{YX}$, with p variables, there are, in general, $p(p - 1)$ nonredundant, off-diagonal correlation coefficients. For this reason, some computer

EXHIBIT 17–4

Sample Output for SPSSX
Correlation Analysis

```
                              --Correlation Coefficients--
                     SIZE      COVERAGE      OUT       SALE      RATIO

SIZE               1.0000       .9040**    -.9031**    .2552     .1440
COVERAGE            .9040**    1.0000      -.8548**    .2970     .1529
OUT                -.9031**    -.8548**    1.0000     -.2864    -.0549
SALE                .2552       .2970      -.2864     1.0000     .3593
RATIO               .1440       .1529      -.0549      .3593    1.0000
** - Signif. LE .05   ** - Signif. LE .01   (2-tailed)
"".'' is printed if a coefficient cannot be computed
```

statistical software programs for correlation analysis provide only those correlation coefficients appearing in either the lower or upper triangular portion of the correlation matrix.

If the 20 firms listed in Table 17–2 are considered a sample from a larger population, then the correlation coefficient computed on the basis of the sample information can be regarded as an estimate of the population correlation coefficient, which, as is customary, will be denoted as ρ_{XY}. To statistically test the association between two variables, it is possible to perform a hypothesis test of whether the population correlation coefficient between these two variables is zero. This hypothesis test follows the general guidelines discussed in Chapter 16. The null hypothesis is

HO: $\rho_{XY} = 0$

The alternative hypothesis is generally one-sided:

HA: $\rho_{XY} > 0$

or

HA: $\rho_{XY} < 0$

depending on whether positive or negative correlation is expected.

The test statistic

$$t = \frac{r_{XY} \sqrt{n-2}}{\sqrt{1 - (r_{XY})^2}} \qquad (17\text{-}2)$$

follows the t-distribution. As is standard procedure, to find the critical value of the test statistic, you set α and calculate the degrees of freedom, which in this case are equal to $n - 2$, where n is the sample size.

To illustrate let us consider Exhibit 17–5 and the correlation between sales-force size and out-of-stock items. Because it is reasonable to suspect that these two variables should be negatively correlated, the alternative hypothesis is

HA: $\rho_{XY} < 0$

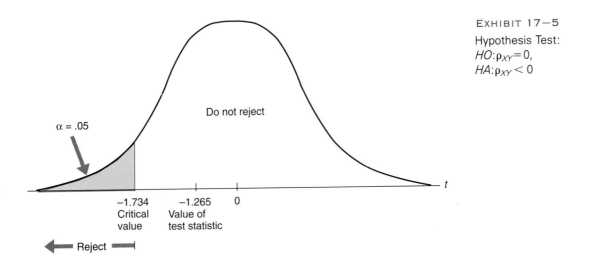

Exhibit 17—5
Hypothesis Test:
$HO: \rho_{XY} = 0$,
$HA: \rho_{XY} < 0$

Following equation 17–2 the test statistic is

$$t = \frac{-.286\sqrt{18}}{\sqrt{1 - (-.286)^2}}$$

$$= \frac{-1.212}{0.958}$$

$$= -1.265$$

Setting $\alpha = 0.05$, the critical value of the test statistic with df $= 20 - 2 = 18$ is -1.734. Because the value of the test statistic (-1.265) is greater than the associated critical value (-1.734), we cannot safely reject the null hypothesis. Thus the correlation between sales-force size and out-of-stock items is not large enough, in absolute value, to reject the notion that the true population correlation between these two variables is zero.

Ordinal Variables

Suppose you now are asked to determine the relationship, if any, between rankings on technical assistance and rankings on service. The correlation coefficient given in equation 17–1 does not apply since the variables being correlated are ordinally scaled. When variables have ordinal rank-order properties, the appropriate measure of correlation is the *Spearman rank-order correlation coefficient*. Letting r_s denote Spearman's rank-order correlation we have

$$r_s = 1 - 6 \sum_{i=1}^{n} \frac{d_i^2}{n(n^2 - 1)} \qquad (17\text{-}3)$$

where d_i represents the difference in the ranking between the two variables for the *i*th object or person, n is the number of objects or people ranked, and the number 6 is a constant that is needed to ensure that the sample-based estimate is unbiased.

Table 17–4 contains summary manual computations. Applying equation 17–3 we find

$$r_s = 1 - 6\left[\frac{56}{20(20^2 - 1)}\right]$$

$$= 1 - 6\left[\frac{56}{7980}\right]$$

$$= 1 - .042$$

$$= 0.958$$

Though the correlation between industry ranking on technical assistance and service is quite high, we can nonetheless effect a statistical hypothesis test of its significance. If once again the 20 firms listed in Table 17–2 are considered a sample from a larger population, then the correlation coefficient computed on the basis of the sample information can be regarded as an estimate of the population correlation coefficient, which we denote as ρ_s. It is possible to perform a hypothesis test of whether the population correlation coefficient is zero. The null hypothesis is

HO: $\rho_s = 0$

The alternative hypothesis is generally one-sided:

HA: $\rho_s > 0$

or

HA: $\rho_s < 0$

depending on whether positive or negative correlation is expected.
The test statistic

$$t = \frac{r_s\sqrt{n - 2}}{\sqrt{1 - r_s^2}} \tag{17-4}$$

follows the *t*-distribution. To find the critical value of the test statistic, you set α and calculate the degrees of freedom, which in this case are equal to $n - 2$, where, again, n is the sample size.

Because it is reasonable to expect that industry ranking on technical assistance and service should be positively correlated, we state the alternative hypothesis as

HA: $\rho_s > 0$

Following equation 17–4 the test statistic is

$$t = \frac{0.958\sqrt{18}}{\sqrt{1 - (0.959)^2}}$$

$$= \frac{4.064}{0.283}$$

$$= 14.34$$

Technical Assistance	Service	d_i	d_i^2
1	3	−2	4
8	9	−1	1
15	14	1	1
6	7	−1	1
12	12	0	0
3	2	1	1
5	6	−1	1
11	10	1	1
14	11	3	9
10	13	−3	9
4	4	0	0
9	8	1	1
2	1	1	1
7	5	2	4
13	15	−2	4
20	18	2	4
16	19	−3	9
19	20	−1	1
17	17	0	0
18	16	2	4
		0	56

TABLE 17−4

Calculation of Spearman's Rank-Order Correlation Coefficient

Setting $\alpha = 0.05$, the critical value of the test statistic with df = $20 − 2 = 18$ is 1.734. Because the value of the test statistic (14.34) is greater than the associated critical value (1.734), we can safely reject the null hypothesis (see Exhibit 17−6). Thus, the correlation between industry ranking on technical assistance and service is large enough, in absolute value, to reject the notion that the true population correlation between these two variables is zero.

Nominal Variables

Suppose you want to determine the relationship, if any, between delivery time performance and whether the firm offers computer-assisted ordering. Both of these variables are nominally scaled. In Table 17−2 the firm receives a value of 1 if its average delivery time is greater than the industry average, 0 if its average delivery time is the same as the industry average, and −1 if its average delivery time is less than the industry average. If the firm does not offer computer-assisted ordering, a 0 appears in Table 17−2, whereas if the firm does provide this option, a 1 appears.

The first step in computing the correlation coefficient for two nominally scaled variables is to form a cross-tabulation. The most widely used correlation coefficient between two nominally scaled variables is the **Cramer**

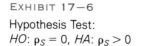

EXHIBIT 17—6

Hypothesis Test:
$HO: \rho_S = 0$, $HA: \rho_S > 0$

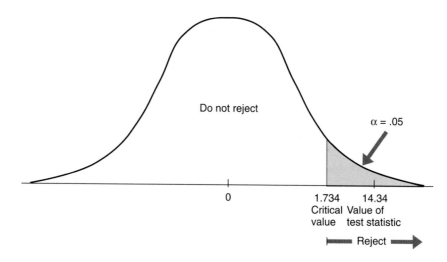

CRAMER'S CONTINGENCY
COEFFICIENT (V)

Measure of the degree of
association between nominal
variables, which is appropriate for any size contingency
table.

CHI-SQUARE STATISTIC

A measure of the difference
between what we observe
from the sample and what
we should have observed in
the sample if the two variables were not associated.

contingency coefficient. This correlation coefficient is referred to as Cramer's V and is derived from the chi-square statistic as follows:

$$V = \sqrt{\frac{X^2/n}{q-1}}$$ (17-5)

In equation 17–5 n is the sample size, q is the number of rows or columns of the cross-tabulation, whichever is smaller, and X^2, is the **chi-square statistic.**

$$X^2 = \sum_{k=1}^{K} \frac{(O_k - E_k)^2}{E_k}$$

where O_k are the observed counts appearing in each cell of the cross-tabulation and E_k are the corresponding expected counts derived under the assumption that the null hypothesis of no association is true.

Table 17–5 presents the cross-tabulation of the data on delivery time performance and computer-assisted ordering given in Table 17–2. Panel A gives the observed counts and Panel B the expected counts. Expected counts are calculated by taking the row total times the column total divided by the total sample size for the cell in question. To illustrate, consider the first cell in Table 17–5 Panel A. The row total is 12. The column total is 7. Thus, the expected count is

$$E_1 = \frac{12(7)}{20} = 4.2$$

Having computed the expected count, let us now compute the chi-square statistic:

$$X^2 = \sum_{k=1}^{K} (O_k - E_k)^2 / E_k$$

$$= (2 - 4.2)^2/4.2 + (6 - 4.8)^2/4.8 +$$
$$(4 - 3.0)^2/3.0 + (5 - 2.8)^2/2.8 +$$
$$(2 - 3.2)^2/3.2 + (1 - 2.0)^2/2.0$$
$$= 4.46$$

A. Observed Counts

Computer-Assisted Ordering	Delivery Time			Row Total
	Below Industry Average	Equal to Industry Average	Above Industry Average	
No	2	6	4	12
Yes	5	2	1	8
Column total	7	8	5	20

B. Expected Counts

Computer-Assisted Ordering	Delivery Time			Row Total
	Below Industry Average	Equal to Industry Average	Above Industry Average	
No	4.2	4.8	3.0	12
Yes	2.8	3.2	2.0	8
Column total	7	8	5	20

According to equation 17–5, the correlation between delivery time performance and computer-assisted ordering is

$$V = \sqrt{\frac{4.47/20}{2 - 1}}$$
$$= 0.47$$

We can use the chi-square test statistic to perform a test of the statistical significance of Cramer's V. The null hypothesis is

$$HO: \rho_V = 0$$

The alternative hypothesis is generally one-sided:

$$HA: \rho_V > 0$$

or

$$HA: \rho_V < 0$$

depending on whether positive or negative correlation is expected. In this case, state the alternative hypothesis as

$$HA: \rho_V > 0$$

since we expect that delivery time performance and computer-assisted ordering are positively correlated.

The test statistic, X^2, is distributed as a chi-square random variable with $(r - 1)(c - 1)$ degrees of freedom, where r is the number of rows and c is the number of columns in the cross-tabulation. As you saw in Chapter 16, the chi-square distribution is not symmetrical and its shape varies with the degrees of freedom. To find the critical value, you locate

EXHIBIT 17—7

Hypothesis Test:
HO: $\rho_V = 0$,
H_A: $\rho_V > 0$

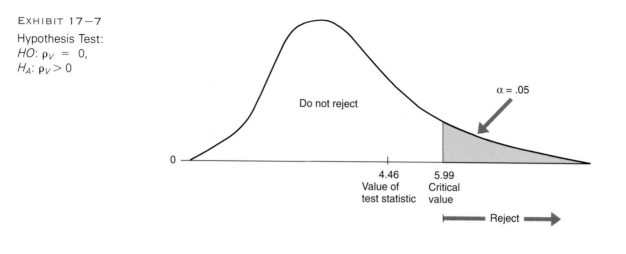

the row corresponding to the appropriate degrees of freedom and move across to the column corresponding to the level of significance.

Setting $\alpha = 0.05$, the critical value of the test statistic with $(2 - 1)(3 - 1) = 2$ degrees of freedom is 5.99. Because the value of the test statistic (4.46) is less than the critical value (5.99), we cannot reject the null hypothesis of no association between delivery time performance and computer-assisted ordering (see Exhibit 17–7). On the basis of this test, we must conclude that an observed correlation coefficient as large as 0.47 could be obtained when in fact the correlation between these two variables in the population is zero.

Mixed Scales

What happens when the two variables being correlated have different measurement properties? In the remainder of this section, we consider two frequently encountered situations.

Dichotomous and interval variables. It can happen that one of the variables is dichotomous, assuming only two values, whereas the other variable is intervally scaled. In this case, the appropriate correlation coefficient is called the **point biserial correlation coefficient,** which is generally denoted as ρ_{PB}.

POINT-BISERIAL
CORRELATION
COEFFICIENT

Coefficient that measures the association between a dichotomous variable and an interval-scaled variable.

Manual computation of the point biserial correlation is rather tedious. Fortunately, however, application of the Pearson product moment correlation formula to a dichotomous variable assuming the values of 0 or 1 and an intervally scaled variable will yield the same value as application of the point biserial correlation formula.

Suppose you want to determine the relationship between computer-assisted ordering and the number of items out of stock. Table 17–6 presents summary manual computations. Applying the Pearson product moment correlation coefficient formula (see equation 17–1), we find that

TABLE 17−6

Summary Calculations for Computing Correlation Coefficients between Computer-Assisted Ordering and Number of Items Out of Stock

Firm	Computer-Assisted Ordering X_i	$(X_i - \bar{X})$	$(X_i - \bar{X})^2$	$[(X_i - \bar{X})(Y_i - \bar{Y})]$	$(Y_i - \bar{Y})^2$	$(Y_i - \bar{Y})$	Number of Items Out of Stock Y_i
1	0	−0.40	0.16	−7.28	331.24	18.20	30
2	0	−0.40	0.16	−4.08	104.04	10.20	22
3	0	−0.40	0.16	−2.08	27.04	5.20	17
4	0	−0.40	0.16	−1.68	17.64	4.20	16
5	0	−0.40	0.16	−0.88	4.84	2.20	14
6	1	0.60	0.36	4.32	51.84	7.20	19
7	0	−0.40	0.16	−1.28	10.24	3.20	15
8	1	0.60	0.36	1.32	4.84	2.20	14
9	0	−0.40	0.16	−0.48	1.44	1.20	13
10	0	−0.40	0.16	0.72	3.24	−1.80	10
11	1	0.60	0.36	−0.48	0.64	−0.80	11
12	1	0.60	0.36	−1.68	7.84	−2.80	9
13	1	0.60	0.36	0.12	0.04	0.20	12
14	0	−0.40	0.16	2.32	33.64	−5.80	6
15	0	−0.40	0.16	3.92	96.04	−9.80	2
16	0	−0.40	0.16	0.72	3.24	−1.80	10
17	1	0.60	0.36	−3.48	33.64	−5.80	6
18	1	0.60	0.36	−5.88	96.04	−9.80	2
19	0	−0.40	0.16	3.52	77.44	−8.80	3
20	1	0.60	0.36	−4.08	46.24	−6.80	5
			4.80	−16.40	951.20		

$$\rho_{PB} = \rho_{XY} = \frac{\dfrac{-16.4}{19}}{\sqrt{\dfrac{4.80}{19}}\sqrt{\dfrac{951.20}{19}}}$$

$$= \frac{-0.863}{(0.503)(7.076)}$$

$$= 0.243$$

The algebraic sign of the point biserial correlation coefficient is arbitrary in the sense that a change in the coding of the dichotomous variable, for example, no = 1 and yes = 0 instead of no = 0 and yes = 1, changes the algebraic sign of the resulting correlation coefficient.

To statistically test the significance of a point biserial correlation, you use the same procedure as for the Pearson product moment correlation

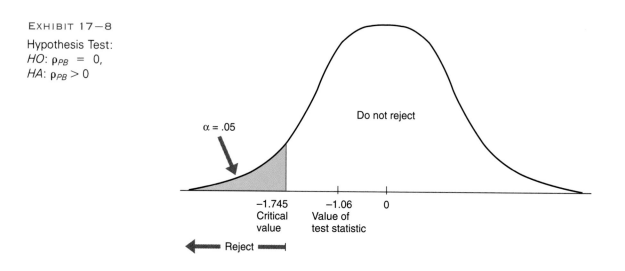

coefficient. The null hypothesis states that the two variables are uncorrelated in the population:

HO: $\rho_{PB} = 0$

The alternative hypothesis depends on whether positive or negative correlation is expected. In the case of computer-assisted ordering and the number of items out of stock, it is reasonable to expect that computer-assisted ordering will decrease the number of items out of stock. Thus the appropriate alternative hypothesis is

HA: $\rho_{PB} < 0$

The test statistic is the same as that shown in equation 17−2, except we substitute ρ_{PB} for ρ_{XY}. Thus,

$$t = \frac{r_{PB}\sqrt{n-2}}{\sqrt{1-r_{PB}^2}}$$
$$= \frac{-.243\sqrt{18}}{\sqrt{1-.06}}$$
$$= -1.06$$

The test statistic follows the t-distribution with $n - 2$ degrees of freedom. Setting $\alpha = .05$ and the critical value for df $= n - 2 = 18$ is -1.745. Because the value of the test statistic (-1.06) is larger than the associated critical value (-1.745), we cannot safely reject the null hypothesis that in the population computer-assisted ordering and the number of items out of stock are uncorrelated (see Exhibit 17−8).

Categorical and interval variables.   Suppose you are interested in determining the relationship between a categorical variable and an intervally scaled variable. Unfortunately, there is no formal correlation coefficient appropriate for this case. There are, however, several informal approaches.

One popular informal approach is to transform the interval-scaled variable into a smaller number of categories, cross-classify the transformed variable with the categorical variable, and then use Cramer's V as a measure of correlation. There are no hard rules for collapsing the intervally scaled variable into categories, although the sample size will clearly play a role in this decision. With a small sample size, the resulting contingency table may be very sparse if the intervally scaled variable is broken down into a large number of categories. In such cases, each cell of the table will have only a small number of observations, and many cells may even have no observed counts. It is difficult to handle contingency tables in which many of the cells have few or no observations. A generally accepted practice is to have at least five responses per cell. This suggestion (at least five observations per cell) is, however, only a guideline, not a hard-and-fast rule.

REGRESSION ANALYSIS

Correlation analysis investigates the extent to which two variables are associated. When correlating two variables, the variables are treated symmetrically—there is no attempt to specify the relationship between the variables. In contrast, in **regression analysis** one of the variables is designated as the *dependent variable,* while the other variable is designated as the *explanatory variable,* and the aim is to predict the mean or average value of the dependent variable on the basis of the known values of the explanatory variable. Regression analysis attempts to answer two important questions:

1. What is the change in the dependent variable for a unit change in an explanatory variable?
2. Given a specific value of an explanatory variable, what is the most likely value of the dependent variable?

REGRESSION ANALYSIS
Procedure that determines how much of the variation in the dependent variable can be explained by the independent variable.

As an illustration consider Exhibit 17–9, which presents a scatter diagram for two variables: the number of people entering the showroom, hereafter referred to as *ups,* and the dollar amount of advertising expenditures for an automobile dealership. The Pearson product moment correlation between the two variables is 0.857, indicating that these two variables show a systematic relationship. Though this information is useful, a manager might also want to know

1. For each $100 in advertising expenditure, how many more people will visit the dealership?
2. If advertising expenditures were, say, $5,500 next year, how many people will visit the dealership?

These questions are important to the manager because they quantify the magnitude of the relationship between advertising expenditures and the number of people visiting the dealership. If there is a large responsiveness to a dollar spent on advertising, then the manager may feel more comfortable in recommending that advertising budgets be increased.

EXHIBIT 17—9

Scatter Diagram for
Number of Ups and
Advertising Level

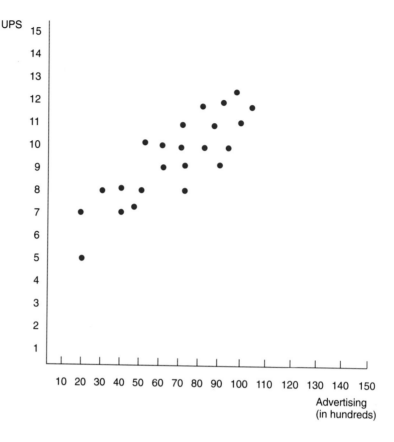

The terms *simple regression analysis* and *multiple regression analysis* are used to describe the kind of regression model being fit. When only a single explanatory variable is being considered, we refer to this procedure as **simple regression analysis.** When two or more explanatory variables are being considered, we call this procedure **multiple regression analysis.** In this section, we introduce the simple regression model. In the section that immediately follows, we discuss multiple regression analysis.

SIMPLE REGRESSION
MODEL

Model that considers the
case of a single independent
variable.

MULTIPLE REGRESSION
MODEL

Model that considers the
general case of more than
one independent variable.

THE SIMPLE TWO-VARIABLE REGRESSION MODEL

Simple regression analysis considers the relationship between a dependent variable and a single explanatory variable. Following convention, the dependent variable will be denoted as Y and the explanatory variable as X. The purpose of regression analysis is to develop an equation that can be used to predict the value of Y on the basis of the known values of X. Looking at the scatter diagram shown in Exhibit 17–9, the problem can be solved by fitting a straight line through the data points. In general, the equation for a straight line is

$$Y = a + bX$$

In the context of the regression model, the estimated **regression line** is written as

$$\hat{Y}_i = \beta_0 + \beta_1 X_i \qquad (17\text{-}6)$$

REGRESSION LINE
A line fitted to the data that in some sense best captures the functional relationship.

where the subscript i denotes the observation number, $\hat{Y}_i$ is the estimated value of Y, β_0 is the intercept (that is, the value of Y when $X = 0$), and β_1 is the slope coefficient that gives the rate of change in Y for a unit change in X.

There are, however, many different straight lines that can be fit to the data shown in Exhibit 17–9 by varying the values of β_0 and β_1. For any specific values of β_0 and β_1, we have an estimated value $\hat{Y}_i$. The difference between the actual and estimated Y-values is called the *residual,* which we will denote as e_i:

$$e_i = Y_i - \hat{Y}_i \qquad (17\text{-}7)$$

$$= Y_i - \beta_0 - \beta_1 X_i \qquad (17\text{-}8)$$

Among other things, the residuals reflect the fact that rarely will all of the variation in Y be explained by X—there are other factors, perhaps unknown to the researcher, that possibly influence the dependent variable.

It is reasonable to want the differences between the actual and estimated Y-values to be small. In the extreme case, if all of the residuals are zero, then each estimated value of Y is exactly equal to its corresponding actual value. To this end, the regression model adopts the following criterion: Choose values for β_0 and β_1 in such a way that the sum of the squared residuals

$$\sum e_i^2 = \sum (Y_i - \hat{Y}_i)^2$$

is as small as possible. This criterion is known as the *least-squares criterion.*

Estimation of the Regression Coefficients

The simple two-variable regression model is

$$Y_i = \beta_0 + \beta_1 X_i + e_i \qquad (17\text{-}9)$$

where β_0 and β_1 are determined such that Σe_i^2 is minimized. Having found sample-based estimates for the regression coefficients, we can write the estimated regression function as

$$Y_i = \hat{\beta}_0 + \hat{\beta}_1 X_i + e_i \qquad (17\text{-}10)$$

$$= \hat{Y}_i + e_i \qquad (17\text{-}11)$$

where the "hat" indicates an estimate.

We still are faced with the problem of which $\hat{\beta}$ values to choose. Applying the least-squares criterion, the following estimates are obtained:

$$\hat{\beta}_1 = \frac{\sum_{i=1}^{n} (X_i - \overline{X})(Y_i - \overline{Y})}{\sum_{i=1}^{n} (X_i - \overline{X})^2} \qquad (17\text{-}12)$$

$$\hat{\beta}_0 = \overline{Y} - \hat{\beta}_1 \overline{X} \qquad (17\text{-}13)$$

TABLE 17—7

Manual Computations for Estimating β_0 and β_1

Advertising Expenditure ($hundreds) X_i	$(X_i - \bar{X})$	$(X_i - \bar{X})^2$	$[(X_i - \bar{X})(Y_i - \bar{Y})]$	$(Y_i - \bar{Y})^2$	$(Y_i - \bar{Y})$	Ups Y_i
1.00	−4.53	20.52	20.84	21.16	−4.60	4.00
2.00	−3.53	12.46	5.65	2.56	−1.60	7.00
2.00	−3.53	12.46	12.71	12.96	−3.60	5.00
10.00	4.47	19.98	10.73	5.76	2.40	11.00
9.00	3.47	12.04	1.39	.16	.40	9.00
6.00	.47	.22	.66	1.96	1.40	10.00
7.00	1.47	2.16	3.53	5.76	2.40	11.00
6.00	.47	.22	.19	.16	.40	9.00
6.00	.47	.22	−.28	.36	−.60	8.00
4.00	−1.53	2.34	2.45	2.56	−1.60	7.00
3.00	−2.53	6.40	1.52	.36	−.60	8.00
5.00	−.53	.28	.32	.36	−.60	8.00
5.00	−.53	.28	−.74	1.96	1.40	10.00
8.00	2.47	6.10	3.46	1.96	1.40	10.00
9.00	3.47	12.04	11.80	11.56	3.40	12.00
		107.72	74.30	69.60		

NORMAL EQUATIONS/ORDINARY LEAST-SQUARES

Formulas that produce a regression line such that Σe_i^2 is minimized.

The $\hat{\beta}$ estimates obtained produce a regression line such that the sum of squared residuals is minimized. There are no other estimates that provide "better" estimates of Y, or, alternatively, smaller residuals. These equations have a long history and are derived from what are referred to as the **normal equations.** The estimates are commonly referred to as the **ordinary least-squares (OLS)** estimates of β_0 and β_1.

Table 17–7 presents manual computations for estimating β_0 and β_1 for the data shown in Exhibit 17–9. Applying the estimation formula we find

$$\hat{\beta}_1 = \frac{74.3}{107.7}$$
$$= 0.689$$
$$\hat{\beta}_0 = \frac{129 - 0.689(83.0)}{15}$$
$$= 4.79$$

The estimated regression line therefore is

$$\hat{Y}_i = 4.79 + 0.689X_i$$

From the estimated regression line we find that every $100 in advertising generates about 0.689 visits, so that every $200 spent on advertising would result in approximately one additional person visiting the dealership. We can also use the estimated regression line to ascertain the number of people expected to visit the dealership for any level of advertising. For instance, if the advertising expenditure is set at $500, the estimated number of people visiting the dealership is 4.79 + 0.689(5), or roughly eight people.

Evaluating the Regression

It seems reasonable to want to find out how well the estimated regression line fits the data. As we indicated earlier, it is presumptious to think that all of the actual Y-values will lie on the estimated regression line—rarely will a perfect fit be obtained. More likely there will be some positive e_i-values and some negative e_i-values. What we hope for is that these residuals around the estimated regression line are as small as possible.

How well the estimated regression line fits the data is determined by how much variation in Y is explained by X. The total variation of the actual Y-values about their sample mean, which may be called the total *sum of squares* (TSS), is

$$TSS = \sum_{i=1}^{n} (Y_i - \overline{Y})^2$$

The total sum of squares can be partitioned into two components. The first represents the variation of the estimated Y-values about their mean, which may be called the *sum of squares due to regression* [i.e., due to the explanatory variable(s)], or *explained by the regression,* or simply the *explained sum of squares* (ESS), and is given by

$$ESS = \sum_{i=1}^{n} (\hat{Y}_i - \overline{Y})^2$$
$$= \hat{\beta}_1^2 (X_i - \overline{X})^2$$

The second component of variation represents the residual or *unexplained* variation of the Y-values about the regression line, or simply the *residual sum of squares* (RSS), and is given by

$$RSS = \sum_{i=1}^{n} e_i = \sum_{i=1}^{n} (Y_i - \hat{Y}_i)^2$$

Thus,

$$TSS = ESS + RSS$$

These various sums of squares are graphed in Exhibit 17–10.

Exhibit 17–10
TSS, ESS, and RSS

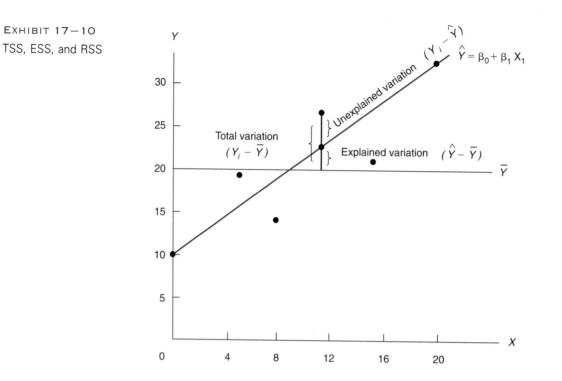

COEFFICIENT OF
DETERMINATION (R^2)
The ratio of explained to total
variation.

The ratio of explained to total variation is called the **coefficient of determination (R^2).**

$$R^2 = \frac{\text{Explained variation}}{\text{Total variation}} \tag{17-14}$$

$$= \frac{\sum\limits_{i=1}^{n} (\hat{Y}_i - \overline{Y})^2}{\sum\limits_{i=1}^{n} (Y_i - \overline{Y})^2} \tag{17-15}$$

$$= \frac{\hat{\beta}_1^2 \sum\limits_{i=1}^{n} (X_i - \overline{X})^2}{\sum\limits_{i=1}^{n} (Y_i - \overline{Y})^2} \tag{17-16}$$

The coefficient of determination is a measure of goodness of fit. It does not, however, indicate the percentage of correct predictions or the likelihood of correctly predicting the value of Y given a specific value of X. The coefficient of determination simply tells us how much of the variation in the dependent variable is explained by the independent variable. The range of R^2 is 0 to 1. The closer R^2 is to 1, the stronger the linear relationship between the two variables.

We can use the manual computations appearing in Table 17–7 to calculate R^2 for the data on advertising expenditures and ups. From these summary computations we have

$$R^2 = \frac{(0.689)^2(107.70)}{69.60} = 0.735$$

Thus advertising expenditures explain 73.5 percent of the variation of people visiting the dealership.

Simple two-variable regression can be performed with the use of statistical software packages. Exhibit 17–11 presents sample output from SPSSX. The sample output from regression analysis software packages provides a number of statistical tests and summary diagnostics. Notice first that the output presents the explained sum of squares (ESS) and the residual sum of squares (RSS). SPSSX labels these two sums of squares components *regression* and *residual*, respectively. Associated with any sum of squares are its degrees of freedom. For simple regression, ESS has 1 df, RSS has $n - 2$ df, and TSS has $n - 1$ df. The various sums of squares are displayed in what is referred to as the *analysis of variance*. Recall we discussed ANOVA in Chapter 16. The *mean square* column is obtained by taking each sum of squares component and dividing by its df.

Testing the significance of a regression model amounts to testing whether there is a statistically significant relationship between Y and X. If the explanatory variable X has no linear influence on the dependent variable Y, then $\beta_1 = 0$. Thus, the appropriate null hypothesis for testing the significance of a regression model is

HO: $\beta_1 = 0$

The alternative hypothesis is generally stated as two-sided:

HA: $\beta_1 \neq 0$

although a one-sided test is appropriate when information on the expected algebraic sign of β_1 is available.

This test can be performed in one of two alternative but complementary ways. One approach is to form the F-ratio defined by

$$F = \frac{ESS/df}{RSS/df} \tag{17-17}$$

$$= \frac{ESS/1}{RSS/(n - 2)}$$

The alternative approach is to perform a t-test on the β_1 coefficient itself. The null hypothesis and alternative hypothesis are the same as before. The appropriate test statistic is

$$t = \frac{\hat{\beta}_1}{\hat{\sigma}_{\beta_1}} \tag{17-18}$$

where $\hat{\sigma}_{\beta_1}$ is the estimated standard of β_1. Assuming that the disturbances, 1_i, are normally distributed and HO: $\beta_1 = 0$, the t-statistic follows the Student's t-distribution with $n - 2$ df. As shown in Exhibit 17–11, computer programs for regression analysis provide standard errors, the values of t and F, and also the corresponding p-levels for the null hypothesis.

From the summary information provided in Exhibit 17–11, we see that there is a statistically significant relationship between advertising expenditures and the number of people visiting the dealership. The F-value of

EXHIBIT 17—11

Sample Output for SPSSX
Simple Regression
Analysis

```
             **** MULTIPLE REGRESSION ****
Listwise Deletion of Missing Data
Equation Number 1   Dependent Variable..  UP

Block Number  1.  Method: Enter    AD

Variable(s) Entered on Step Number
  1..    AD

Multiple R              .85689
R Square                .73426
Adjusted R Square       .71382
Standard Error         1.19279

Analysis of Variance
                     DF      Sum of Squares   Mean Square
Regression            1         51.10433        51.10433
Residual             13         18.49567         1.42274
F =     35.91956    Signif F = .0000


            **** VARIABLES IN THE EQUATION ****
   Variable        B         SE B       Beta        T      Sig T
AD              .688738    .114918    .856888     5.993    .0000
(Constant)     4.788985    .706536               6.778    .0000
```

35.92 is significant at the $p<0.0001$ level. The p-level is given by Signif F = .0000. The explanatory variable, denoted by AD in the output, is also statistically significant. The t-value is 5.993, which is significant at the $p<0.0001$ level.

For the two-variable regression model there is really no need to perform both of these tests. When multiple regression is considered, however, these tests provide different information. Because computer programs for regression analysis do not distinguish between two and more than two explanatory variables, both tests are always routinely provided.

MULTIPLE REGRESSION

Multiple regression predicts the value of the dependent variable on the basis of the known values of two or more explanatory variables. Assuming that p explanatory variables, $X_1, X_2, \ldots, X_p$, are used, the estimated regression function is written as

$$Y_i = \hat{\beta}_0 + \hat{\beta}_1 X_{1i} + \hat{\beta}_2 X_{2i} + \ldots + \hat{\beta}_{pi} X_{pi} + e_i \qquad (17\text{-}19)$$

where the "hat" again indicates an estimate.

Frequently the explanatory variables are measured in different units. One explanatory variable may, for example, be measured in dollars while another is measured in hours. When the explanatory variables are measured in different units, it is usually difficult to compare regression coefficients because the magnitude of each β is affected by the scale used in measuring each X. Stated somewhat differently, the regression coefficients are not independent of the change of scale—measuring an explanatory variable in terms of cents rather than dollars will change the magnitude of the resulting β. To remove the effects of scale, the standardized regression coefficients, often called *beta coefficients,* are computed. The beta coefficient associated with the kth explanatory variable, denoted by $\hat{\beta}_k^x$, is

$$\hat{\beta}_k^\star = \hat{\beta}_k (S_{X_k}/S_Y) \tag{17-20}$$

where S_{X_k} and S_Y are the standard deviations of X_k and Y in the sample. The beta coefficients can also be obtained by standardizing X and Y prior to estimating the regression function. Beta coefficients are bounded by -1 to $+1$; hence the larger the magnitude (in an absolute sense) of a beta coefficient, the more important is that explanatory variable.

When more than one explanatory variable is used, computations become quite tedious. For this reason, computer software is almost always used when estimating the β values and measures of goodness to fit. To illustrate, Exhibit 17–12 presents SPSSX output from a concept test study. The study focused on a new cold remedy concept. Three hundred respondents indicated the likelihood that they would purchase the new concept if it were available. Respondents also rated the new concept with respect to their perceptions of the ability of the new concept to relieve cold-related symptoms without producing any undesirable side effects. The purpose of the regression analysis is to investigate the extent to which the product attribute perceptual ratings on relief and gentleness can explain a respondents' likelihood of purchase.

In the exhibit the dependent variable, likelihood of purchase, is denoted as *ATTP,* and the two explanatory variables, relief and gentleness, are denoted by *LK1* and *LK2,* respectively. Notice first that there is a statistically significant relationship between likelihood of purchase and ratings on relief and gentleness. The F-value of 80.34 is statistically significant at the $p < 0.0001$ level. In terms of explained variation, the two perceptual attribute ratings explain a little over 35 percent of the variation in likelihood of purchase. You may not think this amount of explained variation is very high, but remember the hypothesis test is one of *no* relationship between the dependent variable and the two attribute rating explanatory variables. Both explanatory variables are statistically significant at the $p < 0.0001$ level. The beta values shown in Exhibit 17–12 indicate that *LK1* is more important than *LK2* in influencing purchase likelihood.

Effects of Multicollinearity

The term *multicollinearity* was apparently first coined by Ragnar Frisch.[2] Originally it was used to describe the existence of a "perfect", or exact, linear relationship among some or all explanatory variables of a regression model. If one or more exact linear relationships exist among a set of explanatory variables, then at least one of the explanatory variables can be

EXHIBIT 17—12

Sample Output for SPSSX
Multiple Regression
Analysis

```
                          **** MULTIPLE REGRESSION ****
Listwise Deletion of Missing Data
Equation Number 1     Dependent Variable..   ATTP

Block Number  1.  Method: Enter     LK1     LK2

Variable(s) Entered on Step Number
1..   LK2
2..   LK1

Multiple R               .59250
R Square                 .35106
Adjusted R Square        .34669
Standard Error          2.73917

Analysis of Variance
                        DF        Sum of Squares   Mean Squares
Regression               2          1205.51489      602.75744
Residual               297          2228.40511        7.50305
F =      80.33502    Signif F = .0000


Variables in the Equation
Variable      B            SE B        Beta        T       Sig T

LK2          .881134      .152062     .289143     5.795    .0000
LK1         1.383171      .162099     .425782     8.533    .0000
(Constant)  7.942291     1.007959                 7.880    .0000
End Block Number  1  All requested variables entered.
```

written as a linear combination of the remaining explanatory variables. For
example

$$X_1 = aX_2 + bX_3 \ldots + wX_p$$

MULTICOLLINEARITY

Correlation among independent variables. Multicollinearity causes problems in interpreting the individual regression coefficients because the values are affected by the amount of association between the independent variables themselves.

where a, b, . . . , w are weights. Today, the term **multicollinearity** is
more broadly used to include the case of perfect linear dependence as well
as the case where the X variables are intercorrelated but not perfectly.

No multicollinearity is an assumption underlying the proper use of
multiple regression analysis. No multicollinearity means none of the explanatory variables can be written as a linear combination of the remaining
explanatory variables. What this means can be seen from the Venn diagram, or the *Ballentine* shown in Exhibit 17–13.[3] (The name *Ballentine* is
derived from the well-known Ballentine beer emblem with its circles.) In
this figure, the circle Y represents the variation in the dependent variable Y
and the circles X_1 and X_2 represent the variation in the explanatory variables X_1 and X_2, respectively. In Panel A, there is a single explanatory
variable and area 1 represents the variation in Y that is explained by X_1.
With a single explanatory variable we do not need the assumption of no
multicollinearity. In Panel B, area 2 represents the variation in Y that is
explained by X_1 and area 3 represents the variation in Y that is explained by
X_2. In Panel C, areas 4 and 5 show the variation in Y explained by X_1 and
areas 5 and 6 show the variation in Y explained by X_2. Because area 5 is

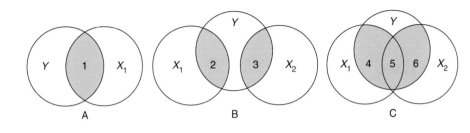

EXHIBIT 17–13

Ballentine Showing No
Multicollinearity and
Multicollinearity

common to both X_1 and X_2, there is no way to assess which part of area 5 is due to X_1 and which part of area 5 is due to X_2. In other words, there is no way to apportion the common area to the explanatory variables. The common variation in area 5 represents the situation of multicollinearity. The assumption of no multicollinearity requires that X_1 and X_2 do not overlap.

The logic behind the assumption of no multicollinearity is intuitive. Suppose that Y is the amount invested in the stock market and X_1 and X_2 are wealth and income of the consumer, respectively. In postulating that the amount invested in the stock market is linearly related to wealth and income, the presumption is that wealth and income have some *independent* influence on investment. In the extreme case, if wealth and income are perfectly correlated, then we have, in effect, only a single explanatory variable, not two, and there is no way to assess the *separate* effects of wealth and income on investment. In essence this is the problem of multicollinearity. When explanatory variables are correlated, the β estimates can be highly misleading and there is no way to assess the individual influence of each X on Y.

To reinforce the concepts we have been discussing in this chapter, consider Table 17–8, which presents the data relating sales volume Y to shelf space X_1 and in-store coupons distributed X_2 for 10 brands of hand soap. Table 17–9 presents β estimates derived by regressing Y on each explanatory variable separately (simple regressions) and regressing Y on X_1 and X_2 simultaneously (multiple regression). The table also reports the beta coefficients as well. Notice that the estimate of the influence of X_2 on Y varies rather dramatically depending on whether X_1 is included in the regression function. In the multiple regression it appears that the influence of coupon activity has little to do with sales volume—both the unstandardized and standardized coefficients are relatively small. In the simple regression, however, the influence is relatively strong, and, in fact, the product moment correlation between coupon activity and sales volume is equal to 0.76. This apparent inconsistency is due to the fact that coupon activity and shelf space are themselves highly correlated—there is more coupon activity for those brands that have larger amounts of shelf space.

Multicollinearity is an extremely difficult problem to deal with. Many approaches to reducing multicollinearity have been suggested. Sometimes increasing the size of the sample may attenuate the multicollinearity problem. For example, in the example just discussed, to assess the individual

TABLE 17—8

Regression of Sales
Volume *(Y)* on Shelf-Space
(X₁) and Coupons
Distributed *(X₂)*

	Sales Volume Y_i	Shelf-Space X_{1i}	Coupons Distributed X_{2i}
1	50	13.0	12
2	57	13.0	14
3	65	14.0	18
4	72	15.0	15
5	77	14.5	13
6	84	15.0	16
7	88	16.0	20
8	90	17.0	18
9	93	17.5	22
10	97	18.5	19

TABLE 17—9

Estimated Regression
Coefficients

	Unstandardized		Standardized	
	β_1	β_2	β_1	β_2
Simple regression	8.00	3.75	.94	.76
Multiple regression	7.52	.35	.88	.07

effects of shelf space and coupon activity on sales volume, what we need is a sufficient number of brands that have relatively large shelf space and low coupon activity, and brands that have relatively small shelf space and high coupon activity. Multivariate statistical techniques such as *factor analysis* and *principal components analysis* or techniques such as *ridge regression* have been used to "solve" the problem of multicollinearity. These techniques are, unfortunately, beyond the scope of this book.[4]

Model Assumptions

There are other assumptions concerning the proper use of regression analysis. These assumptions concern the distribution of the residuals $e_i = (Y_i - \hat{Y}_i)$. One assumption is that at each of the various X-values the Ys have the same variance. Technically, this assumption is referred to as the assumption of *homoscedasticity,* or equal (homo) *spread* (scedasticity), or *equal variance.* Another assumption, one that is needed in order to test the overall significance of the regression model as well as individual β coefficients, is that the residuals are normally and independently distributed.

Often plots of residuals and other types of residual analysis can provide useful information on whether these assumptions are in place. Residual plots, which are usually available in standard software packages (such as SPSSX), are used to determine whether the residuals exhibit any systematic pattern. If the residual plots show a systematic pattern, then the homoscedastic assumption and the normality assumption may be suspect.[5]

SUMMARY

Assessing the level of association (correlation) between two variables is a common practice in marketing research. In this chapter we have seen that the method used for calculating the correlation between two variables depends on the measurement properties of the variables. Correlation coefficients for nominal, ordinal, and interval variables were discussed and illustrated. We also considered the case of two variables having different units of measurement. This chapter also considered simple two-variable and multiple regression analysis. Regression analysis is a model for predicting the values of a dependent variable on the basis of the known values of one or more explanatory variables. Various aspects of regression analysis were discussed including the problem of multicollinearity and the assumptions underlying the proper use of the regression model.

KEY CONCEPTS

Pearson's Product Moment Correlation

Spearman's Rank-Order Correlation

Cramer's V

Point Biserial Correlation

Regression Analysis

Explained Variation

Coefficient of Determination

Multicollinearity

REVIEW QUESTIONS

1. The following table shows data on sales, advertising expenditures, and the number of salespersons for 10 regional divisions of a large national distributor of hardware.

Sales ($000)	Advertising ($000)	Number of Sales-persons
120	20	8
200	50	13
235	47	14
174	37	11
187	41	12
196	33	13
149	27	10
169	31	11
172	35	11
153	40	9

a. Compute an appropriate correlation coefficient for each pair of variables.
b. Interpret each correlation coefficient and determine which pairs of variables exhibit statistically significant association.

2. The following table shows data on the sales rankings and rankings of salesperson expertise for the 10 regional divisions shown in Question 1. In the table a 1 denotes the highest ranking.

Sales Ranking	Salesperson Expertise Ranking
1	2
9	7
10	9
6	6
7	5
8	10
3	4
4	3
5	8
2	1

a. Compute the correlation between sales and salesperson expertise.
b. Interpret this relationship and determine whether it is statistically significant.

3. Each of 14 respondents were rated accordingly to their exercise habits. Each respondent was classified as either above average (1), average (0), or below average (-1). The following table shows these data along with the gender of the respondents (coded 1 for males and 0 for females).

Gender	Exercise
1	1
1	0
1	-1
1	0
1	0
1	1
1	0
0	0
0	0
0	1
0	-1
0	-1
0	0
0	-1

a. What correlation coefficient is appropriate for these data?

b. Compute the correlation between gender and exercise behavior.

c. Interpret this correlation and determine whether it is statistically significant.

4. For the data shown in Question 1, regress sales on advertising expenditures.

a. How do you interpret the intercept and slope of the regression line?

b. Plot the regression line of the estimate of advertising expenditures and sales.

c. What percent of the variation in sales is explained by advertising expenditures?

d. Is the regression model statistically significant?

e. Compute the residual for the first regional division.

f. What is the predicted sales volume for the first regional division?

5. For the data shown in Question 1, regress sales on advertising expenditures and number of salespersons.

a. Does the inclusion of the number of salespersons in the estimated regression model explain more of the variation in sales?

b. Is the model significant?

c. Interpret the regression model.

d. Which explanatory variable is more important in explaining sales?

ENDNOTES

1. D. Gujarati, *Basic Econometrics* (New York: McGraw-Hill, 1978), p. 12.

2. Ragnar Frisch, *Statistical Confluence Analysis by Means of Complete Regression Systems* (Oslo University, Institute of Economics Publication no. 5, 1934).

3. See Peter Kennedy, "Ballentine: A Graphical Aid for Econometrics," *Australian Economics Papers* 20 (1981), pp. 414–16.

4. The interested reader can consult Samprit Chatterjee and Beatrice Price, *Regression Analysis by Example* (New York: John Wiley & Sons, 1977), for a readable account of these techniques.

5. Excellent discussions of residual analysis can be found in N. Draper and H. Smith, *Applied Regression Analysis* (New York: John Wiley & Sons, 1966).

CASE 1: KENTUCKY FRIED CHICKEN

The following provides details on a Kentucky Fried Chicken (KFC) concept study. Based upon the information provided and any statistical tests you feel are appropriate, prepare a statement of findings.

Purpose

The objective of the research is to assess two alternative concept positionings for Kentucky Fried Chicken ("Chicken Superiority" and "Good For You") through a battery of evaluative scaled measurements that address (1) appeal and (2) relevance.

Method and Scope

Two hundred respondents were recruited via central-location shopping mall intercept. Qualified respondents were screened to meet the following requirements:

— Age 18-49
— Household income *under* $35,000.
— At least four visits to a fast-food restaurant in the past month.
— Past six month KFC visitor.
— Not negative to future KFC visit

Sample quotas were set to provide for a respondent sample that conformed to the following conditions:

— One-half male; one-half female.
— One-half with a child aged 6–18 at home; one-half without a child aged 6–18 at home.

Detailed Findings

Findings are listed in Tables 1–8.

TABLE 1

Overall Rating of Kentucky Fried Chicken

Base: Total respondents	"Chicken superiority"	"Good for you"
	200 %	200 %
Excellent/very good	45	65
Excellent	20	40
Very good	25	25
Good	15	15
Fair	25	10
Poor	15	10

TABLE 2

Summary of Mean Score
Agreement Levels
(7-Point Scales)

Base: Total respondents	"Chicken superiority" 200 $\overline{X}$	"Good for you" 200 $\overline{X}$
Appeal		
The way they described Kentucky Fried Chicken was appealing to me personally	3.80 (1.21)*	5.87 (.98)
I really like the way she talked about Kentucky Fried Chicken	3.77 (1.12)	4.74 (1.01)
Listening to what she said could really make me hungry for Kentucky Fried Chicken	3.45 (1.01)	5.41 (.95)

*Numbers in parentheses give variances.

TABLE 3

Summary of Mean Score
Agreement Levels

Base: Total respondents	"Chicken superiority" 200 $\overline{X}$	"Good for you" 200 $\overline{X}$
Relevance		
The Kentucky Fried Chicken experience described here is something I'd like to have more often	3.45 (1.45)*	3.52 (1.21)
She was talking about some things that matter to me when it comes to fast food	3.63 (1.23)	5.87 (1.01)
She described what I really like about eating Kentucky Fried Chicken	3.60 (1.5)	4.89 (1.01)

*Numbers in parentheses give variances.

TABLE 4

Summary of Top-Box
Agreement Levels
(Strongly Agree)

Base: Total respondents	"Chicken superiority" 200 %	"Good for you" 200 %
Appeal		
The way they described Kentucky Fried Chicken was appealing to me personally	12	36
I really liked the way she talked about Kentucky Fried Chicken	14	36
Listening to what she said could really make me hungry for Kentucky Fried Chicken	15	40
Relevance		
The Kentucky Fried Chicken experience described here is something I'd like to have more often	8	15
She was talking about some things that matter to me when it comes to fast food	14	38
She described what I really like about eating Kentucky Fried Chicken	13	18

	"Chicken superiority"	"Good for you"	
Base: Total respondents	200	200	
Appeal			
The way they described Kentucky Fried chicken was appealing to me personally	−.154	.654	
I really liked the way she talked about Kentucky Fried Chicken	.200	.589	
Listening to what she said could really make me hungry for Kentucky Fried Chicken	.107	.761	
Relevance			
The Kentucky Fried Chicken experience described here is something I'd like to have more often	−.140	.641	
She was talking about some things that matter to me when it comes to fast food	−.200	.742	
She described what I really like about eating Kentucky Fried Chicken	.109	.451	

TABLE 5

Simple Correlation of Attributes to Overall Rating of KFC

	"Chicken superiority"	
	Regression coefficient	Standard error
Eating Kentucky Fried Chicken is a more enjoyable experience than eating most other fast foods (X_1)	2.89	.50
It made me look forward to the next time I get Kentucky Fried Chicken (X_2)	.56	.42
The way they described Kentucky Fried Chicken was appealing to me personally (X_3)	−1.85	1.01
I really liked the way she talked about Kentucky Fried Chicken (X_4)	−1.01	1.25
This reminds me of a lot of other Kentucky Fried Chicken commercials I've seen in the past (X_5)	−.025	.32

$R^2 = .262$; RSS = 16543.21; ESS = 46542.3

TABLE 6

Multiple regression (Overall Rating Regressed on Specific Attribute Ratings)

Correlation matrix

	y	X_1	X_2	X_3	X_4	X_5
y	1.0					
X_1	.67	1.0				
X_2	.23	.45	1.0			
X_3	−.36	−.42	−.67	1.0		
X_4	−.31	−.38	−.42	.50	1.0	
X_5	−.15	−.09	−.16	.25	.10	1.0

TABLE 7

Multiple Regression (Overall Rating Regressed on Specific Attribute Ratings)

	"Good for you"	
	Regression coefficient	Standard error
Eating Kentucky Fried Chicken is a more enjoyable experience than eating most other fast foods (X_1)	2.25	.87
It made me look forward to the next time I get Kentucky Fried Chicken (X_2)	1.32	.35
The way they described Kentucky Fried Chicken was appealing to me personally (X_3)	.87	.25
I really liked the way she talked about Kentucky Fried Chicken (X_4)	1.01	.87
This reminds me of a lot of other Kentucky Fried Chicken commercials I've seen in the past (X_5)	−1.25	.65

$R^2 = .433$; RSS = 19911.394; ESS = 26063.432

Correlation matrix

	y	X_1	X_2	X_3	X_4	X_5
y	1.0					
X_1	.59	1.0				
X_2	.58	.65	1.0			
X_3	.46	.23	.32	1.0		
X_4	.40	.21	.29	.89	1.0	
X_5	−.09	.05	.01	−.14	−.25	1.0

TABLE 8

Demographics

	"Chicken superiority"	"Good for you"
Base: Total respondents	200 %	200 %
Age		
18–24	31	26
25–29	24	26
30–34	17	19
35–39	15	14
40–49	13	15
Household size		
One	9	12
Two	19	24
Three	34	22
Four	20	21
Five or more	18	21
Income		
Under $15,000	21	25
$15,000 to under $25,000	38	35
$25,000 to under $35,000	41	40
Race		
White	72	66
Black	25	26
Other nonwhite	3	8
Markets		
Atlanta	15	15
Chicago	14	14
Detroit	13	13
Houston	23	22
Los Angeles	21	22
Seattle	14	14

CASE 2: AN EVALUATION OF ONE PRINT ADVERTISEMENT FOR VELVET LIQUEUR

The following case exercise is used as an interviewing tool by Perception Research, Inc., Englewood, New Jersey. The instructions and materials that follow appear as they would if you were interviewing at Perception Research, Inc. Following, for a short print ad study, are:

1. A background and objectives statement.
2. Discussions of methodology.
3. Tables of results.

Your assignment is to discuss detailed findings in writing, as if the next step were to give it to the typist. You may include a short summary and conclusions, if you wish.

Our purpose is simply to aid in the evaluation of your ability to organize your thoughts, to draw insights from the data, and to express yourself in writing.

You may type a rough copy or handwrite as you normally might do. Please take as much time as you need to produce what you feel is a representative sample of your work.

Background and Objectives

White Palace Partners, Inc. is currently considering a new advertising execution for a proposed new liqueur product called Velvet.

They have requested that PRS evaluate the new execution to determine if it appears to be a viable introductory vehicle for this new product. The *key* objectives of the new execution were

— An unaided recall score of at least 30 percent.
— A purchase intent top-box level of at least 15 percent.
— A "someone-like-me" level of at least + 25 percent (see user image).

Sample Composition

A total of 75 interviews were conducted among purchasers (past year) and drinkers (past month) of a proprietary liqueur. One-half of the participants were men and one-half of them were women. In addition, one-half were of legal drinking age to 34 and one-half were aged 35–49.

Test Date and Locations

Interviewing was conducted at the PRS test facilities in New Jersey, Florida, California, and Minnesota.

Research Procedures

Participants were screened at each shopping-mall location. They were not, however, prealerted as to the category under consideration.

Qualified respondents were seated in an interviewing booth that contained a slide projector. Participants were informed that they would be viewing a series of advertisements taken from a magazine. They were allowed to spend as much or as little time as they wished viewing each ad.

Unaided and aided recall was then obtained.

Participants were then reexposed to the test ad and asked to examine it in detail. A brief verbal interview was then conducted. Questioning focused on

— Future purchase intent and reasons.
— Product and user image.

Detailed Tables

Tabulated information from the questionnaire is listed in Tables 1–6.

TABLE 1
Unaided Recall (left)

TABLE 2
Total ad recall
(unaided or aided)
(right)

	Total Base: (75) %		Total Base: (75) %
Amaretto di Saronno	69	Kahlua	97
Kahlua	69	American Express	95
Volkswagen Jetta	65	Kool Lights	93
American Express	63	Amaretto di Saronno	91
Hilton Hotel	60	Citizen Watches	91
CocoRibe	59	Hilton Hotel	91
Pentax	52	CocoRibe	87
General Electric	47	Volkswagen Jetta	85
Citizen Watches	40	Pentax	84
Kool Lights	40	General Electric	75
Velvet	33	Grand Marnier	69
Grand Marnier	31	Velvet	61
Test Average*	54	Test Average*	87

Q. Thinking of the ads you just saw, which ones can you remember? Do you recall any other products or companies? Tell me the names of the products and companies you just saw advertised.

*Excluding Velvet.

Q. Here is a list of brand names. Some of these brands appeared in the ads you just saw, while others did not. Please tell me those which you definitely remember having seen, even though you may have mentioned them before.

*Excluding Velvet.

TABLE 3
Purchase Intent

	Total Base: (75) %
Definitely would buy (5)	7 ⎤
Probably would buy (4)	27 ⎦ 34
Might or might not buy (3)	33
Probably would not buy (2)	24 ⎤
Definitely would not buy (1)	9 ⎦ 33
Mean rating	3.0

Q. Assuming Velvet were available at your liquor store, how likely would you be to buy a bottle based on what this ad shows and tells you about the brand? Please tell me the statement on the card that comes closest to describing how you feel about buying Velvet?

	Total			Total
Base:	(75) %		Base:	(75) %

Favorable	51		Other favorable	20
Product attributes	37		Curious/try new products	12
Taste/flavor	33		Would buy for company/guests	4
Almond and orange flavor	20		For special occasions	4
Like almond	7		Unfavorable	28
Would taste good	4		Taste/flavor	23
Would taste similar to Amaretto	3		Dislike almond	11
Other product attributes	13		Wouldn't like orange and almond flavor	8
Like cordials/liqueurs	7		Would be too sweet	5
Italian/imported from Italy	5		Dislike coconut	3
Like the color of the liqueur	3		Visual	5
Visual	16		Bottle	3
Bottle	13		Other visual	3
Like the shape of the bottle	4		Dark color ad	3
Attractive bottle	4		Other unfavorable	4
Cut glass bottle	3		Neutral/conditional	39
Unusual shape bottle	3		Satisfied with current liqueur	11
Other visual	8		Not familiar with it	9
Almonds in the ad	7		Wouldn't buy a bottle until I've tasted it	9
Like the glass	3		Depends on price	9
			Don't drink much liqueur	5

Q. Why do you say that?

TABLE 4

Reasons for Purchase Intent

	Total
Base:	(75) %

Product Image

High quality (versus low quality)	+69
Good after dinner (versus not)	+65
Good for serving to guests (versus not)	+52
Good straight or on-the-rocks (versus not)	+47
An Italian liqueur (versus not)	+44
Has a light orange taste (versus strong)	+43
Would make a good gift (versus would not)	+43
Good tasting (versus is not)	+33
Has a light almond taste (versus strong)	+23
Different from other liqueurs (versus similar)	+21
More expensive than other liqueurs (versus less)	+ 5

User Image

For selective drinkers (versus drink almost anything)	+68
For people who really know liqueurs (versus don't)	+35
For women (versus not for women)	+27
For men (versus not for men)	+24
For someone like me (versus not)	+ 1

Q. On this card are pairs of phrases that could be used to describe a product such as Velvet or the types of people who might buy a product such as this. For each pair of phrases, please indicate how this ad makes you feel about Velvet by placing an "X" in the space that best reflects your feelings.

*Percent selecting the two boxes closest to the description appearing first, minus the percent selecting two boxes closest to the description shown in parentheses, utilizing a five-point semantic differential scale.

TABLE 5

Product and User Image Net Differences*

TABLE 6

Summary for Key Dimensions

| | Previously tested Velvet ads | | | | | | New product liqueur norm |
| | Velvet | A | B | C | D | E | |
Base:	(75) %	(150) %	(151) %	(149) %	(150) %	(151) %	%
Unaided recall	33	15	17	26	28	27	32
Total recall	61	47	50	42	52	38	53
Likes and dislikes							
Any likes	NA	71	75	79	80	75	79
Any dislikes	NA	37	44	48	51	51	49
Net difference	NA	+34	+31	+31	+29	+24	+30
Purchase intent							
Definitely would buy	7] 34	1] 23	9] 31	6] 35	5] 26	5] 29	8] 38
Probably would buy	27	22	22	29	21	24	30
Product image—net differences*							
High quality	+69	+57	+72	+54	+55	+57	+51
Good after dinner	+65	+75	+76	+70	+70	+74	NA
Good for serving to guests	+52	+67	+60	+62	+62	+72	+68
Good straight or on-the-rocks	+47	+71	+72	+71	+66	+69	+65
An Italian liqueur	+44	+49	+89	+68	+81	+68	NA
Has a light orange taste	+43	+39	+23	+32	+39	+39	NA
Would make a good gift	+43	+39	+46	+40	+45	+42	NA
Good tasting	+33	+46	+39	+46	+42	+45	+55
Has a light almond taste	+23	+48	+47	NA	NA	NA	NA
Different from other liqueurs	+21	−3	−8	−7	−5	−13	+18
More expensive than others	+5	+17	+17	+9	+27	+19	+17
User imagery—net differences*							
For selective people	+68	+54	+43	+53	+54	+47	+40
For people who really know liqueur	+35	+48	+47	+50	+51	+54	+41
For women	+27	+46	+58	+57	+65	+64	+65
For men	+24	+27	+19	+29	+34	+35	+15
For someone like me	+1	+25	+34	+29	+28	+27	+29

*Top two boxes minus bottom two boxes, based on a 5-point scale.

CASE 3: CONSUMER ATTITUDES AND PERCEPTIONS TOWARD SEAFOOD WHEN EATING OUT—POSITIONING PHASE

In earlier Case Studies, we introduced details on a study designed to collect information about consumers' attitudes and perceptions toward nontraditional fish consumption when eating out (in particular, see Part II, Case 4). Following is the executive summary for the focus-group phase of this study.

Executive Summary

Overall participants in these focus groups have a favorable attitude toward fish. They are eating more fish today than they ever have in the past, and they expect that consumption to increase. These consumers are more willing and more likely to try fish when eating out than they are at home. In fact, on many occasions they seem to relate eating out with eating fish.

On the other hand, despite the high propensity to eat fish in restaurants, there is significant resistance to trying the nontraditional species that were suggested to the participants in this study. Some participants are familiar with less traditional fish, if only by name, but none speak highly or very favorably about any of them. In some cases perceptions are negative; in many cases they are inaccurate.

In general, it might be said that there is an outright "suspicion" of nontraditional species, that is, that they project an unpleasurable experience. Those who are not familiar with the species mentioned seem to base their perceptions solely on the name. Other influential negative factors are the image of fish as an animal, its eating habits, its appearance, and its social behavior. Those who hold these perceptions are not influenced by those who do not, or by those who have had good experiences with nontraditional species.

Participants agree that they eat fish because they like the way it tastes. Health factors are also mentioned as reasons for consuming fish, particularly by the men. That fish is light and easily digested is mentioned more by the women. Fish is considered a good alternative to red meats, but generally it is not served at home. Many participants say they eat fish in restaurants because it is a change from what is prepared at home. This also depends on the amount of trust they put in the reputation of the restaurant and/or chef.

Factors that can either inhibit or promote the selection of fish include the method of preparation, previous experience, and cost. Although fish is not considered to be inexpensive, it is generally seen as a good food value. Yet some group participants said price prevents them from trying an unfamiliar fish. The risk of disliking the fish is too great relative to the cost in both dollars and the dining experience. A few participants feel that low-priced fish are of poor quality. Others complain about fish being "smelly," "bony," "oily," "slimy," or "too strong."

The consumption of fish in restaurants does not appear to have a direct correspondence with childhood, geographic, ethnic, or religious exposure or experience.

Several ideas for promoting nontraditional fish were suggested. Both men and women agreed that a description of the fish, its type, taste, and method of preparation enhances the likelihood of their trying it if it is unfamiliar.

Other frequently mentioned suggestions were to serve these fish as appetizers or "specials," or to include them in a combination plate. Free samples give people an opportunity to try an unfamiliar fish without the risk. Media suggestions include food preparation programs or morning talk shows with respected authorities like Julia Child.

Also mentioned was the implementation of an industrywide program, one comparable to the American Dairy Association, to promote fish in general. This was considered a good strategy to make consumers more aware of fish as an alternative to other foods.

Other means suggested to promote unfamiliar fish included:

— Make clear that the fish is fresh and prepared to order (but do not overdo, which causes suspicion).

— Offer in a "specialty" restaurant setting, especially a seafood restaurant.

— Price attractively — lower than steaks, for example, but not radically lower than other well-known fish.

— Have recommendations come from the restaurant — that is, from the chef, not from waiters or waitresses.

In addition, focus-group participants were also asked to provide similarity/dissimilarity ratings for eight traditional species of fish:

Fillet of sole	Blue fish	Halibut
Scrod	Salmon	Swordfish
Haddock	Cod	

In the next phase of this research study, interest centered on consumers' attitudes and perceptions of nontraditional fish. Specifically, the objectives were to explore:

— Current eating-out habits of consumers in non-fast-food restaurants.

— Attitudes, beliefs, and intentions of consumers concerning the ordering of fish when eating out.

— Consumers' perceptions of nontraditional fish.

— Consumers' willingness to try nontraditional fish.

— Perception of nontraditional fish species' attributes held by consumers. Familiarity of and satisfaction with selected nontraditional fish.

— Different promotional techniques that might increase consumers' willingness to try nontraditional fish when dining out.

— The relationship among "ideal," perceived, and actual attributes of specific nontraditional fish.

— Characteristics of consumers who would be more willing to try nontraditional fish.

Each of the eleven nontraditional fish species

Butterfish	Squid	Eel
Hake	Pollock	Cusk
Mackerel	Whiting	Tilefish
Monkfish	Skate	

were evaluated on eleven attributes and a "willingness to try" measure, as shown below:

Criteria	Range of Variation	
	(1)	(2)
Willingness to try	Not very	Very
Body	Soft	Firm
Flavor	Mild	Strong
Fat content	Low	High
Oily	Not oily	Very oily
Flaky	Not flaky	Very flaky
Color	White	Dark
Boniness	Not bony	Very bony
Odor	Mild	Strong
Moisture	Dry	Moist
Fleshiness	Lean	Meaty
Fishiness	Not fishy	Very fishy

Table 1 provides mean and percentage rating on "willingness to try" for each nontraditional fish species. Figure 1 presents the profile for the ideal fish, and Figures 2–12 (pages 492–94) present perceptual maps for three user groups ("not willing to try," "uncertain," "very willing to try") for each type of nontraditional fish.

Species	Willingness to try (mean responses)	Not willing (1 & 2)	Uncertain (3)	Very willing (4 & 5)
Butterfish	3.39	27%	22%	51%
Hake	2.96	39	21	40
Mackerel	3.22	35	16	49
Monkfish	2.91	42	18	40
Squid	2.49	57	12	31
Pollock	3.52	24	21	55
Whiting	3.27	28	25	47
Skate	2.52	51	22	27
Eel	2.07	67	12	21
Cusk	2.81	43	21	36
Tilefish	2.41	51	26	23

TABLE 1

Willingness to Try Nontraditional Fish [Scale (1) not very willing to (5) very willing]

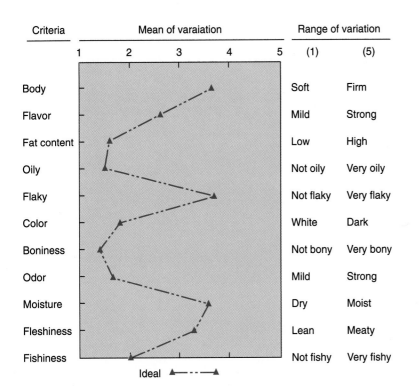

FIGURE 1

Profile of the Ideal Fish

Case Questions

Based upon the results provided in Table 1 and in the perceptual maps that follow, answer the following questions.

1. What are consumers' general attitudes and perceptions of consuming fish when eating out?
2. Recommend a strategy for increasing the consumption of nontraditional fish when eating out.

FIGURE 2
Discriminant Analysis of Butterfish

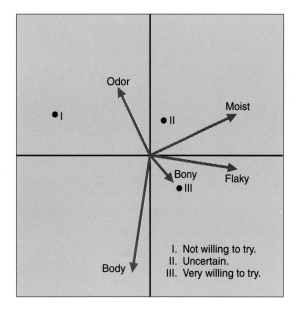

FIGURE 3
Discriminant Analysis of Cusk

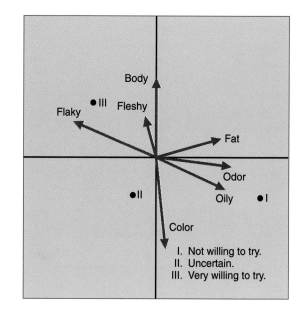

FIGURE 4
Discriminant Analysis of Eel

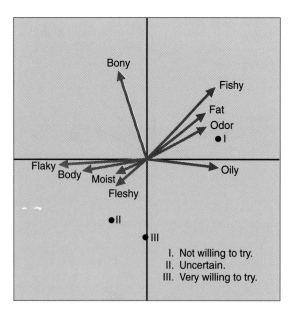

FIGURE 5
Discriminant Analysis of Hake

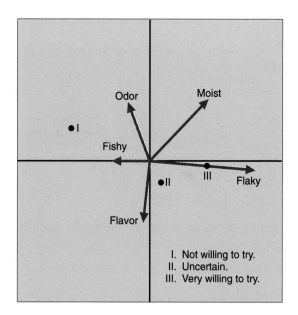

FIGURE 6

Discriminant Analysis of Mackerel

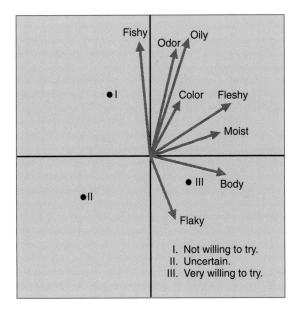

I. Not willing to try.
II. Uncertain.
III. Very willing to try.

FIGURE 7

Discriminant Analysis of Monkfish

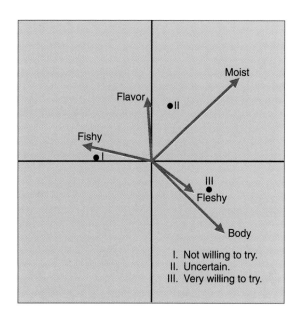

I. Not willing to try.
II. Uncertain.
III. Very willing to try.

FIGURE 8

Discriminant Analysis of Pollock

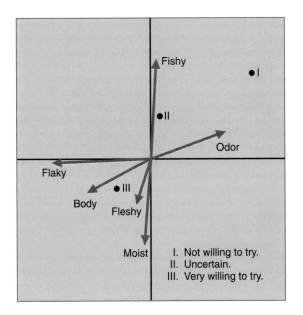

I. Not willing to try.
II. Uncertain.
III. Very willing to try.

FIGURE 9

Discriminant Analysis of Skate

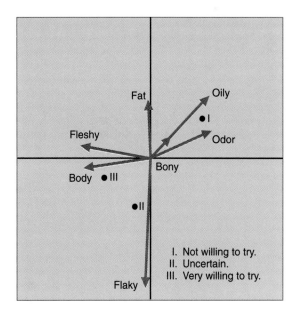

I. Not willing to try.
II. Uncertain.
III. Very willing to try.

FIGURE 10
Discriminant Analysis of Squid

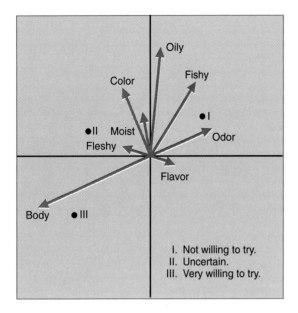

I. Not willing to try.
II. Uncertain.
III. Very willing to try.

FIGURE 11
Discriminant Analysis of Tilefish

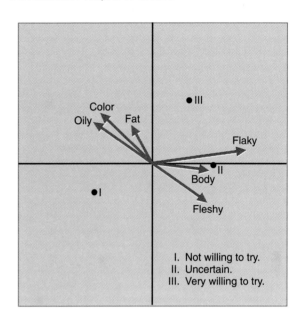

I. Not willing to try.
II. Uncertain.
III. Very willing to try.

FIGURE 12
Discriminant Analysis of Whiting

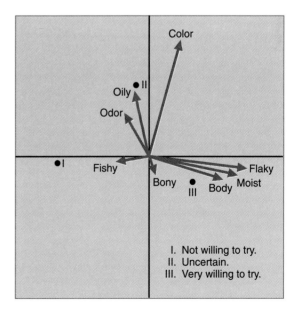

I. Not willing to try.
II. Uncertain.
III. Very willing to try.

CASE 4: BANKING SEGMENTATION STUDY

The YMA advertising agency recently received a request by one of the leading banks in a medium-sized metropolitan area to present its approach to handling the bank's advertising program. The account executive assigned to the account was very interested in obtaining the bank as a client. To formulate the advertising strategy, the account executive decided to commission a research study to assess what consumers thought were the most salient characteristics of banks. The research objective was to obtain information for the design of advertising messages to specified segments.

The research would be conducted in two phases. Phase one would be a series of focus groups that would identify the salient attributes, and phase two would survey the importance that consumers placed on the salient attributes.

The series of focus groups identified 19 characteristics of banks that are important to consumers when choosing a bank or when switching their business to a new bank. The identified attributes are listed below.

1. Variety of services.
2. Reputation for quality service.
3. Convenient locations.
4. Convenient hours.
5. Quick service.
6. Friendly atmosphere.
7. Ease of parking.
8. Senior-citizen privileges.
9. Drive-thru tellers.
10. Banking by phone.
11. No minimum balance required.
12. No service charge for checking accounts.
13. Overdraft protection for checking accounts.
14. Level of interest rates for savings accounts.
15. Level of interest rates on loans.
16. Credit cards available.
17. Automatic Teller Machines (ATMs).
18. No fee for ATM usage.
19. Financial stability.

A mall-intercept study conducted by a local research supplier provided data for phase two. Quotas were specified for sex (50 percent female and 50 percent male) and age (60 percent less than age 35 and 40 percent age 35 or older). Eligible respondents were surveyed to determine (1) the importance of each of the attributes, (2) the usage patterns, and (3) the demographics. The appendix that follows (see pp. 496–97) contains the coding sheet utilized to punch the data.

Case Question

You have been assigned the task of tabbing the data, that is, generating tables for analysis. Prepare the relevant table specifications so that the tab house can generate the tables that you think would be required.

APPENDIX FOR CASE 4

Part One: Importance Ratings

	Not at All Important						Very Important	
Variety of services	0	1	2	3	4	5	6	(1)
Reputation for quality service	0	1	2	3	4	5	6	(2)
Convenient locations	0	1	2	3	4	5	6	(3)
Convenient hours	0	1	2	3	4	5	6	(4)
Quick service	0	1	2	3	4	5	6	(5)
Friendly atmosphere	0	1	2	3	4	5	6	(6)
Ease of parking	0	1	2	3	4	5	6	(7)
Senior citizens privileges	0	1	2	3	4	5	6	(8)
Drive-thru tellers	0	1	2	3	4	5	6	(9)
Banking by phone	0	1	2	3	4	5	6	(10)
No minimum balance required	0	1	2	3	4	5	6	(11)
No service charges for checking	0	1	2	3	4	5	6	(12)
Overdraft protection	0	1	2	3	4	5	6	(13)
Checks returned with statement	0	1	2	3	4	5	6	(14)
Level of interest rates for savings	0	1	2	3	4	5	6	(15)
Level of interest rates for loans	0	1	2	3	4	5	6	(16)
Credit cards	0	1	2	3	4	5	6	(17)
Automatic Teller Machines (ATMs)	0	1	2	3	4	5	6	(18)
No fee for ATM usage	0	1	2	3	4	5	6	(19)
Financial stability	0	1	2	3	4	5	6	(20)

Part Two: Usage:

Frequency of use for banking transactions:

In-bank tellers	_____ times per month	(22–23)
Drive-thru tellers	_____ times per month	(24–25)
ATM	_____ times per month	(26–27)

In an average month, approximately how many checks do you write?   (28)

[ ] 1–10   [ ] 11–20   [ ] 21–40   [ ] 41 +
(1)   (2)   (3)   (4)

In an average month, number of deposits/withdrawals: (29–30)

Deposits	(29)		Withdrawals	(30)
_____	(1)	0–3	_____	(1)
_____	(2)	4–10	_____	(2)
_____	(3)	11 +	_____	(3)

Part Three: Demographics

Are you:	(1)	[ ]	Married	(3)	[ ]	Divorced/separated	(31)
	(2)	[ ]	Single, never married	(4)	[ ]	Widowed	
Are you:	(1)	[ ]	Male	(2)	[ ]	Female	(32)

Into which of the following age categories do you fall? (33)

(1) [ ] 19–24   (4) [ ] 45–54
(2) [ ] 25–34   (5) [ ] 55–64
(3) [ ] 35–44   (6) [ ] 65+

Do you rent or own your home? (34)

(1) [ ] Rent   (2) [ ] Own

Please mark the income category that best matches your total annual
household income. (35)

(1) [ ] Under $15,000   (4) [ ] $45,000–$59,999
(2) [ ] $15,000–$29,999   (5) [ ] $60,000–$74,999
(3) [ ] $30,000–$44,999   (6) [ ] over $75,000

Which category below best describes the level of education you have completed? (36)

(1) [ ] Some high school   (5) [ ] Graduate work/degree
(2) [ ] High school graduate   (6) [ ] Technical school graduate
(3) [ ] Some college   (7) [ ] Community college graduate
(4) [ ] College degree

PRESENTING THE RESEARCH AND ETHICAL ISSUES

BERT DECKER
FOUNDER AND CHAIRMAN
DECKER COMMUNICATIONS

The use of computer technology is ubiquitous in the business world today. The best speakers will take advantage of it to present information.

Unfortunately, there is a hidden flaw in that strategy, says Bert Decker, founder and chairman of Decker Communications in San Francisco. "It is not enough to just present facts," Decker asserts. "People buy on emotion and justify with fact."

Often, the technology can overwhelm the most important part of the presentation—the behavior of the presenter. "You have to connect emotionally with people, or they will tune you out no matter how brilliant your technology is," says Decker, whose 12-year-old company does communication training for business executives, managers, and salespeople throughout the country.

The most popular visual aid is the slide show. But Decker advises against that form because "the big detriment is [that] you get caught up in a scripted slide show and can't interact" with your audience.

For the mechanically adept, live computer graphics on a TV screen are effective visual aids, allowing the presenter to control the visual aid while speaking. However, "the higher the level of technology, the greater the chance of Murphy's Law coming into play," Decker warns.

Decker's visual aid of choice is overhead transparencies that are in color and developed on a computer. "With overhead transparencies, you can have the lights up and control them yourself in a less formal manner," he says.

Overall, Decker urges speakers to use video technology when practicing for a

presentation. "The most important communication tool is yourself—what you do when you're nervous," Decker says. "With camcorders readily available, it is essential to use them and get feedback on how you come across to an audience."

While viewing the tape, be aware of behavioral patterns such as eye contact, nervous gestures, and pauses.

"Use natural animation and energy," Decker says. "Get rid of non-words like 'ums' and 'ahs'. All you have to do is pause, leave a three-second pause, while you think of what to say next. And whatever you say next sounds like a great, momentous statement."

Decker, whose book, *You've Got To Be Believed To Be Heard,* came out in 1992, also cautions speakers to never, except in rare instances, read a speech or stand behind a lectern or podium.

"You are still the most important element in the presentation, not the facts, figures, and information," Decker believes. "You give me a confident, likable, natural presenter who has energy with no inhibition—with no visual aids—and that presenter will always win."

Bert Decker holds a B.A. degree in psychology from Yale University. From his experience as a filmmaker and media consultant to dozens of political candidates (such as Robert Kennedy and Edwin Muskie), he designed a program integrating the latest research findings on speaking, communicating, appearance, and making favorable impressions. His company, Decker Communications, is the fastest-growing communications training company in the United States today.

Presenting the Research

POWER-UP PRESENTATIONS

Every day we are bombarded with images from television, magazines, billboards, books, flyers, and signs. These images have been created by professional artists and designers, and they set a standard that people start to expect from all sources—including business publications and presentations.

It wasn't all that long ago that corporations hired outside graphics houses to create and output their sales and marketing presentations. The process was expensive and time consuming. Marketing executives often felt at the mercy of a group of graphic technologists who were not intimately aware of the nuances of the goods and services for which they were creating presentations. By the time that a presentation was delivered to a field person, the information was often displayed in a format that did not suit the product.

The time and expense of using these graphics houses prevented many companies from creating internal presentations that were visually stimulating and easily comprehensible. Peer meetings were marred by low quality, out-of-focus transparencies and executives were constantly inundated with reams of boring tabular information that was difficult to assimilate and utilize when decisions needed to be made.

The business people creating those publications and presentations often have little or no training in graphic design, and have to meet real-world budgets and deadlines. How can these people produce attention-getting transparencies, slides, newsletters, and other materials?

The introduction of computer graphics a few years ago brought promises of a solution. But the combination of underpowered computer systems, immature software, and low-resolution clip art kept the performance of computer graphics from meeting the promise. Until now.

A new generation of powerful PC's, a revolution in graphic user interfaces, and a new generation of powerful graphics software is allowing busy executives, managers, and secretaries to create professional artwork that informs, persuades, and gets attention.

CHAPTER
OBJECTIVES

EXPLAIN
the considerations involved in
communicating research
findings to management.

DISCUSS
general guidelines for writing
the research report.

EXPLAIN
the organization of the
research project.

DISCUSS
general guidelines for the oral
presentation.

ILLUSTRATE
the use of visual aids.

New graphics software is taking advantage of today's powerful computer systems to provide business people with easy-to-use tools for creating high-quality transparencies, slides, and other materials on a daily basis. The premise behind this revolution is graphics composition: the belief that while not everyone can draw, everyone can assemble graphic forms into coherent compositions.

Because some new software packages allow people to bypass the often insurmountable step of drawing images from scratch, they have become a tool that everyone can use.

The key to these graphic composition systems are their collection of flexible art forms. Many graphics programs include clip art in the form of completely finished illustrations, and woe upon the person who wants to make changes. The more flexible programs, on the other hand, are open in design. Art forms can be mixed and manipulated to quickly create original illustrations.

Today it is common to see executives, mid-level managers, and secretaries utilizing graphics software packages to "power-up" their presentations. The advantages of the "do it yourself" trend are staggering: marketers have more control over the look of their presentations, data can be updated rapidly, middle managers and executives have access to graphically animated data at their desks, and production costs have been greatly reduced.

Source: *Marketing Insights,* Summer 1991, pp. 109–11. Reprinted with permission.

INTRODUCTION

Marketing researchers do not work for themselves. The results of their research must be effectively communicated to company managers. As we have seen, there are some interesting ways to communicate research results.

Research results are usually provided to managers in an oral presentation and a formal written research report. The report and presentation are important for three reasons. First, the research report is tangible evidence of the research project—after the study has been completed and a decision is made, there is very little physical evidence of the resources in time, money, and effort that went into the project. Second, the written report and oral presentation are typically the only aspect of a study that many marketing executives are exposed to—management's evaluation of the research project rests on how well this information is communicated. Third, the effectiveness and usefulness of the material contained in the written report are critical in determining whether that particular supplier will be used in the future.

Every research firm has its own style, and each person writes differently. Nevertheless, there are some basic principles for writing a clear research report and for making a good oral presentation. The principles we discuss in this chapter provide a perspective on style that can help you to communicate the critical essence of your marketing research study.

WRITTEN REPORT

We have said that the written report is critical because (1) it is the basis upon which decisions are made, (2) it serves as a historical record, and (3) it is critical in determining whether the supplier will get future research projects. Preparing a research project involves more than writing, which is the last step in the process. Before writing can take place, the results of the research project must be fully understood, and some thought given to how the results are best presented. Thus, preparing a research report involves three steps: *understanding, organizing,* and *writing.*

Usually, the marketing research supplier will review the data and discuss specific requirements with a marketing person from the sponsoring firm. This "meeting" can be by telephone or in person. The first step is to outline the major findings and to arrange them in order of priority. All report requirements are clearly explicated at this time. The meeting confirms specific dates for the report to be delivered and for other data, if requested, to be available.

The marketing research supplier is responsible for report writing. What the client (sponsoring firm) wants is a well-analyzed, tersely written report. Typically, either the marketing research analyst or another marketing executive at the sponsoring firm will be responsible for the final editing and for writing the "Marketing Implications and Recommendations" section. Whether you write research reports at a supplier house, are a marketing research analyst who must edit and write specific sections of the research report, or are a brand manager or other marketing executive who must react to and use the information communicated in written research reports, there are several aspects of report writing that you should be aware of.

General Guidelines

The guidelines you would follow in writing any report or research paper should be followed when you write a marketing research report.

Think of your audience.   Marketing researchers are primarily involved in planning and conducting marketing research studies. Marketing managers use the results of a study to make decisions, and it is they who must understand the report. Don't be overly technical or use too much jargon; in other words, the tone and content of the research report must be appropriate for the audience that will read it.

Understand the results and draw conclusions.   The marketing managers who read the report will expect to see interpretive conclusions about the information presented in the research report. Thus, before you write, you must have an overall understanding about what the results mean, and you must be able to describe the results in a few sentences. Simply reiterating facts that are presented in tables and exhibits won't do.

Be complete yet concise.   A written report should be complete in the sense that it stands by itself and needs no additional clarification. Remember that for the majority of people who read the report it will be their only exposure to the project. On the other hand, the report must be concise: It must focus on the critical elements of the project, leaving out minor issues and findings. The "Background and Objectives" section of the proposal provides a guideline for deciding what is important and what is not.

Report Format

The organization of the written report essentially follows the format used in developing the research proposal. Exhibit 18–1 presents a typical organizational structure.

Title page.   The title page should contain:
1. A title that accurately conveys the essence of the study.
2. The date.
3. The agency (typically, a marketing research supplier) submitting the report.
4. The organization that has sponsored the study.
5. The names of those persons who should receive the written report.

Table of contents.   The table of contents lists:
1. The sequence of topics covered in the report, along with page references.

EXHIBIT 18–1

Report Format

The organization of the written research report essentially follows the format used in developing the research proposal. The following outline is the suggested format for writing the research report:

 I. Title page.
 II. Table of contents.
 III. Introduction.
    A. Background and objectives.
    B. Methodology.
       — Sample.
       — Procedure.
       — Questionnaire.
    C. Action standards.
 IV. Management summary.
    A. Key findings.
    B. Conclusions.
    C. Marketing implications and recommendations.
 V. Detailed findings.
    A. Evaluative measures.
    B. Diagnostic measures.
    C. Profile composites.
 VI. Appendices.
    A. Questionnaire.
    B. Field materials.
    C. Statistical output (supporting tables not included in body).

2. The various tables and exhibits contained in the report, along with page references.

Introduction. The introduction section of the report gives details on the research project regarding (1) background and objectives, (2) methodology, and (3) action standards. This section closely follows the research proposal, except that any technical jargon that might have been used in the research proposal should be translated into everyday terms. This section tells the reader why the study was conducted, how it was conducted, and how the results were evaluated.

Management summary. The management summary is perhaps the most important component of the written report because many managers who are designated to receive the report will read only this section. For this reason, the management summary must be clear and concise. It presents findings, accompanied by interpretive conclusions. The conclusions should answer research questions derived from the study objectives, and they should be supported by study findings. Exhibit 18–2 provides a prototypical management summary.

EVALUATIVE MEASURES

Research findings that help answer the question, "What happened?"

Detailed findings. The detailed findings section provides information about key measures collected in the study. Typically, findings are reported for: (1) **evaluative measures** such as purchase-intent, which help answer

EXHIBIT 18—2

Management Summary

The revised edition of the Westbank Access Account commercial, "Money Crazed II" performs somewhat better than its predecessor, "Money Crazed." Money Crazed II generates greater brand-name recognition on an unaided basis (while performing at parity on total recall) and communicates a broader spectrum of benefits (combined accounts, banking ease, higher interest rates, fee savings) than the earlier version (convenient access and check-bouncing protection). Both versions are seen as relevant, creating positive attitudes toward Westbank, entertaining, and realistic, while being deficient in news value area and for generating purchase motivation.

— Money Crazed II is at least as intrusive as Money Crazed. Although no differences emerge between the two ads for total recall (with nearly 9 in 10 viewers recalling the Westbank Access Account brand name), the revised execution (Money Crazed II) achieves levels of unaided brand-name recall (64 percent) that are significantly higher than levels realized for the original Money Crazed execution (50 percent).

— Although Money Crazed II is not an improvement over Money Crazed, the executional device is still prominent in communication playback (40 percent mention at least one executional element in Money Crazed II, 52 percent for Money Crazed). Most important, nearly 7 in 10 Money Crazed II viewers and better than half of all Money Crazed viewers recall some services. Key areas of playback for each execution are outlined below.

Money Crazed	Money Crazed II
24-hour banking	Checking/savings in one account
Easy access to money	Interest rates (high/er)
Checks won't bounce	Transferring money
Get cash fast	Fee savings

Responses to the bank service recall and main-point questions were quite similar to those cited above.

— Consumers evaluated the Westbank Access Account ad on a series of viewer response profile characteristics in order to yield information on entertainment value, empathy, confusion, familiarity, relevance, and brand reinforcement. Money Crazed II is rated at parity on most items vis-à-vis Money Crazed, although Money Crazed was described as more entertaining and realistic, and it provided a message individuals could identify with.

On the positive side, both executions were relevant, reinforcing favorable brand attitudes, providing entertainment value, and presenting their respective messages in a realistic manner. Also, both commercials were judged as weak in providing news value and a message that bank customers would identify with.

— Interest in opening a Westbank Access Account (after exposure to the ad) is relatively low, and both versions performed at parity on this measure: 44 percent of Money Crazed viewers said that they "definitely/probably would open an Access Account," whereas 41 percent of Money Crazed II respondents made the same assertion.

the question, "What happened?"; (2) **diagnostic measures** such as likes/dislikes and attribute ratings, which help answer the question, "Why did it happen?"; and, finally, (3) **profile composites,** of heavy users, for instance, which help answer the question, "To whom did it happen?" In all cases, detailed findings are reported in order of importance with the unaided-question format results reported first, followed by the aided-question format results. This section, which usually is written by the sponsoring firm, specifically focuses on the marketing problem at hand and, more importantly, uses the research findings and conclusions to provide alternative actions that can potentially solve the problem.

DIAGNOSTIC MEASURES

Like/dislike and attribute ratings that help answer the question, "Why did it happen?"

PROFILE COMPOSITES

Research findings that answer the question, "To whom did it happen?"

Appendices.   The appendix, or appendices, contains information that will not be of primary interest to all readers of the research report. The sampling plan, copies of the questionnaire, details on the interviewing procedures and general field instructions, and in-depth statistical tables generally are relegated to the appendix.

Presenting the Data

Easy-to-understand tables and graphics will greatly enhance the accessibility of the written research report. All tables and figures that appear in the report should contain: (1) an identification number to permit easy reference; (2) a title that conveys the contents of the table; and (3) table banner heads (column labels), table stub heads (row labels), and **legends,** which define specific elements in the exhibit. Tables should be labeled consistently and appear in a logical, meaningful order for the reader. For example, the column of data that shows the "control" product in a five-cell product test should be placed either first or last, so that the reader can readily compare the four "test" products to it. A table that summarizes data that are multidimensional (likes/dislikes, attribute ratings, usage occasions) should be ordered so that the characteristic that has the highest frequency of response appears first.

Exhibit 18–3 displays typical illustrations of how data can be presented in tabular and graphic form. Three commonly used graphic presentations are shown: the pie chart, the bar chart, and the line chart. (You will recall that we have already discussed graphic representations of data in Chapter 14).

LEGENDS
Explanations of specific elements in a figure.

Pie chart.   A pie chart is a circle divided into sections, where the size of each section corresponds to a portion of the total. Part B of Exhibit 18–3 displays the market share data, given in Part A of the figure, in the form of four pie charts. Notice that each section of each pie reflects a brand's market share in the respective region.

Bar chart.   A bar chart displays data in the form of vertical (or horizontal) bars, where the length of each bar reflects the magnitude of the variable of interest. Parts C and D of Exhibit 18–3 display two types of bar charts for the market-share data given in Part A.

Line chart.   A line chart is a graph. Part E of Exhibit 18–3 presents a line chart for the market-share data given in Part A. Line charts are superior to bar charts when (1) the data involve a long time period; (2) several series are involved; (3) the emphasis is on the movement rather than the actual amount; (4) trends of frequency distributions are presented; (5) a multiple-amount scale is used; or (6) estimates, forecasts, interpolation, or extrapolation will be shown.

EXHIBIT 18—3
Three Commonly Used Graphic Presentations: The Pie Chart, The Bar Chart, and The Line Chart

Part A: Market shares by region

Brand	Region			
	North	South	East	West
A	.10	.35	.12	.30
B	.15	.25	.18	.05
C	.30	.08	.35	.11
D	.20	.12	.10	.14
E	.25	.20	.25	.40

Part B: Market shares by region (pie chart)

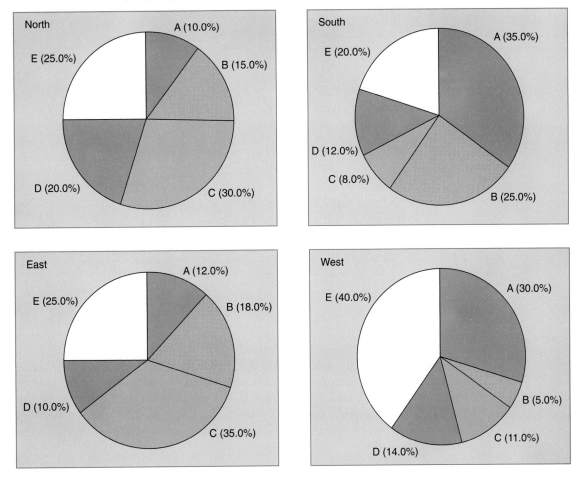

EXHIBIT 18–3   (*continued*)

Part C. Market shares by region (bar chart)

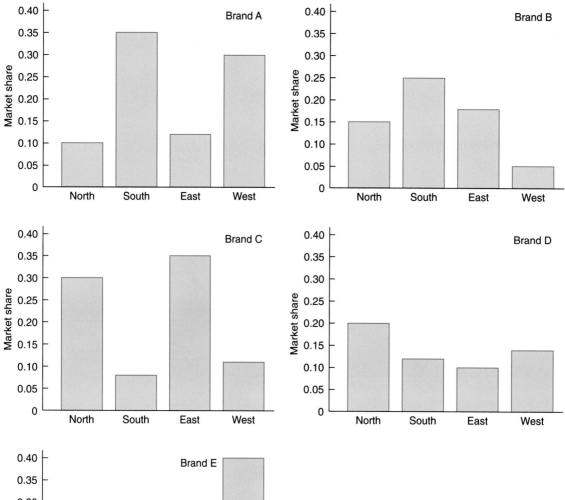

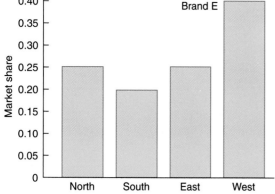

EXHIBIT 18–3 *(continued)*

Part D. Market shares by region (bar chart)

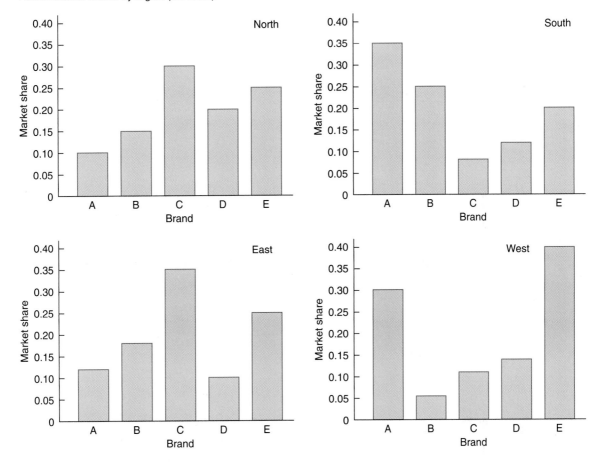

ORAL PRESENTATION

In many instances, the oral presentation is as important in determining how the overall project is received as the written report. It provides the management team with opportunities to ask questions and to have points clarified; most importantly, it allows managers to think aloud about their interpretations of the research findings. Typically, major projects require a series of informal oral reports as well as a formal oral presentation given at the conclusion of the study. The concluding oral presentation by the sponsoring firm can take place before or after the written research report has been distributed.

General Guidelines

The general guidelines for written reports apply equally well to oral presentations. In addition, the following suggestions may prove useful:

1. Prepare a written script or detailed outline for the presentation.

EXHIBIT 18–3   *(concluded)*

Part E. Market shares by region (line chart)

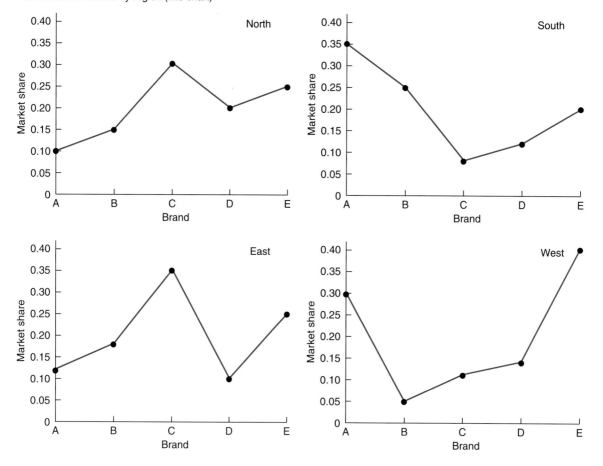

2. Begin the presentation with a discussion of the background of the study, the research objectives, and the method used.
3. Make extensive use of visual aids.
4. Practice the presentation several times in front of a live audience.
5. Check audiovisual equipment thoroughly before the presentation.

Exhibit 18–4 presents guidelines by Decker Communications, Inc., a consulting firm that specializes in giving seminars about effective communication techniques.

Visual Aids

Visual aids are critical to the oral presentation. Exhibit 18–5 lists several considerations in the use of visual aids.

EXHIBIT 18—4

Seven Secrets to a
Memorable Oral
Presentation

1. **The "So-What Test"**

   What are three benefits to my listeners?

2. **Attention-Getting Opening**

   What will grab my listeners' attention and focus their interest on my topic?

3. **Two Experiences, Brief Stories, or Examples**

   What personal or business-related experiences support my key points?

4. **Quote(s)**

   What did somebody else say that is relevant to my topic or situation?

5. **Analogies**

   How can I compare my ideas with examples that are familiar to my audience? What about: statistical comparisons? Humorous stories? Metaphors? Future projections—"what ifs—"? Can I use vivid descriptions that are easily visualized?

6. **Pictures in My Visual Aids**

   How can I help my audience to picture and to remember the situation?

7. **Strong Closing**

   A day, a week, a month from now, what do I want my listeners to *do*? What do I want them to *remember?* To *know?* What lasting *feeling* do I want them to *feel?* If all they remember is my last statement, *what counts most?*

Source: Decker Communications, Inc. (San Francisco, 1982).

EXHIBIT 18—5

Principles in Using Visual
Aids

Support your *point of view.*

Give only what listeners *need to know.*

Discuss information in *bite-size pieces.*

Remember, visual means *visual* (not just letters and numbers).

Apply *big, bold, and brilliant.*

Always *appropriate.*

Use *rule of threes* (maximum of six).

Don't *read* (look at visual, then talk to listeners!).

Source: Decker Communications, Inc. (San Francisco, 1982).

Overhead projector acetates, graphic poster boards, and 35-mm slides can be effective for communicating the research findings. Exhibit 18–6 presents several different 35-mm slide formats. Today, visual aids like the ones shown in Exhibit 18–6 can be constructed on a personal computer by using computer-graphics software packages.

By way of summary, Exhibit 18–7 provides pros and cons and do's and don'ts of using flip charts, overheads, and slides.

EXHIBIT 18—6

35-mm Slide Formats for
Oral Presentations

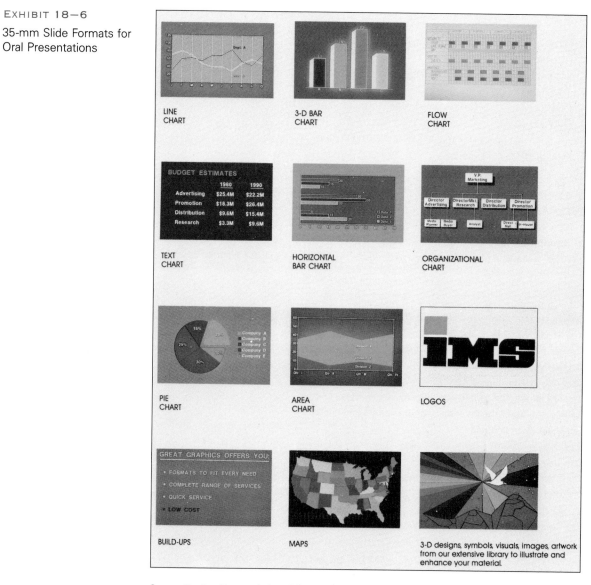

Source: Reprinted by permission of Great Graphics.

EXHIBIT 18—7

Visual Aids: Pros and
Cons and Do's and Don'ts

Flip Charts—Best for Smaller, More Informal Groups

Pro:

Quick and easy to prepare.
Inexpensive.
Easy to use.
Flexible.
Interactive with group.

Con:

Limited audience size.
Limited control.
Quality is limited or costly.
Bulky to carry.

Techniques:

Do:
Consider visibility/readability.
Prepare in advance, fill in data.
Speak to listeners, *not chart!*
Pencil notes lightly on side.
Remove after use.
Use color.
Use to record sensitive questions.
Turn page to reach conclusion.

Don't:
Put too much information/detail on.
Talk to the chart.
Play with marking pen or pointer.
Write too small or too light.

Overhead Projector—Most Versatile

Pro:

Quick and easy.
Fully lit room.
You can turn it on and off.
Face your listeners.
Portable.
Almost any size group.
Use overlays.
Inexpensive.
Easy last-minute changes.

Con:

Limited full-color effect.
Poor photo projection.
Screen placement.
Sometimes it is less professional.

Techniques:

Do:
Use revelation.
Turn light on and off.
Have a friend change transparencies.
Locate transparency in advance.
Use pencil as a pointer.
Place screen in corner.
Make notes on frame.
Use overlay technique.

Don't:
Put too much information/detail on the screen.
Talk to machine.
Leave light on.
Be married to machine.

Slides—Best for Formal, Structured Speeches

Pro:

Excellent visual effect.
Directed light.
Very professional.
Colorful and creative.
Portable.
Any size group.
Easily reproducible.

EXHIBIT 18—7
(concluded)

Con:	Lack of control (canned). Limited eye contact (lose eye contact). Lead time required (last-minute changes difficult). Cost factors.
Techniques:	*Do:* Keep a light on *you.* Reveal one line at a time. Show in six-slide segments. Show five seconds per slide. Dry run for sequence. *Don't:* Think that slides are your presentation—*You are!* Read slides. Fidget with remote control. Beware . . . early morning or after lunch.

Source: Decker Communications, Inc. (San Francisco, 1982).

SUMMARY

The written report and the oral presentation are the culmination of the months of work involved in any marketing research study. They are the final product of the study, not an incidental byproduct. Both the written report and the oral presentation must be prepared with care and attention to detail. They should follow the general guidelines that apply to any report or presentation in the social sciences. Elements that are specific to a marketing research report, moreover, require special attention; the management summary is an example. Good reports and presentations will get the attention they deserve, and most likely they will get more business for the supplier. In conclusion, remember to:

— Think of your audience.

— Be concise, yet complete.

— Understand the results and draw conclusions.

— Begin an oral presentation with a discussion of the study, the research objectives, and the methodology used.

— Use visual aids appropriately.

KEY CONCEPTS

Research Report   *Management Summary*   *Visual Aids*

Report Format   *Oral Presentation*

REVIEW QUESTIONS

1. What general guidelines would you follow in writing a research report and in preparing an oral presentation?

2. In Chapter 16 you performed several different types of hypothesis tests. For review questions 2–5 in that chapter, recast your results in language that a manager would easily understand.

3. Comment on the statement: "Although visual aids are critical to the oral presentation, it doesn't matter whether one uses flip charts, an overhead projector, or slides."

4. Go through *The Wall Street Journal* or other business publication such as *Business Week* or *Fortune* and pick out three graphic illustrations. For each graphic

	Quarterly Income (000) Fiscal Quarter Ending					
	06/30/91	03/31/91	09/30/90	06/30/90	03/31/90	09/30/89
Net sales	$26,982,000	$30,193,000	$28,826,000	$25,669,000	$26,383,000	$23,432,000
Cost of goods	14,129,000	15,578,000	15,683,000	13,389,000	11,424,000	12,287,000
Gross profit	12,853,000	14,615,000	13,143,000	12,280,000	14,959,000	11,145,000
R&D expenditures	193,000	185,000	261,000	212,000	190,000	211,000
Selling, general, and administrative expenses	9,750,000	9,947,000	9,734,000	8,864,000	11,161,000	7,730,000
Income before depreciation and amortization	2,910,000	4,483,000	3,148,000	3,204,000	3,608,000	3,204,000
Depreciation and amortization	1,188,000	1,205,000	1,185,000	1,323,000	1,286,000	1,205,000
Nonoperating income	285,000	492,000	191,000	309,000	330,000	225,000
Interest expense	173,000	248,000	240,000	321,000	391,000	373,000
Income before tax	1,834,000	3,522,000	1,914,000	1,869,000	2,261,000	1,851,000
Provision for income taxes	662,000	1,181,000	781,000	769,000	910,000	667,000
Minority interest (income)	47,000	101,000	58,000	n.a.	71,000	74,000
Net income before extraordinary items	1,125,000	2,240,000	1,075,000	1,100,000	1,280,000	1,110,000
Net income	$ 1,125,000	$ 2,240,000	$ 1,075,000	$ 1,100,000	$ 1,280,000	$ 1,110,000

n.a. = Not available.

illustration determine what type of chart or graphic presentation is being used and discuss its positive and negative features.

5. The above table provides information on the operating income of Exxon, Inc.

a. Develop a visual aid to present Exxon's quarterly gross profit.
b. Develop a visual aid that would compare the change in net income to the change in net sales.
c. Develop a visual aid that would present information on how expenses change over the six quarters.

Ethical Issues

RIGHT TO PRIVACY ISSUE PITS CONSUMERS AGAINST MARKETERS, RESEARCHERS

Big Brother is no longer watching you. He's accessing you.

Just about anyone in any facet of sales and marketing with a computer and a checkbook can not only buy names of consumers, but also information regarding everything from their finances to their favorite flavors. Whether or not consumers pop up as part of a marketing research study or, more often, a telemarketing campaign is beyond their control.

The question is whether the marketing research, telemarketing, and direct marketing communities infringe on each other to the point that their own self-regulating policies are insufficient to provide comfortable levels of consumer privacy.

"Where it becomes an issue," said Larry Chiagouris, senior vice president and director of strategic planning at the Bozell ad agency in New York, "is where people don't know that when they buy a car, subscribe to a magazine, respond to an 800 (telephone) number solicitation, etc., their name goes into a file. Marketing professionals sell those names to other professionals."

It has become an accepted way of doing business, and "there's nothing wrong with that," he said. "We never give a name that's been generated under research to a direct marketing organization."

Despite his assertion, and similar ones from his peers, Chiagouris and his colleagues know that the public holds somewhat different perceptions.

And the public seems to have a friend in the government, at least with the privacy issue.

Bonnie Guiton, director of the U.S. Office of Consumer Affairs and special adviser to President Bush on the matter, told a congressional subcommittee last month that the 1970 Fair Credit Reporting Act (FCRA) is no longer sufficient to guarantee respect for consumer privacy, at least not in regard to "the business community's need to base credit and other business decisions on adequate and relevant information."

She hinted at changes in the FCRA, or new laws altogether.

Consumers, she told the subcommittee, "would be surprised to learn that financial information they generally regarded as confidential is used as a criterion to put them on lists that are subsequently sold to marketers for a myriad of uses," despite what she described as "the efforts of dedicated consumer educators," such as the Your Opinion Counts (YOC) Public Education Program.

"Consumers need to understand all the methods companies use to get their

CHAPTER

19

CHAPTER
OBJECTIVES
—

DEFINE
ethics

DISCUSS
the factors leading to
business ethics.

DISCUSS
ethics in marketing research.

DISCUSS
ethical issues relating to
respondents, clients, and the
general public.

PRESENT
a behavioral decision model
of ethical/unethical decisions.

PRESENT
possible solutions to control
current unethical marketing
research practices.

"The proliferation of telemarketing hurts our efforts. YOC is pretty much funded by other associations, including the Marketing Research Association (MRA), the Council of American Statistical and Research Organizations (CASRO), and the AMA."

And although the AMA, CASRO, MRA and other organizations have codes of ethics, "We have to make the public aware that we have a code of ethics," said William D. Neal, senior executive officer at Sophisticated Data Research in Atlanta, and a former vice president of the AMA's Marketing Research Division. "Everyone who calls is put in the same group, whether it is a marketing researcher or a telemarketer."

Neal called state certification programs a "disaster" because marketing research operators who conduct telephone surveys nationwide would have to be certified in every state. He said Florida, California, Georgia, and others have taken the initiative ahead of the federal government and passed their own privacy laws, short of certification.

Source: Howard Schlossberg, *Marketing News,* October 23, 1989, pp. 1, 19. Used with permission.

names, addresses, and telephone numbers with or without their permission," Guiton added.

"There is confusion in the consumers' minds," said Corinne Maginnis, a vice president at MARC research in Irving, Texas, and chairman of the YOC Public Educational Program.

"That is the problem we deal with," she said. "We're associated with those [direct and telemarketing firms]. Marketing research is different. Marketing research is 99% done off of random sampling or client-supplied lists.

INTRODUCTION

This final chapter broaches the subject of ethics in general terms, then focuses on the ethical and unethical practices of marketing research. Following a general definition of ethics—specifically ethics in business situations—a model depicting the internal and external influences on the decision to behave in an ethical or an unethical manner is presented and discussed. The chapter then addresses the concerns of ethical/unethical marketing research practices from the perspective of customers, clients, and the general public. The chapter closes with some recommendations for assuring ethical practices in marketing research.

ETHICS DEFINED

Throughout history many scholars have devoted their time to the development of a theory of ethics. Some have advocated a normative perspective in which the theorists construct moral standards and codes that one ought to follow. Other scholars have followed a positive perspective of ethics, which attempts to describe and explain how individuals actually behave in an ethical situation.

A major preoccupation of many ethical theories has been an attempt at providing a universal definition of ethics. After reviewing many definitions of ethics, John Tsalikis and David Fritzsche concluded that the term ethics is often considered synonymous with morals. And, therefore, ethics refers to the study of moral conduct.[1]

In a major study, Phillip Lewis reviewed 158 textbooks and 50 articles on business ethics from the period 1961 to 1981.[2] In addition, a survey was randomly distributed to 359 blue-collar workers and white-collar executives. The survey simply asked, "What is your definition of business ethics?" Based on the results of the study, four concepts emerged as integral to a definition of business ethics:

1. Rules, standards, codes, or principles.
2. Morally right behavior.
3. Truthfulness.
4. Specific situations.

Lewis noted that in addition to the four concepts, business ethics also may be defined in terms of the following:[3]

1. Focus on social responsibility.
2. Emphasis on honesty and fairness.
3. Emphasis on the Golden Rule.
4. Values that are in accord with common behavior or with one's religious beliefs.
5. Obligations, responsibilities, and rights toward conscientious work or enlightened self-interest.
6. Philosophy of what is good and bad.
7. Ability to clarify the issues in decision making.

8. Focus on one's individual conscience and/or legal system.

9. System or theory of justice questioning the quality of one's relationships.

10. Relationship of means to ends.

11. Concern for integrity, what ought to be, habit, logic, and/or principles of Aristotle.

12. Emphasis on virtue, leadership, character, confidentiality, judgment of others, placing God first, situationalness, temporalness, and publicness.

As defined by Lewis, "Business ethics is moral rules, standards, codes, or principles which provide guidelines for right and truthful behavior in specific situations."[4]

ETHICS IN MARKETING RESEARCH

As early as 1962, Leo Bogart identified four possible ethical/unethical situations in marketing research:[5]

— The extent of the researcher's honesty in doing what he/she purports to do.

— The manipulation of research techniques in order to produce desired findings.

— The propriety of business judgement exercised in undertaking research (e.g., when a client chooses to define a problem in terms the researcher cannot accept).

— The forthright relationship of the researcher to those interviewed regarding the study's true purpose and sponsorship.

These situations are still prevalent today and highlight the potential ethical/ unethical practices and dilemmas facing the marketing researcher and between the researcher and (1) the research respondent, (2) the researcher's client, and (3) the general public. These constituencies are discussed in the sections that follow.

Research Respondents

Marketing researchers must have integrity. After all, they expect respondents to be willing participants who honestly and accurately respond to their questions. Presumably, respondents agree to provide information because they believe it is a valuable commodity and that the exercise is in their best interest. However, they are entitled to expect marketing researchers to respect their rights.

Alice Tybout and Gerald Zaltman introduced what they called the respondent's bill of rights.[6] These rights included the:

— Right to choose. There should be no forced compliance.

— Right to safety. If confidentiality is promised, then respondents must remain anonymous. That is, they are not identified with their responses.

— Right to be informed. Respondents should be debriefed at the end of the study, especially if an experimental manipulation is used.

AN AD AGENCY GOES TO COURT IN BOSTON

A David and Goliath courtroom fight is starting in Boston, and the outcome could shake the loyalty some advertisers have to their agencies.

At issue is how aggressively an agency can promote its past experience for a competitor when going after a potential new client.

Apart from advertiser concerns regarding the ability of agencies to keep proprietary information confidential, the Boston case also is raising questions about the procedures agencies have to protect such information.

The issue may get a full airing, courtesy of Rossin Greenberg Seronick & Hill, a $26 million agency that is about to countersue Lotus Development Corp., a $200 million computer software marketer.

Cambridge, Massachusetts-based Lotus sued the agency earlier this month, after software rival Microsoft Corp., Redmond, Washington, forwarded a copy of a flier it had received from Boston-based RGS&H, which was pitching the $10 million-plus Microsoft business.

The court granted Lotus a temporary restraining order barring RGS&H from revealing any trade secrets, effectively barring the agency from pitching the Microsoft or any other Lotus competitors' account.

The flier sent to Microsoft said: "You probably haven't thought about talking to an agency in Boston. . . . But since we know your competition's plans, isn't it worth taking a flier?

"The reason we know so much about Lotus is that some of our newest employees just spent the past year and a half working on the Lotus business at another agency.

"So they are intimately acquainted with Lotus' thoughts about Microsoft and their plans to deal with the introduction of [Microsoft] Excel."

Rob Lebow, Microsoft director of corporate communications and the coordinator of its agency review, said he was "horrified" by the RGS&H flier.

"And I'm no choirboy," Mr. Lebow added.

RGS&H President Neal Hill said he will wait to determine what kind of countercharges to file until after a December 23 hearing in Suffolk Superior Court, when Lotus presents its case. He acknowledged, however, that a protracted—and costly—legal battle could effectively close down the agency.

Lotus contends it is protecting its proprietary corporate information by enforcing a confidentiality clause in its contract with its agency, Leonard Monahan Sabaye, Providence, Rhode Island.

Whereas Tybout and Zaltman focused primarily on experimental research,[7] Kenneth Schneider discussed ethical issues with respect to respondents in both survey and experimental research.[8] His ethical/unethical issues centered on respondent abuse concerning:

1. Deceptive/fraudulent practices—for example, fake sponsorship, or not keeping responses anonymous.
2. Lack of consideration for subjects—for example, poorly conducted surveys, or failure to debrief.
3. Invasion of privacy—for example, undisclosed one-way mirrors, or projective techniques.

"If a client fires an agency, in my view it's perfectly appropriate for an agency to go after a client in the same category, and the quicker the better," said Jack Bowen, chairman-CEO, D'Arcy Masius Benton & Bowles, New York.

But, he adds, it is "despicable" for an agency to try to sell confidential information about the old client to the new one.

Many shops have informal policies governing exchange of proprietary information.

Other agencies say ethical considerations and ordinary judgment determine how and when to capitalize on prior experience in a category.

"When we have confidential information for a client and they resign us or we resign them, it's still confidential as far as I'm concerned," said Marvin Sloves, chairman-CEO of Scali, McCabe, Sloves, New York.

"The general rule is to protect clients," said John McNamara, president-chief operating officer of McCann-Erickson Worldwide, New York.

"There's a thin line between experience and first-hand, recent knowledge (of a competitor's business). I can't imagine a new-business presentation in which the agency didn't introduce people who worked on the prospect's kind of business," Mr. McNamara said.

He said some agency/client contracts call for a period of time in which the agency cannot do business with a competitor.

"After a brief period of time, the kind of information an agency might have, about new strategies or campaigns about to break, becomes unusable," he said.

Young & Rubicam's "conduct of business policy" is issued to new employees and covers privileged information from both clients and prospects, said R. John Cooper, executive VP-general counsel.

Mr. Cooper said an agency would not want to betray a prospect's trust because, even if the agency did not get the business this time, it might want to get it sometime in the future.

Besides, trading on other companies' secrets would irritate an agency's current client, he said.

"It would be like cutting off your nose to spite your face," Mr. Cooper said.

Source: Cleveland Horton, "Ethics at Issue in Lotus Case," *Advertising Age*, December 21, 1987, p. 6.

Client Concerns

In terms of suppliers servicing clients, there also are a number of ethical considerations. Marketing research suppliers, for example, must ensure that information about their clients remains confidential. Suppliers often have access to confidential client information about specific projects. Consider, for example, the relationship between advertisers and their agency.

Marketing research suppliers also are ethically obligated to provide unbiased designs and honest and objective fieldwork, whether results confirm or contradict their client's expectations about the outcome of a study. Finally, marketing researchers are ethically obligated to not pirate research designs and other relevant information that is obtained, say, through requests for proposals, as these are seldom legally protected.

The General Public

Even though marketing research practices are grounded in social science methodology and statistics that are based on well-established guidelines and principles, the collection of information has a subjective element because it is vulnerable to distortion both by the people who have the responsibility of collecting and disseminating the information and by those who provide the answers. The possibility of distortion raises ethical questions.

Consequently, the outcome of the research may affect the general public. Errant practices of marketing research suppliers and other practitioners can have harmful effects on consumers, clients, and the general public.

From the general public's point of view, there are a number of practices that can lead to deception. Two examples, the pseudo poll and result misrepresentation, are on the rise.

Pseudo poll

"We're conducting a survey," reads the letter from XYZ Survey Research Company.

The "survey," which will be sent to 50 million homes, is a questionnaire asking for respondents' preferences for consumer products and their names, addresses, telephone numbers, occupations, and family income. For the respondents' cooperation, the sponsoring company offers them free samples and discounts from consumer products companies.

What the material *doesn't* say is that the personal information will be compiled onto data tapes and sold to marketers to help them promote their products.

Pseudo polls use the public's willingness to be surveyed in order to accomplish something other than survey research. It is a misrepresentation to the consumer when a selling or marketing activity uses the forms, language, and aura of survey research to mask the real nature of the activity. Selling under the guise of marketing research is known in the industry as *sugging*. In 1982, 15 percent of the people surveyed in a study tracking trends in the marketing research industry said that they had been exposed to a sales pitch disguised as a survey. By 1988, 22 percent reported that they had been sugged.[9]

Result misrepresentation

A local television news program asked whether or not the United States should provide additional funding for space exploration. Sixty-eight thousand viewers called in their opinion by using a "900" number. Of those, 59 percent wanted additional funding. This result is in marked contrast to the results of another survey, also reported on the program, indicating that over 60 percent of the sample opposed additional support.

Result misrepresentation frequently occurs with call-in, write-in, or other forms of volunteer surveys in which the researcher has no control over who participates in a study. People participating in the poll conducted

EXHIBIT 19—1

Errant Marketing Research
Practices

— A person answers a few questions only to find him/herself suddenly eligible to buy a specific product or service. This misuse of the survey approach as a "blind" for sales canvassing is by no means new, and it shows no sign of abating.

— Questionnaires about products and brands are sent to households, and response is encouraged by the offer of free product samples to respondents. The listing firms compile their information by implying to the prospective customer that he or she has been interviewed in an opinion or market study. Although the components of questionnaires vary by sponsor, in each case respondents are asked to specify their name, addresses, and telephone numbers. Presumably, to the individual, these data are requested in order to provide the respondent with an incentive. However, the consumer is not told that the company conducting the survey is in business other than research. A brochure for one of these consumer database companies describes their business as "the reporting of name, address, phone number, demographics, and results to client customized questions," to potential clients such as "advertising agencies, distributors, wholesalers" and others.

— A telemarketing company uses "surveys" to promote services offered to broadcasters. Contacts occur during audience measurement periods. According to the company's literature, hundreds of thousands of computerized telephone calls are placed that not only promote a specific broadcast but also poll audience opinions about program subject matter. Here, the "poll" is used to raise broadcast audience ratings.

— Because marketing principles have been applied to nonprofit organizations and political candidates, the survey approach has been misused to generate donations. The incentives for response are the opportunities to provide information, to receive a report of findings, and, at the same time, to contribute financially to an association or to a candidate.

— Newspaper questionnaires are frequently printed as an insert or as part of the paper. In these polls, readers are asked to express their opinions by completing the questionnaire and sending it to the paper; results of the poll are often reported in a later issue. A variation is the use of insert questionnaires by public officials in their newsletters to their constituents; the results of these polls also are reported to the public in a later newsletter.

— Automated polling devices are often placed in recreation centers, retail outlets, airports, and other locations that have substantial pedestrian traffic. The hardware typically includes a computer, a monitor screen, and a keyboard. Through graphics, music, taped messages, and other techniques, passers-by are attracted to these devices, which invite participation in a self-administered survey. The results of "polls" using this equipment have appeared in hundreds of newspapers.

Source: "Phony or Misleading Polls," Advertising Research Foundation, *ARF Position Paper,* September 1986.

by the local telephone news program may not be representative of the entire community. The reason for the disparate results is simply that different groups of people responded to the two surveys. A "survey" where the respondents can self-select is not a legitimate survey because it is unlikely to be representative of the population at large, no matter how many people respond. Misrepresentation occurs when self-selected survey results are reported as "true" about anyone other than those who have responded.

Exhibit 19–1 provides additional illustrations of errant marketing research practices that lead to consumer deception and mistrust.

Errant marketing research practices have serious implications for the general public and public policymakers. Among other consequences, unethical practices can:

EXHIBIT 19–2

Behavior Model of Ethical/Unethical Decision Making

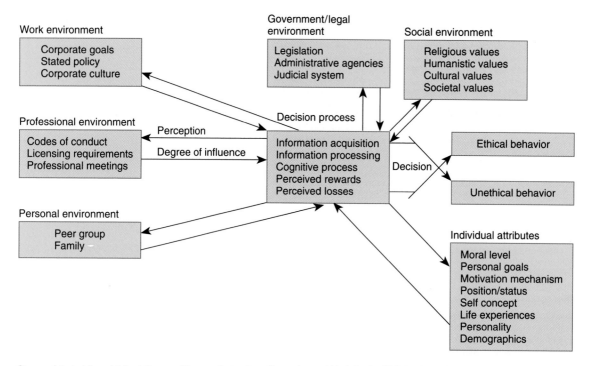

Source: Adapted from Michael Boomer, Clarence Grato, Jerry Gravander, and Mark Tuttle, "A Behavioral Model of Ethical and Unethical Decision Making," *Journal of Business Ethics* 6 (1987), p. 266.

1. Impair legitimate research activities by diminishing the public's willingness to participate in survey research. This affects response rates; statistical reliability; and, ultimately, response quality.

2. Distort the policymakers' perceptions of public opinion and business-related issues. Dangerous feedback can result if policy makers misread consumer sentiment due to invalid research procedures.

3. Lessen the public's ability to distinguish valid from invalid research findings. Even valid polls with inconsistent results may render the public indifferent to, confused about, or distrustful of what they read, see, or hear from survey research. Phony polls do worse, as they result in miseducation.

A Model of Ethical/Unethical Decisions

The model depicted in Exhibit 19–2 describes the various influences that can affect the cognitive process, resulting in the decision to behave ethically or unethically in a given situation.[10] Individual characteristics such as goals, morals, and self-concept that constitute the individual's life experiences and personality interact with external influences such as the work environment as well as legal and social environments. This highlights the fact that the interpretation as to whether the decision was ethical or un-ethical is influenced by a variety of factors, many of which are outside the control of the individual.

ORGANIZATIONAL PERSPECTIVES

The organization to which managers belong is an important determinant of their perspectives on ethics. Organizational norms play a crucial role in the practice or acceptance of ethical or unethical behavior. In other words, the current set of norms that pervade an organization determine what is or is not appropriate behavior. Because members of an organization, or for that matter a department, are known to share organizational values and beliefs, existing company norms, whether stated or implicit, determine the ethical environment and guide the thoughts and actions of decision makers.

Other factors can influence managers' adherence to ethical practices. There is evidence to suggest that referent and significant others play a role in determining ethical or unethical behavior.[11] The terms *referent* or *significant others* simply identify those individuals that serve as a reference for executives when making decisions. Peers and top managers often assume the role of referent or significant others. Evidence also indicates that job demands are an important factor.

Job demands are particularly relevant when comparing marketing research jobs with marketing management jobs. Research jobs, in general, require greater adherence to rules and standards as they relate to scientific methods of inquiry and data collection, while marketing management jobs are more likely to be evaluated in terms of profit and loss. A recent survey designed to elicit marketing professionals' opinions about ethical issues in marketing research asked a group of marketing researchers and marketing executives to indicate their approval/disapproval of the action(s) of the marketing research director in 11 different scenarios relating to different marketing research practices.[12] The results (see Exhibit 19–3) showed marked differences in the opinions of marketing researchers and marketing executives. In particular, executives have higher disapproval rates than researchers concerning the use of ultraviolet ink (item 1), one-way mirrors (item 2), advertising and product misuses (item 4), and the provision of potentially damaging information (item 6). On the other hand, marketing researchers have higher disapproval rates than executives concerning possible conflict of interest (item 3) and sharing information with trade associations (item 5).

Solutions

The problems generated by errant marketing research practices are complex, and they are not easily solved. One way to curb abuses is to establish guidelines and regulations to educate, ensure consistency, and protect. Historically, such standards and regulations have been established by the federal government or by the industry.[13]

Exhibit 19—3

Comparison of Responses to the Ethical Scenarios (items)

Scenario (item)	Percentage of Disapprovals*	
	Marketing Researchers Present Study ($n = 205$)	Marketing Executives Present Study ($n = 215$)
Confidentiality		
1. Use of ultraviolet ink. A project director went to the marketing research director's office and requested permission to use an ultraviolet ink to precode a questionnaire for a mail survey. The project director pointed out that although the cover letter promised confidentiality, respondent identification was needed to permit adequate cross-tabulations of the data. The marketing research director gave approval.	57	69
2. One-way mirrors. One of the products of X company is brassieres. Recently, the company has been having difficulty making decisions on a new product line. Information was critically needed regarding how women put on their brassieres. The marketing research director therefore designed a study in which two local stores agreed to put one-way mirrors in the foundations of their dressing rooms. Observers behind these mirrors successfully gathered the necessary information.	94	97
Conflict of interest		
3. Possible conflict of interest. A marketing testing firm to which X company gives most of its business recently went public. The marketing research director of X company had been looking for a good investment and proceeded to buy some $20,000 of their stock. The firm continues as X company's leading supplier for testing.	54	44
4. Advertising and product misuse. A recent study showed that several customers of X company were misusing product B. Although this posed no danger, customers were wasting their money by using too much of the product at a time. But, yesterday, the marketing research director saw final comps/sketches on product B's new ad campaign, which not only ignored the problem of misuse but actually seemed to encourage it. The marketing research director quietly referred the advertising manager to the research results, well known to all of the people involved with product B's advertising, but did nothing beyond that.	39	55
Social issues		
5. General trade data to center-city group. The marketing research department of X company frequently makes extensive studies of their retail customers. A federally supported minority group working to get a shopping center in their residential area wanted to know if they could have access to this trade information. Since the marketing research director has always refused to share this information with trade organizations, the request was declined.	13	10
6. NMAC request for recent price study. The National Marketing Advisory Council (formed of top marketing executives and marketing educators to advise the Commerce Department) has a task force studying inner-city prices. The head of this study group recently called to ask if they could have a copy of a recent X company study that showed that inner-city appliance prices are significantly higher than in suburban areas. Since X company sells appliances to these inner-city merchants, the marketing research director felt compelled to refuse the request.	20	26

*To simplify the table, only disapproval rates ("disapprove somewhat" or "disapprove") are reported.

Source: Ishmael P. Akaah and Edward A. Riordan, "Judgments of Marketing Professionals about Ethical Issues in Marketing Research: A Replication and Extension," *Journal of Marketing Research*, February 1989, pp. 112–20.

Government regulation. The Federal Trade Commission (FTC) has considered the unethical or illegal use of research. Specifically, Section 5 of the FTC Act declares unfair or deceptive acts to be unlawful. The FTC considers the use of research as a sales ploy to be deceptive, and it has ruled in this manner in several court cases. It is clear that the FTC considers using research as a "door opener" illegal.

The Federal Communications Commission (FCC) has addressed the practice of misrepresenting results. The FCC recognizes the threat associated with the reporting of results of phone-in polls in its Public Notice to Licensees, which states:

> Broadcast facilities should not report the results of polls they have conducted without making clear to the public the nature of the poll, and specifically that the poll does not purport to be conducted upon a scientific basis where, in fact, it is not so based.

Local communities, states, and Congress also have considered legislation. The recent advent of electronic interviewing techniques has led to proposals for the regulation of this type of interviewing as well as proposals for the regulation of telemarketing.

Industry standards. Industry standards that guide and regulate the practice of marketing research exist because they serve several important functions. First, a code of ethics provides objective criteria upon which to judge the behavior of the profession. Second, a professional code of ethics provides a potential counterbalance to interests within a company that may attempt to compromise an individual's integrity. Third, a professional code of ethics provides guidelines to companies that may not have the resources to develop their own code.

A number of industry groups in the marketing research field have developed codes of ethics to guide researchers. Among the industry groups with published codes of ethics are the American Marketing Association (AMA), the American Association for Public Opinion Research (AAPOR), the Marketing Research Association (MRA), and the Council of American Survey Research Organizations (CASRO). Although each set of guidelines is somewhat different, they are in consensus regarding many marketing research practices. For example, the various codes agree on (1) the respondent's right to privacy, (2) the respondent's right to anonymity, and (3) the public's right to know how a survey was conducted at the time the results are reported.

SUMMARY

In this chapter we have discussed a variety of ethical issues facing the marketing researcher. We began by presenting factors that are integral to the definition of ethics. To define ethics we must incorporate (1) rules, standards, codes, or principles (2) morally right behavior, and (3) truthfulness in specific situations. Consequently, unethical actions minimally violate one or all of these factors. The marketing researcher must consider these factors when interacting with clients and with the respondents that provide the data. In addition, marketing researchers must consider the results and effects of their decisions on the general public.

The chapter closes with a discussion of organizational perspectives and sanctions for ethical/unethical behavior and some recommended solutions to control errant marketing research practices.

KEY CONCEPTS

Definition of Business Ethics

Ethical Situations in Marketing Research

Ethical Concerns of Respondents

Ethical Concerns of Clients

Ethical Concerns of the Public

ENDNOTES

1. John Tsalikis and David J. Fritzsche, "Business Ethics: A Literature Review with a Focus on Marketing Ethics," *Journal of Business Ethics* (1989), pp. 695–743.

2. Phillip V. Lewis, "Defining 'Business Ethics': Like Nailing Jello to a Wall," *Journal of Business Ethics* 4 (1985), pp. 377–83.

3. Ibid, p. 382.

4. Ibid.

5. Leo Bogart, "The Researcher's Dilemma," *Journal of Marketing* (1962), pp. 6–11.

6. Alice M. Tybout and Gerald Zaltman, "Ethics in Marketing Research: Their Practical Relevance", *Journal of Marketing Research* (1974), pp. 357–68.

7. For a comment on the general ability of Tybout and Zaltman, see Robert L. Day, "A Comment on Ethics in Marketing Research," *Journal of Marketing Research* (1975), pp. 232–33.

8. Schneider, Kenneth C., "Subject and Respondent Abuse in Marketing Research," *MSU Business Topics* 25, pp. 13–20.

9. Randall Rothenberg, "Surveys Proliferate but Answers Dwindle," *New York Times,* October 5, 1990, p. D4.

10. For an in-depth discussion of the model shown in Exhibit 19–2, see Michael Boomer, Clarence Grato, Jerry Gravander, and Mark Tuttle, "A Behavioral Model of Ethical and Unethical Decision Making," *Journal of Business Ethics* 6 (1987), pp. 265–80.

11. See for example, O. C. Ferrell and Larry G. Gresham, "A Contingency Framework for Understanding Ethical Decision-Making in Marketing," *Journal of Marketing* 49 (Summer 1985), pp. 87–96; and Linda Klebe Trevino, "Ethical Decision Making in Organizations: A Person-Situation Interactionist Model," *Academy of Management Review* 11 (July 1986), pp. 601–17.

12. Ishmael P. Akaah and Edward A. Riordan, "Judgments of Marketing Professionals about Ethical Issues in Marketing Research: A Replication and Extension," *Journal of Marketing Research,* February 1989, pp. 112–20.

13. The following discussion is taken from "Phony or Misleading Polls," Advertising Research Foundation, *ARF Position Paper,* September 1986.

CASE 1: LEADING RESEARCHERS INVITE CRITICISM—AND THEY GET IT

ST. PETERSBURG, FLA.—Pollsters are taking notice of critics who say self-serving marketing research and an explosion of political polls get too much attention.

"It hasn't been hard to find people in the research business who readily concede there's a lot of junk masquerading as studies these days," said Cynthia Crossen, who investigated the survey industry for *The Wall Street Journal.* "Of course, it's always the other guy."

Instead of polls being a quest for truth, "many today are little more than vehicles for pitching a product or opinion," Crossen said in a speech at the annual meeting of the American Association for Public Opinion Research.

Christopher Hitchens, Washington editor of *Harper's Magazine,* said polls no longer just measure public opinion, but influence it.

Leading pollsters invited this criticism and listened intently because their profession is perpetually at the mercy of the kindness of strangers: More people than ever are unwilling to take time to answer surveys.

"We need to face the problem squarely and solve it," Norman Bradburn, director of the National Opinion Research Center, said in a speech marking the end of his term as president of the pollsters' professional association.

James Beninger, a University of Southern California professor who invited Crossen and Hitchens, said public confidence in surveys will erode if people feel they are being spoon-fed cooked data, even if the numbers are pulled from legitimate polls.

Likening such partial results to campaign sound bites, Stanford University professor Herbert Clark dubbed them "poll bites."

As examples of self-serving polls, Crossen cited a study sponsored by Chrysler that found test-drivers preferred Chryslers to Toyotas, and one sponsored by the paper-bag industry that found shoppers prefer paper bags.

Other junk polls are based on tiny samples or self-selected groups or have loaded questions, pollsters say.

Crossen said editors push reporters to get statistics, even from sloppy studies. Even more troubling, she said, reporters and editors promise good, uncritical play for studies promised as exclusives.

Sheldon Gawaiser, a polling consultant for both marketers and the media, said it is the reporter's responsibility to treat an advocacy poll critically.

"If you got any other information from someone who has a vested interest, you're going to treat that information differently than if you get it from a subject that's independent," Gawaiser said.

Harry O'Neill, vice chairman of the Roper Organization, said a few reporters have learned to differentiate between good polls and bad, but many have not. It is the polling company's responsibility to make sure an advocacy group releases its data completely and accurately, "but once the media get hold of it, that's where my control ends," he said.

The New York Times' survey director, former Princeton University professor Michael Kaguy, said his department screens polls before they are cited in stories. Other major media organizations also have in-house experts, but they regularly swap stories about the bad polls that got by them.

Hitchens said political reporters have an especially "overwarm" relationship with pollsters, sometimes paying more attention to polls than to candidates.

Source: *Marketing News,* June 22, 1992, p. 5. Used with permission.

"Their shoe leather can remain intact Gucci. They can punch up a few numbers on the screen and say they have taken the temperature of the nation," Hitchens said. "The same can be said for politicians."

He says polls are so influential that people who used to be opinion makers now swap the latest poll findings rather than talking about issues. "There is a danger of surrogate democracy taking place in a political vacuum," he said.

Case Question

A number of industry groups have specified criteria that constitute ethical from unethical practices. Assume that Mr. Kagoy of *The New York Times* has asked you to create guidelines for discriminating between ethical and unethical polls. Prepare this set of guidelines.

Statistical Tables

TABLE 1

Random Number Table

Line/Col.	(1)	(2)	(3)	(4)	(5)	(6)	(7)	(8)	(9)	(10)	(11)	(12)	(13)	(14)
1	10480	15011	01536	02011	81647	91646	69179	14194	62590	36207	20969	99570	91291	90700
2	22368	46573	25595	85393	30995	89198	27982	53402	93965	34095	52666	19174	39615	99505
3	24130	48390	22527	97265	76393	64809	15179	24830	49340	32081	30680	19655	63348	58629
4	42167	93093	06243	61680	07856	16376	39440	53537	71341	57004	00849	74917	97758	16379
5	37570	39975	81837	16656	06121	91782	60468	81305	49684	60072	14110	06927	01263	54613
6	77921	06907	11008	42751	27756	53498	18602	70659	90655	15053	21916	81825	44394	42880
7	99562	72905	56420	69994	98872	31016	71194	18738	44013	48840	63213	21069	10634	12952
8	96301	91977	05463	07972	18876	20922	94595	56869	69014	60045	18425	84903	42508	32307
9	89579	14342	63661	10281	17453	18103	57740	84378	25331	12568	58678	44947	05585	56941
10	85475	36857	53342	53988	53060	59533	38867	62300	08158	17983	16439	11458	18593	64952
11	28918	69578	88231	33276	70997	79936	56865	05859	90106	31595	01547	85590	91610	78188
12	63553	40961	48235	03427	49626	69445	18663	72695	52180	20847	12234	90511	33703	90322
13	09429	93969	52636	92737	88974	33488	36320	17617	30015	08272	84115	27156	30613	74952
14	10365	61129	87529	85689	48237	52267	67689	93394	01511	26358	85104	20285	29975	89868
15	07119	97336	71048	08178	77233	13916	47564	81056	97735	85977	29372	74461	28551	90707
16	51085	12765	51821	51259	77452	16308	60756	92144	49442	53900	70960	63990	75601	40719
17	02368	21382	52404	60268	89368	19885	55322	44819	01188	65255	64835	44919	05944	55157
18	01011	54092	33362	94904	31273	04146	18594	29852	71685	85030	51132	01915	92747	64951
19	52162	53916	46369	58586	23216	14513	83149	98736	23495	64350	94738	17752	35156	35749
20	07056	97628	33787	09998	42698	06691	76988	13602	51851	46104	88916	19509	25625	58104
21	48663	91245	85828	14346	09172	30163	90229	04734	59193	22178	30421	61666	99904	32812
22	54164	58492	22421	74103	47070	25306	76468	26384	58151	06646	21524	15227	96909	44592
23	32639	32363	05597	24200	13363	38005	94342	28728	35806	06912	17012	64161	18296	22851
24	29334	27001	87637	87308	58731	00256	45834	15398	46557	41135	10307	07684	36188	18510
25	02488	33062	28834	07351	19731	92420	60952	61280	50001	67658	32586	86679	50720	94953
26	81525	72295	04839	96423	24878	82651	66566	14778	76797	14780	13300	87074	79666	95725
27	29676	20591	68086	26432	46901	20849	89768	81536	86645	12659	92259	57102	80428	25280
28	00742	57392	39064	66432	84673	40027	32832	61362	98947	96067	64760	64584	96096	98253
29	05366	04213	25669	26422	44407	44048	37937	63904	45766	66134	75470	66520	34693	90449
30	91921	26418	64117	94305	26766	25940	39972	22209	71500	64568	91402	42416	07844	69618
31	00582	04711	87917	77341	42206	35126	74087	99547	81817	42607	43808	76655	62028	76630
32	00725	69884	62797	56170	86324	88072	76222	36086	84637	93161	76038	65855	77919	88006
33	69011	65795	95876	55293	18988	27354	26575	08625	40801	59920	29841	80150	12777	48501
34	25976	57948	29888	88604	67917	48708	18912	82271	65424	69774	33611	54262	85963	03547
35	09763	83473	73577	12908	30883	18317	28290	35797	05998	41688	34952	37888	38917	88050
36	91567	42595	27958	30134	04024	86385	29880	99730	55536	84855	29088	09250	79656	73211
37	17955	56349	90999	49127	20044	59931	06115	20542	18059	02008	73708	83517	36103	42791
38	46503	18584	18845	49618	02304	51038	20655	58727	28168	15475	56942	53389	20562	87338
39	92157	89634	94824	78171	84610	82834	09922	25417	44137	48413	25555	21246	35509	20468
40	14577	62765	35605	81263	39667	47358	56873	56307	61607	49518	89656	20103	77490	18062
41	98427	07523	33362	64270	01638	92477	66969	98420	04880	45585	46565	04102	46880	45709
42	34914	63976	88720	82765	34476	17032	87589	40836	32427	70002	70663	88863	77775	69348
43	70060	28277	39475	46473	23219	53416	94970	25832	69975	94884	19661	72828	00102	66794

TABLE 1 *(concluded)*

44	53976	54914	06990	67245	68350	82948	11398	42878	80287	88267	47363	46634	06541	97809
45	76072	29515	40980	07391	58745	25774	22987	80059	39911	96189	41151	14222	60697	59583
46	90725	52210	83974	29992	65831	38857	50490	83765	55657	14361	31720	57375	56228	41546
47	64364	67412	33339	31926	14883	24413	59744	92351	97473	89286	35931	04110	23726	51900
48	08962	00358	31662	25388	61642	34072	81249	35648	56891	69352	48373	45578	78547	81788
49	95012	68379	93526	70765	10592	04542	76463	54328	02349	17247	28865	14777	62730	92277
50	15664	10493	20492	38301	91132	21999	59516	81652	27195	48223	46751	22923	32261	85653
51	16408	81899	04153	53381	79401	21438	83035	92350	36693	31238	59649	91754	72772	02338
52	18629	81953	05520	91962	04739	13092	97662	24822	94730	06496	35090	04822	86774	98289
53	73115	35101	47498	87637	99016	71060	88824	71013	18735	20286	23153	72924	35165	43040
54	57491	16703	23167	49323	45021	33132	12544	41035	80780	45393	44812	12515	98931	91202
55	30405	83946	23792	14422	15059	45799	22716	19792	09983	74353	68668	30429	70735	25499
56	16631	35006	85900	98275	32388	52390	16815	69293	82732	38480	73817	32523	41961	44437
57	96773	20206	42559	78985	05300	22164	24369	54224	35083	19687	11052	91491	60383	19746
58	38935	64202	14349	82674	66523	44133	00697	35552	35970	19124	63318	29686	03387	59846
59	31624	76384	17403	53363	44167	64486	64758	75366	76554	31601	12614	33072	60332	92325
60	78919	19474	23632	27889	47914	02584	37680	20801	72152	39339	34806	08930	85001	87820
61	03931	33309	57047	74211	63445	17361	62825	39908	05607	91284	68833	25570	38818	46920
62	74426	33278	43972	10119	89917	15665	52872	73823	73144	88662	88970	74492	51805	99378
63	09066	00903	20795	95452	92648	45454	69552	88815	16553	51125	79375	97596	16296	66092
64	42238	12426	87025	14267	20979	04508	64535	31355	86064	29472	47689	05974	52468	16834
65	16153	08002	26504	41744	81959	65642	74240	56302	00033	67107	77510	70625	28725	34191
66	21457	40742	29820	96783	29400	21840	15035	34537	33310	06116	95240	15957	16572	06004
67	21581	57802	02050	89728	17937	37621	47075	42080	97403	48626	68995	43805	33386	21597
68	55612	78095	83197	33732	05810	24813	86902	60397	16489	03264	88525	42786	05269	92532
69	44657	66999	99324	51281	84463	60563	79312	93454	68876	25471	93911	25650	12682	73572
70	91340	84979	46949	81973	37949	61023	43997	15263	80644	43942	89203	71795	99533	50501
71	91227	21199	31935	27022	84067	05462	35216	14486	29891	68607	41867	14951	91696	85065
72	50001	38140	66321	19924	72163	09538	12151	06878	91903	18749	34405	56087	82790	70925
73	65390	05224	72958	28609	81406	39147	25549	48542	42627	45233	57202	94617	23772	07896
74	27504	96131	83944	41575	10573	03619	64482	73923	36152	05184	94142	25299	84387	34925
75	37169	94851	39117	89632	00959	16487	65536	49071	39782	17095	02330	74301	00275	48280
76	11508	70225	51111	38351	19444	66499	71945	05422	13442	78675	84031	66938	93654	59894
77	37449	30362	06694	54690	04052	53115	62757	95348	78662	11163	81651	50245	34971	52924
78	46515	70331	85922	38329	57015	15765	97161	17869	45349	61796	66345	81073	49106	79860
79	30986	81223	42416	58353	21532	30502	32305	86482	05174	07901	54339	58861	74818	46942
80	63798	64995	46583	09785	44160	78128	83991	42865	92520	83531	80377	35909	81250	54238
81	82486	84846	99254	67632	43218	50076	21361	64816	51202	88124	41870	52689	51275	83556
82	21885	32906	92431	09060	64297	51674	64126	62570	26123	05155	59194	52799	28225	85762
83	60336	98782	07408	53458	13564	59089	26445	29789	85205	41001	12535	12133	14645	23541
84	43937	46891	24010	25560	86355	33941	25786	54990	71899	15475	95434	98227	21824	19535
85	97656	63175	89303	16275	07100	92063	21942	18611	47348	20203	18534	03862	78095	50136
86	03299	01221	05418	38982	55758	92237	26759	86367	21216	98442	08303	56613	91511	75928
87	79626	06486	03574	17668	07785	76020	79924	25651	83325	88428	85076	72811	22717	50585
88	85636	68335	47539	03129	65651	11977	02510	26113	99447	68645	34327	15152	55230	93448
89	18039	14367	61337	06177	12143	46609	32989	74014	64708	00533	35398	58408	13261	47908
90	08362	15656	60627	36478	65648	16764	53412	09013	07832	41574	17639	82163	60859	75567
91	79556	29068	04142	16268	15387	12856	66227	38358	22478	73373	88732	09443	82558	05250
92	92608	82674	27072	32534	17075	27698	98204	63863	11951	34648	88022	56148	34925	57031
93	23982	25835	40055	67006	12293	02753	14827	23235	35071	99704	37543	11601	35503	85171
94	09915	96306	05908	97901	28395	14186	00821	80703	70426	75647	76310	88717	37890	40129
95	59037	33300	26695	62247	69927	76123	50842	43834	86654	70959	79725	93872	28117	19233
96	42488	78077	69882	61657	34136	79180	97526	43092	04098	73571	80799	76536	71255	64239
97	46764	86273	63003	93017	31204	36692	40202	35275	57306	55543	53203	18098	47625	88684
98	03237	45430	55417	63282	90816	17349	88298	90183	36600	78406	06216	95787	42579	90730
99	86591	81482	52667	61582	14972	90053	89534	76036	49199	43716	97548	04379	46370	28672
100	38534	01715	94964	87288	65680	43772	39560	12918	80537	62738	19636	51132	25739	56947

Source: Abridged from *Handbook of Tables for Probability and Statistics,* second edition, edited by William H. Beyer (Cleveland: The Chemical Rubber Comnpany, 1968). Reproduced by permission of the publishers, The Chemical Rubber Company.

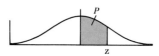

TABLE 2

Cumulative Standard Unit
Normal Distribution

Values of P corresponding to Z for the normal curve. Z is the standard variable. The value of P for $-Z$ equals one minus the value of P for $+Z$, e.g., the P for -1.62 equals $1 - .9474 = .0526$.

Z	.00	.01	.02	.03	.04	.05	.06	.07	.08	.09
0	.5000	.5040	.5080	.5120	.5160	.5199	.5239	.5279	.5319	.5359
.1	.5398	.5438	.5478	.5517	.5557	.5596	.5636	.5675	.5714	.5753
.2	.5793	.5832	.5871	.5910	.5948	.5987	.6026	.6064	.6103	.6141
.3	.6179	.6217	.6255	.6293	.6331	.6368	.6406	.6443	.6480	.6517
.4	.6554	.6591	.6628	.6664	.6700	.6736	.6772	.6808	.6844	.6879
.5	.6915	.6950	.6985	.7019	.7054	.7088	.7123	.7157	.7190	.7224
.6	.7257	.7291	.7324	.7357	.7389	.7422	.7454	.7486	.7517	.7549
.7	.7580	.7611	.7642	.7673	.7704	.7734	.7764	.7794	.7823	.7852
.8	.7881	.7910	.7939	.7967	.7995	.8023	.8051	.8078	.8106	.8133
.9	.8159	.8186	.8212	.8238	.8264	.8289	.8315	.8340	.8365	.8389
1.0	.8413	.8438	.8461	.8485	.8508	.8531	.8554	.8577	.8599	.8621
1.1	.8643	.8665	.8686	.8708	.8729	.8749	.8770	.8790	.8810	.8830
1.2	.8849	.8869	.8888	.8907	.8925	.8944	.8962	.8980	.8997	.9015
1.3	.9032	.9049	.9066	.9082	.9099	.9115	.9131	.9147	.9162	.9177
1.4	.9192	.9207	.9222	.9236	.9251	.9265	.9279	.9292	.9306	.9319
1.5	.9332	.9345	.9357	.9370	.9382	.9394	.9406	.9418	.9429	.9441
1.6	.9452	.9463	.9474	.9484	.9495	.9505	.9515	.9525	.9535	.9545
1.7	.9554	.9564	.9573	.9582	.9591	.9599	.9608	.9616	.9625	.9633
1.8	.9641	.9649	.9656	.9664	.9671	.9678	.9686	.9693	.9699	.9706
1.9	.9713	.9719	.9726	.9732	.9738	.9744	.9750	.9756	.9761	.9767
2.0	.9772	.9778	.9783	.9788	.9793	.9798	.9803	.9808	.9812	.9817
2.1	.9821	.9826	.9830	.9834	.9838	.9842	.9846	.9850	.9854	.9857
2.2	.9861	.9864	.9868	.9871	.9875	.9878	.9881	.9884	.9887	.9890
2.3	.9893	.9896	.9898	.9901	.9904	.9906	.9909	.9911	.9913	.9916
2.4	.9918	.9920	.9922	.9925	.9927	.9929	.9931	.9932	.9934	.9936
2.5	.9938	.9940	.9941	.9943	.9945	.9946	.9948	.9949	.9951	.9952
2.6	.9953	.9955	.9956	.9957	.9959	.9960	.9961	.9962	.9963	.9964
2.7	.9965	.9966	.9967	.9968	.9969	.9970	.9971	.9972	.9973	.9974
2.8	.9974	.9975	.9976	.9977	.9977	.9978	.9979	.9979	.9980	.9981
2.9	.9981	.9982	.9982	.9983	.9984	.9984	.9985	.9985	.9986	.9986
3.0	.9987	.9987	.9987	.9988	.9988	.9989	.9989	.9989	.9990	.9990
3.1	.9990	.9991	.9991	.9991	.9992	.9992	.9992	.9992	.9993	.9993
3.2	.9993	.9993	.9994	.9994	.9994	.9994	.9994	.9995	.9995	.9995
3.3	.9995	.9995	.9995	.9996	.9996	.9996	.9996	.9996	.9996	.9997
3.4	.9997	.9997	.9997	.9997	.9997	.9997	.9997	.9997	.9997	.9998

Source: Taken with permission from Paul E. Green: *Analyzing Multivariate Data* (Hinsdale, Illinois: The Dryden Press, 1978).

TABLE 3

Upper Precentiles of the *t* Distribution

v^*	.75	.90	.95	1 − α .975	.99	.995	.9995
1	1.000	3.078	6.314	12.706	31.821	63.657	636.619
2	.816	1.886	2.920	4.303	6.965	9.925	31.598
3	.765	1.638	2.353	3.182	4.541	5.841	12.941
4	.741	1.533	2.132	2.776	3.747	4.604	8.610
5	.727	1.476	2.015	2.571	3.365	4.032	6.859
6	.718	1.440	1.943	2.447	3.143	3.707	5.959
7	.711	1.415	1.895	2.365	2.998	3.499	5.405
8	.706	1.397	1.860	2.306	2.896	3.355	5.041
9	.703	1.383	1.833	2.262	2.821	3.250	4.781
10	.700	1.372	1.812	2.228	2.764	3.169	4.587
11	.697	1.363	1.796	2.201	2.718	3.106	4.437
12	.695	1.356	1.782	2.179	2.681	3.055	4.318
13	.694	1.350	1.771	2.160	2.650	3.012	4.221
14	.692	1.345	1.761	2.145	2.624	2.977	4.140
15	.691	1.341	1.753	2.131	2.602	2.947	4.073
16	.690	1.337	1.746	2.120	2.583	2.921	4.015
17	.689	1.333	1.740	2.110	2.567	2.898	3.965
18	.688	1.330	1.734	2.101	2.552	2.878	3.922
19	.688	1.328	1.729	2.093	2.339	2.861	3.883
20	.687	1.325	1.725	2.086	2.528	2.845	3.850
21	.686	1.323	1.721	2.080	2.518	2.831	3.819
22	.686	1.321	1.717	2.074	2.508	2.819	3.792
23	.685	1.319	1.714	2.069	2.500	2.807	3.767
24	.685	1.318	1.711	2.064	2.492	2.797	3.745
25	.684	1.316	1.708	2.060	2.485	2.787	3.725
26	.684	1.315	1.706	2.056	2.479	2.779	3.707
27	.684	1.314	1.703	2.052	2.473	2.771	3.690
28	.683	1.313	1.701	2.048	2.467	2.763	3.674
29	.683	1.311	1.699	2.045	2.462	2.756	3.659
30	.683	1.310	1.697	2.042	2.457	2.750	3.646
40	.681	1.303	1.684	2.021	2.423	2.704	3.551
60	.679	1.296	1.671	2.000	2.390	2.660	3.460
120	.677	1.289	1.658	1.980	2.358	2.617	3.373
∞	.674	1.282	1.645	1.960	2.326	2.576	3.291

$^*v$ = Degrees of freedom.

Source: Taken with permission from Table III of R. A. Fisher and F. Yates: *Statistical Tables for Biological, Agricultural, and Medical Research,* published by Oliver & Boyd Ltd., Edinburgh, 1963, 1978).

TABLE 4

Selected Percentiles of the χ^2 Distribution

v^*	$\chi^2_{.005}$	$\chi^2_{.01}$	$\chi^2_{.025}$	$\chi^2_{.05}$	$\chi^2_{.10}$	$\chi^2_{.90}$	$\chi^2_{.95}$	$\chi^2_{.975}$	$\chi^2_{.99}$	$\chi^2_{.995}$
1	.000039	.00016	.00098	.0039	.0158	2.71	3.84	5.02	6.63	7.88
2	.0100	.0201	.0506	.1026	.2107	4.61	5.99	7.38	9.21	10.60
3	.0717	.115	.216	.352	.584	6.25	7.81	9.35	11.34	12.84
4	.207	.297	.484	.711	1.064	7.78	9.49	11.14	13.28	14.86
5	.412	.554	.831	1.15	1.61	9.24	11.07	12.83	15.09	16.75
6	.676	.872	1.24	1.64	2.20	10.64	12.59	14.45	16.81	18.55
7	.989	1.24	1.69	2.17	2.83	12.02	14.07	16.01	18.48	20.28
8	1.34	1.65	2.18	2.73	3.49	13.36	15.51	17.53	20.09	21.96
9	1.73	2.09	2.70	3.33	4.17	14.68	16.92	19.02	21.67	23.59
10	2.16	2.56	3.25	3.94	4.87	15.99	18.31	20.48	23.21	25.19
11	2.60	3.05	3.82	4.57	5.58	17.28	19.68	21.92	24.73	26.76
12	3.07	3.57	4.40	5.23	6.30	18.55	21.03	23.34	26.22	28.30
13	3.57	4.11	5.01	5.89	7.04	19.81	22.36	24.74	27.69	29.82
14	4.07	4.66	5.63	6.57	7.79	21.06	23.68	26.12	29.14	31.32
15	4.60	5.23	6.26	7.26	8.55	22.31	25.00	27.49	30.58	32.80
16	5.14	5.81	6.91	7.96	9.31	23.54	26.30	28.85	32.00	34.27
18	6.26	7.01	8.23	9.39	10.86	25.99	28.87	31.53	34.81	37.16
20	7.43	8.26	9.59	10.85	12.44	28.41	31.41	34.17	37.57	40.00
24	9.89	10.86	12.40	13.85	15.66	33.20	36.42	39.36	42.98	45.56
30	13.79	14.95	16.79	18.49	20.60	40.26	43.77	46.98	50.89	53.67
40	20.71	22.16	24.43	26.51	29.05	51.81	55.76	59.34	63.69	66.77
60	35.53	37.48	40.48	43.19	46.46	74.40	79.08	83.30	88.38	91.95
120	83.85	86.92	91.58	95.70	100.62	140.23	146.57	152.21	158.95	163.64

$^*v$ = Degrees of freedom.

Source: Adapted with permission from *Indtroduction to Statistical Analysis,* 2nd ed., by W. J. Dixon and F. J. Massey, Jr., McGraw-Hill Book Company, Inc., 1957.

TABLE 5
Selected Percentiles of the F Distribution

$F_{.90(v_1, v_2)}$ α = 0.1

v_1^* / v_2^{**}	1	2	3	4	5	6	7	8	9	10	12	15	20	24	30	40	60	120	∞
1	39.86	49.50	53.59	55.83	57.24	58.20	58.91	59.44	59.86	60.19	60.71	61.22	61.74	62.00	62.26	62.53	62.79	63.06	63.33
2	8.53	9.00	9.16	9.24	9.29	9.33	9.35	9.37	9.38	9.39	9.41	9.42	9.44	9.45	9.46	9.47	9.47	9.48	9.49
3	5.54	5.46	5.39	5.34	5.31	5.28	5.27	5.25	5.24	5.23	5.22	5.20	5.18	5.18	5.17	5.16	5.15	5.14	5.13
4	4.54	4.32	4.19	4.11	4.05	4.01	3.98	3.95	3.94	3.92	3.90	3.87	3.84	3.83	3.82	3.80	3.79	3.78	3.76
5	4.06	3.78	3.62	3.52	3.45	3.40	3.37	3.34	3.32	3.30	3.27	3.24	3.21	3.19	3.17	3.16	3.14	3.12	3.10
6	3.78	3.46	3.29	3.18	3.11	3.05	3.01	2.98	2.96	2.94	2.90	2.87	2.84	2.82	2.80	2.78	2.76	2.74	2.72
7	3.59	3.26	3.07	2.96	2.88	2.83	2.78	2.75	2.72	2.70	2.67	2.63	2.59	2.58	2.56	2.54	2.51	2.49	2.47
8	3.46	3.11	2.92	2.81	2.73	2.67	2.62	2.59	2.56	2.50	2.50	2.46	2.42	2.40	2.38	2.36	2.34	2.32	2.29
9	3.36	3.01	2.81	2.69	2.61	2.55	2.51	2.47	2.44	2.42	2.38	2.34	2.30	2.28	2.25	2.23	2.21	2.18	2.16
10	3.29	2.92	2.73	2.61	2.52	2.46	2.41	2.38	2.35	2.32	2.28	2.24	2.20	2.18	2.16	2.13	2.11	2.08	2.06
11	3.23	2.86	2.66	2.54	2.45	2.39	2.34	2.30	2.27	2.25	2.21	2.17	2.12	2.10	2.08	2.05	2.03	2.00	1.97
12	3.18	2.81	2.61	2.48	2.39	2.33	2.28	2.24	2.21	2.19	2.15	2.10	2.06	2.04	2.01	1.99	1.96	1.93	1.90
13	3.14	2.76	2.56	2.43	2.35	2.28	2.23	2.20	2.16	2.14	2.10	2.05	2.01	1.98	1.96	1.93	1.90	1.88	1.85
14	3.10	2.73	2.52	2.39	2.31	2.24	2.19	2.15	2.12	2.10	2.05	2.01	1.96	1.94	1.91	1.89	1.86	1.83	1.80
15	3.07	2.70	2.49	2.36	2.27	2.21	2.16	2.12	2.09	2.06	2.02	1.97	1.92	1.90	1.87	1.85	1.82	1.79	1.76
16	3.05	2.67	2.46	2.33	2.24	2.18	2.13	2.09	2.06	2.03	1.99	1.94	1.89	1.87	1.84	1.81	1.78	1.75	1.72
17	3.03	2.64	2.44	2.31	2.22	2.15	2.10	2.06	2.03	2.00	1.96	1.91	1.86	1.84	1.81	1.78	1.75	1.72	1.69
18	3.01	2.62	2.42	2.29	2.20	2.13	2.08	2.04	2.00	1.98	1.93	1.89	1.84	1.81	1.78	1.75	1.72	1.69	1.66
19	2.99	2.61	2.40	2.27	2.18	2.11	2.06	2.02	1.98	1.96	1.91	1.86	1.81	1.79	1.76	1.73	1.70	1.67	1.63
20	2.97	2.59	2.38	2.25	2.16	2.09	2.04	2.00	1.96	1.94	1.89	1.84	1.79	1.77	1.74	1.71	1.68	1.64	1.61
21	2.96	2.57	2.36	2.23	2.14	2.08	2.02	1.98	1.95	1.92	1.87	1.83	1.78	1.75	1.72	1.69	1.66	1.62	1.59
22	2.95	2.56	2.35	2.22	2.13	2.06	2.01	1.97	1.93	1.90	1.86	1.81	1.76	1.73	1.70	1.67	1.64	1.60	1.57
23	2.94	2.55	2.34	2.21	2.11	2.05	1.99	1.95	1.92	1.89	1.84	1.80	1.74	1.72	1.69	1.66	1.62	1.59	1.55
24	2.93	2.54	2.33	2.19	2.10	2.04	1.98	1.94	1.91	1.88	1.83	1.78	1.73	1.70	1.67	1.64	1.61	1.57	1.53
25	2.92	2.53	2.32	2.18	2.09	2.02	1.97	1.93	1.89	1.87	1.82	1.77	1.72	1.69	1.66	1.63	1.59	1.56	1.52
26	2.91	2.52	2.31	2.17	2.08	2.01	1.96	1.92	1.88	1.86	1.81	1.76	1.71	1.68	1.65	1.61	1.58	1.54	1.50
27	2.90	2.51	2.30	2.17	2.07	2.00	1.95	1.91	1.87	1.85	1.80	1.75	1.70	1.67	1.64	1.60	1.57	1.53	1.49
28	2.89	2.50	2.29	2.16	2.06	2.00	1.94	1.90	1.87	1.84	1.79	1.74	1.69	1.66	1.63	1.59	1.56	1.52	1.48
29	2.89	2.50	2.28	2.15	2.06	1.99	1.93	1.89	1.86	1.83	1.78	1.73	1.68	1.65	1.62	1.58	1.55	1.51	1.47
30	2.88	2.49	2.28	2.14	2.05	1.98	1.93	1.88	1.85	1.82	1.77	1.72	1.67	1.64	1.61	1.57	1.54	1.50	1.46
40	2.84	2.44	2.23	2.09	2.00	1.93	1.87	1.83	1.79	1.76	1.71	1.66	1.61	1.57	1.54	1.51	1.47	1.42	1.38
60	2.79	2.39	2.18	2.04	1.95	1.87	1.82	1.77	1.74	1.71	1.66	1.60	1.54	1.51	1.48	1.44	1.40	1.35	1.29
120	2.75	2.35	2.13	1.99	1.90	1.82	1.77	1.72	1.68	1.65	1.60	1.55	1.48	1.45	1.41	1.37	1.32	1.26	1.19
∞	2.71	2.30	2.08	1.94	1.85	1.77	1.72	1.67	1.63	1.60	1.55	1.49	1.42	1.38	1.34	1.30	1.24	1.17	1.00

$F_{.95(v_1, v_2)}$ $\alpha = 0.05$

v_1* v_2**	1	2	3	4	5	6	7	8	9	10	12	15	20	24	30	40	60	120	∞
1	161.40	199.50	215.70	224.60	230.20	234.00	236.80	238.90	240.50	241.90	243.90	245.90	248.00	249.1	250.10	251.10	252.20	253.30	254.30
2	18.51	19.00	19.16	19.25	19.30	19.33	19.35	19.37	19.38	19.40	19.41	19.43	19.45	19.45	19.46	19.47	19.48	19.49	19.50
3	10.13	9.55	9.28	9.12	9.01	8.94	8.89	8.85	8.81	8.79	8.74	8.70	8.66	8.64	8.62	8.59	8.57	8.55	8.53
4	7.71	6.94	6.59	6.39	6.26	6.16	6.09	6.04	6.00	5.96	5.91	5.86	5.80	5.77	5.75	5.72	5.69	5.66	5.63
5	6.61	5.79	5.41	5.19	5.05	4.95	4.88	4.82	4.77	4.74	4.68	4.62	4.56	4.53	4.50	4.46	4.43	4.40	4.36
6	5.99	5.14	4.76	4.53	4.39	4.28	4.21	4.15	4.10	4.06	4.00	3.94	3.87	3.84	3.81	3.77	3.74	3.70	3.67
7	5.59	4.74	4.35	4.12	3.97	3.87	3.79	3.73	3.68	3.64	3.57	3.51	3.44	3.41	3.38	3.34	3.30	3.27	3.23
8	5.32	4.46	4.07	3.84	3.69	3.58	3.50	3.44	3.39	3.35	3.28	3.22	3.15	3.12	3.08	3.04	3.01	2.97	2.93
9	5.12	4.26	3.86	3.63	3.48	3.37	3.29	3.23	3.18	3.14	3.07	3.01	2.94	2.90	2.86	2.83	2.79	2.75	2.71
10	4.96	4.10	3.71	3.48	3.33	3.22	3.14	3.07	3.02	2.98	2.91	2.85	2.77	2.74	2.70	2.66	2.62	2.58	2.54
11	4.84	3.98	3.59	3.36	3.20	3.09	3.01	2.95	2.90	2.85	2.79	2.72	2.65	2.61	2.57	2.53	2.49	2.45	2.40
12	4.75	3.89	3.49	3.26	3.11	3.00	2.91	2.85	2.80	2.75	2.69	2.62	2.54	2.51	2.47	2.43	2.38	2.34	2.30
13	4.67	3.81	3.41	3.18	3.03	2.92	2.83	2.77	2.71	2.67	2.60	2.53	2.46	2.42	2.38	2.34	2.30	2.25	2.21
14	4.60	3.74	3.34	3.11	2.96	2.85	2.76	2.70	2.65	2.60	2.53	2.46	2.39	2.35	2.31	2.27	2.22	2.18	2.13
15	4.54	3.68	3.29	3.06	2.90	2.79	2.71	2.64	2.59	2.54	2.48	2.40	2.33	2.29	2.25	2.20	2.16	2.11	2.07
16	4.49	3.63	3.24	3.01	2.85	2.74	2.66	2.59	2.54	2.49	2.42	2.35	2.28	2.24	2.19	2.15	2.11	2.06	2.01
17	4.45	3.59	3.20	2.96	2.81	2.70	2.61	2.55	2.49	2.45	2.38	2.31	2.23	2.19	2.15	2.10	2.06	2.01	1.96
18	4.41	3.55	3.16	2.93	2.77	2.66	2.58	2.51	2.46	2.41	2.34	2.27	2.19	2.15	2.11	2.06	2.02	1.97	1.92
19	4.38	3.52	3.13	2.90	2.74	2.63	2.54	2.48	2.42	2.38	2.31	2.23	2.16	2.11	2.07	2.03	1.98	1.93	1.88
20	4.35	3.49	3.10	2.87	2.71	2.60	2.51	2.45	2.39	2.35	2.28	2.20	2.12	2.08	2.04	1.99	1.95	1.90	1.84
21	4.32	3.47	3.07	2.84	2.68	2.57	2.49	2.42	2.37	2.32	2.25	2.18	2.10	2.05	2.01	1.96	1.92	1.87	1.81
22	4.30	3.44	3.05	2.82	2.66	2.55	2.46	2.40	2.34	2.30	2.23	2.15	2.07	2.03	1.98	1.94	1.89	1.84	1.78
23	4.28	3.42	3.03	2.80	2.64	2.53	2.44	2.37	2.32	2.27	2.20	2.13	2.05	2.01	1.96	1.91	1.86	1.81	1.76
24	4.26	3.40	3.01	2.78	2.62	2.51	2.42	2.36	2.30	2.25	2.18	2.11	2.03	1.98	1.94	1.89	1.84	1.79	1.73
25	4.24	3.39	2.99	2.76	2.60	2.49	2.40	2.34	2.28	2.24	2.16	2.09	2.01	1.96	1.92	1.87	1.82	1.77	1.71
26	4.23	3.37	2.98	2.74	2.59	2.47	2.39	2.32	2.27	2.22	2.15	2.07	1.99	1.95	1.90	1.85	1.80	1.75	1.69
27	4.21	3.35	2.96	2.73	2.57	2.46	2.37	2.31	2.25	2.20	2.13	2.06	1.97	1.93	1.88	1.84	1.79	1.73	1.67
28	4.20	3.34	2.95	2.71	2.56	2.45	2.36	2.29	2.24	2.19	2.12	2.04	1.96	1.91	1.87	1.82	1.77	1.71	1.65
29	4.18	3.33	2.93	2.70	2.55	2.43	2.35	2.28	2.22	2.18	2.10	2.03	1.94	1.90	1.85	1.81	1.75	1.70	1.64
30	4.17	3.32	2.92	2.69	2.53	2.42	2.33	2.27	2.21	2.16	2.09	2.01	1.93	1.89	1.84	1.79	1.74	1.68	1.62
40	4.08	3.23	2.84	2.61	2.45	2.34	2.25	2.18	2.12	2.08	2.00	1.92	1.84	1.79	1.74	1.69	1.64	1.58	1.51
60	4.00	3.15	2.76	2.53	2.37	2.25	2.17	2.10	2.04	1.99	1.92	1.84	1.75	1.70	1.65	1.59	1.53	1.47	1.39
120	3.92	3.07	2.68	2.45	2.29	2.17	2.09	2.02	1.96	1.91	1.83	1.75	1.66	1.61	1.55	1.50	1.43	1.35	1.25
∞	3.84	3.00	2.60	2.37	2.21	2.10	2.01	1.94	1.88	1.83	1.75	1.67	1.57	1.52	1.46	1.39	1.32	1.22	1.00

*v_1 = Degrees of freedom for numerator. **v_2 = Degrees of freedom for denominator.

TABLE 5 (concluded)

$F_{.975(v_1, v_2)}$ $\alpha = 0.025$

v_2 \ v_1	1	2	3	4	5	6	7	8	9	10	12	15	20	24	30	40	60	120	∞
1	647.8	799.5	864.2	899.6	921.8	937.1	948.2	956.7	963.3	968.6	976.7	984.9	993.1	997.2	1001	1006	1010	1014	1018
2	38.51	39.00	39.17	39.25	39.30	39.33	39.36	39.37	39.39	39.40	39.41	39.43	39.45	39.46	39.46	39.47	39.48	39.49	39.50
3	17.44	16.04	15.44	15.10	14.88	14.73	14.62	14.54	14.47	14.42	14.34	14.25	14.17	14.12	14.08	14.04	13.99	13.95	13.90
4	12.22	10.65	9.98	9.60	9.36	9.20	9.07	8.98	8.90	8.84	8.75	8.66	8.56	8.51	8.46	8.41	8.36	8.31	8.26
5	10.01	8.43	7.76	7.39	7.15	6.98	6.85	6.76	6.68	6.62	6.52	6.43	6.33	6.28	6.23	6.18	6.12	6.07	6.02
6	8.81	7.26	6.60	6.23	5.99	5.82	5.70	5.60	5.52	5.46	5.37	5.27	5.17	5.12	5.07	5.01	4.96	4.90	4.85
7	8.07	6.54	5.89	5.52	5.29	5.12	4.99	4.90	4.82	4.76	4.67	4.57	4.47	4.42	4.36	4.31	4.25	4.20	4.14
8	7.57	6.06	5.42	5.05	4.82	4.65	4.53	4.43	4.36	4.30	4.20	4.10	4.00	3.95	3.89	3.84	3.78	3.73	3.67
9	7.21	5.71	5.08	4.72	4.48	4.32	4.20	4.10	4.03	3.96	3.87	3.77	3.67	3.61	3.56	3.51	3.45	3.39	3.33
10	6.94	5.46	4.83	4.47	4.24	4.07	3.95	3.85	3.78	3.72	3.62	3.52	3.42	3.37	3.31	3.26	3.20	3.14	3.08
11	6.72	5.26	4.63	4.28	4.04	3.88	3.76	3.66	3.59	3.53	3.43	3.33	3.23	3.17	3.12	3.06	3.00	2.94	2.88
12	6.55	5.10	4.47	4.12	3.89	3.73	3.61	3.51	3.44	3.37	3.28	3.18	3.07	3.02	2.96	2.91	2.85	2.79	2.72
13	6.41	4.97	4.35	4.00	3.77	3.60	3.48	3.39	3.31	3.25	3.15	3.05	2.95	2.89	2.84	2.78	2.72	2.66	2.60
14	6.30	4.86	4.24	3.89	3.66	3.50	3.38	3.29	3.21	3.15	3.05	2.95	2.84	2.79	2.73	2.67	2.61	2.55	2.49
15	6.20	4.77	4.15	3.80	3.58	3.41	3.29	3.20	3.12	3.06	2.96	2.86	2.76	2.70	2.64	2.59	2.52	2.46	2.40
16	6.12	4.69	4.08	3.73	3.50	3.34	3.22	3.12	3.05	2.99	2.89	2.79	2.68	2.63	2.57	2.51	2.45	2.38	2.32
17	6.04	4.62	4.01	3.66	3.44	3.28	3.16	3.06	2.98	2.92	2.82	2.72	2.62	2.56	2.50	2.44	2.38	2.32	2.25
18	5.98	4.56	3.95	3.61	3.38	3.22	3.10	3.01	2.93	2.87	2.77	2.67	2.56	2.50	2.44	2.38	2.32	2.26	2.19
19	5.92	4.51	3.90	3.56	3.33	3.17	3.05	2.96	2.88	2.82	2.72	2.62	2.51	2.45	2.39	2.33	2.27	2.20	2.13
20	5.87	4.46	3.86	3.51	3.29	3.13	3.01	2.91	2.84	2.77	2.68	2.57	2.46	2.41	2.35	2.29	2.22	2.16	2.09
21	5.83	4.42	3.82	3.48	3.25	3.09	2.97	2.87	2.80	2.73	2.64	2.53	2.42	2.37	2.31	2.25	2.18	2.11	2.04
22	5.79	4.38	3.78	3.44	3.22	3.05	2.93	2.84	2.76	2.70	2.60	2.50	2.39	2.33	2.27	2.21	2.14	2.08	2.00
23	5.75	4.35	3.75	3.41	3.18	3.02	2.90	2.81	2.73	2.67	2.57	2.47	2.36	2.30	2.24	2.18	2.11	2.04	1.97
24	5.72	4.32	3.72	3.38	3.15	2.99	2.87	2.78	2.70	2.64	2.54	2.44	2.33	2.27	2.21	2.15	2.08	2.01	1.94
25	5.69	4.29	3.69	3.35	3.13	2.97	2.85	2.75	2.68	2.61	2.51	2.41	2.30	2.24	2.18	2.12	2.05	1.98	1.91
26	5.66	4.27	3.67	3.33	3.10	2.94	2.82	2.73	2.65	2.59	2.49	2.39	2.28	2.22	2.16	2.09	2.03	1.95	1.88
27	5.63	4.24	3.65	3.31	3.08	2.92	2.80	2.71	2.63	2.57	2.47	2.36	2.25	2.19	2.13	2.07	2.00	1.93	1.85
28	5.61	4.22	3.63	3.29	3.06	2.90	2.78	2.69	2.61	2.55	2.45	2.34	2.23	2.17	2.11	2.05	1.98	1.91	1.83
29	5.59	4.20	3.61	3.27	3.04	2.88	2.76	2.67	2.59	2.53	2.43	2.32	2.21	2.15	2.09	2.03	1.96	1.89	1.81
30	5.57	4.18	3.59	3.25	3.03	2.87	2.75	2.65	2.57	2.51	2.41	2.31	2.20	2.14	2.07	2.01	1.94	1.87	1.79
40	5.42	4.05	3.46	3.13	2.90	2.74	2.62	2.53	2.45	2.39	2.29	2.18	2.07	2.01	1.94	1.88	1.80	1.72	1.64
60	5.29	3.93	3.34	3.01	2.79	2.63	2.51	2.41	2.33	2.27	2.17	2.06	1.94	1.88	1.82	1.74	1.67	1.58	1.48
120	5.15	3.80	3.23	2.89	2.67	2.52	2.39	2.30	2.22	2.16	2.05	1.94	1.82	1.76	1.69	1.61	1.53	1.43	1.31
∞	5.02	3.69	3.12	2.79	2.57	2.41	2.29	2.19	2.11	2.05	1.94	1.83	1.71	1.64	1.57	1.48	1.39	1.27	1.00

$F_{.99(v_1, v_2)}$ $\alpha = 0.01$

v_2 \ v_1	1	2	3	4	5	6	7	8	9	10	12	15	20	24	30	40	60	120	∞
1	4052	4999.5	5403	5625	5764	5859	5928	5982	6022	6056	6106	6157	6209	6235	6261	6287	6313	6339	6366
2	98.50	99.00	99.17	99.25	99.30	99.33	99.36	99.37	99.39	99.40	99.42	99.43	99.45	99.46	99.47	99.47	99.48	99.49	99.50
3	34.12	30.82	29.46	28.71	28.24	27.91	27.67	27.49	27.35	27.23	27.05	26.87	26.69	26.60	26.50	26.41	26.32	26.22	26.13
4	21.20	18.00	16.69	15.98	15.52	15.21	14.98	14.80	14.66	14.55	14.37	14.20	14.02	13.93	13.84	13.75	13.65	13.56	13.46
5	16.26	13.27	12.06	11.39	10.97	10.67	10.46	10.29	10.16	10.05	9.89	9.72	9.55	9.47	9.38	9.29	9.20	9.11	9.02
6	13.75	10.92	9.78	9.15	8.75	8.47	8.26	8.10	7.98	7.87	7.72	7.56	7.40	7.31	7.23	7.14	7.06	6.97	6.88
7	12.25	9.55	8.45	7.85	7.46	7.19	6.99	6.84	6.72	6.62	6.47	6.31	6.16	6.07	5.99	5.91	5.82	5.74	5.65
8	11.26	8.65	7.59	7.01	6.63	6.37	6.18	6.03	5.91	5.81	5.67	5.52	5.36	5.28	5.20	5.12	5.03	4.95	4.86
9	10.56	8.02	6.99	6.42	6.06	5.80	5.61	5.47	5.35	5.26	5.11	4.96	4.81	4.73	4.65	4.57	4.48	4.40	4.31
10	10.04	7.56	6.55	5.99	5.64	5.39	5.20	5.06	4.94	4.85	4.71	4.56	4.41	4.33	4.25	4.17	4.08	4.00	3.91
11	9.65	7.21	6.22	5.67	5.32	5.07	4.89	4.74	4.63	4.54	4.40	4.25	4.10	4.02	3.94	3.86	3.78	3.69	3.60
12	9.33	6.93	5.95	5.41	5.06	4.82	4.64	4.50	4.39	4.30	4.16	4.01	3.86	3.78	3.70	3.62	3.54	3.45	3.36
13	9.07	6.70	5.74	5.21	4.86	4.62	4.44	4.30	4.19	4.10	3.96	3.82	3.66	3.59	3.51	3.43	3.34	3.25	3.17
14	8.86	6.51	5.56	5.04	4.69	4.46	4.28	4.14	4.03	3.94	3.80	3.66	3.51	3.43	3.35	3.27	3.18	3.09	3.00
15	8.68	6.36	5.42	4.89	4.56	4.32	4.14	4.00	3.89	3.80	3.67	3.52	3.37	3.29	3.21	3.13	3.05	2.96	2.87
16	8.53	6.23	5.29	4.77	4.44	4.20	4.03	3.89	3.78	3.69	3.55	3.41	3.26	3.18	3.10	3.02	2.93	2.84	2.75
17	8.40	6.11	5.18	4.67	4.34	4.10	3.93	3.79	3.68	3.59	3.46	3.31	3.16	3.08	3.00	2.92	2.83	2.75	2.65
18	8.29	6.01	5.09	4.58	4.25	4.01	3.84	3.71	3.60	3.51	3.37	3.23	3.08	3.00	2.92	2.84	2.75	2.66	2.57
19	8.18	5.93	5.01	4.50	4.17	3.94	3.77	3.63	3.52	3.43	3.30	3.15	3.00	2.92	2.84	2.76	2.67	2.58	2.49
20	8.10	5.85	4.94	4.43	4.10	3.87	3.70	3.56	3.46	3.37	3.23	3.09	2.94	2.86	2.78	2.69	2.61	2.52	2.42
21	8.02	5.78	4.87	4.37	4.04	3.81	3.64	3.51	3.40	3.31	3.17	3.03	2.88	2.80	2.72	2.64	2.55	2.46	2.36
22	7.95	5.72	4.82	4.31	3.99	3.76	3.59	3.45	3.35	3.26	3.12	2.98	2.83	2.75	2.67	2.58	2.50	2.40	2.31
23	7.88	5.66	4.76	4.26	3.94	3.71	3.54	3.41	3.30	3.21	3.07	2.93	2.78	2.70	2.62	2.54	2.45	2.35	2.26
24	7.82	5.61	4.72	4.22	3.90	3.67	3.50	3.36	3.26	3.17	3.03	2.89	2.74	2.66	2.58	2.49	2.40	2.31	2.21
25	7.77	5.57	4.68	4.18	3.85	3.63	3.46	3.32	3.22	3.13	2.99	2.85	2.70	2.62	2.54	2.45	2.36	2.27	2.17
26	7.72	5.53	4.64	4.14	3.82	3.59	3.42	3.29	3.18	3.09	2.96	2.81	2.66	2.58	2.50	2.42	2.33	2.23	2.13
27	7.68	5.49	4.60	4.11	3.78	3.56	3.39	3.26	3.15	3.06	2.93	2.78	2.63	2.55	2.47	2.38	2.29	2.20	2.10
28	7.64	5.45	4.57	4.07	3.75	3.53	3.36	3.23	3.12	3.03	2.90	2.75	2.60	2.52	2.44	2.35	2.26	2.17	2.06
29	7.60	5.42	4.54	4.04	3.73	3.50	3.33	3.20	3.09	3.00	2.87	2.73	2.57	2.49	2.41	2.33	2.23	2.14	2.03
30	7.56	5.39	4.51	4.02	3.70	3.47	3.30	3.17	3.07	2.98	2.84	2.70	2.55	2.47	2.39	2.30	2.21	2.11	2.01
40	7.31	5.18	4.31	3.83	3.51	3.29	3.12	2.99	2.89	2.80	2.66	2.52	2.37	2.29	2.20	2.11	2.02	1.92	1.80
60	7.08	4.98	4.13	3.65	3.34	3.12	2.95	2.82	2.72	2.63	2.50	2.35	2.20	2.12	2.03	1.94	1.84	1.73	1.60
120	6.85	4.79	3.95	3.48	3.17	2.96	2.79	2.66	2.56	2.47	2.34	2.19	2.03	1.95	1.86	1.76	1.66	1.53	1.38
∞	6.63	4.61	3.78	3.32	3.02	2.80	2.64	2.51	2.41	2.32	2.18	2.04	1.88	1.79	1.70	1.59	1.47	1.32	1.00

Source: Adapted with permission from *Biometrika Tables for Statisticians*, vol. 1, 2nd ed., edited by E. S. Pearson and H. O. Hartley, Cambridge University Press, 1958.

PHOTO CREDITS

NAME
INDEX